Wildlife Politics

Attitudes toward charismatic animals such as tigers, lions, bears, and wolves vary greatly and change over time, resulting in bitter political debates. This comprehensive book identifies and analyzes the factors that influence policies across the globe, highlighting how these impact conservation as a whole.

Issues such as overexploitation, hunting, ecotourism, and the struggle to prevent illegal wildlife trafficking are examined, and science's role in policymaking are assessed. The conflicting forces behind legislation, including institutions, interest groups and the media are analyzed, with particular focus on the significance of the U.S. Endangered Species Act. The book covers over forty-five species that have become matters of political debate in sixty-seven different countries.

Case studies and conceptual frameworks provide a clear understanding of the key topics, shedding light on this important yet overlooked area of environmental politics.

Bruce Rocheleau is Professor Emeritus in the Department of Public Administration, Northern Illinois University, USA.

Wildlife Politics

BRUCE ROCHELEAU

Northern Illinois University

CAMBRIDGE
UNIVERSITY PRESS

University Printing House, Cambridge CB2 8BS, United Kingdom

One Liberty Plaza, 20th Floor, New York, NY 10006, USA

477 Williamstown Road, Port Melbourne, VIC 3207, Australia

4843/24, 2nd Floor, Ansari Road, Daryaganj, Delhi – 110002, India

79 Anson Road, #06–04/06, Singapore 079906

Cambridge University Press is part of the University of Cambridge.

It furthers the University's mission by disseminating knowledge in the pursuit of
education, learning, and research at the highest international levels of excellence.

www.cambridge.org
Information on this title: www.cambridge.org/9781107187306
10.1017/9781316941218

First published 2017

Printed in the United Kingdom by Clays, St Ives plc in 2017

A catalogue record for this publication is available from the British Library.

Library of Congress Cataloging-in-Publication Data
Names: Rocheleau, Bruce A.
Title: Wildlife politics / Bruce Rocheleau, Northern Illinois University.
Description: Cambridge : Cambridge University Press, 2017. | Includes bibliographical references and index.
Identifiers: LCCN 2016047635 | ISBN 9781107187306 (Hardback : alk. paper)
Subjects: LCSH: Wildlife conservation–Political aspects. | Wildlife conservation–Social aspects. |
Animals–Effect of human beings on.
Classification: LCC QL82 .R63 2017 | DDC 333.95/416–dc23 LC record available at
https://lccn.loc.gov/2016047635

ISBN 978-1-107-18730-6 Hardback

Contents

Preface and Acknowledgments

I retired from the Public Administration Department at Northern Illinois University in 2007. During my thirty-three years as a professor at NIU, I researched and published many articles, chapters, and three books in the areas of governmental information management and health policy. By the 1980s I had become interested in nature and wildlife, and traveled and read about these topics as an "avocation" joining the Audubon Society, Sierra Club, and National Wildlife Federation, among other organizations. In the years before my retirement, I formed the idea of undertaking research on political and public policy issues concerning wildlife as a retirement project. I had noticed that there was very little systematic research about wildlife done by political scientists and public policy researchers in general, outside of a few books that concentrated on case studies involving the Tellico Dam, Spotted Owl, and the subject of wolves. I found the topic fascinating and decided to do a book that covers broadly wildlife politics that will, I believe, make a significant contribution to understanding a topic that has been neglected and is likely to become more contentious in the future. I began the research before my retirement and have continued it for more than nine years with this volume. It has been a liberating experience to work on a project that I will not be reporting on my "faculty activity report" and thus able to research with no time limits pressing me to publish. Although my previous topics (governmental information management and health policy) were of great intellectual interest to me, I think that wildlife politics are much more inherently interesting and I loved doing this research. I simply worked until I had achieved what I think is a useful and interesting analysis of an important topic. I hope that this work will stimulate more research on wildlife politics. I would like to thank Professors Susan Clark, Rosaleen Duffy, and Christopher McGrory Klyza for their helpful comments on a previous draft. I owe special thanks to Dominic Lewis for his interest and support, which made this book possible. Any weaknesses and limitations of the book are the results of purely my own efforts.

1 An Introduction to Wildlife Politics

In April of 2011, after months of bitter struggle, Democrats and Republicans finally agreed to a budget compromise to avert the shutdown of government in the United States. One of the key compromises was to remove Rocky Mountain gray wolves from the Federal Endangered Species Act (ESA) protection and also to block judicial review of this decision [1; 2]. The compromise was sponsored by a Democratic Senator (Jon Tester) from Montana and a Republican representative (Mike Simpson) of Idaho. This is an example of how important wildlife issues are in politics in the United States. Wildlife politics sometimes reflect partisan divides, such as between the Republican and Democratic parties in the United States, with Democrats tending to be more protective of wildlife. However, the association with partisan politics is far from perfect. Republican Teddy Roosevelt placed higher priority on protecting wildlife than any other president and the ESA, the single most important legislative act to preserve wildlife, was developed and passed during the Nixon Administration. Conservative Texas community members became strongly supportive of efforts to preserve whooping cranes because of their "passion to protect these natural resources because it's part of Texas" [3 p. 7]. There are numerous examples of Democrats in the West opposing protections for wildlife, as occurred in the above case where Senator Tester was about to face an opponent associated with an extreme anti-wolf proposal. Kamieniecki's review of the relationship among party, ideology, and environmentalism found only "weak relationships" among them [4 p. 165]. Governments often become engaged in wildlife politics throughout the world. For example, in China, tigers were almost extinguished but the government has attempted to change attitudes toward the predators and banned the trade of tiger bones in 1993 [5].

There is substantial evidence that wildlife species are increasingly threatened with extinction due to human activities in this Anthropocene age that may rival the five major previous extinction periods [6]. For example, "bottom trawling" by fishing fleets destroys coral and the sea floor in a manner reminiscent of clear-cutting of forests, but this form of trawling covers 150 times the area compared to the forests [7 p. 196]. Likewise, 34 of 175 species of sharks are threatened with global extinction [7 p. 200]. A worldwide group of researchers documented increased numbers of protected areas for species but nevertheless pressure on species has continued to build because of "overexploitation of species, invasive alien species, pollution, climate change, and especially the degradation, fragmentation, and destruction of habitats" and especially "due to the growth of agriculture which comes at the expense of biodiversity" [8 p. 1299]. Another group of scientists reported increased threats to vertebrate species that play "vital roles in the ecosystems" [9 p. 1503].

1

Similarly, Butchart *et al.* report declines in the populations not only of vertebrates but birds, corals, and crucial habitats such as mangroves and sea grass beds [10]. A comprehensive study of the "State of Birds" reported that 230 bird species are in danger of extinction [11]. Stephen Meyer, an MIT political scientist, wrote a book titled *The End of the Wild* which claims that "nothing" can save nature and that "prohibitory regulation is aimed at ghosts" that have virtually no chance of survival [12 p. 43]. In short, the preservation of wildlife diversity is a worldwide problem that we face and consequently it is important to examine how governments and politicians are dealing with this challenge.

Wildlife politics are characterized by high levels of intensity. This is especially true of policy struggles over charismatic animals that people love (e.g., whales, elephants, baby seals, manatees, wild mustangs) and those that have "negative" as well as positive charisma (e.g., wolves, sharks, and grizzly bears) that lead to bitter political battles. Moreover, attitudes toward wildlife can change and create new political conflict. Formerly, the U.S. Federal and state governments rewarded bounty hunters for killing animals they considered "vermin," such as wolves and coyotes, but now the Federal government has made significant investments to return wolves to the West over the protests of powerful groups in these states [13]. Intense struggles over non-predators such as deer occur in urban "liberal areas" on the East Coast as well as rural states [14]. The strong attachment (and sometimes antagonism) that humans feel for animals brings more passion to policy struggles over wildlife than most political issues.

The political strife observed in the United States is reflected in other countries, demonstrating the universal salience of wildlife politics. Many westerners resent Federal government efforts to protect species such as owls or carnivores with the view that outsiders are making unwarranted intrusions on their livelihoods and customs. Similarly, a major challenge in many developing countries is the attempt to get local communities to "buy in" to international goals of protecting wildlife. Local residents often poach wildlife that threaten their agriculture or in order to sell animal parts. Despite similarities, there remain intriguing differences between countries in how they approach wildlife, even when they are similar in other respects. For example, the approaches of the United States and Canada to preserving endangered species are different – given the latter's emphasis on voluntary and discretionary efforts [15]. This book seeks to identify and analyze the broad range of forces that affect the politics of wildlife. This book proposes that wildlife politics represents a significant subgenre of environmental politics due to people's emotional attachment to wildlife and the unusual coalitions that form, cutting across traditional political divides. Below I outline the categories of influences in order to develop a broad framework for understanding of wildlife politics.

Basic Constraining Variables: The Context of Wildlife Policy

Habitat Size and Richness, Human Population, and Development

There are some key variables that are either fixed or slow to change that affect wildlife politics. One concerns the area of land available to wildlife. Conservation biologists theorize ("island theory") that the larger an area is, the more species that it can support [16]. Even parks as large as Yellowstone are inadequate to ensure the survival of wide-ranging species such as grizzlies over long time periods [17]. Development and associated infrastructure such as roads create obstacles to wildlife corridors and thus reduce the effective habitat available to species. Roads often lead directly to mortality for wolves and Florida panthers – Gaydos reports that 45 percent of Florida panther deaths were due to auto-accidents [18 p. 156]. In the United States, early conservationists placed emphasis on creating national parks as a way of conserving wildlife but now research points to the need to link these areas [16]. As human populations grow and develop, the habitats of wildlife are cut back or made inhospitable. For example, Ackerman, Powell, Maehr, Noss, and Larkin report that 24 percent of manatees are killed by collisions with boats – manatees can detect but not avoid approaching boats [19 p. 315]. Manatees are also killed by "entanglement in lines, canal locks, flood gates, pipes, culverts and other human-development causes" [19 p. 314–15]. The same is true internationally – for example, in Africa, most wildlife exist outside of parks [20]. On continents such as Europe, there is no possibility of huge parks – European countries have relatively small parks due to long-established "legitimate economic constraints" [21 p. 120]. The quality of land, not just its size, affects the ability to support wildlife. The parks that do exist in the United States tend to consist of poor-quality land in terms of richness of soil, or otherwise these areas would have been settled. For example, the creation of Denali National Park in Alaska succeeded partly due to the fact that it was viewed as being "unsuitable for agriculture and had few useable resources" [22 p. 29]. Alaska's growing season is short, flora such as trees grow very slowly, and Alaska's lands have less fish and wildlife per acre than Oregon's [23 p. 274]. Foreman characterizes much of the park land in the West as being of "unproductive habitat" consisting of "rocks and ice" chosen to avoid conflicts with farming and extractive industries [24 p. 579]. In the continental United States, it has been shown that although riparian areas constitute only 1 percent of the total area, nevertheless they support more species than all of the rangelands of the West [25 p. 163]. Tobin says that "nearly one-third of vertebrate species depend on riparian areas" but these lands and waters are "most prized by humans" and that the competition for water "ended with humans on top and native species left high and dry" [26 p. 66]. Since public lands are generally poor in terms of biodiversity, the majority of wildlife exists on private lands but these lands are not often studied [27 p. 681–2]. Noss, O'Connell, and Murphy similarly state that "in all countries" the lands used for economic areas include "coastal areas, fertile grasslands, riparian areas, low elevation sites in mountainous areas, and well-watered sites in arid regions" [28 p. 11]. By way of contrast, these rich and watery lands are poorly represented in areas reserved for wildlife protection [28 p. 11]. They go on to point out that human recreational uses of these conservation areas are often given priority over conservation goals [28 p. 185]. Consequently, extremely large areas may be needed to support diverse wildlife because of the nature of the land. Mangun says that the history of the [U.S.] West has been "shaped by" who "gets access to land and water resources" and that wildlife were not represented in this political process" [29 p. 110–11]. Indeed, Eric

Dinerstein states that we can predict that animals that prefer rich habitat will be threatened by humans [30]. In short, land and water availability are underlying constraints for attempts to address wildlife issues.

The impact of development on wildlife is complex. Although development usually destroys habitat, others point out that when human populations become wealthier, their affluence may encourage them to give attention to the vanishing wildlife and scarce wilderness areas [31 p. 14]. Still, there is a consistent association between the emergence of "human overpopulation" and the consequent loss of biodiversity [32]. Edward Wilson points to Hawaii as an example as it has lost a huge portion of its species, many of the existing species are threatened, and he says the survival of several remaining species is due to the fact that they live in remote, relatively uninhabited areas [33]. Nyhus and Tilson state that on islands such as Bali and Java "there were simply too many people and too few forests" and thus the tiger disappeared by 1980 [34 p. 129]. Wilson uses the acronym HIPPO to outline key forces that human overpopulation brings: habitat destruction, invasive species, pollution, and overharvesting [33 p. 50]. Population expansions inevitably impinge on wildlife habitat, leading to conflict such as that in northeast India which has resulted in threats to the tiger, rhinoceros, and elephant populations in this area. Choudhury concludes that unless the growth rate of human populations is controlled, there are no solutions to the human-elephant conflicts [35].

Another emerging uncontrollable factor is climate change. Worldwide analyses by Parmesan and Yohe find evidence that some 1700 species had exhibited changes such as shifts in their ranges that match the predictions of climate change [36]. Incorporation of climate change into wildlife policy has been muted so far with the exception of a few species such as polar bears. For example, the U.S. government "did not acknowledge climate change as a significant issue until 2008" and the few conservation plans that mention climate change just point to the need to be aware of it and conduct "adaptive management" [37 p. 1104–5]. However, along with the spread of invasive species due to globalization and the increase in pollution, climate change is another factor that will increasingly affect wildlife policy and is another one that requires international cooperation.

Human Customs, Attitudes, and Ethical Values Concerning Wildlife

Human customs and attitudes toward animals can intervene between population size and its impact on wildlife. Humans have often eliminated wildlife that they perceive to be a nuisance. But people may also come to tolerate inconvenience from wildlife and impose restrictions on consumption of them. For example, in the 1990s, several statewide initiatives passed in states such as Alaska, Colorado, Washington, and Michigan restricting or abolishing trapping, baiting, and hunting of wildlife [38]. In part, these results may reflect the fact with the increasing urbanization of the United States the numbers of hunters and trappers have become a smaller percent of the U.S. population. Bixby claims that there has been a major reversal in attitudes toward predators [39]. Manfredo too argues that humans have become more accepting and less utilitarian in their perception of animals [40]. Decker *et al.* posit the existence of a "wildlife acceptance capacity" of local residents in their attitudes toward bears [41]. Some wildlife organizations such as Defenders of Wildlife have tried to increase acceptance by humans by providing compensation for damage caused by predators.

Customs such as the wearing of fur and feathers led to the endangerment of several species. The origin of the Audubon Society can be traced to the attempt of Augusta Hemenway and others to combat the feather trade in order to preserve egrets and other birds [42]. Asian delight in eating shark fin soup has caused sharks to be threatened and some governments are taking action to attempt to change consumption patterns [43]. The threats to large mammals such as tigers is partly due to their association with male virility and their use in oriental medicine. But these threats may possibly be lessened by the development of new drugs such as Viagra which Roman says led to the decreased sale of some animal parts such as seal penises [44]. One change in customs is a decreasing tendency (based on per capita figures) of U.S. citizens to visit nature parks – the decline began in the mid 1980s and has been steady since then. One hypothesis is that the public and particularly children are preoccupied with electronics and Kareiva worries that this change in habits is undermining support for wildlife conservation [45].

The past century has witnessed the growth of a strong animal rights movement that challenges the primacy of human interests over those of animals [46]. This movement works with environmentalists in supporting protections for wildlife. However, environmentalists are concerned with the preservation of diverse species, not necessarily with protection of individual animals, and most environmentalists accept the need for "sustainable use" of wildlife. Indeed, many environmentalists encourage hunting especially of invasive species that threaten native animals. Natives in Alaska and countries such as Norway view the hunting of whales as a right and integral to their culture and customs. All fifty states have passed laws forbidding the harassment of hunters [47]. On the other hand, the percentage of hunters in the United States has been declining while the percentages of people involved in bird-watching and other non-consumptive uses of wildlife has been rising in part due to the aging of the U.S. population [48 p. 210]. Thus debates over wildlife policies involve struggles among different value systems and changing customs and interests of human populations.

Over the past fifty years, humankind has become aware of the threats to vanishing wildlife species and there has been a worldwide movement to protect and preserve species. But the question remains as to how humans should intervene with nature. Indeed, intervention or the failure to intervene can both become hot political issues. For example, beginning in 1968 in Yellowstone National Park, a "natural regulation policy" has been employed in which wildlife such as elk and bears are no longer fed but are allowed to live or die based on natural factors such as weather, disease, and the availability of natural food sources [49 p. 209]. However, passive "non-intervention" strategies are hard to maintain in the face of public opinion. For example, Smith discusses the policy of feeding elk in the National Elk Range and notes that having "droves of dead and dying elk within sight of thousands of people" would be politically unacceptable [49 p. 209–10]. Indeed, hunters of elk in Colorado and caribou and moose in Alaska have been assisted by official policy of sustaining larger numbers of these game animals through feeding or the elimination of competitors to human hunters such as wolves. Likewise, animal rights groups are loath to let charismatic animals such as elk or wild horses die – they demand that no-kill methods be used to control populations such as immunocontraception [49 p. 207].

The theory of community-based natural resources management (CBNRM) holds that attitudes of humans in poor developing countries can become more accepting of wildlife if local residents can be shown to benefit from them. Hackel points out that Africa's population is expected to double by 2025 to 1.5 billion people and this increase will almost certainly isolate protected lands, turning them into small islands of unconnected wildlife [50]. Hackel also says that it is difficult to show that material benefits from wildlife conservation exceed those of agriculture [50]. If the economic value of wildlife cannot be shown to exceed the value that can be derived by destruction of wildlife habitat or poaching of wildlife, then the preservation of species may be doomed unless humans adopt a less utilitarian attitude [51]. In short, human perceptions and values can affect and intervene in the relationship between population growth and wildlife diversity.

Adaptability of Wildlife and Their Attractiveness to Humans

Humans have won the battle for survival of species and the challenge to wildlife is to adapt to a world dominated by humans [52]. Matthiessen points out that some birds like mourning doves consume wide varieties of food and are willing to nest in a variety of trees and consequently they flourish while birds like the red-cockaded woodpecker that only nest in certain pines vanish [52]. Some conservationists refer to species that flourish in proximity to humans as "weed species" (e.g., raccoons). Matthiessen acknowledges that the lack of adaptability of many species make them losers in the struggle for survival but he points out that humans greatly speed up extinction for these less adaptable species [52]. A recent example of the problem has occurred in San Francisco, where a Salt Pond Restoration project attracted masses of California gulls which feasted on endangered snow plovers, a species that is much less adaptable [53]. Dinerstein found that the blue-winged warbler is not threatened but the very similar golden-winged warbler is in danger – the difference being that the former is more flexible, willing to make use of woods in different phases of growth [54]. Human developments often change habitats to favor one species over another, such as the fact that artificial water bodies give red foxes an advantage over endangered kit foxes [55 p. 264]. Some species such as deer and peccaries have populations that consist of large numbers of short-lived individuals with short gestation periods and are less threatened by poaching and overhunting than others such as carnivores and primates [56 p. 105]. Animals that are appealing to humans acquire interest groups that fight for policies to preserve them. The importance of this principle is demonstrated by the U.S. General Accountability Office's (GAO's) study of the implementation of the ESA [57]. GAO found that most of the "discretionary recovery funds have been directed toward a small percentage of species generally acknowledged as having high public appeal." In short, it is not only the adaptability of wildlife that helps to foster their preservation but also their ability to attract the support of humans.

Technology and Its Use

Advances in technology have contributed to decline of wildlife. Both Native Americans and white settlers were able to slaughter thousands of caribou in Alaska with ease, which would have been impossible in the years prior to widespread use of guns and ammunition [58]. Matthiessen says that although tigers were killed by thousands for centuries that they were not "seriously threatened" until the advent of firearms [59 p. 64]. The development of transportation has endangered species. For example, the Great Indian Bustard was "never easy to shoot" before the advent of jeeps in India but is "foolishly unafraid of jeeps" and vanished in areas frequented by hunters in jeeps [60 p. 119]. Kaye points out how difficult it was for humans to threaten wolves in Alaska due to the difficulty of hunting them prior to the introduction of aerial hunting [61]. Theberge says that the "snowmobiles and the airplane have extinguished remoteness" [62 p. 47]. Nash argues that the automobile has been the major threat to wilderness and thus to wildlife that depend on wilderness [23]. The case of ocean life illustrates the importance of technological changes. Ocean fish once were perceived to be an infinite resource but the development of fishing technology (e.g., long nets) along with global markets has turned fish into an exhaustible resource over which humans exert control [63; 64]. For example, Rigney cites statistics that the waters off Maine have "lost 97 to 99 percent of finfish and bivalve mollusks" over the past 150 years [65 p. 5]. Roberts says that modern fishing technology leaves "fish with no place to hide" and hence large unfished reserved areas must be created [66 p. 364]. Recently, it has been estimated that gillnets drown more than 400,000 seabirds annually – seabirds used to be able to spy the nets and avoid diving after fish in them but the modern monofilament nets are mostly invisible to them [67]. Regulations and advances in technology may alleviate some of the harmful effects of technology. For example, restrictions on the hunting of whales and exclusion devices for fishing nets have decreased somewhat the destructive effects on whales and other mammals [68]. Rigney reports that proponents of aquaculture have an "almost religious faith in technology" as the way to replace the shortage of wild fish [65 p. 143–4]. Hames cites examples of how the introduction of guns to the Plains Indians led to "local extinctions of bison," though he holds that it is the development of external markets that drives changes in aboriginal culture [69 p. 173]. While technological advances have contributed to threats to species, at the same time, there are also reports of the development of new technologies that may help to control some threats such as poaching. Scientists have developed "fingerprint readers" for "dozens of species" that may be able to track much of the wildlife and assist in anti-poaching efforts [70]. Overall, advances in hunting and fishing technologies have greatly exacerbated threats to wildlife.

Markets and the Politics of Wildlife

Markets are central to the politics of wildlife. The growth of global markets has been a major factor as to why many species such as fish and mammals are threatened. For example, Nyhus, Tilson and Hutchins argue that the "commoditization" of privately owned tigers should concern everyone interested in their preservation [71 p. 237]. Geist argues that emphasis on the commercialization of wildlife and the misapplication of the tragedy of the commons have led to the ignoring of the substantial achievements that public ownership and management have achieved for conservation [72]. Hames's studies of aboriginal tribes in South America show that by far the most dramatic change in their behavior occurs when demand is driven not by local subsistence needs but "opportunities presented by the external market" so that game value increases as they are used as "pets, skins, feathers, furs" and ingredients in medicines often "in species that had no previous value" [69 p. 179 & 192]. The end result is that the spread of the market is "undoubtedly the most potentially devastating change in aboriginal environmental relations" [69 p. 192].

The International Context of Wildlife Politics

Wildlife often cross governmental boundaries. This is especially true of birds and fish which has led to many disputes and the development of international treaties and organizations, such as the International Whaling Commission, to deal with these. But land animals are also affected by illegal trade of wildlife or products from killed wildlife that represent a significant threat to many species. Treaties, most notably CITES (Convention on International Trade in Endangered Species of Wild Flora and Fauna) have been adopted that are aimed at controlling illegal wildlife trade, but Duffy points out that Western countries have blamed developing nations for poaching and illegal animal trade but the West has not put many resources into lessening the demand for wildlife by not rigorously enforcing laws such as the United States's Lacey Act [73 p. 51, 183, & 185]. The politics of poorer countries with rich wildlife systems such as those in Africa and Latin America are very much influenced by ecotourism and non-governmental organizations such as the World Wildlife Fund (WWF). The consequence is that the preservation of many species depends upon international agreements and support from Western countries and international NGOs (non-governmental organizations). Even the most powerful countries such as the United States need cooperative international action to achieve their biodiversity goals.

Concepts and Frameworks for Understanding Wildlife Politics

The Time Dimension in Wildlife Politics: Policy Cycles, Media, and Disasters

In the above paragraphs, I pointed out that there are several important constraints that are either fixed (e.g., amount of land and water) or difficult to control (e.g., technology, economic development, and globalization of trade) that influence the survival of wildlife.

Thus governments that attempt to encourage wildlife conservation must cope with these powerful constraints if they are to be effective. In this book, I employ concepts and frameworks that help to explain the forces and dynamics of wildlife politics. One set of concepts concerns the time dimension of wildlife politics and related concepts such as policy cycles, the role of media, and environmental disasters. Wildlife politics were virtually invisible or slow to change for centuries but change has been rapid over the past fifty years throughout the world. The implementation of new policies for wildlife conservation often involves attempts to overcome strong forces such as deeply held customs and attitudes (e.g., fear and hatred of wolves). Progress in wildlife conservation may not be linear. Research shows that public policies tend to follows cycles in which problems are discovered, and major attention is devoted to the crisis with the passage of legislation that takes a long time to implement with eventual decline of public interest in the issue [74]. Media can bring wildlife issues to the forefront but the focus on them tends to be fleeting. Over the past fifty years, the passage of environmental laws has been spurred by environmental disasters such as an oil spill in Santa Barbara in 1969 and the catching fire of Ohio's Cuyahoga River [75]. Some policy analysts refer to this public policy pattern of sudden action followed by a longer, quiet period as "punctuated equilibriums" [76]. Anthony Downs, an American economist, predicted shortly after the first Earth Day (in 1970) that environmental problems "would ... have a brief moment in the sun" but fade once the public "realized the cost of ... progress" as well as due to "boredom with the issue" and "decline in media attention" [77 p. 65]. The 1960s and early 1970s were marked by several major legislative acts such as the National Environmental Policy Act and Endangered Species Act that introduced notable policy innovations [78]. But the ESA has not been reauthorized since 1992 despite Congressional efforts to do so in the 109th, 110th, 111th, and 112th Congresses. Instead, the same ESA remains in force and "funds have been appropriated to implement the administrative provisions of ESA in each subsequent fiscal year despite its lack of reauthorization" [79 p. 1]. However, interest in the ESA remains strong. For example, a conservative group, the Pacific Legal Foundation, argues that it represents the most contentious of environmental laws supported more consistently by Federal courts than the Patriot Act [80 p. 22]. Thus the lack of reauthorization of the ESA has not been due the Downs policy cycle factor of disinterest but rather because it has both strong support and opposition and no compromise has developed that suits both sides [79]. Reversals of policies and priorities can and do occur in wildlife conservation. For example, the Park Service had been worried about Indians killing too many elk in Glacier National Park for many years but then later changed to the position that they were not killing enough [81]. Wildlife politics is complex and does not conform to easy explanations offered by any single public policy model but attention to policy cycles, media, and disasters will help to understand some of the major dynamics.

Market Incentives: The Problem or Solution to Problems?

A second set of useful concepts to understand wildlife politics involves markets and economic incentives. Although the growth of markets for endangered wildlife products has been a major cause of their endangerment, some believe that the intelligent use of market incentives can be structured to support wildlife. Governments have sought to protect animals endangered by "command and control" approaches such as international treaties like CITES to prevent trade in wildlife deemed to be threatened, and through "protected areas" (e.g., parks) to preserve wildlife. But the effectiveness of these government-controlled efforts has been questioned, especially with respect to developing countries. For example, Rasker, Martin, and Johnson argue that a superior approach is to allow commercialization of wildlife so that landowners can benefit from hunting and thus have an incentive to preserve wildlife [82 p. 339]. They acknowledge that there are problems with the private property incentive approach. For example, wildlife are mobile and fences may have to be constructed in order for a commercial approach to be effective; this would have deleterious effects such as leading to small islands of wildlife.

One of the chief criticisms of the ESA has been its lack of incentives for land owners to cooperate and there have been several attempts to make government compensate landowners for restrictions on the use of their property. For example, Republican Representative Richard Pombo called for a revised ESA that would "protect and incentivize private property owners" [83 p. 3]. Actually, major changes made to the ESA since its enactment have been aimed at providing reassurance to landowners through mechanisms such as habitat conservation plans (HCPs) that allow commercial projects to be undertaken in areas with threatened species if they develop a plan to mitigate harmful consequences that meets the standards of the U.S. Fish and Wildlife Service (USFWS) [84]. Critics such as Donahue point out a number of weaknesses to incentive approaches, arguing that monetary incentives are never enough and that they have to be "backed up by regulations with teeth" if they are to be effective [85 p. 147]. Moreover, economic incentives do not necessarily dominate human interest in wildlife. Pasquini, Cowling, Twyman, and Wainright studied the use of private incentives in South Africa to preserve wildlife and found that the owners engaged in the programs for personal enjoyment and conservation reasons, not economic benefits [86]. CBNRM approaches employ incentives to enable local communities to keep benefits but there have been many problems in trying to implement incentives. For example, benefits are to be given to the community but, as Duffy notes, "community" is a complex term and there is disagreement over who should get what [87]. Gibson points out the need to look at individual incentives because there are big differences in the perspectives of different groups of individuals such as residents, scouts, and chiefs [88 p. 120].

The most recent emphasis in the use of market incentives for conservation concerns the use of PES (Payments for Environmental or Ecosystem Services) in which the "beneficiaries" (e.g., the public or groups that value biodiversity) reimburse the "providers of these services" (e.g., farmers or ranchers who make modifications of their practices to encourage biodiversity) through a contract that is "performance-based" (e.g., rewarding them according to how well the provider scores on measures of implementation and outcomes of desired practices) [89 p. 1135]. Their rise in popularity is illustrated by the fact that the number of publications about PES in Google Scholar increased from 12 during 1996–8 to over 500 during the period from 2006 to 2008 [89 p. 1135]. PES appear to be especially attractive for developing countries where central governments are weak and unable or unwilling to enforce regulatory approaches to preserving wildlife. They are also popular because they provide a vehicle for meeting the huge costs of preserving species estimated at 75 billion [90]. However, the PES trend has been challenged by critics who contend that nature values are "hard to convert to economic terms" and that "by handing it over to the market you are in effect handing it over to corporations and the very rich" [90]. One of the requirements for PES to work is clear property rights, though the "property" does not necessarily have to be private property [91 p. 1]. In developing countries, land is often "government owned or the private land is regulated but these de jure statutes are not enforced" and thus land tenure is "ill defined" [91 p. 6–7]. For example, a PES is being planned for the buffer zone around a park in India (Bandhavgarh National Park) known for its tigers [92 p. 408–10]. Most of the land in the buffer zone is "overgrazed with cattle" and thus necessitates the involvement of the entire village in the PES and, in making payments, decisions have to be made as to whether to give it in a lump sum to the entire village or to individual households [92]. Performance indicators under consideration include the number of "tree saplings without bite marks," "number of felled trees," "lack of cow dung in adjacent areas" (i.e., to test for displacement of grazing to nearby areas), and absence of poaching in adjacent areas [92 p. 408–10]. Data on indicators selected have to be consistently collected and used to determine the amount of payments. Thus development of valid and reliable measures for judging the effectiveness of PES can be a difficult and possibly costly process.

With respect to hunting, Geist argues that commercialization of wildlife has failed in practice to conserve, contrasting the successes of public ownership of wildlife in the U.S. with failures in countries such as Germany that employ a commercialization approach [72 p. 48–66]. Geist argues that allowing markets for dead wildlife products harms conservation and makes enforcement costly and ineffective. Another critique of market approaches is that use of monetary incentives may undermine non-economic (e.g., complying with the norms of the community and "contributing to the common good") reasons for achieving conservation and thus result in less satisfaction and causing people to withdraw their previous voluntary efforts [93 p. 1605–7]. It is open to question whether economic incentive approaches are sustainable in poor developing countries because their success may depend on continuing contributions from non-governmental organizations (NGOs) and advanced industrial countries.

Oceans present special difficulties for preservation of species and market solutions. Overfishing has been combated by the establishment of quotas. Systems to allocate percentages of the total take to fishermen of the quota such as "individual transferable quotas" have been developed to implement a market-based approach to preserving fish [94]. These systems can be run by government, private companies, or "common property ownership systems" that must deal with problems such as "free riding" in which individuals fish without contributing to the costs of the regulatory system [95]. Such systems are likely to be more successful when certain situations exist such as the common area being small enough to monitor and assurance compliance with rules. For example, in Maine, "harbor gangs" enforce regulations, warning offenders and "molesting" their gear if they break rules [96]. Dolsak and Ostrom state that there is no consistent evidence that shows one of these three different types of regulation systems is superior to the others [95]. The question remains whether these market-based approaches can offset the negative effects that globalization of markets has had on endangered species. To summarize, there is no doubt that markets and economic incentives are a central factor in causing threats to wildlife. Market incentive policies may in some cases assist in preserving species but their effectiveness is a complex and contentious issue that I will explore in this book.

Implementation of Wildlife Conservation Policies

A third set of concepts for understanding wildlife politics concerns policy implementation. Although many countries have adopted ambitious laws with respect to protection of wildlife, these laws are often not effectively implemented. Public policy research shows that implementation of public programs has been a generic problem and is not peculiar to wildlife programs. Pressman and Wildavsky's study showed how difficult it was to implement economic development programs aimed at assisting low income persons in the United States [97]. They found that success depended on a complex series of steps, and failure often resulted. If aiding humans is so difficult, one might expect it to be even more difficult to implement policies that run counter to the interests of humans in favor of wildlife. Indeed, implementation failure has been a common outcome in wildlife conservation. For example, Rabinowitz says that the Sumatran rhino was well protected "on paper" but the existence of laws did not stop poaching or result in the prosecution of offenders [98 p. 486–7]. Lack of enforcement of laws concerning wildlife is a general theme for many countries and species such as Serengeti rhinos and elephants [99 p. 510], tigers in India [100 p. 82], and spectacled bears in Peru [101]. Consequently, wildlife legislation and regulations need to be examined concerning the degree to which they are implemented and enforced – "paper-only" policies are common. In this book, I analyze factors that affect the success of wildlife conservation policies. Recently, the USFWS is placing major emphasis on reaching agreements with private landowners (including extractive industries such as oil and gas companies) in return for not listing endangered species. The success of these agreements is based on the degree to which they are adhered to but critics charge that the agreements are often not public, that the land is private and not accessible to independent verification, and that compliance is not monitored. Likewise, payments for environmental services (PES) noted above are based on "conditionality" – payment is made only if the services are provided and hence PES "require monitoring and quantifying of the service as well as enforcement for noncompliance" [91 p. 5]. Thus analysis of implementation will grow even more important in both advanced countries like the United States and developing countries as they move to employ economic incentives and voluntary agreements for conservation. Chapter 3 will specifically focus on implementation issues.

Interest Groups, Institutions, Subgovernments, and Wildlife Politics

The fourth set of concepts are interrelated: interest groups, institutions, and subgovernments. The importance of people united by common "interests" was recognized by James Madison who tried to design a political system that would not be dominated by any particular faction. Interest groups are examples of organizations acting on behalf of their members who use their assets such as money, numbers, and public relations to gain favors from policymakers. Political scientists such as Arthur Bentley viewed public policy as the result of "balance of competing interests" [102 p. 11]. Over time, group theorists believed that "countervailing" interest groups would rise to act on behalf of unrepresented interests if they were adversely affected by existing interest groups. For example, Zeigler describes how smaller retailers pooled forces to fight the growing power of "chain stores" in the United States in the 1930s [102 p. 44]. By the 1970s, environmental and conservation groups represented "countervailing forces" to traditional interest that affect wildlife such as ranchers and farmers [103 p. 67]. It is important to note that the rise of countervailing groups does not necessarily result in a "balance of forces" and some interests may continue to be unrepresented [103 p. 58].

Interest groups sometimes are able to "join forces" with legislative committees and executive agencies to form "iron triangles" that research has shown to dominate many policy areas [104]. Later analyses of this process expanded the iron triangle concept to include a wider variety of actors and relabeled them as "subgovernments." One of the secrets to the successes of these subgovernments was their "monopoly of information" concerning the policy area [103 p. 71]. The rise of environmental and conservation groups during the 1960s and 1970s interfered with existing subgovernments that had dominated policies regarding national forests and public lands and challenged their monopoly of information [105 p. 58]. The rise of the environmental movement was accompanied by new laws protecting wildlife, new agencies (e.g., Environmental Protection Agency) to implement laws, and "increased judicial scrutiny of administrative actions" [105 p. 60]. Thus, while subgovernments continue to exist and exert important influence, they are now much more likely to face countervailing groups and hence public scrutiny.

Subgovernmental institutions are important determinants of wildlife conservation at both the Federal and state levels. For example, many wildlife supporters have attempted to reform the grazing of cattle on Federal lands that create problems for predators and other species through degradation of the environment but Western ranchers and agricultural interests dominate legislative committees that have oversight concerning these policies [106 p. 242–51]. One of the reasons for their dominance is that they were put into office with the financial support of energy and resource extraction industries so they control the House Committees on Interior and Insular Affairs [107 p. 207]. Many state wildlife commissions are dominated by hunting-fishing interests [108 p. 223]. and county commissions in states like Florida are dominated by developers [109 p. 142]. that fight wildlife protection proposals. Although many developing countries have "strongman" governments that are dominated by "personal politics," nevertheless Gibson found that institutions had a significant impact on wildlife policy in African countries [88]. In some cases such as Kenya, a strong president (Moi) was able to shift wildlife policy by appointing Richard Leakey to reorganize the state wildlife agency but Gibson cites several other cases of strongmen such as Mugabe of Zimbabwe who were unable to control wildlife policy due to the resistance of the parliament, state wildlife agencies, and local chiefs. Concerning interest groups in developing countries, the key forces in relation to wildlife issues tend to be international NGOs rather than domestic groups. Overall, both in the United States and other countries, it is crucial to study how interest groups and other institutions influence wildlife policies.

Coalitions, Compromises, Advocacy Coalition Framework, and Collaboration Mechanisms

Battles over wildlife politics involve complex alliances and struggles among interest groups. Until the 1960s, there was hardly any need for compromise because forces such as ranchers, extractive interests, development interests, and hunters dominated policy. Environmental interest groups were relatively small until the 1960s – for example, the Sierra Club had only about 15,000 members in 1960 but grew to 113,000 by 1970 [110 p. 97]. Groups like the Sierra Club and the Natural Resources Defense Council have been especially successful in mobilizing members (and raising funds) when they have confronted actions they view as unfriendly, especially during the Reagan and Bush Administrations [110 p. 99]. With the rise of the environmental movement, coalitions and compromise have become central to studying wildlife politics. In traditional politics over "bread-and-butter issues" (e.g., unions versus corporations), there is often a negotiation that concerns economic costs and benefits. However, studies of environmental groups have found that they are "purposive" organizations that do not conform to Mancur Olsen's theory that groups are rational and exist because they provide "selective benefits" to their members [111 p. 117, 121, & 137]. Rushefsky cites research that environmental groups were less likely to change their positions than groups with a "material" orientation. Interest group alliances in wildlife politics can be fluid [112 p. 295]. There has been much internal strife between long-time national groups like the Sierra Club and the Wilderness Society and newer groups (e.g., Alliance for Wild Rockies and Earth First!) with the latter pursuing "more ambitious" goals and less disposed to compromise [113]. Environmentalists and hunters are often at odds over protections for predators. For example, many hunters see the wolf as a competitor for caribou and moose and support aerial hunting and other measures to reduce wolf numbers, but hunters and fishermen often join with environmentalists to fight developers and corporations over the protection of habitat for wildlife [114]. Animal rights groups join environmentalists to support measures to protect wildlife including predators such as wolves but battle them over the attempt to kill and remove invasive species such as feral mouflon sheep in Hawaii while hunters supported the animal rights position because they like to hunt the sheep! [115]. In short, the line-up of forces in battles over wildlife varies by issue and is often unpredictable. There can be much more fluidity in wildlife policy advocacy coalitions than in most environmental politics.

One early form of coalition formation has been labeled as "co-optation," in which organizations bring outside elements, especially those that loom as potential threats, into policy decision-making bodies [116 p. 279]. The classic case was the Tennessee Valley Authority described by Phillip Selznick, in which the Authority incorporated members from the local communities into the decision-making process at the expense of achieving their goals fully [117]. Thomas describes the attempt of the Bureau of Land

Management (BLM) in San Joaquin Valley (California) to "co-opt" local county supervisors into a consortium to protect biodiversity in the region [116 p. 227–47]. However, in this case, although the county officials pretended to go along with the joint effort, they had decided to seek changes in the ESA rather than agree to a compromise plan. Co-optation represents an early form of what has become known as "collaborative management."

The Advocacy Coalition Framework (ACF) is useful for studying wildlife politics because it helps us understand the difficulty of achieving compromise. It holds that opposing coalitions involved in political struggles over policy issues are dominated by core beliefs that are stable [118]. For example, conservatives believe in the primacy of property rights and market incentives as requisites that should constrain attempts to protect wildlife. Conservationists place conservation of biodiversity as their top priority and encourage government efforts that will support this goal. ACF posits that coalition belief systems are "hierarchically structured," ranging from deep core beliefs that are almost "religious" in the fervor with which they are held, to "secondary belief systems" that are more susceptible to alteration due to learning through experiences which create "dissonance" [119 p. 484–6]. One of the strengths of the ACF is that it focuses on the possibility of change that can occur despite the attachments of coalition members to their beliefs. For example, despite disagreement on core beliefs, it is possible that opposing coalitions may agree on the desirability of certain goals like the maintenance of endangered species such as grizzlies and salmon. If agreement on such goals can be established, then opposing coalitions may propose alternative methods to achieve these desirable results and it then becomes possible for "learning" to take place by studying the effects of these alternative approaches. It is possible that the accumulation of scientific knowledge can provide a means for achieving consensus and progress in conserving wildlife.

ACF's emphasis on learning is particularly appropriate to wildlife politics because the ESA and other mandates such as those of international organizations like CITES and the International Whaling Commission are based on the idea that science should be relied upon to make policy decisions. Jenkins-Smith, Silva, Gupta, and Ripberger say that ACF has "had relatively little to say *a priori* about the substantive content, scope, and generality of these core beliefs, relying instead on case studies to tease them out" [119 p. 484]. Although ACF theory has been employed in the study of many environmental issues, it has not been used extensively to explore wildlife politics so this study will contribute to analyzing how useful the framework is, especially because wildlife conservation organizations tend to be "purposive" organizations that do not fit well into the models of economists like Olson. The ACF framework may be especially useful for analyzing wildlife policy because, beginning with the Clinton Administration, wildlife agencies at the Federal and state levels have sought to achieve compromise between opposed coalitions (e.g., farmers and ranchers vs. environmentalists and conservationists). These methods have been generally based on procedures that bring together advocates of opposing coalitions in a problem-solving framework. These "collaborations" may work by helping the opposed coalitions to achieve trust and eventually agreement through compromise. The "Quincy Library Group" in California was one such effort to preserve forest for spotted owls and it achieved some degree of success although only after a long-involved process [120]. In this book, I give extensive attention to the attempts to reach compromise. Compromise is difficult to achieve when the group's values are non-economic and "intrinsic" in nature – for example, one of the environmentalists who fought the opening of the Arctic National Wildlife Reserve to oil exploration explained that most people would never "never go to the refuge" but he would "get some peace of mind knowing that there is an area of naturalness on such a scale" [121].

The extreme difficulty in securing compromise in Congress over wildlife policy for the last forty years has caused Democratic administrations (i.e., Clinton and Obama) to seek devices to solve impasses between opposed coalitions. Klyza and Sousa have developed the concept of the "green state" to describe and help explain how a complex combination of conflicting laws, adversarial interest groups, and government institutions caught in the middle have created and sustained "gridlock" over environmental policymaking since the 1980s [122]. As a result of frustration with "excessive adversarialism" on the part of both pro- and anti-wildlife conservation coalitions, there arose a desire to find "common ground" through collaborative decision-making that was initiated by the Clinton Administration which wanted to escape the war "between environmentalists seeking more aggressive species protections ... and ascendant conservatives seeking to gut the ESA" [122 p. 81]. The goal of the Clinton Administration was to bring the opposing coalitions together in negotiations to reach "common ground" in the "radical center" and achieve a "Win-Win" result [123 p. 426]. The Clinton Administration achieved substantial success by creating 400 HCPs compared to only 14 that had been created between 1982 and 1992 [123 p. 385]. Both the Bush II and Obama Administrations have sought to continue this emphasis on collaboration, albeit with much less friendly (to wildlife) approaches during the Bush Administration. More radical organizations such as the Center for Biological Diversity (CBD) have opposed what they view as over eagerness on the part of national organizations to compromise. Consequently they have pursued aggressively litigation often contrary to the wishes of large mainstream environmental organizations like the Sierra Club and Audubon Society. Bevington has shown how CBD and similar radical environmental organizations have explicitly rejected the "insider strategy" employed by large nationals, and argues that their more "muscular" strategy forced stalemates overseen by the Federal courts that eventually did result in compromise but one much more favorable to environmentalists than if they had pursued a softer agreement without the threat of litigation [124 p. 179].

Klyza and Sousa contend that these collaborative methods exemplify what Theodore Lowi has referred to as "policy without law" that hands over public authority to private interests instead of incorporating "new ideology of collaboration and consensus into the [revised] laws" though they acknowledge that given the structure of political forces now the hopes for such a breakthrough are "dim" [122 p. 137, 381, & 424]. Consequently, policymakers seek ways around gridlock using vehicles such as administrative negotiations, Congressional riders, the Antiquities Act (which does not require Congressional approval) that can provide short-term achievements. However, policy changes made through these mechanisms can be overturned by subsequent presidential administrations or Federal courts, thus resulting in "unstable policy" because virtually "no decision is final" but can be challenged in other "venues" [122 p. 30]. The United States is not the only country to face gridlock on wildlife issues, as other Western democracies find it challenging to enact policies that preserve, for example, carnivores in a way that is satisfactory to farmers, ranchers, and landowners who must live with them. Consequently, a key focus is how governments and wildlife agencies attempt to solve "wicked problems" that have no easy solution.

Organizational Behavior and Wildlife Politics

Understanding how government agencies behave is crucial because the manner in which they implement policies can support or harm wildlife. Organizational theory offers insights that I use to study how wildlife agencies attempt to deal with their complex tasks and disparate "customers." One basic concern is how agencies interact with their "environments" such as the people they serve and/or regulate. Clarke and McCool point out that the job of natural resource agencies is regulatory in nature and they are saddled with the "thankless task" of imposing restrictions on "economic, political, and social activity" and thus tend to act timidly [125 p. 12]. By way of contrast, "politicians and bureaucrats love distributive policies" that work "in harmony with Congressional committees" to produce benefits for some favored interest" [126 p. 203]. This is how agencies such as BLM (e.g., handing out grazing rights to ranchers) and the U.S. Forest Service (give timber allocations to lumber companies) operated before the rise of environmentalism.

Organizations try to minimize uncertainty and threats to what they consider as their "core missions" [127]. For example, the Forest Service viewed providing logs to industry as a central goal. Thomas points out that when Judge Dwyer shut down the logging operations of the Forest Service over the spotted owl, it forced other agencies such as the BLM to protect "their autonomy" and change their behaviors by attempting to avoid threats to endangered species in areas they controlled [116 p. 240–1]. Thus agencies concerned with "clients" such as ranchers, extraction industries, and park visitors suddenly had to take into consideration needs of "non-commodity" species they had previously neglected [128 p. 236]. Another point made by Thomas is that agencies like the National Park Service and BLM are "multiple-use" agencies that have strong constituencies whose interests run counter to those of wildlife [116 p. 10]. According to Thomas, even the USFWS tries to "generate political support" for its Wildlife Refuges by permitting "competing usages" including grazing and recreation [116 p. 15].

Agencies vested with protecting wildlife such as USFWS are now often forced to act as a regulatory agency and have to give bad news to powerful groups such as cutbacks in grazing, lumber allocations, or restrictions on how farmers and ranchers manage their farms or herds [129 p. 230]. It is perhaps understandable that these agencies behave "timidly." A good example of timid behavior, according to Allin, is how the Forest Service implemented the 1964 Wilderness Act by making the "least possible change" [78 p. 144]. New or weak agencies that exist in threatening environments have often sought the support of powerful interests they are supposed to regulate [120]. For example, Michael J. Robinson labeled the agency that has had several names but is now known as "Wildlife Services" and resides in the Department of Agriculture responsible for killing "undesirable predators," such as wolves and coyotes, a "predatory agency" [130]. He details how it developed a constituency in the West by exterminating predators that bothered ranchers. Thus this agency operated with strong political and virtually unchallenged support from farmers and ranchers for decades. However, the rise of the environmental movement created an entirely new set of interest groups that fought against consumptive uses of wildlife. As a result, agencies such as BLM now often have to position themselves as "intermediaries" between environmentalists and traditional users of their services, giving them some leeway in selecting policy options [129 p. 244]. McFarland hypothesizes that the existence of countervailing power "enhances agency autonomy" and also may encourage greater professionalism and the "impartial enforcement of standards" [103 p. 67–8]. Today, it is necessary to study the agencies' behaviors in order to determine the relative strength of these different groups and how they affect policy regarding wildlife [131]. Weakness of agencies in charge of wildlife conservation is a worldwide phenomenon. For example, Saberwal and Rangarajan state that the Indian Forest Department and the Ministry of Environment and Forest have been "consistently weak players within the Indian bureaucracy" and lack "clout to oppose development projects" [132 p. 18]. Saberwal says that in conflicts with the more powerful [Indian] Revenue Department, the Forest Department was denied the authority to enforce bans on people from entering protected areas [133 p. 245].

A major limitation is that wildlife agencies such as the USFWS and agencies with similar functions in other countries have relatively few resources compared to the enormous tasks they are supposed to achieve and the powerful interest groups they must deal with [134 p. 104]. The sources of funding of agencies have a big impact on their behavior. In the United States, many agencies overseeing wildlife derive a majority of their funds from taxes and fees on hunters and anglers which greatly affects their approach to wildlife conservation [135]. These traditional interest groups have sometimes opposed attempts to broaden support such as tax checkoff systems because they fear this change would give "non-consumptive users" (e.g., animal rights groups) power over the agencies. For developing countries such as Kenya, the interests that most affect governmental wildlife agencies are often external, such as Western NGOs (e.g., WWF) and organizations involved in tourism since they make major contributions to the economies and wildlife agencies in these countries [88 p. 156]. In short, it is important to study the web of interests that attempt to influence agencies and how they respond to conflicting demands.

Federalism

For the United States and other democratic nations, federalism is a crucial factor that affects wildlife politics. A nation's division of power between its central and other governments plays an important role in the politics of wildlife. Fights between interest groups often involve attempts to overcome defeats at one level of government by pursuing interests at another. For example, when large-scale chain stores arose in the 1930s, independent retailers sought relief at the state level by successfully passing "special taxes on chain stores" and they were initially successful because of "home town sentiment" at the state level against "foreign big businesses" [102 p. 44–6]. Later on, when the chain stores counterattacked successfully in some states, the retail stores sought Federal legislation but found that they did not have the resources to match the chains at the national level and the chains recruited other interest groups (e.g., the American Farm Bureau) to support their position [102].

Many of the major battles over wildlife issues in the United States have pitted the Federal government's Fish and Wildlife Service (USFWS) against state and local governments. For example, according to Yaffee, Wyoming "repeatedly downplayed" the danger to black-footed ferrets because of the strength of local ranching and agricultural interests that viewed the species as a nuisance [136]. Yaffee goes on to say that the USFWS took a position of trying to "avoid controversy" by delaying listing decisions. Clark concluded that the USFWS passed along the responsibility for the ferrets to the Wyoming Fish and Game Department, which provided money to the state's Department of Agriculture to poison "pests" near the ferret area [137]. Yaffee also concludes that the existence of overlapping state and Federal agencies can lead to "fragmentation of authority" in which no agency is willing to take the responsibility for making politically sensitive decisions [134 p. 337]. A recurring theme in wildlife politics policy concerns the fight over the venue for decision-making. Often environmentalists want to "nationalize" issues because they believe the national agencies and courts are more favorable to them than many state and local courts [138 p. 40]. Opponents of wildlife protection measures generally prefer state and local controls. Federal–state relations are especially prominent in Western states because, as Cawley and Freemuth point out, about 46 percent of 12 Western states (excluding Hawaii) are owned by the Federal government compared to only 4 percent in the remainder of the states [139 p. 69]. In short, Federalism looms large in wildlife politics in the United States and other countries.

The Courts and Wildlife Politics

In the United States, the Federal courts have played a central role in interpretation of the ESA. The ESA is an act that contains such strong language that it has been referred to as a "macho law" and allows environmentalists to bring lawsuits to force implementation that is favorable to their interpretation [140]. The power of the courts is well illustrated in the twists and turns of policy on wolves. In 2007 and 2008, the USFWS delisted wolves in the Western Great Lakes and Northern Rockies but was forced to relist the wolves by Federal courts in 2008 [79 p. 12–13]. Martin Nie states that the so-called iron triangle dominated by Congressional committees, interest groups, and agency staff has been replaced by a judicial iron triangle in regard to public lands management [141]. In a study comparing U.S. and Canadian environmental policies, VanNijnatten says that "litigative avenues have provided interest groups with formidable means to influence public policy" as a major reason why interest groups in the United States play a stronger role in environmental policy [142 p. 269–70]. Courts have played an especially important role over wildlife policy in the United States but they remain significant in many other countries, especially as to how seriously they enforce penalties for violations of wildlife protection laws.

Conservatives have long complained about the oppressive effects of ESA that pay no consideration to the burdens put on individuals to conserve species. A basic question concerns how important is the strong prohibitory language of the ESA to protecting species [143]. Above, I pointed out that the USFWS is understaffed and perceived as a weak agency, but environmental activists such as the CBD have been willing and able to use the ESA to challenge powerful economic and political interests without the direct participation of the USFWS. Thomas conducted case studies on collaborative efforts to preserve biodiversity in California and concluded that reliance on voluntary efforts of private (and public) organizations was "invalid" – that only the regulatory threat of listing provided the "necessary incentive for participation" [116 p. 193–219]. In short, although great emphasis is now placed on collaboration, the threat of Federal court action based on the ESA lies at the heart of many of actions to preserve wildlife in the United States.

Forces for Change: Elections and Learning

Over the long term, forces such as population growth, changes in human customs and attitudes, and urbanization that are largely outside the control of government bring about important change that can protect or threaten wildlife. Thus it instructive to look at what forces can effect changes in the status quo and bring about policy change that is potentially within the control of policymakers. Elections such as Reagan's 1984 victory can bring about important change in the leadership of agencies like the Department of Interior and the U.S. Fish and Wildlife Service that develop, implement, and monitor wildlife policies [144 p. 81]. Hoberg details the huge change in the major Congressional committee with oversight over public lands due to the Republican takeover after the 1994 election [105 p. 64–5]. The average "League of Conservation scores" (0 represents anti-environmental votes, 100 pro-environmental votes) for the five committees overseeing wildlife policies dropped from 75 percent to 3 percent as a result of that election [105 p. 65]. The ESA law has not been reauthorized since 1992, but nevertheless change in administrations has had a great impact on agency behaviors. The number of new listings of endangered species has been much lower in the Reagan and Bush (both Bushes) Administrations than in the Clinton and Obama Administrations and those that occurred during the former were often due to court cases brought by environmental organizations. Inaction by presidential administrations can cancel out rules that have been negotiated such as Clinton's "roadless rule" – the Bush Administration chose not to defend it in courts [122 p. 122]. Such deadlocks are not only common in the United States, but occur in many other countries. The Antiquities Act has allowed presidents since Theodore Roosevelt to set aside huge areas for conservation without the need for Congressional approval, and these actions are often taken at the end of a president's term right before elections. To sum, elections can have major impacts on wildlife policies.

ACF theory posits that science is a major mechanism for "policy learning" that may change policy options considered by opposing coalitions even if it does not result in modification of their underlying values. Wildlife policy is the perfect vehicle for testing the impact of science on policy learning because the ESA and other laws explicitly state that policies should be based on the "best available science." Thus many hope that science will facilitate compromise that can produce "win-win" solutions that achieve conservation measures but also minimize costs to humans. Learning also can bring about changes in customs and beliefs of the general public through educational efforts by government and media. For example, many governments have attempted to reduce demands for products made from species such as elephants and tigers. In this book, I devote attention to the role of science and learning in regard to wildlife politics.

"New" versus Traditional Conservation

A major controversy in the conservation area today is the dispute between "new conservationists" and traditional conservationists concerning the best way to conserve biodiversity. Led by Peter Kareiva, the lead scientist for The Nature Conservancy, the new conservation movement has disputed many accepted "postulates" of traditional conservation such as the need to focus efforts on protected areas, holding that "pristine nature does not exist" and asserting that more attention needs to be given to "areas that have been and that will likely continue to be affected by human activities" [145 p. 964–5]. Moreover, they cite evidence from Gallup polls that a much smaller percentage of the public support the environment compared to economic activities than was the case in the past when major environmental laws were passed. They also critique traditional conservation's reliance on "doomsday" predictions despite the evidence that nature is actually "resilient" to harmful effects of humanity. They argue that, rather than relying on arguments about the "intrinsic value" of nature, conservationists need to give more attention to how conservation can help humans and work with corporations if they are to win needed political and societal support for conservation. They conclude that the new conservation by "embracing development and advancing human well-being will almost certainly not be the conservation that was imagined in its early days" but "it will be more effective and far more broadly supported, in boardrooms and political chambers" [146]. New conservationists also tend to have a strong belief in "technology enthusiasm" that will allow us to "resolve problems well in advance of the doom we are prone to see" [147 p. 47]. Traditional conservationists respond that "the intrinsic value argument has not failed conservation" but "it is conservationists' failure to organize enough people willing to act on behalf of biodiversity that has limited realization of conservation goals" [148 p. 33]. Johns argues that it is often difficult to prove the benefits of nature and consequently intrinsic values need to be emphasized along with political pressure to protect the interests of wildlife. In short, one of the core differences between the two groups concerns politics – what strategy is most effective at encouraging preservation of wildlife and biodiversity? To what extent can conservation be motivated by intrinsic values or should more emphasis be placed on the utilitarian value created by wildlife? Will this divide among the conservation coalition weaken their political efficacy? These are some of the questions addressed by this book.

Literature on Politics and Wildlife

There are relatively few works that have focused specifically on political issues related to wildlife. Political science and public policy researchers have focused most of their attention on "environmental politics" that directly affect humans, such as clean air and water policy as well as energy policy. For example, wildlife issues and the ESA are not even mentioned in standard public policy texts such as those of James Anderson [149]. and Thomas Dye [150]. and generally occupy only a small portion of books on environmental politics [110]. Soulé cites Dave Foreman's distinction between the "goals of environmentalism" that are "anthropocentric," aimed at the "health and welfare of people," and those of conservationism that are "biocentric or ecocentric" [151 p. 74]. An exception is the work of Klyza and Sousa who have provided an explanation for gridlock in wildlife conservation policy and its implications [122]. Another exception is Douglas Bevington's work that explores what he calls "grassroots activist" organizations like the CBD that have challenged the insider approach of large national environmental organizations and have successfully employed a "sue the bastards" approach [124]. There are many works that discuss politics and wildlife in regard to certain topics such as the ESA. For example, there are books describing the effects of the ESA such as Goble, Scott and Davis's *The Endangered Species Act at thirty* [152] that contains a chapter on how politics influenced decisions to list or not list species [153]. There have been books on the contentious politics that pertain to efforts to reestablish or protect certain charismatic species like wolves [154], whales and elephants [155], and tigers [156]. Nie is also among those who have contributed to understanding the role of institutions such as state wildlife commissions to wildlife policy [157]. Some research has examined legal aspects of the ESA, such as Doremus and Tarlock's *Water war in the Klamath Basin: Macho law, combat biology, and dirty politics*, which also contributes to an understanding of how science interacts with politics in wildlife policy [140]. Research by Michael Manfredo and others has analyzed how public attitudes and ballots have influenced wildlife policy [40]. There have been fascinating case studies of legal and political conflicts over species such as the snail darter [134]. and spotted owl [158] that demonstrate the key role of politics in the outcomes. There is also a literature that discusses political aspects of wildlife policy in developing countries such as Fred Nelson's *Community rights, conservation and contested land: The politics of natural resource governance in Africa* [159], and Clark Gibson's *Politicians and poachers: The political economy of wildlife policy in Africa* [88], that bring out the difficulties of preserving species in countries where the poor predominate. There have been books devoted to international aspects of wildlife politics such as Duffy's *Nature crime: How we're getting conservation wrong* [160]. There have been a few (though not nearly enough) accounts by politicians who have played an active role in wildlife policy struggles such as those by Bruce Babbitt [161], the head of the U.S. Department of Interior during the Clinton Administration, and Richard Leakey [162], who took over Kenya's wildlife agency in 1989. I have drawn on a large literature of academic research on conservation biology (and related areas) in which wildlife politics plays a significant role. Despite the existence of these valuable sources, few academic books and articles focus specifically on wildlife politics and of necessity I have drawn heavily on periodicals (e.g., publications of the Audubon Society and High Country News) and other sources that report on conflicts over wildlife policy that do not appear in academic literature. Of course, these publications may have biases and I have taken pains in each case to present alternative viewpoints and focus on factual accounts – the reader is provided with links to the specific articles to make their own assessments.

This is the first work to attempt to focus on wildlife politics throughout the world. Although the most information is available for wildlife politics in the United States and thus the majority of the book pertains to the United States, this book contains discussions of the impact of wildlife on politics of more than sixty countries worldwide, including chapters on comparative and international aspects. One major theme is that wildlife politics engenders strong human passions and due to the intensity and unpredictability of coalitions over these issues, these politics are fascinating and worthy of analysis. For example, there are many attempts to preserve forests but when proponents are able to associate it with the preservation of a species, there is an added emotional impact – both positive and negative (e.g., the ridicule associate with the attempt to protect the snail darter). In short, I argue that wildlife politics is a significant aspect of politics that has not received the attention that it deserves.

Conclusion

Politics involving decisions about wildlife are important not only in the United States but throughout the world. Although wildlife politics are significantly affected by traditional political divisions such as conservative–liberal differences, the strong attachments (and sometimes antipathies) that humans feel for animals have resulted in a politics of wildlife that is complex and often unpredictable, and thoroughly worthy of study that will be pursued in this book. Sanderson has bemoaned the fact that conservationists have tried to lead "the political load of conservation by themselves" and that conservation gains "have come without much help" from "political science" [163 p. 470]. I hope that this book will contribute to understanding the politics of wildlife and thus assist in conserving species. This book is an exploratory effort aimed at identifying a significant subgenre of environmental politics.

In the sections above, I have shown that wildlife policy is affected by a variety of forces that are slow to change and, indeed, may be beyond the control of government. Nevertheless, individuals, parties, and interest groups have succeeded in passing and implementing laws that do affect wildlife. One of the aims of this book is to focus on the dynamics of wildlife politics and, in particular, to identify the variables that lead to change or reinforce the status quo. I employ the ten sets of concepts and frameworks outlined above, drawn from the study of political science and public policymaking, that are helpful in explaining different aspects of wildlife politics.

Plan for the Book

Chapter 2 examines the role of science in wildlife policymaking. Perhaps more than any other policy area, the major legislation and international treaties on wildlife mandate the use of the best available science. Thus it is appropriate to begin the book with a look at the extent to which science has been able to bring about change and resolve contentious wildlife conservation issues. Chapter 3 focuses on the challenge of implementing policies because wildlife policies have often not been implemented effectively. Hence I find it useful to clarify at the beginning the difficult problems faced by those who try to design policies that will be effective. Chapter 4 studies the forces behind the passage of legislation in the United States, with a particular focus on the ESA because of its immense importance. In addition, I study in detail the opposing coalitions that exist in wildlife politics and the difficulties faced in trying to achieve some sort of middle ground compromise. Chapter 5 reveals how humans have strong emotional ties to charismatic wildlife that have been the source of many of the most bitter and long-lived wildlife politics. One of the major themes of this book is that this strong emotional involvement justifies the treatment of wildlife politics as an important subgenre of environmental concerns. Chapter 6 analyzes in depth the effects of the ESA, the centerpiece of U.S. wildlife politics, and one of the most contentious laws over the past forty years, including the controversies over how to evaluate its impacts. Chapter 7 undertakes comparisons of wildlife politics, including differences among developed nations and the evolution of wildlife politics in developing nations. Particular emphasis is given to the difficulties of preserving wildlife without adversely affecting poor populations in native countries through mechanisms such as CBNRM. Chapter 8 studies the international aspects of wildlife, including the attempts to prevent illegal trafficking and overexploitation of wildlife. Chapter 9 explores the evolving values and ethical systems with which humans have viewed wildlife, including contentious issues over "invasive species" and what rights should be extended to them. Chapters 10 and 11 concern hunting and ecotourism respectively, two of the major ways in which humans derive utility from wildlife. Both help to stimulate efforts to preserve wildlife but also can cause them damage. Chapter 12 reviews findings and examines the status of the wildlife conservation coalition today.

2 Science and the Protection of Wildlife

Science is the major vehicle for "policy learning," in which objective information can contribute to a better understanding of policies affecting wildlife. Science can create the potential for advancement in policy debates between opposing coalitions [1]. For example, if these coalitions can come to agreement on some goal such as the need to preserve a species, then empirical data may be gathered to test alternative ways of achieving this goal so as to meet the objectives of the wildlife conservation coalition while minimizing cost to groups such as ranchers, farmers, hunters, and extractive industries. Science has played an especially crucial role in wildlife conservation policy because many of the major laws, such as the Endangered Species Act (ESA) and Marine Mammal Protection Act, require that critical activities such as the listing of endangered species be based on the "best available" science [2 p. 89–90]. Furthermore, members of conservation organizations have often used science as the basis of lawsuits protecting endangered species like wolves [3 p. 136]. At the same time, developers and property rights advocates have criticized what they call "junk science" used by conservation organizations and have demanded that regulatory decisions be made only on the basis of "sound science" [4]. Below I explore the role that science has played in the development of wildlife policy.

Scientific Explanations

The essence of scientific information, as used here, refers to information gathered using methods that are public and open to be tested by persons other than the original "investigators." Thus science stands in contrast to purely subjective information that is the "property" of those who "possess" it. The results from scientific studies often disagree with the perceptions of non-scientists based on their personal experiences. For example, a scientist-constructed model based on sources of data from catch records and research trawlers found a shortage of cod off Massachusetts, while at that same time fishermen claimed they were seeing more cod than they had in years [5]. Similarly, the head of the Maine Lobstermen's Association, in the face of restrictions, claimed that "lobsters have been making damned fools out of scientists" [6 p. 16]. In the cod case, scientists responded that catching fish does not mean that the population of fish is large, but rather that fishermen may just be more efficient at taking the few fish that remain [5]. Sutherland and Gill report that cod have a "wide range of densities" and that fishermen did not notice a problem because their fishing was "concentrated in the most . . . high density aggregations" [7 p. 264]. Moreover, scientists say that population drops can occur unexpectedly and rapidly (the "Allee effect") which refers to the "decline in survival rate" that occurs in smaller populations due to a number of "behavioral factors" such as inability to find mates and less vigilance from predators due to smaller numbers [7 p. 264]. Another example is the distrust that livestock farmers have for official figures gathered about wolves killing livestock – the farmers do not believe governmentally collected information [3 p. 106]. Distrust of data that conflict with personal perceptions is common in many situations. For example, the head of the Colorado Wildlife Commission refused to believe survey results that showed that a substantial proportion of Coloradans opposed hunting, saying that "People in Colorado . . . love hunting" [8 p. 192]. In the Yukon, Clark, Workman, and Slocombe reported that there grew two competing "narratives" on the number of grizzly bears – the Yukon government's estimates said they were declining by 3 percent a year, though with "wide point estimates" due to the difficulty of counting them, but the local populace perceived there to be an abundance of the bears and thought that the government results had been obtained by "questionable methods" [9 p. 114]. Although both the government and local populace believed in the "motherhood" goal of continued grizzly-bear existence, the attempt to build a compromise floundered because the "devil was in the details" and disagreement on the data made it impossible to build a consensus [9 p. 117]. Zac Unger, author of a book on polar bears, cites personal accounts to challenge alarm over threats to polar bears from climate change, and, though he admits that "management decisions must be driven by scientific data," he goes on to say that "the experience of people who know bears best can't be entirely discounted," and that he "found that people who actually live in polar-bear country say, by a wide margin, that they're seeing more bears than ever before" [10]. Another example is disagreement concerning the size of habitat required to protect species. Scientists, including those who support the hunting of wolves, argue that Alaska's harsh environment means that it requires far more acreage to support predators and prey than in "more productive" land in the lower forty-eight states [11]. But Nash cites a member of the Alaskan Independence Party stating that anyone who says that "the ecology [of Alaska] is fragile is an ignoramus or a goddamn liar" [12 p. 274]. Bjerke, Retan, and Kellert found that the impact of giving scientific information about the number of wolves was small in Norway and that, although the information did have a general impact on attitudes of a majority of people, those with negative attitudes were skeptical and resisted the scientific information and thus the authors conclude that scientific information alone is insufficient to change beliefs [13]. Ames says that wolves travel far and wide in their foraging and thus they can create the perception that "wolves are everywhere" in the minds of locals who are actually seeing the same wolves "in different locations" [14 p. 110]. In short, sharp differences are common between the views of scientists and people who live among wildlife.

Disagreements over science have bedeviled the development of habitat conservation plans (HCPs) created under the ESA. For example, Alagona and Pincetl describe how the attempt to develop the Coachella Valley Multiple Species Habitat Conservation Plan got dragged out for more than a decade because of disagreements over science between a "homegrown Scientific Advisory Committee" and officials from the USFWS who felt that the local planners had not "adequately incorporated ... the principles of conservation into their plan" [15 p. 7]. Alagona and Pincetl conclude their case study by stating that "there is no universal ideal of 'sound science'" but that it requires a "negotiated agreement" among parties and "requires mutual trust and effective communication" that were lacking in this case [15]. Klyza and Sousa point out that a large number of scientists protested the "no surprises" rule adopted by the Clinton Administration that guaranteed that no changes would have to be made for very long time periods (e.g., fifty years) even if new science showed threats [16]. They point out that this rule was not based on "science" but was "a political necessity" for landowners to have an incentive to participate in HCPs [16 p. 186]. Disagreements over wildlife science occur throughout the world. For example, in Sweden, officials recently resumed wolf hunts that were to be targeted on the "most inbred" wolves with the argument that this was a "conservation measure" that could be effective in the short run but Chapron, Lopenz-Bao, Kjellander, and Karlsson claim it was a "misuse of science" because only immigration (of outside wolves) would solve the problem of inbreeding [17 p. 1521].

The development of a "collaborative approach" to solving environmental–wildlife issues that became popular during the Clinton Administration has often conflicted with the "strict definition" of science. For example, Edward Weber says that though the new collaborationists do not advocate "an outright rejection of science," they demand that "practical knowledge" be acknowledged as a "legitimate claimant" to defining the public interest and helping to "correct for the nondemocratic bias of the ... bureaucratic expertise model" [18 p. 250]. Furthermore, Brick and Weber say that "collaboratives are also less certain that scientific information can or should be insulated from the political arbitration of conflicting values" but believe that we must "integrate scientific knowledge and technical expertise with local knowledge, a community perspective, and local talents" [19 p. 19]. Thus, while "the best available science" dominates the ESA and Federal courts' approaches to wildlife conservation, emphasis on compromise and collaboration often conflict with this priority.

Disagreements Among Researchers

If consensus can be obtained among most, if not all, wildlife researchers, then this consensus can be a powerful source for change in wildlife conservation policy. However, there is often disagreement among wildlife researchers. For example, three researchers who are employees of the Alaska Department of Fish and Game, Boertje, Keech, and Paragi, published a study in the *Journal of Wildlife Management* with data to show that wolves and bears in Alaska kill healthy prey in significant numbers and thus lessen the number of moose available for human hunters [11]. By way of contrast, opponents of wolf-hunting have often argued that wolves take old and unhealthy prey and thus conservationists contend that wolves perform a useful function for their prey populations. Scientists have found that it is difficult to measure the impact of predators on the population size of their prey for several reasons, including the probability that the prey may have died anyway due to other reasons such as disease or starvation – thus they could be part of what ecologists called the "doomed surplus" [20 p. 172]. Also, some prey such as mallard ducks "compensate" for predation by "renesting" several times if necessary [20 p. 172]. Boertje and his colleagues maintain that their own and other empirical studies demonstrate that reducing the number of predators has a beneficial impact on the number of moose available to hunt and does not endanger the predator population. Furthermore, Boertje et al. note there is an Alaskan state legislative mandate to boost harvests of moose and thus predator control such as aerial wolf hunts are justified [11]. They claim that Alaskan predator control policy is based on a "balanced" policymaking system. In a 2007 issue of the Journal of Wildlife Management, researchers similarly challenged the long-held assumption that there high degree of competition between prairie dogs and livestock, arguing that the degree of competition between the two species was "highly situational" and thus concluding that prairie dogs populations should not be kept too low to perform their ecological function [21]. Miller, Schoen, Faro, and Klein argue that the 1994 Alaskan statute to reduce predators has resulted in "politically-driven," not scientific, management and research [22 p. 1250]. In short, opposing sides concerning the conflict between species such as bears and wolves versus moose or prairie dogs versus cattle claim science supports their positions.

It is even possible for the same scientific study to be used by both environmentalists and their skeptics to support opposed positions. For example, a 2012 study showed that polar bears have existed for five times longer than has previously been thought to be the case [23]. Skeptics about the supposed bad effects of climate change on polar bears pointed out that the finding shows that the bears have survived previous warming periods and thus throws doubt on the need to view the bears as being threatened by global warming [23]. But conservationists argue that this research also shows that previous warming periods were slower to develop than previously thought and thus it shows bears had longer to adapt to these changes [23]. Scientific disputes related to the climate issue are at the heart of other debates such as "ocean acidification," with some scientists arguing that increased acidification due to increased carbon emissions threatens sea species such as oysters [24]. Another controversy concerns whether decreasing native vegetation due to the greater area covered by monoculture farming is causing the decline in species such as monarchs and honey bees [25]. These controversies over climate, ocean acidification, and the effects of decrease in native culture help to demonstrate the increasingly important role that science will play in future political struggles over the preservation of wildlife.

Science is often at the heart of Federal lawsuits over controversial species such as wolves. The national Farm Bureau and its western affiliates such as the Wyoming Farm Bureau brought suit against the reintroduction of gray wolves (transferred from Canada) to the Yellowstone area, arguing that it would doom the Rocky Mountain subspecies of wolf (*canis irremotus*) to extinction, thus violating the ESA; they originally had some support from some environmental organizations such as the National Audubon Society [26 p. 147 & 217]. But by 1986, the National Audubon Society switched sides and joined the USFWS and other environmental organizations in opposing the lawsuit to outlaw the introduction of the Canadian wolves because they contended (and ultimately the courts agreed) that there was no solid evidence of a continuous breeding population of the *canis irremotus* existing on a continuous basis. Environmentalists viewed the lawsuit to outlaw the introduction of the Canadian wolves in order to save a hypothetical still-existing Rocky Mountain subspecies as a cynical attempt to use science to prevent or long delay the establishment of any significant wolf population in the region.

Science and the Dispute Between New and Traditional Conservationists

One of the sharpest current debates over science in the conservation area is not between conservationists and their historical opponents such as developers, extractive industries, and ranchers but among conservationists themselves. Recently, the "new conservation movement" has challenged some tenets of conservation biology. The new conservationists contend that all baselines are arbitrary and artificial – for example, there is nothing sacred about the time that Europeans invaded an area [27 p. 24–5]. Likewise, they cite evidence that humanity has touched all areas and that there are no purely "pristine" areas and that land can be managed to "make more nature" and "better, not just less bad" and also asserts that exotic introduced species can enhance biodiversity – not necessarily harm it [27 p. 56 & 109]. "Traditional conservationists" have responded to these arguments by critiquing the reductionism of new conservationists by noting that there are "degrees of wildness" such as the "difference between the City of Los Angeles and the Arctic National Wildlife Reserve" [28 p. 169]. Similarly, Johns says that the Wilderness Act's definition refers to wilderness as "untrammeled" but "not necessarily pristine" [29 p. 34–5]. Foreman [30 p. 123]. and others claim that the new conservation movement, by arguing that there is no pristine environment, is undermining the ESA and support for the use of protected areas to redirect natural resources to "more humanitarian" goals [31 p. 76]. The debate between new and traditional conservationists extends to scientific interpretations of environmental history. New conservationists point to evidence that there were millions of people in the pre-Columbian Americas and they affected and helped to structure nature in the Americas so that all of even so-called pristine areas of nature are really "cultivated, man-made" [27 p. 70–1]. But Foreman argues that there is a huge difference between 2 million people and the current population of 300 million, and cites research that contends there is no way this historical population spread sparsely over the entire continent armed with primitive tools could have "domesticated the whole continent" [30 p. 117]. There is also disagreement between the two groups on how resilient nature is to the harmful effects of humanity. For example, new conservationists point to the recovery of cod off the coast of Newfoundland from the effects of overfishing as an example of such resilience, and criticize conservationists' use of "environmental apocalypse" alarms for political purposes [32 p. 155]. Locke counters with evidence that cod in the greater Newfoundland area have not rebounded and their numbers remain "a shadow of what they were" [32 p. 155]. Still another point of disagreement concerns the ecological effects of invasive species. It is the contention of traditional conservationists that "non-native species" are "driving biodiversity loss ... and a host of other ecological disruptions"; though they acknowledge that some may have "positive conservation effects," they warn that others could have "disproportionately large effects" [33 p. 884]. They warn that those species that appear innocuous for decades may eventually become harmful perhaps in "subtle" ways "but nonetheless great, and remain unrecognized until damage is incurred and containment is impossible" [33 p. 884]. By way of contrast, Schlaepfer, Sax, and Oldens point to several cases of non-native species "contributing to the achievement of conservation objectives" and they argue that many scientists are biased against non-natives and automatically count them as negatives with respect to biodiversity; they also critique the use of "military language" such as "war on invasives" [34 p. 429]. Schlaepfer et al. point to invasives' positive functions such as "substituting for extinct" species, and use the example of "Aldabra giant tortoises ... introduced to several small islands surrounding Mauritius" to replace extinct native tortoises [34 p. 430–1]. In addition, new conservationists argue that introduced species can provide "food and shelter" for natives species. In contrast, Ricciardi and Simberloff warn that "invasion science has not developed a predictive capacity sufficient to engage in frequent introductions without harming biodiversity and ecosystems" and thus contend that we should err on the side of caution to avoid "unanticipated consequences" [33 p. 884]. Schlaepfer et al. acknowledge that underlying the dispute is a difference in values, with traditionalists putting their "premium on the integrity of native ecosystems" while others "value the ecosystem function provided by a non-native species" [34 p. 434]. Another example of a dispute within the conservation coalition concerns the National Park Service over grizzly bears in Yellowstone. John and Frank Craighead, well-known grizzly bear researchers, criticized the National Park Service decision to stop abruptly feeding bears in Yellowstone, arguing that it should be done over a period of ten years [35 p. 21]. Alston Chase, in a book titled *Playing God in Yellowstone*, argues that "believing garbage is artificial" is not "a scientific hypothesis but a cultural bias" [36 p. 177]. Chase goes on to say that ancient nomadic people just left their garbage behind and that "intervention" is needed for these animals to exist because they are trying to exist in an area that is a fraction of the size they used to occupy. In short, disputes over science occur within coalitions as well as between them.

Underlying Goals and Values

There is agreement that key decisions in the policymaking process concerning preservation of wildlife are of necessity based on values that are not subject to scientific research. For example, Doremus [4 p. 438] and Vucetich, Nelson, and Phillips [37] say that a goal such as whether to restore the wolf to its full historical range or just maintain it in the few areas that it now resides is a value question that science cannot answer. More recently, Vucetich and Nelson express alarm at the decision by USFWS to provide ESA protections "only if a species is at risk of extinction in a vital ... portion of its range where its loss would put the entire species at risk of extinction" [38]. The "range" referred to is now considered to be "its current range," not its historical range [38]. This interpretation is crucial with respect to species such as wolves which currently occupy only 15 percent of their historical range. The USFWS defended their proposal to delist the gray wolf in the entire forty-eight lower states with the following rationale [39]:

The ESA does not require us to restore the gray wolf (or any other species) to all of its historical range or even to a majority of the currently suitable habitat … The Service's role in wolf management is limited to the authorities under the ESA, which directs us to ensure that the gray wolf is no longer in danger of extinction.

Vucetich and Nelson argue that this interpretation amounts to limiting the purpose of the ESA to "keeping the minimum number of species" to survive rather than broader goals such as restore ecosystems and "mitigating harm" to species like wolves that had been extirpated [38]. They point out that the USFWS argues that their interpretation is "reasonable" but it also admits that "there is no single best interpretation." Underlying the entire ESA law is the basic value presumption that species should be preserved and that this goal should have a very high priority, though the law does not assist in determining how widely a species such as wolves should be restored in the United States. Disputes over science and politics also occur in other countries. For example, in India, there was a debate over culling of elephants and lions. Saberwal and Rangarajan say that "the decision as to whether to cull them is a political decision," but they argue that biological science can identify which animals to cull because in both cases much of the damage is caused by a small group of males [40 p. 7]. In short, despite the fact that conservation legislation requires that the best available science be employed in making decisions, the interpretation of the goals of the laws are in the hands of policymakers – not scientists.

Another aspect that is subject to debate concerns the baselines that are to be used to set goals for restoration of species as these can have a big effect on the numbers and range of the species to be preserved [2 p. 148]. "Scientific goals" are clearly influenced by the pragmatics of the political context of a decision. For example, the decision to delist wolves as endangered species in the Yellowstone area involved tradeoffs by the USFWS in deciding what numbers to use as a recovery goal. The USFWS scientists discuss their reasoning in their Final Environmental Impact Statement [41 appendix 9, p. 38–40]. They state that a goal of a minimum of 50 wolves (thus suggesting a range between 46 and 150 wolves) would be required to ensure short-term population viability but that an estimate of 500 wolves was required for long-term viability [41 appendix 9, p. 38]. The report proceeds to state that "finding an area to support 500 wolves in the lower 48 is unlikely" as this "would equate to a population in the thousands" [41 appendix 9, p. 40]. By way of contrast, the minimum number of fifty was already accommodated by the number thought to exist in the Yellowstone ecosystem at the time and consequently this was selected as the recovery goal. Disagreement over goals led the Arizona representative, Jim Heffelfinger, to resign from the Mexican Wolf Science and Planning Committee in 2012 [42]. Heffelfinger and the Arizona Department of Game and Fish Department said that the number of wolves proposed by the committee "exceeds the number for wolves to no longer be in danger" and referenced "divergent opinions" on the "scientific under-pinnings used to develop the criteria." The Department also said that the proposed numbers were more appropriate for "restoration" than "recovery." Thus, although goal-setting employs scientific tools such as historic data and modeling, these tools do not necessarily achieve consensus. The time interval employed affects the minimum size of the population needed to guarantee survival. For example, Mace and Reynolds point to conservationists who calculate "sustainability based on time intervals of over thousands of years" which, they point out, are much longer than any "commercially based resources manager would consider relevant" [43 p. 8].

Probabilities, Uncertainties, and Costs versus Benefits

Scientific research usually results in findings that are subject to probability, and uncertainty that can result in disagreement. One issue concerns what population size of an endangered species "is enough" to ensure its survival [44]. Wilhere points out that the probability of ensuring that endangered species do not go extinct is generally set at 90 or 95 percent levels by scientists though sometimes it may be placed as high as 99 percent [44 p. 514–15]. Moreover, he says that the marginal cost can increase greatly as the probability is set at a higher level. For example, he cites a study that raising the Northern Spotted Owl survival chances from 90 to 91 percent would cost an estimated 1.4 billion dollars. Thus there are tradeoffs between the goal of ensuring survival with other societal goals and, he argues, these choices cannot be determined scientifically. In 2006, several scientists who reviewed the status of the ESA admitted that parameters were based on how important policymakers viewed the risk of extinction, but they cited the view of the International Union for Conservation of Nature and Natural Resources that this probability should be kept at less than 10 percent within a hundred-year period [45 p. 172].

An illustration of how scientists can disagree based on differing assumptions and methods occurred concerning counts done by the Interagency Grizzly Bear Study Team (IGBST) of the U.S. Geological Survey. Biologists Doak and Cutler (in a study financed by the National Resources Defense Council) contend that the disappearance of traditional grizzly food sources such as pine nuts (a major grizzly food) due to the spread of the pinebark beetle, the decline of cutthroat trout, and the spread of wolves have forced grizzlies into open areas in search of food and this change has made them easier to "sight" and thus biased the counts toward a larger number than justified [46]. Doak and Cutler contend that estimates of population by the IGBST are based upon faulty assumptions and question the accuracy of sampling efforts (based on counts of grizzlies from planes during flyovers) and they claim that the estimate of 700 bears in the Yellowstone ecosystem is likely to be an overestimate due to failure to account for senescence (loss of fertility in aging female brown bears) [47]. The IGBST researchers responded to the critique by stating that "no two investigators are likely to make the exact same choices in dealing with complex data" and they did not necessarily reject the point about senescence but said it would increase "model complexity," and Doak and Cutler had not provided evidence to warrant changes in their model [48 p. 324–9]. The grizzly estimates of IGBST were used to support the delisting of grizzlies but the *New York Times* editorialized that the uncertainty about these numbers shows that the move to delist these grizzlies was premature [49]. The case demonstrates that population estimates for endangered species are often based on complex models involving a number of key assumptions that are open to challenge and change.

There are recurring battles over the number of an endangered species that should be maintained. The USFWS set a "wolf recovery floor" of 100 to 150 wolves for Montana, Idaho, and Wyoming as the minimum number of wolves that states must accept in order to have the wolf delisted. However, there are fears on the part of wolf-supporters that this minimum number will become the maximum for these states and that this population size is far too low to maintain a secure and viable population for the long term [50]. Moreover, there has been controversy among scientists over whether the current population of wolves should be delisted as recommended by experts such as L. David Mech [51 p. 69]. or whether they need the listing protection to provide time to study differences between the "pre-recovery" and recovered wolf populations as suggested by the research of Leonard and Wayne [52 p. 97; 53 p. 67]. Adams cites a study which shows that, although grizzly numbers are sufficient to survive for a century, their odds of survival decline after that and argues that we need to think in terms of assuring their survival for much longer periods of time [54]. According to Mills, the concept of "minimum number" is obsolete and has been replaced by Population Viability Analysis (PVA) because we cannot determine a "single number of individuals that will be viable for the long term" due to uncertainty in nature and management [20 p. 254]. In place of a "futile focus on a single number" we should assess a "range of possibilities" [20 p. 254].

A related concept is "maximum sustainable yield" which is employed to refer to the number of wildlife that can be "taken" without endangering their long-term population. Walker says that although "normal variation" is usually taken into consideration in calculating it, its calculation often "ignores extreme events" and assumes that changes in populations will be "linear and incremental" [55 p. 27]. Another key concept in wildlife conservation is "carrying capacity," which refers to the maximum number of a species that a habitat is able to support. However, as implemented by USFWS Grizzly Coordinator, Bob Servheen, this number is as much a question of "human behaviors and values as a scientific one" [56]. Servheen says that some people want only 800 while others want 1400 in the "primary conservation area" covered by Glacier National Park, the Bob Marshall Wilderness, and other parts of Montana and that he is trying to strike a "balance" for "what humans can tolerate" [56]. He points out that most grizzly deaths are due to humans from moving them, illegal killings, and killings due to self-defense and thus carrying capacity is not just dependent on factors such as the number of prey and other food sources available to the bears. The attitudes and actions of humans are crucial.

What levels of probability should be required before taking action to protect a species? Conservatives and developers tend to hold that "sound science" requires that high levels (e.g., 99 or 95 percent) be employed before taking preservation actions that would stop or prevent development. Conservationists believe that the USFWS should give the benefit of the doubt ("the precautionary principle") to the side of the potentially threatened species and thus not require such stringent levels [4 p. 415]. However, Doremus observes that the interpretation of this principle can cover a range of positions from a mere willingness to consider regulations up to an unreasonable demand for certainty that endangered species will not be harmed. Rigney argues that the precautionary approach should be taken to preserve bluefin tuna off the U.S. east coast – that the maximum sustainable yield (MSY) is not adequate because of uncertainty partly due to corruption in enforcement of "illegal, unregulated, and unreported fishing" [57 p. 278]. Since data are inadequate, rough estimates become part of the decision process, as in the case of the spotted owl. Yaffee says that the original estimate of 300 acres as the minimum needed for each spotted owl was discovered to be inadequate later when telemetry data became available [58 p. 23]. Thus the concept of the "best available science" is not stable – it can become antiquated and incorrect as newer information is gathered. The National Research Council (NRC) says, given the lack of information and uncertainty about calculating population viability, the key question is "who has the burden of proof" for listings – those who are trying to protect species or those who claim that not enough data are available to justify them [59 p. 167–8]. The NRC argues that given the magnitude of the danger of making a decision that will lead to the extinction forever of a species, that the burden should not be on those seeking to protect species.

Although certainty in science is impossible to attain, virtual certainty has been demanded for some decisions related to wildlife. One such case concerns the threat of the brucellosis disease that led Montana to slaughter bison leaving Yellowstone because of the possibility that the bison might infect livestock of ranchers. Wilkinson cites expert opinion that there has never been a documented case of bison infecting cattle [60]. In 2007, cattle in Montana were infected and thus the state lost its brucellosis-free designation that is crucial to selling beef [61 p. 153]. But the cause of infection in this case was not bison but elk. Nevertheless, the states insisted on killing all bison leaving the park, including male and uninfected bison. Bruce Babbitt, then the Secretary of the Interior, requested that the National Academy of Sciences undertake a study of the threat of brucellosis [60]. Likewise, when more than fifty members of Congress asked Secretary of Interior Salazar to look into BLM's controversial roundup of wild horses using helicopters that resulted in the deaths of 100 horses, Salazar asked the National Academy "to conduct a technical review of the program" [62]. Peacock discusses how the Clinton Administration tried to achieve a compromise solution to the slaughter of bison leaving Yellowstone but failed [63]. More recently, Montana is considering some options that allow buffalo to roam more freely [64]. The Wildlife Conservation Society's Dr. Keith Aune's study showed that brucellosis bacteria only linger for two weeks and thus the risk of infection of cattle is very slight. He goes on to say that if the date for extending the hazing of buffalo were extended for only two weeks, it would obviate the need for hazing bison back into Yellowstone [64]. But the state's director of the Department of Livestock says that such a delay would "could create an undue burden on his constituents" and that even if the risk of transmission is "slight, it still persists" – implying that only certainty was acceptable. The political controversy engendered over "free-roaming" bison case is illustrated by a Montana State Senator who has introduced many "anti-bison" bills, contrasting "heathen wild buffalo" with "Christian" domesticated buffalo. [64; 65]. Calculations of costs and benefits of preserving a species are also subject to great debate. A 2007 U.S. House of Representatives Committee on Natural Resources report questioned the validity of the conclusion that a rare species of frog was too expensive to protect because the study did not consider the monetary benefits of protecting the land [66 p. 30].

An issue distinct but related to uncertainty concerns multiple causation of threats to wildlife. For example, the state of Idaho has been concerned with significant declines in mule deer herds. Utah has focused on reducing predators, coyotes and wolves, which have been blamed for the decline. In 2012, Utah legislators approved two laws to deal with this decline: Predator Control Funding to collect money to kill predators and the Mule Deer Protection Act that spends $500,000 ($50 per coyote) on bounties to "remove coyotes from areas where they may prey on mule deer" [67]. In 2014, Utah's Division of Wildlife Resources published a report detailing the program's "success" [68]. The program resulted in the killing of more than 25,000 coyotes and represented a 59 percent increase over the previous yearly take of coyotes. However, the Division reported that the fawn:doe ratio actually decreased in 2014. The Division said the decrease "could be due . . . factors in addition to predator control that can influence numbers . . . like weather and habitat conditions" [68]. Indeed, scientific research is being conducted in neighboring Wyoming concerning the decline in mule deer and is focusing on the roles of "spreading energy development, increasing traffic, human encroachment, and drought" [69]. Most people are banned from BLM land in Pinedale Mesa where many mule deer spend their winters grazing but "energy development continues year round" and negatively affects the deer because research shows that the deer avoid energy development areas and must overcome the effects of energy and other development (e.g., that blocks the path of their migrations) [69]. It is likely that drought is affecting the deer but the researchers were careful not to relate the drought to climate change in this "energy dependent state." A researcher said: "Leave it to somebody else to evaluate why we're seeing more frequent drought. We're not addressing those questions. We're addressing 'What does it mean for mule deer?'" [69]. The general point is that there are often several causes to declining game species numbers but policymakers often direct their wildlife departments and public policies to focus on those that are most politically acceptable such as killing coyotes leaving more important causes unaddressed.

Science aims at discovering causality in order to understand phenomena such as threats to endangered species. However, often knowledge about causality is limited. In Federal court cases involving agencies such as the National Marine Fisheries Service (NMFS) and the USFWS, judges give "deference to agency expertise" but "the presumption of agency expertise may be rebutted if its decisions, even though based on scientific expertise, are not reasoned" [70 p. 16]. In a case involving threats to the Steller sea lion (SSL) from the fishing industry in Alaska, the fishing industry presented evidence from scientists that Greenpeace's evidence about the threats posed by large fish trawlers "did not establish a cause/effect relationship between the fisheries and the

SSL decline" [70 p. 20–1]. Judge Zilly "acknowledged that the evidence was not conclusive," but referred to the ESA, which requires only that decisions be made on the basis of "the best scientific and commercial data available." In this case, Judge Zilly accepted NMFS's "competition theory," which suggests that SSL and the fisheries competed with each other for available prey and thus affects SSL population [70]. The judge said that he was impressed by NMFS's consideration and rejection of "alternative threats" to SSL decline such as "predation, toxic substances, research, natural environmental changes, and prey quality." The judge allowed "declarations" about SSL from experts of the plaintiffs and defendants but gave the most weight to the plaintiff's expert, "a pinniped specialist for some thirty years," who emphasized the threat of reduction of the prey of the SSL due to the trawlers [70 p. 32–3]. Thus, in his review of four successive cases involving the SSL, McBeath concludes that the NMFS does not have to have "certainty" because the law "tolerates uncertainty" but "requires institutional caution and consistency in agency implementation" [70 p. 41–2].

The Complexity of Science

Scientific research on species involves a complex set of variables, and this complexity often results in modification or even refutation of initial generalizations by later studies. For example, one assumed benefit of restoring wolves to Yellowstone was based on the fact that wolves are hypothesized to save aspen trees, thus assisting other species that depend on them such as beavers because elk browse the trees less in the presence of wolf packs [71 p. 3]. This phenomenon is often referred to as an example of a "trophic cascade" in which the presence of an apex predator bring about changes in the number and behaviors of their prey that in turn impacts the vegetation eaten by the prey and hence helps provide habitat for other species [72]. Recently, Kauffman, Brodie, and Jules found that that the impacts of elk browsing were not reduced in areas where elk were at high risk of predation by wolves [73]. Likewise, L. David Mech considered the supposed ecological benefits of wolves and concluded that most of them could be due to other factors and suggests that wolves are neither "saints nor sinners" [74 p. 147]. However, Ripple and Beschta reexamined the hypothesis and again found support for the positive effects of wolves on elk browsing of aspens [75]. Ripple and Beschta suggest that the difference between their findings and those of Kauffman et al. may be due to methodological differences in measuring aspen, the fact that aspen were just beginning to increase, or other variables [75]. Other explanations include the fact that the number of wolves is simply not large enough to have the impact they had in the past. Eisenberg found that it was the effects of fires and wolves together that produced trophic effects [72 p. 51]. It is notable that the experience of ranchers, perhaps the wolves' biggest opponents, support the trophic hypothesis by claiming that cattle fearful of predation "reduce the time they [the cattle] spent foraging from 88 to 44 percent" [76 p. 26]. A study by Marshall, Hobbs and Cooper states that there is no doubt that wolves had acted in the past (prior to their extirpation seventy years ago) to sustain the area's ecology but that "the loss of wolves from the food web caused multiple changes in the ecosystem's biological and physical processes, creating an alternative state where herbaceous vegetation dominated riparian corridors … where beaver, once abundant, were absent" [77 p. 1 & 5–6]. They employed an experimental study to show that the presence of wolves, in the seventeen years since they have been restored, has not been able to restore the former ecology because their absence for such a long time had created conditions that were impossible "to quickly repair the effects of predator removal" [77 p. 1]. They conclude that their "results amplify the fundamental importance of conserving intact food webs because changes in ecosystems caused by removal of apex predators may be resilient to predator restoration" [77 p. 5–6]. Rooney and Anderson summarize research on trophic cascades in the Great Lakes by concluding that whether these effects on vegetation will be "important" depend on a number of factors including climate, human activity, and habitat productivity" [78 p. 211]. Estes et al., in an article in *Science*, emphasize the need to look at very long-term impacts such as decades to judge the importance of top-down predation and note the "irony" that by the time their impact is appreciated, the species may have been eliminated "from the ecosystem and the ability to restore top-down control has been lost" [79 p. 302]. They point to the Scottish island of Rum where wolves were eliminated 250 years ago as showing how their absence over the long run turned a "forested environment into a treeless island" [79 p. 306].

The entire "trophic cascade" hypothesis has been turned on its head with some scientists such as William Murdoch positing that it is the low-level ("bottom-up") forces that most influence biodiversity and a debate has ensued between those who emphasize the importance of top-down (e.g., apex predators) and bottoms-up forces [72 p. 46]. Although the extent of impact of trophic cascades on land is still being debated, marine cascades have been strongly backed, especially by the example of the disappearance of sea otters leading to the destruction of kelp forests because they controlled the number of sea urchins [80 p. 64]. Indeed, the sea otter case illustrates the complex interactions of the "food chain" because whaling led to the decline of this prey for orcas who then began to feast on otters and greatly reduce otter numbers [80 p. 74]. Boutin suggests that the evidence shows "trophic cascades are less pronounced in terrestrial systems" [81 p. 274]. Ray points out that there are reasons why such effects are easier to detect in marine areas due to the "small sizes" of the species "along with their limited mobility and range" that make it easier to do "manipulations and experimental studies" that detect "top-down impacts" [82 p. 404]. In Patagonia, Novaro and Walker found that carnivores such as pumas can have a negative effect on the biodiversity by preying on endangered species such as guanacos, though this happens because pumas (and other predators such as the culpeo, a South American wild dog) are also able to eat sheep, deer, and other mammals introduced by humans and thus are not constrained by elimination of the native species [83 p. 283]. In the far east of Russia, an argument used by environmentalists to natives for preserving the tiger is that tigers drive out wolves which "are worse than tigers" [84 p. 204]. The importance of the debate over trophic cascade effects revolves around the fact that supporters of the restoration of carnivores such as wolves would like to have a scientific, biodiversity-related argument for reintroducing them because, due to the fear and dislike of many humans for them, the desire to regain a lost species itself will not seem a strong argument for many [82 p. 39]. A volume devoted to the study of how carnivores affect biodiversity revealed more than anything else the complexity of science and difficulty making strong generalizations because "the relationship between predation and numbers of species is not tight ... because a number of other factors, including colonization, extinction, productivity, and refuge and habitat complexity, can interact to either increase or decrease the effects of predation" [85 p. 265]. Another example of change in science concerns the assumption for many years that frogs and other amphibians function as "canaries" that warn us of threats to species and thus provide a useful indicator species for the health of the environment. But recently Kerby, Richards-Hrdlicka, Storfer, and Andrew found that there is actually little evidence to show that amphibians are especially sensitive to chemical contamination [86 p. 66]. The cases of wolves and frogs demonstrate that science is complex and there are so many factors that affect biodiversity that it is often difficult to draw firm conclusions to assist decision makers. Our understanding of wildlife changes with new findings and theories so that there is always the possibility that "existing explanations will have to be changed" [87 p. 73].

Nevertheless, policy decisions such as how many wolves should be allowed must be made. Tolerance by humans is not directly considered in scientific models but is always relevant. Weber contends that populations of wolves and grizzlies should only be considered recovered when they are able to control the overabundant populations of elk or moose, but that this number would be far beyond the "few dozen breeding females" mandated by the Federal government [88 p. 238]. However, Weber acknowledges that such a large number of predators would be "far beyond" the tolerance of Yellowstone area ranchers. Decisions must be made and scientists openly acknowledge that political considerations often predominate. For example, L. David Mech, a renowned wolf expert, was concerned when decision making on the numbers of wolves to be targeted for Minnesota, was made by a "roundtable of stakeholders" because he believed that their recommended numbers were too high and would lead to wolf depredations on cattle resulting in a backlash against the species, thus, in effect, arguing that wolf population recommendations should heed political considerations [89 p. 8–9].

Data Availability and Quality

Another limitation of science is that frequently the data available for making decisions are inadequate or may be of questionable quality. For example, Gehring and Ruffing discuss the case of the white shark – Australia and Madagascar wanted to have the shark listed in the Appendix II of CITES but Japan opposed the listing on the basis that there was not enough available trend data to show that this action was needed and hence the shark was not listed [90]. Metrick and Weitzman's study found that (in 1993) there was "insufficient data" to list 3000 of the 3600 species that "were candidates" for listing and the availability of data was clearly linked to non-scientific factor of the "charisma" of the species – the more interesting a species is to humans, the more likely it is to be studied [91 p. 18]. Funding of research to gather information on endangered species runs into obstacles because developers do not want to collect these data because they might result in costly restrictions for them [92]. Yaffee quotes a manager for the Georgia-Pacific Corporation complaining that when they provided USFWS information about the numbers of spotted owls living on their timberlands, that "it backfired on them" and they were "penalized" for providing this information [58 p. 221]. ESA debates often wind up in Federal courts where judges have to decide which scientists to believe. Swedlow provides a detailed account of the use of science in the spotted owl case by the USFWS, the Federal judges, and both environmental and industry-affiliated scientists [93]. Swedlow concludes that the Federal judges (especially Judge Dwyer) consistently "barely even acknowledged industry experts" in opinions, but rather "lent a sympathetic ear to scientists testifying on behalf of environmental groups" [93 p. 277–8]. According to Swedlow, the basic problem about using science was there simply was not enough solid empirical research as to what "constituted adequate owl habitat" [93 p. 258]. Faced with this inadequate data, scientists developed models from limited data that were extrapolated to derive conclusions on the extent of threat to the owls [93 p. 275–6]. Although some academic and industry experts questioned the validity of these model-driven conclusions, the judges employed them.

Due to the lack of rigorous data, rules of thumb such as "50 and 500" have been used as guidelines for minimum numbers of individuals to survive for the short and longer term [20 p. 250]. But these rules are not scientifically based, and models are needed to provide a more accurate assessment, taking into consideration variables such as population growth rates and inbreeding "depression" [20 p. 251]. The International Union for the Conservation of Nature and Natural Resources (IUCNNR) has developed a Red List for threatened species that is based on the species "reductions or fluctuations in their geographic range or populations," and "very small size coupled with fluctuations or declines" [20 p. 267]. PVA can also be used to justify listing but is commonly not done due to the lack of sufficient data to enable its use [20 p. 267]. Data are often inadequate to use precise and sophisticated analyses and thus, with time pressure for making decisions, government officials such as in the spotted owl case have to rely on "subjective expert panel type of approach" to assess threats which amounts to "educated guesses" [20 p. 265]. A good example of the difficulty of calculating PVA concerned the Florida Panther Recovery team that reviewed a variety of PVAs calculated for the endangered panther, including one "consensus" model that pooled and averaged results from five different models that employed differing initial estimates and parameter values that surprisingly agreed on viability estimates in four of the five cases due to "drastically differing, but fortuitously offsetting, assumptions between modelers" [94 p. 74–93]. Among the key assumptions were kitten mortality (different model assumptions ranged from 20 to 50 percent) and rate of habitat loss (ranging from no loss to 1 percent per year). The Panther Recovery Team decided on using the one model that they thought represented the "best available science" but they acknowledged the need for sensitivity analysis due to questionable assumptions such as "no change in amount, quality, or configuration of habitat; no difficulty finding mates; no catastrophes; no additional human-induced mortality" [94 p. 83].

Another example of the importance of assumptions concerns models to predict crab populations on Chesapeake Bay. Suri says that the model assumed a lifespan of eight years for crabs and, though this figure was "long derided by fishermen," further research found that it was "too high" and consequently had "attributed too many crab deaths to harvesting" [95]. Moreover, despite improved sophistication and inclusion of more variables into the models, the population of crabs has fallen and risen by hundreds of millions that could be possibly due to causes such as "unusual weather patterns, predation of young crabs by the red drum fish, or loss of eel grass habitat" and consequently Suri characterizes model numbers as "educated guesses" [95].

One of the most important emerging forms of conservation involves the use of Payments for Environmental Services (PES) in which landowners are compensated for providing "environmental services" (e.g., wildlife-friendly practices) by governments or other "beneficiaries" such as non-governmental organizations (NGOs) that want to preserve species [96 p. 2]. However, in order for these contracts to work, Naeem et al. say that the "science has to be right" to ensure that services have been provided and are working but their review of 116 PES projects found that 60 percent failed to adhere to one or more basic principles required for scientific integrity [97 p. 1206]. Alston, Andersson, and Smith found that technology such as satellite imaging can assist in providing data for certain outcome measures such as land use, but it is more difficult to use technology to determine changes in populations of rare species [96 p. 8]. For example, Sommerville, Milner-Gulland, and Jones attempted to measure the success of a PES project in Madagascar targeted on "three of the species of highest conservation interest (flat-tailed tortoise, Madame Berthe's mouse lemur, and striped mongoose)" and concluded they were not encountered frequently enough to allow us to compare measures because the "services" are "elusive" and difficult to measure [98 p. 2834]. PES efforts are still relatively young and thus far few have attempted to determine "additionality" that is whether the changes would have occurred anyway in the absence of the program [99 p. 260].

Jackson reports that the number of tigers estimated by the governments of Bangladesh and India have been much overstated and much smaller estimates were found when camera-trap surveys methods were employed by researchers [100 p. 12]. There are cases in which the lack of data has been used as the rationale to take no action to protect species. Tobin cites a case that took place in the 1970s where the USFWS did not take action to protect spiderlike invertebrates from a dam on the basis that data were "insufficient" to support a listing [101]. Beatley says that lack of knowledge about what conditions affect the fringe-toed lizard and Bell's vireo affected HCP deliberations [102 p. 62]. For example, noise from automobile traffic or farm equipment could affect vital activities such as establishment of territory and mating. In such cases, Beatley argues that HCPs should err on the side of "caution." Even after a species has been listed as endangered, a U.S. General Accountability Office (GAO) study showed that the USFWS does not have the budget or staff to monitor the "take" of most listed species – only about 10 out of nearly 500 listed species were being monitored [103].

Another cause of insufficient information is that a large portion of endangered species live on private lands and developers often resist giving the USFWS data that are requested such as for the gnatcatcher in California [101 p. 100]. In a study of 43 HCPs, Kareiva et al. found that in only about one-third of the cases was there enough information to determine the impact of the proposed take (e.g., from a development) on the threatened species [104 p. 41]. Kareiva et al. conclude that, lacking adequate scientific information, officials should employ a "precautionary" principle but also found that there was no relationship between the amount of information available and the use of this precautionary approach in the plans [104 p. 41]. Mace and Reynolds say that "direct censuses of most exploited populations are very difficult, time-consuming, and expensive" [43 p. 9]. They cite the case of caribou in Alaska as an example of a species that would seem "to be straightforward" but turns out to be impossible in reality to accurately count and thus we must rely on estimates and assumptions [43 p. 10].

There are often simply not enough data or resources available to monitor the effects of policy changes, despite the fact that there is a major emphasis on the use of "adaptive management" of wildlife in which monitoring is done to detect the effect of changes. Thomas studied the implementation of HCPs and found that once a compromise agreement is reached to establish an HCP, participants in the process did not want to gather new data on the state of the endangered species for fear that the difficult negotiation process would be reopened [105]. The NRC's review of the ESA concluded that "population viability analysis" is the cornerstone of "recovery planning" but that the genetic and population data to conduct these analyses are lacking for most species and thus "educated guesswork" has to be employed and that "confidence intervals have to be placed around projections" to be defensible [59 p. 82]. However, the NRC also states that better tools (e.g., geographic information systems) are becoming available to increase the precision of analyses. At the international level, the data are often of questionable validity [59 p. 117]. For example, Tilson, Nyhus, Franklin, Bastoni, and Yunus distinguish between "paper tigers" versus actual tiger occupancy. They say that tiger reserves in Sumatra claim tiger habitat for areas that are "close to or bisected by roads, towns, cities, and agriculture" unprotected from poaching [106 p. 282].

Fishery managers have developed concepts such as MSY "based on mathematical analyses of fish population and fisheries" but Punt and Smith say that fisheries management is more about the "management of people than fish" and that "total allowable catch" determinations are made in a "political context" with pressure not to reduce catches "especially when there is uncertainty" [107 p. 54]. Punt and Smith cite the UN's Food and Agricultural Organization's "precautionary approach" to fishing that includes guidelines such as "being more cautious when the information is uncertain" and "not using the absence of information to postpone conservation measures" [107 p. 56–7]. Certain activities such as recreational fishing are "diffuse in nature" and are assumed to be "benign" until research is conducted about them [108 p. 52]. Sanderson notes that some concepts such as MSY have the appearance of science but have been "politically appropriated" with the result that they "invite compromise around the least demanding constraint" such that "minimum viable population becomes the maximum population worried about, or minimum critical size becomes the most acreage policy-makers must leave intact" [109 p. 471–2]. In recognition of the limitations of data, the 1992 Rio Declaration on Environment and Development contains a principle that desire for "full scientific certainty should not be used as a reason for postponing cost effective measures to prevent environmental degradation" [110 p. 105].

The controversy over bans on whaling and the International Whaling Commission (IWC) have involved a debate over science and demonstrates how the gathering of data is subject to disagreement and values. The IWC has a Scientific Committee that is vested with the job of determining whether the stocks of different whale species are sufficient for resuming commercial whaling and have determined that certain species (e.g., minke whales) have recovered enough to do so [111]. There are disputes over the validity of the estimates. British representatives argued that the Norwegian figures had "dropped recently" though that could have been due to the fact that Britain did not allow Norway to count whales in "the British Area of the North Sea." However, according to the New Zealand commissioner, the underlying problem is that their "attitudes were not based entirely on science" but "the view that killing whales is inherently cruel" [111]. In short, data quality concerning threatened wildlife are often subject to question and consequently policy decisions often rely on guidelines such as "burden of proof" assumptions and non-scientific political factors.

Scientific Models and Assumptions

Adaptive management is the philosophy that many conservationists seek to adhere to in preserving species. Adaptive management involves making predictive models, then making policy changes based on those models, and revising the models as monitoring data become available [112 p. 22]. Thus the adaptive management approach helps to cope with the issues of inadequate data and changes in science. Scientific management of wildlife often depends on models that make assumptions that are subject to disagreement. For example, there was disagreement over the use of models of climate change as the basis for putting wolverines on the endangered species list. Recently, the USFWS proposed listing the wolverine due to research that "wolverines rely on snow [cover] for survival" [113] and a model [114] that predicted that warming due to climate change would threaten wolverine habitat and thus they required protection under the ESA. The USFWS sent the proposed rule out to seven reviewers for comment and two of the reviewers (Audrey Magoun and Robert Inman) argued that the rule was based on faulty science. Curiously, Magoun was one of the coauthors for both publications and Inman was a coauthor of the Copeland et al. article that was used to support the listing [115]. Magoun agreed that wolverines are dependent on persistent late spring snow but said that in order for the model to be used as "best available science" justification, that it "must show the ecological/biological reasons that wolverines must have snow cover until May 15" and show that without this snow cover, wolverines cannot occupy (i.e., "feeding, breeding, and sheltering") the landscapes or "demonstrate that snow cover … that is proposed to disappear" will result in the lack of "suitable wolverine habitat" for feeding, breeding, and sheltering [116]. Magoun goes on to say that there had been no evidence presented to show that these either of these conditions was true. Inman states that "While I am a coauthor on that paper, I have, after further thought and new information, come to the conclusion that this hypothesis is not based in sound theory, is not actually supported by the observed correlation, and is not proving to be true upon subsequent real-world assessment" [117]. He proceeds to say "There is no reason to believe that wolverines are incapable of using non-snow structures as dens. In fact there is now evidence of wild wolverines successfully using non-snow dens" [117]. It is notable that three of the seven reviewers selected by USFWS were authors of articles used as the basis for the proposed listing, demonstrating the small universe of researchers in this area. The response of the USFWS to the disagreement was to delay the listing and seek further comments with questions such as the following: (1) whether the basis for defining wolverine habitat based on persistent spring snow is valid and/or whether the use of other dates would be "more defensible" or produce different results than the McKelvey model's use of May 15; (2) whether the McKelvey model adapted an invalid habitat model so that its projections of climatic impact would also be invalid. As a result of the listing, the Montana Department of Fish, Wildlife and Parks initially suspended trapping of wolverines but then resumed it [118]. On August 12, 2014, the USFWS published the final rule rescinding the original plan to list the wolverine [119]. The three regional USFWS directors involved made their decision "based on a synthesis of the entire body of scientific evidence" and because "climate change models are unable to reliably predict snowfall amounts and snow-cover persistence in wolverine denning locations" [119]. However, the Society for Conservation Biology and the American Society of Mammalogists viewed this as an example of "disregard for the best available science" [120]. This case illustrates how controversial the use of predictive models can be when they concern issues such as climate change's effects on mammals.

Another good example of disagreements based on differing assumptions concerns the impact of delisting of Northern Rocky Mountain Distinct Population Segment of gray wolves. The USFWS issued a report that concluded that renewed hunting of wolves in the region did not result in "increased risk" to this population of wolves, noting that the total population of wolves in the area had remained constant [121]. Creel et al. took issue with the research and conclusions of the USFWS [122 p. 1475]. They pointed to the fact that a 14 percent decline occurred in the "take of wolves in Idaho and Montana" despite extended hunting periods and relaxed limits on takes. They suggested that these data point to a decline in the wolf populations of these states. They also emphasize that the USFWS conclusion based on overall wolf populations ignores the fact that the area had been expanded to include Washington and Oregon and ignored individual state changes such as the decline in pack size in Idaho and decline in the survival rates of Idaho pups from 60 to 38 percent [122 p. 1475]. The USFWS emphasized an increase in the Montana wolf population but Creel et al. question the validity of this conclusion because Montana increased staff and time to count wolves and the USFWS numbers are adjusted (upward) to account for unseen wolves living outside of packs. They also critique the USFWS for failing to distinguish between replacement from local sources and "immigration from an external population," thus leading to a false conclusion. Indeed, Creel et al. assert that there is no scientific basis for wolf populations goals "other than avoiding relisting" [122 p. 1475]. In short, differing assumptions can in some cases lead to wholly different conclusions by scientists looking at the same data.

Conservative skeptics challenge the assumptions that models can make valid predictions long into the future. Indeed, in 2014, the U.S. District Court of Alaska vacated the listing of the distinct population "Beringia" (i.e., in the areas of the Bering Strait, Bering Sea, and Chukchi Sea) segment of the bearded seals because, the court contended, the listing was based on a model projecting fifty years into the future and "too speculative and remote" to justify the decision to list [123 p. 4]. These cases illustrate the difficulty of making decisions about threatened species based on predictions of models, and points out that the criterion of "best available science" does not necessarily lead to consensus on the part of scientists.

Sound Science versus "Junk Science"

The debate over what constitutes "junk science" overlaps the discussion on uncertainty and lack of information. In 2002, House Republicans proposed amending the Endangered Species Act with a provision titled "Sound Science for Endangered Species Act Planning" that required any petition to list a species under ESA prove that any change in the population is "beyond the normal fluctuation for the species and meet the criteria of "clear and convincing evidence" [124]. Opponents of this amendment said that it would shift the burden of proof to the petitioner and create delay in the listing of species. Some equate "sound science" with the publication of studies in peer-reviewed journals but the accumulation of such studies may take several years which could be too late to save the endangered species and scientists are unlikely to respond to requests for "regulatory reviews" in a timely manner [4]. In response to a 2014 USFWS decision to list the Gunnison sage-grouse as a threatened species, Colorado and Utah state agencies criticized the listing decision for not being based on peer-reviewed research and the Federal agency responded as follows [125]:

Under the standards of the ESA, we are required to base our determinations of species status on the best available information. Our first choice is information from recent, peer-reviewed publications that is specific to Gunnison sage-grouse. However, sometimes the only available information may be based on studies of greater sage-grouse. Additionally scientific data are sometimes limited, studies are conflicting, or results are uncertain or seemingly inconclusive. Scientific information includes both empirical evidence, and expert knowledge or opinion.

Disagreements over assumptions underlie many disputes over the legitimacy of "science." For example, a Canadian workshop was held to involve stakeholders involved in areas frequented by grizzly bears. Some industry representatives did not trust the "assumptions made on limited data" that they thought were biased to "make the grizzly bear population appear more vulnerable than it was" and thus this "bias could increase the cost of environmental mitigation for their companies" [126 p. 314].

The quality of "scientific reports" are routinely questioned by opponents and must survive scrutiny. For example, Hamilton describes how Jack Ward Thomas, a USFWS scientist, compiled a report that proposed a logging ban on "30 to 40 percent of public timberland in the Northwest" to preserve the spotted owl habitat, but that his report was criticized by both environmentalists (it would sacrifice as much as half of the spotted owl population) and loggers [127 p. 22]. The Council of Economic Advisors asked a "team of four university scientists" to review the Thomas report and this group concluded that the report was one of the "finest reports on environmental issues" and consequently the report changed the "tenor of the debate" on logging [127 p. 23–4].

In addition to uncertainty, the term junk science also covers the validity of the data such as the "fudging of numbers." Duffy cites the case of a non-governmental organization accusation that Zimbabwe was "double-counting" their elephants to boost the reported population numbers by counting them before they moved to neighboring Botswana and again when they returned [128 p. 164]. Matthiessen cites a case from India where a park estimated that there were forty-five tigers but upon further study the number was revised to twenty-eight with experts stating that it actually was only fifteen [129 p. 83]. Some key assumptions about species are based on dated studies that experts say are not valid. For example, there has been a long-term debate concerning whether prairie dogs reduce the "carrying capacity" of land for livestock [21]. This assumption was based on a 1902 study whose validity they question. USFWS scientists in Florida used a model to calculate areas used by panthers but this model did not include tracking panthers during their nighttime travels – thus reducing the amount of area with development restrictions and consequently producing a map that conservationists viewed as biased in favor of developers [66 p. 30 & 130]. The decision as to what animals should be included to calculate population size of threatened species can be another point of contention. For example, the Bush Administration modified a report on the size of wild salmon populations in the Pacific Northwest by combining the numbers of hatchery-raised salmon with wild salmon [66]. Conservationists do not believe that hatchery fish should be included – only wild salmon should be counted. Hybrid and "introduced" species are not valued by the ESA – quite the contrary. For example, Carbyn describes a struggle between "purist" conservationists who wanted to replace "hybrid" wood buffalo with "pure" wood bison while the natives in the area acted to protect the hybrids [131]. The issue of hybridization continues to beset the Red Wolf Recovery Program begun in 1987 in North Carolina. A review of the program by the Wildlife Management Institute (WMI) states that the USFWS should consider whether "the current red wolf genome reflects excessive introgression of coyote genes due to interbreeding" because that would disqualify them "for protection under the Endangered Species Act," and notes that there exists "disagreement among geneticists regarding the appropriate methods to determine what constitutes a species or subspecies" [132 p. 17–19]. WMI also point out the difficulty of making a "nontrivial" decision on the basis of "taxonomic uncertainty" to terminate a program that has been going on for more than three decades [132]. Likewise, "introduced species" (often referred to as "invasive species" by conservationists) are viewed negatively by environmentalists while some observers question the supposed harmful effects of non-native species such as feral cats in Australia. They assert that claims about the bad effects of the cats are overstated [133 p. 165–70].

Still another point of contention among scientists concerns the criteria that should be employed to determine whether a subpopulation of a species is genetically different enough to be designated a "subspecies" and thus worthy of being protected. Carolan describes the case of "Preble's jumping mouse" which, supporters argued, should be listed while opponents said it should be considered merely a member of other existing subspecies and thus not deserving to be listed [134]. According to Carolan, one study showed that Preble's mouse shared 99.5% of its genetic code with other subspecies but this finding raises the question of how different a subspecies must be in order to be protected [134]? The NRC states that the Florida panther is "no longer genetically distinct from other panthers in the southeastern states" [59 p. 64]. In 1978, the USFWS combined four subcategories of wolves into gray wolves and, according to Yaffee, this reclassification allowed Minnesota to change the status of depredating wolves from endangered to threatened; thus they could be killed [135 p. 77]. The NRC says that the "distinctiveness" that marks a subspecies can be based on genetic, molecular, behavioral, morphological, or ecological characteristics and that "any single method will often be inadequate" [59 p. 5]. The NRC says that some designations such as "brown bear" and its protection status depend more on "political boundaries, management and aesthetic criteria" rather than whether they constitute an "evolutionary unit." Since protecting a subspecies as a threatened or endangered species can affect the economic wellbeing of landowners, disputes are likely to arise over these definitions and values become important in making decisions about them. For example, the Secretary of the Interior during the George H.W. Bush Administration, Manual Lujan, questioned whether "every subspecies has to be saved" [59 p. 55].

Symanski discusses how Michael Blake, the author of *Dances with Wolves*, sponsored a census of wild horses that came to radically different (much smaller) numbers than those gathered by the Bureau of Land Management [136]. The discrepancy was due to a number of factors including the areas studied, the method (helicopter versus fixed-plane) and experience of the surveyors. Symanski believes the numbers collected by the "environmental fringe" represented by Blake are invalid. Recently, conservative critics of the ESA, Schiff and MacDonald claimed that the USFWS and National Oceanic and Atmospheric Administration "no longer base decisions on what the law calls for" but instead "invent squishy standards" like "best professional judgment" [137].

In the absence of adequate data, the USFWS sometimes base their goals for endangered species on arbitrary figures. One such case concerns the Mexican wolf. In proposing a rule making revisions to USFWS regulations for the "Nonessential Experimental Population of the Mexican Wolf," one of the expert reviewers commented that "there needs to be some justification presented why 100 Mexican wolves was once determined to be biologically warranted goal or why that number rather than 50 or 200 is not the goal for Mexican wolf restoration in its historical range of the purported subspecies in Arizona and New Mexico?" The USFWS responded with the following statement [138]:

The prime objective of the 1982 recovery plan was to conserve and ensure the survival of the Mexican wolf by maintaining a captive-breeding program and reestablishing a viable, self-sustaining population of at least 100 Mexican wolves in the wild ... This number was not intended to be a recovery goal. It was a ***starting point*** [emphasis added] to determine whether or not we could successfully establish a population of Mexican wolves in the wild that would conserve the species and lead to its recovery ... however, we recognize the need to revise the 1998 Final Rule so that we can improve the effectiveness of the reintroduction project to achieve the necessary population growth, distribution, and recruitment, as well as genetic variation within the Mexican wolf experimental population so that it can contribute to recovery in the future. We acknowledge that a ***scientifically based population goal, as a component of future objective and measurable recovery criteria, is needed*** [emphasis added] in order to help determine when removing the Mexican wolf from the endangered species list is appropriate.

Thus key goals can be arbitrary, rough estimates and/or the result of pragmatic politics. Overall, scientific data are subject to questions of validity, definitions, and assumptions, and thus can fail to achieve consensus among scientists and, even more, opposed coalitions. In short, many important decisions are based on arbitrary and rough estimates.

Science, Contentious Issues, and Peer Review

Despite all of the limitations of science outlined above, when major conflict occurs over wildlife, politicians often turn to scientists with the hope they will solve the problem. The National Academy of Sciences (NAS) is one organization that is often asked to conduct inquiries in disputes such as whether predators should be controlled in Alaska [3]. Alaska's governor wanted the NAS not only to evaluate the ecological impacts of controlling predators but also to consider the costs and benefits of such policies. Although the NAS conducted a study, it did not resolve the conflict [3]. Recently, when some people were mauled and killed by grizzlies, there was a call for the NAS to determine the cause of the sudden increase in fatal grizzly attacks [139]. Doremus and Tarlock describe a case where a NRC report undercut the position of environmentalists in a conflict over whether water should be diverted in the Klamath Basin for agricultural interests [140]. The NRC report contradicted the position of the USFWS and NMFS that this diversion would threaten Coho salmon and consequently the Bureau of Reclamation used the report as justification to maintain the status quo on irrigation.

Peer review is supposed to be the *sine qua non* of the scientific process and the best way to ensure that science rather than politics dictates decisions. But the recent case of the gray wolves demonstrates that even peer review does not insulate science from politics. When gray wolves were proposed by the USFWS to be listed in all forty-eight lower states, a peer review was supposed to be conducted to provide an impartial review of the proposed action [141]. A private consulting firm (AMEC) was hired to select a review panel of experts. According to news accounts, USFWS was able to identify the panel members selected by AMEC even though they were supposed to be anonymous by reviewing their resumes [142]. USFWS asked that three be removed because they had signed a letter expressing concern about the "scientific basis of removing wolves" from Federal protections [143]. The USFWS suspended the process because "it did not meet their standards" [142]. A *New York Times* editorial claimed that the removed experts "did not meet up with the agency's anti-wolf bias." Moreover, the USFWS had trouble finding experts who had not already taken a position on the removal of wolves from protections [143].

The USFWS frequently encounters challenges that their actions, such as proposed listings and critical habitat, have not undergone public review. For example, one recent comment concerning the designation of critical habitat for the Fluted Kidneyshell and Slabside Pearly Mussel criticized the agency for publishing a rule that "had not undergone peer review" and relied on "decades-old data" [144]. The USFWS responded to this comment by stating that they "solicited expert opinion from eight knowledgeable individuals" in accordance with their peer review policy established in 1994 and received comments from two of the peer reviewers. They subsequently published the comments on the Internet and reviewed all of the comments concerning them before proceeding [144]. Thus, the agency of necessity often relies on solicited comments. One of the complaints of critics of the ESA and some professionals in the USFWS itself is that the flood of lawsuits by environmental organizations have taken away from the authority of the knowledgeable experts in the USFWS to make decisions. But Greenwald, Suckling, and Pimm conducted a study that found that "court-ordered peer reviews" were "better than those conducted by the USFWS" [145 p. 689]. Hodges and Elder found that court-ordered cases employed not only more criteria than non-court-ordered cases but also used "more challenging criteria" [146 p. 2665–7]. In short, a consensus based on peer-reviewed studies is often unavailable which leads to substitutes such as "expert judgment" and rough estimates. Although peer review is supposed to be objective, the values of researchers as reflected in their policy positions are assumed to affect their judgments.

The Role of Scientists

The role that scientists play in policymaking concerning wildlife has often been controversial. The Bureau of Biological Survey in the Department of Interior was an agency that was originally created to conduct research, but that through time focused on the mission of eradicating wolves and other predators that preyed on livestock [147]. The Biological Survey built a strong supportive constituency through its extermination of the wolf and efforts to do away with other predators such as grizzlies, and coyotes. However, by the 1930s, "leading members" of the American Society of Mammologists disputed the Survey on the value of wolves and the annual meetings of the society were the scene of "pitched battles over the perpetuation of large carnivores" [148 p. 3]. However, according to Robinson, these scientific societies were "no match for the powerful livestock interests" [147 p. 242]. More recently, a 2007 U.S. House of Representatives report cited a survey of USFWS scientists that 42 percent of the scientists did not feel that they could "express concerns about the needs of species … without fear of retaliation" [66]. The same report listed several cases in which they contended that a George W. Bush Administration USFWS-appointed official (Julie MacDonald) replaced scientifically based recommendations with political decisions – the cases included both the Greater and Gunnison Sage-Grouse and Trumpeter Swan, among others [66 p. 28–30]. Republican defenders of Ms. MacDonald on the committee made several arguments on her behalf, including that policymakers must take into consideration economic considerations and sometimes make decisions that disagree with those of scientists [66 p. 160–2].

Up until the 1960s, the accepted model of decision making for wildlife resource managers was a top-down model with the assumption that professional wildlife managers were best equipped to decide policies [149 p. 27]. But with the growth of the environmental movement, wildlife managers now routinely employ a "stakeholder management" approach in which their focus is on making sure that all major groups are incorporated into the decision-making process and then try to develop a constructive dialogue among participants that can reach agreement that all major actors will accept. In this model, information from scientists is essential but the decision is generally based on a "political compromise" among opposed interests and thus science plays a supportive but not necessarily deciding role. Richie, Oppenheimer, and Clark discuss the case of the Canadian national parks organization's (Parks Canada's) attempt to develop a "collaborative" stakeholder approach in 2005 to supplant their traditional reliance on hierarchy of science professionals in order to deal with resentment and resistance to measures they adopted [150]. The authors cite attacks by citizens on scientific reports that critics characterized as "scare tactics" to provide grizzlies unwarranted stronger protections [150 p. 271]. Although the collaborative approach had some initial successes, it ultimately failed and Parks Canada returned to the more traditional superintendent-dominated process though it now emphasizes "visitor experience" over ecology [150 p. 271].

There are several cases when scientists have opposed policies of the agencies and been punished or even fired as a result. For example, Andy Eller, a biologist with the USFWS charged his agency with failing to protect Florida panthers and was fired [151; 152; 153 p. 1615–17]. Some scientists were afraid to attach their name to research on the bad effects of lead shot and refused to take a public position on banning lead shot for fear of losing their jobs and threats to their personal safety [154]. Adolph Murie conducted research that showed that wolves and coyotes did not have any major deleterious effects on ungulate populations in Alaska, but his research was not accepted by the Biological Survey [155 p. 41]. Scientists such as Murie learned that they had to moderate their policy recommendations to deal with political realities. Rawson cites a letter in which Murie suggests that some killing of wolves should be allowed in McKinley (now Denali) National Park in order to avoid creating even more hatred of the wolf and thus, by allowing some killing of them, wolves would have a better chance for survival [155 p. 142 & 197]. More recently, according to Hull, the USFWS now supports efforts to delist grizzlies for the same reason – they fear that grizzlies preying on livestock and encounters with humans will cause "ill will among ranchers and hunting groups" [139]. The desire to build political compromises can lead to less influence of scientists over policymaking. For example, Bruce Babbitt and the Clinton

Administration developed a process for achieving compromise between environmentalists and their opposing coalitions of livestock owners and farmers [156]. Babbitt did so by creating state-level "Resource Advisory Councils" which worked on the basis of interest group liberalism which, according to Wagner, took away discretion from scientists and conservation professionals, replacing expert-dominated decisions with political compromises among these various constituencies represented on these councils [156].

Conservation groups often make use of science. For example, former Sierra Club President David Brower fought against a dam by emphasizing "facts and figures" more than "aesthetic arguments" [157 p. 165]. Nie says that The Center for Biological Diversity (CBD) believes in the use of science as the only effective method to fight "entrenched" interests such as ranchers whose cows graze on public lands [3 p. 136]. Klyza and Sousa point out that CBD has won a large number of lawsuits through the use of science despite having a "lean budget" [16 p. 142–9]. John Buse, Senior Council and Legal Director for the CBD, communicated to me on April 27, 2015 that, "looking solely at the court cases that have been concluded, and counting successful settlements as wins, their record 'stands at 525 wins and 106 losses' for an 83.1 percent success record." Thus, for laws such as the ESA that specify decisions should be made on the best available science, scientific expertise is the major resource – more important than assets usually cited as crucial in traditional interest group research such as money, numbers, organization, and access.

The Interagency Grizzly Bear Study Team, a coalition of scientists from the National Park Service, USGS, USFWS, and the U.S. Forest Service plus the wildlife departments of Idaho, Montana, Wyoming, and the Wind River Reservation, is charged with impartially tracking grizzly numbers and claim to go out of their way to present unbiased information. Both conservationists and ranchers have sometimes rejected their findings when they do not like their substance. For example, when grizzly numbers were reported by IGBST to be very low, ranchers and loggers claimed their data were "bunk" but when they reported strong recovery numbers conservationists questioned their data [158 p. 31]. Decker and Chase discuss a case where state biologists said that some "antlerless" deer must be harvested in order to manage the herd size effectively but hunters rejected the biologists' recommendations and then were successful in removing the biologists' authority over the decision, leading to what the authors call a "quarter century" of ineffective deer management [159 p. 136].

A current case concerning the "lesser prairie chicken" illustrates how science can become a central focus of a policy dispute over wildlife. Avian ecologists are undertaking multimillion dollar research projects (about three dozen individual studies) covering the five states where the species has been listed as threatened [160]. The purpose is to figure out what areas will be accepted by the birds for mating and reproduction. There are many conditions that affect their ability to reproduce, including some that are due to nature such as long droughts that occur in the West. However, many human-made structures such as oil pumps and other noise-generating activities (e.g., noise from vehicles) disturb the birds and fragment their habitat. They are also affected by the presence of tall structures and farming practices such as the use of pesticides [160]. One current GPS (global positioning system) study shows that female birds travel as far as

70 km which may suggest that they, according to the researcher, may be able to "move between widely separated swaths of habitat in fragmented landscapes" despite the fact that they are weak flyers [160]. Such studies have implications for how much habitat they need and whether they can survive fragmentation. Consequently, the results of these studies will be used (depending on their substantive conclusions) as "ammunition" by the sides in the controversy (conservationists versus extractive industries and farmers) [160]. To summarize, although scientists prefer to view their data as objective and non-political, their findings are interpreted in a political context.

Decisive Impacts of Science

Sometimes scientific research does have a decisive impact on policymaking, though it often requires the existence of a crisis for it to have such an effect. Ernst describes how the Virginia Fish Commission faced with record "low blue crab harvests" finally followed the prescriptions of "overwhelming scientific evidence" [161 p. 109–11]. In 1935, the director of the National Park system ended the policy of predator control, despite strong objections from Congress and Western stockmen on the basis that it was not supported by scientific findings [155 p. 148]. Durbin discusses how the U.S. Forest Service finally changed their policy toward logging in the Tongass national forest due to scientific findings though they did this reluctantly [162 p. 306]. Gehring and Ruffing report that countries such as Indonesia supported the listing of the humpback wrasse despite the fact that they had formerly opposed it and had significant economic interests involved [90 p. 140–1]. The change in positions came when new scientific information was presented that supported its endangered status. Goodall cites the case of the banning of DDT and the subsequent Supreme Court case supporting the ban as an example where scientific data presented concerning its harmful effects on birds of prey "could not be refuted" [163 p. 86]. Scientific evidence has often been decisive in courts. For example, the expert opinion of scientists convinced the judge in the spotted owl case to require that the USFWS review its decision not to list the owl, leading the agency to eventually reverse its position in 1990 [164 p. 88]. Hunter Jr., Bean, Lindenmayer, and Wilcove view science as setting the basis for later political bargaining which may or may not result in "ecologically sound" decisions [165]. As Keiter concludes, although scientific data alone cannot determine policy decisions, it does provide trend data and make clear tradeoffs so that decision making is not done solely in an ad hoc manner based on political power alone [164].

More often, the use of scientific data can be a necessary condition for achieving change in wildlife policies, but it is usually not sufficient. A case study of the first federally protected wildlife corridor for pronghorn in Wyoming details the steps that were necessary to achieve success [166]. First, the researchers used GPS technology to document pronghorn migration and prove that they used "a single invariant migration route" that crossed private and public lands with "noteworthy bottlenecks" due to "human development" and presence of rivers [166 p. 1142–4]. After gathering this data, the researchers approached an energy company (The Shell Exploration and

Production Company) for support of further research on pronghorns, and this company funded a project on pronghorn ecology. Although this funding was not aimed at conservation, the association of the researchers with an energy company helped open the door for the scientists to approach Wyoming's conservative Governor David Freudenthal and convince him to support the researchers' proposed "Path for Prong-horn" corridor [166 p. 1145–8]. The researchers were careful not to link this corridor to more controversial species such as wolves, bison, or elk that might threaten ranchers and farmers, and the researchers also avoided association with "controversial" conservation groups [166 p. 1147]. They concentrated their energies on the county that appeared to be more receptive to the corridor (Teton County) and hoped that the other involved county (Sublette County) would go along if they were successful with Teton. The researchers concluded that their success was achieved through their willingness to "engage" politicians and make presentations and "targeted communications" as well as to be "thick-skinned" in the face of "barrages in sensitive meetings" [166 p. 1149]. They found that the role of science was "surprisingly small" compared to their engagement on the front lines of politics in establishing this wildlife corridor.

Conclusion

To summarize, many people place high hopes and expectations on science to solve debates over wildlife conservation. This is the case because, perhaps more than any other law, the ESA emphasizes that "the best available science" should be used to make decisions [72 p. 69]. However, there are strong limitations to the impact of science. First, policy goals for wildlife conservation are set by politicians, not scientists, but research shows that "when conservation targets are based on the research and expert opinion of scientists they far exceed targets set to meet political or policy goals" [167 p. 18]. In this chapter, I have focused on cases where there were disputes over science related to endangered species but many listings based on science are implemented without significant controversy. Political controversy generally occurs when species protections threaten the interests of corporations and landholders. Since the ESA was passed, controversial decisions often wind up in Federal courts, where the "best available science" as determined by the presiding judge has been decisive. For interest group theory and also the Advocacy Coalition Framework, the ESA is a fascinating case because it illustrates how organizations with scientific expertise concerning wildlife (e.g., Center for Biological Diversity) have a competitive advantage over the "opposing coalition" and thus has led to many victories in Federal courts – scientific evidence is more important than numbers and cash.

However, reliance on science has major limitations. Science does not necessarily provide conclusive evidence to one side of conflicts because, as I have shown, there are often many legitimate points of disagreement among scientific researchers. Uncertainty and probability allow for a wide range of estimates about key policy variables such as the minimum population needed to sustain a species. Often there are not good empirical data and studies on which to base decisions and reliance is often made on the basis of expert judgments which may be considered subjective and "soft." Increasingly, scientists employ predictive models to assess threats to endangered species and there are disagreements about the assumptions and accuracy of these models. Indeed, as illustrated in the bitter dispute between "new" and traditional conservation camps, disputes over science occur within the conservation movement itself. Questions about the validity of data and accusations about "junk science" now often occur. Scientific findings are subject to change and current models and assumptions may be found to be invalid later. Likewise, due to the number of variables involved, limitations of time and lack of variation in key variables, it is often impossible to rigorously test competing hypotheses. My review of research on the trophic cascade shows that science most often reveals complexity that makes it difficult to draw clear conclusions for public policy, leaving a big role for assumptions and hence values. These limitations often allow opposing sides on contentious issues to argue that science supports their position. In such cases, there is debate over which side "has the burden of proof" and whether to employ the "precautionary principle" to give the benefit of the doubt to preservation of species. Because of the fact that use of the best available science is an integral part of the ESA, it provides a good test for the role that science plays in policymaking. The Advocacy Coalition Framework specifically recognizes the role that new information can play in "policy learning" by bringing change to coalition positions at least on their "secondary" policy positions but also posits that such change is difficult and usually requires years [168]. Indeed, when there is a strong consensus among researchers, science has had major impacts on policymaking and has changed attitudes toward risk factors (e.g., DDT) and respected scientific organizations like the National Academy of Sciences often are turned to when controversy exists in order to reach a consensus that is unbiased. But in recent years, in the face of difficult decisions, emphasis is placed on reaching a political compromise among actors with conflicting objectives and science plays a supporting rather than decisive role in this process. By way of contrast, in the Federal courts, science has predominated.

3 Implementation and Enforcement Issues in Preserving Wildlife

The United States has been a leader in wildlife issues, both in creating national parks and in passing the Endangered Species Act (ESA) and other laws to protect wildlife. Many other countries have followed the United States in creating their own parks and passing similar wildlife protection legislation. However, there is the important question: how effective has conservation legislation been in preserving wildlife? It is a basic fact that the passage of legislation does not necessarily mean that these laws are effectively implemented and enforced. Wildlife conservation legislation exists in most countries, but may actually provide little help to preserve endangered species. The political science literature is full of examples where legislation is passed but merely serves as "symbolic politics" that is not intended to result in meaningful action [1]. Even when programs and activities are undertaken, in many cases the implementation of these programs is so ineffective that the programs accomplish little, if anything, of what was intended [2]. The classic case of legislation not being effectively implemented is the Prohibition (18th) Amendment to the U.S. Constitution that was followed by a decade-long flouting of the law [3]. More recently, Maryland, Virginia and the Federal government all experienced repeated failures in trying to solve dangers to crabs and fish in the Chesapeake Bay that led one official with the Chesapeake Bay Foundation to state that "We have the science and the solutions ... All we need is the implementation and the dollars" [4]. Below I study implementation and enforcement issues concerning wildlife preservation.

Williams points out that the United States rarely enforces the ESA on taking of endangered species on private lands and, on the rare occasion they do try to bring a case, they are often lambasted by the property rights movement, the media, and the public for persecution of the individuals doing the taking [5 p. 38]. The National Marine Fishery Service (NMFS) failed in the past to establish recovery plans for threatened species under its purview, but Congressional reviews of the NMFS did not take the agency to task for this failure, suggesting, according to Tobin, that Congress had no real interest in this aspect of the legislation [6 p. 259]. Tobin also points out that there is evidence that Section 7 of the ESA, requiring other agencies to consult with the USFWS, was intended to be symbolic rather than substantive because only a brief vague discussion of it exists in the House and the conference reports on this section [6 p. 149]. The Bureau of Land Management (BLM) refused to enforce rules against year-long grazing because it would harm "the financial condition of livestock operators" [7 p. 53]. Schorger found that states did not effectively implement wildlife protection laws that were on the books, so that species such as the passenger pigeon became extinct [8 p. 228]. For example, Pennsylvania had a law to protect the pigeon, but despite the fact that it had been "notoriously violated" "in all of the years it was in effect" "not one offender had been arrested" [8 p. 228]. Chase, Lamber, and Decker cite research that found that only 15 percent of hunters in Northwest Alaska obtained hunting licenses and the inhabitants of this area rebelled when out-of-season hunting regulations were enforced [9 p. 159]. In short, the existence of wildlife protection legislation and parks creates only the possibility that they may have some impact, but their effectiveness depends on the extent to which they are implemented.

The ESA now relies heavily on voluntary agreements (e.g., habitat conservation plans) between the USFWS and states, private property owners, developers, and extractive industries to implement habitat conservation plans (HCPs) that allow development that does not threaten endangered species. I document these agreements extensively in Chapter 5. The USFWS and the Obama Administration have touted these agreements as "win-win" agreements for conservation and industry alike. However, there are serious questions as to whether adequate oversight is conducted to determine if the terms of these agreements are actually being followed. In 2012, there was discussion by USFWS staff about the possibility of listing the sagebrush lizard "found only in New Mexico and West Texas' oil and gas country" [10]. The Texas State Comptroller at the time was Susan Combs, who "developed a plan to avoid federal regulations through voluntary pacts with landowners" [10]. USFWS had to approve the plan and the top official in Texas at the time was Gary Mowad, who proposed his "two most experienced biologists" to review the plan; they were rejected by Mowad's boss, Joy Nicholopoulos, who was in charge of the region. Instead, she requested that an "inexperienced biologist" named Allison Arnold be appointed to the review committee and subsequently Arnold reported directly to Nicholopoulos, cutting Mowad out of the review process [10]. The plan stated that "no more than one percent" of the sagebrush lizard's habitat "in the first three years of the plan could be disturbed" but the agreements were voluntary and did not require that landowners adopt "specific measures" to protect the lizards [10]. Moreover, the USFWS was "not allowed to see the agreements with specific landowners" thus making it impossible "to check to see if the plan was working" [10]. Mowad objected that the plan was not only "unenforceable but not even verifiable" [10]. Moreover, the then Southwest Regional Director for USFWS, Benjamin Tuggle, stated that "there was no way we were going to list a lizard in the middle of oil country during an election year" and, when Mowad spoke with USFWS's officer for scientific integrity about his concerns, he was reassigned to another job with no duties and subsequently retired, but brought a whistleblowing suit against the agency [10]. Tresaugue states that the Inspector General's Office concluded that Tuggle and the head of the USFWS (Dan Ashe, appointed by President Obama) had ignored warnings to discipline supervisors who "retaliated against biologists" and concludes that ultimately these supervisors received promotions while the whistleblowers suffered reprisals [10]. The sagebrush lizard's denial of listing is still being tested in courts by the Center for Biological Diversity [11]. The case reveals two significant issues. First, although the new collaborative devices offer ways of achieving compromises that reach agreements that appear to be conservation friendly, some of these agreements make it extremely difficult, if not impossible, to monitor whether they are being implemented. Secondly, a politically weak agency like USFWS, especially when it operates in hostile environments like the state of Texas, will not want to see agreements that they have touted as successes in working with conservative states challenged, even if the challenges raise valid scientific concerns. This is true of the conservation-friendly Obama Administration. Thus the emphasis on voluntary agreements makes the issue of implementation more important than ever.

Lax Enforcement Worldwide Problem

There are a multitude of studies that show that enforcement of wildlife protection is lax in many, if not most, countries. Fred Nelson studied natural resource management in Africa and concluded that wildlife policy changes are often espoused but rarely implemented [12 p. 25]. Steinhart studied the status of the spectacled bear in South America and found that, although it is illegal to shoot the bears "in all Andean nations," that the law "is not enforced" [13 p. 95]. Steinhardt goes on to note that in the United States, the solution would be to create a park to protect these bears but in South America, national parks have "no constituency" and often no staff [13 p. 95]. Only ten of Columbia's thirty-three parks have any staff at all, though he notes there are nation-to-nation differences – for example, Ecuador is more protective than Columbia [13 p. 100]. In Mexico, the vaquita (a small porpoise) is rapidly disappearing. Mexico instituted a two-year ban on the use of gillnets which trap the vaquita and there was a "strong law enforcement presence when a refuge for the vaquita was established in 2008" but now fishermen are still using gillnets and the control efforts have shrunk to virtually nothing [14]. This emphasizes one of the problems with implementation – efforts often dissipate through time. The Sumatran rhino is endangered, despite legislation to protect it, in Indonesia and Malaysia because the actions needed were "never implemented" [15 p. 129]. Similarly, Duffy found that Belize brought few cases "of environmental violations" despite the fact that it has an extensive set of environmental legislation [16 p. 40]. The root causes of the failure to forcefully implement programs are often due to demands from customers in wealthy countries. For example, Duffy says that threats to lemurs in Malagasy due to illegal mining for gemstones must be controlled by attacking the demand for the illegal gemstones in rich Western countries [16 p. 178]. Tilson, Nyhus, Rubianto, and Sriyanto report that, although some eighty-six poachers of tigers were arrested in Sumatra, only a few were convicted because the civil service was afraid of "repercussions" and also because powerful military and bureaucrats were involved in the poaching [17 p. 108]. Duffy places most of the blame for the problem on rich Western countries that have failed to enforce their restrictions on wildlife trade, pointing out that there were only eighty U.S. officers in 1993 to contend with 70,000 shipments of wildlife [16 p. 146].

In areas such as the Serengeti, Arcese, Hando and Campbell found that the budget of agencies to protect against poaching is subject to the rises and falls in tourism and that tourism decline during the 1986 time period resulted in only a single vehicle being available for poaching patrols [18 p. 510]. Rigney provides detailed accounts of the difficulty of enforcing international fishing quotas and bans [19]. According to him, reported records of catches are widely falsified and the efforts to enforce the rules are limited and of questionable effectiveness, due to the lack of resources as well as widespread corruption. Gibson provides a detailed case study of poaching in Zambia that illustrates the problems of enforcement [20]. He reports that although President Kaunda was the head of the government and favored strict enforcement of wildlife regulations, he was ineffective due to a number of reasons including the fact that the public did not view poaching as a problem, and that the implementation of the policies depended on others (including his own party members) who had little interest in antagonizing "their electorates." The agency responsible, the Zambian National Parks and Wildlife Service (NPWS), had inadequate budgets and personnel and their scouts rarely made more than one arrest per year for poaching [20 p. 38]. A similar situation prevailed in Kenya under President Moi. However, Moi was pressured by international forces (the World Bank) to preserve wildlife which led Moi to hire Richard Leakey as the Kenya Wildlife Service director, resulting in a renewed emphasis on preservation.

Weak Government and Weak Implementation

One of the factors that affects enforcement is the strength of the governments and the agencies involved. Williams found that a "hump-backed antelope" known as the saiga nearly became extinct in the former USSR by 1917 but under strict protection from the country's new Communist government, it recovered so that there existed about 2 million by the time of the breakup of the USSR in 1990 [21]. But the subsequent years under the weak new Russian government led to a huge drop in numbers down to 4,000 in 2002. Chivers examined the status of threatened sturgeon in the Caspian Sea area and found that developing countries such as Azerbaijan fail to enforce laws against poaching of sturgeon due to official corruption [22]. Buchori and Ardhian argue that the orangutan is threatened due to illegal logging in Indonesia due to the weakness of the bureaucracy [23 p. 278–81]. They found that nominally "illegal" logging is openly and regularly observed by both the police and military. Onishi points out that the Forest Ministry of Indonesia blames Indonesian local governments for ignoring national laws, thus allowing cutting of trees in parks aimed at protecting orangutans [24]. Similarly, Sturm states that the Costa Rican bureaucracy responsible for maintaining biodiversity is "understaffed and demotivated" so that destruction of woodlands is tacitly accepted by farmers [25 p. 243]. Gibson found that after achieving independence, many African countries did not enforce wildlife regulations because enforcement would hurt their political fortunes and their publics did not view these infractions as serious crimes [20 p. 38].

Many of the national parks in Africa are "paper parks" according to Duffy because park boundaries have been "breached" by local people as well as poachers [26 p. 24]. International enforcement actions such as those prohibiting trade in CITES (Convention on International Trade of Endangered Species of Wild Fauna and Flora) listed species depends primarily on nation states to do their own enforcement – there was only about a five million dollar budget for CITES enforcement in 1999 [27 p. 197]. Countries such as Canada are reluctant to take action against nations violating CITES because it could incur foreign trade reprisals [27 p. 198; 28 p. 173]. Outside pressures, such as from the World Bank, were required for many countries to place a higher priority on enforcement [20 p. 74].

The problem of ineffective implementation is even greater when it concerns international areas such as the world's oceans. Marine protected areas (MPAs) covering more than 1.6 million square kilometers have been established throughout the world as a major method to protect fish species that have been depleted over the past century [29]. However, a recent study reports that a large percentage of these MPAs are "paper parks" that do not enforce rules on no take or allow recreational and "hook and line" fishing [29]. Edgar et al. state that only about 10 percent of the MPAs have at least four of the five characteristics to be effective in protecting "marine biodiversity" [30].

Threats to Government Workers and Conservationists

A significant reason why agencies are often reluctant and weak in their implementation and enforcement activities is the fact that agency personnel and citizens sympathetic to the laws are often threatened with violence. Bielski gives an account of how U.S. Forest Service workers were threatened by a rancher resisting restrictions on grazing in the national forest [31 p. 34]. The rancher threatened the rangers with "100 people with guns to meet you" if they tried to enforce the rules. Williams gives an account of a woman named Midge Erskine who pursued a twelve-year personal campaign to prevent illegal dumping of oil that threatened migrating birds [32 p. 29]. Erskine said that she was threatened, her dog poisoned, and a wildlife sanctuary she had constructed was firebombed, among other reprisals, before action was finally taken. USFWS officials attempting to reintroduce wolves to the Southwest near the Gila National Forest were told that "someone is going to get shot over this," according to Robinson [33 p. 158]. Robinson [33] says that consequently the USFWS got "cold feet" and delayed their implementation plan. Shrimpers who employed TEDS (Turtle Excluder Devices) were threatened with being shot and other reprisals such as having their boats burnt [34 p. 30]. Donahue provides an account of how a couple in Oregon who spoke out against overgrazing on a wildlife refuge were socially ostracized and warned to leave the area or "they would be dead" [7 p. 107]. Russell relates how a couple, Denzel and Nancy Ferguson, worked at a field station in the Malheur National Wildlife Refuge and when they complained about overgrazing of cattle, groups associated with cattlemen tried to have them fired and, when that did not work out, they tried to get the state legislature to stop funding of the station [35 p. 17–19]. According to Russell, Don Oman, a Forest Service ranger working in the Sawtooth National Forest, began enforcing standing rules about cattle grazing too close to riparian (e.g., streams) areas that had never been enforced before [35 p. 46–53]. Ranchers in this area sought to have him removed by contacting Congressional and Forest Service officials but these actions failed in this case and he remained with the Service. Another example is the harassment of Center for Biological Diversity (CBD) staff in New Mexico. CBD staff had the tires of their car slashed and a handmade poster put in a courthouse with gun hairs imposed over their pictures [36 p. 59].

The Wise Use Movement begun in the 1990s has been associated with "bombings of Forest Service and BLM offices" as well as a Forest Service Ranger's home [37 p. 124]. Keiter reports that when the Nevada state's national forest director resigned her job after bombings, she called attention in her resignation letter to the "atmosphere of fear and intimidation" directed at Federal employees in these rural areas [38 p. 236]. More than a hundred incidents of violence occurred against employees of the Federal agencies (the Forest Service, BLM, and USFWS) seeking to implement environmental regulations [39]. Helvarg details numerous incidents where anti-environmental activists sought (and often succeeded) in intimidating both Federal employees and environmentalists such as by following Forest Service workers home [39]. One such activist said "You can't reason with eco-freaks but you sure can intimidate them" [39 p. 202]. One environmentalist cited by Helvarg argues that conservationists lose out to anti-environmental groups in public meetings due to this intimidation with the result that a minority view dominates [39 p. 179]. Rick Bass, an environmental writer, related how he visited a gas station in Arizona and, when he mentioned wolves, the owner said that "the only problem with Babbitt" [former Secretary of the Interior under Clinton] is that "he is still alive" [40 p. 162]. Recently, High Country News published an online map with links to documents describing dozens of incidents where "anti-government" persons threatened government officials (e.g., BLM, USFWS, and U.S. Forest Service employees) on public land [41]. Helvarg contrasts the attitude of the FBI in dealing with threats from eco-terrorists and those involving attacks on conservationists – the former are given top priority while the FBI has little or no interest in the latter [39 p. 239]. During the George W. Bush Administration, Wise Use activists became heads of the governmental agencies that they formerly fought such as Gail Norton, Secretary of Interior, and Anne Veneman, Secretary of Agriculture [42]. Threats of violence against environmental agencies are common in other countries, too, such as in Guatemala and El Salvador. McConahay says that not a single source in Guatemala wanted their name used in her environmental reports due to their fear of reprisals [43 p. 45]. However, McConahay also acknowledges that tourism related to wildlife has given the environmental agencies some "political clout" [43 p. 45 & 48].

The best-known recent incident of threats against Federal employees attempting to implement wildlife conservation policy concerns the case of Cliven Bundy and his ranch in Nevada. Bundy stopped paying grazing fees when the BLM "ordered him to restrict grazing" to certain "periods … in order to protect the endangered desert tortoise" [44]. Fifty heavily armed supporters forced the BLM to back down and return the cattle they had removed. Cliven Bundy said later that "they don't have the guts enough to try to start that again for a few years," and one of his sons said "We ran them out of here … We were serious. We weren't playing around" [44]. A deputy assistant director with the Bureau of Land Management announced that they were withdrawing from the area and would now pursue the matter "administratively and judicially" [44]. As of March 2015, Bundy still had "not been charged for the trespassing cattle or the unpaid fines" and his cattle had "all returned back to their normal grazing habitat" [45]. Secretary of Interior Sally Jewell responded to a question about the Bundy prosecution status by stating that "the case is in the hands of the FBI . . . and Department of Justice" but neither agency nor the BLM would comment on the status of the case [45]. Bundy and his son subsequently encouraged nearby counties "to cease engagement with BLM" [45]. A former Superintendent of Lake Mead National Recreation Area, Alan O'Neill, said that he had a similar experience with Bundy in 1994 and he was "told to back off because of concern for violence" and Bundy's cattle remain a problem in the Recreational Area too [46]. O'Neill rhetorically asks "What if other people decide that they are also going to do whatever they want on Federal land regardless of the law and stake claims to that right" [46].

On January 2, 2016, Ammon Bundy (Cliven Bundy's son) and a small group of armed men took over the Malheur Wildlife Refuge in Oregon stating that they intended to stay "for years" "freeing these lands up . . . getting ranchers back to ranching, miners back to mining, and loggers back to logging" [47]. Federal law enforcement officials initially responded tepidly to the takeover. The cautious nature of their response to both Bundy incidents was the result of previous disastrous consequences from armed responses by the FBI to confrontations with radical right extremists at Ruby Ridge in Northern Idaho and Waco, Texas [48], that became "rallying cries for anti-government militants" and may have contributed to incidents like the bombing of the Federal building in Oklahoma City [49]. Thus the FBI took a cautious approach in waiting eighty-one days of negotiations with "Freemen compound" in Jordan, Montana, and eventually secured their peaceful surrender. But others argue that the failure to do anything about the earlier Cliven Bundy standoff after one and a half years "set a bad precedent" and encouraged the Ammon Bundy takeover. Indeed, the spokesperson for the 2016 takeover, LaVoy Finicum, stated that the "government crushes those who will not or cannot fight back" but "they don't go after the strongest wolf" [49]. In the Oregon case, the local Harney County Sheriff David Ward was fully in support of enforcing Federal law but there are many local sheriffs in the West who challenge the authority of Federal and state agencies. For example, the Siskiyou (CA) County Sheriff stated: "Some of your federal and state agencies care more about fish, frogs, trees and birds than (they) do about the human race" [50].

The Malheur occupation ended when Ammon Bundy and four others were arrested when they left the refuge for a meeting and were stopped by a combination of FBI and Oregon State Police. Finicum was shot dead and Ryan Bundy (Ammon's brother) was shot in the arm [51]. Cliven Bundy was also arrested when he left his Nevada compound and flew to Oregon to support the Malheur occupation. Several days later the remaining protesters left the Malheur and the occupation ended.

Taken together, the two Bundy incidents demonstrate why agencies like the BLM and USFWS are reluctant to try to implement wildlife protections when the opposition consists of armed anti-government militants – they are not designed nor equipped to handle such situations and even Federal and state law enforcement officials are reluctant to act. The FBI prefer to rely upon action by the local law enforcement people such as the sheriff as well as state officials [52]. In the Cliven Bundy case, BLM asked for the support of the local sheriff but failed to get it but in the early 1990s, the BLM routinely asked for and often received support from the local law enforcement because BLM staff numbers are small and spread out over huge areas of the West [53]. The role of the local sheriff is key because the militants often view them as the only legitimate law enforcers [53]. Anti-Federal sheriffs have formed an association, the Constitutional Sheriffs and Police Officers Association, that supports the view that the local sheriff can nullify Federal law [50].

It is difficult to think of other cases where U.S. Federal officials are threatened openly and successfully with violence without the government taking action – Cliven Bundy's arrest came one and a half years after his initial standoff. During the standoff with Bundy, Bundy's position was supported by several politicians including Nevada Senator (Republican) Dean Heller who referred to the Bundy supporters as "patriots" [44]. The Bundy case demonstrates the life-threatening difficulties of implementation of wildlife conservation even in an "advanced country" with a strong central government like the U.S., and the fact that resisting forces often have strong local and state support and thus are able to intimidate Federal employees. Nevertheless, it is important to note that, despite the weakness shown in the Bundy cases, the broader perspective is that grazing on BLM-owned Western public lands has declined by 25 percent [54 p. 156].

Delays in Acting

Delay is often a tactic used to weaken enforcement of environmental laws. For example, the Audubon Magazine reports that the delays of listing of species led to the extinction of freshwater mussels during the construction of Tennessee-Tombigbee Waterway [55 p. 8]. The reintroduction of gray wolves was delayed for several years by Congressional members from Wyoming [56 p. 108]. Rules mandating use of TEDs were first delayed by the Commerce Department for a study of the effects of seaweed and later by shrimpers blocking the Houston shipping channel which led again to suspension of these rules [57 p. 156]. Reagan's Commerce Secretary, Robert Mossbacher, himself delayed the implementation of rules requiring TEDs [34 p. 28]. Another problem is that, although a recovery plan may be established for a species, its success often depends on actions of state and local officials who fail to do what was needed, as occurred in the case of the Hawaiian threatened bird, the palila [6 p. 249]. Tobin found no relationship between the establishment of a recovery plan for a species and successful outcomes, because many of the tasks in the plans had not been completed [6 p. 244–5]. The USFWS regularly misses deadlines for making decisions about the listing of species as endangered and, indeed, Congress has placed a cap on the amount of money that can be devoted to listing of species [58 p. 336 & 355–6]. Yaffee cites the case of the designation of critical habitat for grizzly bears as an example of a delay that extended far beyond what was supposed to happen according to the law [59 p. 88]. The lack of cooperation of other Federal agencies is also a problem. For example, Hunt reviewed the impact of Federal water projects on biodiversity and found that Corps of Engineers' consistently opposed USFWS's proposed mitigation activities [60]. The call for more research is another reason often used to delay actions. Knowledge about the causes and extent of endangerment of species can always be improved and thus there can be legitimate reasons for delay due to inadequate knowledge. However, calls for more research often are employed more cynically, as Arha and Emmerich illustrate in discussing how Rocky Mountain states demanded research in order to delay the listing of grizzlies but later these same states criticized environmental organizations' call for more research before delisting the grizzly because they viewed it as ploy to delay the delisting [61 p. 291 & 304].

Inadequate Resources

Implementation and enforcement agencies generally have modest budgets and few personnel to implement and enforce laws and regulations. In the United States, the USFWS is known for being a "timid" agency and also understaffed [62 p. 108 & 119]. There are few agents and small resources devoted to preventing illegal smuggling of endangered birds. For example, on the Texas-Mexico border, there are only two assigned agents, despite the fact that the profits to be derived from the sale of the birds exceed that of drugs. Due to the limited number of USFWS inspectors, the detection of illegal importation of endangered species or parts (e.g., bear gall bladders) depends largely on general U.S. Customs inspectors for whom detection of drugs is the top priority [63]. Consequently illegal smuggling contributes in a major way to decline of endangered species despite the fact that countries such as Venezuela, Brazil, and Ecuador have total bans on the export of these animals [64 p. 74]. Lynn Greenwalt, while she was director of the USFWS, stated that due to their limited resources they were only able to carry out about one-quarter of what they needed to do and thus the USFWS can only deal with high priority species [6 p. 58]. The director of EPA's endangered species program admitted that they have limited staff [65]. In 2014, Vucetich and Nelson criticized the USFWS's decision not to provide protections to endangered species unless the entire species is threatened and "not to take into account its historical distribution" but "only where the species is found now" [66]. The response of USFWS's director, Dan Ashe was as follows [67]:

Among these is that scarce resources [of the USFWS] needed to help species at high risk – such as elephants facing a global poaching and trafficking crisis – would go instead to species no longer facing extinction's peril [i.e., wolves]. Further success, measured by species recovered and taken off the endangered list, would be slowed, and yet that success is critical to sustaining public and political support for this vital law.

Thus the USFWS's head acknowledged that limited resources and concern with public support led to an important policy limiting restoration of species.

In 2015, President Obama announced "an aggressive plan for taking on traffickers that will include using American intelligence agencies to track and target those who benefit from the estimated $20-billion-a-year market" but in reality there will only be a "limited increase in the budget" of "law enforcement arm of the USFWS" [68]. According to Nixon, the budget request for the new fiscal year is $75 million, "an 8 million increase over the previous year" [68]. There has been a long-term decrease in the USFWS law enforcement investigations; they dropped from 13,000 in 2012 to 10,000 in 2014. Moreover, the deputy director of the USFWS law enforcement service says that they have the same number of officers as in the 1970s when the "trade was nothing like it is today" [68]. It is estimated that the chances of being caught are only 10 percent and due to limited resources, the agency focuses on the "biggest smugglers" [68].

There is a clause in the ESA that allows delays for species worthy of being protected due to threats to them. These species are referred to as "warranted but precluded (WBP)." The primary justification for WBP status is that the USFWS has other higher priorities that it is working on that preclude it from giving attention to these new listings. The agency assigns a "Listing Priority Number" from 1 (highest priority) to 12 that is based on the magnitude (of the threat), immediacy, and "taxonomic status" [69 p. 2]. Environmental organizations such as the CBD claim that the assignment of the WBP status is abused in order to "avoid angering industry lobbyists," and cite cases such as the bull trout, which was recognized as a "candidate for listing" in 1985; nothing occurred until 1992 when two conservation groups brought the case to the courts, which ruled that the agency's actions were "arbitrary and capricious" [70]. Environmental organizations have also claimed that the Bush Administration deliberately cut funds for listing in order to be able to use the WBP status as an excuse for not listing species. Despite more than 200 species on the candidate "waiting list," WildEarth Guardians says that the Interior Department only asked for an average of $10 million for listing between 2003 and 2010, a fraction of the $153 million it says that would be required to "address the backlog" [71].

There is evidence that environmental groups more recently have sought to cope with the limited resource problem by avoiding the listing process and working to force extractive industries and landowners to sign "conservation agreements" to set aside habitat for species and investing in restoration such as for the sage-grouse [72 p. 10]. Indeed, the Audubon's policy advisor for the Central Flyway says that the agreement reached "by NOT [Audubon's emphasis] listing" the sage-grouse could be "the Endangered Species Act's greatest success" [72]. Thus the threat of an ESA listing may enable the achievement of goals despite limited resources through compromises, though this presumes that the listing threat is taken seriously.

As far as protection of species on private lands is concerned, in order for developers to have incentives to participate in HCPs, developers must perceive that there is a likelihood of being punished if they fail to do so; this is a hard sell, according to Timothy Beatley, because enforcement officers are so rare (e.g., only one for the entire state of Nevada) [73 p. 217]. One of the few aspects of the ESA to focus on recovery was the requirement that critical habitat be designated for endangered species, but sometimes administrations such as that of the George W. Bush refuse to carry out activities listed in the law. The Bush Administration held that such designations were redundant and would not help [74 p. 76]. Both the USFWS and the most enthusiastic interest groups supporting endangered species have admitted that Congress has only allocated a tiny proportion of the resources that would be necessary to do a full implementation of the ESA. For example, Seelye quotes a USFWS official as saying "there is a disconnect between what we need to do under the Act and the funds we have to do it" [75]. The CBD, one of the most active groups pushing for tougher enforcement of ESA agreed to a compromise in 2001 that would protect twenty-nine endangered species in exchange for a promise that they and other environmental groups would not push for "immediate court compliance" with some other species. A Center spokesperson justified this compromise based on the fact that "Congress had shucked its responsibility to provide money for the mandates of the ESA" [75]. For perspective, it should be acknowledged that virtually every governmental program (with perhaps the exception of the military during a full-scale war) is provided with fewer resources than required to fully achieve its goals. Moreover, protection of wildlife does not have the same associated interest group political strength that is likely to create Congressional support for added resources for agencies such as USFWS compared, for example, with programs for Social Security beneficiaries.

Conflicting Goals and Powerful Opposing Forces

Agencies have goals that may conflict with conservation of wildlife. For example, the U.S. Forest Service argues that "it must keep southeast Alaska loggers and sawmills in business" and thus planned a large auction of timber in the Tongass National Forest, despite the objections of environmental groups who say the logging would threaten the Alaskan wolves that rely on deer whose habitat would be affected [76]. The logging industry has dropped from 4500 to 200 jobs in the Southwest area of Alaska, but one Forest Service ranger said: "Without the mills, there's no timber industry and, without the Forest Service's second-growth sales, there are no mills . . . We've got to keep the mills alive" [76]. Although the relative importance of the timber industry in the area is now small, the industry nevertheless has strong political support because Alaska's Congressional delegation supports logging and Senator Lisa Murkowski could become the head of the Senate Committee overseeing Forest Service's budget [76].

The slow implementation of USFWS's experimental Red Wolf Recovery Program in North Carolina illustrates how agency staff must "walk on egg shells" in trying to implement the program. A previous effort to recover red wolves in the Land Between Lakes area of Kentucky did not work due to the "failure to secure the cooperation of the state and local landowners" [77 p. 30–8]. So when another red wolf recovery effort was made in North Carolina, USFWS took several steps to try to ease acceptance of the program. An outside evaluation of the North Carolina Red Wolf Recovery Program by the Wildlife Management Institute (WMI) found that the agency left the implementation of the program up to local staff (rather directing it centrally) and proceeded with the "best of intentions" in trying to "gain public acceptance for the reintroduction" and "to build constructive relationships" with local landowners [77]. The experimental designation given to the wolves is intended to maximize flexibility for implementation because it gives significant latitude for taking wolves under certain conditions such as [77 p. 35–6]:

(1) Any private landowner or any other individual having his or her permission, may take red wolves found on his or her property when the wolves are in the act of killing livestock or pets provided that fresh kills are evident and the take is reported within 24 hours;

(2) Any private landowner or any other individual having his or her permission, may harass red wolves found on his or her property provided the harassment is by methods that are not lethal or physically injurious to the wolf again if it is reported within 24 hours.

(3) Any private landowner may take red wolves found on his or her property after efforts by project personnel to capture such animals have been abandoned; provided the Service project leader has approved such actions in writing and it is reported within 24 hours.

(4) Public Land: Any person may take red wolves found on lands owned or managed by federal, state, or local government agencies provided that it is incidental to lawful activities; is unavoidable, unintentional, and not exhibiting a lack of reasonable due care.

One part of the program is to prevent hybridization between the red wolves and coyotes in the area. In order to do this, the USFWS has employed what they refer to as a "placeholder strategy" that involves the capture and sterilization of coyotes in nearby areas [77 p. 20]. A significant problem is that when wolves are killed (often due to illegal poaching, auto accidents, poisonings, among other causes), the remaining member of the breeding pair is more likely to interbreed with coyotes. While the strategy has been somewhat effective in preventing hybridization, the WMI report questions whether it can be continued indefinitely because it is time-consuming for the agency with its limited resources. Some wolves are taken by people who claim that they thought they were taking a coyote. In response to a court case, the agency has enforced a five county ban on coyote hunting [77 p. 38]. The WMI report concluded that this ban had lit a "powder keg" of emotion with many people of the area viewing it as a "violation of property rights" and "the right to defend their home" [77 p. 55]. The WMI also found an underlying distrust and dislike for the Federal presence in the area due to the fact that the Federal government "owns much of Dare County" in eastern North Carolina as well as the presence of many Federal employees and their restrictions related to protection of wild horses. As a result, WMI concluded that there appeared to be a "concerted effort" recently to discredit the red wolf program with several landowners making numerous requests for red wolf removals from their lands and claims about negative results of the wolf programs at public meetings such as the lowered number of deer available for hunting – claims that the WMI found to be "not accurate" after studying data [77]. The WMI conducted a survey at public meetings about the red wolf program and found that slightly more than half (53 percent) of the attendees did not agree that restoration of "rare species was important." WMI also found that USFWS relationship with the State of

North Carolina's Wildlife Resources Commission had become tenuous. WMI concludes by advising the USFWS to employ a "comprehensive conflict resolution" approach to deal with stakeholders who have "deeply held and conflicting values and interests" [77 p. 65]. Overall, the red wolf population, which had increased from its introduction in 1987 to 2006, has declined over the last eight years [77 p. 20]. The North Carolina Red Wolf case emphasizes the difficulties of implementation of a wildlife program in the face of state and local opposition.

Social Customs versus Enforcement

There are severe limitations on the resources of wildlife agencies that make it difficult, if not impossible, to enforce regulation; consequently it is essential that the majority of the population accept prohibitions if they are to be effective. Thirgood and Redpath found that legal enforcement of laws protecting hen harriers in the United Kingdom was ineffective because hunters blamed them for drops in grouse populations [78 p. 1551–3]. Thus the authors conclude that a change in attitudes of hunters is the solution – not law enforcement.

China presents an example of a country that has many laws to protect wildlife that are strong on paper but weak on enforcement, rendering the laws ineffective. Recently, China passed a new law to prosecute consumers for "eating protected wild animals" and this legislation was praised by conservationists because "the country's huge appetite for exotic animals" is "the prime driver of illegal trade" [79]. Despite the new legislation, endangered species such as the pangolin are still in trouble due to a "catch" in Chinese law – protected species "can be eaten if they were bred in captivity" [79]. Thus farmers can raise the species for a fee of about 5 percent of the sale price and payment of a "conservation management fee." Critics maintain that restaurants "pass off" illegal wild animals as "legal" and consequently "enforcement is difficult," rendering the new law of questionable utility [79]. In China, businesspeople often offer eating of exotic (and preferably wild) animals as a "part of business culture" [79]. In short, when laws run counter to important social and cultural expectations held by important businesspeople, they are likely to fail.

Weak Legal Penalties

Fines and punishments for violating the ESA have been limited in number and weak, though they were increased in 1988. Tobin reports that during the Reagan Administration, the number of investigations and agents declined [6 p. 267]. According to Williams, judges often do not view taking of endangered species such as butterflies as serious offenses and give light penalties to those convicted of this crime [80 p. 33]. Evidence shows that strict enforcement can deter poaching. According to Schueler, after a Texas man was convicted for illegally shooting eagles from a helicopter, "there were no reports of illegal killings of eagles for some time" in Texas [81 p. 97]. Democratic as well as Republican Administrations are often hesitant to enforce rules. James Baca, a former head of the BLM under Clinton, criticized the Administration's failure to back up employees enforcing regulations because of the fear that it will lead to a loss of votes, thus resulting in appeasement that leads to more threats [82 p. 85]. Bass states that the Federal government had not prosecuted any hunters or ranchers for killing wolves in Montana by 1992 because they did not want to bring a case until they were confident that they could win it because a loss would send "a message" that it was open season on wolves. In short, caution makes the government reluctant to act [83 p. 144].

Federalism and Enforcement

The U.S. government is based on the institution of federalism, which means that state and local governments play an integral role in implementation and enforcement. But Mathiessen's history of wildlife in the United States says that states were unable to enforce their own laws and it was "only Federal agencies, cooperating with private agencies that slowed the decline of native species" [84 p. 184]. Williams found that enforcement of rules against illegal oil waste pits varies greatly by the state, with Colorado and Texas conducting serious enforcement in contrast to many other states [32 p. 26]. Beatley, Fries, and Braun report that the Balcones Canyonlands HCP had to rely upon expensive purchase of land as a solution to save cave invertebrates because the state of Texas does not allow land use controls [85 p. 77]. U.S. county governments are often key to the control of developments and how they affect wildlife. Wortman-Wunder found that some county governments passed "land preservation subdivision ordinances that aim to concentrate on certain areas of the development leaving the rest of the area as free open space" [86]. However, a study of such developments in the Boulder, Colorado area found no significant differences in the preservation of biodiversity in most cases between the new developments and more dispersed housing and both forms of housing developments had less biodiversity than undeveloped areas [87]. Inslerman tells of how the New York State Department of Environmental Conservation felt they had to adhere to local laws, even though they viewed their agency as being beyond local control, such as laws "prohibiting the transportation of dangerous animals including wolves" [88 p. 30]. Lenth, Knight, and Gilgert argue that planning on a regional level is required to protect biodiversity. Federalism affects wildlife conservation in many other countries [87]. For example, Australia has a law similar to our ESA but its enforcement depends largely on states and territories and its protections mainly apply to federal lands (which make up only 1 percent of the continent) [89 p. 959].

State wildlife conservation departments tend to have budgets that are heavily based on fees from hunters and fishers, and historically these constituencies have had a dominant control over department policies. This is perhaps best illustrated by the case of the Alaska Department of Field and Game (ADFG) which has undertaken the goal of boosting caribou populations by killing competitors to human hunters such as wolves and bears [90 p. 223]. Critics of this approach have labeled the ADFG policy as a "game farm" approach to wildlife conservation. A counterforce was exerted against this approach when the state was threatened with tourism boycotts. The controversy over wolves illustrates the problems of relying on state policies to regulate a far-ranging species. While Idaho and Montana developed management plans considered satisfactory by the USFWS to protect wolves, Wyoming resisted and the judge stated that he could not take the wolf off the endangered species list on a "state by state basis" – that it would take all three Northern Rocky states to "assure its well-being" [91].

In recent years, Hawaii, Oregon, Washington, Illinois, California, Maryland, New York, and Delaware have passed laws banning the use of shark fins, but these bans are "hard to police" because of the limits on staff – for example, California has thirty-five fewer "ground wardens than they did in 1990" [92]. It is difficult to determine the effectiveness of bans. There were only seven citations for violating the ban in the seven states in 2013, which makes it difficult to know if the small number reflects the effectiveness of the ban or if violators are able to get around it by going underground [92]. The same issue applies to other bans, such as the international ban on the sale of ivory. The bans are resented by merchants in areas with large numbers of Chinese, such as San Francisco, where a Chinese advocacy group is "fighting the ban in federal court" claiming "discrimination." Some of the staff vested with the responsibility of enforcing the bans complain "about the piling on of new bans" to protect "critters" [92].

The Bureau of Land Management historically was dominated by ranchers and agricultural interests that favored grazing on Federal lands because Congressional committees that oversaw BLM were dominated by members from Western states [93 p. 240]. According to Debra Donahue, the organizational structure of the BLM is another reason why it was reluctant to enforce rules "against year-long grazing" on public lands in Nevada [7]. Donahue says that the BLM implementation of rules was dominated by state directors whose power base depends on state and local interests such as the grazing industry. She cites a BLM employee who says that changes that ranchers did not like were postponed or modified [7 p. 72]. By way of contrast, the U.S. Forest Service's multi-state regional structure made it less subject to state and local pressures. From the perspective of the agencies involved, they are now often looking for compromise among the interest groups that present competing demands to them. Koontz and Bodine found that "political obstacles" were the "most frequent" barrier to implementing ecosystem management, based on a survey of Forest Service and BLM employees [94 p. 66]. In particular, they cited "pressure to use BLM lands for a particular" use as the top obstacle and an "inability to get different interests to work together" as the third most important obstacle [94 p. 66].

There have been extreme and indefinite delays in implementing policies. When President Clinton set aside "1.9 million acres of forests, canyons and mesas as Grand Staircase-Escalante National Monument in 1996," many assumed that grazing would be greatly reduced if not eliminated in the area [95]. However, grazing was "grandfathered in" and it was only in 2015 that BLM was finally seriously considering implementation of a grazing "management plan" [95]. A 2002 memorandum required that BLM first declare that lands within grazing districts are no longer "chiefly valuable for grazing" before allowing a permit to be retired" but BLM has been very reluctant to do this [95].

Moreover, there is a dispute over how rigorous the standards for grazing should be, with some studies indicating that 65 percent of grazing lands did not meet "rangeland health standards" but in 2008 a more lenient standard found that only 20 percent did not meet the standard [95]. Utah's two senators (Hatch and Lee) have introduced the Grand Staircase-Escalante National Monument Grazing Protection Act, which would "preserve the grazing rights that Utah families have used for generations, and prohibit BLM from reducing grazing" [95]. Peterson cites comments by representatives of the non-profit Grand Canyon Trust that "the ranchers and county governments are running the monument" and that the BLM is "frightened and paralyzed" [95]. In short, though national monuments and other Federal public lands are nominally under the direct control of Federal agencies, powerful state and local groups and politicians are able to intimidate and indefinitely delay implementation of policies to protect public lands for wildlife.

The Courts and Enforcement

The role of courts in the ESA is controversial. Some contend that reliance on courts is counterproductive and ineffective. Wyman argues that it is unlikely that USFWS can "list let alone protect" species and believes that court suits by environmental organizations are overburdening the agency and forcing them to spend time on less important and less threatened species [96 p. 495]. Wyman concludes that the ESA has been mostly unsuccessful in achieving goals of restoring endangered species, and suggests that the current goals of ESA are too ambitious to be achieved and should be made more realistic by making them "time-limited" and "probabilistic," such as, for example, to "reduce the danger of extinction to a certain percentage over a 100 year period" [96 p. 518]. Wyman proposes solutions, such as the need to set priorities, to make the most of limited resources and focus on "hotspots" and tailor protections to specific species, supplementing the "old standby" ESA measures (e.g., designating critical habitat and prohibiting taking of endangered species) with other alternatives such as conservation banking and payments to state and local governments as well as private landowners [96 p. 520–1].

Despite Wyman's contentions, the evidence shows that the courts have been central to the protection of species in the United States. In particular, the ESA allows citizens to petition the USFWS to list species as endangered and, if the agency does not do so, to challenge the agency in Federal courts. One of the arguments against citizen lawsuits is that they prevent agency professionals who have greater knowledge of endangered species from making the decisions [97]. Congress has been aware of USFWS's dilemma with listings for some time and consequently forced them to adopt a set of priorities for listing species that included the following four factors: (1) the extent to which a species is threatened; (2) the probability that the species can be saved; (3) the "taxonomic uniqueness" of the species; and (4) the extent to which the preservation of the species would conflict with economic development [58 p. 335]. A recent article by Biber and Brosi compared listings initiated by petitions from the public with those originated by the agency and found the former were more endangered than those due to the USFWS [58]. Biber and Brosi also found that public-initiated listings were more likely to conflict with an economic development project [58]. These results suggest that these third-party suits force USFWS to take controversial actions they would not otherwise take. Achterman and Doermann reviewed the case of Coho Salmon in Oregon and observed that the National Marine and Fishing Service "rarely took enforcement actions" concerning the listing of fish but "the primary effect of the listing was the ability of third parties to bring citizen suits" which was "a large concern for both landowners and local governments" [98 p. 236]. The spotted owl case illustrates how the Federal agency most involved (the U.S. Forest Service) "did nothing to protect spotted owl habitat" until they were forced by the court case to reduce "old growth harvests enough" to preserve the spotted owl population [99 p. 154–5]. There are several instances where judges have forced the USFWS to reconsider its listing decisions such as the case of the greater sage-grouse. When the USFWS decided not to list the grouse, a judge ordered them to reconsider because their decision was based on "faulty science" that favored "oil and gas interests" [100 p. 22].

BLM's behavior has also been strongly influenced by the courts. Environmental non-governmental organizations (ENGOs) have found that their most successful challenges to grazing are through the courts, which have "generally favored the application of environmental laws" [93 p. 250]. Cashore and Howlett make the same point about the U.S. Forest Service and the spotted owl – the "key causal mechanism" that successfully protected old growth and hence the owl were the "strict legal" rulings of Judge Dwyer in the case [99 p. 155]. Hoberg provides data on the magnitude of change due to the role of courts [101 p. 31]. In the early 1960s, the Forest Service had to deal with only one lawsuit per year, compared to more than ninety cases per year throughout the 1990s. Keiter states that by late 1992 the courts "were essentially running the Northwest federal forests" and also stepped in to protect other species such as the grizzly bear and California gnatcatcher [38 p. 96 & 118–19]. He concludes that it is necessary to have the ESA "threat" to induce those involved to take difficult but necessary actions [38 p. 257]. Indeed, Nie goes further and states that a "judicial iron triangle" has replaced the previous "iron triangle" dominated by Congressional committees, interest groups, and Federal agencies [102 p. 73].

Congressional Riders

Congress has counteracted judicial rulings by passing riders and taking other actions that block the enforcement of ESA protections for species. The first rider took place in the well-known Tellico snail darter case when a mostly empty House passed a funding bill that exempted the Tellico project from ESA review [103 p. 173]. More recently, Congress forced the delisting of wolves [104; 105]. and passed a 1995 rider that allowed logging that had previously been banned – thus affecting the protections of the spotted owl and also the grizzly bear [38 p. 106–7]. Recently, Congress passed a budget rider that prohibited USFWS from protecting the sage-grouse as an endangered species for at least one year [95].

Conclusion

To summarize, laws and rules to preserve wildlife are generally hard to implement and enforce. Few resources are given to agencies responsible for implementation and enforcement, and thus the laws often remain "symbolic" rather than substantive. Actions to protect wildlife often interfere with powerful interests, and these forces resist and sometimes threaten Federal officials. Many people resent humans losing control of their land in order to protect wildlife – a form of redistribution they cannot accept. Consequently, the wildlife and conservation agencies are in a tenuous situation politically and are hesitant to take action. Cooperation is generally needed between the national and subnational governments to be successful, but this is often difficult to obtain. In many cases, public sentiment is against the strict enforcement of regulations. For many developing countries, only external pressures by non-governmental organizations and institution such as CITES, the World Bank, and ecotourism businesses provide these governments with the incentive to act. Wealthy countries, in their weak enforcement of illegal trade in endangered species, create the demand that causes some of the major problems in poorer countries. Even in wealthy countries such as the United States, implementation has faced numerous obstacles and often met with limited success, with much burden placed on the legal system due to the limitations and political weakness of the agencies involved. However, since the 1960s, the rise of environmental organizations along with organizations devoted to (often charismatic) species have changed the politics so that there is now a significant "advocacy coalition" on behalf of wildlife that was lacking previously. Nevertheless, given the limited resources of enforcement agencies such as USFWS, the emphasis on implementation has switched to voluntary agreements with the expectation – or at least hope – that they will be implemented as promised.

4 The Development of U.S. Wildlife Policies and Legislation

Policymaking concerning wildlife is influenced by a wide variety of forces including actions by legislative and executive institutions, interest groups, popular opinion, media coverage, and courts. In this chapter, I review the major forces in the United States that result in the enactment of wildlife policies, as well as those forces that block or defeat attempts at policy change. I begin with the crucial example of the Endangered Species Act (ESA) and then proceed to other wildlife conservation measures.

How the ESA Was Passed

The ESA is a good place to begin because it is the single most important legislation to influence wildlife preservation in the United States and this law has spurred similar legislation in many other countries. Scott views the development and passage of the ESA as the result of "timing" and "luck" due to the fact that the Nixon Administration had an Interior Department that was run by Republicans such as Rogers C. Morton who had strong interest in conservation [1 p. 41]. Robinson states that Nixon "despised environmental activists" but nevertheless wanted to build a reputation as an environmentalist with young people as a result of the passage of the constitutional amendment in 1971 guaranteeing the vote to those eighteen years or age or older [2 p. 314–15]. Russell Train confirms that Nixon had no personal interest in the environment and thus delegated oversight of it to staff; his disinterest may have made the development of such comprehensive legislation possible [3 p. 79–80]. According to Roman, the potentially "revolutionary" implications of the ESA resulted from language inserted by a scientist (Talbot) working for the Council on Environmental Quality and counsel (Potter) for the Merchant Marine and Fisheries committee – they eliminated the word "practicable" from the legislation, thus providing unqualified protection for species [4 p. 52]. Nixon and his senior staff did not notice the implications of the wording that made the ESA a "zero tolerance" law [4 p. 58; 5 p. 158–9]. Robinson says that the rancher "establishment" had just completed a full-scale war on proposed legislation to outlaw poisons for controlling "pests" and was not prepared to conduct a struggle against "a vaguer threat" – neither the "Farm Bureau nor the Woolgrowers" groups testified against it [2 p. 321]. Indeed, the discussion of the bill in the House raised no significant controversies with only short discussions on minor topics such as whether the Act would force Alaska's subsistence hunters to meet the requirements of Marine Mammal

Protection Act with regard to native handicrafts and the Senate discussed matters such as alligators in Louisiana [6 p. 198 & 384]. The vote in the House was 390 yeas to 12 nays; in the Senate 92 yeas and 0 nays.

Indeed, the fact that it was ignorance of a law's implications that enabled its passage was testified to by former Republican Senator Pete Domenici in a Senate hearing concerning the ESA in 2003 [7 p. 4–6]:

I have been here long enough to have voted for the ESA. I came here in 1972. At that time, I did not know very much about what I was voting on, but even if I did, I probably would have voted for the ESA. It is a great sounding piece of legislation. Obviously, when you look at it, and look at the kind of people who were then sponsoring it, you would for vote it. Back then, you had people like Scoop Jackson proposing the ESA and proposing other environmental laws of the days. You usually would vote for them. That is not to say that those same senators sitting here today would agree with the laws that they passed. Nonetheless, they were giants who were trying to make some sense out of what could end up being a very environmentally confused part of our country. Did any of us who voted for the ESA intend for it to apply retroactively? I do not think so. Did any of us who voted for it intend that through the courts you could achieve super status to the point of abrogating pre-existing contracts as has happened here? I did not.

Conservative Republican Don Young of Alaska made a similar assertion in a 2007 House hearing concerning the ESA [8 p. 98]:

And if I can, Mr. Chairman, my concern here is, and of course, I am probably the only person on this Committee that has ever voted for the Act itself, and it is probably the worst vote I made because we were misled at that time in what the Act was supposed to do, and the Act has been implemented and used by groups to try not to preserve species, but to impede any type of development or growth, and that is the unfortunate thing.

Some other important pieces of conservation legislation also owe their passage to ignorance of their implications. For example, Douglas Strong says that the 1891 Act that enabled public lands to be "set aside as public reservations" would "certainly have been defeated by Western congressmen" if its "true importance" had been recognized at the time [9 p. 65]. Allin says that opposition to the establishment of Yosemite National Park may have been deliberately undermined by its "misleading forest designation" [10 p. 33]. Likewise, many in Congress did not realize the importance of the passage of the National Environmental Policy Act that required consideration of any negative effects on the quality of the human environment" resulting from Federal actions [10 p. 157].

After the passage of the ESA, its revolutionary impact became clear, and subsequent attempts at changes in the ESA became much more difficult as both sides were aware of their implications. Since the 1970s, a wide array of policy organizations representing both environmentalists and those often opposed to conservation legislation, such as the business community, now closely monitor all proposed legislation for potential implications contrary to their interests so that surprises are less likely to occur. For example, the number of wildlife-related organizations increased from less than 50 in 1945 to 400 by the mid-1980s [11 p. 13]. Likewise, groups often opposed to wildlife conservation such as those affiliated with the Wise Use Movement are well organized, funded, and represented by organizations such as the Pacific Legal Corporation, People for the West, and Oregon Lands Coalition [12]. As a consequence, a virtual stalemate has occurred concerning the ESA and other wildlife conservation-related acts. For example, in 1982 during the Reagan Administration, both "pro" and "anti-ESA" factions were unable to come to agreement on a reform of the law [13 p. 133].

Nevertheless, the ESA continues to exert great policy importance, as is illustrated by the reaction of Western states like Montana to the possibility of the listing of the sage-grouse as an endangered species. The range of the grouse extends over 165 million acres and 11 states, much of it in areas rich with sources of fossil fuels [14]. An environmentalist said: "The sage-grouse issue may finally put the brakes on the fossil-fuel industry in a way that no other factor has been able to" [14]. In order to forestall the listing, there has been a "mad scramble among the unlikeliest of allies including western states, the energy industry, and federal officials inspired by the fear of loss of profits and revenues from projects that would have been prohibited if the listing occurred" [14]. Thus the ESA remains as important as ever.

The passage of the ESA represents not only the keystone event in wildlife politics but also a major deviation from the usual process of policymaking. For most of U.S. history, politics related to wildlife changed incrementally and was dominated by "policy subsystem" actors composed of "interest groups, public management agencies, and political representatives, which ... reward each other with favorable decisions ... to create a self-reinforcing cycle of support for a particular policy and to exclude opposing interests" [15 p. 10]. An example of such a policy subsystem concerns Western ranchers who graze their cattle on public lands. The subsystem includes "the House Resources Committee and the Senate Energy and Natural Resources Committee" with member-ships that "typically represent western districts or states" [16 p. 251]. Policies concern-ing grazing on public lands were formalized in 1934 by the Taylor Act and the combination of these committees, governors and legislators of Western states, and a friendly Federal agency (the Bureau of Land Management) maintained a status quo that was not challenged until the Clinton Administration [15 p. 19]. The demographics of the West have been changing over the last generation – the 2000 census showed that overall the West is nearly as urban as the East with about three-quarters of the population living in urban areas; environmentalists hope that these shifts will decrease the power of ranchers [17]. The actual number of ranchers who graze on public lands is quite small – 23,000 in sixteen Western states and the number of "permittee" ranchers in Wyoming is smaller than the "membership of the Wyoming Wildlife Federation" [18]. Despite these changes, the political influence of the livestock industry upon the Bureau of Land Management (BLM) and other agencies continues to be enormous.

The ESA which suddenly provided strong protections for species can be character-ized as an example of "punctuated equilibrium" in which a sudden "breakthrough" occurs after decades of little policy change with respect to wildlife. Repetto cites several forces that can lead to such change, and the relevant ones here include a "bandwagon effect" due to the rise of the environmental movement, the emergence of new science such as the threat to species from chemicals documented by Rachel Carson, and political entrepreneurship (Nixon's desire to coopt environmentalism as a campaign issue in the 1972 election) [15 p. 10–11]. The fact that the law emerged from the Nixon Administration was particularly important and allayed the fears of traditional forces who normally would oppose environmental legislation. Since its passage, groups threatened by the law such as ranchers and extractive industries have responded with forty years of "negative feedback" to try to limit the effects of the law, with the consequence that a deadlock has occurred with the law altered but avoiding major changes. Thus, the ESA appears to be a "once-in-a-lifetime" occurrence due in large measure to the naiveté of traditional forces that did not realize the threat posed by the law.

Developing Winning Coalitions: Multiple and Vague Goals

In order to pass legislation, proponents must appeal to a broad array of interests. Legislation is often designed to have multiple and often contradictory purposes within the same law in order to satisfy varied and often opposed interests. For example, Gilbert Pinchot was able to develop the U.S. Forest Service by promising ranchers and mining companies that they would have access to these resources [9 p. 70]. George Hartzog, one of the former heads of the National Park Service, discussed in his memoir how he had to craft language to attract hunter support to overcome resistance to the formation of a National Scenic Riverways in the Ozarks in 1964 by coming up with wording that was vague – because hunting traditionally had not been allowed in national parks [19 p. 67–8]. Hartzog describes how the "multiple use" theme was successful despite the fact that it had built-in contradictions [19 p. 66]:

> The theory of multiple use holds that forest lands may be used for a variety of benefits including water, forage, wildlife habitat, wood, recreation, wilderness and minerals. The extent of the area within which these mostly incompatible multiple uses may occur is never mentioned. On the contrary, the concept is packaged, locally, to leave the impression that one may have all of these goodies at the same time from the same acreage. Moreover, revenues received by the forest service from uses on the national forests are shared with the local governments in whose jurisdictions the forest lands are located ... Skillfully wedding the special interests seeking to exploit America's natural bounty with local politicians receiving a bonanza of public funds without the pain of local taxation, the forest service is, indeed, a powerful political force.

The Organic Law of 1916 promoted the conservation of wildlife but also had the goal of providing for human use and enjoyment of these areas that often conflicts with the wildlife preservation goal [20 p. 10; 21 p. 52]. The legislation creating the National Wildlife Refuges contains language that is subject to multiple interpretations such as "sound professional judgment" and "principles of sound fish and wildlife management." According to the U.S. General Accountability Office (GAO), incompatible secondary uses like hunting, grazing, recreation, logging, and gas and oil extraction are often overdone due to "pressures from local economic interests" [22 p. 3]. This GAO report discusses sixteen cases of incompatible uses such as grazing allowed in the Malheur National Wildlife Refuge. Visitors complained about overgrazing of cattle that damaged the population of Sandhill Cranes [22 p. 63–5]. In short, conservation legislation has often been able to be passed because of the vagueness of how it will work in practice and also due to the fact it has multiple and often conflicting goals that emerge over the course of implementation and enforcement of these laws.

The Effects of Institutionalism

Legislative institutions and processes play an important role in determining what legislation passes. One informal but strong norm in Congress is that when legislation affects particular areas of the country, that the Congressional representatives of these districts deserve deferment to their interests. An example of this process occurred when representatives from New York State (Carolyn Maloney) and Massachusetts (Joseph Kennedy) introduced a Northern Ecosystem Protection Act that would "prohibit development in 16.3 million acres of Rocky Mountain high country" [23]. This proposal had ninety co-sponsors "but not a single one from the districts affected" [24]. Democratic Senator Max Baucus of Montana responded by threatening to take away money targeted for cleaning up Boston Harbor, one of Rep. Kennedy's projects. The influence of westerners is bolstered by the institution of the committee system of Congress. The chair and membership of the Senate Committee on Energy and Natural Resources as well as the House Resources Committee are dominated by members of Western states, increasingly conservative Republicans who "are aligned with extractive industries" and who generally oppose new environmental legislation [25 p. 30]. Fleishner cites studies to show that livestock grazing on public lands is "the single most widespread and pervasive threat to riparian habitats in the arid West" and that the removal of livestock to save this habitat would be "relatively simple logistically" but difficult because of the "uniquely privileged role that ranchers play in U.S. politics and policy" [26 p. 238–9]. Indeed, ranchers virtually wrote the Taylor Act that created the BLM [26 p. 238]. Congressional representatives from other parts of the country do not seek out committees that set grazing policy and media have fostered a "romantic view of cowboys and ranching" [26 p. 250]. Astute users of institutions can facilitate or attack wildlife legislation. An example of the latter occurred when Senator Jesse Helms in 1995 "offered an amendment" to the FY1996 Interior Department budget that would terminate the North Carolina Red Wolf Reintroduction Program [27 p. 72]. Schlickeisen says that supporters of the red wolf program had to scramble to get support in the space of two hours and were barely successful with a 50 to 48 vote.

Public Opinion versus Organized Interest Groups

A theme of the "new conservation movement" is that there has been an erosion of public support for the environment and conservation. Marvier and Wong cite ABC and American Enterprise Institute surveys that show a big drop in the percentage of Americans who regard themselves as "environmentalists" from about 79 percent in 1989 to 41 percent in 2008 [28 p. 282]. They also cite a big drop in the percentage of people who favored the environment over the economy from 61 percent in 1985 to 41 percent in 2012. However, viewing the results available from Gallup of historical trends in attitudes toward the environment, I found that there were some consistent patterns behind the drops [29]. With respect to support for the environment over the economy, the percentages remained high (around 70 percent) from 1985 to 2000 but then dropped markedly to mid-40 to 50 percentage range since then. Surprisingly, the percentage of population stating that they care a great deal about "extinction of plant and animal species" dropped after 2000 from the mid-40 percent to mid-30 percent ranges but has remained about the same since then even during the "Great Recession." Likewise, the percentage of the population stating that the environment should be given priority over the development of U.S. energy supplies has remained fairly steady since 2001 with the exception of the Great Recession years of 2010–12. When asked if the U.S. government is doing "too much" in terms of protecting the environment, the Gallup polls show that the percentage saying "too little" has consistently exceeded those who say "about the right amount" or (far exceeding) "too much" and this has been the case even during the Iraq War and the Great Recession.

There is abundant survey evidence to show that the majority of the general public supports efforts at wildlife conservation. For example, a March 2005 NBC/Wall Street Journal poll found that 80 percent of the public supported protecting "endangered species even if some people may not be able to develop the land they own" [30] while a 2008 Gallup survey found that "loss of natural habitat for wildlife ranked fourth of eleven environmental problems that people said they "personally worry about" [31]. In some surveys, results suggest that people are less willing to sacrifice for wildlife. For example, a March 1990 survey found that 37 percent of the public would oppose development of energy sources in the Arctic National Wildlife Refuge (ANWR) while 57 percent thought that we could permit development and still protect wildlife [32]. Opinion data on these issues clearly can be affected by wars and serious economic events such as recessions and rapid increases in the price of oil, but it also varies strongly by partisanship. For example, a 2011 survey by Gallup found that overall 49 percent of the public favored "opening the ANWR for oil exploration" but there was a huge partisan divide with Republicans strongly in favor (67 percent) versus only a minority of Democrats (31 percent) [33]. There is also good evidence that general support for conservation of wildlife does not lead to effective action when well-organized interests oppose legislation. For example, surveys [34 p. 1237] show that 84 percent of the public believes "in protecting the marine environment for future generations" but Brailoskova [34 p. 1238] points out that this general support was insufficient to achieve marine conservation measures in the face of opposition from the New England fishing industry.

Popular support sometimes does result in conservation action. Groups such as visitors to national parks were found to be strongly (by a six-to-one margin) in favor of measures such as reintroducing wolves into the Yellowstone [35 p. 60; 36 p. 32–4]. Even in states such as Wyoming, the percentage favoring wolf reintroduction was about fifty percent, a third were neutral, and only sixteen percent were opposed and this evidence of popular support may explain why conservative Republican Senator Alan Simpson decided to consider wolf reintroduction that he previously had opposed [37 p. 316]. Bruskotter et al. surveyed the attitudes of conservative State of Utah's residents and found that the majority favored "non-lethal control of wolves" [38 p. 126]. Keiter states that there were over 160,000 mostly positive comments on the environmental impact statement on wolf reintroduction which helped spur the USFWS to take action to import Canadian wolves into Yellowstone [25 p. 132]. In recent years, there have been several bans on trapping that have been successfully passed in states such as Massachusetts (to protect beavers) [39]. Individual citizens can have an impact on wildlife issues. In Arizona, a citizen whose dog had been caught in a leghold trap succeeded (on a second try) in passing the ban on the traps by a 59 to 41 percent victory [40 p. 60–4].

Although general support for wildlife conservation is broad, nevertheless this support is often insufficient to overcome resistance from groups opposed. Part of the reason is that the intensity of the support from the mass public is not very strong. The situation is similar in Canada, where some researchers characterized public support for wildlife conservation as a "mile wide" (94 percent) but only "an inch deep" in terms of engendering action [41 p. 144–6]. When action is dependent on showing up and participating in meetings, environmentalists and conservationists are often outnumbered by groups such as hunters, ranchers, and agricultural interests. For example, Wisconsin's Department of Natural Resources held sessions open to the public concerning annual wolf hunts in 72 counties across the state and they were packed by hunters, resulting in a vote of 4482 to 772 in favor of the hunts [42]. David Helvarg cites an environmentalist who complains that conservationists tend to be "meek and subdued" when they face strong pro-development forces, with the consequence that majority opinion is dominated by a small fraction [43 p. 179]. Hamilton refers to the case of the ranchers whose cattle graze on public lands to make the same point: though their numbers are small (28,000 nationally), she says the determination of the majority of Americans to impose higher fees for grazing "is weak compared to the gritty determination of those whose profits and livelihoods might be affected" [44 p. 57]. Interest group theory views the outcome of policy as a result of "struggles among … organized groups" and who wins and who loses is dependent on "how well organized" they are and "how effectively they press their case [45 p. 62]. In most cases, ranchers, landowners, and hunters have a stronger and more persistent active base at the state and local levels than wildlife conservationists.

Disasters and Wildlife Policy

Environmental disasters can lead to passage of legislation. The development of the "North American Model of Conservation" took place when the disappearance of bison and other game made it impossible to deny the threat and because near extinctions proved that wildlife resources were not "inexhaustible" [46 p. 449]. Controls over hunting were passed and acceptance grew with the use of science to determine how much hunting should be allowed [46 p. 455]. Another good example of disaster leading to action concerns the extinction of the passenger pigeon. In 1900, Republican Congressman John Lacey of Wisconsin introduced the "nation's first wildlife protection law" (known as the Lacey Act) that "banned the interstate shipping of unlawfully killed" game. Lacey specifically cited the disappearance of the passenger pigeon as "a warning to all of humankind" and later its demise was used as a major argument to take action to cope with the threat in the 1960s to another bird, the dickcissel [47]. The other side of the equation, the recovery of formerly threatened species, can also lead to demands for policy change. For example, in 1966, the International Whaling Commission imposed a moratorium on hunting humpback whales that was successful in restoring the population to more than 20,000 in U.S. waters. Fishermen in Hawaii and Alaska's Fish and Game Department petitioned to delist the Northern Pacific humpback whales after their population recovered [48]. According to Goldfarb, conservationists resisted the delisting, not just because of concern with the whales but because the listing has been their major tool to block other projects such as drilling in the Arctic and (for Canada) the construction of oil pipelines [48].

Federalism and Wildlife Policy

Wildlife policy in the United States and other democratic countries is only partly determined at the national level. States control policy over state-owned areas and also strongly influence the way that Federal policy is carried out. Thus federalism is a major force in shaping wildlife policy. A key factor is that wildlife conservation policy in the states is made by state natural resource departments, wildlife commissions, and legislative committees; and that these institutions are in turn generally dominated by groups unfriendly to actions that threaten the status quo concerning hunting, agriculture, ranching, and extractive industries. There is evidence that administrators of state wildlife agencies pay closer attention to their "natural constituencies," such as hunters and ranchers, than to the general public. For example, in Arizona, a 1987 survey of attitudes showed support by a strong majority (77 percent) of the public for reintroduction of the Mexican wolf, but the director of the state game agency requested that a plan to bring back the wolves "be put on the backburner for several years" [2 p. 352–3]. Mattson points out that almost none of the Arizona Game and Fish Department's budget comes from general funds and that its members are appointed for five-year terms by the governor [49 p. 41]. In addition, the general public has little knowledge about the agency with most not even aware of what government agency was responsible for wildlife management [49]. Pacelle says that hunter and trapper control of wildlife agencies is often mandated by law, such as in Massachusetts where five of the seven seats on the State Fisheries and Wildlife Board must consist of hunters and trappers, despite the fact that they make up only 3 percent of the population of the state [50 p. 47]. In 1996, nearly 60 percent of Alaskans voted to prohibit same-day airborne hunting of wolves by the public and also to prohibit the state from using aircraft in government wolf-control programs except in the case of emergencies. However, in 1999–2000, the Alaska legislature used its constitutional powers to reverse these decisions and renew the banned practices. In addition, the state introduced a constitutional amendment that would prohibit all future policymaking by the initiative process, but this attempt failed [51]. Some states have made it more difficult to pass all types of initiatives, such as Oregon, Florida, and Idaho, in part due to concerns about "ballot-box biology" in which the public votes to institute bans on activities such as hunting and trapping [52]. Thus the combination of federalism and control of key state institutions has led to the formation of effective policy subsystems which have been often able to dominate wildlife policy even in the face of general public opinion.

Struggles over "ballot-box biology" have become common in many states. From the perspective of hunters and many wildlife managers, initiatives that ban hunting and trapping take away decision making from knowledgeable professionals that run state wildlife agencies. Susan Recce, the director of National Rifle Association's Conservation, Wildlife and Natural Resources Division, states that such initiatives take management decisions out of the hands of trained wildlife professionals and place them at the will of the general public [52]. Recce points to a 1996 ban on leghold and body gripping traps as leading to a huge increase in the beaver population in Maine that, according to her, resulted in flooded basements and roads as evidence of the bad effects of such initiatives [52]. Other major successful ban initiatives include a ban on mountain lion hunting in California in 1980 that survived an attempt to reinstate hunting of lions in 1996. Hunters successfully resisted an attempt to ban dove hunting in Ohio but, in order to do so, they had to raise a large amount of money from hunting supporters across the country because such initiatives necessitate a great deal of advertising and voter outreach. In the dove ban vote, their strategy, according to Rob Sexton, vice president of government affairs for the United States Sportsmen`s Alliance (USSA), was not to focus on dove hunting because "doves don't eat people and they don't spread disease" but instead to portray the initiative's animal rights supporters as radicals opposed to farming and medical practices too [52]. In Wisconsin during 1971 the state legislature designated the mourning dove as a "symbol of peace" and consequently, the state Department of Natural Resources (DNR) took the bird off the list of game to be hunted [53 p. 77]. In 1999, hunter-dominated advisory groups to the DNR proposed dove hunts which were then approved by the DNR and finally by a Natural Resources Board set up by the governor. The hunters' strategy in the political struggle was to argue that the banning of dove hunting was just a prelude to the outlawing of all hunting [53 p. 77–88]. In studying survey data on public attitudes toward predators such as wolves, grizzly bears, and mountain lions, it is striking that the survey data show the public in states like Alaska, Montana, and other Western states are much more accepting of these carnivores than the legislatures and state wildlife departments. For example, Kellert's study in 1980 found that Alaska's population ranked low on the utilitarian scale of attitudes toward wildlife [54 p. 117]. But the state legislatures in these states have repeatedly taken harsh measures toward carnivores. One explanation for the divergence between public attitudes and state policy is that those who hold negative attitudes care much more about the issue than those who favor the predators and thus are more effective in influencing their state legislators' votes on these issues.

Coalitions and Compromise

Politics is often defined as "the art of compromise," but the process of seeking compromise over wildlife conservation has not proven easy for the USFWS or any other major actors. As a result of the rise and growth of the Wise Use and environmental movements, wildlife agencies have sought a method for trying to develop consensus among these varied and often bitterly opposed groups. Vaske, Fulton, and Manfredo state that wildlife managers now routinely employ "a stakeholder approach" that brings "diverse interests into direct communication with one another" such as "citizen task forces and stakeholder planning teams" to develop solutions to difficult problems [55 p. 92]. This kind of approach was emphasized by the Clinton Administration and was used by the Forest Service in New Mexico in order to mediate disputes between the Friends of the Gila River, a group concerned about the decline of the river due to harmful effects of grazing, and ranchers in the area [56 p. 30–41]. The Forest Service formed what they called an "Integrated Resource Management" (IRM) team that included a biologist from the state Fish and Game department, a hunter, representatives from the Audubon, Nature Conservancy and Wilderness Society, and a professor representing the interests of the New Mexico Cattlemen's Association, among others [56 p. 30]. The process worked on members such as Steve Johnson, an organizer of the Friends of the Gila River, who said that he felt like a "member of the team" and wanted a consensus that would provide a lasting decision [56 p. 34]. Johnson acknowledged that some environmentalists accused him of "being coopted by ranchers" but he saw it as "cooperation" and that any approach that ignores the "long-established customs" like ranching could result in "peril" [56 p. 37]. The IRM committee managed only to come up with a draft plan but the Forest Service went ahead and implemented it to address some of the major complaints of the Friends of the Gila River and environmentalists. However, there was concern that their "solutions" were just to move cattle from the areas that committee members complained about to other wilderness areas and that overtime, despite assurance of the ranchers, some of the bad practices of "trespassing cows" and "broken fences" returned, leading Steve Johnson to wonder if the IRM process had been a "bit of sham" to make him and other environmentalists happy [56 p. 41]. As noted above, the state of Minnesota formed a "roundtable" to come up with a plan for wolves in the state that contained a variety of actors representing environmentalists, hunters, trappers, governmental agencies, and interested citizens [51 p. 115]. Although the Minnesota DNR had promised to support the roundtable plan, the state legislature rejected it but came up with a revised plan that achieved compromise by dividing the state into zones and treating wolves differently depending on the zone – giving the wolf "leeway" in wilderness zones but giving landowners and agricultural interests leeway to rid themselves of problem wolves in their areas [51 p. 116]. These stakeholder approaches have thus achieved some significant successes but there is no simple method for designing them [57]. Nie rhetorically asks: "should the stakeholder table be balanced if the state isn't?" when, for example, "public opinion is 80 percent pro-wolf and 20 percent anti-wolf" [51 p. 194]. This is especially problematic because, as seen above, the intensities of the interest vary greatly with the minority often caring much more about the issue than the nominal majority. Utilizing devices such as "experimental" populations and zones have proven invaluable in producing flexibility to achieve compromise in difficult situations.

Gaining the trust of stakeholders is not an easy task. The stakeholder approach has been used in other countries such as Canada. In a Canadian workshop aimed at stakeholders in areas frequented by grizzly bears, Vredenburg discusses how he used personal relationships to try to get an industry representative to attend but the representative refused because he believed that it would be a chance for "bear enthusiasts to gang up on the beleaguered tourism industry" and some of industry representatives who did attend "felt like strangers at the party" [58 p. 314]. The only industry representatives who attended and made use of the workshop were those who had already participated in previous efforts. Richie, Oppenheimer, and Clark describe how Parks Canada moved to a collaborative decision-making stakeholder approach from a traditional top-down process dominated by park superintendents in 2005 [59 p. 271–2]. The process began with "skill-building workshops" that openly discussed perspectives and biases of the participating groups which included tourism-based industries, recreational groups, wildlife scientists, local citizens, First Nation, and park representatives, among others [59 p. 273]. According to Richie and Oppenheimer, the group achieved some successes such as developing plans for managing grizzlies in certain areas during its early period [59]. One method used by the facilitator to achieve consensus was to summarize the group discussions and ask whether everyone could live with the conclusions based on a 1 to 5 scale where "5" represented total "heartburn" [59 p. 229]. If anyone reported a "5," they resumed discussion of the issue. However, with the passage of time, the group membership turned over and difficult new issues were raised concerning a road (the Bow Valley Parkway) that passed through the grizzly habitat area. Trust among members of the group declined and several members felt they now had no say in the decision-making process and the group process came to an end in 2009. It was replaced by a revised stakeholder approach in which superintendents no longer gave up their decision-making role to the group but used the stakeholders to try to find points of consensus. Richie, Oppenheimer, and Clark found that the fact that the new members and new superintendents did not participate in the skill-building exercises was a significant reason for the failure of the original process [59 p. 275]. According to the authors, the role of the facilitator is important because they seek to find common ground during conflicts [59 p. 278]. Based on this case, it appears that a key question is whether the sense of trust and commonality of purpose developed by the groups is strong enough to forge a compromise position that key groups will be willing to accept, rather than trying to achieve a better result (from their perspective) by other methods. Richie, Oppenheimer, and Clark cite [59 p. 278] "core beliefs" such as different "normative stances," "languages," and "constructions of reality" as being difficult to overcome which is in keeping with advocacy coalition theory [60]. There were some successes. Olson describes how in one such process, a representative of the governmental Department of Environmental Quality did not feel that his expertise about water quality was respected by representatives of irrigators but through many meetings and field trips, members of the group developed trust in each other's knowledge [61 p. 76]. In the Banff (Canada) collaborative management case about grizzlies, trust was harmed when one participant shared confidential information with the media contrary to the accepted "ground rules" [62 p. 234]. Change is possible when the two sides' positions are not totally opposed as in the Alberta Canada case concerning wolves in which ranchers on the advisory group (Oldman Basin Carnivore Advisory Group) "settled for a reduced level of wolf removal while the biologists and conservationists agreed to a moderate level of lethal wolf [killing] ... targeted wolves that repeatedly preyed on livestock" [63 p. 164]. But compromise is impossible when "one side wants to expand the protected population and others want to restrict or remove the population" [64 p. 278]. The challenge for these stakeholder groups is to get the participants to commit to "common ground" positions and hope that they can persuade their organizations to go along. Oppenheimer and Richie describe how members would often revert to their organizational positions because they felt "that was their job" [62 p. 277].

A stakeholder approach is showing some promise in developing compromise over grazing in Utah's three national forests (the Dixie, Fishlake and Manti-La Sal) where 97 percent of the land has been grazed without regard for "ecosystem needs," resulting in damage to water quality and the destruction of aspen stands [65]. In 2011, Utah's agricultural and natural resources department heads picked a group of stakeholders to "seek common ground" to find ways of making "grazing better" with representatives from "universities, state, federal, and local agencies, woolgrowers and cattlemen's associations, hunting and conservation groups such as the 'moderate environmental organization' Grand Canyon Trust" [65]. One of the precepts was to "build social capital to get beyond stalemate" that was bolstered by "field trips" where they viewed damage from cattle but also visited areas where "riparian areas had been improved by ... simply changing the grazing regime." The report of the group recommended grazing changes, monitoring regimes, the need to manage from a "landscape level," and the need to "rest pastures especially during growing season" [65]. The national forests are installing "tanks, troughs, and extra fence" with "watered pastures" that will allow them "to move livestock more often" and "in theory protect streams and high-elevation pastures" [65]. However, this solution was dependent on significant infrastructure development paid for by the government, and may not be transferable to other areas. Moreover, other "less moderate" conservation groups such as the Western Watersheds Project question why we "should subsidize public lands for livestock production?" [65]. Nevertheless, Mary O'Brien, the "moderate conservationist" representative, says that the approach may "produce real results" that the public will consider worthwhile supporting [65].

However, another case from Utah concerns the Grand Staircase-Escalante National Monument created by President Clinton in 1996 that demonstrates the great difficulty in developing common ground and trust when core belief systems clash. A group called "the Escalante River Watershed Partnership (ERWP), comprised of residents and representatives from government agencies and environmental groups" is trying to figure out ways to "restore the riparian areas in the Escalante watershed" which have been harmed by overgrazing by cattle [66]. Group members are trying to seek common ground with powerful local rancher "insiders" and say that they do not want to eliminate cattle but rather to focus on solutions such as changing their grazing practices and eliminating "invasive Russian olive trees" that are absorbing much of the water; but the ranchers will not for the most part participate because they do not trust ERWP [66]. Many of the insiders agree that the area has been overgrazed in the past but refuse to work with the group due to deep underlying differences in values as described by one rancher [66]:

"My main focus," he says, "is to live a good life centered on my religious beliefs. For me, the way I see it, the earth and the environment are based in the biblical story of creation – God created the earth for man, and man is the steward over the land. But, for them, God *is* the earth, God *is* the environment.". . . "So that means you can't do anything that threatens or damages the earth or the environment. What I don't understand is, just the fact that you live on the earth damages it. I mean, if you're going to take the cows off the monument then why not put up a sign that says 'No humans past this point'?"

The ERWP has emphasized science and learning tools but they so far have been unsuccessful in establishing a common goal.

The Habitat Conservation Planning (HCP) process was introduced in a 1983 revision of the ESA in which "incidental takes" of threatened species are permitted if an adequate plan is developed to minimize and mitigate impacts. The HCP process employs a stakeholder type of approach in which a group is formed composed of a wide variety of interests including developers, local and national environmental organizations, landowners, local government officials, and relevant state and Federal officials [67 p. 41]. Although HCPs were introduced in 1983, they did not take off until the Clinton Administration – the model clearly conforms to its emphasis on developing a process that encourages compromise and consensus. Beatley gives an account of the successful use of an HCP in Coachella Valley California to preserve the Coachella fringe toed lizard [67 p. 208]. Though the process failed to convince many of the group that the lizard was worth all of the trouble, many of the non-environmental group accepted it based on the support for recreational benefits that would be derived from preserving open space. Chase, Lauber, and Decker cite examples of the successful use of employing citizen participation to solve disputes [68]. In one case, the citizen group came up with a solution for managing an "abundant deer" herd in Indiana. The group included wildlife ecologists, hunters, and environmentalists, among others, and also worked to ensure its successful implementation. Failure to include representatives of all key constituencies was the reason for the failure of an early 1975 attempt to do collaborative planning in Grays Harbor, Washington, in an attempt to preserve wetlands [69 p. 4]. Neither environmental nor development interests were involved in the "official planning" process. Some HCP participants described it as a "balance of terror approach" in that participants were afraid of "liability" if they should "walk away from the process" [70 p. 58]. One difficulty is deciding on the relative number of members from opposed coalitions to be included in the HCP process. Beatley describes how the one environmental group included in the steering committee of the desert tortoise HCP in Clark County (California) was outnumbered by several representatives of "resource users" and developers and that this number advantage affected the outcome of the HCP deliberations [70 p. 68]. The role of media can be potentially important in stakeholder approaches. McCreary and Adams studied a collaborative commission process in Oregon in 1973 and found that opening the negotiating process to media coverage had a positive impact on moving the process forward because "recalcitrant parties were apt to be depicted in a bad light" [71 p. 126].

The collaboration approach often requires mediators to make the effort successful. Beatley points out the importance of consultants to the HCP process [70 p. 39]. In the early years of HCPs, a small number of consultant organizations prepared most of the HCPs in California and developed expertise in working with groups made up of opposed coalition members. According to Lauber, Decker, Leon, Chase, and Schusler, collaboration approaches take time to develop the trust and belief in the process necessary to achieve success and they cite the case of the Florida Fish and Wildlife Commission's stakeholder group formed to deal with the gopher tortoise [72 p. 148]. Lauber et al. say that the process began with the stakeholder group serving first to provide for information exchange but over time turned into a "cautious co-manage-ment" approach with the group helping to make significant decisions [72 p. 148]. They also say that the process was not a straightforward success but had its ups and downs, eventually winding up as successful in the longer term. Lauber et al. go on to point out that wildlife departments use a variety of mechanisms to achieve stakeholder input such as surveys of the public, focus groups, workshops, advisory groups, among others. These inputs can often surprise wildlife departments as occurred when a survey done by the Montana Fish, Wildlife, and Parks Department showed that public attitudes toward mountain lions were "more favorable than expected" [72 p. 145]. A closely related approach used to seek compromise is referred to as "adaptive management" in which management actions are viewed as "experiments" and empirical data are gathered to determine if the actions worked as intended and if adaptations need to be made [73 p. 282–3]. The National Academy of Sciences recommended this approach to solve the debate over the wild horse and burro program of BLM. The essence of the problem is that the underlying differences in core values of the different stakeholders make it hard to get the participants to "buy into the process" [73 p. 284]. The adaptive management approach attempts to bring together these opposed groups to get them to recognize each other's viewpoints and to have confidence in the empirical information gathered. The essence of success is when participants feel a stake in the group process enough so that they will want it to succeed and go beyond just representing their single stakeholder viewpoint.

Attempts at compromise can be undermined by the forceful language of the ESA. Indeed, Cashore and Howlett state that in the spotted owl case "even the Federal government was attempting to find a solution that permitted the most harvesting" of forests and that the key "causal mechanism" for the "punctuation" was the "rigid legal requirement" that protected old growth forests without regard to "economic impacts" [74 p. 155]. Another example of the importance of the legal requirements occurred when the USFWS sought to defuse the controversy over wolves in Rocky Mountain states by delisting the wolves with the idea that the states would maintain sustainable populations of wolves despite takings by hunters. However, the initial attempt to do this was overruled by the U.S. District Judge Donald Molloy who ruled that USFWS's decision was a "pragmatic" and "political solution" that did not conform to the letter of the ESA law [75]. Major methods of achieving compromise between developers and environmentalists include establishing different "zones"and "grandfathering" devices. For example, in negotiations to establish Maryland-Chesapeake Bay Area "Critical Areas Program," a 25-member commission devised three different types of areas: (1) intensely developed areas where residential, commercial, and industrial uses dominate;

(2) environmentally sensitive areas with more protections such as prohibition on road and bridges crossing "habitat protection" areas unless there was no alternative; (3) resource conservation areas that are dominated by nature with the highest level of protection [76 p. 191]. Using different zones for different levels of protection has been employed in other cases, such as in Minnesota over how wolves were to be controlled. The Critical Area Program also allowed grandfathering of projects that had "substantially advanced toward development" as well as allowing landowners in critical areas to build a single house if none already existed [76 p. 195]. Such mechanisms can mitigate the fury of landowners and developers toward new protections for habitat and wildlife but were the subject of the most controversy in the process.

Porter and Salvesen studied collaborative planning efforts and found that they are rarely employed until the situation becomes intolerable for both development and conservation forces such as every permit becoming involved in a bitter battle [77 p. 275]. In order to work, developers have to set aside large areas for preservation and conservation forces must be willing to permit "selective destruction of natural resources" [77 p. 276]. President Clinton was devoted to the idea that compromise was the only way to resolve bitter impasses that had developed between environmental and opposing interests, stating that he did not want to see "the situation go back to posturing" and "the politics of division" [43 p. 76]. Bruce Babbitt describes a meeting attended by Clinton in Portland concerning the spotted owl early in his Administration with "labor leaders, mill owners, scientists, conservationists, elected officials and others" to discuss how "to strike a balance between protecting the owl and letting loggers" have access to the forests" [78 p. 56]. Helvarg cites evidence that Clinton gave up on reforms of fees for grazing, mining, and logging on public lands because of opposition from Democratic Senator Baucus of Montana [43 p. 287]. However, Baucus's aide said later that Baucus had been willing to compromise on these reforms before Clinton's "cave-in." Environmental issues had a lower priority for Clinton than jobs, trade, and health care issues. He only spoke about environmental issues on Earth Day [79 p. 103]. Clinton's approach to the struggle to preserve the spotted owl sought compromise – in this case based on certain principles that included that the "needs of the logger and timber industries" had to be addressed [80 p. 143]. Environmentalists complained that despite having a Democratic majority in the first two years of the Clinton Administration, the California Desert Protection Act was the only major environmental act passed due to a coalition of Republicans and "resource industry Democrats" blocking other reforms [43 p. 289]. Hamilton describes how Clinton's Secretary of the Interior's (Bruce Babbitt's) efforts to increase fees for grazing on public lands were undercut by Clinton himself after being pressured by Senators such as Ben Nighthorse Campbell (then a Democrat from Colorado) [44]. Hamilton quotes a representative of the National Cattlemen's Association as saying that they were trying just to get some reduction in the increase in fees and were surprised to see the entire proposal "gone." Hamilton describes Babbitt as trying to move a "reform agenda" without "alienating the opponents of reform" [44 p. 57]. Bruce Babbitt's account of the early days of the Clinton Administration discusses how they proposed a "biological survey" but that when the proposal hit the floor both Democrats (who controlled

Congress at this time) and Republicans "assailed the bill as threat to property rights" of Americans and likewise opposed the concept of "Federal land use planning" which they viewed as a local function [78 p. 59–60].

More radical organizations such as Earth First! rejected the compromise approach and employed methods such as monkeywrenching and civil protest rather than negotiation. Indeed, Bevington argues that Babbitt and the Clinton Administration dragged their feet by failing to designate critical habitat – they used it only for six species compared to fifty-seven during the Reagan Administration [81 p. 86]. Also, Bevington says that USFWS under Babbitt and Clinton failed to ask for enough funds for listing critical habitat and enforced a rule that would not allow transfers of funds from other areas for it [81 p. 197]. Babbitt did this, Bevington says, in an overreaction to "protect the ESA" from Republican attack. Bevington goes on to cite Center for Biological Diversity (CBD) leaders as saying that CBD set up a Washington office not to lobby Congress but rather to persuade the large national environmental organizations to oppose "compromises that would weaken biodiversity protection" [81 p. 213]. The CBD view the nationals as "habitually" and "reflexively" agreeing to compromises that "lead to irreversible degradations" [81 p. 5]. Their point is that the term "compromise" implies that neither side gets all that they want but thus covers a wide range of outcomes that differ radically in how much biodiversity is achieved.

It was only in the waning days of the Clinton Administration that he discarded the emphasis on compromise when he set aside large tracts of land (so-called "monuments") for preservation using the Antiquities Act which delighted environmentalists but antagonized most other parties given its "top down" and "unilateral" style of decision making [51 p. 160]. The negative reactions to monuments are exemplified by the action of Congress that exempted Wyoming from further applications of the Act after Franklin Roosevelt created the Jackson Hole National Monument in 1940 [78 p. 163]. Also, Babbitt, commenting on the creation of the Grand Escalante Monument during the Clinton Administration, says that creating parks by taking away land from the BLM and giving it to the Parks System was not a sufficient strategy for conservation of landscapes [78 p. 166]. However, Babbitt now is encouraging President Obama to use the Antiquities Act aggressively by establishing several new monuments as well as using other executive authority (without the need for Congressional approval) to "add lands to our national refuge system" [82]. This change in approach reflects the impossibility of passing any major new expansion of protections for wildlife through Congress. The resentment by Congress, especially Republicans, over the use of the Antiquities Act is reflected by the House of Representatives passage of a bill to "gut the Antiquities Act" [82]. Babbitt's argument is that by using it vigorously, the popularity and broad political support for conservation would be proven once again. Thus the Antiquities Act, like the ESA, is a good example of another law that is "hard to imagine passing today" [83 p. 111]. Moreover, despite the heated opposition to use of the Act to create monuments, nonetheless monuments have proven popular over the longer term. For example, Republicans complained about the designation of the "Missouri Breaks monument in Montana" but Gale Norton, Bush's Secretary of Interior, declined to reverse the designation, perhaps because the monument allowed hunting and grazing [83 p. 111].

Disputes over how much to compromise are at the heart of many struggles within the environmental movement. An example of such a struggle occurred during the campaign to return the wolf to the Yellowstone area between the Wolf Fund and the Greater Yellowstone Coalition (GYC) [84 p. 194–9]. The Wolf Fund was willing to have the wolf reintroduced by allowing them to be designated as an "experimental population" while the GYC opposed this approach because it would allow killing of wolves [84 p. 194]. The Wolf Fund (and Defenders of Wildlife) held that in allowing the experimental designation to be used so that some killing of wolves could take place, they would ultimately weaken the opposition of "wolf haters" and get "wolves on the ground" [84 p. 264]. A similar debate took place over the treatment of grizzlies in the Northern Rockies, with Defenders of Wildlife willing to give authority over them to a citizen-led commission. Seven regional conservation groups said this would be "bad for bears" and set a "dangerous precedent" [84 p. 263]. Even Bruce Babbitt, Clinton's Secretary of the Interior, told the Audubon Society that before reintroducing wolves, he was "very sensitive to the perceptions of westerners about livestock issues" and would only proceed "with a great deal of care" [85 p. 83]. The unwillingness of more radical environmental organizations such as Earth First! to compromise was successful in forcing action for the Balcones Canyonlands HCP in Austin, Texas – their threat to sue developers and local governments spurred action to save invertebrates living in caves according to Beatley, Fries, and Braun [86 p. 86]. Some accounts of HCP deliberations report a process that is dominated by the private landowners and USFWS with environmental and citizen groups in a very secondary position. For example, Sousa and Klyza cite descriptions of the Plum Creek Native Fish HCP process as being dominated by the "top layer" of U.S. Fish and Wildlife Service, National Marine Fisheries Service, and consultants hired by the Plum Creek Timber Company followed in importance by participants from Washington State Department of Fish and Wildlife and Natural Resources, the Environmental Protection Agency (EPA), and local tribes [87 p. 395–6]. Finally, the bottom layer consisted of "environmental and recreational groups" [87 p. 395–6]. Critics of the process said that the timber company was "pleasant and smiling" but "did not change the substance of the agreement" in response to the other participants [87 p. 396].

Accounts of legislation often show that a successful compromise of necessity will make "both sides" unhappy. The passage of the Alaskan National Interests Act (ANILCA) got through despite the unhappiness with it on the part of both the Carter Administration and the Alaskan Congressional delegation [88 p. 1487]. Beier cites evidence that this was a "tenuous compromise" and ascribes its success due to the huge size of the reserves that allowed compromises "with only minor losses for conservation" along with some clauses that gave flexibility due to the "special conditions" of Alaska, though these clauses later on led to disputes over their interpretation [88 p. 1488–94]. However, the more immediate factor that forced environmentalists to compromise was due to the fact that Carter lost the 1980 election to Reagan; thus, environmentalists who had favored stronger legislation were forced to compromise before a conservative president and more conservative Congress took office.

Although compromises are integral to politics, in many cases neither side is willing to compromise, nor is a "winning coalition" able to be formed so that wildlife conservation can pass. This situation has frustrated both those interested in preserving species and those who find such legislation threatening. For example, the Sierra Club criticized the 1994 Congress for achieving very few legislative victories despite the existence of a Democratic majority along with a Democratic president [89]. The Club ascribed this failure to "minority rule run amok" in which filibustering over appointments to committees and a coalition of "conservative Republicans and western Democrats" blocked environmental bills that "had majority support" from passing [89 p. 20]. In the next few years of the Clinton Administration, conservatives gained control of Congress and attempted to pass rollbacks to environmental legislation but were frustrated by the willingness of Clinton to veto this legislation [43 p. 287]. In 1982, as pointed out above, the ESA was reauthorized with only minor changes despite unhappiness with the Act by both supporters and opponents because "both sides" were "unwilling to work out a compromise" [13 p. 133]. Male and Donlan point out that there is always going to be an "inherent contradiction" between "maximizing conservation benefits" and securing "widespread participation necessary for landscape-level benefits" [90 p. 222]. Commitment to core coalition values is often too strong to overcome this contradiction.

Riders versus the ESA

The strong language of the ESA has made compromises difficult. Indeed, organizations like the CBD proved that "blocking by the courts is more effective than direct action" by radical organizations like Earth First! [81 p. 35]. One of the few mechanisms to undercut the ESA and the Courts is the Congressional rider in which wildlife legislation is attached to other legislation crucial to the operation of the government (e.g., budget acts funding programs) which both sides are reluctant to reject. Sometimes, riders have been used to advance wildlife concerns such as in 1991 when a rider was added to the Department of Interior's budget appropriation requiring an environmental impact statement concerning the reintroduction of wolves to the Yellowstone area – which was ironic because opponents of reintroduction had blocked previous attempts at doing this through the use of riders [25 p. 131]. More often the rider has been used to overcome restrictions posed by the ESA. For example, in 1995, Congress passed a budget bill for compensating victims of the Oklahoma bombing with a rider that allowed logging for eighteen months in areas previously restricted due to the ESA and other laws. This rider "prohibited any administrative and any judicial review for compliance with environmental laws" [25 p. 106]. When ESA protections of red squirrels living in an area where a University of Arizona telescope was to be built, after a great deal of struggle, the matter was brought to an end in June 1990 when "a rider was passed on the last day of 100th Congress without any public hearings," overriding ESA protections in this case [91 p. 56]. A more recent example of the use of the rider concerns removal of wolves in the northwest Rockies from protected listing status under the ESA [92]. The USFWS wanted to bring to an end its continued strife with Wyoming, Idaho, and Montana and the Obama Administration undoubtedly saw this as a way to help preserve the Senate seat held by Democratic Senator Jon Tester of Montana by defusing the wolf controversy.

Conclusion

The passage of key wildlife legislation in the 1960s and 1970s supports the views of Kingdon [93] and Cohen, March, and Olsen [94] that policymaking can be an "anarchic" process in which most participants are unaware of the significance of events and thus "policy entrepreneurs" can achieve policy adoptions that, in retrospect, appear remarkable. Progressive environmentally oriented administrators did exactly this during the Nixon Administration. "Messy legislation" with unclear and often conflicting goals enabled the advancement of conservation measures. This anarchic period quickly ended when the implications of the legislation became apparent and policymaking since then has become largely not just stable but stalemated with entrenched lines of battle between opposed advocacy coalitions. Threats to charismatic species such as the bald eagle and bison helped to stimulate the development of the wildlife conservation coalition and acceptance on the part of the general public concerning the need for protecting them. However, despite general popular support, groups such as hunters and ranchers have been able to defeat wildlife conservation forces on many issues such as prohibition of lead ammunition and fishing tackle, and grazing on public lands, through effective control of institutions such as state and Federal legislative committees and state wildlife agencies. Thus institutions (e.g., committees and wildlife commissions) have continued to play a dominant role especially at the state level, though the rise of conservation coalition has disrupted key "subsystems" at the Federal level such as those affecting public lands.

The rise of the conservation movement has led to tension between states and the Federal government over wildlife policy. Due to the political and economic strength of the opposition to the ESA and, perhaps more importantly, the fact that environment is secondary to issues such as the economy and employment, moderate Democratic (Obama and Clinton) Administrations have emphasized mechanisms to achieve compromise such as through the use of stakeholder groups. Indeed, the emphasis on habitat conservation plans has, in effect, institutionalized a stakeholder approach to conservation. These stakeholder approaches have achieved some notable successes but have proven difficult for both advocacy coalitions since meaningful compromise means sacrificing interests for both conservationists and their opponents. Some devices have been employed to facilitate compromise and defuse opposition such as "experimental populations designations for carnivores" and areal differences in protections for wildlife. Still, the singular resource for the wildlife conservation coalition remains the strong language of the ESA and the willingness of Federal judges to enforce a strict interpretation of it. Despite the emphasis on collaboration in HCPs, Federal legislation has been frozen due to legislative gridlock. Consequently, the major advances in protecting major new conservation areas have been accomplished through executive action (via the Antiquities Act) which avoids any need to compromise. Although there has long-term stability in these coalitions, significant "within group" conflict has marked many attempts to compromise due to hardliners on both sides.

5 Charismatic Animals, Carnivores, and the Politics of Wildlife

What Animals Are Charismatic?

There are thousands of species of animal life but a relatively small proportion of them capture the attention of the public and politicians. In this chapter, I focus on so-called "charismatic" animals and carnivores (these two categories overlap heavily) because they generate the emotion that inspires passions of love or hatred that are likely to lead to political battles over wildlife. The labeling of animals as charismatic or, on the other side of the coin, as undesirable such as "vermin," is a subjective process based on a human being's perception of the species. The primary factor in determining how a species is perceived depends on whether it is viewed as harming the interests of humans. For example, Cioc defines vermin as "any animal that deserves eradication because it competes in some way with the spread of human settlements or agricultural growth" [1 p. 6]. Some animals can be considered charismatic because they are (in the eyes of humans) beautiful and/or graceful. For example, Yaffee distinguishes between the outrage expressed at the blocking of the Tellico dam in Tennessee over an "obscure fish" called the snail darter with the situation that occurred when a Nebraska water project was stopped because it threatened Sandhill cranes. In the Tellico case, most politicians in Tennessee expressed outrage at the stoppage of the dam while in the latter case, the state of Nebraska acted to oppose the project [2 p. 101]. Beatley describes how many Coachella Valley (in southern California) officials viewed the spending of a large amount of money for saving a small fringe-toed lizard as "preposterous" and consequently the matter became the "butt of jokes" [3 p. 3]. By way of contrast, the threat of the vanishing of the iconic buffalo helped the passage of the law that established Yellowstone National Park [2 p. 32]. Generally, fish tend to be characterized as less charismatic than land mammals. When the state of Florida resisted the attempt to make the Biscayne National (underwater) Park off limits to fishing, the director of the park said that there would no debate over the matter if a terrestrial "parkland were involved" [4]. A crucial factor distinguishing charismatic animals is whether they have interest groups advocating for them. For example, an organization, Project Seahorse, was established by volunteers specifically to save this species. Before the seahorse ruling in 2004, fish were considered "food items" not to be dealt with by CITES (Convention on International Trade in Endangered Species of Wild Fauna and Flora) [5].

People's devotion to charismatic species may help preserve others. For example, the measures taken to protect seahorses force ships to be more careful about "bycatch" in shrimp-trawler nets – a major threat to seahorses but also other marine life [5]. Greenberg says that people will never feel the same way about tuna as they do about whales because whales are mammals with large brains who "nurse their young" but he suggests that we should act against industrial fishing of the "lions and tigers" of the sea like the Bluefin tuna [6]. Mooallem says that the true value of the polar bear is its "magnetism" that "inspired enough public gushing" to make it impossible for the Bush Administration to "bury the issue of climate change yet again" [7 p. 59]. Letters to the Department of the Interior about whether polar bears should be designated as threatened or endangered, "normally quiet . . . ordeals," elicited thousands of handwritten notes from schoolchildren begging that the bears be saved [7 p. 53]. The whooping crane's charismatic status in the Gulf Coast area near Aransas National Wildlife Refuge was indicated by the "multiple images of cranes; they were hung from doorways, displayed in windows of retail establishments, and appeared on road signs" [8]. The ability to identify individual members of a species also can help to personalize human identification with them – for example, some people were able to identify certain whooping crane members and couples [8 p. 5].

At the international level, certain mammals (elephants and whales) have proven to attract intense support and allegiance of humans and organizations aimed at preserving them. Barcott illustrates the power of charisma: a salt factory in Belize was not stopped by concerns about mangroves or scallops but by "two words: baby whales" [9 p. 126]. However, the perception of charisma varies by country with nations such as Japan and Norway continuing to press their rights to harpoon and harvest whales. Chadwick cites Iceland as another country that stopped and then resumed whaling in 2008 despite the fact that whale-watching is a million-dollar industry in the country [10 p. 54]. Defenders of commercial whale hunting such as Kalland criticize the anthropomorphizing of whales into "caring, playful, family-oriented, singing, kind" humanlike creatures, lumping together the characteristics of several different whales (blue: largest, humpback: singing, sperm: largest brain) into one "super whale" in an attempt to invalidate the consumption of them [11 p. 159–63]. Likewise, although elephants draw tourists and are viewed favorably by most, they often destroy crops and "attack" villages in Africa and the villagers retaliate by killing elephants so often that elephant researchers now study "human-elephant conflict" in order to determine how to lessen it [12 p. 135]. Perhaps the best example of a charismatic animal is the panda. An Englishman, Sir Peter Scott, founded the World Wildlife Society and carefully selected the panda for its logo which has been integral to the organization's successful fundraising efforts [13 p. 4]. As Schaller details it, China has employed the charisma of the panda as a "political tool," giving pairs of panda to certain countries such as the United States as a "gesture of friendship" [13 p. 8–9]. The popularity and tourist draw of the panda helped conservationists to convince the Chinese government to set aside thousands of acres of land such as the Wolong reserve [14 p. 335]. These reserves also help preserve other threatened animals including bird species, wild goats, and monkeys, and thus this is another example of a charismatic animal's positive effects on other species. The importance assigned to pandas is reflected in Chinese law – the punishment for killing a panda is now the death penalty [14 p. 335]. China makes millions of dollars over pandas given to zoos – for example, the Atlanta Zoo paid one million dollars a year and pandas "boosted attendance and donations" that help to justify the payment to the Chinese government [15 p. 14]. Another example of the power of a charismatic animal is the "Pink Dolphin" (actually Chinese white dolphin) which was selected by Hong Kong to be its "official mascot" in 1997 and which has been described as a "treasure of national heritage" by the head of the Hong Kong Conservation Society [16]. Their numbers had been dwindling due to pollution which led to a ban on trawlers by the government to preserve fish and thus assist the dolphin. While many of the most charismatic animals are perceived by humans as friendly and cuddly, even the greatest predators have attracted the devotion of humans. This is illustrated by the case of "Cecil," a lion who lived in the Hwange National Park in Zimbabwe but was lured and shot (first by bow then by guns) – the lion was beloved by locals and tourists and the shooting ignited a firestorm of invective against the U.S. dentist who killed it [17].

Non-governmental organizations (NGOs) play a key role in determining which species are protected by the Endangered Species Act (ESA) and other governmental laws. Humans have formed NGOs around a relatively small proportion of species. Kareiva et al. state that fifty-seven NGOs are dedicated specifically to birds but only four represent invertebrates [18 p. 178–80]. A significant portion of interest in wildlife does not concern admiration for its charisma, beauty, or grace but is due to consumption-oriented interests like hunting. The strength of interest in much of wildlife is affected by whether a species is a "game" animal and thus of interest to hunters. For example, according to Czech and Krausman, Ducks Unlimited has a membership of 550,000, largely consisting of hunters, outranking seven of the top ten environmental NGOs and outnumbering memberships of organizations dedicated to reptiles and amphibians taken together [19 p.72–3]. DiSilvestro says that black bears were treated more leniently by Alaska's Fish and Game Department than wolves because they were "popular game animals" [20 p. 102]. Krausman describes mountain sheep as "charismatic" and suggest one way to determine the value of a resource is by the amount of money people are willing to pay to "use it" – he cites data that permits for shooting mountain sheep ranged from $56,000 in Colorado to $405,000 in Alberta, Canada [21 p. 231]. Similarly, Gugliotta found that cougars are much more tolerated by ranchers than wolves because they are a more "manageable nuisance" and are "easier to hunt and control" [22].

Still, much of human interest is based on non-selfish goals, as illustrated by the high interest in protecting turtles and tortoises. Czech and Krausman point out that the resources and organizational skills of the Desert Tortoise Council resulted in the fact that the vast majority of funds spent on endangered reptiles in 1993 (98 percent) were devoted to turtles and tortoises [19 p. 73]. They note that the underlying reason for this support is that turtles and tortoises are "associated with positive cultural" symbols. McClenachan, Cooper, Carpenter, and Dulvy point out that the amount of research and thus information about threats to populations is based on the charisma or popularity of a species [23]. They state that marine turtles have had ten times more research devoted to them than "any other charismatic taxonomic group"– an average of 194 published papers per turtle species compared with 10 for sharks and rays (per species) and only 0.1 for invertebrates [23]. Howard, Shogren and Tschirhart studied the number of court opinions per species between 1973 and 1995 and found that the most cases involved either species that humans view as charismatic such as the bald eagle, bears, and wolves, or those that had become viewed as obstacles to human interests such as the snail darter and spotted owl [24 p. 13]. Rauber discusses how the anti-ESA coalition focuses on non-charismatic animals [25 p. 31]. For example, the American Farm Bureau claimed that it was being "victimized" by species such as "toads, chubs, rats, bugs and weeds" [25]. Rauber goes on to say that biologists would say that the glamorless species such as microorganisms, insects, and fungi "keep an ecosystem alive" but this fact has held little or no sway over public opinion [25]. The National Research Council noted that although there was an overwhelming bias toward protection of mammals and birds compared to invertebrates, changing this situation was an "enormous challenge" but that from 1985 to 1991, 59 percent of the proposed listings were for mammals and 40 percent for birds – so the bias was somewhat less than had been the case in prior years [26 p. 46].

The beauty of an animal such as the scarlet macaw led to a major effort to preserve its habitat in Belize, as described by Barcott [9 p. 147]. Posner discusses how despite the fact that pigs are much smarter than koalas, the pig's face "is the wrong shape" and thus we slaughter pigs but "form societies to preserve koalas" [27]. By way of contrast, vultures are viewed negatively even though they perform useful functions for humans by stopping infectious diseases in wildlife such as botulism and anthrax [28 p. 79]. The subjectivity of charisma is reflected in a comment by an official in the U.S. Fish and Wildlife Service's (USFWS's) Endangered Species unit: "Would you feel bad if you ran over it"; the same official knew that mussels would be difficult to list because they would fail this test [29 p. 262]. Charisma is subjective and can be affected by a variety of factors. For example, Bass says that a grizzly with a radio collar "does nothing for me" while one without a collar does "everything" – the former brings to mind "computers" and helicopters – not mystery [30 p. 92]. Hunting can bring about changes in natural selection that affect the traditional characteristics and hence charisma of a species. For example, Smith claims that there is much less bugling in areas where elk are hunted than in areas where they are protected, and that elephants are increasingly becoming "tuskless" due to the selection caused by poaching [31 p. 208]. Kellert's 1980 survey showed that people would be willing to "forego a variety of benefits" in order to save species such as the Silverspot butterfly, porpoises, foxes, squirrels, and raccoons but that they showed little interest in preserving spiders, unspecified "blackbirds," rats, and bats, among others [32 p. 31]. On the other hand, as Barcott notes too, the beauty of animals such as the scarlet macaw leads to poaching, so beauty can be a double-edged sword. Similarly, there is much interest in butterflies compared to a dislike or indifference or antipathy for most insects, but "this charisma may contribute to their demise by over-collecting" such as in the case of rare "fritillaries and blues" [33 p. 102].

Deer illustrate the complexity of human perceptions of animals. A large proportion of the public hold positive perceptions of deer because they are non-threatening mammals and are associated with positive cultural symbols (e.g., Bambi), plus most humans enjoy observing them. Hunters value deer as game. More recently, with the growth of deer populations in suburban locations, a smaller but significant proportion of the public views them as a pest because they eat valued vegetation and also, from an environmentalist perspective, may deprive some endangered species of food they need. A recent book details other harmful effects of deer such as forcing foresters to "bud cap" trees to prevent deer form eating the buds off every seedling, as well causing more than one million deer–vehicle crashes, and spreading Lyme disease [34]. Consequently, Brant reports that "deer have created the most difficulties of any wildlife species with three-quarters of the states having problems with them" [35 p. 102]. Deer also arouse intense feelings [35 p. 102]. Brant tells of one incident in North Haven (New York) which involved two parties, one in favor of controlling deer by hunting and another opposed to hunting (and in favor of the use of immunoception as the method of control). Brant says that one Village Board member was told that if "a deer dies . . . one of your family will die" [35 p. 58].

The concentrations and habits of animals can affect humans' perceptions of them. Most people view egrets as attractive birds but when they nested in masses in certain areas such as Conway, Arkansas, they became perceived as a nuisance due to the noise and bad odor emanating from the area [36 p. 197]. Likewise, The majority of people tend to view beavers positively but, due to protections, beaver populations in the East rose greatly since the 1990s and have led to a number of problems for humans such as flooded basements. Siemer, Jonker, Merchant and Brown report that the New York State Department of Environmental Conservation received almost 11,000 "nuisance beaver" complaints between 1993 and 1997 [37]. Still, their survey revealed that most people continued to view them positively except for those who had experienced "beaver damage" directl,y and thus most people found "lethal controls" of beavers only acceptable if human health were at stake [37 p. 9–11].

The bias toward familiar animals such as mammals is not restricted to the United States – Freedman et al. state that Canada's vertebrates are vastly overrepresented in their list of protected species [38 p. 26]. Brailovskaya states that fish are viewed differently than land animals as illustrated by the fact that they would be "outraged to find blue herons or raccoons" in the supermarket but accept new species of fish for sale without comment [39 p. 1237]. Willison finds biases even within the fish category – bottom-dwelling marine life lose out to more visible surface-dwelling fish [40 p. 94]. McClenachan et al. state that the "extinction risk" to marine life is much higher than for land animals such as 100 percent for sea turtles, mackerel sharks (80 percent threatened), and eagle rays (50 percent threatened) [23]. Game fish like the Atlantic Cisco that are "exciting" to catch and tasty to eat draw more attention (e.g., being featured on a Canadian postage stamp), though of course these "positive" characteristics from the human perspective can also lead to overfishing and threatened status. Still, it is usually concern with some charismatic species that provides the spur to preserve habitat that may help other species. For example, Wilcove [41 p. 187] points out that because most "rare plants and obscure little animals" do not elicit sympathy from the public that the preservation of habitats such as scrub in Florida will be due to the interest of birdwatchers in species like the scrub-jay "whose bizarre behavior" has made them into a "flagship species" which Verissimo, MacMillan, and Smith define as those "that have the ability to capture the imagination of the public and induce people to support conservation action and/or to donate funds" [42 p. 2]. Thus a flagship species as defined do not have any necessary "ecological significance" – the concept is based on their "marketability" [42 p. 2].

Many researchers have criticized too much focus and resources being spent on charismatic species. Graham argues that too much is spent on "megavertebrates" like the bald eagle and grizzly bear and not enough on less glamorous species that ecosystems need [43 p. 39]. Boutin points out that the [total] "biomasses of small mammals like squirrels can equal a moose" and that the mass of tent caterpillars in a forest can equal that of 175 moose, concluding that mammals and their predators "do not necessarily dominate ... the trophic levels of the boreal forest" [44]. Tobin holds that, despite the Reagan Administration's expressed preference for support of "higher life forms," "lower life forms" such as snails, insects, and crustaceans did well in terms of finalized recovery plans (under the ESA) during the mid-1980s [45 p. 240]. But the U.S. General Accountability Office's (GAO's) review of the USFWS use of recovery funds found that it has been concentrating on certain "highly visible species" such as the Aleutian goose and bald eagle and thus were deviating from the priority system that the USFWS itself had set up [46 p. 5]. The USFWS said that part of the reason for this was due to Congressional earmarking of funds but admitted that it was also partly due to the "desire for a positive view of the program." Anderson argues that the focus on "charismatic megafauna" has resulted in greater spending for less endangered species that is inefficient – more should be spent on "more unique species" [47 p. 114]. Thus spending on species is very much influenced by an animal's charisma and political support.

Wild horses illustrate the complexity of problems presented by a charismatic species. They represent a species that has attracted intense and loyal support, and Kellert and Berry report that horses ranked second after only dogs as the most liked animal in the United States. Indeed, their appeal is worldwide, as shown by surveys in New Zealand and Australia that found that, although some viewed wild horses as pests, most people desired to have free-ranging horses and would not accept culling of them [48 p. 276]. Consequently, a recent report by the National Academy of Sciences recommended abandonment of the "roundup" of wild horses and use of fertility control drugs instead [49; 50]. The complexity of attitudes toward certain wildlife is also illustrated by the status of dingoes in Australia. They are at one and the same time a "declared pest legally required to be controlled" and a "protected species in conservation lands" [51 p. 136]. However, according to an environmentalist writer for Audubon Magazine, Ted Williams, wild horses and burros have ruined "ecosystems" for threatened species such as sage-grouse and desert tortoises [52 p. 28–36]. Williams holds that their impact is worse than that of cows because they are not moved to new areas when the grass is low and they are not "wintered" off the range. Environmentalists like Williams refer to them as "feral horses" and an "alien species." Similarly, Gulliford speaks of their "voracious appetites and hefty hooves" that endanger native plants and dominate water holes "that other mammals need" [53]. Yet they have strong popular support as evidenced by the passage of the Wild Free-Roaming Horse and Burro Act of 1971 that banned lethal controls of them [54 p. 1]. The Act declared that the horses were "living symbols of the historic and pioneer spirit of the West; that they contribute to the diversity of life forms within the Nation and enrich the lives of the American people" [54 p. 1]. The number of these horses had dwindled to an estimated 9500 by 1971 and the passage of the legislation demonstrates the salience of the issue for the public and its political representatives. However, by the late 1970s, it was determined that a large increase in wild horses and burros was causing overgrazing of the range they occupied. Consequently, in 2004, Congress amended the 1971 legislation to allow for adoption of the horses that are over ten years of age or that have been offered three times for adoption without success "for any reason" which could potentially include "sale for slaughter." The goal of the legislation was to achieve an "optimum number of horses" (the so-called "appropriate management level") that would not cause a deterioration in the range. Beginning in 2001, the Bureau of Land Management (BLM) has removed an average of 10,600 animals per year [54 p. 2–3]. When the horses are removed, they are put into "short-term holding facilities" where they are supposed to be either adopted or sold. BLM, under the influence of horse advocacy groups, required that purchasers sign an agreement that they were not to be sold for slaughter [54 p. 4]. On average, the GAO reports that 6300 horses were sold per year. However, because not enough horses are adopted or sold, BLM pays private contractors to keep the excess horses in long-term holding facilities. The revised 2001 Act also allowed BLM to "euthanize" those unable to be adopted but BLM "had not destroyed any since 1982" [54 p. 3–4]. BLM's reluctance to euthanize is undoubtedly due to their public popularity and the actions of groups such as the Humane Society that oppose euthanizing animals. In addition, wild horses have also spurred the growth of interest groups dedicated specifically to them, such as American Wild Horse Preservation Campaign and the Cloud Foundation (an organization dedicated to "preservation of wild horses on public lands"). On the other side, interest groups such as the National Cattlemen's Beef Association and the Nevada Bighorns Unlimited view wild horses and burros as competitors for their livestock and work to control their numbers. In Wyoming, "ranchers won a lawsuit" that mandated removal of wild horses from public and private lands and the BLM had to comply even though they had virtually no room to "store" them [55]. The Humane Society of the United States agrees with BLM's goal of having only a sustainable number of wild horses, but wants to achieve it by the use of contraceptives. The problem is similar to that of deer: the only way to control the population that is acceptable to their fervent supporters is through "birth control," but Schirtzinger points out that this approach would be hard to implement on the 32 million acres they inhabit in the West, unlike its successful use on contained populations such as Assateague Island off the coast of Maryland and Virginia [56 p. 20]. The methods used to gather the wild herds in the West include helicopters to achieve these "gathers" that result in panic among the horses and often injuries and thus are unacceptable to wild horse enthusiasts [53].

Carnivores and Negative Charisma

Charisma as used here refers to the ability of a species to evoke the interest and enthusiasm of humans. In reviewing the history of animals, and especially carnivores, it can be said that some animals have what I refer to as *negative charisma* – the ability to evoke passionate dislike and hatred on the part of humans that goes beyond rational concern with economics alone. A significant cause of human dislike of animals such as wolves is rational, in that they are seen as depriving humans of resources, such as the taking of livestock and game that lead to lower takes for humans. The first bounties for wolves in the colonies were begun by 1630 because of their competition with human hunters for deer [57 p. 31]. Even when species have characteristics associated with positive charisma, they can be viewed as a pest if they are perceived as competitors to human interests. For example, Alaskans put a fifty-cent bounty on golden eagles in 1917 because they ate salmon and sometimes preyed on foxes raised for fur [58 p. 100]. With the expansion of human populations and developments, there is "less and less space for the wild" increasing the "number of unwanted human encounters" with a variety of creatures including egrets with their bad odors, otters that compete with anglers for fish, and deer that eat flowers, shrubs, and hit cars (#36 p. 205–219). For example, Conway, Arkansas and the USFWS worked jointly to scare away the egrets.

Buffalo are another example of charismatic animals that have posed difficult problems for wildlife managers and politicians. Many buffalo leave the protection of Yellowstone Park during periods when it is covered by a heavy snow layer, in order to find grass. Because buffalo can possibly infect cattle with the dread disease of brucellosis, these buffalo are killed when they leave the park. If brucellosis is discovered in cattle in a state, that state loses its "brucellosis free" status and its cattle would have to be tested individually which would be expensive. In 2008, nearly 1200 buffalo were killed [59]. Some other measures have been tried, such as "hazing," but reliance on culling has been the major alternative. Buffalo have drawn protectors from a variety of organizations. For example, Amy McNamara of the Greater Yellowstone coalition holds that the buffalo are "an American icon" that should not wind up in someone's freezer [59].

Although dislike of predators such as wolves has a rational basis due to their impact on livestock and game, many humans form negative anthropomorphic images of them that go beyond mere rational conflict of interest. Nie describes how people did not just kill wolves but sometimes tortured them such as setting them on fire or "pulling their jaws out" and setting their dogs on them [60 p. 37]. Coleman describes how humans were "dissatisfied with mere annihilation" of wolves but "persecuted them" with a "ferocity" that was "horrendous" and "inexplicable" [61 p. 72]. They viewed them as "fearsome monsters" [61 p. 37]. Sharman Apt Russell says that some people dislike wolves because of their "excess killing" and other behaviors such as eating their prey "before they are properly dead" and killing of wounded wolves by their packs [62 p. 149]. Parsons also relates how cattlemen were outraged that wolves killed more than they could eat and thus were "wasteful of meat" [63 p. 186]. Smith points out that wolves share this characteristic with humans [31 p. 173]. Robinson describes the evolution of the program that eventually became known as Animal Damage Control (ADC) that was aimed at exterminating wolves and other species viewed as noxious to ranchers and farmers [64 p. 48]. The agency conducting this program has had a variety of names and bureaucratic locations in the Federal government; it is currently known as "Wildlife Services" and is now located in the Department of Agriculture. The agency's leaders and supporters (most strongly ranchers and farmers) developed political support for the agency not only by emphasizing losses of livestock due to wolves but also by depicting wolves as "killers," "criminals," and like "gangsters" [64 p. 153]. According to Robinson, the killing of wolves and other carnivores was seen as progress of civilization in the West [64 p. 48]. The agency was restrained by the growth of the environmental movement in the 1970s but "regained momentum" during the Reagan Administration and the agency was transferred from the Department of Interior to the Agricultural Department due to "pressure from the livestock industry" [65 p. 80]. In 1990, the agency killed more than 800,000 animals in Western states including more than 91,000 coyotes [65 p. 80]. Counting all animals (e.g., raccoons, etc.), almost five million animals were killed in 2008 [66 p. 12]. From 2000 to 2007, more than 250,000 animals were shot from the air with coyotes constituting the majority (210,000) often with the aim of increasing game for hunters [66 p. 9]. However, rigorous research by two Idaho Fish and Game researchers determined that the chief cause of death of game such as mule deer was severe winters, and that the shooting of coyotes did not produce more mule deer [66 p. 64]. Shivik notes that hunters blame carnivores for declines in game but the real culprits are humans [66 p. 62]. For example, the human population of Utah nearly doubled between 1980 and 2010, and consequently the deer population is now as large as can be expected but hunters "remember that there were 500,000 deer in the 1960s" and "want something done about it now." Shivik reviews a wide range of non-lethal methods for predator control that have been used effectively, such as animal-activated alarms, aversive stimuli, altering the timing of breeding, animal armor, guard dogs, and other guard animals, fladry (ropes with flags attached to them), landscape design, and shock collars, and rhetorically asks: "If there are so many non-lethal methods available … why are guns still the overwhelmingly go-to method?" [66 p. 142]. The USFWS itself describes the wolf as having been "pursued with more passion and determination than any other animal in U.S. history" [67]. The Federal agency responsible for removing wolves suffered a setback in its reputation when a widely distributed photo was taken of eleven dismembered mountain lions being "mocked" by the ADC hunters and trappers, which is an example of how media can affect the politics of wildlife [65 p. 84]. The long history of antipathy toward carnivores is evidenced in Douglas Brinkley's biography of Theodore Roosevelt, who loved birds and wildlife, but who referred to predators such as wolves and mountain lions as "varmints" deserving of being shot if not poisoned, though he did moderate his views later in life [68 p. 411–13 & 512]. Though the attitudes of a large portion of the population toward carnivores has changed, many still hold strong negative views, including Urbigkit who, in her book on the controversy of introducing wolves to Yellowstone, refers to the predation of wolves on sheep as a "terrorist attack" [69 p. 252–8]. One example of public support of mountain lions occurred in Arizona:

when the Arizona Game and Fish Department sought to remove mountain lions perceived as threatening hikers near Flagstaff and Tucson, the agency was surprised by a "maelstrom of media coverage" and support by the public opposed to killing the lions or removing them; it also elicited criticism by the then governor (Janet Napolitano) about the agency's performance [70 p. 34]. However, Mattson notes that the agency's response was to hire a public relations firm and the agency wound up taking "measures that would have no impact on harvest levels of the lions" [70 p. 37].

Other Federally protected species such as prairie dogs are also disliked by ranchers because of their supposed negative effect on cattle, and extensive amounts of poisons such as Rozol and Phostoxin have been targeted for them [71 p. 66–72]. Indeed, Williams cites one example in Kansas where the county authorized officials to enter private lands and eradicate prairie dogs and then send a bill to the landowner [71 p. 69–70]. Snakes are another species that have been vilified and have been threatened in some areas due to "snake roundups" that result in the killing of thousands of snakes directly through "public slaughtering" or indirectly due to the rough handling such as broken ribs and jaws that can result in death even if they are released at the end of the roundup [72 p. 154]. Rattlesnakes have been the primary species targeted by roundups but other venomous snakes such as copperheads and sometimes non-venomous snakes such as "black rat snakes" are also brought in. Franke recounts how the decapitation of the snakes at some of these roundups is justified by references to the Bible as being "biblical serpents" or "cursed among all animals" [72 p. 158]. Franke cites evidence of some recent positive changes in attitudes toward snakes but observes that "the biggest impediments to reform are the political connections" of influential roundup organizers who often use the events to raise money for organizations like the Jaycees or Lions Club [72 p. 158]. Texas has been one of the states that has large rattlesnake roundups in which gasoline is used to flush the snakes from their burrows but recently the state's wildlife agency proposed to ban the use of gasoline for this purpose [73]. The state agency said that the purpose of the gasoline ban "wasn't to end roundups" but due to the fact that the gasoline "vapor exposure impaired or killed seven species of snakes, toads, and lizards" [73]. Sweetwater, Texas has hosted "one of the largest snake roundups" and claims that the ban would endanger their economy and harm the local Jaycees fundraising supporting local projects such as feeding the poor [73]. One licensed snake hunter cited the Bible as proving that "snakes have intimidated people" and held that you wouldn't want "restrictions on how to get them off" your land [73].

Attitudes toward animals are subject to change due to influences such as scientific findings (e.g., about the ecological benefits of predators) but also due to cultural influences. For example, bats used to have negative connotations for many people, but the growing recognition that bats feast on mosquitoes plus the popularity of a children's book series featuring a "loveable bat" ("Stella Luna") have modified views of them – now some people even purchase bat houses to encourage them nesting on their property [74]. Wallace states that manatees did not use to be a popular species in Florida but became so popular that it became the "official Florida state mammal" and special auto licenses with the mammal on them led to more than $1.2 million into the Save the Manatee trust fund in 1992 [75 p. 144–5]. Cultural and commercial events can contribute to attitude change. For example, Farley Mowat's book "Never Cry Wolf" (and the subsequent movie) had a positive impact on perceptions of wolves [76 p. 152]. Farquhar quotes Dave Freudenthal, former (Democratic) governor of Wyoming, as saying that he knew they had lost the war against wolves when he visited a "Cracker Barrel and saw ... cute stuffed ... wolves on sale to be put in a baby's crib" [77]. The 1975 film Jaws had a devastating impact on sharks, spurring tournaments and contests for the biggest fish landed and helping to result in a steep drop in shark populations according to DuPree; historically sharks have been considered a pest by fishermen and an "impediment" to fisheries [78]. Ferretti, Myers, Serena, and Lotse [79] and DuPree [78] and others have attempted to rehabilitate the shark's image by pointing out their positive functions for ocean ecology of cleaning up the carcasses of dead whales and keeping the lid on species that have no other predators. Recently, in Australia, there were seven human deaths due to sharks over a period of three years that resulted in a "shark culling" in which "172 sharks were caught and 68 were shot" but none of them was a great white shark [80]. Australia's Environmental Protection Authority did not grant the states the authority to continue the program because of its potential threat to the great white population. According to Baird, a poll found that over 80 percent of Australians believe that sharks should not be killed and she argues that they suffer from an "international bad public relations" image in which they are portrayed as "being somewhere between a psychopath and a member of an outlaw motorcycle gang" [80]. As with wolves, many humans not only fear their ferocious ability to kill but also view them as evil and out to get humans. Actually, as Baird notes, they frequently swim near humans in Australia but fatal encounters are very low and usually a result of sharks making a "mistake" [80]. She concludes that those most likely to encounter sharks must learn to take precautions such as "by not swimming in murky waters, at dawn or dusk, far from shore, or near schools of fish" and accept the risk of nature rather "than to try to kill sharks haphazardly."

There are several causes that reduce the prey populations for hunters but nevertheless they focus their resentment on carnivore competitors. In Sweden, Bergman found that, because the restrictions on the numbers of moose allowed to hunters had been decreased by lumber companies, the addition of a restored wolf pack was "the final straw" and attitudes toward wolves grew more hostile after their reintroduction [81 p. 13–17]. Similarly, attempts to build tolerance for wolves in Alberta (Canada) encountered problems due to poor market conditions in the area – because of the discovery of a bovine disease, Canadian cattle had been banned as imports to the United States and other countries, thus financially pressuring the ranchers [82 p. 159]. Attitudes may take several years to change. Peterson found a positive change in attitudes toward wolves in Michigan by 2000 compared to when the first four wolves were released twenty-five years previously [76 p. 159]. These wolves were shot, but wolves eventually proceeded to "naturally recolonize" Michigan which, according to Schadler, made them more accepted by deer hunters and landowners because they had not been forced upon them by the Federal government – Michigan did not even offer any compensation for livestock lost to wolf predation but attitudes improved [83 p. 168]. Goodall says that the reintroduction of the red wolf in North Carolina was due to a successful education program aimed at changing attitudes toward wolves [84 p. 59]. However, it should be noted that between January 2012 and November 2013, USFWS reported that nine wolves have been illegally shot and another is suspected of dying due to "illegal take" and the program continues to face severe challenges, as discussed in Chapter 3 [85]. The challenge of protecting wildlife such as wolves is never assured. Jane Goodall argues that social influence can help change attitudes and help to save the lynx when it becomes a "symbol of prestige to have a lynx on your property" [84 p. 155]. Preserving predators involves not only protecting them but also their prey – the conservationists first had to stop landowners from shooting rabbits to help lynx survive.

The extreme passions of those on either side of the wolf debate make compromise difficult. Those who hate wolves often express delight in showing their contempt for those who like them. McAllister tells of an incident in which an Alaskan outfitter wrote to him after McAllister had assisted a National Geographic film crew to film wolves, telling McAllister that he had discovered where the crew's "precious wolves" were and had killed as many of these wolves "as he could" [86 p. 186]. A significant portion of the current hatred of wolves can be ascribed to the fact that many people resent the Federal government "imposing" wolves on them through reintroductions and protections afforded them under the ESA. This was evident to Audubon's Ted Williams, who attended an Alaskan "summit" on wolves with anti-wolf protesters holding signs that said "Environmentalists: Kiss my Alaska Ass" and "Outsiders: Shit in your own nest – don't try it in ours" [87 p. 44]. In the Upper Michigan case noted above, shortly after four wolves were released, all four were shot and one of the carcasses of the dead wolves was left on the doorstep of the local game warden [88 p. 169]. When grizzly bears were proposed to be delisted by USFWS, one outfitter said that he planned to kill "Bear 399," famous for leading her cubs near roadsides in the Grand Teton area because of his "hatred for the federal government, bear-loving environmentalists and the Endangered Species Act" [89]. These stories serve to reinforce Tolmé's point that one has to be a "sociologist" (or perhaps, psychiatrist?) to understand the struggle over species such as wolves because of intensity of passions on both sides that it makes it so difficult to find "common ground" [90].

The "Kill Wolves to Make Them More Acceptable" Hypothesis

The hatred of reintroduced wolves in the West among important groups such as ranchers and farmers has been so strong and consistent that it has engendered an informal but widely prevalent hypothesis on the part of USFWS staff and other conservationists that wolves must be killed in order for these key groups to tolerate their existence. Indeed, this "kill wolves to make them acceptable" idea is one of the central rationales for delisting the reintroduced wolves from the Endangered Species List. The Final Environmental Impact Statement of the USFWS discusses how a variety of activities ranging from "harassment" to "take" of wolves either by "authorized agencies" or the public would "aid in wolf recovery" because they would "likely reduce landowner frustration" and thus prevent "indiscriminate and unnecessary killing of wolves" where they are not bothering livestock [91 appendices, p. 5]. Indeed, the same approach was proposed by the Interagency Grizzly Bear Committee in what they refer to as the "North American Model of Wildlife Conservation," which emphasizes the role that humans play and thus favors delisting of the grizzly and "regulated hunting" to improve their coexistence with humans [92]. The committee held that "unchecked grizzly populations" would compromise the "tolerance people have for grizzlies" [92]. Mech predicts that the numbers of wolves taken by hunters will decline "once the novelty wears off" [93 p. 1422]. When wolves were initially delisted by USFWS in 2009, Montana set a quota of 220 that would cut the state's wolf population by 25 percent and the tags to hunt them sold out quickly, which, according to some, was due to anger that had built up about them [94]. In June of 2013, the USFWS proposed a rule that would end Federal protections for wolves in the lower forty-eight states [95]. Thus the USFWS sought to defuse the controversy with a policy of allowing states to make decisions concerning predators with the proviso that the number killed cannot threaten the sustainability of the species. In response, the *New York Times* asked if wolves "can't get a fair hearing at the Federal level, what chance do they have at the state level?" [95]. The assumption of the USFWS is that the killing of individual species members will lead to decreased anger and increasing acceptance. They believe that without such a policy in place, illegal killings of species like grizzlies and wolves will escalate, resulting in a worse outcome for them.

Recently, the Wyoming Fish and Game Department released a plan to cut its wolf-hunting quota in half [96]. The major reason for doing so was that more wolves had been killed than planned and fewer pups born than anticipated. The department and key stakeholder groups such as outfitter organizations want to make sure that the population stays above 141 – the minimum number needed to support ten breeding pairs if they are to avoid having the wolf placed on the endangered list again [96]. The proposed cutback so far has generated little public controversy in statewide meetings on it, which may support the hypothesis that delisting has defused hatred of wolves. If states continue with this approach, the minimum number of wolves set by USFWS could, in effect, become the maximum and thus not necessarily lead to a secular upward trend as expected by some. Treves and Martin's research questions the assumption that allowing hunting of wolves will necessarily increase tolerance for them and promote their conservation [97]. In their surveys of Northern Rocky Mountain and Wisconsin hunters, they found that a majority (60.3 percent) of wolf and bear hunters opposed wolf conservation and also opposed any restrictions on hunting such as the banning of baiting, prohibiting use of dogs, or restricting hunting to wolves that had caused "property damage" [97 p. 990–1]. Finally, Treves and Martin argue that research shows that these attitudes will take "generations" to change. Wuerthner contends that "science" contradicts the hypothesis concerning grizzlies because hunters tend to kill the dominant members of the species that can survive without attacking livestock while they are "replaced" by bears that are more likely to kill livestock [98]. He cites studies of the impact of killing black bears and mountain lions that found more human–predator conflicts resulted. Schanning summarizes a variety of studies on attitudes toward wolves in the Great Lakes Region and concludes that there has been little change in attitudes during the period from 1970 to the early 2000s, but that the major change and improvement in attitudes toward wolves occurred during the period from 1930s to 1970 when the wolf had been "virtually extirpated" [99 p. 253–5].

The actions of Idaho show little change in attitudes toward wolves there. Recently, the Idaho Department of Fish and Game hired a professional wolf hunter to kill a pack of wolves in the remote area of Frank Church River of No Return Wilderness because the area is so remote that they cannot rely on hunters to kill wolves [100]. The reason behind the hunt, according to the Idaho Department, is that wolves are killing too many elk calves. The goal is to kill the entire pack of wolves because, says the Idaho Department's Bureau Chief, "If you're looking for cost benefits you remove an entire pack … It's going to have a longer-term benefit than removing members of the pack" [101]. The U.S. Forest Service allowed the Idaho Department to use its airstrip to fly in the wolf hunter after the University of Idaho turned down a request to use their landing facility. Zuckerman describes a "wolf and coyote killing derby" in Salmon, Idaho – carcasses will be weighed at the conclusion of the event to determine the winner [102].

Askins makes the point that wolves take at most only about one percent of livestock in areas where they exist, a smaller number than due to other causes such as losses due to storms and dogs [103 p. 15–18]. Nevertheless, ranchers have successfully focused public attention on the losses due to wolves with the result that millions of public tax dollars are spent on "public lands to kill predators so that private industry can make a profit" [103]. They have been able to accomplish this, according to Askins, because "emotions, not facts, have controlled the debate" and for many the wolf remains a symbol of evil and of the intrusion of the Federal government [103]. In responding to a public comment criticizing its removal of wolves depredating livestock, the (Mexican Wolf) Adaptive Management Oversight Committee stated that "wolves that are a chronic threat to livestock … are removed to address negative impacts and to promote tolerance for other wolves on the landscape" as has been done in other wolf recovery efforts – their goal is to "manage wolves within the framework of practices that were in place prior to reintroduction or expansion of wolves" [104 p. 5]. In short, they argue that killing depredating wolves is "a reasoned response to wolf/human conflicts that arise" and that restoration efforts must not disrupt the welfare of ranchers who have livestock near the restoration areas. Goble points out that because of the experimental designation for the Mexican wolf, people could take wolves as a result of "car accidents or trapping" and if they attack livestock [105 p. 133]. Also, "no critical habitat" was designated for them and there were no restrictions on altering their habitat. Thus the Mexican wolf reintroduction took a conservative approach in order to minimize human resentment. Still, despite all of these concessions, Goble notes, it took fifteen years to get them introduced as an experimental species because of the "emotional component" of the opposition that was little affected "by the concrete statutory provisions" [105 p. 135].

More recently, a "Mexican Wolf Coexistence Council" has been formed to try to develop a plan that will increase the number of wolves in the Southwest while at the same time minimizing alienation of ranchers. A major method is to "fund wolf presence" by "reducing the number of wolf removals" and by providing payments to offset losses that ranchers suffer. The fund is allocated among potential livestock producers on a number of criteria including the following: (1) Is the producer in core wolf territory? (2) Is the producer implementing proactive conflict avoidance measures? (3) Are there wolf pups that have survived to December 31 in the core area? [106 p. 12]. The difficult task is to accurately monitor how well producers are adhering to the plan guidelines. This task is assigned to the Mexican Wolf Interagency Field Team that monitors data including the minimum number of wolves, the number of packs and breeding pairs, the area of each pack's territory, and the minimum number of pups that survived to December 31 of the year of their birth. These data will be used to determine the allocation of funds to each eligible applicant, according to a formula [106 p. 16]. Techniques of problem avoidance such as increased human presence, timed calving, range riders, use of alternate pastures, supplemental feeding, and turbo-fladry approaches that have proven effective will be encouraged. Ranchers will be compensated based on the following schedule: calf: $800, lamb: $225, yearling: $1,200, ewe: $225, cow: $1,450, ram: $750, and bull: $2,500 [106 p. 22]. Another approach being attempted by the environmental group WildEarth Guardians is to buy out rancher's permits to graze cattle on wolf habitat. The group has offered one rancher "several hundred thousand dollars" in exchange for his permit to graze on about 25,000 acres [107]. However, there have been hold-ups in working out the deal – funders want the "retirement" to be permanent and that would require a Congressional bill that has not passed yet [107]. Similar deals have worked in the Yellowstone area but there are differences from the Gila National Forest controlled by the U.S. Forest Service, where the grazing occurs throughout the entire year, while grazing in the Northern Rockies only happens during summers. Rancher organizations like the New Mexican Cattle Growers Association do not oppose one-time deals but oppose permanent "permit retirement." Moreover, the Forest Service ranger in charge of the area has to approve the deal and the Forest Service moves very carefully in taking any actions that are opposed by the rancher industry. Recently, they approved new management practices increasing the areas where they are allowed "to roam," but their "experimental population" designation was retained that allows taking of them [108].

The perceptions that people hold about charismatic animals in general and especially predators such as wolves and grizzly bears are complex. The USFWS, in its environmental impact statement on the reintroduction of wolves to Yellowstone, makes the following statements about human attitudes [109 appendices, p. 65]:

Public opinion surveys, public comments on wolf management planning, and the positions of elected local, state, and federal government officials consistently indicated they and the public will repeatedly and fervently resist any attempts to reintroduce wolves without assurances that current uses of public and private lands would not be disrupted by wolf recovery activities, that wolves that attack livestock will be controlled, and that in the rare instances where wolf predation may significantly impact big game populations that the state wildlife management agencies can resolve those types of conflict.

Ed Bangs, the USFWS agent in charge of the wolf delisting in Yellowstone, is quoted by Joe Roman as stating that the delisting of wolves in 2010 followed by the selling of many licenses to shoot wolves "had improved dramatically" the local view of wolves [29 p. 177]. Recently, the USFWS has proposed to delist wolves from ESA protection in all forty-eight lower states – a step that Klinkenborg claims has "little to do with science and everything to do with politics." In short, one of the foundational arguments for the delisting of wolves is based on the hypothesis that killing of wolves (and grizzlies) is a necessity if humans in the area are to tolerate this species [110].

Survey research literature actually shows that in recent decades the majority of the population holds generally positive attitudes toward wolves and grizzlies. Kellert and Barry found, surprisingly, that Alaskans expressed "far greater willingness than other regions to forsake benefits in order to protect wildlife and ecosystems" [32 p. 59]. These results are supported by the reaction of Alaskans to former Governor Hickel's proposal to shoot wolves from helicopters – Hickel received more than 100,000 negative comments [111]. Brown and Decker found that Alaskans accept lethal predator control only when Alaskans who rely on moose or caribou cannot find enough [112]. Bruskotter, Vaske, and Schmidt discovered that in the conservative state of Utah, most residents favored "non-lethal controls of wolves." Although hunters and the agricultural sector were somewhat more likely to favor lethal controls, the general finding of opposition to lethal controls nevertheless was common across all stakeholder groups including hunters [113 p. 130]. Pate found strong support (about 71 percent) in favor of wolf reintroduction to Colorado even in the rural western areas of the state [114 p. 421]. A survey of public opinion in Idaho conducted in March of 1992 found that 72 percent of Idaho residents favored having wolves in the state's wilderness areas [115 p. 550]. Willcox reports that 99.9 percent of the 210,000 comments submitted to the USFWS concerning their decision to delist grizzlies were negative to the proposal [116]. Williams reviewed studies of attitudes toward wolves conducted between 1972 and 2000 and found an overall favorable attitude of 51 percent toward wolves with 60 percent favoring wolf "restoration" [117 p. 575]. The positive symbolism attached to grizzlies is evidenced by their use as "mascots" of teams such as the University of Montana [118]. A 2001 survey conducted for the Wyoming Fish and Game Department found that 74 percent of residents felt that grizzlies "were a benefit to Wyoming" (44 percent strongly agreed) [119 p. 5]. However, there was an even split between those who thought that the grizzly should be removed from the Endangered Species List (36 percent) and those who opposed their removal, and only 3 percent had no opinion on this issue. Furthermore, most of those who supported removing grizzlies from the list "strongly agreed" with this position, while similarly most of those opposed to removing them strongly agreed with that position. Thus, despite the overall positive view of grizzlies, there is strong polarization on the issue as to whether they should be protected by listing [119 p. 5]. Survey results are subject to change due to various factors – for example, they found that support for reintroduction of grizzlies fell from 62 percent in 1995 to 46 percent in 1997 [120 p. 210–11]. Nevertheless, the results of survey research show that a large majority of the public in the Western states holds positive attitudes toward wolves and grizzlies, which raises the question of why the political debate over them in these states has been dominated by groups who fear and hate them.

Certain groups are negative toward wolves and their reintroduction – only 35 percent of the ranchers and only14 percent of those using public lands permits (in Utah) were favorable [117 p. 575 & 578]. A survey of Greenlee County (Arizona), a potential release site for Mexican wolf reintroduction, found that only 22 percent supported their reintroduction, 58 percent opposed it, and the remainder were undecided [121 p. 42]. However, according to one report after the release, anxiety about the wolves lessened in the county [122 p. 181]. Major national media tend to be supportive of wolves: The *New York Times* editorialized concerning the need for the USFWS to monitor and modify its deals with Western states concerning the delisting of wolves [123; 124]. The *Chicago Tribune* editorialized that they would "love to see wolves re-establish packs throughout the Midwest, including Illinois" [125]. Films such as the 1971 Canadian film "Death of a Legend" had such an "emotional impact" that it is credited with "eliminating the wolf bounty" in much of Canada [126 p. 979]. However, despite the support from these national media outlets, the overall coverage of media is quite different. Houston, Bruskotter, and Fan analyzed evaluative comments about wolves in more than 7000 stories in the Lexis-Nexis database and found that stories in the news media became increasingly negative during the period from 1999 to 2008 [127 p. 399]. Enck and Brown's study of attitudes toward wolf restoration in New York State found that largely negative media coverage of wolf restoration during the 1998–9 period affected Adirondack Park residents' attitudes toward wolves [128 p. 26]. More generally, Enck and Brown found that the amount of media coverage was the only variable in their study that correlated negatively with these attitudes [128 p. 22]. Overall, those studies show that those who have the most to lose hold very different views from the majority. Thus, despite the surveys that show positive attitudes toward predators such as wolves, the political reality is that an impassioned, well-organized group of well-to-do and influential residents who oppose wolves can have far more impact on the politics of wolf restoration than an amorphous majority who do not have a major stake in the issue. This point is illustrated by Dizard's study of attitudes toward possible wolf restoration in the Adirondack Park in New York in which a survey revealed high levels of support for the possible reintroduction even among hunters (about two-thirds favoring) but that the organization representing elected officials inside the park area voted "overwhelmingly to oppose the reintroduction" [129 p. 83 & 89]. Enck and Brown's study showed that overall that 60 percent of New York State residents approved the restoration of wolves, but Adirondack residents (where the wolves would be reintroduced) were split, 42 percent approving and 41 percent disapproving – a result that again emphasizes the difference between attitudes of general public versus those most affected by conservation measures [130]. Despite the survey cited above that a large majority Idahoans favored wolves, Idaho politicians such as former Governor C. L. "Butch" Otter, a rancher turned governor, have made a career of aggressively opposing wolves and, more importantly, he succeeded in being elected and reelected. Otter was cheered by hunters and groups representing them such as Idaho Sportsmen and Fishermen, a non-profit group opposing wolves, when he proposed that 80 percent of wolves in Idaho be killed and that he wanted to shoot one himself [131]. In 2010 while running for reelection, Otter wrote to Ken Salazar, head of the Interior Department, that Idaho would no longer "manage wolves as the designated agent of the Federal government" [132]. Also, in 2010, Otter "ordered Idaho wildlife managers to relinquish their duty to arrest poachers or even to investigate when wolves are killed illegally" [133]. In 2011, Otter signed a bill declaring the wolves a "disaster emergency" in the state and proposed to strip the animal of Federal protections in the state [134]. In 2012, when an Idaho hunter killed an Oregon wolf, Otter offered to provide Oregon with as many Idaho wolves as they would take [135]. Houston et al. found less negative discourse in news media in states like Alaska with permanent wolf populations and the survey research by Kellert found a positive attitude among the general population to be hopeful signs for wolves [127 p. 400]. But as discussed elsewhere, Alaska's key institutions (e.g., Game Commission that sets rules for hunting of wolves) have been determined to reduce the wolf population so as to enhance the number of game like moose and caribou available to hunters. Likewise, the Alaska State Legislature in 1994 passed a statute that mandates "consumptive use of ungulates by hunters over other resource values" [136 p. 1244]. Indeed, Kellert, Black, Rush, and Bath make the point that, although most hunters and trappers are favorable toward predators, a "small minority rabidly anti-predator" sub-group have an "outsized impact" [126 p. 987]. Thus the "killing wolves hypothesis" depends not on changing the attitude of the general public but those of this small but important segment that holds antipathy for them. The "killing wolves to make them more acceptable" hypothesis has been challenged by researchers studying Wisconsin hunters' attitudes which showed a drop in tolerance of wolves "after a culling of wolves program" was implemented from 2001 to 2009 [137; 138]. This hypothesis is an example of how a major policy is undertaken based on expectations, assumptions, and politics.

Many people fear and dislike wolves and other predators such as mountain lions because they view them as a threat to humans. Negative experiences can form or change views on animals. For example, Hudenko, Decker and Siemer reviewed the effects of personal experience with coyotes and found its impact was complex though unsurprisingly negative experience resulted in negative attitudes toward the species [139]. Manuel wrote about the fears of wolf attacks on humans prior to the reintroduction of red wolves to North Carolina [140 p. 25]. Likewise, Congressman Pearce from New Mexico cited fears that a baby's cry is "the most provocative thing for a wolf"and asked "what is being done to protect humans?" [141 p.104–5]. However, wolf expert L. David Mech has stated that no such attacks have occurred other than some bites by lone wolves seeking handouts in Algonquin Park in Canada at a campsite [140 p. 24]. Indeed, Carroll, Noss, Schumaker, and Paquet state there is substantial evidence that, given habitat available, wolves select areas with low human density, whether due to human-caused mortality or behavioral avoidance" [142 p. 28]. In particular, roads "negatively affect wolf populations" at all levels by increasing human access. Duke et al. report that human presence in the Banff National Park such as highways, secondary roads, and recreational areas broke up their habitat and the wolves avoided the human presence and thus abandoned "high quality habitat" [143 p. 262]. Consequently, Parks Canada used an unusual strategy – they removed "all human structures" such as buffalo corrals, barns, an airstrip, and this reduced human activity led to an increase in wolf use of the Cascade Corridor [143 p. 271]. Maehr, Hoctor, and Harris point out that, although the missions of national parks have grown to include the protection of biota, that the parks "remain primarily set-asides for human recreation" [144 p. 294]. Harris et al. found that wildlife refuges such as the Arthur R. Marshall Loxahatchee National Wildlife Refuge have focused completely on wading birds and created a "river of grass" that is low in diversity and useless for the mammal population [145 p. 322]. In short, the juxtaposition of humans and wolves and other wildlife presents much more danger to these species than to humans.

Mountain lions, on occasion, have attacked humans and researchers have hypothe-sized that the expansion of humans living in lion habitat leads to "habituation" of the animals to humans and thus danger of increased attacks [146 p. 225]. Linn reports that mountain lion attacks in the past twenty years (prior to 2003) had exceeded those in the past eighty years and ascribes this to the fact that people are "moving into the ranges of elk and deer – the cougar's favorite meals" [147 p. 23–4]. She asks rhetorically whether people value their wildlife experiences enough to allow this risk. Beier reported that all of the fatalities in his survey involved children "unaccompanied by adults" [148 p. 410]. Manfredo, Zinn, Sikorowski, and Jones studied mountain lion populations near Denver and found that human population growth was concentrated in the foothills where the lions live due to increasing numbers of prey such as mule deer in the area and wildlife management such as restrictions on trapping [149]. Meyer points out that there are 350,000 deer–auto collisions each year causing "10,000 serious injuries and 150 human deaths annually" compared to only 50 confirmed deaths due to cougars over the past 100 years [150 p. 69]. The visibility of a species affects how dangerous we perceive it to be. Although coyotes can be a threat to livestock, deer, and pets, people do not notice them like lions, and despite now being prevalent throughout the East, there has been no "general cry for their extermination" [151 p. 20]. On the other hand, impressive size such as the existence of bears as "large as geysers" in Yellowstone attracted more attention than any other animals in the park, making them a prime tourist attraction but also perceived as a threat to humans [152 p. 79].

One of the points that opponents of conservation of predators such as cougars and wolves make is that supporters in Eastern states and urban areas are hypocritical and would not allow dangerous predators in areas close to them. One recent example occurred in Illinois when a cougar was shot by an Illinois Department of Natural Resources officer after a farmer complained that they felt threatened by it [153]. However, there is evidence that there is support in states such as Illinois for allowing the presence of such predators. The *Chicago Tribune* editorialized in favor of "giving cougars protection under the Illinois Wildlife Code" – they have lacked protection until now because there was no evidence of a breeding population in the state. Shortly afterwards, Marc Miller, the Director of the Illinois Department of Natural Resources, wrote that "there is room . . . for apex predators"(cougars and wolves) but they will have to be managed because it is too late to curb human occupancy and that the reintroduc-tion of these predators will require "new ethics" [154]. The difference between urban and rural states is illustrated by the contrast between the state of Washington and nearby states like Wyoming and Idaho. Washington's legislature approved a plan "allowing the wolf population to expand ... the goal was 15 packs in three zones spread across the state, with five to 10 wolves typically in each pack" [155]. A spokesperson for a group called Washington Residents Against Wolves criticized the plan by the "urban-dominated legislature" that would most affect rural residents in eastern Washington where most wolves would reside [155]. Attitudes are also affected by the degree to which an area relies upon agriculture and livestock, as illustrated by the state of Michigan where there is a "lower tolerance for wolves" in the northern Lower Peninsula (NLP) compared with the Upper Peninsula (UP) due to the greater density of livestock farms in the NLP than UP [156 p. 79].

There is a large discrepancy between risk perception and reality. Knuth et al. found that only about 5 percent of Montanans did not think that they were under risk of a cougar attack even though the actual risk for most was one in a million [157 p. 224]. According to Knuth, though they appreciate the "lions in wildlife settings," they have no tolerance for those living near people. Rauber reports that interviews with people who had survived bear attacks revealed that they did not blame the bears for the attacks, admitting that it was "their own fault" [25 p. 50]. In 2012, in response to four grizzly attacks on humans in Yellowstone, the USFWS as well as the Wyoming and Idaho Fish and Game departments wanted grizzlies delisted, as wolves had been, in order to avoid fueling hatred by local ranchers and hunters and because grizzlies had reached the population targets set in their recovery plan by USFWS [158]. Part of the reason for the increase in attacks was the greater number of grizzlies, but another factor could be loss of food because of depredation of white bark pine trees due to beetles. Opponents of the delisting point to the fact that a large proportion of grizzly victims fail to follow basic rules such as not hiking alone and failure to carry bear spray [158]. Thus the question arises whether attacks in situations where the humans behaved foolishly should be considered at all as evidence of the need to control the wildlife?

The Paradox of Fear

One of the paradoxes of charismatic predators such as grizzlies is that a significant part of their "magical charisma" is due to the thrill that humans obtain of seeing an animal that is capable of killing them. They like the thrill presented by these predators. I have visited parks with grizzlies such as Glacier National Park in Montana and the major topic of conversation during hikes concerns the possibility of seeing and encountering grizzlies. Edward Abbey had a predilection for predators because, as he quoted his friend Doug Peacock, "it isn't wilderness" "unless there is a critter out there that can kill you and eat you" [159 p. 167]. Abbey enjoyed "the element of danger" that such animals brought. Similarly, William Hornaday, a famous conservationist and zoologist, said that a Rocky Mountain without a bear was "half a mountain" and that merely adding a grizzly cub to it would immediately add "uncertainty and thrills" [160 p. 177]. Mooallem talked to Churchill (Canada) polar bear tour operators after a man was mauled and killed by a polar bear and the operator reported that the killing, far from detouring tourists, had "the opposite effect" – if there "was a chance of being ripped apart," "people were into it" [7 p. 32]. The tension between wanting to have fearsome predators and fear of them is illustrated by Romo's report on the debate of reintroducing wolves to the Southwest. She relates how one child told how she saw a wolf tear apart her dog outside her home while two teens told of how they like to hike the same (Gila) area, were not afraid of the wolves, and loved the "uniqueness" of it due to the presence of wolves [161]. More recently, when the USFWS proposed that most Mexican wolves receive ESA protections, opponents showed pictures of "chicken coop" type of structures they said would be needed to protect children from wolf attacks [162]. Supporters of the wolf-ESA protections participated in a "Save the Lobo" demonstration financed by the Defenders of Wildlife, while nearby opponents financed by the Koch brothers' Americans for Prosperity showed a film that equated dangerous wolves with "an out-of-control Federal government" [162]. Siemer, Decker, and Merchant studied risk and perception of bears in New York and found most people were thrilled to see a bear "once in a while" and didn't want them harmed in any way [163 p. 12]. On the other hand, they reported that "if they [bears] were showing up on a regular basis" they "wouldn't be happy." These New York residents were often surprised to learn that the New York State Department of Environmental Conservation did not generally respond to calls about bears such as requests to remove them humanely from the area [163 p. 17–18]. Still, many people are attracted to moving to areas where predators such as bears live. Perceptions of danger and risk are subject to rapid change and Siemer et al. note that the mauling and subsequent death of a child in 2002 due to a bear attack in New York received huge media coverage and affected their risk perception [163 p. 21]. But experience shows that most people also are reluctant to change other than on a short-term basis human behaviors that affected their likelihood of encountering bears, such as putting out bird feeders and "smelly garbage."

In short, people are conflicted in their attitudes toward dangerous predators and the tradeoffs between their appreciation for these charismatic animals and the excitement they lend to the outdoors and their own safety from attacks. The paradox between wanting to have the excitement of encountering a deadly predator while not allowing humans to actually die from encounters with them leads USFWS officials (e.g., in Yellowstone and other parks with deadly predators) to employ a curious process of conducting "criminal investigations" of bears that kill or injure humans. Jessica Grose studied the decision to "execute" a grizzly (Wapiti) sow in October of 2011 [164]. This same sow was found to have killed a hiker (Brian Matayoshi) on July 6, 2011 when he and his wife encountered the sow with its two cubs. Brian and his wife ran from the sow – a behavior that is not advised – and the sow chased him down and severed his femoral vein and he died from loss of blood. The park's bear manager, Kerry Gunther, and others including Chris Servheen, the USFWS's Grizzly Bear Coordinator, conducted an investigation of this death and determined that the grizzly sow "had acted naturally" defending her cubs and decided not to euthanize her or even put a collar on her [164]. On August 27, 2011, another man (John Wallace) was found to have been killed and an investigation showed that the same sow had encountered Wallace and may have killed him; thus the bear was judged again and this time the decision was to execute her. Grose summarizes the rules: "If a grizzly hurts someone while acting in a naturally aggressive way, then the bear goes free. If a grizzly acts unnaturally aggressive, though, and injures a person, it must be euthanized. It all comes down to the animal's state of mind" [164]. The failure of humans to take proper precautions such as not hiking alone and being without bear spray, as well as not to turn and run are taken into consideration in judging the bears. However, these rules are not necessarily followed in all parks. In Denali National Park in 2012, a solo backpacker was killed by a grizzly sow after photographing the bear for 8 minutes from 60 yards when he had been warned to stay 300 yards from bears and not backpack alone [165 p. 96]. Nevertheless, the bear was shot the next day. Another implicit rule is that the park and USFWS officials have to err on the side of safety for humans. Grose points out that Interagency Grizzly Bear Team is being sued due to the death of a man who died after "bear managers had removed a warning sign from the area where he was killed" [164].

Other than threatening of humans, charismatic species can have other negative effects. In Britain, hunters have been shooting hen harrier birds because they decrease their take of grouse [166 p. 1551]. Dangers can be health-related. For example, beavers increased the possibility of giardia presence in water systems [129 p. 87]. Wolves kill livestock, game animals, and pets. In Alaska, wolves have been blamed for not having enough moose to "meet the consumptive needs of Alaskans" [167 p. 917]. Part of the issue with Alaskan wolves is the desire on the part of State Game Board to have "high levels of human harvest" – higher than would exist without taking wolves that compete with human hunters. As noted in Chapter 2, the impact of wolves and grizzlies on the numbers of ungulates is subject to dispute and there are other causes such as the takings of white and native hunters as well as overgrazing of the ranges but Rawson states that wolves were a cause they could "do something about" [58 p. 99]. A similar dispute concerns the supposed negative effect of wolves on elk available for sports hunters in states such as Idaho [168 p. 271]. The Idaho Department of Fish and Game claimed that elk numbers were down but the USFWS disputed that the decline was due to wolves [168 p. 292]. In Wyoming, elk are fed on grounds "operated by the state" and wolves are not only blamed for taking too many elk but also for scattering these elk, which sometimes have the brucellosis disease feared by ranchers. USFWS official Ed Bangs responded that the take of wolves had not been large and that increased difficulty in shooting elk may be due to the secondary effect that wolves have on elk, making them more alert and thus harder to hunt [169].

Many "popular" charismatic animals such as elephants can cause damage that negatively affects humans and sometimes other species. Raymond Bonner says that Amboseli Park in Kenya looks like "napalm was dropped on it" due to the destruction of trees by elephants. This destruction harms other wildlife such as monkeys, kudzus, and impala [170]. Bonner goes on to argue that NGOs such as the African Wildlife Federation and World Wildlife Fund have used the charisma of the elephant and advertisements that highlight the slaughter of them to raise huge funds without taking into consideration the need to keep their numbers at a sustainable level because their contributors will not accept the need to cull these charismatic animals [170]. When charismatics block development, people's self-interest can overwhelm the attractiveness. For example, Williams says that the appearance of Florida panthers near a development where children lived led the Fish and Wildlife commission to have them removed [171 p. 28–9]. The attempt to establish other populations of the cats in Arkansas was refused by the Arkansas Fish and Game Commission due to their fear of negative impact on deer hunters. Another population was attempted to be established in northern Florida but also failed due to the opposition of deer hunters and people frightened for the safety of their children. In the latter case, some panthers were killed due to being shot or snared and when the remainder were evacuated, many died "in transit" or wound up in a caged hunting preserve [171]. In Hawaii, recently, several monk seals, an endangered species, have been slain, reportedly by local subsistence fishermen who resent their taking of fish [172]. Mooallem says that resentment against not only the seals but also the Federal government first appeared in 2006 when President Bush declared Papahānaumokuākea Marine National Monument that blocked some fishermen from using the area they had previously access to. Due to proposals to protect other species, such as humpback whales and sea turtles, as well as the seals, some local residents said that the government was creating a sea aquarium and thus taking away the rights of fishermen and divers [172].

Positive Impacts of Predators

In order to argue against the rush to eliminate them, conservationists point to positive ecological impacts on the environment that result from predators. Goodall says that wolves can lead to an increase in game birds such as wild turkeys and quail because they prey upon raccoons [84 p. 59]. Sharpe, Norton, and Strachan found that the wolf population on Isle Royale had increased tree density through its predation of moose on the island [173 p. 130]. However, some of these purported positive ecological effects have been called into question recently as Mech reports that other factors may explain effects originally hypothesized due to wolves [174]. Sea otters are often disliked by fishermen but they eat sea urchins, thus helping to maintain high levels of kelp necessary for flourishing fish and bird populations [175 p. 4]. McGrath says that one otter can consume "4500 pounds of shellfish a year" and that is why many fishermen "cheered when they heard that the Exxon Valdez oil spill was killing hundreds of sea otters" in Alaska [176 p. 45]. But a researcher on the Aleutian Islands noticed a "pattern that … islands with sea otters had kelp forests and those without … only had pebbly green carpets of sea urchins" [176 p. 45]. This researcher, Jim Estes, argues that this finding supports the proposition that when you remove "the apex predator, the landscape changes and typically becomes more impoverished" [176 p. 45]. Coyotes can help to keep down local geese populations, thus minimizing their damaging effects such as water pollution and avian influenza due to overpopulations of geese [177 p. 77]. Recently, Gehrt, Wilson, Brown, and Anchor found evidence that the presence of coyotes in urban parks helped to "buffer natural areas" from the effects of predation by feral cats [178]. Foreman makes the more general point that the absence of the top predator results in "ecosystem simplification accompanied by a rush of extinctions" [179 p. 124]. Judson reports on the same phenomenon – the "landscape of fear" where prey cannot "go where they like" and thus the prey "tend to grow more slowly and reproduce less" which can be positive for the biosystem [180]. Dugelby et al. cite research that the presence of all large carnivores (e.g., pumas) encourage "herding" of elk and deer and that without their presence, foragers tend to be stationary, which alters vegetation negatively and can lead to desertification [181 p. 68]. Ripple, Wirsing, Beschta, and Buskirk found evidence that the endangered lynx would be aided by the presence of wolves due to their effects on lowering coyote populations as evidenced by the high numbers on Isle Royale and rarity in the wolfless Yellowstone area during the same periods [182]. They admit that other factors are involved, such as climate change, since deep snow gives hares an advantage over coyotes, and that restoration of wolves must be in sufficient numbers to be effective. These predator effects occur not only for mammals but also for invertebrates like grasshoppers that are more numerous if spiders are absent. Similarly, "meadow communities" lose biomass when there are no lizards to eat grasshoppers [183 p. 349].

A more politically potent argument is that charismatics have significant positive effects on matters of immediate importance to humans, such as increased tourism. Rauber says that tourism "is now more important" to Wyoming's economy "than timber" and that most people come to the state to view wildlife, not kill it [184 p. 33–4]. Rauber cites one Wyoming Tourism official as saying that Glacier "park naturalists get more questions about wolves" than any other topic and tourist shops sell loads of wolf memorabilia [184]. Similarly, Seideman reports that 40,000 people lined up the previous (1995) summer for ranger-led talks about wolves and that a University of Montana economist estimates that $110 million will be brought to the state by "wolf watchers" [185 p. 70–1]. Duffield, Neher, and Patterson compared the costs of wolves (including livestock losses and losses of game to hunters) with the positive benefits of tourist spending and concluded that wolves bring a net benefit of $58 million in Wyoming, Montana, and Idaho [186 p. 25]. Johnson cites data that the population growth in areas near Yellowstone have been double the rate for other parts of Wyoming [187]. He also quotes the head of Wyoming's Fish and Game Department as saying that the new residents "do not see wolves as the older residents do" and are more interested in vistas than "the price of grain and calves." He goes on to say that many of the new landowners have banned hunting on their property, in effect creating "wolf sanctuaries." Dax cites data that income from professional and services industries in the West increased from $250 million to $1 billion while agriculture and mining remained below $50 million [188]. Dax says that in Montana, for example, professional, business, and service industry employment "increased by 30,000 jobs between 1998 and 2008" while farming and ranching lost jobs [188]. In Utah, Dax says that only about 4 percent were employed in agriculture or mining. In addition, recent research by Rob Wielgus found that a wolf control program actually contributed to more livestock predation, possibly because of "compensatory breeding" following the killing of wolves [189].

Studying these developments, including the positive economic impacts as well as the generally positive attitudes of the general public even in Western states cited above, one would think that wolves and grizzlies would have significant positive supporters to counter the heated opposition of ranchers and hunters but, up until now, Western state and local politics concerning wolves has been strongly anti-predator. For example, Phillips, Edward, and Arapkiles cite a 1994 survey that showed 71 percent of registered voters favored wolf reintroduction to Colorado but nevertheless the Colorado Game Commission (in 1989) approved a resolution against reintroductions and even authorized a bounty on wolves [190 p. 242–4]. Dax notes that despite the changes in the economy of the West, its politicians such as Wyoming Senators Mike Enzi and John Barasso continue to tie themselves into the old "cowboy" culture, putting grazing horses and pickup trucks on their Congressional websites [188]. Part of this may be due to one of the rules of "political economy of regulation": the costs of regulations are much more concentrated than the benefits [191 p. 38]. The argument is that losses due to predation make ranchers more militant in their opposition to predators than those who appreciate and support them. Thus those in control of wildlife management agencies remain more concerned with their traditional constituencies of hunters and ranchers than the general population.

The Difficult Politics of Charismatic Wildlife

Due to the intense passions of both haters and defenders of charismatic wildlife, it has proven difficult to find middle-of-the-road compromise solutions. Clearly, the USFWS is tired of being put in the position of fighting rancher-hunter-dominated administrations of Western states and now refers to state wildlife management agencies as "their partners." In a 2012 article in the *Billings Gazette*, Dan Ashe, the newly appointed Director of the USFWS, stated that wolves have the ability to flourish "despite high mortality rates" and describes "regulated hunting" as a "valuable tool for reducing conflicts with humans." This desire to end conflict over predators with dominant constituencies is as true of the liberal Obama Administration as well as the previous conservative Bush Administration. As Nie has pointed out, due to the reintroduction and ESA listing, the wolves for many rural citizens came to represent an intrusive Federal government [60 p. 77]. Democratic leaders are aware that crucial Senate and House seats could be lost if controversies over wolves and grizzlies were to determine election outcomes and this helps to explain why they accepted the budget compromise rider to limit the scope of the ESA. Democratic senators supporting the delisting included Montana's Max Baucus and Jon Tester, as well as the liberal Amy Klobuchar of Minnesota [192 p. 22]. Brian Schweitzer, the former two-time Democratic governor of Montana, threatened in 2011 to defy the Federal government by encouraging livestock owners to kill wolves even in areas where killing "is not allowed" [193]. The major opponents of the delisting are environmental NGOs including the Alliance for Wild Rockies, the Center for Biological Diversity, Wild-Earth Guardians, and Friends of the Clearwaters. Their major argument against the rider was that it "violated the Separation of Powers doctrine" because this action "repealed a previous federal ruling without amending existing law" [194]. L. David Mech argues that public participation in the wolf debate can have a harmful impact such as when animal welfare and wolf advocacy groups inflamed public opinion that wolves were being threatened in Denali National Park despite scientific evidence to the contrary [195 p. 18]. On the other side of the politics, Parker cites a case where local politics scuttled a plan to introduce red wolves into the Land Between-the-Lakes Kentucky [196 p. 73].

Examples of Public Participation: The Case of Mexican Wolf Reintroduction

It is instructive to look at public comments made concerning the five-year review of the reintroduction of the Mexican wolf to understand the nature of the feedback that wildlife managers face over controversial issues. The Adaptive Management Oversight Committee (AMOC) is an interagency group composed of members from the Arizona Game and Fish Department, the USFWS, the Wildlife Services of the Department of Agriculture, and other agencies. They published their responses to 611 written and 345 oral comments – the responses include sizeable percentages of questions from both pro- and anti-wolf groups. Here are some examples.

Pro-Wolf Comments

USFWS attendance at closed political meeting: One comment criticized the USFWS's attendance at a meeting sponsored by Congressman Steve Pearce (Republican, New Mexico), a wolf reintroduction opponent, with members of livestock and landowner "interests." The questioner said that "USFWS should avoid the appearance of favoritism by not attending such meetings unless they are announced ahead of time and open to the public." **Response:** The AMOC replied that "when a standing member of Congress asks a Federal agency such as USFWS to attend a meeting, that agency generally does not decline the invitation. Regardless, neither AMOC nor its individual agency members can dictate with whom a Congressman and/or his staff meet. Any group or individual can request a meeting with a Congressman by contacting him or his staff directly" [104 ARPCC-3].

Mexican Wolf Reintroduction Does Not Provide Enough Protections for the Wolves: **Comment:** "We question the appropriateness and scientific validity of imposing secondary boundaries on this small population of endangered wolves and we see no reason why highly endangered Mexican wolves should receive lower standards of protection and tolerance than more abundant wolves elsewhere in the USA." **Response**: "The Mexican wolf is protected under ESA consistent with the law itself and the Final Rule under which reintroduction is occurring. The Final Rule, issued under Section 10 (j) of the ESA, designates the AZ-NM population as "experimental nonessential," meaning that wolves released to the wild within the 10(j) boundary are not essential to recovery. That is, even if all wild Mexican wolves in the BRWRA [Blue Range Wolf Recovery Area in Arizona] died, elimination would not occur because there are now sufficient Mexican wolves in captivity" [104 ARPCC-29].

Critique of Financial Incentives for Livestock Industry: **Comment**: "Any proposed financial incentives to livestock producers should be conservatively and realistically selected to maximize the success of the reintroduction program. Describing the desired return on incentives as 'an increased level of tolerance' is unacceptably vague. Given that years of political compromise and taxpayer funded subsidies to the livestock industry have produced continued intolerance, legislative sabotage, lawsuits against USFWS to terminate the reintroduction, and illegal wolf killings, what is the realistic hope for adequate return on further incentives?" **Response:** "AMOC believes that financial incentives can contribute to wolf recovery in the Southwest. A compensation subcommittee of AMOC has been established to evaluate alternative incentive and compensation programs. Updates on progress have been reported during quarterly AMOC meetings. Ultimately, authorization for a compensation program would require legislative action" [104 ARPCC-65].

Anti-Wolf Comments

Attack on Rural Culture: A comment said that "inherent in the Mexican wolf program is the 'opinion' that the various rural cultures are not valuable. This is our home and our world and it is being attacked by outsiders in a very sophisticated but insensitive and war-like manner by these transient outsiders from their transient homes, worlds, and careers. The Mexican wolf program if persisted in, will inevitably lead to cultural and material disasters – the rural cultures are threatened by wolf recovery and cannot survive it." **Response:** The AMOC response was that "the AMOC Lead Agencies wish to make clear that by law, policy, regulation, ethics and action, they do and always will value rural cultures. The fact is wolf reintroduction and recovery are infinitely more compatible with rural than with urban culture" [104 ARPCC-14].

Environmentalist bias: One comment criticized the AMOC for being biased in favor of wolves: "The program sides with environmental extremists. Key employees' attitudes may be jaded for love of the wolf over other wildlife. It is common knowledge that one or more key players on the USFWS Wolf Recovery Team are on record of wanting to stop multiple-use and in particular, grazing on federally managed lands. That makes it hard for your team to be objective and obvious that the program has always been about more than just reintroducing wolves." **Response:** The AMOC responded as follows: "Agency employees in the Reintroduction Project do not have anti-grazing or anti-multiple-use agendas. As government employees and public servants, our job is to implement the Project consistent with all applicable Federal, State, and Tribal laws, and help recover the Mexican wolf, not make judgments regarding the appropriateness of grazing or other multiple-use activities on public lands. Grazing of public lands is a lawful activity, subject to regulations that AMOC does not establish or administer. It is, however, just one of the multiple-uses of public lands that we must consider in adaptively managing the Reintroduction Project" [104 ARPCC-3].

Impact on elk: Once comment stated that "wolves in the Gila are having a big effect on the elk's behavioral patterns. They are being pushed into higher heavier timber and don't use the wet meadows and open ridges anymore. If wolves continue to reproduce as they are, they will have a definite impact on elk herd sizes and State Game and Fish Departments will reduce licenses and hurt outfitter and other businesses." **Response**: "Unquestionably, wolves will eventually redistribute prey within the BRWRA through predation pressure and mere presence. State and Tribal wildlife agency monitoring of elk numbers and distribution will help determine when (and the extent to which) this occurs but no detectable changes to big game populations as a result of wolf reintroduction have occurred to date ... If unacceptable negative impacts on prey base are ever identified, the State and Tribal wildlife agencies have the authority to implement remedial wolf management action. Unacceptable impacts to game populations are defined within the experimental population rule as '2 consecutive years with a cumulative 35% decrease in population or distinct herd segment compared to the pre-wolf 5-year average.' The Final Rule also encourages wildlife management agencies to develop their own definitions of unacceptable impacts for approval by USFWS. Thus, both AGFD [Arizona Fish and Game Department] and WMAT [White Mountain Apache Tribe] have set that standard at 25% reduction attributable to wolf depredation" [104 ARPCC-57].

Whose Opinions Should Count: "Those that live in the recovery area want the wolves out. The only private sector opinions that should be considered are from those living inside the recovery area. Those that want the wolves that live in cities don't have to deal with a dangerous animal in their midst or threats to their livelihoods." **Response:** The AMOC response was that it "is committed to ensuring that the voices of those most directly affected by wolf reintroductions are heard and heeded as decisions are shaped and implemented, but all other opinions and voices must be heard" [104 ARPCC-14].

Mothers Worried about Children: One comment said that "mothers in the Catron County area have seen wolves in their yards and keep their children in their homes when they should be allowed to at least roam their yards or stand at bus stops." **Response:** The response by the AMOC was: "Observations of wolves in proximity to areas or structures occupied by humans do not of themselves mean the wolves might attack humans or domestic animals. Although some situations ... have caused concern among local residents, no incidents of Mexican wolves attacking children have been documented anywhere in AZ or NM" [104 ARPCC-93].

Mechanisms to Seek Acceptable Compromises

Faced with these difficult politics, wildlife managers have developed some approaches to secure compromises that facilitate reintroduction of wolves. Povilitis, Parsons, Robinson, and Baker say that the Mexican Wolf AMOC led by the Arizona Department of Game and Wildlife selected areas to release wolves less likely to result in "potential livestock conflict" rather than those with high-quality habitat where wolves would be likely to flourish [197 p. 943–4]. It is more difficult to restore predators like wolves in some areas. Povilitis et al. point out the difficulties faced in the Mexican wolf restoration were due to the fact that there was a lack of livestock free habitat where the wolves could be "lightly managed," in contrast to the situation in Yellowstone [197 p. 942]. DiSilvestro discusses the zone approach used in Minnesota for wolves as a method to facilitate coexistence of wolves and humans [20 p. 98]. Different rules are used depending on the zones so that "core areas" (Zone 1) put emphasis on species and no trapping is allowed while in zones 4 and 5 "human priorities take precedence over conservation of wolves." Linn describes how Montana proposed similar zones concerning mountain lions in order to find a "balance" between human and predator needs [147 p. 24]. Their three zones would include a zone where "lions are supported," a second zone where lions and humans would "live together," and a third zone where "lions would not be tolerated." The zone approach does not satisfy everyone and it was criticized by groups such as Fund for Animals [147 p. 25]. Bixby says that the zone approach allows states to deal with "hard decisions" on how much "space humans are willing to yield to other species" but that the zones have "relegated species to the most remote and least . . . desirable locations" [198 p. 206]. In Wyoming, an area labeled the predator zone constitutes about 80 percent of the state and is a heavily grazed area. Mech says that Wyoming authorized the killing of seventy wolves in this area which meant that "no packs could persist there." Thus the killing of wolves in this zone remains a bone of contention [199].

Removal of threatening wolves is a management tool that has been used heavily for the Mexican wolf reintroduction. Cart reports that the USFWS allowed Arizona and New Mexico officials to use a "three strike" policy to remove, kill, or place them in lifelong captivity when they killed three cattle [200]. Cart cites some former USFWS officials as saying that the wolves were being heavily managed in a "revolving door" situation, being moved from captivity to the wild repeatedly which could have bad effects on pack dynamics. There is concern about inbreeding of Mexican wolves due to the fact that removals of wolves had led to the predominance of wolves from one pack [201]. USFWS hoped to solve the problem by proposing a new rule that wolves would able to roam a larger area and new reintroductions to wolves would be made to New Mexico while previously reintroductions were limited to a small area of Arizona. However, New Mexico's Republican governor, Susana Martinez, has refused to go along with this proposal and New Mexico has also "refused to renew the permit for a captive wolf facility" on Ted Turner's New Mexico ranch – a facility that is "regarded as crucial" for the overall recovery of Mexican wolves [201]. The Mexican wolf experience illustrates the importance of federalism – states have the ability to frustrate Federal programs. It also shows that party control does have influence – the previous New Mexico governor Democratic Bill Richardson was supportive of the recovery program [201].

Enck and Brown outline a "social feasibility" approach to restoring wildlife. In this approach, a series of steps are followed in which an "intervention agent" (which can be a trained individual, an NGO, or governmental organization) helps to facilitate discussion of the issues and the collection of information [130 p. 314–24]. The emphasis is on finding a path to restoration that combines social feasibility with "mitigation plans" to deal with those who may suffer from it. After Congress passed the rider to delist wolves, some environmental groups became alarmed and decided they had better try to forge alliances with ranchers to salvage the situation and formed a non-profit called "People and Carnivores" that emphasizes prevention of conflicts such as to build electric fences and install flags to protect calves [94]. Many other preventive measures have been attempted, such as horse riders, guard dogs, and noise aversion, with some degree of success. However, success is not easy and Kaufman reports that though one group appeared to accept the preventive approach, they wound up using monies originally intended for a horse rider program instead to rent a helicopter to shoot wolves.

Does Compensation Affect Attitudes Toward Predators?

Since the killing of livestock is the major reason why ranchers and farmers fear and hate wolves, compensation for losses has been attempted by both environmental groups (notably Defenders of Wildlife) and some governments as a way to lessen opposition. The Defenders compensation program was well-known – it was their iconic program to which many wolf lovers contributed. Urbigkit summarizes the negative views held by many ranchers and farmers concerning the Defenders program: they claimed that the program only paid for livestock that had been found and inspected by Federal officials – not for missing cattle "even though only a small percentage of kills are ever found" [69 p. 276–8]. She contrasts the Defenders' program with that of the state (Wyoming) program which provided compensation for up to two and a half animals that could not be found. Urbigkit also emphasizes the negative attitude with which many ranchers viewed the Defenders program – some ranchers refused to apply for the Defenders' compensation because they did not want "the group to get any more good publicity" – they viewed the program as a publicity stunt [69 p. 257]. Schlickeisen defended the program, stating that they often paid for half or all of the market value even when the losses are suspected but "cannot be verified" [202 p. 69]. Difficulty of verification is a significant issue for compensation programs. Conover and Dinkins cite a Utah project that was only able to locate carcasses of 112 of the 898 lambs that were missing, and they argue that compensation programs are not a good alternative to lethal control because they are too expensive for public wildlife agencies due to the fact that money paid out in compensation exceeds that brought in by hunting licenses and other revenues [203 p. 186]. Musiani et al. report that private compensation programs are less likely to be criticized by taxpayers [204 p. 66]. However, Vynne reports that a survey of livestock producers in the Southwest found that "although fifty percent were satisfied with the amount of compensation," all of them were unhappy with the "process" due to their mistrust of the Defenders program which most (72 percent) viewed as a publicity stunt [205 p. 456–7]. Interestingly, more than 50 percent of these same livestock producers supported "proactive measures" such as fencing and tax credits, among others. Treves, Jurewicz, Naughton-Treves, and Wilcove conducted a study of Wisconsin's compensation program and found that, although the program was popular, it did not change the tolerance for wolves as much as expected – only 26 percent of Wisconsin respondents said that their tolerance would decrease if the compensation were not available [206 p. 4016]. The Wisconsin compensation program draws money from a combination of sources including a voluntary "checkoff" contribution on the annual state income tax form, a surcharge for "wolf license plates," and money from state general revenues [206 p. 4006–7]. Overall, the Wisconsin wolf compensation takes about 10 percent of the funds devoted to "endangered resources" and competes with other activities such as preserving habitat and restoring trumpeter swans, among others. Treves et al. found that compensation for the killing of hunting dogs was unpopular but nevertheless was retained because of "vocal interest groups" and due to the fact that the Wisconsin Department of Natural Resources did not want to be accused of being "indifferent" to these constituencies [206 p. 4017]. Naughton-Treves, Grossber, and Treves report that, although compensated hunters and livestock owners were no more tolerant of wolves than others, all of them approved of compensation as a "strategy" [207].

Using compensation to attempt to preserve carnivores and other wildlife that damage the interests of humans (e.g., elephants) has been used for a number of other species throughout the world. However, evidence shows that *ex post facto* (i.e., after the depredation has already occurred) compensation systems have not worked well in the United States or other countries. For example, McGregor tells of how compensation was paid to farmers and fishermen to turn in crocodile eggs but it did not change attitudes toward the crocodiles because the amounts paid were not sufficient [208]. Jonsing, Pandav, and Madhusudan characterize compensation payments in India for losses due to tigers as being too small, "tedious" and involving "complex paperwork" and befuddled by "corruption and inefficiency" so that there exists much resentment at wildlife conservation [209 p. 326]. Likewise, Nyhus and Tilson found that compensation programs have "varying degrees" of success depending on problems similar to those involving wolf programs including problems of verification, sustainability of funding, and delays [210]. Bulte and Rondeau report that compensation programs in areas such as Kenya's Masailand require that those receiving compensation take steps toward prevention of the depredations such as bomas (an African term for livestock enclosures) and dogs [211 p. 16]. Without such required behavioral measures, they argue that compensation may be bad for conservation. A related approach is to pay for outcomes such as encouraging the propagation of predators. Zabel and Holm-Muller describe a "performance payments system" to preserve lynx, wolves, and wolverines in Sweden in which landowners receive payments based on how many "carnivore reproductions" occur on their property [212]. Perhaps because of the problems outlined above, Defenders of Wildlife abandoned its iconic wolf compensation program and instead is now focusing on "preventing conflicts between wolves and wildlife before any animals are harmed" by encouraging actions such as non-lethal hazing of wolves, riders to protect livestock, and fences with flags to scare off wolves [213]. Defenders points to the Omnibus Public Lands Management Act of 2009 sponsored by Senators Tester (Democrat, Montana) and Barrasso (Republican, Wyoming) that gives funds to state-initiated compensation programs as the chief mechanism to replace the Defenders program. Research in Brazil found that negative attitudes toward jaguars extended even to farmers who did not own livestock (and thus did not suffer depredation) leading them to conclude that hostility to them is "socially ingrained and cultural"and thus very difficult to solve by material means alone

[51 p. 138]. A study of Brazilian ranchers found they regarded jaguars as the "most detrimental species" to humans and estimated that they lost 11 percent of their livestock to jaguars but a study by biologists found that less than 1 percent were lost to them [66 p. 61]. In short, conflict between humans and carnivores occurs across the globe and has proven difficult to resolve everywhere.

Conclusion

The strong passions that humans commit to wildlife have led to political struggles over legislation and its implementation; this is a major reason why wildlife politics constitutes a significant area of political research. Charismatic animals have been instrumental in bringing wildlife issues to the forefront of the political agendas of all levels of government. While the passion for charismatic species has helped to enable the passage of conservation legislation, at the same time, it encourages a "species-by-species" perspective on wildlife rather than an ecosystem approach regarded as optimal by scientists. Back in 1976, the then director of USFWS endangered species program admitted that he was concerned not to lose the ESA due to "a couple of spiders" [45 p. 44]. A conservative Republican, Jake Garn (Republican, Utah) once complained about the ESA protecting "animals that nobody cares about" and distinguished them from "some really fine endangered species" worth protecting" [45 p. 103–4]. Metrick and Weizman's quantitative analysis found that "visceral" charismatic factors far outweighed objective factors of biodiversity importance (e.g., threat to the species and biological uniqueness of the species) in both listing and especially conservation spending decisions [214]. Thus human emotional attachment to wildlife is a dominant factor in wildlife politics. There is some evidence that an increasing percentage of citizens now realize the equal importance of all species, not just those with charisma, to preserving biodiversity. Czech points to survey data that the public "considers the conservation of all types of species important, regardless of how they are prioritized" which, he says, shows "public understanding and appreciation for biotic diversity is at an all-time high" [19 p. 68]. Jasper and Nelkin comment on the wide variety of species that now have defenders such as, for example, the banana slug of Northern California [215 p. 51]. Still, strong emotions about a limited number of species have remained consistently at the core of political struggles. Most scientists would prefer emphasis on preservation of habitats that preserve a wide variety of species (plants and animal) to foster the maximum biodiversity. Indeed, John Muir deliberately focused on non-charismatic animals such as the rattlesnake in talking about the right of animals to exist [216 p. 77]. However, charismatic species like grizzlies require "thousands of acres of habitat" and Tobin argues that politics dictates that it is easier to justify measures to protect species like grizzlies than to emphasize protection of habitat that supports them [45 p. 77]. As I have shown, negative charisma associated with certain species, notably wolves, has powerful effects on wildlife politics. The 2011 U.S. Federal budget compromise in which Western senators and representatives forced the delisting of wolves from ESA protection shows that emotional antipathies and attachments to individual species remain the core of wildlife politics. The same point is true internationally where certain species such as whales, panda, elephants, and tigers have been at the center of political controversies related to wildlife.

The relevance of traditional interest group theory is supported by wildlife politics, demonstrating that most public funds are spent on species that have organized groups of humans dedicated to them. However, the wildlife case also demonstrates that these interest groups are based primarily on emotional attachment to these charismatic species, not the economic self-interests of members. At the same time, economic losses and personal fears and hatred of certain species has led many traditional interest groups (e.g., farm bureaus and hunter groups) to oppose protective policies for both economic and emotional reasons. Predators such as wolves helped to inspire what I have referred to as "negative charisma," characterized by hatred of them that exceeds merely rational economic calculations. Likewise, species such as wild horses have inspired strong attachments that make political compromises extremely difficult, if not impossible, from the perspective of their admirers. In the wild horse case, the BLM's response to a National Academy Report noted that "leaving the control to nature" such as letting the horses roam freely and starve if they cannot find enough food requires a "laissez faire style" of management that they did not think Congress or the American people would support [50]. The strength of passions over wildlife has made compromise difficult.

Agencies such as the USFWS have sought to find methods to achieve compromise such as assigning "experimental status" to species so they may be killed if they threaten human interests, making differentiations among zones where species are often highly protected in some areas, and emphasizing preventive measures. The USFWS is in a difficult position – it does not have enough resources to protect species and must rely on the cooperation of state agencies. The hatred of having policies forced upon them by the Federal government is the widely held emotion shared by members of the anti-ESA coalition. There is a striking paradox in the politics of wildlife that has resulted in the maintenance of status quo politics in the West over predators, despite growing evidence of general population support for them as well as economic benefits from them such as ecotourism. The explanation behind this paradox is that an aroused, well-organized group protective of its interests can prevail over a larger body of people whose interest in the issue is more remote. Institutionalism also helps to explain the outcomes of wildlife politics due to the fact that policy-making organizations such as wildlife departments and commissions and legislative committees governing wildlife have been dominated by ranchers and hunter members. Thus the priority for the USFWS is to defuse the controversy which it believes is overwhelming their agency and preventing it from achieving other priorities and also politically risky for the future of the ESA.

The Advocacy Coalition framework contributes to understanding of the dynamics of the politics of charismatic animals. There are consistent coalitions that form the basis of those wishing to preserve and protect species including environmentalists and animal rights advocates. The opposing coalition that views endangered species as threats to their interests include ranchers, farmers, and extractive industries. One pivotal group is sportsmen such as hunters and fishermen who have sometimes opposed predators such as wolves but who also sometimes join with environmentalists to protect habitats that support these species. Science has led to changes in some of the secondary beliefs of both sides such as research showing the positive benefits of predators. However, the core beliefs of most of the anti-ESA group remain consistent such as the belief in the primacy of human interests over those of wildlife and an antipathy for Federal laws that they view as intruding on their rights to farm, ranch, or hunt.

6 The ESA: Evaluation and Politics

The Endangered Species Act (ESA) was path-breaking legislation when it was enacted by Congress in 1973 for several reasons: (1) It pertained to all life except some bacteria, viruses, and insect pests; (2) It defended "critical habitat" as well as animals; and (3) It covered private as well as public lands [1 p. 176–7]. The law has been described as "prohibitive policy" because it prohibited actions that would threaten the existence of species. It passed easily with broad legislative support at the time because it appeared to have "few associated costs" and "it was not obvious whom it would hurt" [2 p. 47]. The law protects species that are "listed" because they have been determined to be endangered. It is enforced by the U.S. Fish and Wildlife Service (USFWS) for land and fresh water species while the National Marine Fisheries Service (NMFS) oversees salt water species. There have been significant changes to the law and/or policies that govern the management of it including the following: (1) the God squad; (2) habitation conservation plans; (3) experimental population provision; (4) candidate conservation agreements (CCAs); (5) candidate conservation agreements with assurances; (CCAAs) (6) the no-surprises policy.

In 1978, the law was amended to create the so-called God Squad committee consisting of seven Cabinet-level members to consider exemptions from the law's requirements. In 1982, the law was amended to allow permits to "take" listed species if approved mitigation steps were taken to protect these species. This step led to what are known as "habitation conservation plans" (HCPs), to be discussed below. At the same time, a new "experimental population provision" was added to the law to allow species to be introduced to areas without the legal protections for endangered species, in an attempt to lessen resistance to wildlife that threatened landholders, such as wolves. The other major changes are administrative policies based on interpretations of the ESA by the USFWS. CCAs are voluntary conservation agreements between the Service and one or more public or private parties [3; 4]. These agreements focus on species that have not been formally listed as endangered but are "candidates" for listing. The goal is to identify threats to candidate species, plan the measures needed to address the threats and conserve these species, and find landowners who are willing to form agreements with conservation measures. CCAAs go beyond the traditional CCA by providing non-Federal landowners with additional incentives for engaging in voluntary conservation through assurances that limit future conservation obligations. The no-surprises policy was established during the Clinton Administration in 1994 and guarantees that if a landowner participates in an approved HCP that they will not have to pay additional monies if the needs of the species change through time. In short, over time, the ESA has undergone significant changes from strictly prohibitive policy to one in which negotiated agreements can be reached with states, local governments, and private landowners.

In the major early judicial case involving a small fish, the snail darter, the decision by the Chief Justice emphasized the lack of qualifying language in the ESA legislation – a big contrast with previous wildlife conservation laws [5 p. 130]. The ESA was used to challenge the construction of the Tellico Dam in Tennessee because it threatened the snail darter. One of the arguments made by ESA opponents was that Congress had already authorized expenditures for the Tellico Dam but the Supreme Court ruled that neither the Congressional budget appropriations process nor cost-benefit calculations could affect the priority given in the legislation to "the incalculable value of preserving endangered species" [5 p. 132].

Controversies over Effectiveness

Although the ESA passed with almost unanimous consensus in 1973, since the snail darter case, the law has been enveloped in a debate between detractors, who think that it has been ineffective as well as harmful to economic development, versus supporters who believe that it has been successful in preserving species. Mann and Plummer criticize the forceful language of the ESA, arguing that to save "every species every-where would cook our society to death" [6 p. 113]. They note that we "discard useless pieces of paper" so "why not useless species" and describe this logic as "compelling" though they acknowledge that "most people have rarely embraced it" [6 p. 133]. They criticize biologists who emphasize that they "just are doing science" because "scientists have no claim to represent the values of other people" and argue that "as imperfect as it is, politics has a more legitimate claim to that representation than does science" [6 p. 208]. In short, Mann and Plummer argue that the ESA has been ineffective and costly to society.

Wyman argues that the small number of recovered species shows the infeasibility of the law's goal of "recovering all imperiled species" [7 p. 495]. Consequently Wyman believes that rather than trying to save every species, efforts should be targeted so as to get "more bang for the conservation buck" [7 p. 502]. Wyman says that the failures are due to most listed species being in such desperate straits that they are "conservation dependent," which is a major problem because the USFWS does not have enough resources "to list let alone protect" them [7 p. 495–6]. Her conclusion is that the ESA's stated objective to preserve all species is not feasible, that we should admit that every species cannot be saved, and that efforts have to be targeted on certain species. Tobin emphasizes the dilemma for those implementing the ESA – should they focus on those most in danger or those "most recoverable?" [8 p. 235–6]. Tobin quotes one USFWS employee as saying their focus on recovering species most in danger will lead to inability to "recover and delist a species" [8 p. 235]. This debate raises a more basic question: Is maximizing the number of recovered species the most important goal or the avoidance of extinction? For example, Tobin said that it would cost only a small amount (e.g., $8,000) to save some species (e.g., the endangered Borax Lake Chub in Oregon) but the USFWS prefers to save those most in danger even though the Senate Committee on Environment and Public Works preferred an approach focusing on species "closest to recovery" [8 p. 247].

Wyman also says that the law should be made more realistic by making it time-limited, such as guaranteeing only that a species will not become extinct over three human generations. The time dimension is important in determining the size of population needed in order to avoid deleterious inbreeding and other, unexpected threats – the longer the time period to be secured, the larger the population needed. How many years into the future should be used as the goal for calculating the minimum number of a species to preserve? For example, a study by VonHoldt et al. found low levels of inbreeding among gray wolves in Yellowstone National Park [9 p. 268–9]. They describe measures taken by wolves to avoid inbreeding such as avoidance of breeding with related pack members and male "dispersal to other packs where they breed with nonrelatives." They speculate that the unexpected diversity could be due to the nature of the reintroduction into a "prey-abundant habitat" devoid of wolves. Due to this diversity, they calculate that a "population size of 170 individuals" is adequate for "short-term retention of genetic variability" of these wolves. The USFWS has used such findings to support the delisting of the wolves. However, VonHoldt et al. caution that "over the long term, genetic variation will decrease" without "migration" such as from "corridors" that they describe as "currently low quality" [9 p. 269–70].

The criteria to be used to judge the success of the program are at issue. Critics especially focus on the number of delistings, species that had been endangered but have recovered enough to be removed from listing, as the major criterion of success. The lack of delistings has been emphasized by critics of the ESA such as former Republican Senator Bob Smith (New Hampshire) who said that (as of 2001) there had been 1243 listed species but only 9 had been delisted due to recovery, and thus the failure to delist many species is used to support the argument that the ESA has failed [10]. There have been more delistings since then. In 2015, the USFWS announced the delisting of the Oregon Chub (a minnow fish) with a press release stating that "The Endangered Species Act Scores Another Success" and noted that it was the first fish and twenty-ninth species to be delisted [11]. Just 1000 of the fish existed when it was listed in 1993 but due to restoration and acquisition of habitat, promotion of natural river flows, the Oregon Chub population now totals 140,000 at some eighty locations.

Defenders of the ESA such as Biologist Edward O. Wilson criticized the logic of using delisting as the main criterion of success because this is "akin to calling for closing of hospital emergency rooms because many people die there" [12 p. 34]. The USFWS emphasizes that 98 percent of species that have been listed as endangered or threatened continue to exist [13]. Some critics believe that implementation of the ESA has not been ambitious enough. For example, Maile, Leidner, Haines, Goble and Scott looked at the "recovery objectives for 1173 species with recovery plans" and found virtually all of them "too low to ensure the species long-term persistence" [14 p. 656]. Tobin says that the ESA could either be considered a "modest success" or "massive failure" [8 p. 256–7]. He points out that species listed are already endangered and because their habitat often is being destroyed, "effective solutions" may not be available given the limited resources of the USFWS and NMFS. The ESA was used as the "last line of defense" against the poisoning of animals by Animal Damage Control, a Federal agency. In 1986 when the U.S. Environmental Protection Administration (EPA) was considering reauthorizing the use of strychnine for rodent control, environmental organizations successfully sued the government, arguing that the poison would threaten "endangered species" [15 p. 330]. Martin Nie says that it was not until the passage of the Federal ESA in 1973 that the "wolves began their successful recovery in the upper Midwest" [16 p. 18]. He goes on to argue that he believes states will do an adequate job of managing delisted wolves because of the "threat of Federal relisting" – that states would rather have "wolves back than Federal bureaucrats involved in their affairs" [16 p. 147]. Nie states that lack of habitat and the fact that red wolves are constricted to their refuge means that the species "will probably never be delisted" [16 p. 16].

One limitation of the ESA has been that species are generally not listed until they are in serious danger. There is a movement to emphasize "pre-listing" approaches that achieve voluntary cooperation before their existence is in imminent threat through "market-based incentives" and the use of tools such as conservation banks [17]. However, Male and Donlan acknowledge that such "early intervention" strategies face a "'chicken and egg' dilemma" [emphasis added] – that the USFWS is not likely to act unless a species is a "candidate for listing" nor are participants such as developers or ranchers likely to want to participate until the threat of "regulatory activity" is real [18 p. 222].

The desire to emphasize the successes of the ESA can affect policy decisions. In 2014, the USFWS announced that listing will be applied only if a species is at risk of extinction in a vital portion of its range where its loss would put the entire species at risk of extinction and that range no longer takes into account its historical distribution but defines the concept in terms of where the species is found now [19]. In a letter to the *New York Times* defending their decision, USFWS officials claim that if they used the criteria such as historical range, there would be far fewer species removed from the endangered species list and thus the public's perception and political support for the law would be harmed [20]. Thus choice of evaluation measures for assessing the ESA are affected by politics and can influence wildlife policies.

Some experts such as Stephen Meyer of MIT say that the large battle for biodiversity has already been lost and that our world is already dominated by wildlife that are compatible with human beings such as "weedy" species like raccoons that flourish in suburban settings much more so than in the "wild" [21 p. 6 & 10]. Meyer argues that almost "all regulatory efforts are focused on ghosts" and that "true recovery" which many consider the chief goal of the ESA is virtually impossible [21 p. 46]. Meyer goes on to say that in order to maintain some biodiversity that humans will have to continually intervene such as by transferring threatened species like the Great Basin pika to locations not threatened by human development [21 p. 85]. The magnitude of the difficulty of recovering species is exemplified by the Mexican wolf. Udall relates how James Brown, a biologist who describes himself as being "all for the lobo," nevertheless declined to sign a petition favoring the reestablishment of the Mexican wolf because "there are only 39 adults left" and "their former habitat is so fragmented" that a "viable population may not be possible" [22 p. 77].

The protection of species viewed as a threat or pest without "charisma" has been one of the marked accomplishments of ESA because it is possible that only charismatic species would have enough support to survive without the ESA. An example of such a species is the "midget faded rattler" that exists in western Colorado [23]. The Bureau of Land Management (BLM) and private developers paid no attention to it until some dead midget rattlers were found near a new gas well area. The possibility of the snake being listed under the ESA led BLM and the Wyoming Game and Fish Department to map and try to preserve key den and foraging areas of the snake. A biologist from a reptile preservation group stated that the agencies were spurred to protect the species "despite the fact that it has often been vilified" because "no one wanted the species to end up on the endangered species list" with "its onerous land restrictions" [23]. Likewise, Zollinger and Daniels describe the difficulties involved in trying to preserve the prairie dog because it had been viewed as a pest and that it was only the threat of its listing under ESA that convinced many livestock owners to go along with the conservation plan for the species [24 p. 266].

A few species such as alligators and brown pelicans have had dramatically quick recoveries and been delisted, but they are the exception, the reason being that the major threats to them, such as poaching, are fairly controllable compared to more difficult issues such as disappearance of habitat [25 p. 66]. Watkins argues that the main purpose of the Act should be to prevent extinction. Since species are only listed when they are endangered or threatened, he argues that the fact that 41 percent of the 909 species listed (in 1996) were improving or stable is a sign of success [26 p. 40]. Similarly, Doremus and Pagel argue that because so many listed species are in extreme danger of extinction and that many of the threats they face (e.g., habitat degradation due to exotic species and pollution) are difficult to control so that many "listings will be forever" [27 p. 1258]. Moreover, they go on to say that the ESA's primary stated goal is the avoidance of extinctions, which, they argue, must be "the ultimate measure of the law's success or failure" [27 p. 1261]. Indeed, Doremus and Pagel caution that the USFWS in its desire to demonstrate the successes of the ESA to critics may be delisting species too soon and thus threatening them in the longer term [27 p. 1262 & 1267].

There have been systematic attempts to assess the law's success. The National Research Council reviewed the effects of the ESA and concluded that "although it is impossible to quantify the ESA's biological effects," that the ESA has prevented some species from becoming extinct [28 p. 15]. However, they proceed to state that the ESA "by itself cannot prevent all extinctions" even if it were modified – that other methods and the efforts of state and local governments as well as private organizations will be needed. The National Research Council also argued that it was too soon to judge most recovery plans because they take a long time to work or fail [28 p. 198].

Experimental methods are impossible to employ in evaluating the effects of the ESA. Thus calculations of its effect involve estimations of what would have happened had the ESA not been passed. Causality is complex and there are causes other than the ESA that may have contributed to the improvement of some species. In particular, the banning of DDT in 1972 by the EPA had a huge impact on saving species such as the bald eagle and it is difficult to distinguish the effects of these other causes from the passage and implementation of the ESA [29 p. 1]. Roman cites a USFWS report that thirty-five species had been extinguished since the ESA passed but one estimate by supporters is that 262 species would have died out between 1973 and 2003 if the ESA had not been passed [30 p. 131]. The USFWS also emphasizes that it takes "considerable time to reverse a specie's slide toward extinction" [13]. They go on to say that declines have often taken place over decades and will require "considerable time, resources, and even luck" to recover. They suggest that the number of species that are reclassified from "endangered" to "threatened" is another indicator of success and that twenty-seven species had been so upgraded in their latest five-year review. The wood stork is an example of a species that has been proposed for upgrading.

A study by Ferraro, McIntosh, and Ospina matched listed and unlisted species and found that only listings combined with substantial funding for recovery efforts showed positive results, but that listed species without funding support actually did worse than unlisted species [31]. An econometric study by Kerkvliet and Langpap found that designation of critical habitat did not have an impact on species survival, but increased spending on species reduced the probability that "the species is extinct or declining" [32 p. 508]. They also found that species that "conflict with economic objectives are more likely to be extinct." Other aspects of the ESA such as the designation of critical habitat are contentious. The George W. Bush Administration put a disclaimer on critical habitat designations, stating that they provided "little additional protection to species" [33 p. 401]. But Greenwald, Suckling, and Pimm cite evidence that the designation of critical habitat made a species twice as likely to recover [34 p. 686]. However, when they then studied all of the proposed critical habitat decisions made between 2002 and 2007, they found in a "majority of instances" the USFWS did not follow the expert peer review in making critical habitat designations [34 p. 689]. The National Research Council expressed concern that critical habitat was designated in only a limited fraction of listings and suggested that "survival habitat" defined as that needed to ensure the survival of the existing population for a "short time" (e.g., twenty-five to fifty years) be designated without being constrained by economic criteria [28 p. 76].

Another aspect of the ESA is the development and implementation of recovery plans for species. Although they are supposed to be done, recovery plans often are not developed for some listed species. The U.S. General Accountability Office's (GAO's) review found that "a significant number of species" they studied were helped by the establishment of recovery plans under the ESA [29 p. 3]. However, the GAO also notes that USFWS biologists are unable to help many species because "they can't secure the needed habitat" or "don't know enough about the threats or how to mitigate them" [29 p. 3–4]. The GAO report provides case studies of successes of recovery plans such as for the Rio Grande silvery minnow that proposed to change the river from being "deeply channeled" and "isolated from the surrounding floodplain" to a more gently flowing, broader river with "eddies and slack water for juvenile minnows" [29 p. 11–12]. They describe the complexity of this recovery plan that will involve coordinating a "myriad of property owners and water rights interests." Work to change the nature of the river's bank would involve the Bureau of Reclamation and the Army Corps of Engineers. Thus the effort would require a "broad coalition" of Federal agencies, tribes, local governments, and property owners, and consequently take a long time to be effective. Rachlinski systematically tested the hypothesis of ineffectiveness of the ESA based on analysis of data presented by the USFWS in biannual reports submitted concerning the biological status of endangered and threatened species [35 p. 379–86]. One of Rachlinski's tests was to study the length of time a species has been on the list and its status. He found that for each additional year of listing, it was "1.5 percent more likely to be improving or stable" [35 p. 377]. He also found that species with recovery plans "were doing much better than those without plans" and designation of critical habitat "appeared to benefit species" but the evidence for this last point "was weak" [35 p. 380 & 384]. Rachlinski concludes that the main weakness of the ESA is a lack of resources, making it difficult to form and implement recovery plans and designate critical habitat for species [35 p. 386]. Some species such as marine life are especially complex and difficult to protect, and information on them has been difficult to collect. For example, Armsworth, Cappel, Micheli, and Bjorkstet found that the "median delay in reporting marine extinctions was 53 years" [36 p. 40–1]. The same authors state that saving marine species involves a "Byzantine patchwork of Federal and state regulations." Moreover, regulators are reluctant to specify the locations of critical habitat for fear that doing so would "encourage poaching." For threatened species like the "right whale" the GAO states that the causes of the threats are well known, such as high takes by commercial whaling and entanglements with fishing lines. International agreements have protected the whale since 1935 and more recently, agreements to modify fishing gear and avoid collisions with ships are expected by National Marine Fishery Services biologists to have an impact; however, they will take a long time to recover because of their small population and slow reproduction rate [29 p. 16]. Finally, the GAO states that some species like the Florida panther are "unlikely to recover" because of their loss of habitat combined with lack of public support for increasing their population due to fears of their predation on pets and livestock [29].

Many threats to endangered species derive from the mundane general effects of development. For example, turtles are more likely to head toward beachfront house lights than the ocean and "mistake floating plastic bags for their much-loved jellyfish" [37 p. 159]. Roads can be a major threat to endangered species. Yet, Allin points out that both the National Park Service and the Forest Service favored road-building for many years in national parks and forests. For the Forest Service, roads provided a better means to fight fires while they provided better access to the tourists desired by the National Park Service [38 p. 68].

Most likely a large majority of environmentalists and ecologists would agree that the ESA should be more focused on saving entire ecosystems and their habitat rather than individual species. Important court decisions have allowed ESA to protect habitats, not just individual animals. A 1995 court decision (Babbitt *v.* Sweet Home) upheld the right of ESA to protect habitat, but Wolf says that the emphasis is still mostly on individual species [39 p. 248]. The importance of this decision is illustrated by the fact that, before this decision, state and Federal officials had been reluctant to challenge Pacific Lumber in order to save a "shy seabird" called the marbled murrelet [40]. Pacific Lumber planned to clear-cut old growth forests but a Sierra Club official admitted that before this decision, the ESA was a "slender reed on which to rely" because the courts were "split over whether destruction of habitat alone can violate the act." One of the ways the USFWS and conservationists have dealt with the ESA's focus on individual species within the limits of the current law is to list species whose preservation helps save many other species. Sometimes these species are referred to as "focal" or "umbrella species" [41 p. 305–6]. A major example is the attempt to preserve the northwest spotted owl which was transformed from being an "owl-only issue" in the 1970s to "ecosystem protection" in the 1990s [42 p. 51]. Colburn notes that the 1979 regulations required USFWS to identify "indicator species" that would act as "surrogates for a given animal or plant community as a whole" and the spotted owl was employed as a surrogate for species requiring old forest habitat [43 p. 165]. However, using an umbrella species is less effective than an "assemblage of species" [44 p. 129]. For example, Noss, Maehr, and Larkin cite research that although the grizzly bear habitat is large and does cover 65 percent of vertebrate habitat in Idaho, nevertheless certain species such as reptiles would be harmed by relying only on grizzly habitat [44 p. 129]. Similarly, Boutin [45 p. 378–9] and Linnell et al. [46 p. 396] argue that, while setting aside areas for large mammals is useful as a "coarse-filter" support of biodiversity, that a "fine-filter" approach that focuses on other species is required for conservation. Noss agrees that the bison is a keystone species whose impacts are disproportionately large compared to their numbers because the bison selects areas that are dominated by grasses and "converts them into species rich sites" [47 p. 3–4]. Tear says that the individual species planning is especially inappropriate for invertebrates where thousands of species can be involved and thus a habitat approach is required [48 p. 192]. Holt argues that too much focus has been put on saving a single species, whales, when the goal should be to preserve all marine species [49 p. 451–2]. On the other hand, Abbitt and Scott, although they agree multispecies planning is valuable, suggest that "individual species plans may still be required" because of the unique problems faced by each species [50 p. 1281]. Naeem and Jouseau state that "studies have demonstrated that multispecies plans are less effective than the single-species models at increasing and maintaining the populations of listed species" [51 p. 95]. In a few cases, conservation activities for one species can threaten another species, as occurred with the recovery program for the San Clemente Shrike which may endanger the San Clemente fox [52 p. 1251]. Thus Roemer and Wayne argue that a "balanced ecosystem approach" that considers needs of all taxa is required [52 p. 1253]. The complex interplay that can occur among species is illustrated by the San Joaquin kit fox. Clark Jr. et al. describe how kit foxes were often killed when they ate poison left out for wolves, and now compete with coyotes and red foxes which harass and often kill the kit foxes [53 p. 119–21].

Politics and the ESA

Although the ESA has strong language in favor of species conservation, political forces can sometimes overcome it. One example is the Tellico Dam *v.* the snail darter case that led to the momentous Supreme Court decision interpreting the law in a forceful manner. This decision was ultimately overridden by politics via a Congressional action to exempt the Tellico Dam from the ESA [54 p. 162]. The politics of ESA have worried environmental groups who feared strong negative reactions to steps taken to protect species such as the spotted owl. They feared that such actions could be used to picture the ESA as a "train wreck" leading Congress to weaken the law [55 p. 138]. As noted elsewhere, gray wolves were removed from the protections of the ESA via a rider on a budget bill compromise passed by Congress in 2011 [56]. Plater, Abrams, Goldfarb, and Graham ask the question "why is the ESA so much more embattled than other environmental statutes" like the regulation of pollution and toxic wastes [57 p. 706]? They argue that the reason is that the benefits to humans are less direct and obvious for the ESA than the others.

Maile et al. state that political factors such as the nature of the species affect USFWS decisions to delist species [14 p. 655–6]. For example, they point out that the bald eagle was not delisted until "its range was larger than it was when the first Europeans" reached America while it delisted the gray wolf when it occupied less than 5 percent of its historical range in the lower forty-eight states. They conclude that for most species "ongoing management interventions" will be needed to "prevent their relisting." Bruskotter and Enzler note the significance of the Bush Administration's decision to interpret the ESA as referring to "its current range," not its "historical range" [58 p. 73–5]. They argue that if this interpretation had existed earlier when the gray wolf was listed, the USFWS would have been able to list the wolf only in Minnesota – the only state with a "verified wolf population at the time" [58 p. 80–1]. The locations of proposed restorations are often controversial [59 p. 199]. Adams notes that pumas "could be saved" by preserving them in some "remote corner of the Yukon" and let them be extinguished elsewhere. He criticizes the Clinton Administration for its rush to delist the grizzly so as to be able to show a "success story" to the Wise Users. Another question concerns transplantations – should endangered species be allowed to be relocated to resolve conflicts with developments? Yaffee reports that, though USFWS resisted transplantation in the famous case of the snail darter, they allowed it in some other cases but stopped doing relocations because they feared it would set a precedent that could be applied generally [2 p. 101–2]. Mooallem refers to the phenomenon of "shifting baselines syndrome" which refers to the tendency of scientists (and others) to judge the status of a species based on the population that existed at the beginning of the scientists' lives – not against historical standards. He argues that this phenomenon produces a downward bias in the goals for restoration.

Doremus notes that recovery is supposed to be "in the wild" but says that some animals such as the elk are being preserved in an artificial manner such as the national elk herd in Wyoming which are fed alfalfa throughout the winter [60 p. 14–17]. Similarly Sanderson et al. question whether the recovery of bison has been a success because the restored herds have not been allowed to "play their former role in the environment" because they are not allowed to "compete with other grazers, interact with wild predators, and shape landscapes" [61 p. 254]. Due to the potential threat of brucellosis in cattle, there are strict regulations on where they may roam and, the authors argue, they are treated more like livestock than wildlife. They go on to argue that true restoration returns a species to its former ecological functionality and that currently this is not the case with bison.

A related dispute concerns whether a species should be listed if, although it is endangered in the United States, there is a substantial population of them in adjacent countries such as Canada or Mexico. For example, the George W. Bush Administration did not want to list the wolverine despite the fact that there were only small numbers of them left in Wyoming, Idaho, and Utah [62]. The Administration claimed that there were a large number of wolverines in Canada and this contiguous population was not distinct from the U.S. population as claimed by conservationists [62]. The *New York Times* argued that if this argument were accepted, then the restoration of populations such as the grizzly bear and bald eagle would never have been accomplished.

Another controversy has concerned the listing of "subspecies." There have been several disputes over whether a subspecies warrants listing. When is a subspecies "different enough" to warrant protection? For example, Novak in 1995 lumped twenty-four previous subspecies of wolves into only five [63 p. 15]. Beatley states that while most scientists "believe that the Coachella Valley fringe-toed lizard is a separate subspecies," most "lay persons would have trouble distinguishing it from another fringe-toed lizard" [64 p. 50].

A somewhat related issue concerns hybrids – should hybrids be considered a replacement for purebred species? For example, the endangered west-slope cutthroat trout may hybridize with "introduced rainbow trout" [65 p. 107]. This issue has arisen concerning the red wolf restoration in the Eastern United States. There are reports that coyotes have been breeding with red wolves in locations such as Arkansas, resulting in a smaller "red wolf" and the same phenomenon would likely occur in the Eastern United States [66 p. 52]. Theberge says that it is unlikely that red wolves could replace coyotes fully; nevertheless, the establishment of a hybrid could "pinch hit" for the wolf in the Adirondacks, albeit with some differences, especially with respect to lack of predation of the moose as well as differences in the degree to which they hunt beaver and rabbits [66 p. 61]. The ESA generally aims at protecting purebred species but Theberge argues that "hybridization has always been a major evolutionary force" for biodiversity [66 p. 62].

There have been important changes to the ESA that were passed partly to deal with the perception that it was a "train wreck" hurting the interests of humans, such as the "experimental population" provision added in 1982. With such a designation (e.g., for gray wolves), less protection was offered to the species so as to deflect opposition of landowners and ranchers who feared "economic losses" [67 p. 131]. Goble points out that the experimental designation avoids requirements for "consultation," allows "broad discretion for takings" that would be required for endangered species, and does away with restrictions on altering of critical habitat [67 p. 133]. Still, despite the fact that

USFWS offered to introduce the Mexican wolf as an "experimental species," it took more than fifteen years to introduce them, so strong was the opposition [67 p. 134].

One change in the ESA law that has had little effect concerns the "God Committee" that was created in 1978 as an amendment to the ESA at the instigations of Tennessee Congressmen and Senators who were outraged at the cancellation of the Tellico Dam due to the snail darter. The committee consists of seven Cabinet members: the administrator of the Environmental Protection Agency; the administrator of National Oceanic and Atmospheric Administration; the chairman of the Council of Economic Advisers; a representative from the state in question; the Secretary of Agriculture; the Secretary of the Army; and the Secretary of the Interior. This committee's purpose is to decide controversies such as the Tellico Dam case, and thus have the power to override ESA protections, and thus act like God if they so wished [57 p. 702]. Some liberals and conservationists supported the establishment of the committee because they saw it as a way to save the ESA which was suddenly being attacked. Unexpectedly, this committee ruled in favor of the snail darter in this case and the powers of the committee have been rarely employed. In one case, the committee was used to overrule a decision to protect Coho and Chinook salmon. The committee voted to support the diversion of waters from the Klamath River "to downstream farmers" resulting in 70,000 dead Chinook salmon [68 p. 44].

Although Congress has sometimes asked the USFWS to set priorities and pursue the most cost effective recoveries, Wyman points out that Congress has also "earmarked funding for specific species, usually because they are politically popular" [7 p. 44]. A GAO study found that nearly 25 percent of its discretionary recovery funds had been spent on four popular species: the peregrine falcon, southern sea otter, gray wolf, and Aleutian goose [69 p. 99]. This raises the question of to what extent, if at all, should political and other non-biological factors be heeded? Wyman admits that "it would not be politically wise to allocate ESA resources without paying attention to popular preferences" because "the ESA ultimately depends on public support for its existence" [7 p. 502–3].

Politics affects the implementation of the ESA. For example, the USFWS did not designate some recommended critical habitat for the Cape Sable seaside sparrow living in the Everglades National Park and Big Cypress National Preserve, because of the opposition from an Indian tribe and the Army Corps of Engineers [34 p. 689]. Changes in presidential administrations have had a significant impact on ESA listings. From 1996 to 2000, the number of listed species grew by fifty species per year but, after the election of George W. Bush, only one plant species had been listed by August of 2001 and that was due to a court order [70].

Intergovernmental relations constitutes another significant political aspect of the ESA. There is a consensus that the USFWS lacks the resources to implement the ESA effectively. Thus the preservation of these species depends on accessing resources of private citizens or other government agencies such as state and local governments. However, Ted Williams of Audubon Magazine points to the lack of compliance of states such as Hawaii with the ESA in regard to "non-game wildlife" and thus he concludes that relying on states to do the job is risky [71 p. 38 & 44]. In addition to political factors, one of the reasons why the USFWS is reluctant to push species such as wolves is that it must rely greatly on state resources including "personnel, land, and funds" to implement effective restoration programs [60 p. 24–5]. An indirect effect of the ESA has been to inspire state governments to pass their own endangered species acts, though most are not nearly as potent as the Federal law [72 p. 127]. According to Doremus and Pagel, the state ESA laws do not cover private land use decisions; nor are they "enforceable by citizen lawsuits" [27 p. 1261]. Keiter and Boyce cite examples where only the existence of the ESA forced Park Service employees (e.g., in Yellowstone Park) to stand up to local pressures [73 p. 394–6]. The Park Service often retreats from decisions after initially giving precedence to nature. For example, when local interests protested the Service's decision to close a "fishing bridge" near grizzly country, they changed their position due to pressure from the nearby Cody business community [73 p. 396]. Stokes, Hanson, Oaks, Straub, and Ponio studied the land use planning decisions made by localities in the state of Washington and ranked them according to how many "biodiversity" friendly practices they employed [74 p. 452]. They found that all planning agencies gave significant attention to mandates, especially the ESA, in making their decisions. They found that the lowest-ranked agencies regarded the ESA as the most important "driver of biodiversity management." Although many scientists prefer a habitat focus for the ESA, these planners thought that the term "biodiversity" was too nebulous a term to gain local support and they believed that in order to have political currency mandates require a focus on individual species such as "salmon" [74 p. 457].

Metrick and Weitzman [75 p. 32–3] and Anderson [76 p. 114] cite data that the implementation of the ESA has been cost inefficient, with a disproportionate amount of resources going to protecting charismatic megafauna whose protection conflicts with development. Metrick and Weitzman discovered that "conflict with development" turned out to be the most important of the four criteria implemented by USFWS – even though it was supposed to be less important than the other three according to their priority system (degree of threat, recovery potential, and taxonomy) [75]. A GAO study found that "half of the tasks in the 16 [recovery] plans had not been undertaken" even though they had been approved for an average of four years [77 p. 2]. The response of the USFWS was that they simply did not have enough resources. The USFWS was required by Congress to set priorities in order to deal with this lack of resources but GAO found that USFWS had not adhered to these but had spent more time on species with "high appeal." They discovered that too many recovery plan tasks received the top "1" priority ranking even when they concerned species that were not considered highly threatened [69 p. 32–3]. Among birds, the bald eagle, American peregrine falcon, spotted owls, and red-cockaded woodpecker received a large percentage of the funds annually [78 p. 1296]. A study by Tear examined all of the 1991 ESA recovery plans and found them flawed in that they did not have enough data to support them, did not have clear goals or ambitious enough goals, and did not make "clear distinctions between threatened and endangered species" [48 p. 191–192]. His explanation behind the weaknesses is that "political and social constraints" force them to focus on what is "feasible." He suggests that since political and social constraints are so important, they should be included in the plans themselves.

Although the ESA is viewed as a "macho" law, some aspects were left vague such as the parts on implementation and consultation. Tobin points out that the law "failed to indicate what procedures should be used for the designation of critical habitat" and was vague about the requirements that other agencies have for consultation with the USFWS such as time factors, obligations, and means for enforcing or sanctioning other agencies for not consulting [8 p. 147]. Tobin goes on to claim that the USFWS issued "no jeopardy opinions" for water projects and "relied almost entirely on political considerations," arguing that if they had done so, it could have precipitated requests for exemptions from the ESA concerning projects in the upper Colorado basin and threatened the law itself [8 p. 191].

Still, the ESA's potential is demonstrated in the sage-grouse cases where many conservative Western states and industries in those states have taken significant steps to preserve sage-grouse habitat in order to forestall the listing of the bird [79]. The Gunnison and greater sage-grouse cases discussed below are good case studies that demonstrate difficulties of negotiating compromise between opposed coalitions over a multistate region involving a complex array of Federal, state, local, and private organizations. By 2014, the Federal government has already denied "more than two dozen energy projects in the West due to the [greater sage-grouse] bird" including many wind turbines [79]. Federal officials have cooperated with state and industry officials in order to "preempt the designation" [79]. The state and Federal governments have experienced great difficulty at arriving at suitable compromises. One such compromise was signed by Montana governor Steve Bullock in September of 2014 that created the Montana Sage Grouse Oversight Team (MSGOT) and the Montana Sage Grouse Habitat Conservation Program. The agreement was specifically "intended to preclude the need to list sage-grouse as a threatened or endangered species" [80]. It bans "occupancy" within 0.6 miles of leks (sage-grouse mating areas) and restricts activities that could disturb the grouse between March 15th and July 15th. However, it does not directly affect private lands, and existing land uses are exempt as are "production and maintenance activities, existing oil, gas and power line facilities." The MSGOT is supposed to encourage voluntary efforts on private properties that prevent "conversion of grouse habitat" to agricultural uses [80]. Unlike many other Western states, a high percentage (over 60 percent) of sage-grouse exist on private lands in Montana. The agreement won support from both industry and some environmentalists. For example, the head of the Montana Petroleum Association praised it for ensuring that "grouse management remains in state hands" as did the head of the Montana Stockgrowers Association who said that "continued state management is important ... especially for cattle ranchers" [81]. The program was also praised by the Program Director for Montana Audubon because "business as usual will have devastating effects on sage-grouse" [81].

The Montana plan copied a Wyoming plan by "creating buffer zones around occupied leks and establishing seasonal work stoppages during the bird's nesting season." The Wyoming plan has been accepted by the Federal BLM which helped to convince the head of the Montana Petroleum Association to follow its model because it had Federal approval. The initial plan for Montana required a buffer of 1 mile around leks but the Wyoming plan only restricts development within 0.6 miles. Some environmentalists contend that development within this distance of the leks would harm the bird [79]. The decision of the BLM to accept Wyoming's plan led Wyoming governor Matt Mead to thank the BLM – an agency which he had previously railed against in his reelection campaign earlier that year [82]. The plan has won acceptance from several environmental groups "such as the Wilderness Society, the Wyoming Wildlife Federation and the Wyoming Outdoor Council" for striking "a reasonable balance between conservation and development" [82]. However, the head of the Pew Charitable Trust's Public Lands Project said that it allowed oil and gas development "too close to leks" [82]. Six environmental groups, including the Center for Biological Diversity and Wild Earth Guardians, rejected the plan, saying that it met only nine of thirty-three conservation standards set by the 2011 Sage-Grouse National Technical Team Report which they view as the "best available science" [83]. The Wyoming plan allows "up to 5 percent disturbance per 640 acres" compared to the National Technical Team's 3 percent. Another critique concerns how to measure "density and disturbance" with the environmental critics saying that plan's calculation method allows calculation across "hundreds of square miles" that would "disguise the intensity of local projects" [83]. The BLM responded to these environmentalist criticisms by stating that "Livestock grazing was not identified as a primary threat in the region … grazing is compatible with grouse conservation and may improve habitat" [83]. Moreover, the BLM emphasized that the plan was the result of seven years of discussion among a variety of stakeholders and that the "balancing of all interests and resources is delicate."

From the USFWS perspective and those environmental groups supporting the compromises, blocking too many of these highly profitable projects would expose the ESA to sharp backlash with threats of it being overridden by Congress. Colorado initially resisted accepting such a compromise. Its governor, Democrat John Hickenlooper, was facing a tough election and, according to Williams, tried to "ingratiate himself with the extractive industry" despite the fact that the industry had accepted the Wyoming plan as being good because it gives them "a rulebook" that they could live with [84]. Williams, an environmental writer, accused Colorado (and also Utah) of obstinacy in failing to compromise that could endanger the entire ESA because Congress was "already itching to emasculate it" [84]. The sage-grouse case illustrates the complexity of wildlife coalition politics. Environmentalists are divided based on their willingness to compromise and accept a "deal." One reason for reluctance to accept the compromise is that the Wyoming and other plans emphasize certain "core areas" for protection, thus making the assumption that these actions offset the lack of protection for non-core areas" and will be enough to "sustain population over the long term" [85 p. 179]. They cite a study that predicts that sage-grouse population in Wyoming will decline by anywhere from 14 to 29 percent with this "core area" focus alone.

Another possible alternative solution to protecting the sage-grouse is to kill predators of sage-grouse eggs. Some Western states (e.g., Nevada and Idaho) recently have undertaken campaigns to kill ravens with poison because one study showed they were nest egg predators, and one Idaho county has petitioned to have ravens removed from protection under the Migratory Bird Treaty Act [86]. However, the campaign to kill ravens (and other members of the corvid bird family) has roused controversy because other biologists say that it has not worked; anti-poisoning petitions have been signed by thousands of people [86]. They contend that removal of some nesting pairs merely opens the space to new ones, plus the ravens are so smart they are hard to kill. And others claim that excessive grazing is what has exposed grouse nests to the ravens [86].

In November of 2014, USFWS announced the final rule listing the Gunnison sage-grouse (closely related to the greater sage-grouse) as a threatened species [87]. The decision to list it as a threatened but not endangered species disheartened environmentalists such as Clait Braun, who managed to get it recognized as a distinct subspecies of the greater sage-grouse. He opposed the decision because "threatened status" allows more development, grazing, and oil and gas development in the bird's range than "endangered status" [87]. Ranchers were upset that it was even listed as threatened because, they argued, they had taken many voluntary measures to restore sagebrush habitat in public and private lands in western Colorado (and southern Utah) where the bird resides and they said this listing would dampen their enthusiasm for any future voluntary efforts [87]. The USFWS said that the listing decision would have no impact on landowners who participate in CCAAs [88]. USFWS emphasized that because the species was listed only as threatened, USFWS has "the flexibility to tailor the conservation measures needed to protect the species through a special 4(d) rule," which it intended to propose later "to allow still other ranchers, farmers and other landowners who commit to Gunnison sage-grouse conservation to continue to manage their lands without additional restrictions" [88]. Although the agreement appears to be an attempt to compromise between the opposed environmental and development-rancher forces, the USFWS Mountain-Prairie Regional Director said that the Gunnison decision had no relationship to a [then] pending decision on the greater sage-grouse [89].

The Gunnison sage-grouse decision process demonstrates how the USFWS tries to walk a fine line between opposed forces. Concerning the USFWS's final rule (published in the Federal Register), several commenters complained that listing the Gunnison grouse would "adversely affect the local economy" [90]. The USFWS's response was that the ESA "does not allow them to "consider economic impacts" in listing decisions but that under Section 4(a)(1) of the ESA, these costs "may be considered in the designation of critical habitat" and they would do an economic analysis and thus pay attention to such impacts. Some environmentalists such as the WildEarth Guardians view the use of Section 4(d) that protects landowners who are already taking voluntary steps from "tougher restrictions" as "loopholes" that are being employed to "avoid restricting development when habitat overlaps with politically powerful industries" [87]. Erik Molvar of WildEarth Guardians says that use of Section 4(d) used to be rare but now is employed "with every other listing" and the result is that due to these loopholes the assignment of "threatened status" no longer has any effect [87].

The economic importance of the greater sage-grouse decision was much greater than that concerning the Gunnison grouse. The USFWS had considered listing of the greater sage-grouse as a threatened species since 2010 when it found that the "bird was heading toward possible extinction" [91; 92]. Its listing could threaten 31,000 jobs, more than $5 billion in economic activity, and cost state and local governments more than $250 million [91]. Consequently, a "bipartisan task force" headed by Colorado's Democratic governor (John Hickenlooper) and Wyoming's Republican governor (Matt Mead) was formed to deal with this case. The task force was aimed at avoiding the listing by demonstrating that the states voluntarily "proactive" activities can "do a better job" than USFWS [91]. Opponents of the listing argued that it would "harm state conservation efforts" by taking away incentives to take voluntary steps but the Secretary of the Interior (Sally Jewell) said that the USFWS "must follow the best available science" and noted that if even "one state doesn't play" ball that it would be impossible to avoid the listing [91]. The debate over the greater sage-grouse is similar to that over the spotted owl but the owl case concerned only 24 million acres while the affected grouse habitat is 165 million acres [91]. A Nevada Department of Conservation and Natural Resources official said that "if hunters can't hunt and miners can't mine . . . then you lose" because the user fees pay for land programs [91]. This decision posed a difficult issue for the Obama Administration and for Western Democratic senators like Harry Reid of Nevada and Michael Bennet of Colorado because environmentalists are an important core constituent of their party. The Obama Administration attempted to deal with the politically touchy situation by encouraging private landowners to take voluntary conservation measures for the grouse via CCAs. The Natural Resources Conservation Service invested more than $350 million (from the U.S. farm bill) over eleven states for a "Sage-Grouse Initiative." The desire to avoid the consequences of this threatened species has been the major motivation behind the development of CCAs but the Western Governors' Association reported that "participation in the grouse initiative declined precipitously" in the Nevada-California area when the USFWS proposed listing a "distinct population segment" of the grouse [93]. In Oregon, thirty landowners have joined a CCA in which they agree not to "fragment habitat" by allowing subdivisions and taking other conservation measures such as improving "forage and nest cover" in order to protect the grouse [93].

On September 22, 2015, Interior Secretary Sally Jewell said that the greater sage-grouse would not be listed. The announcement brought praise from those engaged in the conservation efforts aimed at avoiding listing, but criticism from the WildEarth Guardians (the group that brought a lawsuit that forced the 2010 warning by USFWS) because, they contended, "the land use plans" employed to conserve the birds would be "subject to exceptions, modifications, and waivers" that would undermine conservation [92]. Indeed, the agreement is based on "98 land use plans" "across 10 states" [94]. The decision shows a pattern that the Obama Administration has been following of preferring compromises that do not satisfy some in the environmental community. Conservative Republicans such as Rob Bishop, chair of the House Natural Resources Committee, also rejected the compromise because, he said, "The Obama administration's oppressive land management plan is the same thing as a listing" under the Endangered Species Act [92]. The true impact of the effort will be determined by the long-term effects of the implementation of the plans.

The idea of reaching voluntary agreements between conservationists and industry has been referred to as the "preemptive" approach and has been used to resolve disputes over BLM lands in Colorado and Utah in recent years [95]. In Colorado, BLM announced $113.9 million-worth of mineral leases to companies on public land in the "Roan Plateau" in western Colorado, but environmental organizations challenged the sale and a judge ordered BLM to reconsider the sale in order to protect animal (e.g., cutthroat trout and mule deer) and plant species [95]. In November of 2014, Interior Secretary Jewell announced a revised agreement where "16 of the 18 leases were cancelled" protecting 38,000 acres while development would be allowed in the remaining 16,000 acres though with "provisions prohibiting surface disturbance on about half the area to protect wildlife" [95]. A similar agreement had been reached in northeastern Utah. One of the companies involved said that they were happy with the agreement because it ended "a long period of uncertainty" that limited their "ability to invest in development" [95]. Environmental groups were also supportive of the agreements but noted that this "preemptive approach" was "enabled by its successful record of past litigation" [95].

The Costs and Benefits of the ESA

One of the major criticisms of the original ESA was its negative and punitive emphasis, and many believe that "rewards and incentives" should be offered for landowners who practice "good behavior" [96 p. 184]. Others such as Donahue have discussed problems with the incentives approach, such as the limited resources and piecemeal planning often associated with them. Moreover, she argues that these positive incentive approaches only work if they are backed up by "regulations with teeth" [97 p. 147]. Ando notes that political economists such as Stigler hypothesize that, since costs are more concentrated than benefits for programs, legislators are more likely to favor those who have costs forced on them [98 p. 38]. Her empirical study found that political variables such as interest groups and public pressure (e.g., through public comments) have "significant effects on the amount of time that a species" takes to pass through the listing process [98 p. 29]. She found that opponents of listing are successful "at low levels of pressure" but as supporting comments increase, the "pro forces" can overwhelm the initial opposition and thus shorten the time it takes to be listed [98 p. 50].

The costs of preserving species help to explain why recovery plans are not developed or, if developed, not implemented. An example is the plan to save the Aleutian Canadian goose that consisted of twenty-eight tasks [69 p. 48–9]. Some of the major tasks included eradicating arctic foxes (their predators), breeding captive geese, and then releasing them, restricting hunting of the geese in their wintering grounds, and acquisition of habitat. It is estimated that activities undertaken between 1976 and 1987 for this recovery effort would cost more than $9 million. Wilhere says that determining how many members of a species to save is "an ethical and political" question that cannot be answered by science [99 p. 514–15]. Wilhere goes on to cite a study that shows that increasing the chances that the spotted owl will survive from 0.90 to 0.91 probability would be prohibitively expensive ($1.4 billion) and thus extinction risks must take into consideration economics and "cost-benefit tradeoffs."

Congressional hearings on the ESA have regularly featured Congressional representatives complaining about the negative effects it has had on their constituents. Many elected officials have attacked the ESA for taking the side of animals over humans, such as then Senator from New Mexico, Pete Domenici, who criticized a court decision in favor of protecting the "silvery minnow" that lives in the Rio Grande River "over the needs of the people of our state" [100 p. 4–6]. Domenici goes on to describe the ESA as a "Frankenstein monster" run wild over "75 years of existing law ... needs of the burgeoning population of Albuquerque" [100 p. 6]. Similarly, former Senator Mark Hatfield of Oregon said "where I have to choose between a spotted owl and the welfare of humanity ... I am going to choose my fellow human beings" and "I could live without spotted owls" [55 p. 54–5].

The language used to describe actions taken on behalf of the ESA points to radically different perspectives of the law. *Mitigation* is the term used by conservationists to denote actions taken to "offset or avoid" jeopardy to endangered species, but critics such as former Republican congressman Richard Pombo refer to these required actions as *exactions*: "I mean, you required them to mitigate – you don't want to use the word 'mitigation' – you required an exaction out of them in order to do that, and there has been a series of these exactions that have been required" [101 p. 49]. Republican representative Billy Tauzin of Louisiana added that "we are at some point going to have to legislate what is proper mitigation" and "you can't simply ask a few individuals in America to bear all of the costs at the discretion of a biologist" [101 p. 52]. A more recent example of conflict occurred in Texas, where a Federal judge ordered Texas "officials to allocate water supplies to the world's last flock of endangered Whooping Cranes" [102]. One Texas official criticized the decision because it "dismisses the needs of people and industry." The conflict had been brought on by the occurrence of a drought in the area. Cashore and Howlett point out that it was the ESA language that forced the Forest Service to maintain old growth forest for the spotted owl because the ESA had a "rigid legal requirement ... without taking into consideration any resulting economic impacts" [103 p. 155].

By way of contrast, Wyman cites evidence that overall ESA costs are not high due to the lack of enforcement of the law – she describes the law as a "paper tiger" [7 p. 503–5]. This lack of enforcement, she argues, is due not only to the small amount of resources for enforcement but also due to the difficulty of proving that habitat modifications are "significant" and the "proximate cause of death or injury to wildlife" as required by Section 9 of the ESA. In some early cases, when the USFWS tried to enforce the law, they were blasted by the media for picking on private property owners. One such case involved a Taiwanese migrant in California who was required by the agency to obtain "special permits to plow the land occupied by the Tipton Kangaroo Rat" [104 p. 38]. Media sources such as the *Readers Digest*, the *Wall Street Journal*, and Rush Limbaugh depicted the case as "converting private lands into a public trust for rats" and 1000 farmers picketed the Federal building in Fresno [104]. Donahue acknowledges that enforcement of the ESA on private lands is virtually impossible [97 p. 30]. She says that some kinds of actions may be provable, such as "draining the only wetland habitat of an amphibian" but that many actions such as drainage of pesticides downstream, killing endangered fish, would not be able to be prosecuted because the Federal government is "required to prove harm" under the Act and this is difficult to do.

Ted Williams, a writer for the Audubon Magazine, sharply criticizes mitigation efforts for replacement of wetlands, stating that they often are "mere retention ponds" and also conservation banks which, he claims, often "enhance wetlands" by deepening and thus harming them [105 p. 60–6]. Williams goes on to ask, rhetorically, "why should a developer get to compensate for wetlands that he destroys by preserving or restoring wetlands that are supposed to be protected by law?" [105 p. 60–6]. Williams, writing during the George W. Bush Administration, claimed that the USFWS frequently ignored its responsibility to ask the Corps of Engineers not to fill wetlands and that due to lack of resources often "farms out" its responsibility to write biological opinions ("BiOps") on developments that "will affect endangered species" [105 p. 60–6]. Williams says that the BiOps are often written by developers themselves or political pressure is brought on USFWS biologists to write BiOps favorable to developments. He cites one biologist (Eller) who refused to do so and claims that he was subsequently fired, though pressure by the group Public Employees for Environmental Responsibility succeeded in having him reinstated [105]. Beatley points out the problem of a conflict between the time orientations of wildlife biologists and developers – the developers want quick and firm answers, while the former may need "several years to study the biology of a single species" [106 p. 61].

Lueck points out that the ESA can result in negative impacts on threatened species because landowners may (without USFWS knowing) kill threatened species and/or destroy habitat for these species that might be protected under Section 9 of the ESA [107 p. 89]. Lueck cites the case of landowner in North Carolina whose lands had strong restrictions on harvesting of timber in order to protect land already occupied by red-cockaded woodpeckers (RCWs). In response, the landowner harvested a large amount of timber in adjacent areas (not yet occupied by RCWs). Hoffman, Bazerman, and Yaffee report that the RCWs only affected 15 percent of the landowner's property and that the USFWS had offered him "habitat conservation proposals insulating him from future ESA" actions but he refused these offers [108 p. 60]. Lueck and Michael found evidence that these "preemptive" destructive actions regarding RCW's were common, though they acknowledge that it was impossible for them to determine if the RCW land preserved by the ESA exceeded that destroyed due to preemptive destruction [109 p. 54]. Stap reported that in 1984 he completed the first "comprehensive census of Schaus Swallowtails" and "naively reported" their locations to the state [110 p. 23]. One contractor used this information to bulldoze one of the locations. Conover and Messmer cite a study that showed that RCW restrictions caused "opportunity costs" for land-owners in Georgia of about 36 percent of land values [111].

In response to the charges that the ESA can devastate landowners' economic well-being, the USFWS has employed the Safe Harbors Program begun in 1995 to help provide incentives to landowners to preserve RCW habitat; by 1996, 20,000 acres had been enrolled in the program and it was expected the RCW population on these lands "would double by 2005" [111 p. 259]. Tobin says that the employment of conservation banks can make more money for timber companies with RCWs on their property than "if it is reduced to pulp or two-by-fours" [112 p. 323–4]. However, he also notes that the ESA has to be rigorously enforced in order to create "demand for these credits" and to make sure "they don't get off too easy" with the conservation bank terms. The Georgia Pacific Corporation had been using "short rotation cutting methods" which cuts trees before they are thirty-five years old and resulted in habitat loss for the RCWs [113 p. 28]. Some environmentalists criticized the agreement because it "allows the bird colonies to be divided by twice as many feet as allowed by Federal guidelines" and also allows Georgia Pacific to log "old or abandoned cavity trees" and one Florida State biologist said that the agreement "leaves minimal habitat" for the RCWs [113]. In response, the USFWS said that the "for the first time," USFWS "has jurisdiction over private land" and the Audubon Society approved the agreement despite its limitations because it shows that "ESA can work with business" [113 p. 29].

There is disagreement over the impact of conservation in general, and the ESA in particular, on growth and development. Stevens cites a study by the Texas and Southwestern Cattle Raisers' Association that protection of the "golden-cheeked warbler" had depressed real estate prices in "Texas Hill Country" and quotes former Republican representative Richard Pombo as labeling the ESA as a "growth control ordinance" [114]. In contrast, research by MIT's Stephen Meyer contradicted this finding. Meyer conducted a fifty-state study of the relationship between conservation measures and economic development, and found that states with stronger environmental policies outperformed other states on "all the economic measures" [115]. Research has shown that the presence of wildlife and parks can foster substantial growth and revenues in local areas that counter the negative effects of the ESA. However, Prato and Fagre caution that "amenity-based" growth near "gateway communities" such as those surrounding the Yellowstone National Park can cause "landscape fragmentation" in the buffer areas just outside the park as well as lead to increased traffic that can threaten the existence of species like grizzlies [116 p. 38 & 283]. For example, they cite data that there has been a 400 percent increase in rural development in the Montana and Wyoming parts of the Greater Yellowstone Ecosystem [116 p. 247]. Brooks, Jones, and Virginia point out that the U.S. National Park Service (and other Federal agencies) have had to "retrofit the management of our parks" to mesh with the new emphasis on ecosystem management and they have to try to "accommodate human interests and occupancy" with this new philosophy [41 p. 203].

Even "green development projects" supported by groups like the Sierra Club can threaten endangered species. Solar projects in the Mojave Desert have threatened "sand-colored desert tortoises" [117]. According to Wells, the Sierra Club and Natural Resources Defense Council have "supported industrial-scale wind and solar installations on public land" [117]. Other conservationist groups have objected to locating projects on "pristine desert." Reportedly, the Sierra Club had "lobbied for changes to protect the tortoises" but nevertheless decided to support the project [117]. Wells also reports that the Audubon Society fought a wind farm that it claimed would threaten endangered birds such as the "snail-eating Florida Kite" [117]. Initially, solar developers received the green light to develop projects wherever they wanted in the West but later environmentalists have modified this to "appropriately-sited lands" [117]. Cart relates the difficulties of BrightSource, the developer of one Mojave solar project, to design it without endangering tortoises [118]. The company reduced the number of planned towers from seven to three, giving up 10 percent of its "expected power output" [118]. It also installed "extensive fencing" to prevent relocated tortoises from returning to the project area. Initial surveys only found a small number (sixteen) of the tortoises but later many more turned up exceeding the number (thirty-eight) that the company had been approved to "move." Cart reports that at the same time, there was a big increase in off road vehicle (ORV) traffic that killed tortoises, as well as an increase in trash dumps that attracted ravens, one of the chief predators of tortoises [118]. There is also the problem that moved "tortoises nearly always attempt to plod home." Consequently, Bright Source and other solar developers are having to "pay to close off ORV routes, fund public education, and rehabilitate degraded habitat" [118]. Some argue that ranches with cattle grazing in the West are preferable conservation-wise to development projects. But Sullivan says that, although this may be true in the short run, over the longer term, ranchers sell out to developers if they are in areas surrounded by development [119 p. 1048]. Moreover, he argues ranches are "hotspots for endangered species" because they exist in "optimal habitats" near water sources in an otherwise arid area – that is why so much of endangered species exist on private lands.

Negotiation and the ESA: HCP, CCA, and Other "Incentive" Policies for Conservation

According to Scott, Goble, and Davis, the ESA has changed from "prohibitive law to a flexible permitting statute" [120 p. 8–9]. In particular, the 1982 amendment to the take provisions allowed individual endangered animals to be taken as long as projects did not threaten "the existence of the species" and the applicant submitted a conservation plan to obtain an "incidental take permit under Section 9" [120 p. 10]. Safe harbor agreements and CCAs were aimed at allowing landowners and developers to have "certainty to make economic decisions" [120 p. 10]. According to Burgess, the concept of safe harbor agreements was originated by the head of the Environmental Defense Fund (Michael Bean) who feared that landowners in the Southeast were incentivized to "liquidate their forestland" before reaching "USFWS's minimum threshold" [121 p. 126]. Likewise, the use of the category of "experimental, non-essential" has been employed for wolves (both the gray and Mexican wolves) in order to give "government and landowners flexibility in treating troublemaking wolves" [16 p. 13]. The experimental designation in Section 10(j) of the ESA allows the release of "an experimental population that is totally separate from non-experimental populations of the species" [16 p. 13]. The USFWS is only required to "confer," not consult when it releases experimental non-essential populations and thus does not have to "insure that its actions will not jeopardize the species" [122 p. 133].

One of the key limitations of the ESA is that, although it theoretically covers private as well as public lands, accessing and implementing rules on these private lands is difficult if not impossible without the agreement of the landowners. Nie says that some environmentalists argue that greater protections should be given to species like grizzlies to compensate for the loss due to development of habitat on private lands [16 p. 217].

Long before the passage of the ESA, legal rulings had established that "wildlife is publicly owned," but the complexity of enforcing the law is due to the fact that most of the habitat in which the wildlife reside is privately owned by people who have goals other than "producing wildlife" [111 p. 255]. Maehr says that because there are "insufficient funds" available to the government to "recover or expand" Florida panther habitat, that conservation is highly dependent on private lands and their owners' decisions [123 p. 189]. Cioc states that the "massive depletion of wetlands" has far outstripped the public bird reserves and other public protected areas over the past 100 years [124 p. 100]. A report by GAO stated that 517 of the 781 species listed at that time had 60 percent (or more) of their habitat on non-Federal lands and 264 of these listed species existed *only* on non-Federal lands [125 p. 100]. Thus incentives such as HCPs and other inducements (e.g., no surprises) to secure landowner cooperation are a necessity [126 p. 386–7 & 397].

The 1982 amendments that led to the creation of HCPs made an important change to the ESA – before these amendments, the protection of species was "the sole purpose of the ESA," while after it, the law allowed for "balancing by agencies and courts" [41 p. 212]. Until the Clinton Administration, few HCPs were enacted. Bruce Babbitt describes one of the reasons for slow development of HCPs was that "biologists" in the USFWS had been trained for research on wildlife and lacked the skills to "negotiate between angry landowners and hostile environmentalists" [127 p. 62–3].

Early HCPs often focused on only one or two species: Coachella Valley HCP on the area's fringe-toed lizard, the Clark County Desert Tortoise HCP, and San Diego's Least Bell Vireo HCP [64 p. 34]. By way of contrast, the Plum Creek Native Fish HCP in Montana covers more than 1 million privately owned acres and "17 different fish species" [128 p. 216]. One hoped-for advantage of HCPs is that these plans would cover a larger area rather than small individual projects and thus will help to lower costs of complying with the ESA [64 p. 168]. Hierl, Franklin, Deutschman, Regan, and Johnson found that the number of HCPs that "cover more than one species" has "increased through time" and that 40 of the more than 480 HCPs that had been approved by January of 2007 "covered 10 or more species" [129 p. 166–7]. Hierl et al. cite the San Diego Multispecies Plan that covers more than eighty-five threatened or endangered animal and plant species [129]. The complexity of setting up such an HCP is great because it covered not only the city of San Diego but eleven other jurisdictions. This complexity is the reason why many multispecies HCPs take more than a decade to complete, with the delay having a negative effect on the species [130 p. 1]. Alagona and Pincetl looked in depth at the development of the Coachella Valley Multiple Species HCP and found two major reasons for the delay: (1) Tensions developed between the local sponsor of the plan, the Coachella Valley Association of Governments (CVAG), and the state and Federal regulatory agencies; (2) As delays mounted, some local governments deserted the plan, such as City of Desert Hot Springs which became opposed to "land use planning" [130 p. 2]. The opposition of Desert Hot Springs was attributed in part to the influence of national forces such as the negative attitude of the Bush Administration and its lack of enthusiasm for HCPs [130 p. 8]. They also argue that the parties in the Coachella Valley case needed help with the process because CVAG lacked the authority and skills to manage such a complex process but were loath to hire facilitators because of the cost.

One of the principles of conservation planning enunciated by Noss et al. is that ecology, not political boundaries should determine conservation plans but they acknowledge that adherence to this principle is difficult in practice [44 p. 108]. The development of HCPs can be slow and political. In one case, the steering committee for the HCP consisted of seventy members and the process was described as an "exercise in obfuscation" [131 p. 102]. Keiter cites the case of then Oregon governor John Kitzhaber's attempt to develop a plan to restore salmon habitat as containing "voluntary and thus unenforceable agreements" as evidence that the hammer of a possible ESA listing is essential to get "interest groups to invest the time and energy" required to solve environmental problems [128 p. 253–7].

Tobin discussed how even apparently successful HCPs like the one in the Austin, Texas area are likely to lose a significant proportion of their protections for species due to subsequent development and usage of the open space areas created [112 p. 317]. The manager of the city's portion related how residents "loved the open space so much that they built barbecue pits, extended their patios into the habitat" and cyclists blazed new paths and that "most biologists" with whom he spoke said the "preserve was made far too small." Luoma cites both positives and negatives about HCPs [132 p. 36–9]. They can cover species that are not yet endangered and do so without "banging somebody over the head" – the best of them go "way beyond the ESA." The major negative, says Luoma, is that the plans are prepared in private by the developer – that is how the law is written and they do not become public until after they are completed.

The environmental group Defenders of Wildlife critiques HCPs for providing inadequate public input and the fact that the no-surprises rule limits "the ability of the HCP to improve the agreement if subsequent harmful consequences are discovered" [116 p. 135]. Donahue argues that this policy is directly contrary to the "adaptive management" emphasis that is supposed to be employed by conservation planners which requires gathering of new information and modification of conservation measures depending on the new information [97 p. 46]. Noss et al. thus point out that given that major changes are not likely to be made in agreements involving HCPs with no-surprises guarantees, the science used to establish the boundaries and rules for these agreements is crucial to avoid locking in to arrangements that will do irreversible damage not foreseen at the time of the agreement [44 p. 16]. Noss et al. note that relatively new techniques such as modeling with geographic information systems and the use of sensitivity analyses can assist in such planning [44 p. 173]. However, they caution that the knowledge that "informs" these models is often very inadequate and consequently it is often better to rely on "streamlined approaches" such as trend estimates from local experts [44 p. 173].

Perspectives and reference points determine one's view of the success of HCPs. Tobin discusses two alternate views of the success of the Sonoran Desert Conservation Plan (SDCP) in Pima County Arizona [112 p. 327]. He says the SDCP "identified" 141,000 acres of "valuable habitat" for endangered species but estimated that about "40 percent would be lost to development" over thirty years [112 p. 327]. Initially, such a loss makes the SDCP appear to be a failure, but given the "expected growth of population in southern Arizona and the dominance of human interests overall," he says that saving 60 percent "is no small feat" [112 p. 327]. Another possible difficulty with making agreements is that assumptions about threats to species can change with new scientific research.

Greer identified the long-term issues that HCPs face including the following: (1) long-term funding issues must be resolved – where will the money come from – local governmental budgets or bond issues? (2) "monitoring for effectiveness" – who will conduct follow-up studies on how the HCP is affecting the threatened and endangered species? [133 p. 234–6]. A small number of consultant organizations guided early HCP implementations [106 p. 39]. Much of the early funding of HCPs has come from "development mitigation fees" – thus the costs are passed along to future homeowners because this is "more politically acceptable than taxing existing residents," and thus developers see them as a way to pass on part of the costs of development to the general public [106 p. 57]. From a political perspective, Beatley says that HCPs provide a "pressure valve" to promote compromise between development and environmental interests [106 p. 57]. Theoretically, HCPs contribute to "no net loss" of habitat because habitat losses are compensated for by restorations elsewhere. However, Beatley notes that habitat may be difficult if not impossible to recreate [106 p. 60]. Beissinger and Perrine cite research that questions the "scientific rigor of many HCPs" and fears that they may "facilitate destruction of habitat rather than its protection" [25 p. 67].

A study of forty-three HCPs found that only seven contained "monitoring programs sufficient for determining success" [134 p. 114–15]. Thomas also found that HCPs such as that in the Coachella Valley overlooked critical habitat in their agreement, but all parties including the USFWS did not want to reopen the agreement for revision because they did not want to threaten an agreement based on difficult political negotiation and also because the USFWS has limited resources [134]. Goldstein describes in detail how Federal regulatory biologists wanted to use a new model-based map for monitoring Coachella Valley lizards but this was resisted by local biologists who feared that it would upset the existing consensus [135]. Noss et al. admit that it is difficult to "revise reserve design" once it is committed to because changing boundaries would likely require Congressional approval and acquisition of new funds [44 p. 148]. Thus they state that coping with need for changes will likely have to depend more on changes in management practices than reserve redesigns (e.g., rules for use by humans for recreation and hunting).

Dixon et al. studied the implementation of the "Multiple Species Habitat Conservation Plan, a plan to conserve 500,000 acres of the 1.26 million acres in the western part of the Riverside (California) county" that was finalized in 2004 – the planning process for this HCP began in 1999 [136 p. xvi–xx]. They found that by mid-2007 very little acreage "had been conserved through the development review process because the developers had mostly avoided projects that would require contributions" [136 p. xix–xx]. They noted that the plan was still in its early phase of implementation and the situation could change. However, they state that if contributions continued to be delayed, the price of land would rise substantially and thus less land would be able to be purchased from developer contributions at later dates. The authors also studied the funding of nineteen large (more than 1000 acres) HCPs and found that thirteen out of nineteen were funded by grants, mitigation fees, or a combination, while six relied entirely on sales of "timber or water" [136 p. 110].

Noss et al. state that funding is available for HCPs involving private lands that otherwise would not be present, and thus HCPs can preserve habitat that otherwise "would be destroyed" [44 p. 68]. Brook, Zint, and De Young studied the impact of ESA listing on landowner actions concerning Preble's mouse and found that about the same percentage (25 percent) sought to hurt the mouse as help it due to the listing [137]. Nevertheless, as a result of their research, they conclude that although critics question CCAs and Safe Harbor Agreements because they lack adequate protections, nevertheless such policies may be necessary to allay landowners' fear of regulators that lead them to harm listed or "candidate" species.

Fox, Scott, Goble, and Davis argue that in the past HCPs "generally" resulted "in small, disconnected and uncoordinated reserves" but that conservation banking can make up for these deficiencies by offering "landowners the prospect of selling conservation credits," and speed up the process, allowing the assembling of reserves more quickly [138 p. 228–31]. The shortening of the HCP process reduces costs and thus "mitigates political resistance." However, Fox et al. also emphasize that for conservation banking to work as intended, the USFWS has to "aggressively enforce ESA" or there will not be sufficient demand for conservation banks and they will not be "financially successful" [138 p. 239]. Li and Male say that conservation banks are most appropriate for situations where the USFWS lacks a "clear understanding" of "future adverse impacts" from projects [139 p. 81].

According to Roman, Bruce Babbitt (Secretary of Interior during the Clinton Administration) saw measures such as no-surprises agreements as a means of undercutting the outcry against the ESA [30 p. 143]. Roman says that Babbitt's "brilliant" strategy was to negotiate individually with timber companies, developers, and the water industry, and thus divide them. For example, the president of the Murray Pacific Corporation, which owned a hundred thousand acres of spotted owl habitat, signed an agreement in order to secure "certainty" [30 p. 143]. Roman says that California "tradable" credits for land "had little development potential" but resulted in 6000 acres for three threatened species (the San Joaquin fox, Tipton kangaroo rat, and blunt-nosed leopard lizard) [30 p. 150].

Beatley's analysis of the San Bruno and other HCPs found that the agreements were based on a "series of negotiated compromises" with plenty of room for "subjective interpretation" of what actions are necessary to meet Section 10(a) standards of the ESA [64 p. 63]. He goes on to say that the nature of the agreement depends on the "political standing and resources" of the various actors involved but "credible scientific expertise" played a key role in facilitating successful HCPs [64 p. 68]. Beatley described an HCP as involving a "balance of terror" in which both sides "fear walking away from the process" because if they do, they will have to incur legal expenses in courts or go through many individual project by project negotiations [106 p. 57]. Thus the HCP can be viewed as an "efficient solution" for developers. Another positive aspect is that the developers can get "higher prices" for developments near protected open space areas [64 p. 212].

One of the primary reasons for developing the CCAA program was to address landowner concerns about the potential regulatory implications of having a listed species on their land. The CCAA program specifically provides them with the assurance that if they implement various conservation activities, they will not be subject to additional restrictions if the species becomes listed under the ESA. Ted Williams describes the potential advantages of CCAA as a better way of protecting species like the prairie chicken than the Safe Harbors Program because participants get to work with state wildlife agencies that they know better and are more knowledgeable than the USFWS are concerning their land [140]. He quotes a Texas Parks and Wildlife official as saying that they had signed up 115,000 acres for the CCAA program. However, Williams cites Audubon officials, who note that the USFWS oversight continues to be needed in a case like the prairie chicken which covers five states and faces problems of habitat fragmentation.

"Credit exchange programs" such as Utah Prairie Dog Credit Exchange are similar to conservation banks in that landowners protect endangered species on their property and then sell the credits to developers wanting to build elsewhere but the credit exchange "goes further by acting as broker and removing delays and financial risk in setting up" the banks [141]. It also provides assistance from biologists and inspections to make sure that "it's done right." The credits cost somewhere between $4800 and $8000 to offset impacts to one acre of prairie dog habitat [141]. The aim is to change farmers' perception of the prairie dog from a pest to an asset. Some localities such as Enoch, Utah have outlawed "conservation easements on private land," thus making such exchanges impossible [141]. Opponents view the program as imposing costs that should not exist in the first place.

There are other Federal programs that encourage conservation such as the "swampbuster" provisions in the agricultural bills dating back to 1985 that take away benefits from farmers who "plow prairie potholes" [127 p. 111]. This law was passed through a coalition of Ducks Unlimited and environmentalists concerned about a decline in duck numbers. Other related programs include the Conservation Reserve Program that provides financial incentives for farmers to take land out of production and planted with grasses. Although these programs have been successful in encouraging conservation, Babbitt points out that the effects of these programs are "randomly scattered" and do not provide planning and linkages needed to create connected ecosystems [127 p. 111–13].

Other options that can contribute to conservation include Land Preservation Agreements that several counties around the United States have adopted that are aimed at preserving open space in areas where development is occurring [142]. The basic idea of these ordinances is to encourage housing to be "clustered in a certain portion of the land" so that "40 to 80 percent is left as open space." The idea is that these developments will be able to charge higher prices due to their closeness to attractive recreational areas for residents. Wurtman-Wunder [142] cites a study of these "conservation developments" (CDs) that found that houses located in these developments enjoyed an increase of 20 percent in price compared to similar housing not located in CDs [143 p. 162–3], but the expected conservation benefits did not occur. The land located in CDs was no better protected than developments not located in CDs – so-called "exurban sprawl areas" [142]. They explained that due to key factors such as the small size of most CDs – only the huge ones (e.g., thousands of acres) had significant ecological impacts.

Prato and Fagre cite data that even our largest protected areas such as the Greater Yellowstone Ecosystem are too small to ensure the long-term survival of species like the grizzly bear – it can only support 500 bears while 2,000 are needed to "ensure survival from challenges of weather, diseases, and other threats" and thus "continental scale conservation" planning is needed [116 p. 221]. Encouraging regional planning is a difficult process, as illustrated by the fact that when the concept of "Yellowstone Ecosystem" planning was proposed, governors of three states (Wyoming, Montana and Idaho) condemned the "vision" and both the U.S. Park Service and U.S. Forest Service "forbade . . . employees from using the term" [131 p. 179 & 219]. Also, few CDs "sponsored land stewardship" or assigned specific responsibility for "post-development oversight" – these activities are left to the homeowner associations. Also, the open space was often not planned to be contiguous and often was located on the periphery of the development. Certain counties (e.g., Routt County, Colorado) required that developers "identify and avoid areas inhabited by endangered or threatened species" and Tooele County (Utah) requires that 75 percent of its open space be located in contiguous tracts, while some other counties are attempting to develop provisions that strengthen the ecological planning done before construction [142]. The creation of corridors to connect habitat areas has been an increasing focus of many experts as a way of maintaining and improving biodiversity. However, Beatley cautions that corridors can also transmit "disease and pests" and may be used as a justification for the fragmentation of habitat and thus of questionable value to endangered species [64 p. 204]. Morrison and Boyce point to the problem of trying to create corridors for mountain lions who are increasingly passing through narrow corridors near urban areas [144 p. 281]. They believe that plans like California's Natural Communities Conservation Planning Program have potential to get beyond the typical "parcel" planning to take a broader view necessary to create and protect such corridors.

The Courts and the ESA

Despite the fact that since the Clinton Administration has emphasized negotiation using mechanisms such as HCPs, no surprises, CCAs and CCAAs, conservation banks, and credit exchange programs, the courts have continued to play a central role in the implementation of the ESA – the incentive to negotiate depends on the existence of the threat of listing with its attendant restrictions. There are many examples attesting to the power of a listing. For example, Wilcove states that the turning point in protecting the northwest salmon came in 1991 when the NMFS placed it on the endangered species list so that the northwest salmon "could no longer be ignored" [145 p. 133]. Keiter describes how Oregon was forced to preserve salmon habitat by the NMFS and that voluntary plans were rejected by the courts and environmentalists as being "too vague and untested" to be relied upon [128 p. 253–7]. The importance of the power to place a species on the endangered list is central to the ESA. Bruce Babbitt, Secretary of the Interior during the Clinton Administration, relates the story of how Pete Wilson, then governor of California, was angry that the delta smelt fish was placed on the list and that he vowed that water would never be "diverted from farms" to protect it since it was a species that "only a few biologists" cared about [127 p. 49–50]. However, subsequently, the USFWS forced pumps diverting water to farms shut down in order to aid the fish during its "spawning cycle." Eventually, Wilson and Babbitt negotiated an agreement to dismantle some dams and take other steps to maintain water flow and wetlands to preserve the fish and other species [127 p. 51].

The threat of ESA legal action was the key that allowed a "few biologists with few political or financial" resources to bring the developers "to the table" in the Coachella Valley case [134 p. 120]. Babbitt similarly says that it was the ESA and the listing of the ferruginous pygmy owl that achieved the Las Cienegas National Conservation Area supported by state and local officials who (unlike the cases in California) had been opposed to the ESA [127]. Babbitt points to programs like the Natural Community Conservation Planning, passed by California in 1991, as spurring the kind of land use planning incorporating a broad ecosystem viewpoint necessary to protect species that may not be achieved by most HCPs or other conservation programs. Several studies cited by Doremus and Tarlock found that conservation agencies did not list species when they conflicted with economic development "unless they are forced to do so" [146 p. 354]. Thus lawsuits by organizations such as the Center for Biological Diversity often force the issue. An example of the successful use of the threat of listing occurred in Montana Big Hole Watershed during the 1990s. The grayling (a fish) was in danger due to water taken from streams by ranchers. When the USFWS "determined that the grayling was threatened," it led to the formation of a "Watershed Committee," consisting of ranchers, outfitters, and conservationists as well as local governmental officials, that took conservation steps such as shutting down of irrigation ditches for cattle at certain times of the year.

However, there is some evidence that the threat of a listing may be counterproductive in certain cases. In 2013, the USFWS had to decide whether to list the lesser prairie chicken whose numbers had been cut in half. The problem was that its habitat was mostly on private property in Texas, a state that resents Federal regulations on private land use. Indeed, land use controls are such "an anathema in Texas, that many counties don't have any enabling legislation to adopt land use controls" [106 p. 77]. The Texas Parks and Wildlife Department has developed a "Range-Wide" plan in which landowners would be "paid to preserve the birds' habitat" and thus avoid Federal listing [147]. Governor Perry supported the plan but those running the program often omit mention of the chicken and the threat of the proposed listing because they fear that many would refuse to participate in the program if they know it is tied into a threatened listing and thus "synonymous with . . . Federal regulation" [147].

The Federal courts have played an enormous role in the implementation of the ESA. Plater et al. describe the ESA as a "roadblock statute" because it contains a "stark flat prohibition provision" that provides "particular effectiveness" because of its "directness" and "lack of ambiguity" [57 p. 671–3]. Plater et al. go on to state that endangered species protections confront "strong marketplace resistance" and because wildlife protections do not have "overt human importance" that "without tough legal standards," it could be expected to be "honored in the breach" [57 p. 671–2]. They note that the courts have been generally "more attentive to Act's requirements" than presidential administrations – the Reagan and the George H.W. Bush Administrations both engaged in a slowdown of listing of species [57 p. 693]. Part of the reason for the numerous court battles over listings was the slowness in the listing process. The process to list the flycatcher began in 1992 but the rule did not come out until 1995 and the final ruling happened in 1997; and it only occurred then because the Center for Biological Diversity sued the USFWS over it [131 p. 89].

The centrality of the courts to some of the key events in the history of the ESA is illustrated by the controversy during the 1990s over the preservation of spotted owl. There was a dispute between BLM, which managed the forests, and the USFWS that wound up in the Federal courts. Robert Keiter says that the intransigence of agencies like BLM and the "hopelessly stalemated Congress" forced Federal courts to take over implementation of the ESA [128 p. 94–5]. In particular, during the 1990–2 period, he says that BLM refused to consult as required with USFWS over the newly listed spotted owl concerning its logging practices that environmentalists contended threatened its habitat. The Ninth Circuit Court ruled that BLM must consult with USFWS – in effect, the Federal courts "were running northwest federal forestlands" [128 p. 96]. However, the situation changed in 1995 when a rider was attached to a major budget bill which contained moneys for the Oklahoma bombing victims. The "salvage rider" temporarily removed the ESA consultation requirements and judicial review and made the Forest Service the sole manager of logging operations [128 p. 94–5]. Still, despite the temporary rider, as a result of the stalemate in Congress, Keiter says that the Federal courts deserve "much of the credit" for introducing ecosystem management, because they forced the designation of critical habitat when the USFWS was reluctant to do so in controversial cases like California gnatcatcher and northern spotted owl, and that the threat of the "ESA hammer" is essential to get interest groups to collaborate in difficult natural resource conflicts [128 p. 257]. The Interior Department complained that it had "lost control over the listing process" and had been overwhelmed by court orders. The Nature Conservancy and other environmental organizations bargained with the Bush Administration and reached a compromise agreement that they would take action to protect twenty-nine threatened animals (e.g., the pygmy rabbit) and plant species as long as the environmental organizations agreed to delay actions such as mapping of critical habitat for four Hawaiian invertebrates [70]. The argument in support of legal action is that without these proceedings, many threatened species would not be protected. Doremus and Tarlock state that "the most effective combination is likely to be a statutory hammer big enough to bring the status quo interests to the table, together with a forum for negotiation that encourages broad thinking and allows some trade-offs" [146 p. 148]. CCAs formed the basis of a negotiation between the USFWS and the Center for Biological Diversity and WildEarth Guardians – these two environmental organizations agreed to "curtail many lawsuits and petitions" if the USFWS would "process its candidate backlog" [148].

The other side of the debate was articulated in Congressional hearings by Gary Frazer, a Bush Administration official in charge of endangered species who said in 2001 that "virtually our entire listing budget is dedicated to complying with court-ordered actions most of which are for species that are already listed" and thus they are unable to undertake discretionary actions [10 p. 15]. He went on to say that as of March 2001 that the USFWS was involved with "75 active section 4 lawsuits covering 400 species" and "36 lawsuits covering over 354 species regarding critical habitat" and has received "86 notices of intent to sue which involve another 640 species" [10 p. 17]. Lowell Baier, a critic of environmental litigators, says they "ignore the social and economic impact" of their lawsuits and characterizes them as a "real threat to the traditional way of life in the West" [149 p. 251]. At the same hearing, Zeke Grader, Executive Director of the U.S. Federation of Fisherman's Association, a defender of the need for lawsuits, said that the lawsuits were necessary because of the refusal of agencies to act [10 p. 40]. He goes on to say that in California the joke was that their biggest river was the "river of denial" and that he would like to see the agencies listen to their own scientists.

The USFWS estimated "in its 2012 budget that it would only be able to make decisions on four percent of species that had been petitioned for listing" and the agency asked Congress to "impose a cap on the amount of money it could spend on listing" [150]. The Agency "routinely" misses deadlines to make determinations as to whether petitions deserve to be further investigated [150]. The Agency believes that it is being besieged by lawsuits from organizations like the Center for Biological Diversity that make it unable to do its other work. Representatives of these organizations argue that we are in an "extinction crisis" that justifies the large number of petitions and that the agency should adopt a "streamlined process" such as listing by geography to speed the process [150].

Biber and Brosi emphasize that the ESA has very broad "citizen suit provisions" aimed at prohibiting "agency capture" [151 p. 332]. As pointed out above, these provisions have enabled many lawsuits every year over listings (and failures to list) that have had a major impact on agency actions and sometimes have seemingly overwhelmed the USFWS. In response to claims that they agency was overwhelmed by these suits, beginning in 1998, Congress imposed a limit on the "amount of USFWS's budget that can be spent on listing decisions" [151 p. 335–6]. The debate over the burden of listing petitions begun during the late 1990s has persisted into the Obama Administration. For example, during February of 2011, the Administration declared the Pacific walrus "at risk of extinction" but "declined to list the mammal as endangered" because it said that there was a "backlog" of other animals that were in even greater danger [150]. Obama's USFWS said that the barrage of lawsuits has created a "backlog of 254 species" whose protection they agree is "warranted but precluded" by a lack of resources. Two environmental groups, the Center for Biological Diversity and WildEarth Guardians, have filed "90 percent of the petitions since 2007" [150]. Biber and Brosi empirically studied the hypothesis that listings due to legal petitions by outside groups such as environmental organizations result in listings that are inferior to those begun by the professionals of USFWS [151 p. 363]. They systematically compared the two sets of listings and the only significant differences were that outsider-initiated listings had more conflicts with "development projects." They go on to argue that the outsider petitions help to compensate for the lack of budgetary and personnel resources that make it impossible for USFWS to keep up with deadlines. They note that the ESA imposes "significant data collection requirements" and they argue that the technical expertise of the outside groups has been shown to be comparable to those of USFWS. They also argue that these "citizen suits" ensure that the agency will not be "captured" by powerful interests that oppose listings of "controversial species" [151 p. 371]. They note that USFWS "regularly misses ... statutory deadlines for listing species" and plaintiffs charge that they have been doing this unlawfully [151 p. 347].

The debate over whether the citizen lawsuit provision of the ESA is being abused has continued with the Obama Administration. Recently, Republican legislators have accused USFWS of actively encouraging lawsuits by environmental organizations when the agency does not want to take the blame for a controversial action [152]. A *Wall Street Journal* editorial labeled these lawsuits the "sue and settle" approach by the government and argued it was not about saving species but "restricting land use on thousands of acres of private and state land" thus ending most oil and gas development in the United States. Coincidentally, during the George W. Bush Administration environmentalists suspected the same type of collusion between the Administration and lawsuits by extractive industries [152].

Recently, Ruhl has argued that the Supreme Court has, in effect, "eviscerated" the Hill ("snail darter") decision and that the court is skeptical about it (and other environmental laws) especially when they regulate private lands with no attention to cost-benefit calculations of the costs to private landowners [153 p. 532]. He supports this argument with analysis of six cases since the Hill decision where the court directly faced issues concerning the ESA. In Lujan *v*. Defenders of Wildlife (1992), the court rejected the extension of the ESA agencies' authority to foreign nations [153 p. 499–500]. In another (1995) case, Babbitt *v*. Sweet Home Chapter of Communities for a Great Oregon, although the court ruled that habitat (not just individual animals) was protected under the ESA, they added requirements that the government must prove "proximate causation, foreseeability, and injury to particular animals" that are difficult to prove [153 p. 502]. In the 2007 case of National Homebuilders *v*. Defenders of Wildlife, the court's decision significantly restricted the presumption that other governmental agencies must consult with ESA agencies in matters of "discretionary decisions" [154 p. 278]. Ruhl notes that these six decisions came within a different context from the Hill case, which was the first instance of the ESA invoked against a development project. Listed species had increased from a few dozen to more than a thousand by 1995 and projects were being challenged across the nation [153 p. 518]. He notes that the administration of the ESA by the Clinton-Babbitt Administration had implemented an "administrative reform agenda" that successfully warded off "congressional assault" on the ESA but the resulting HCPs look like other environmental "permitting programs" and not the unique "macho" statute as interpreted by Burger in the Hill case that held ESA did not need to heed "cost-benefit" calculations [153 p. 519]. Thus it appears that the leadership role that the Federal judiciary played in enforcing ESA may be challenged.

Unusual weather patterns can increase the dilemmas posed by the ESA. Recently, serious droughts in Western states have led to disputes over water that has been allocated to saving endangered fish and other species. Recently, a Republican representative from California (Tom McClintock) proposed changes in the ESA by replacing draining of rivers to aid endangered fish by taking other measures such as "promotion of fish hatcheries" and "predator control" [155]. McClintock complained that "while homeowners parch their gardens and clog their showerheads with flow restrictors to save a few extra gallons of water, their government thought nothing of wasting water" to reduce the temperature a few degrees. Environmental groups such as The Wild Earth Guardians are threatening to sue "federal and state agencies because water users in Colorado and New Mexico are siphoning off too much water" and thus harming the "Rio Grande silvery minnow" which has been listed as endangered since 1994 [102]. Farmers say that due to the extreme drought they "cannot afford a drop to spare" [102]. A similar struggle has taken place in California between farmers and water reserved to "protect the threatened delta smelt" fish [102]. Campoy quotes a New Mexico state official as saying that they had "done everything they could for the species . . . under the resource constraints" [102]. In short, compromises reached under normal or good conditions may break down when extreme events such as droughts or other natural disasters occur.

Implementation, Monitoring, and Outcome Evaluation Issues

Some environmentalists are not pleased with the results of the "bargaining approach" to ESA because they do not have confidence in the way the HCPs and other agreements will be implemented and monitored. The Interior Department of the Obama Administration (as with the Clinton Administration) has used the threat of ESA listing to obtain concessions in a bargaining process over the sagebrush lizard in Texas and New Mexico, claiming that they had won voluntary agreement from landowners of 640,000 acres of land to take steps to protect the lizard without actually listing it as a threatened species and thus allowing oil and gas development to proceed in the Permian Basin [156]. Salazar claimed that this agreement was an example of "how the ESA should be used." However, Root has questioned the agreement because the group responsible for overseeing the implementation of the conservation plan are all members of the Texas Oil and Gas Association [157]. A representative of the Center for Biological Diversity calls the situation "a case of the fox guarding the hen house" and is planning to sue in state and Federal courts over it [157]. The sage brush lizard lives in the western Texas Panhandle and southeastern New Mexico. The Interior Department decided not to list the lizard "once landowners in Texas and New Mexico agreed to take steps to protect its habitat" [156]. Denny says that this CCAA is like no other one because for the "first time it has the provision to be rolled over into a Habitat Conservation Plan if the species gets listed" [158]. According to Denny, the plan "maintains that the needs of the lizard are just too unclear to specify conditions" [158]. The Center for Biological Diversity will challenge the agreement because they say it "only vaguely describes the conservation measures required" leaving these to be "spelled out" in "certificates between each participant and the State of Texas" but that Texas has prevented Federal officials and members of the public from viewing these certificates. The Defenders of Wildlife published a "white paper" in which they also point out weaknesses of the agreements: (1) Since the USFWS does not have access to certificates they cannot directly "verify the level of compliance" with the CCAA so they have to depend on self-reporting and a contractor to be hired by the Texas Comptroller's Office; nor does the agreement discuss how access will be obtained to the private lands on which the lizards live; (2) No public input is required if the CCAA route is taken [159 p. 9–14].

Wyman cites a series of 2005 articles in the *Seattle Post-Intelligencer* by Robert McClure and Lisa Stiffler [160] that found the USFWS "invests very little time and staff resources in monitoring implementation of HCPs and thus many plans are probably not properly implemented" [7 p. 505]. McClure says that many liberals (e.g., Clinton Administration) and conservationists support HCPs because they see it as the only way to minimize "harm to species on private lands" – that more will be gained by "getting landowners to sign up to protect species than going after violators" according to a USFWS official because the government simply lacks the resources to prosecute except in a few of "the most flagrant cases." McClure and Stiffler's series was based in part on a 1999 study by Peter Kareiva and other researchers at National Center for Ecological Analysis and Synthesis that analyzed 208 HCPs. Kareiva et al. found that "barely 50 percent of the agreements contain clear monitoring plans" and few contained monitoring sufficient to determine the plan's success [161]. They point out that monitoring is essential if "adaptive management" is to be employed. They also point out that lack of adequate data about threatened species makes it difficult to use a "precautionary approach"– precaution did not appear evident in most HCPs they studied.

Li and Male state that "while monitoring and periodic reevaluation are a stated component of CCAA, HCPs, and other ESA tools, they have *rarely been used* [emphasis added] to their full potential" [139 p. 93]. This author has only been able to find one published study in a peer-reviewed journal that evaluates the outcomes of implementation of HCPs – a study by Schweik and Thomas of the Coachella Valley (California) HCP aimed at saving the fringe-toed lizard [162]. They employed Landsat satellite images and found no evidence of non-compliance with the plan, but the images revealed that the majority of the habitat for the lizard was outside the HCP preserve system [162 p. 255]. They point out that these satellite images are easily available for such use – their evaluation cost $10,000 which they noted was small compared to the "seven million dollars collected in developer fees for the main preserve." The USFWS did commission "an Independent Evaluation of the U.S. Fish and Wildlife Service's Habitat Conservation Plan Program" conducted by Management Systems International [163]. One limitation of this evaluation is that (due to the number and variety of HCPs) it is based heavily on case studies of twelve large HCPs. They make some important points such as the fact that there were (in 2009) 584 HCP plans but over 99 percent of the land covered by them is in only 57 HCPs while 34 percent of HCPs are tiny and cover only one acre or less [163 p. ii]. The report concludes that virtually every large

HCP is effective in the sense of avoiding or minimizing take of listed species, and establishing "acceptable mitigation" steps that compensate for species that are taken [163 p. ii–iii]. They emphasize the HCPs have been effective in terms of "leveraging funding" and thus "habitat lost to development was being replaced with conserved land at a ratio of two acres for each acre of land lost, and in several cases the replacement ratios were higher in order to compensate for habitat quality concerns" [163 p. iv]. The report also points out that HCPs are not responsible for "recovering species," though it concludes that most HCPs are assisting species such as through setting aside about one million acres of land (in 2009) "exclusively for protection of endangered and threatened species" [163 p. 53]. The evaluation did note a number of limitations and weaknesses in the HCP program. They state that the HCP program is "understaffed and underresourced" and devotes most of its time to HCP development with little time left for monitoring or responding to HCP applicants' needs [163 p. 1]. Related to this is the fact that ECOS (Environmental Conservation Online System) database is "incomplete and inaccurate ... Performance data are not tracked ... data that are supposed to be collected often are not" [163 p. 5]. The report states that there are no standards for gathering of scientific data and conducting peer reviews [163 p. 24 & 34]. They acknowledge that HCP applicants cannot control many factors that affect species survival (e.g., climate change). Li and Male acknowledge the problem of limited resources of the USFWS and suggest that monitoring and evaluation could be done by other actors such as academicians, non-governmental organizations, state agencies, and "proponents of the project" [139 p. 93].

The USFWS requires that monitoring of HCPs be done [164]. This should include periodic accountings of take, surveys to determine species status in project areas or mitigation habitats, and progress reports on fulfillment of mitigation requirements (e.g., habitat acres acquired). Monitoring plans for HCPs should establish target milestones to the extent practicable, or reporting requirements throughout the life of the HCP, and should address actions to be taken in case of unforeseen or extraordinary circumstances [164]:

In addition, the U.S. Fish and Wildlife Service must monitor the applicant's implementation of the HCPs and the permits terms and conditions; the biological conditions associated with the HCP to determine if species' needs are being met, and must determine if the biological goals that are expected as part of the HCP mitigation and minimization strategy are being realized.

Consequently, there are many documents across the country submitted by organizations responsible for the HCPs and ITPs (Incidental Take Permits), though there is no central database of these reports maintained by USFWS according to Trish Adams, National Habitat Conservation Planning Coordinator (personal communication, April 30, 2015). It is instructive to examine some actual monitoring reports. One such report concerns the endangered scrub jay bird in Indian River (Florida) County [165]. The report notes that Indian River County has been undertaking significant habitat restoration efforts that should help the scrub jay in the long term but notes that they found twelve families – one less than the prior year – and only five successful fledglings. Moreover, even if the restoration is successful, the report acknowledges that it may take "several years for the jay population to respond positively" [165 p. 5–6]. A major emerging problem is predation due to "feral and unleashed cats" that needs to be dealt with by the city of San Sebastian through public education, trapping, and "fining" of cat owner households under the local leash law if they do not keep their cats controlled. The report also notes the impact of road kills with "road-naïve immigrants" (scrub jays) suffering "extremely high annual mortality during their first 2 years as breeders ... in many cases not even surviving long enough to attempt nesting." The report recommends placement of "slow, wildlife/scrub-jay crossing" signs and rumble strips in the areas. Another example of a monitoring report is that submitted by Monroe County (Florida) Department of Planning and Environmental Resources concerning its HCP for Key Deer [166]. The report focuses on the number of deaths due to vehicles (the major cause of death for the deer) and notes that the number of such deaths first exceeded 100 in 2003 and reached its maximum in 2012 at 161 but declined to 117 in 2013. The other major focus of the report concerns a comparison of habitat acquired versus that lost due to development (a ratio of about 7.48 to 1 in 2013). The report does not provide any information on attempts to deal with the deaths due to accidents. The USFWS does have ECOS links to reports including five-year reviews, summary and evaluation for listed species (these are not directly related to specific HCPs and ITPs.) The USFWS is required by the ESA to conduct a status review of each listed species at least once every five years to evaluate whether or not the species' status has changed since it was listed. For example, USFWS issued a 2013 report on the spectacled eider (bird) that was first listed in 1993. It assigned a priority of 5 to the species on a scale where 1 is most endangered and 18 is the least threatened. A "5 priority" means that the "species faces a high degree of threat and has a low probability of recovery" [167 p. 3]. There are three main populations of the bird, two in Alaska (Yukon-Kuskokwim Delta and Arctic Coastal Plain) and one in Russia, about which little is known. This species forages during winter for prey such as clams, and relies on ice to save energy (estimates are that swimming in water consumes as much as 1.9 times as much energy) and there is concern that climate change could harm them, though there is no empirical evidence on this yet. Major threats are predation by arctic foxes and gulls. However, a proven threat that increases their mortality rate is lead shot that resides in the ice. In 2006 and 2007 the State of Alaska Board of Game passed regulations prohibiting the use of lead shot for upland game bird hunting on the Arctic Coast and Delta areas where the bird resides and conducted education efforts with mixed success. Up until now, development has not been a threat in these areas of Alaska.

Overall, these HCP monitoring reports reveal how idiosyncratic and varied are the threats to hundreds of endangered species that exist in the United States, though there are common themes, especially with the regard to human developments and their associated occurrences such as taking of habitat for development and threats posed by increased use of roads, lights, and human pets. I was impressed with the evident effort at monitoring and attempt to take steps to protect endangered species in the reports reviewed. However, it is clear that many of the most important causes such as loss of habitat due to development along with traffic will persist and actually increase in the future.

Conclusion

The paradox of the ESA is that its supporters admit to basic underlying failures and limitations in the statute but want to keep it. For example, Dwyer, Murphy, and Ehrlich, who were associated with the Center for Conservation Biology, made several devastating critiques of the ESA including the following: (1) "No one suggests that the Federal ESA is realizing Congressional intent or has been implemented rationally or responsibly"; (2) "Everyone complains about the single species focus of the law that doesn't adequately protect biodiversity"; (3) "Everyone recognizes that certain provisions" "serve as real disincentives to real conservation of species" [168 p. 736]. But the authors proceeded to state "it is not time for a major overhaul of the ESA"! Why not? Writing during the Clinton Administration, they emphasized the flexibility introduced by the HCP modifications to the law as being able to address the problems. However, the resolution of the paradox also concerns politics – the likelihood is that any attempt to overhaul the law would likely either lead to a political debate and stalemate or result in a new ESA law that would be much weaker than the 1973 Act. There have been many failures to "overhaul" the Act. For example, during the 103rd Congress (during Bill Clinton's first term, January 1993–January 1995), both proponents and opponents of the ESA pointed to its problems and reauthorization hearings were held but no "viable policy solutions" or compromise emerged [169 p. 133]. Pro-ESA Democratic representative from California, George Miller, introduced several bills to strengthen the ESA but none passed [170 p. 11]. The *Economist* wrote an editorial that approved of how the George W. Bush Administration was "taming" the Act by using a "habitat-trading scheme" that "infuriates environmental purists" but is the "best hope" for protecting nature "with the need to keep the water running" [171].

The effectiveness of the ESA has been judged based on a variety of methods, and the degree of success found depends on the criteria employed. The number of delistings is one major criterion primarily emphasized by its opponents and, based on this criterion, the ESA appears to be a failure. Supporters and most researchers argue that using this single criterion is invalid because many of the species listed are in dire straits and merely preventing them from becoming extinct can be counted as a success; and that many species will need to be listed forever. There are many disagreements over how to assess the ESA, such as the time periods to be employed in determining minimum populations, and whether to include subspecies and hybrids in counts. Overall, most of the research cited tends to show that the ESA has helped to prevent extinctions and stabilized the populations of many threatened and endangered species. The text of the ESA does not require the consideration of costs in preserving species, but critics of law have identified economic costs incurred while supporters have pointed to economic benefits received by areas near protected lands.

The Act's species-by-species approach has, in effect, been modified by the heavy use of multispecies HCPs. But it is the strong attachment to charismatic species that has helped to achieve popular support for the legislation. Although there has been no major overhaul of the legislative Act, there have been major changes in its operation and impact due to the heavy expansion of the use of tools such as HCPs, CCAs, and experimental status (of threatened species). These tools have transformed the law in a way that many conservative critics have called for, though these critics would like to defang it much more. The use of these tools has allowed the USFWS to deal with its limited resources and minimize political threats such as the use of Congressional riders. Some environmentalists approve of the usage of these tools and view them as a necessity to achieve actions that otherwise would be unobtainable, as well as heading off threats to wholescale weakening of the ESA. Indeed, without compromises such as over the greater and Gunnison sage-grouse, there would have been a massive political outcry over the ESA. However, some view the compromises as giving in without obtaining any major benefits to species. Perhaps the most serious issue concerning the current operation of the ESA concerns the need to monitor these agreements to ensure that they are protecting species as promised. This task is difficult since some of the major recent agreements have been reached without public overview or clear compliance standards on private land HCPs. Likewise, staff and resources to monitor the agreements have to be provided, and often this does not appear to be the case. Thus, while the flexibility of these new tools has helped the ESA to survive, whether these voluntary agreements are being effectively implemented and preserving biodiversity remains open to question.

7   Comparative Wildlife Politics

A major theme of this book is that the intensity of human attitudes toward wildlife makes wildlife politics a salient issue not only in the politics of the United States but in nations throughout the world. In this chapter, I explore commonalities and differences among wildlife politics across nations. Are there any generalizations that hold true throughout the world? To what extent are wildlife politics dependent on the individual political institutions and cultures of nations?

U.S. Wildlife Politics Comparisons with Other Developed Nations

The comparison of U.S. and Canadian wildlife politics is especially appropriate to begin with, since these two nations share many fauna and flora as well as a similar colonial political and cultural heritage from Great Britain. There are several cases of Canada following the United States's example, such as the fact that they copied "word for word" U.S. legislation when they passed the Canadian National Parks Act of 1930 that the parks should be "left unimpaired for the use of future generations" [1 p. 361]. Lack of personnel and resources with expertise in wildlife also led Canada to rely on U.S. examples and experts. Sandlos says that Canada relied upon USFWS expertise for monitoring waterfowl in Manitoba during the 1950s and consulted with U.S. conservationist William Hornaday in devising their policy for protection of species such as bison. But Sandlos also notes some important differences between the two nations due to climate [1 p. 367]. In particular, the aridity of the U.S. West led to a much larger Federal presence in the United States than in Canada due to the need for Federal action to conserve water.

There are also significant historical differences. Foster points out that Canada lacked the influence of strong environmental organizations like the Sierra Club and Audubon Society during the nineteenth century, as well as individual champions of preservation like John Muir, and these differences help to explain why Canada encouraged development in their Rocky Mountain Park while the United States took more of a "preservationist" approach to Yellowstone [2 p. 4 & 25]. Foster acknowledges that another major reason for this difference is that the threats of development were much greater in the United States than in Canada, and this rapid development helped to stimulate the organization of preservationist movements [2 p. 220]. Amos, Harrison, and Hober ask why Canada was so far behind the United States in species protection given the fact that

Canada had signed the Convention on Biodiversity in 1992 but still did not have national endangered species legislation and their Species at Risk law (SARA) was not enacted until 2002 [3 p. 137]. They argue that, although species protection had high approval, the support for it was very shallow in Canada and that "businesses and landowners" felt that the proposed legislation went too far [3 p. 144]. However, as pointed out in other chapters, support for environmental and wildlife issues in the United States also tends to be "broad but shallow." Illical and Harrison state that the delay in the passage of the Canadian species protection legislation and differences between it and the U.S. Endangered Species Act (ESA) were due to "negative lessons that Canadian businesses and agricultural interests drew from the U.S. ESA experience" [4 p. 373]. As discussed in Chapter 4, in the United States, the private sector and most legislators did not realize the significance of the ESA and consequently this very forceful legislation was passed with almost unanimous support. That was no longer the case when it came time to pass the Canadian species protection law. Consequently, the Canadian and U.S. species acts are significantly different: the Canadian Species at Risk Act sought to achieve its goals through cooperation and governmental spending rather than regulatory coercion, and SARA gives the executive more "discretion" and flexibility, allowing the Cabinet to veto recommendations made on the basis of science "due to socioeconomic reasons." However, Canada does not always trail the United States in its conservation efforts. For example, Johns [5 p. 287–8] cites Canada's greater adherence to biological conservation while the Yellowstone ecosystem has suffered from "reversals" such as the "roadless rule rescission," referring to the reversal by the Bush Administration to curtail the Clinton Administration's plan to designate 59 million roadless acres in national forests, as well as the delisting of wolves in the United States, and the allowance of snowmobiles in Yellowstone backcountry. These U.S. policy reversals were supported by conservative groups like the Federalist Society [6].

Interest groups of sportspersons and anglers have been influential in both countries. For example, Willison says that Atlantic salmon were not listed as "vulnerable or threatened" in Canada due to the political influence of anglers [7 p. 108]. Likewise, Canadians failed to list species such as the porbeagle shark despite losses of 90 percent in "abundance" due to desire to avoid economic losses to one or two fishers dependent on the species [8 p. 574–5]. Constitutional and legal differences also matter. Illical and Harrison point to the fact that Canadian environmental groups are more limited in their role because the Canadian ESA did not include any citizen suit provision that has been the basis for so many listings and so much controversy in the United States [4 p. 379].

In both countries, the division of powers between the Federal government and states (for the United States) and provinces (for Canada) is a key issue. Provinces have greater control over wildlife than the states have in the United States when it involves international treaties [2 p. 140]. For example, British Columbia received a ten-year exclusion from a treaty mandating a "closed season on swans, cranes, and curlews" and Foster says that this exemption was "absolutely necessary for the success of the treaty" [2 p. 140]. Bocking also says that provinces have more authority than U.S. states over natural resources because the Canadian Federal government's authority was "circum-scribed" to "national parks, reserves, and the territories" and thus negotiation of international agreements concerning endangered species by Canada were dominated by Federal-provincial relations [9 p. 127]. Salazar and Alper point to the fact that environmental groups have been able to achieve "substantial protection" of wildlife in the United States through Federal laws and Federal control of natural resources, but there is "little in Canadian Federal law" that would allow similar actions [10 p. 3–21]. Cioc cites a case where the New Brunswick legislature repealed "all of its waterfowl regulations" to protest Federal legislation and the Nova Scotia and Prince Edward Island legislatures refused to hire game wardens to enforce the act, though this latter example is not so different from U.S. Western state resistance to protection of wolves [11 p. 81]. The implications of provincial influence are significant because only seven out of ten of the provinces had passed endangered species legislation and the acts that did pass generally do not require listing even if scientists recommend it – listing is at the discretion of the Cabinet and those that are listed are not often protected [12 p. 963]. The grizzly has not been listed under the Federal Species at Risk Act and the "provincial governments have vehemently" resisted "any attempt" by the Federal government "to expand its authority into ... fields the provinces perceive as properly under provincial jurisdiction such as wildlife management" [13 p. 8]. In Alberta (Canada), property owners can shoot wolves "at any time of the year," can use poisoned bait, and some townships still offer "bounties" for wolves [14 p. 19]. Although the United States has generally led Canada in passing environmental legislation, there are some cases where Canada has been a leader, such as their establishment of the Wood Buffalo Park in 1922 to protect the "largest free roaming herd of larger and darker wood buffalo" [1 p. 363].

A comparison of the United States and Britain reveals significant differences due to their histories. Nash argues that the United States had much less interest in the "rights of nature" than the British because nature seemed to be "inexhaustible" in the United States while Britain by the nineteenth century lacked wilderness and focused their "environmental ideals" on the protection of domesticated animals [15 p. 35–6]. There tend to be consistent differences between U.S. conservation practices and European countries in general. Prato and Fagre state that there are generally more limitations in North American national parks on human "habitation and resource use" than there are in European parks [16 p. 39]. Ray and Ginsberg compared "endangered species acts" of Western nations and noted that Australia, like Canada, has "blurred lines" between Federal and provincial or state responsibilities due to the fact that the Australian Endangered Species Protection Act (ESPA) is restricted to Federally managed land (about 1 percent of the continent) [17 p. 956–8]. In one respect, the implementation of Australia's ESPA and the United States's ESA are similar: recovery plans have been completed and implemented for only a fraction (about 22 percent) of the listed species. The role of the Australian states (like Canada's provinces) is much more powerful than the authority of U.S. states [18 p. 960]. According to Woinarski and Fisher, these constraints on Federal authority have made it impossible to fight the "tide of biodiversity decline" [18 p. 959].

There are differences in national policies toward wolves between two neighboring Scandinavian countries: Sweden and Norway. Although the two countries have had a formal "joint recovery plan" for the wolves, the "comeback of wolves" has been generally welcomed in Sweden but strongly opposed by rural Norwegians [19]. The wolves are blamed for the killing of sheep, though defenders argue that more sheep are killed by other predators such as wolverines and lynx. A survey showed that 52 percent of Norwegians did not accept scientists' assurances that wolves were not a threat to people [19]. However, Monbiot cites a survey that about 80 percent of Norwegians want to keep wolves at their current population [20]. As in the U.S. experience with wolves, the influence of rural livestock owners and hunters who live in the area where wolves reside tends to dominate. The sheep-owners (and hunters) form a powerful group that have attracted support of the right-of-center (Norwegian) Centre party that controls environmental policy in the ruling coalition. Only three new litters of pups per year are permitted in Norway and the current population of twenty-five is insufficient to protect the species from the effects of inbreeding [20]. Indeed, a hunting quota of twelve for the winter of 2012 was adopted. By way of contrast, Sweden's environmental minister criticized the Norwegian actions toward wolves. Scandinavia currently has a population of seventy to eighty wolves but Sweden's goal is to have a "population of 500 that straddles the two countries" [19]. More recently, with the increase in wolves in Sweden, farmers have complained about losses of livestock to wolves and the fact they consider government compensation inadequate, while hunters complain about competition for prey and wolves became a significant issue in the last election, demonstrating that successful restoration can lead to more controversy [21]. Similar problems occurred with respect to brown bears between the two countries. Sweden managed successfully the growth of their brown bear population which led to individual bears migrating to Norway (where the brown bear had been exterminated by 1930) and the bears caused problems because livestock producers in Norway had "adopted less intensive husbandry leaving sheep unattended" and consequently led to great pressures for the problem bears to be killed [22 p. 76]. There is also a contrast between formal environmental policies and actions with respect to wolves in Norway. Norway signed a plan to preserve biological diversity at the Convention on Biological Diversity in 2012 and the wolf is on Norway's endangered species list. In both Sweden and Norway, there is evidence of a big discrepancy between attitudes of urban and rural residents (especially those living near the carnivores), and both countries have been seeking ways of decentralizing policies to regional "game management delegations" as a method of dealing with these strains [23 p. 391]. Norway has also had problems with predation of sheep by lynx, which have emerged due to the near-historical extinction of large predators such as wolves and bears, which led to a decline in "close shepherding" and the use of fences in Norway [24 p. 143]. Thus as predators make a comeback, loss of sheep has become a problem. This discrepancy between urban and rural attitudes is similar to the tensions in the U.S. Western states and the attempt of Sweden to find "collaborative management techniques" to reduce these tensions is reminiscent of the compromises proposed by the Clinton and Obama Administrations concerning spotted owls and wolves [23]. Italy is a country where wolves have enjoyed a renaissance. There are now some 500 wolves in Italy – they were first legally protected in 1976 [25 p. 8]. McNamee says many wolves live on the outskirts of major cities such as Florence and Milan – a situation that would be unthinkable in the United States. He cites one Italian wolf scientist as explaining the greater acceptance of wolves in Italy is a result of "ancestral culture" [25 p. 8]. The "restoration" of wolves in France was, according to a 1995 opinion poll, welcomed by 79 percent of the general public [26 p. 99]. But, as in the United States and Scandinavian countries, livestock owners (mainly sheep-owners in France) did not want wolves in their areas, and the government began to have different policies in pastoral areas where "control of wolves" was allowed versus total protection in some park areas [26 p. 102–3]. According to Campion-Vincent, the local agents of the county and agricultural departments as well as personnel hired by the environmental department heeded the views of the sheep-owners despite "noisy complaints" from national forces [26 p. 117]. Again, this same dilemma is faced in the United States by employees of the USFWS faced with implementing policies disliked by ranchers and hunters.

Valerius Geist hails the "North American model of wildlife conservation," comparing it favorably with the commercial, privatized model common in European countries such as Germany [27 p. 48]. He acknowledges that originally wildlife in the United States was treated as a "commons," and this fact led to its decimation, but that "a small elite" terminated the commons policy by putting effective controls over the exploitation of public resources [27 p. 50]. The North American model is based on certain key principles including the "public ownership of wildlife" and the elimination of "markets" for meat from game animals [27 p. 52]. In addition, it is marked by the dominance of law in prohibiting poaching and the allocation of the "benefits of wildlife." Geist argues that these policies resulted in greater jobs and economic benefits than the German wildlife system which is based on private control [27 p. 54]. Critics argue that Geist ignores the contributions of conservationists including preservationists such as John Muir to wildlife conservation – that setting aside parks helped to protect U.S. endangered species [14 p. 247].

Attitudes toward wildlife in advanced industrialized nations have changed through time – concern with the preservation of most species did not use to be a major concern. Thus Saberwal criticizes policy recommendations by the Wildlife Conservation Society to preserve the tiger through "the eviction of humans from tiger habitat," arguing that the United States would "never treat rights of [its] citizens versus mountain lions like that [28 p. 815–16]. Saberwal asks "where in the Western World would the killing of an animal in defense of life or property be characterized as 'illegal?'" [28 p. 816]. However, Jacoby describes how U.S. state governments passed laws to "protect the wilderness from the recklessness of rural folk" dating back to the late nineteenth century and adopted "European forestry standards" which made subsistence hunting illegal and turned fishermen and hunters into "squatters and thieves," though Jacoby admits that local hunters and fishermen often ignored or resisted the laws with violence [29 p. 198]. Jacoby cites one *New York Times* correspondent as saying that he had not "found a single instance in which the state forestry laws were obeyed" in the Adirondacks State Park that was established in the in the 1890s [29 p. 48]. Prior to the establishment of state parks, wealthy families such as the Rockefellers set up "private parks" that were much resented by the public [29 p. 43–7]. Partly this lack of obedience was due to the "myth of the inexhaustibility of natural resources" [15 p. 35]. As time passed and outside market hunters began to invade their territory, decimating the supply of local game, local people became less overtly resisting of the laws but complained that the laws were "simplistic" and did "take into account their wants and needs" [29 p. 66]. Some of the locals replaced their lost subsistence support by obtaining jobs as guides to outside hunters and fishermen to the area [29 p. 67]. Eventually these guides banded together to form the Adirondacks Guide Association, which supported new laws controlling the hunting of does and bears as well as steps to restore certain species such as beavers to the park [29 p. 70–1]. In short, the history of U.S. wildlife conservation shows that it took a long time for policy to evolve from a "commons" approach characterized by few controls over taking of wildlife to its current state with a multitude of conservation regulations that are generally enforced.

Japan is an advanced country that contrasts with the United States in terms of treatment of wildlife. Williams [30 p. 27] says that the country's "nascent environmental movement" is reluctant to criticize governmental policies and cites the Sierra Club's chairman as stating that Japan is the only "highly developed and prosperous country that doesn't have an environmental movement of any strength" and that environmental researcher Stephen Kellert characterizes the Japanese "as [preferring to be] wards of the environment rather than stewards of it" [30 p. 27].

The Politics of Wildlife in Developing Countries

David Johns states that the most basic difference among countries with respect to conservation policy is "between states that can carry out policy effectively and those which are ineffective" [5 p. 287]. He goes on to argue that in states with "weak centers of power," control over conservation policy largely "lie outside of formal centers of power" such as with "local economic elites" and "international corporations and institutions" [5]. He says that "only engagement in the political realm can . . . reverse the destruction of nature" and thus countries with weak central governments cannot effectively counter the universal commitment of societies to "material growth" and conversion of "nature into commodities" [5]. George Francis also argues that "governance for conservation" is based on the "existence of a strong center for political decision making" as well as "administrative capacity" and a commitment to "sustainable development" [31 p. 230–1]. There are cultural differences between and within nations that affect the treatment of nature. For example, Maasai "do not eat wild animals for food except in dire circumstances" plus their "maintenance of grazing lands" through fire rather than agricultural cultivation helps to support the richness of wildlife in much of East Africa [32 p. 272]. Still, many Africans hunt wildlife for subsistence needs. In West African countries like Ghana, bushmeat hunting of fruit bats has become a threat to these species and also a threat to the health of populations because consumption can introduce "pathogens" that can cause illnesses in humans [33]. African wildlife researchers employed Stephen Kellert's typology of three dimensions of attitudes toward animals: naturalistic, utilitarian, and moralistic, but found the need to add another dimension important in "most African cultures: fatalism" [34 p. 58].

Latin America, according to Steinhart, has "no tradition of conservation." Although all Andean nations have laws against shooting spectacled bears, nevertheless they are not safe even in national parks [35 p. 101]. Steinhart says that "there is no ability to manage or control what happens in parks" and that national parks "have no political constituency." The lack of resources to enforce rules is common in Latin American countries – for example, "only 10 out of Columbia's 33 national parks even have staff" [35 p. 100]. There are differences among Latin American nations such as Ecuador being more "protective of nature" than Columbia. Steinhart emphasizes that in poor countries "there are so many pressing needs that national politicians are unlikely to act on behalf of conservation" [35 p. 102]. Mexico has weak enforcement of their environmental regulations and lacks environmental laws that "explicitly protect grasslands" [36]. Consequently, in Mexico as in many developing countries, it is NGOs (non-governmental organizations) from advanced countries that spur many conservation measures. For example, the Nature Conservancy established a ranch in 2005 in Mexico to "serve as an outdoor laboratory" and "imported 36 bison from South Dakota" [36]. According to Gupta, this example spurred the Mexican government to create a 1.3 million acre "biosphere reserve" [36]. Costa Rica's former minister of environment and energy argues that a significant source of the differences between countries concerns whether their "forest service department resides under the minister of agriculture" or "under the minister of environment" with the former viewing forests as "something to cut down for timber" or other "productive uses" [37].

In Africa, cultural attitudes toward wildlife can vary depending on the particular values of tribal societies. For example, Franklin says that the Nuer in South Sudan "display great love for their domesticated cattle" but have "low regard for wild animals" while Lele society of Zaire "despise" domestic animals but value wild animals for their "goodness, grace, and beauty" [38 p. 9]. Cultural values are subject to change in African countries such as Kenya, where traditional culture revered elephants, but these cultural values have broken down and guns are replacing bows and arrows. Many developing countries' wildlife policies have been strongly influenced by the policies of colonial powers such as Great Britain. Duffy has characterized colonial policy toward African wildlife as viewing wildlife as an "object of leisure," in contrast to the locals who viewed wildlife as a source of meat [39 p. 11]. Colonial authorities acted to exclude locals from "safari areas and national parks" [39 p. 11]. Neumann, writing in 1992, traced the evolution of Tanzania's decision to establish the Arusha National Park in the Mt. Meru area of Tanzania to British colonial administrators who searched for ways to protect African wildlife and focused on the examples of Yellowstone National Park and Kruger National Park (in South Africa), as recommended by an English conservation group [40 p. 85–9]. Both of these parks prohibited human habitation and economic activity in the parks, which, in Tanzania, meant that the establishment of these parks was based on this model that displaced peasant farmers and owners of cattle. Neumann claims that the imposition of these parks alienated the local populations so that they felt that the park was of "no benefit to them" and they had "little interest in cooperating with the state wildlife conservation efforts" [40]. The monies from entry fees to the Arusha National Park went to the national treasuries and did not benefit the local communities.

Although the local Meru residents like the Maasai "did not have a strong tradition of hunting," they did not report outside poachers because of their feeling that they had been "shut out of the political process" [40 p. 85 & 95]. Barrow, Gichohi, and Infield argue that history differentiates East from South Africa because East Africa was inhabited "largely by pastoralists" and "remained under customary land tenure" while "the settler communities in Southern Africa … converted [the land] into private farms and cattle ranches, establishing a tradition of … private ownership that has had a great influence on the evolution of conservation policies in the two regions" [41 p. 60]. Thus supporters of giving full property rights over wildlife to communities and individuals often cite the South African example of the success of this approach to conservation. South Africa has over 10,000 private wildlife ranches and private "wildlife utilization enterprises" that cover nearly 17 percent of the country, compared to only about 6 percent for national and provincial protected areas [42]. There has been a big increase in species that have become threatened in East Africa (e.g., rhinos). However, there are dangers and limitations to the private wildlife approach to conservation including: (1) they sometimes crossbreed and thus create hybrid species; (2) they tend to breed species for trophy hunting and this "intensive captive breeding" can cause "genetic pollution"; (3) alien species may be introduced; and (4) they may allow use of what many regard as unfair chase in hunting such as the use of baiting and floodlights [42]. South Africa has enacted "Threatened and Protected Species" regulations to address some of these issues. However, the result has been the fragmentation of wildlife into a large number of small, fenced-in enclosures that are "too small to support genetically healthy predator populations" [42]. Although trophy hunting has been viewed as a primary source of benefits to African countries, the total amount of spending by these foreign hunters is only a fraction of the value of domestic hunters (about US$450 million compared to about US $130 million in 2005) in South Africa [43 p. 36].

Nash describes the distinction between "nature importing and exporting" nations. Wealthy advanced industrial countries have largely destroyed much of their "wild nature" as a part of the "civilizing process" [44 p. 343]. Consequently the wildlife of some developing countries has the possibility of being the equivalent of an "export industry" as tourists from wealthy countries spend foreign currencies in the enjoyment of wild nature not present in their own countries. Nash points to 1933 as the "high point of global nature protection" when England and other colonial powers signed a convention that encouraged the establishment of national parks [44 p. 360]. In 1962, Nash describes how at the First World Conference on National Parks, then U.S. Secretary of Interior, Stewart Udall, argued that African countries would eventually reap economic rewards from tourists to their national parks even if in the short term they might regret them. In 1968, many African nations signed the "African Convention for Conservation of Nature and Natural Resources" supporting the park policy because they had realized that "nature business was good business" [44 p. 372].

Chinese cultural traditions have created a huge demand for ivory. According to Levin, "ivory carving" has been recognized as an "official intangible cultural heritage" and many "Chinese think that giving a trinket made from elephant ivory confers the highest honor" [45]. He cites the president of the Shanghai Collectors' Association as saying that "the prestige and artistry of ivory outweigh any concern with provenance" [45]. The Chinese government has taken several measures to change attitudes toward consumption of illegal ivory, such as publicizing arrests of smugglers, having Chinese embassies in Africa issue warnings concerning the buying of ivory, and sponsoring campaigns by celebrities such as basketball star Yao Ming against use of poached ivory [45]. But critics say that the Chinese message has often been "muddled" such as allowing Chinese visiting Zimbabwe to return with 22 pounds of "carved" ivory souvenirs and their failure to control the activities of syndicates responsible for large-scale smuggling [45]. Dinerstein claims that some supposed cultural traditions such as Chinese desire for rhino horns are a dangerous myth because there had been little demand for the horns, but the media "misconception" about Chinese demand helps to fuel poaching [46 p. 31].

The Chinese have faced a similar challenge concerning the protection of pandas. Schaller recounts how until the late 1980s, it lacked "comprehensive legislation to protect wildlife" and that penalties for killing pandas (two years of jail) were "no deterrent" to poachers, so valuable were their hides [47 p. 224–5]. Then the Chinese Supreme Court increased the penalties to ten years or even possibly life imprisonment or the death penalty. Harris characterizes the Chinese perception of wildlife as being "utilitarian" in nature, which means that they primarily view wildlife in terms of how it affects human "life and livelihood" – not for its intrinsic beauty or value [48 p. 138–9]. Harris says that, though the Chinese are proud of their nature reserves, they are not "managed appreciably different than unprotected lands" and "staffing levels are low" with little spent "on patrol or law enforcement" and conservation goals are subordinated to "economic land uses favored by local counties" [48 p. 138–9]. Schaller quotes a poacher sentenced to life imprisonment as saying that he still would have poached because "if he hadn't been caught, he would be rich" [47 p. 227]. Schaller says that though habitat loss of bamboo is the major long-term threat to pandas, the control of poaching would help in the short term and should be "easy and inexpensive" but doing the "necessary patrolling is a hard and thankless task" – similar to the situation in other developing countries with large populations of poor people living near the endangered species [47 p. 224–5].

India illustrates how conservation efforts can ebb and flow over time. Teer, writing in 1993, cites data that India's Project Tiger was an initial success increasing the tiger population from 1800 in 1973 to over 4000, but that setting aside reserves that were "formerly used by people" has caused "antipathy towards conservation in the country" and Teer argues that conservation cannot be successful "in spite of human interest" [49 p. 82–3]. Indira Gandhi's Administration stopped many timber operations in tiger reserve areas and illustrates the huge impact that a strong leader can have on wildlife conservation. She had a lifelong interest in wildlife and supported bans on trade in tiger and leopard skins, stating that "foreign exchange was important, but not at the cost of some of the most beautiful inhabitants of the country" [50 p. 196]. According to Rahmani, she played a "crucial role in virtually every step of Project Tiger [50]. However, the effects of strong executive action can be weakened by subsequent leaders who are not so committed and large-scale "infrastructure development" was begun again by her son's (Rajiv's) Administration "in seven of India's finest wildlife reserves" that were supposed to be a "model for preserving biodiversity while helping local inhabitants" [51 p. 305]. Saghal and Scarlott argue that this new policy was based on the false assumption that tigers and people "could live in close proximity with no harm to either" and that this policy was supported by some "pliable wildlife experts" who had argued the opposite in earlier times [51 p. 306]. Saghal and Scarlott conclude that "from 1990 on political support for Project Tiger virtually vanished" [51 p. 310]. Seiden-sticker, Christie, and Jackson say that the "heavy-handed top-down" approach to tiger conservation in India did not work and that the tiger reserve system is in "tatters" except for certain exceptions such as Nagarahole National Park (in southern India) due to their isolation [52 p. 197].

The Gandhi-India case points to an important factor influencing conservation that was not part of the frameworks in Chapter 1. It concerns the values and interests of dominant "political leaders" which case studies have shown to be crucial in countries across the world. In the United States, many of Theodore Roosevelt's conservation actions were not based on popular demands but were rather due to his personal interest. Other more recent cases illustrate the same point. Vladimir Putin has led the movement in Russia to save the tiger and to "reintroduce the Persian leopard to Southern Russia to compensate for the negative environmental impacts" of the Sochi Olympics [53 p. 65]. In Chile during the 1960s, President Eduardo Frei Montalva undertook a conservation campaign comparable to Teddy Roosevelt's and "no other president before or after has created more protected areas, in either number or total area conserved" [54 p. 232]. The despicable dictator Ceausescu of Romania "enacted anti-poaching laws" and "enforced strict hunting regulations" that resulted in "an abundance of wildlife throughout the 1970s and 1980s" [55 p. 214]. When strong leaders or dictators enact conservation based on their own interests, these innovations are subject to quick reversal when they are no longer in charge, as occurred in India, but in the Roosevelt and Frei cases, their impact endured.

Elephants in India also have created controversy. As is the case in most developing countries, habitat for elephants and other wildlife has been rapidly decreasing due to deforestation and booming human populations [56]. Romig cites the founder of the Asian Nature Conservation organization, Raman Sukamar, as saying that although Asian elephants have been on the endangered list since 1986, their numbers (contrary to in the rest of the world) have been increasing in India. However, he fears that this trend may be reversed because recently about 500 people per year have been killed by elephants and elephant–human conflict has been increasing due to the loss of habitat [56]. There are also conflicts over how captive elephants should be treated in India. Romig depicts the harsh life of "celebrity elephants," but Sukamar claims that the net effect of their use in festivals is positive, because people are less likely to kill elephants if "they associate them with Lord Ganesha" [56].

Because wildlife is an industry that brings in revenues from foreign hunters and tourists, the politics of natural resources tend to be externally driven in developing countries. For example, Alexander Songorwa, the director of wildlife for the Tanzanian Ministry of Natural Resources and Tourism, pleaded in an opinion piece for the

New York Times that the USFWS not list the African lion as an endangered species because Songorwa said lions are not threatened in Tanzania and trophy hunters had contributed $75 million to the Tanzanian economy from 2008 to 2011 [57]. However, wildlife researchers found that lion harvests have been decreasing by 50 percent in Tanzania and that the current allotment of 500 lions (and 400 leopards) killed each year was unsustainable and recommended that age restrictions be placed (five years for male lions and seven years for leopards) to "minimize the effects of trophy hunting" [58 p. 150–1]. Osnos finds a dilemma with elephants in Thailand where elephants serve "both as equipment and icon" [59]. Thai laws allow them to be "sold and destroyed like cattle" even though Buddhism gives them "a privileged status" [59]. The elephants are used by some as "income producers" as they parade through the street and their owners collect donations – though the Thai government has tried to ban the practice [59]. According to Osnos, mistreatment of elephants has led to traumatic impacts resulting in males sometimes "lashing out at farmers and loggers" in Uganda, India, and Thailand.

Community-Based Natural Resources Management and Politics

Over the last generation, the major movement to preserve wildlife in developing countries has been the attempt to establish and implement community-based natural resources management (CBNRM). (Note: I will use this term throughout this book but there are many other terms used to denote virtually the same concept, such as community-based conservation, community wildlife management, collaborative management, and integrated conservation and development) [60 p. 13]. CBNRM takes many forms, but there are common themes with the basic idea that people who live around protected areas need to participate in the management of wildlife and other natural resources because these local communities (mainly rural) face the costs of preserving wildlife and the wildlife often threaten their crops and, in some cases, lives. Thus the idea behind CBNRM is to create the incentives on the part of the local communities to preserve wildlife by providing them a share of the benefits derived from tourism and hunting, as well as participation in the management and enforcement of park regulations [61 p. 121]. According to Wilshusen, Brechin, Fortwangler, and West, the 1982 World Congress on Parks and Protected areas was the "turning point" in African conservation with CBNRM approaches being formally encouraged [62 p. 1–2]. Historically, the central governments and other influential groups in these countries as well as foreign companies and foreign corporations have received most of the benefits, and thus the implementation of successful CBNRM is a complex and difficult undertaking as illustrated in the case studies of individual countries in Nelson's book, *Community Rights, Conservation and Contested Land: The Politics of Natural Resource Governance in Africa* [63].

One argument is that state-dominated wildlife conservation fails because, although African states claim "ownership" of wildlife, they are not in fact able to enforce this ownership and hence local users "who do not have rights" over the wildlife exploit the resources in a non-sustainable manner, lacking incentive for conservation [64 p. 8].

Cowlishaw, Mendelson, and Rowcliffe point out that in Ghana, the Congo and the "region in general," there is limited "institutional capacity" to implement "systems" and that public awareness and state enforcement of wildlife laws are "extremely limited" and "good governance" has to be addressed before management can be successful [65 p. 44]. Nelson says that there is a "wealth of evidence" that local management protects forests better than "state-protected areas." However, the degree of success of CBNRM in benefiting local populations and thus changing their attitudes toward local wildlife is open to question. For example, Murombedzi claims that CBNRM can actually increase the "reach of states into local communities" and he uses the example of Zimbabwe which has inherited from colonial powers the idea of state dominance of wildlife derived from the King's game tradition [66 p. 34–41]. He says that CBNRM initiatives such as Zimbabwe's "private freehold wildlife conservancies" are often "dominated by elite interests" of private companies and foreign capital invested in tourist infrastructure [66 p. 45–6]. He proceeds to argue that many locals lose more than they gain from CBNRM and that consultation with local communities is often only "token" [66 p. 48]. There are also limits to the amount of revenues that can be derived from trophy hunting. For example, according to Murphree, the Mahenye region of Zimbabwe's revenues from hunting of elephants had reached a plateau by the early 1990s and was constrained by the fact that they could only have sustained hunting of two to four elephants per year [67 p. 191].

Zimbabwe is the home of one of the first and most famous of CBNRM programs, CAMPFIRE, an acronym for Community Areas Management Program for Indigenous Resources. There were several positive reviews during the early years of the CAMP-FIRE program. For example, Butler described how each CAMPFIRE community had an "animal reporter" to monitor wildlife and detect poachers, and that the community came to understand that a buffalo is worth more if it is killed by a "foreign hunter," though Butler also noted complaints from villages "with no wildlife resources" who do not receive any CAMPFIRE funds [68]. Gibson stated that "nearly all analyses of CAMPFIRE praise its innovation" and agree that there have been "financial gains and enthusiasm" for it by "local level officials" [69 p. 112]. Later reports on CAMPFIRE have been much more critical. Duffy says that CAMPFIRE illustrates an underlying problem of CBNRM approaches: the communities "are organizationally complex" [39 p. 92–104]. She says that theoretically "local District Councils" should make decisions but actually it is often the local chiefs who "allocate land" and they sometimes accept payment in return for "illegal settlement in their areas." Duffy also cites claims by some that CAMPFIRE has protected the interests of "white safari operators over those of rural people." McGregor has described a CBNRM program to incentivize fishermen to collect and preserve crocodile eggs in exchange for payments to local communities [70]. But, according to McGregor, these community payments were not sufficient to substitute for "individual income" to change fishermen's attitudes toward crocodiles, so other payments such as reparations for crocodile damage to fishermen nets are being considered. Rihoy, Chnirozva, and Anstey note that CAMPFIRE was "once the darling of the international donor community" but later became a pariah due to the overall political and economic disorder that began in Zimbabwe during the 1990s and has continued since [71 p. 177–8]. Robert Mugabe, a despotic leader, has headed the government since 1980. Under his leadership, the country became isolated and suspended from participation in the Commonwealth of Nations due to "election tampering" and forced land seizures [72]. Thus the success of CBNRM is dependent on a stable political system if it is to attract ecotourists. However, Balint and Mashinya report that trophy hunting in Zimbabwe has suffered much less loss of income due to Mugabe because "trophy hunters are less bothered by bad politics than ecotourists" [73 p. 792–5]. They go on to state that poaching continues to be controlled in the Mahenye and Nyaminyami areas despite drops in CAMPFIRE benefits because the locals have appeared to "internalize" the CAMPFIRE goals. However, Murombedzi [66 p. 253] states that local trackers are not valued by foreign hunters and that (as of 2001) no trainee from the CAMPFIRE training programs had qualified as a guide while Hulme and Murphree [74 p. 295] cite "anecdotes" that hunters hold "right-wing views" and prefer to be guided by white guides.

Adams uses the example of CAMPFIRE to illustrate the danger of "premature overenthusiastic dissemination of positive outcomes" that lead to "misleading narratives of success" often as a result of people "engaged" with the projects [75 p. 302]. But the opposite problem can also occur. Jones and Murphree cite a case where U.S. Agency for International Development (USAID) officials wanted to end support for a community project in Namibia because it did not produce "rapid results," but project implementers resisted and the project turned out later to be the first to be successful [76 p. 54]. Hulme and Infield also emphasize the importance of taking time before making assessments of the successes or failures of community projects, pointing out that community projects are fragile devices, subject to sudden cessations in funding and dependent on "a small number of key personnel" [77 p. 126]. Although Jones agrees that most benefits of CBNRM programs have been low, he says that when there are only small communities of people living next to the highly valued wildlife (in Namibia) that these apparently small benefits in terms of jobs and benefits can be significant [78 p. 161–8].

Bergin challenges the assumption that CBNRM makes law enforcement unnecessary because both policing and "the community approach" are needed as the "right and left hands of one management strategy" [79 p. 103]. Many studies of CBNRM projects have found small benefits accruing to individuals in the communities, but Hulme and Infield say that "though the sums are small . . . they are larger than those that could be expected from government" [77 p. 118]. Still, they proceed to state that CBNRM benefits are "minute" compared to what could be obtained from grazing and cultivation [77 p. 127]. There are several reasons why agricultural returns would be so much higher, including subsidies given to the agricultural sector, such as duty and tax exemptions on imported agricultural equipment, low interest credit facilities, agricultural price fixing, and protection against imported agricultural commodities [80 p. 222].

Rihoy and Maguranyanga found that Botswana has employed a form of CBNRM using "local trusts" in the form of community-based organizations (CBOs) which were supposed to receive the benefits from wildlife by applying for "user rights" to the Botswana Department of Wildlife and National Parks [81 p. 55–8]. Rihoy et al. report that some of these CBOs did receive several hundred thousand dollars from hunting and tourism and that they contributed to keeping wildlife numbers stable during the 1990s [81 p. 58–9]. However, they also found that the implementation of CBNRM in Botswana "has been problematic" and that the "high visibility of expatriate staff" has led to the view that CBNRM is being imposed upon them by a foreign "environmental paradigm." Nelson and Agrawal point out that Botswana's "conservancies" are based on administrative policies rather than legislative provisions as is the case with Namibia's (see below) and thus has proven to be more fragile [82 p. 567–8]. They go on to say that despite the fact that Botswana's civil servants are "high quality," its policymaking is largely "top down" and patrimonial with local communities benefiting only "marginally." Mordi says that the growing population of cattle, goats, and sheep and consequent "overgrazing" are primarily responsible for the "degradation of wildlife habitat" especially in the Kalahari area of Botswana [83 p. 109–10]. This development was, he says, spurred by the "sinking of thousands of wells" and the commercialization of land in the Kalahari [83]. He contrasts the "exalted status of cattle" due to the fact they are owned by the people, with the indifference to wildlife, which are owned by the state, and cites the lack of "internal tourism" as indicative of the lack of a "humanistic attitude towards wildlife" [83 p. 138]. He notes that the lack of a welfare system in Botswana means that many poor hunt wildlife in order to survive and argues that the requirement that wildlife "justify their existence" is a long-term threat to the goals of conservation [83 p. 144].

In Kenya, tourism is "second only to agriculture as a source of foreign currency" and a review of the country's conservation efforts shows how complex it is to protect wildlife and attempt to implement CBNRM [84 p. 2]. In 1989, Kenya's President Moi appointed Richard Leakey as head of Kenya's Wildlife Service (KWS). Leakey and Morell have described Leakey's efforts to improve the KWS's relationships with local communities by giving them "a share of revenues" as well as fencing some of the parks (e.g., Tsavo West) in order to protect nearby residents from attacks by animals [85]. Leaky's most famous action was to burn ivory and help initiate an international ban of the market sales of ivory (to be discussed extensively below). However, his effectiveness was dependent on support from President Moi but, as described by Gibson, Leakey did not "construct alliances with other politicians" and when Moi removed his political support, they moved to attack Leakey [69 p. 109]. The crucial importance of political stability to ecotourism is again shown by the sharp drop in tourism revenues following "the 2007/2008 election disturbances" in Kenya [86 p. 352]. Despite the importance of elephants and wildlife to Kenya's economy, "Kenya's Mombasa port" is the "continent's ... primary trafficking hub" for ivory due to the great degree of "corruption," the "marginalized status" of rural populations, and the easy availability of "small arms" [87 p. 58]. Despite relatively (compared to other central African countries) good resources, Kenya's patrols are not nearly sufficient to patrol areas with elephants, such as Tsavo, and the Kenyan judicial system sent only 4 percent of "offenders convicted to prison" [87 p. 59].

Kabiri found that when the KWS implemented a plan to share benefits from wildlife with communities, the amount received was minimal and the communities "lost faith" in the program [88 p. 131]. Nelson and Agrawal describe the attempt of the KWS to establish CBNRM during the 1990s, but argue that part of the reason for the failure of the reforms was due to an "alliance between foreign animal welfare groups and the tourism industry" that benefits from lack of "competition" due to the "ban on hunting" [82 p. 573]. Hackel points to the rapid growth of African populations as a threat to wildlife conservation in sensitive areas such as the Kajiado District of Kenya, which lies between the Amboseli and Tsavo national parks, from "15,000 in 1927 to 250,000 in 1989 and to 405,000 in 1999" [89 p. 728–31]. Campbell et al. report intensifying conflicts between humans and wildlife in this area with changes occurring with fewer problems proportionately from lion and buffalo but more from elephants, hyenas, and antelope [84 p. 6]. Hackel claims that even revenue-sharing from CBNRM cannot nearly match the money that natives could get from conversion of their land from rangeland to agriculture – he cites a study that Maasai in the area could get anywhere from three to twenty-three times as much in resources if they fully converted their land [89 p. 731]. Du Toit [90 p. 33] suggests that it might be worthwhile experimenting with making direct payments to Maasai to remain herders, since this is their cultural preference, but some research suggests that direct payments are successful for "those committed to a pastoralist way of life" but not for those without this tradition [91 p. 159]. The spread of agriculture is very evident. For example, the slopes of Mt. Kilimanjaro are now being cultivated for agriculture at the expense of forest [84 p. 3]. As a result of these conversions, Hackel reports that protected areas become isolated, surrounded by lands that will not support wildlife. The Tanzanian President (in 2006) Kikwete is quoted as saying that Maasai should "settle down" such as in cities and do "zero grazing" [92 p. 948]. Norton-Griffiths says that the Kenya government "must compensate the Maasai for not developing their land" and that young Maasai want "more value from their land and resources" [93 p. 598 & 602]. He says that it is crucial that compensation go directly to the landowners and "not to the county council" where the monies are "plundered" or even to community projects [93 p. 602]. According to him, landowners only received 1.6 percent of the tourist revenues in the Mara area of Kenya [93 p. 594]. As with Kenya, wildlife has provided significant tourist revenues to Tanzania but, according to Vira and Ewing, though Tanzania used to have a "strong reputation for conservation," in recent years, there has been a large escalation in poaching of elephants and evidence of corruption, "inadequate oversight", and a "high level of complicity" on the part of officials [87 p. 92]. The role of NGOs in limiting or banning trophy hunting has been major. Disputes over the role that hunting should play are common throughout Africa. Animal rights groups formed the Kenya Coalition for Wildlife Conservation that consisted of supporters from environmental groups such as the David Sheldrick Wildlife Trust, as well as ecotourism operators who feared hunting would harm their tourism business [88 p. 132–6]. This coalition has been successful in "selling its [anti-hunting] case" to the government [88].

Lubilo and Child describe one CBNRM program in Zambia, LIRDP (Luangwa Integrated Resource and Development Project) that was implemented by Zambia's President Kaunda and strongly supported by the Norwegian government. It achieved a degree of success with 80 percent of revenues "controlled within villages" [94 p. 204]. But the program was subsequently recentralized in 2003. Zambia's CBNRM program, known as ADMADE (Administrative Management and Design for Game Management), was established in 1987 in order to decentralize wildlife management [95 p. 61–2]. According to Lewis and Alpert, ADMADE's chief innovation was to hire local scouts "to monitor local wildlife" – formerly scouts were hired by the National Parks and Wildlife Service [95]. However, Lubilo and Child cite evidence the ADMADE program was ridden with "fraud," that communities did not know how much money they were getting, that few benefits reached the local level except "employment as local scouts," and that "elite capture" and "lack of transparency" characterized the program [94 p. 205–6]. Gibson says that "ADMADE's data on animal populations was unreliable and sketchy" and it had failed to give "local proprietorship over wildlife to local communities" [69 p. 103]. Gibson claims that, although ADMADE increased the number of arrests for poaching, that poaching continued to occur but was targeted on "smaller animals" [69 p. 112]. Lewis and Alpert estimate that local communities received about 12 percent of the benefits in 1994 from trophy hunting in ADMADE game management areas [95]. Lubilo and Child conclude that CBNRM programs in Africa fail because "personalized and informal" politics overwhelm attempts at devolution and local participation [94 p. 223]. Nelson and Agrawal likewise state that Zambia's governance institutions are "perceived as highly corrupt and neo-patrimonial" with only about 6 percent of the ADMADE "reaching communities" [82 p. 571]. Astle argues that Zambia's populations of elephants and rhinos dropped precipitously during the 1970s and 1980s because they relied too much on wildlife for development and should have emphasized agriculture more so that local people did not need to resort to poaching [96]. Another limitation of CBNRM concerns the fact that the term "community" tends to imply that all locals will benefit from CBNRM, but Homewood and Thompson in studying Wildlife Management Areas in Tanzania state that "even when benefits do flow to the community overall, individual households do not tend to perceive themselves as direct beneficiaries" [86 p. 357–60]. Thus those residents who do not benefit from tourism revenues are more likely to cultivate their land rather than retain it for conservation.

Nelson and Agrawal state that Tanzanian wildlife policy (like several other African nations) is based on "proscribing wildlife uses" as well as establishing "national parks and game areas" with some 30 percent of the country devoted to such areas [82 p. 562]. However, in 1996, Tanzania initiated a move to CBNRM because there was no incentive to preserve wildlife outside of the parks and game areas by establishing "Wildlife Management Areas" (WMAs) that were to be managed by local communities [82 p. 561]. According to Nelson and Agrawal, many communities have not been able to fulfill the multiple conditions required to "gazette a WMA" and they claim that consequently "wildlife has continued to decline" [82 p. 562]. Nelson and Agrawal state that wildlife policy is dominated by elites and external donors, with little grassroots participation [82 p. 563]. Schroeder says that the national Wildlife Division of the Ministry of Environment and Natural Resources undertook steps to undermine and "gut" the "community wildlife management areas" (CWMAs) established in northern Tanzania in the late 1980s [97 p. 590–3]. These were run by "mostly small-scale, tour operators for tourists who prefer walking and wilderness camping trips" [97 p. 590].

Among the changes were "cumbersome regulations" to discourage community involvement and also oversight that "strips the CWMAs of all local control" [97 p. 593]. Recently, Nelson et al. describe a "payment for ecosystem services" (PES) program aimed at encouraging the preservation of wildlife outside of state-protected areas. They point out that even large parks like the Serengeti have wildebeest migrations that depend significantly on surrounding areas outside the park, and also that there are trends that are threatening areas that used to be favorable to wildlife due to the changing customs of the Maasai [98 p. 81]. Maasai are being forced by population increases and increasing scarcity of land so that many former pastoralists are becoming agriculturalists, thus further decreasing habitat for wildlife. According to Nelson et al., PES systems are characterized by "conditionality" – the community promises to adhere to certain conditions in return for payments from a "purchasers" such as tourism companies [98 p. 69]. The conditions in the north Tanzanian case described by Nelson et al. include bans on "charcoal burning" and "unlicensed hunting" in the "concession area" in return for payments, and also hiring of local persons to enforce these conditions [98 p. 83]. The authors note that PES systems conflict with centrally-managed trophy hunting in countries like Tanzania and that there have been attempts to take control of them or banish them. Moreover, Nelson depicts Tanzania's development of wildlife resources as typical of much of Africa due its "personalized" governance in which politicians award contracts and benefits to private persons based on personal relationships and corruption rather than "impersonal rule of law" [63. p. 12]. These developments, Nelson argues, have continued to occur despite "the narratives of decentralization" that have dominated conservation about natural resources since the 1990s. Thus, though reforms have been attempted in Tanzania to increase local control, bureaucrats and other advantaged individuals have continued to seek the rewards through "rent-seeking behavior" because control over revenues from wildlife and hunting are valued resources [99 p. 96].

Brockington has criticized "fortress conservation" where central conservation authorities give "handouts" or "services" but retain control over the protected areas [100 p. 107–17]. An example he describes is Mkomazi Game Reserve in Tanzania in which evictions of natives were carried out – there were over 50,000 people living outside the borders of the reserve. Foreign charities such as the George Adamson Wildlife Preservation charity have played an important role in restoring the reserve and establishing "sanctuaries" for African wild dogs and the black rhinoceros. Brockington argues that "even if wealthy tourists flocked to the Reserve," there would not be enough funds to compensate the natives for the loss of access, and he argues only an arrangement that allows the native populations to access the reserve would make up for the losses. Brockington said that the indigenous population had strongly felt grievances about their eviction and pursued them (unsuccessfully) in legal cases [100]. But Fraser et al. report a successful CBNRM effort in central Tanzania when the Wildlife Conservation Society cooperated with the local villagers to increase local benefits from hunting [101]. Before this effort, in this area, hunters negotiated with the central government's Ministry of Natural Resources and Tourism to secure licenses and villagers generally did not have any say over who hunted there and received few revenues from the hunters. Fraser et al. report that in the first year of the project, hunting revenue increased 800 percent, despite the fact that the area they hunted had been cut only by 75 percent [101 p. 51]. Jones argues that even though benefits in terms of dividends or jobs "are generally low, particularly in the very large communities where income was shared between many people ... the dividend to households still may be significant" [78 p. 161].

According to Nelson and Agrawal, Namibia provides the best example of successful CBNRM, achieved in 1996 when its wildlife laws were changed to "create community conservancies" that gave local communities broad powers over most wildlife as well as contingent authority over rarer species [82 p. 565–6]. Unlike many other CBNRM programs, locally elected committees "retain 100 percent of the revenue from tourist operations." Nelson and Agrawal argue that the success of Namibia is largely due to the "high quality" and "transparency" of the nation's "governance institutions" [82 p. 565–6]. Similarly, Vaughan and Long state that Namibia is a case that clearly illustrates that "governance is at the heart of addressing sustainable wildlife management" [102 p. 137]. The Namibian Association of Community Based Natural Resource Management Support Organizations (NACSO) is an association comprising fourteen NGOs that has undertaken aerial surveys that found big increases (from a beginning point of almost zero) for springbok, oryx, and mountain zebra, and also increases in the number of elephants in the areas of the conservancies [103 p. 20]. These Namibian conservancies were supported by outside donors including USAID, the World Wildlife Fund, European governments, and United Nation's programs. Boudreaux and Nelson cite data that many jobs have been created related to the tourism industry. However, during the same period, due to the increase in predators, the number of human–wildlife conflicts has increased greatly (from about 300 in 2001 to over 7000 in 2008) – most of them due to livestock losses [103 p. 22]. Bryan Jones cites a survey of Namibians with two major conclusions: (1) Namibians "don't want wildlife to disappear," and (2) They wanted something done about "predators that killed livestock" and elephants that ate crops [104 p. 111]. The native Namibian farmers wanted the same rights to benefit from wildlife that white farmers had during the colonial period. Recently, Conniff has praised Namibia as "about the only place on earth that has gotten conservation right" because in the 1990s "they turned over conservation" "to communal conservancies ... not run by white do-gooders but by black ranchers and herders, some of whom, until then, had been poachers" [105]. He contrasts Namibia with nearby South Africa where rhino "poachers have slaughtered almost a thousand rhinos last year alone" – while "Namibia lost only two." However, Conniff admits that a significant advantage and reason for less poaching in Namibia is that it is a large, sparsely populated country.

Uganda illustrates one example of a reported successful case of changing attitudes toward protected areas and wildlife. Hamilton, Cunningham, Byarugaba, and Kayanja describes how the Bwindi area of Uganda was designated as a forest preserve in 1932 and an "animal sanctuary" in 1964 but the area outside of the reserve lost most of its forest [106]. Hamilton et al. said that "at first there was little local support for the new park" because of the loss of access of local people to medicinal trees that only existed in the park and were needed to treat parasites that afflicted much of the population such as "whipworm." Consequently, comments such as "gorillas should be put in cages" were common during the early years of the park but in 1994 and later, three major reforms were made: (1) Villagers were given access to specified resources in the park; (2) Resources from park income were shared with the villagers for "community development"; (3) A "trust fund for forest conservation" in Uganda was established and some of the funds were used to train park staff as well as for community projects [106 p. 1724]. These helped to achieve a notable change in attitudes revealed by a survey as well as the fact that in meetings about the establishment of the park in the 1990s, "not a single voice was raised" in favor of "transferring forest to agricultural land" [106 p. 1723]. Uganda also illustrates the importance of regime stability and order to the preservation of wildlife because of the breakdowns in wildlife protection during the Idi Amin regime in the 1970s. During this period, there was widespread poaching of elephants in the Queen Elizabeth Park and the elimination of the rhino [107 p. 212–14]. However, problems still exist – recently, Uganda reported the theft of 3000 pounds of ivory from the Uganda Wildlife Authority vaults – five staff members under suspicion have been suspended [108].

Wildlife tourism is of great importance to the South Africa, contributing "8.5 percent of Gross Domestic Product" in 2008 [109 p. 153]. The approach of the South African National Parks Administration is to convert locals who are poachers to jobs related to the tourism industry. Still Whande says that the Parks Administration and private investors have more influence than local governments and consequently local communities often face "forced withdrawals" [109]. Booth and Cumming have documented how South African countries have developed a "privatized model" of wildlife that contrasts sharply with the North American model based on the following precepts: (1) The governments do not have the resources to centrally manage wildlife effectively, and thus both conservation and financial returns are better with privately run game ranches; (2) The mostly rural populations of these countries are willing to give up their hunting rights in return for good monetary gains from "commercial sport hunting" [110 p. 292]. However, Booth and Cummings admit that the fenced ranching approach restricts wildlife movements and thus create genetic isolation of populations and has "reduced sustainable densities" of wildebeest populations [110 p. 286]. South Africa alone has 10,000 private reserves [111].

In Mozambique, a CBNRM project was begun in 1999 by the Ministry of Agriculture in the Mahel area that had suffered from "heavy logging, heavy poaching and human–wildlife conflicts" [112 p. 230]. As with many CBNRM projects, its impetus came from outsiders, including the government of the Netherlands and the United Nation's Food and Agriculture Organization. In Mozambique, the "government's own security forces" have often been implicated in poaching and trafficking of ivory [87 p. 75]. Botswana also began a CBNRM effort in the 1990s with the aid of external donors modeled on projects in Zimbabwe and Namibia [113 p. 249]. "Village Trust Councils" were set up to manage "Wildlife Management Areas" and "controlled hunting areas" [113 p. 249]. But Madzwamuse says that local communities and natives have received few of the intended benefits from tourism because most tourism "facilities" are owned by foreigners and "safari operators" tend to hire "non-community members" due to poor literacy of locals leading local residents to complain that "animals are more important than humans" [113 p. 253–8]. Rosaleen Duffy, a critic of "fortress conservation," describes what she views as "draconian regulations" enforced by the government of Botswana in the Khwai area of the Okavango Delta. It was a wildlife area that was "owned by the local community" but "leased to a private safari operator" who demanded no hunting by local people so that "foreign tourists can shoot the wildlife with a camera or a gun" [114 p. 76–80].

Kellert, Mehta, Ebbin, and Lichtenfeld conducted comparative case studies of the implementation of CBNRM in three countries: Nepal, Kenya, and the United States [115]. The Nepal case looked at two sites in the Himalayas (the Annapurna and Makalu-Barun Conservation areas). In Kenya, they studied the Kimana Community Wildlife Sanctuary in southern Kenya. In the United States, they studied the Puget Sound area in Washington State and the Kuskokwim River Watershed area in Alaska. Their overall conclusion was downbeat – the successes achieved concerned "socio-economic objectives" but the projects failed on "biodiversity and conservation goals" [115 p. 709]. In both Kenya and Nepal, they found that the authority over wildlife and forests remained with the state and decentralization was not achieved. Likewise, in both of these countries, "most of the work focused on community development" and "little time" was spent on "protecting biological diversity" [115 p. 711]. Kellert et al. speculate on why the U.S. efforts were more successful and argue that the main reasons were the "focus on a single resource" (salmon) and the existence of strong legal and organizational support including financial infrastructure [115 p. 712]. Hulme and Murphree summarized the findings of several detailed case studies of community projects in Africa and concluded that "community conservation has only made official conservation policy marginally more acceptable to rural people in Africa" and though "it is a step in the right direction," that communities are far from viewing "conservation and wildlife management as preferred forms of land use" [74 p. 281]. Hill reviewed several CBNRM efforts and pessimistically concluded that there was "little empirical evidence for the effectiveness" of CBNRM and "integrated conservation and development" projects [116]. They challenge the idea of "community" arguing that "assuming common needs, beliefs, and actions among community members is naïve" [116 p. 119]. They also say that these efforts need to be periodically reassessed due to the fact that immigration into the area may change the composition of the community and thus affect who should be included in the initiatives. Dinerstein argues that the population threat to wildlife is much greater in Asia than in Africa [46 p. 25–6]. For example, he says that remote areas in Africa where rhinos live are "sparsely populated" compared with most rhino ranges in Asia. The number of firearms is also important in differentiating countries, with rhinos safer in Nepal than Somalia or India due to presence of many fewer firearms [46 p. 26].

CBNRM strategies have been used to save species in China. In Chongzuo China (in Guangxi Province), white-headed langurs had become very endangered by 1996 due to villages depleting their forest homes for firewood and hunters taking them. According to McKenna, the booming Chinese economy in the 1990s led to those with money wanting to "eat wildlife to show how powerful there are" [117]. Pan Wenshei, a Chinese biologist, established the Nongguan Nature Reserve and hired "wardens to protect the remaining animals" but also undertook strategies to change attitudes of the locals toward the langurs [117]. Dr. Pan achieved a "breakthrough" in 1997 by helping the locals to build a pipeline to provide access to clean water and received a small grant to build "biogas systems" derived from animal waste that provided cooking fuel to the locals and made it unnecessary to cut down trees [117]. He also helped build schools and health clinics. As a result of these efforts, local residents now help to free trapped langurs and stop outsiders from coming into poach them [117].

A controversial issue is whether economic development can coexist with conservation goals. In India, the World Bank spent $68 million on "infrastructure projects" such as roads, and buildings in "seven of India's finest wildlife reserves" and their buffer zones are a "model for conserving biodiversity through local participation" but Sahgal and Scarlott report that these projects led to "increased pressure on local wildlife" and diverted attention from the more important priority of "patrolling the forest" [51 p. 305]. Indeed, Gratwicke, Shrestha, and Seidensticker state that tigers are "very susceptible to ecological traps created by roads" because tigers are drawn to them due to "their long sight lines" and the fact that their prey are drawn to the fauna that grow along them so that poachers can drive along these roads with scoped rifles and easily kill the tigers [118 p. 192]. Gratwicke et al. hold that one of the necessary tiger conservation steps is to "create incentives for those who live in tiger conservation areas to value live tigers more than dead tigers" [118 p. 192]. Bennett argues that across "South-East Asia, the spread of roads leads to commercialization of wildlife" resulting in a situation where it can no longer serve as "a source of income" and she illustrates this with the example of China where logging roads in the interior led to "fresh meat every night in Chinese restaurants" [119 p. 243–4]. She says that in countries such as Laos and Cambodia "not even small birds remain" and that in Sarawak, wildlife were "depleted rapidly" when roads came into an area [119 p. 244]. Overall, higher population relative to areas of forest as well as their tie into traditional medicine mean that the situation for wildlife is direr in Asia than in tropical Africa [119 p. 248]. Oates makes the argument that the movement to aim at economic development as a mechanism to make local populations near protected areas accept wildlife has been counterproductive [120 p. 143]. He cites cases such as Cameroon's Korup National Park project where "agricultural development was a major goal" but he reports that direct efforts at protecting wildlife were not a high priority of the project and that the park rangers were not effective because they returned to their villages at night and thus were "unable to arrest or even deter poachers" [120 p. 169]. Oates cites not only the Cameroon case but also his experiences in Ghana and Nigeria to argue that "development oriented projects" attract new immigrants who have "no commitment to the resources they are exploiting" including the use of bush meat and that the planners of these projects are "economists, geographers, agriculturalists, and professional bureaucrats" who "rarely cared for nature" or had much knowledge about it [120 p. 198–200]. Poulsen, Clark, and Mavah, in a study of wildlife management in the Northern Congo, point out that the effectiveness of village controls over poaching depend on strong "interpersonal relations" which "fail when large numbers of outsiders immigrate into an area" [121 p. 142]. They go on to say that these immigrants do not "identify with the area" but often have influence over wildlife policy because they are affiliated with logging companies and possess more wealth and prestige than locals.

The Korup National Park (in Cameroon) illustrates the importance of foreign governments and NGOs as prime instigators of conservation attempts in developing countries. After the park was established in 1986, it was supported by the World Wildlife Fund (WWF) and the European Union. When this funding ended in 2003, protection for wildlife weakened but then the government of Germany took on funding of anti-poaching patrols [122]. In the Democratic Republic of the Congo, the Frankfurt Zoological Society "stepped in to pay the salaries of park staff" when the country's economy collapsed during conflict [123 p. 268]. Milner-Gulland says that the often dominant role played by international NGOs raises difficult ethical questions because "any intervention, no matter how successful … has winners and losers" and there is no clear accountability for them [124 p. 107–8]. However, he also acknowledges that most governments are weak with few resources and that NGOs naturally consider their major accountability to be to their supporters in the West [124 p. 109]. Moreover, he concludes that the NGO, operating within the context of poorly governed and corrupt nations, may provide the singular opportunity for an "envelope of good governance" [124 p. 109–10]. Cobb, Ginsberg, and Thompson point out that in many developing countries, the NGO budgets exceed those of the departments regulating wildlife and forestry [125 p. 151]. The big role that foreign NGOs play in conservation of developing countries leads to complex organizational adaptations. For example, in Gabon, the WWF pays "ecoguards" in Central Africa to protect wildlife. These guards wear a government-affiliated "patch on one sleeve and a WWF patch on the other" and the vehicles they use have only a WWF "logo" [126 p. 165]. Moreover, the WWF effectively fought government attempts to "commercialize bushmeat hunting" [126 p. 169]. NGOs can dominate CBNRM projects. Barrow et al. point that most of the national parks in Uganda have the support of an "international NGO" and the projects they sponsor "bypass the Uganda National Parks administration" [41 p. 69].

The tensions between wildlife conservation and local populations is illustrated by DeChant, who cites the case of the Virunga National Park where gorillas were killed as a warning "to the rangers not to crackdown on the charcoal trade" [127]. Poulsen et al. say that population increases in the Congo create a demand for "animal protein" that is higher than what can be provided for by imported fish and meat and thus "pressure on wildlife is high" [121 p. 151]. Wittemeyer et al.'s study found that the populations of areas near rural protected areas (for wildlife) grew faster in 245 of 306 parks studied [128 p. 123]. They also found that tourism and foreign investment spurred growth of infrastructure such as roads, schools, and hospitals that improved local standards of living but pressured the parks. Wittemeyer et al. argue that the data show that rather than harming local populations, protected areas (PAs) have benefited rural inhabitants by "providing access to road networks, employment, foreign aid" [128 p. 123]. They note that growth rates were correlated "with the density of PA staff" which indicates that there are "increased economic or occupational opportunities" due to PAs "rather than harm from exclusion from natural resources found in them" [128 p. 124]. However, they acknowledge that growth around PAs is also associated with higher rates of deforestation in these areas that are supposed to serve as last refuge for endangered species, and that efforts need to be made to create "large multi-use buffer areas surrounding the core habitats" as well as corridors to connect them [128 p. 125]. Maddox says that the growth of palm oil industry has led to a major decline in the tiger population of Indonesia [129 p. 396–9]. Tigers avoid the "monoculture" of oil palm areas and the associated influx of people, logging, and roads. Ironically, in the past, when these areas allowed hunting of tigers, the tiger population remained healthier; but despite the installment of "conservation friendly management of the area," the tiger population disappeared. Though some of the problems were due to illegal logging and burning, the major causes are legal daily occurrences such as the conversion of land to plantations so that oil palm plantations cover "six million hectares of tiger impenetrable land" [129 p. 399]. Moreover, Maddox says that the biofuel revolution demand for palm oil means that the expansion will continue and that "despite campaigning by powerful environmental groups" against illegal activities, "the benefits that big business can bring to the local and national economy are just too great to be cancelled out by concerns for tigers" [129 p. 399]. Cutter and Hean found that political stability in Cambodia led to "rapid economic development and land use change" and the decline of wildlife that depend on forests [130 p. 358]. However, the complexity of the situation is further illustrated by the observation of Nyhus and Tilson that based on North American and European experiences the increase in wealth can create more support for the preservation of "large mammals" and we can expect this to occur in countries like China though as previously noted, Japan has remained primarily utilitarian in their views of wildlife [131 p. 514].

Ferraro and Kiss describe projects that try to "integrate conservation and development approaches" as "conservation by distraction" [132 p. 1718–19]. They argue that the indirect nature of these approaches makes them complex, costly, and likely to be ineffective. They recommend "direct payments for conservation" as a better approach in which people are paid to protect "habitat and wildlife," and cite low-cost direct-payment projects in Costa Rica, Guayana, and Kenya as examples of the success of such an approach. They acknowledge one major limitation of these approaches – they require outside funding support and thus may not be "sustainable," but they contend that "self-financing" methods may be an impossible dream [132 p. 1719]. However, these agreements can be difficult to negotiate with locals, as Missrie and Nelson found in an attempt by the WWF to use the direct-payment method to protect monarch butterflies in Mexico that encountered many difficulties and complexities [133]. The project paid local communities to "forego use of logging permits and to perform conservation activities." Some of the complexities included disagreements over the "cubic meters in their contracts" and "inaccuracies in the polygons" and the fact that communities did not understand that payments from the fund were separate from those paid by the government. In addition, many other difficulties occurred such as that lands thought to be private turned out to be "ejido" (community farms), and changes in the Federal government administration of Mexico affected the project. Moreover, they report that "enforcement institutions were ineffective" and illegal logging went on; monitoring was costly and involved a learning curve to figure out how to determine the effectiveness of the project [133 p. 12]. Communicating the goals of the project such as what they were getting paid for was difficult and they conclude that "direct payments strategies can be as complex" as indirect methods.

There is a debate over whether CBNRM strategies or "regulatory systems" should be emphasized in India in order to save tigers. A World Conservation Society report argued for more law enforcement and removal of humans from tiger habitat as top priorities for conservation. Saberwal argues that a cheaper and more realistic plan would be to increase community support for tigers by removing problem tigers that threaten human lives and property, as well as improving the poorly run current system for reimbursing locals for losses due to tigers [28 p. 815–17]. Saberwal points to examples such as the Gujarat, India where he says the Maldhari herders live in coexistence with tigers. However, the tiger–human conflict can explode quickly, as has occurred recently in India where "10 deaths have been attributed to a man-eater" such as a forty-five-year-old worker who "got out of a car to relieve himself" in the Jim Corbett National Park – a nature preserve with "one of the densest concentrations of tigers." The man was attacked and "had his flesh torn from his thighs" [134]. "After the attack, angry villagers surrounded the forestry service outpost, trapping the park service employees inside" [134].

Karanth and Madhusudan respond that, although they "empathize" with the use of incentive approaches over the long run, the breakdown of wildlife protection in India during recent years was so bad that "long-term strategies cannot be relied upon" [135 p. 818–20]. They suggest that community-based approaches are most effective in low human density areas where "stewardship of natural resources allows people to meet their socioeconomic needs" but that it is not too much to ask in a country as large as India to set "aside forest patches for tigers" and their habitat [135 p. 818–20]. They argue that there are no areas of high human density that have been successful without regulatory approaches including the Gir Lion preserve cited by Saberwal, where reductions in "human and livestock densities were required" [135 p. 819]. Ward reported that when a forest area in India was turned into the Ranthambore National Park in an Indian desert state of Rajasthan that "overnight ordinary villagers were turned into criminals" with no provision made for them and they then were "driven to destroy all of the forest around the park" [136 p. 67]. He says that the conversion was done without consulting the locals.

Goering gives an account of one successful conservation program in Nagarjuna Sagar in Southeast India that did win over locals, who had previously been poisoning carcasses in order to kill tigers due to resentment of being evicted from the forests and a government program that paid them only "one-third of the value of livestock killed by tigers" [137]. K. Thulsi Rao, a state forest and biodiversity officer for the area, presented slides and presentation that pointed out that the loss of the forest would doom them as well as the tigers [137]. Using funds from NGOs, the Indian government, and World Bank, Rao paid the villagers $2 a day to replant forests as well as planting grazing areas for cattle outside the forests, combined with an education program for poachers and other locals. The effort has been a success, with poisoning of tigers stopped. However, Goering hesitates to say that this same approach would work elsewhere because many reserves are much smaller and "crushing pressure" from India's burgeoning population may be too much. Rodgers, Hartley, and Bashir contrast Indian and African wildlife conservation and identify major differences: African protected areas have relatively few people living within them [138 p. 343–7]. Also, Indian protected areas are mostly small and thus there does not exist an opportunity for "buffer areas" and zonation where restrictions on humans can be relaxed, thus offering a compromise between native use and wildlife conservation [138 p. 363]. Finally, tourism and trophy-hunting revenues have been small in India compared with Africa, and thus there are few financial benefits for local populations [138]. A survey taken of residents living near Wayanad Wildlife Sanctuary in India found that 93 percent of the respondents perceived "no benefits" from the sanctuary [138 p. 365]. Further analysis showed that there was strong support for protecting the forest (of the sanctuary) but much weaker support for protecting its wildlife.

Dinerstein, Rijal, Bookbinder, Katel, and Rajuria found that rebounding tiger populations in Chitwan area of Nepal were due to "strict protection efforts against poaching" and not due to benefits for the local population living near the park [139 p. 317]. They also point to the need to eliminate "free grazing" by livestock through keeping them in stalls, and they say the way to accomplish this is to provide them with "improved stock" that the locals will view as too valuable to be allowed to graze freely. Indeed, they go on to argue that conservationists should not "place too much emphasis on economic incentives to raise the standard of living" but rather focus on "quality of life" and benefits such as from ecotourism spent on "community goods" [139 p. 333]. Dinerstein describes how the "single most important step in establishing the Royal Chitwan National Park was the removal of all of the villages inside the sanctuary area" to a location north of the Rapti River [46 p. 55]. In 1993, the government established buffer zones around the conservation areas and in 1995 it established a law that shared 50 percent of the revenues with these buffer areas, which reduced pressure on the protected areas and helped to make villagers partners in protecting the reserves [46 p. 57]. Dinerstein identifies the lack of firearms and the "law-abiding nature of the Nepalese people" as significant factors in the restoration of tigers [46 p. 26 & 195]. He describes how a Nepalese NGO (National Trust for Nature Conservation) acted to avoid retribution toward tigers in the Bagmara area by capturing the man-eater and putting him in a zoo as well as using "buffer zone funds" to compensate the dead man's family for their loss. In Malaysia, a WWF project helped select communities to build "paddocks to protect cattle" rather than allow them to roam free at night, but Kawanishi et al. report that there was a problem of project participants ceasing these preventive practices when the support from the NGOs was removed [140 p. 375]. Wikramanayake et al. describe an effort to protect tigers in the Terai Arc Landscape – an area that covers both Nepal and India by "establishing connected corridors" between the protected areas [141 p. 167–8]. Wikramanayake et al. developed a ten-year strategic plan but the program was "set back by a Maoist insurgency" [141 p. 167–8]. However, after five years, the project reported five new tigers in the corridor areas and that "because of their vested interest in community forests" the local communities and anti-poaching units "apprehended over 1000 poachers" [141 p. 172]. Wikramanayake et al. conclude that if "conflict [between humans and tigers] can be maintained at low levels" that the survival of the tiger was possible with the help of "local stewardships" even "in human-dominated landscapes" [141 p. 173]. In 2015, a report was issued by India's National

Tiger Authority that reported populations of tigers rising by more than 30 percent in the last four years [142 p. 17; 143]. The report attributed the growth to reduction in "human pressures, protection, prey availability and good quality habitats" and stated that "political will, conservation commitment by wildlife managers and improved protection have paid dividends" [142 p. 17].

Tensions between wildlife conservation are also common in Latin America. In Peru, Bodmer, Pueretas, and Tang describe how poaching was depleting several species of wildlife such as "tapirs, primates, and carnivores" that are much more "vulnerable to bushmeat hunting" than other species such as peccaries and deer [144 p. 105]. According to Bodmer et al., in 1992, with the support of the United States, a tight guard system was established; however, resentment grew on the part of the locals, leading to a machete attack that killed "two young biologists and a park guard" [144 p. 105–9]. After this event, the leadership of the park changed to an approach in which local people were allowed limited use of park resources, and the researchers claim that the local people have changed their attitudes with poachers now becoming "co-managers" of the park who help to keep poachers out [144 p. 110].

In comparing the successes and failures of African CBNRM efforts, Nelson and Agrawal point out that greater success has been realized in countries like Namibia than in Kenya and Tanzania, in part due to the fact that natural resources were less important (economically) in the successful countries and thus were less a target for domination of elites [82 p. 577–80]. They also note that although donors are often influential in encouraging CBNRM reforms, outsiders are not the "principal forces" for successful adoption of reforms. Rather, the basic political institutions and factors such as transparency are the underlying reasons for success or failure. Thus, they advise donors not to concentrate heavily on "technical issues" but rather to search for new models of achieving institutional change. Nelson concludes though CBNRM reforms in Africa are "variable and non-linear," that overall "the trend has been toward reconsolidating authority over natural resources" because of the growth of revenues from tourism rather than toward the intended decentralization [145 p. 310–11]. Thomas describes two different theories of how to allocate benefits of CBNRM: the "microcosmic view," where only those who directly bear the costs of living with wildlife should benefit, versus the "macrocosmic view," where the benefits should be distributed "district-wide" [146 p. 133–40]. Other factors complicate CBNRM attempts to distribute benefits equitably, such as the fact that benefits from programs like CAMPFIRE go to residents in areas where the "wildlife asset is realized" but wildlife are "produced" over a much wider area for many species like elephants [146 p. 138]. Thomas also describes a strategy to reimburse residents based on how much crop and livestock damage has occurred to them, but notes that this system would require monitoring to avoid abuse of claims. Duffy criticizes "preservationist approaches" and environmental ideologies based on animal rights, and argues that "sustainable utilization is the only approach to saving wildlife in … Sub-Saharan Africa that is workable" because "preservationist approaches" are not "enforceable" [39 p. 174–7].

Despite a large number of studies analyzing CBNRM efforts, nevertheless there exists a "want of good data" on the successes and failures of CBNMR [147 p. 613].

There are case studies usually done at certain points in time which I have described above but, as we have seen, circumstances often change through time because these reforms are often initiated with outside financial support which usually is withdrawn after a period of time. Likewise, as in Zimbabwe, national events can dominate and undermine factors affecting the success of CBNRM efforts, such as sharp declines in tourism.

Conclusion

The overall conclusion of the review of wildlife politics across nations is that most nations have had active political struggles over wildlife often as vigorous as, for example, the controversy over wolves in the United States. Although wildlife struggles may not rival the tensions due to strife over religious and ethnic divisions, wildlife politics are consistently prominent and often contentious issues in countries across the world. Moreover, these issues inevitably will grow in importance as attempts to preserve endangered species come into conflict with habitat loss due to population growth and economic development.

Secondly, there are some striking similarities in the nature of wildlife politics. An urban–rural division on attitudes toward wildlife is common throughout the world, with rural people who live with the wildlife viewing them as competitors or threats, while urban populations tend to view them with less utilitarian attitudes. The United States, due to its early creation of national parks and passage of the ESA, has had an outsized effect on wildlife politics in many other countries because they have often modeled themselves after these U.S. innovations. However, even among advanced industrial countries including those sharing colonial histories, there are significant differences in politics due to institutional differences, such as federalism, and also cultural differences in perceptions of wildlife, as well other factors such as the relative importance of wildlife to the national economy.

There is a significant contrast between advanced industrialized countries and developing countries concerning the protection of endangered species that can threaten the interests of locals who live near them. In the United States and in countries such as Norway, France, and Sweden, despite the passage of legislation to protect wildlife, rural groups such as ranchers and farmers have significant and often dominant power over subnational environmental policies with enough political clout to force compromises from the Federal government concerning species that they view as threats or nuisances. By way of contrast, villagers living near wildlife in developing countries generally have little political power to force compromises by the national government, although they are able to exert impact by undertaking (often) illegal poaching and destruction of habitat through burning of wood and conversion of land to agriculture. Likewise, external forces such as wildlife-related NGOs (e.g., WWF) and foreign national governments play a vastly more important role in forming wildlife policy in developing countries than in industrialized societies. Indeed, critics now refer to the dominant NGOs as "BINGOs" (big international conservation organizations) [148 p. 577].

These BINGOs include the WWF, Conservation International, and the Nature Conservancy [148 p. 597]. They have long been important but have become more dominant since the 1990s when disillusionment with "policy failures" led to the USAID to redirect most of their funds to BINGOs – by 2000, 4 of the 7 billion USAID dollars went to them [148 p. 588]. There arose in the U.S. Congress bipartisan support for these big international conservation NGOs with caucuses created in both the House and Senate to support funding and even a 501C(3) organization (the International Conservation Caucus Foundation) to lobby for assistance [148 p. 593]. One explanation for the conservative support for these caucuses is that biodiversity overseas does not create "conflict with local constituencies" who "call up their congressman" as it does in the United States [148 p. 592]. Along with the dominance of BINGOs, there was a change in the source of U.S. aid to developing countries. In the 1970s, 70 percent of the aid was from the U.S. government, but by 2000, 80 percent of the aid was private [148 p. 590]. Overall, income from wildlife conservation such as ecotourism and trophy hunting is more important in developing countries because they are "wildlife-exporting" countries, and that makes wildlife politics relatively more important than in Western countries. Although conservation policies can have beneficial impacts on local peoples, they also can engender a sense of resentment on the part of locals that can become contentious as it has in India and other countries when locals are forced out of areas protected for wildlife.

The response of many advanced industrial countries and wildlife-related NGOs has been to encourage developing countries to adopt community-based natural resource management in which there is an attempt to ensure that local populations obtain benefits from wildlife. As has been outlined above, these CBNRM programs take on a wide variety of specific forms and differ on key aspects such as to what extent decisions and resources are actually decentralized to the community level, what members of the "community" make decisions on how to allocate benefits from wildlife, and other issues such as how widespread an area should be allocated benefits. Although some projects have been found to be successful for at least part of their existence, overall, CBNRM programs have often been disappointing in their outcomes for both villagers and wildlife; and those which were successful initially have often fallen prey to recentralization and/or corruption over the longer term. A number of political factors influence the nature of CBNRM outcomes, including the degree to which the country is dominated by elites and extent to which their politics are open and not subject to corruption. In many cases, central governments simply do not have enough power to implement laws on the books. Unlike the United States, these countries usually lack strong domestic interest groups to support the maintenance of national parks and other protected areas and thus international NGOs often play a key role in natural resource decision making. China represents another dimension – it has a strong central government. Though domestic NGOs such as student environmental groups are growing, their role is to assist the Chinese government in environmental activities – they are not allowed to "oppose the Chinese Communist party" [149 p. 178]. One fact that inhibits decentralization and CBNRM efforts is that when wildlife becomes very profitable due to the increase in ecotourism, it makes it less likely that national elites will allow decentralization of controls. Nevertheless, despite all of the complexities and idiosyncrasies of cultural and tribal elements, it is notable that good governance, including low rates of corruption and high levels of transparency, are associated with successful CBNRM outcomes. Hence politics (in a very broad sense) is one of the keys to wildlife conservation.

Despite numerous studies of CBNRM and wildlife conservation in developing countries, there remain underlying debates over fundamental issues. One significant disagreement concerns the role that economic development should play in wildlife conservation. CBNRM projects generally try to accomplish both conservation and economic development to provide jobs for villages displaced by protections for wildlife, with the assumption that these dual goals can both be achieved together. The findings of Wittemeyer et al.'s research suggests that protected areas rather than blocking economic development actually create development, but this development eventually destroys wildlife habitat; consequently they argue that buffer zones need to be established to limit these harmful effects [128]. Sanderson and Redford ask rhetorically "if areas of high conservation priority are encroached, or endangered wildlife harvested, can those charged with protected areas management ignore destructive practices so as to avoid negative economic impacts?" [150 p. 146]. They conclude that if economic impacts take priority, we would have to "watch" as "wetlands are drained," "turtles sold to market," and "primates smoked for sale in cities" because these practices add to local incomes [150 p. 146]. There is also a lack of consensus on the role that privatization of wildlife should play given the failures of governments to secure protection of species. Will CBNRM projects be sufficient to preserve wildlife or should more countries emphasize the South African approach with private wildlife ranches despite their limitations? One major "wildcard" concerns leadership – strong leaders with special interest in conservation can have major impacts on policy in both democracies (e.g., Teddy Roosevelt in the United States and Eduardo Frei in Chile) or dictatorships (e.g., Ceausescu in Romania and Putin in Russia).

The underlying forces of development, population growth, and growth of agriculture (to support the growing population) makes the long-term future of conservation of wildlife more tenuous and pessimistic. There are some potentially countervailing forces such as the example in the West where growing wealth and diminishment of wildlife has given rise to more interest in their preservation as well as the growth of ecotourism that furnishes significant revenues and foreign currency for some countries. However, there are doubts whether the economic benefits from ecotourism and trophy hunting can compete with highly remunerative industries like palm oil in Indonesia or extraction of valuable commodities from African countries; such industries have negative effects on endangered species.

8 International Wildlife Politics

This chapter explores how the politics of wildlife has become increasingly international for two major reasons: (1) Wildlife often cross national boundaries (especially birds and marine species) so conservation efforts require international cooperation; (2) International trade and the exploitation of endangered wildlife species have become huge industries that can only be controlled by international action. Without concerted international controls, even the United States cannot protect many imperiled species. However, achieving cohesive international action has been a difficult challenge.

Why Wildlife Politics Has Become Increasingly International

Many species of wildlife cross international borders and thus require international action if they become endangered. For example, Wilcove says that a bird, Swainson's thrush, crosses "ten different countries" in flying from its winter home in Brazil to "its breeding grounds in Manitoba" and thus its protection depends on Brazil, Columbia, Panama, Costa Rica, Nicaragua, Honduras, Guatemala, Mexico, the United States, and Canada [1 p. 10]. The threat to the monarch butterfly requires action by both Mexico and the United States to save it. Mexico needs to stop illegal logging of its forests where they reside in the winter and the United States needs to take action to restore milkweed plants on which their caterpillars feed; these have been greatly reduced due to pesticides such as glyphosate and "the planting of corn in previously marginal areas that would have been covered by milkweed" [2]. Macdonald, Collins, and Wrangham argue that the greatest conservation successes come when a single country encompasses the species because then it is clear who bears responsibility if action is not taken. They use the golden lion tamarin to illustrate the point – the first primate to have its status reduced from "critically endangered" to "endangered" exists entirely within Brazil [3 p. 285]. Wildlife politics has long been involved in international relations including the development of treaties, international agreements enforced by international agencies such as CITES (Convention on International Trade in Endangered Species of Wild Fauna and Flora) and bilateral negotiations and "politicking" with other nations. Brinkley describes how Theodore Roosevelt convened a "North American Conservation Conference" in 1909 at the White House in which the principle was established that "to be practicable, conservation must be international" [4 p. 804]. The Migratory Treaty Act of 1918 protected migratory birds and was agreed to originally by Great

Britain and Canada, but later included agreements with Mexico, Japan, and Russia. One major international issue concerns trafficking in endangered species. For example, Brazil is losing birds such as "Lear's Macaw with only 300 left in the wild" – these birds are bought by traffickers for only a few dollars but can sell for as much as 60,000 dollars in the United States [5]. Problems are caused by both "exporter" and "importer" nations. Brazil has only "meager fines" ranging from $25 to $100 for the crime, which are tiny compared to the potential profit. According to Jones, a "powerful lobby of private animal collectors" has resisted efforts to strengthen penalties and even got them weakened in 1998 [5]. It is estimated that illegal international wildlife trafficking is the third largest behind drug and arms trading and that the United States is often the "prime destination" though the animals are often first sent to Columbia and Mexico [5]. It is impossible to get very precise figures on the value of wildlife trafficking with the United Nations Environmental Program estimating it to be worth between $50 billion to $150 billion in 2014 [6 p. 25]. Another example of the international nature of wildlife conservation concerns the consumption of bushmeat in Africa. Because international fishing has resulted in steep declines in fish available to West Africa (most of it is consumed in Europe), natives in West Africa have less access to fish protein and consequently it "drives up demand for bushmeat" [7 p. 33]. Du Toit says that "attempts to reduce bushmeat consumption" are impossible "without international agreements to regulate marine fishing activities of foreign fleets" [7].

An example of a reportedly successful effort at controlling destructive fishing occurred in San Salvador, Philippines [8 p. 245–7]. Aquarium fish gatherers had employed "sodium cyanide that destroys the reef and juvenile fish," leading to a big drop in the fish caught by other islanders (from 20 kg to 1–3 kg) [8]. The local community voted to create a marine sanctuary and also "banned unsound fishing" techniques [8 p. 238–9]. According to Christie, there were "disputatious politics" between those who used the banned techniques and those who wanted the new management, and the struggle continued until those in favor of managing the resources won control of the local council and government [8 p. 247].

Fish such as bluefin tuna may be the most difficult species to save because the seas are "governed by largely feeble international agreements" and research has found that catches have increased by "700 percent" over the last century in what Greenberg characterizes as "the last great wild-fish gold rush we are likely to see" [9]. Roberts says that in the nineteenth century, "untapped sea exceeded fished areas by 100:1 but that today that ratio is reversed" and that, unlike food from land, "we depend on wild nature to supply the majority of our seafood" [10 p. 297]. One of the most worrisome fears for environmentalists is the possibility that "free trade" agreements enacted by the World Trade Organization (WTO) under the General Agreement on Tariffs and Trade (GATT) would overrule U.S. environmental regulations that protect species such as dolphins and bluefin tuna. According to Public Citizen, in the 1950s, fishermen discovered that they could catch large numbers of tuna by tracking dolphins – because tuna tend to travel with dolphin pods so they "encapsulated both the tuna and the dolphins in giant purse seines" – then drawing them to the surface, resulting in the killing of dolphins [11]. Due to public reaction against the killing of dolphins, Congress passed the Marine Mammal Protection Act in 1972 and later in 1990 "created a dolphin safe program" followed in 1992 by banning the sale of tuna that were not caught by "dolphin-safe" methods. However, Mexico and other nations challenged the U.S. legislation as violating the GATT rules. In 1991, a GATT tribunal ruled that the U.S. law did in fact violate GATT rules but the United States did not immediately conform to GATT because the "Clinton Administration thought that such an action would threaten the passage of the NAFTA (North American Free Trade) treaty" [11]. Eventually, Congress did make changes in the Marine Mammal Protection Act that allowed non-dolphin-safe tuna to be imported, but it held that such tuna could not use the "dolphin-safe" label. Environmentalists feared that agreements such as NAFTA would lead to the nullification of other environmental laws "inconsistent with these agreements" [12]. However, instead, Knox argues that the Appellate Body of the WTO has since then acted to allow the continuation of U.S. environmental laws as being in concordance with the treaties. Knox says that they have done this in two ways: (1) The country with the tougher environmental laws must "impose its restrictions only after it pursues serious efforts" for negotiations with "all interested parties"; (2) The Appellate Body consults independent experts such as environmental organizations about the substantive merits of the treaties [12 p. 45]. The original case in 1987 which the United States initially lost in the WTO concerned the required use of "turtle exclusion devices" (TEDs) in U.S. jurisdictions by shrimp trawlers. Congress had banned the use of shrimp caught without the use of TEDs. The Appellate Body said that the "failure of the U.S. to pursue negotiations of multilateral agreements had led to the kind of unilateralism that the U.S. itself had condemned" [12 p. 38]. In a similar case in 2000, Malaysia accused the United States of "unilateralism" again because, although the countries had negotiated, they had not reached an agreement. But the Appellate Body of the WTO ruled for the United States after reviewing "the U.S. efforts to reach an agreement" [12 p. 40]. Knox says that the WTO had created a Commission for Environmental Cooperation made up of member nations' "environmental ministers," but that this body had failed to "accomplish anything of substance" and thus it was the judicial Appellate Body that accomplished what "governments had failed to do" – the resolution of conflicts between freer trade and environmental regulations [12 p. 1–2].

Regulation of sea fish is perhaps the most international and challenging task for those interested in preserving endangered species. One example is Atlantic bluefin tuna, which have become threatened. The International Commission for the Conservation of Atlantic Tuna (ICCAT) has been vested with the responsibility for regulating international catches of tuna but has been criticized for presiding over the crash of the population. Ted Williams accused the commission of being dominated by the fishing lobby and failing to follow the recommendations of their own scientists concerning the need to cut fishing quotas radically [13 p. 18–20]. Another major limitation of the commission, according to Williams, is that "75 percent of tuna-killing nations" are not members of the commission. Williams quotes a bluefin fish exporter as criticizing those who want to cut back on quotas as being "elite recreationists" [13 p. 19]. Song documented one successful impact of the ICCAT in which Taiwan reduced the size of its bigeye tuna fleet by more than one half, as a result of pressure from Japan, which consumes most of Taiwan's catch of tuna [14 p. 101]. But Song also cites ICCAT's failure to adhere to the recommendations of its scientific committee for "an annual TAC (total allowable catch) of just 15,000 tons" when they set the TAC for 2007–2009 to 29,500 tons – nearly double what the scientists recommended [14 p. 138]. Moreover, Libya and Turkey "rejected their assigned quotas" and set their own limits. The underlying reason for the reluctance and inability of ICCAT to take strong measures is the immense value of IUU (illegal, unreported and unregulated) catches estimated to be worth between $4 billion and $9 billion in 2006. Finally, in 2013, the ICCAT received approbation from environmental organizations like the Pew Foundation for "maintaining catch limits" at 1750 and 13,400 metric tons respectively for western and eastern bluefin tuna [15]. They also praised ICCAT for "mandating that to gain authorization to fish in its convention area, every large fishing vessel has to have an International Maritime Organization (IMO) number," because "to evade authorities, over the years, owners have been able to change vessel names, radio call signs, and flags of registration" thus making it difficult to punish violators of catch limits. However, the Pew Foundation lamented ICCAT's failure to implement an "electronic bluefish document system." According to the World Wildlife Fund (WWF), there had been significant pressure to increase the catch limits but these were successfully resisted due to the strong position taken by the European Fisheries Commissioner [16]. However, the WWF criticized the failure to strengthen protections for sharks that would require that sharks be landed with "fins naturally attached" due to strong opposition from Japan, China, and Korea [16]. Canada successfully opposed protections for the porbeagle shark. Greenberg describes why Japan opposed an Appendix I listing for the Atlantic bluefish tuna because "it was too inflexible" – "once it is listed it will never be delisted" [9]. The difficulties of reaching consensus are great because, Greenberg says, developing countries are aiming to expand their fishing "just as industrialized nations are realizing the need for sensible management" [9]. Ludwig says that the hardest thing to do in fisheries management is to "reduce fishing pressure" and that "governments can seldom resist subsidizing declining industries" [17 p. 35]. Consequently, Ludwig says that governments and fishers overinvest during favorable times and "continue these large harvests" during bad times, with the consequence that despite the fact that fisheries management is the most "sophisticated of natural resources management," nevertheless there has been a "widespread destruction of the world's fisheries" [17 p. 35].

The difficulties of preventing illegal trafficking of fish are illustrated by the case of *Thunder*, a vessel identified by Interpol as one of the "four most wanted" poaching ships in the world [18]. This vessel has been on the most wanted list for years but "no government has been willing" to commit the resources "to go after it." This vessel specializes in illegally catching "Chilean sea bass" renamed from "toothfish" to make it more attractive to consumers. The ship was tracked by the *Sea Shepherd* vessel owned and operated by environmentalists [18]. This "eco-vigilante" group pursued *Thunder* and cut its nets, justifying their actions by pointing out that most nations do not enforce rules against illegal fishing in international waters [18]. Another example concerns a ship illegally fishing Chilean sea bass from the Antarctic that has gone by several different names (*Chang Bai, Hongshui, Corvus, Galaxy, Red Moon*, and *Dorita*) and flown under several different flags (Equatorial Guinea, Indonesia, Tanzania, South Korea, Panama, and Sierra Leone) by several different companies [19]. The ship was tracked to Thailand, which has a reputation for not enforcing laws against illegal fishing, and thus has been threatened with a "seafood embargo if they don't take steps to improve" [19]. Illegal fishing in the Antarctic is "regulated by the Convention on the Conservation of Antarctic Marine Living Resources (CCAMLR)," an Australian organization [19]. However, Thailand has not joined CCAMLR and Thailand's penalties for the ship would be minor compared to the value of the seabass (estimated at $5 million) [19]. In short, it is very difficult to enforce rules against illegal fishing on open seas and the only mechanism that seems to have any effect is to threaten penalties against countries that fail to enforce the rules.

Opponents of CITES use of bans on trade of animals argue that CITES bans only create the "perception" that something is "being done" but actual protection of species can only be achieved by "law enforcement agencies" of individual states [20 p. 3]. Assessing the effectiveness of CITES raises difficulties similar to evaluating the Endangered Species Act (ESA). Kievit says that it is hard to find species that have been removed from the Appendices just as many endangered species remain on the ESA's threatened list [21 p. 88]. Martin states that a review of CITES revealed that only "two of twelve" species had actually improved as a result of their listing on CITES Appendices [22 p. 125]. Martin also criticizes the inflexibility of CITES for lacking "proportionality" – trade in Appendix I species is totally banned while Appendix II can be used "unsustainably without inputs into their management." They also point to differences in the management of charismatic species such as sea turtles that have been protected while the use of crocodiles for consumptive use has "regularly been accepted by parties to CITES" [23 p. 106]. As with the case of assessing the impact of the U.S. ESA legislation, the crucial question is difficult if not possible to determine: What would have happened without the CITES restrictions on trade? Would they be in worse shape?

Macdonald et al. describe fragmentation among five international conventions aimed at preserving biodiversity: (1) the Convention on Biological Diversity (Montreal); (2) the Convention on International Trade in Endangered Species (Geneva); (3) the Convention on Wetlands of International Importance (Switzerland); (4) the Convention on Migratory Species (Bonn); and (5) the World Heritage Convention and Man and Biosphere Program (Paris.) [3 p. 275]. They say the responsibility to "pull these organizations together" lies with the Commission on Sustainable Development (New York) and United Nations Environment Program (Nairobi) but they "have no power or money" to accomplish this task. Moreover, they state that neither these organizations nor any other governmental environmental agency have to the "weight to counterbalance the arguments for unfettered trade coming from the WTO or the World Bank" [3 p. 276].

Controlling Illegal Wildlife Traffic

Actions by the United States and CITES have achieved some cases of apparent success. In 1993–4, after a study by a CITES Standing Committee of the tiger trade, the United

States threatened sanctions [24 p. 218–21]. Coggins says that 1994 was the first time that the United States employed trade sanctions to protect wildlife [25 p. 5]. The United States took action when the Taiwanese government failed to take measures to "curtail trade in rhinoceros and tiger parts." Regional international organizations such as Association of Southeast Asian Nations-Wildlife Enforcement Network (ASEAN-WEN) were established in 2005 to stem illegal trade. Galster, Schaedla, and Redford says that ASEAN-WEN "bolsters cooperation" and "information sharing" among the countries [26 p. 122]. One example of its success came recently when the U.S. Department of Justice announced the arrest of "scores of wildlife traffickers" in an operation that was assisted by ASEAN-WEN. Wildlife officers in Singapore, Thailand, and Indonesia simultaneously ran their own in-country "Operation Wild Web" that targeted illegal wildlife internet sales [27]. The United States of course has no wild rhinoceros but there is nevertheless trade in "antique rhino horns." For example, recently an "illiterate Irish landscaper" was convicted in Brooklyn, New York for hiring another man (a U.S. citizen) to purchase a "black rhino head from a taxidermy auction on his behalf" in Texas for which he paid $18,000 and then resold in New York to an "Asian collector for $50,000" [28]. His lawyer complained about the sentence that he received because he was being treated "like a poacher with a shotgun in Africa" when he had not harmed any rhino.

One way proposed for advanced industrialized countries to provide incentives to developing countries to protect biodiversity is to purchase their debt in return for a commitment to protect habitat and species. Wilson says the idea of debt for nature swaps dates back to the 1970s and that by 1990s, some twenty agreements totaling $110 million had been achieved [29 p. 172]. An example of this "greenbacks for greenery" approach occurred in 1987 when the Weeden Foundation gave Conservation International $100,000 to purchase Bolivian debt when the Bolivian government agreed to "provide maximum protection for the Beni Biosphere Reserve as well as to increase its size by nearly 4 million acres" [30 p. 44]. China has used the panda as both an international foreign policy tool as well as for raising revenue by conducting a "rent-a-panda" program during the 1980s [31 p. 239–44]. There was great demand for the panda with "30 zoos applying for panda rentals" but the rental program was opposed by conservation organizations like the WWF and compromises were made so that only "captive bred animals" could be loaned.

Snow leopards are an example of a threatened species whose habitat lies in remote regions of several different countries including China, Pakistan, Afghanistan, and Tajikistan. Zahler and Schaller identify four underlying reasons for the threat to snow leopards: (1) decline in major prey (marmots that are valued for their pelts and fat in China and thus overhunted, urials or wild sheep that have suffered from competition and diseases transmitted from livestock, and markhors or wild goats also under threat due to transmitted diseases and poaching); (2) poaching for their "skin and body parts"; (3) killing by livestock owners; (4) decrease in their habitat [32]. Zahler and Schaller report successes in building a CBNRM program among some "65 local communities in Pakistan and 55 in Afghanistan" with the incentive of providing "vaccinations to their livestock" in return for their participation in efforts to preserve the snow leopard [32].

However, they note that the vaccination program can result in big increases in livestock numbers and thus constitute threats to the sustenance of the leopards' prey, so the communities are required to "limit their livestock numbers" as well as participate in "monitoring and enforcing anti-poaching" efforts. They note that China also has a CBNRM program to protect habitat and members from all twelve countries with snow leopard populations have met to discuss methods to protect the leopard, demonstrating again the fact that many conservation efforts require international cooperation among many different nations [32]. Although Pakistan has generally banned the hunting of the endangered markhor, a large goat that is the country's "national animal," they have allowed high-priced trophy hunting to gain the support of local people for the maintenance of an abundant supply of the species [33 p. 141].

Polar bears are another charismatic species that has created difficult issues for CITES and international relations. In 2008, the Department of Interior listed polar bears as an endangered species but "41 polar bear pelts" taken in Canada during that year were allowed to be imported to the United States [34]. Moreover, the United States "has pressed for a ban on commercial trade in polar bear parts" that pitted the United States against Canada [34]. but the motion failed with thirty-eight countries voting in favor, forty-two against, and forty-six abstaining [35]. One of the owners of the polar bear pelts said that the ban "made no sense" because "the bears are already dead" and "male bears often eat cubs anyway" thus "killing a few male bears doesn't make a difference" [34]. A major argument made by the United States was that the threat to polar bears will continue to increase from climate change and thus "sustainable trade" is not possible. Canada is the major country exporting polar bear parts. There is disagreement on the part of some polar bear supporters such as the WWF that did not support the ban but instead argued for focus on climate change causing their loss of habitat [35].

Ivory illustrates very well the distinction between wildlife "importing" and "exporting" nations proposed by Nash and the intricacies of pursuing conservation in face of an international market for ivory [36]. Vira and Ewing point out the many advantages that ivory offers for illicit international trading including the fact that it is "portable, cheap to harvest, and does not require static control of territory, while its value ... rivals virtually that of any other bush commodity" thus making it a "lifeline commodity for actors who are otherwise excluded from the global financial system" [37 p. 9]. Lovett outlines the difficulty of protecting the elephant, which he describes as a "bulldozer herbivore" that requires "enormous reserves" and "small armies to police" effectively, while revenues gained from them are limited to tourism and "donations from conservation organizations" [38 p. 129]. The ban on selling of ivory was lifted in 1997 for Botswana, Namibia, South Africa and Zimbabwe where it is now listed under Appendix II of CITES, in contrast to the rest of Africa where it remains under Appendix I [38]. Lovett cites data that the lifting of the ban has led to more poaching.

Recently, the USFWS decided to destroy six tons of ivory held in Denver in order "to help the campaign against killing elephants" [39]. Sas-Rolfes, a conservation economist from South Africa, agrees that the 1989 burning of ivory by Kenya had a beneficial impact by "raising consciousness," and brought about an ivory trade ban. However, he says that "Asian demand for ivory has continued to grow" due to their greater affluence and that consumers are not "always concerned about the source" of their ivory. He goes on to argue that the destruction of ivory by the United States will simply increase perceptions of scarcity and drive up prices but not reduce demand. Consequently, it will increase rewards for poachers. The USFWS says that they had maintained the ivory for over twenty-five years as evidence for prosecuting cases of illegal smuggling but were destroying it because "elephant poaching is now at its worst in decades" and they were showing their commitment to protecting elephants from destruction [40]. They also said they were not going to sell the ivory because "it is extremely difficult to differentiate legally acquired ivory, such as ivory imported in the 1970s, from ivory derived from elephant poaching." They say that their investigations show that "legal ivory trade can serve as a cover for illegal trade" and thus selling the ivory could "stimulate even more consumer demand." According to the USFWS, about "11,000 forest elephants were killed in Gabon's Minkébé National Park alone" with the number of elephants decreasing by 62 percent in Central Africa, with massacres "taking place in Chad, Cameroon and the Central African Republic" just in the past year conducted by "well-armed and organized criminal enterprises" and insufficient protection capacity in remote areas [41]. It is estimated that the global population of elephants declined from 600,000 in 1989 to 472,000 today [42]. Vira and Ewing cite evidence that enhanced protection did have a positive effect on preventing poaching in the Zakouma National Park in 2013 in Chad due to "new management by African Parks" [37 p. 26]. The park has not lost "a single elephant, through a combination of integrated intelligence and rapid-reaction efforts and coordinated patrols with Chadian army brigades" [37].

Some African nations have lost all of their elephants due to poaching such as Sierra Leone while Senegal has only a dozen left [43]. Safina says that the Democratic Republic of Congo has lost 90 percent of its elephant population and that poaching is now intensifying in countries like Kenya and Tanzania where there is a substantial tourist trade and jobs based on elephants. Safina contends that the sale of ivory to China "opened the floodgates" and that only "bitterly won ban of 1990 worked," helping to lead to a "collapse of ivory prices" and an increase, if slow, of the elephant population [43].

Maisels et al. analyzed the results of 80 surveys of elephants in Central Africa ranging from western Cameroon to the eastern border of the Democratic Republic of Congo based on indicators such as the elephant dung density [44]. They found the forest elephant population size declined by 62 percent between 2002 and 2011. They point out that the forest elephant decline is due mostly to poaching, in contrast to the decline of savanna elephants that also suffer major impacts from habitat decline. They found that elephant dung density was greater in areas with "wildlife guards and protected status" and negatively related to an index of corruption they employed (Transparency International's Corruption Perception Index or CPI) [44]. They cite the rapid increase in ivory demand in China and the rapid proliferation of roads that provide access for poachers' transport and trade as underlying causes of the increased poaching. They note that CPI is associated with "the rule of law and good governance" as well as rates of poverty [44]. Strindberg and Maisels report that the poaching affects the behavior of elephants such as their avoidance of unprotected roads and leads to the presence of elephant groupings without elder females and the fact that they are increasingly cut off from their former sources of food and minerals [45]. Thus, time to feed and play has been lost and they are "hemmed in by a shroud of fear" [45]. The occurrence of armed conflicts in several central African countries as well as the weakness of central governments have been the underlying reasons for the magnitude of the poaching. For example, Vira and Ewing state that the central government "has never asserted control over the Central African Republic's remote and under-populated hinterland" and consequently "there has always been raiding from neighboring countries, including Libya, Chad, and Sudan" [37 p. 36]. The number of rangers providing protection is limited and they are often outgunned – for example, "190 rangers have been killed in the Democratic Republic of the Congo (DRC) in the last 15 years" [37 p. 36]. Furthermore, in some countries such as the DRC, the armed forces of the country are among the most common poachers – committing 75 percent of the poaching in "nine of the eleven areas" where elephants roam in the Congo due to the fact that they are undisciplined, poorly trained, and poorly paid [37 p. 37]. Poachers recently have employed the tactic of poisoning vultures as a means of resisting detection by anti-poaching forces in several African countries such as Namibia and Zimbabwe [46]. Vultures detect and flock to carcasses within thirty minutes of killing and thus have served as an alert to rangers because it takes up to seventy minutes for the poachers to hack off the ivory from elephants [46]. Also, body parts of the vultures themselves are valued for medicine as well as "good luck" charms and several are now on the Red List of endangered or vulnerable species [46]. The only solution offered is for African countries to more strictly regulate the sale of pesticides and to enforce stiff prison sentences and penalties for use of poison [46].

The USFWS has described several cases of successful prosecution of individuals for smuggling illegal ivory into the United States [47]. In one case, the conspirator (Victor Gordon) paid an accomplice to purchase raw ivory but have it "carved to specifications" and then stained and dyed so that it would appear to be old. In other cases, the "shipments were accompanied by false shipping and customs documents" that identified the ivory as "wooden furniture and statues" with the ivory painted to look like wood. In still another case, the ivory "included whole tusks hidden inside furniture and concealed in beaded cloth" [47]. The U.S. Department of Justice has described several other successful prosecutions of illegal importation of not only ivory but rhinoceros horn, black corral, South African leopard hides and skulls, cobras, pangolins, hornbills, babirusa (a species of pig), orangutans, Java kingfishers, whale teeth, and narwhal tusks [40]. Despite these successful cases, finding and prosecuting them is a time-consuming and difficult process with relatively few personnel assigned to this task. The difficulty of prosecuting those who participate in illegal international wildlife trade is illustrated by the case of a Laotian (Vixay Keosavang) who is regarded as the single largest known illegal wildlife trafficker in Asia according to the director of an "anti-trafficking" organization called "Freeland" staffed by former law enforcement officials from several Asian countries as well as Britain and the United States [48]. It is "financed partly by the U.S." [48]. He has been convicted (in absentia) and sentenced to forty years of jail in South Africa for hiring petite Thai prostitutes to pose as hunters and shoot rhinos [48]. Fuller says the major part of his illegal activity is "laundering" of animals by smuggling the animal parts into Laos and then exporting them with "Laotian paperwork that says the animals were bred in captivity and thus could be sold legally." Other governments have presented "reams of evidence" to Laotian officials about his illegal activities but he remains free despite his South African conviction and is "untouchable" as long as he remains in Laos, which Fuller says is known for its "widespread corruption" [48]. In 2015, Thailand opened up a Laos-bound ship from the Congo and found it loaded with ivory tusks – Laotian authorities were reportedly furious that Thailand opened the ship's contents [49]. The director of the ASEAN Wildlife Enforcement Network said that while coordination with Vietnam and Cambodia had improved, Laos has been uncooperative [49].

Weak central governments that are unable to enforce regulations are common in several Asian countries such as Mongolia, which is "starved for revenue" and "unable to fund enforcement to stop illegal poaching or grazing" with only a "handful of rangers" patrolling millions of protected hectares of land in eastern Mongolia" [50 p. 333–4]. In Madagascar, a coup in 2009 led to a weak central government that has been taken advantage of by "timber exploiters" from Asia who have cut the forests of endangered lemurs plus used them as meat [51]. Compton and Lee describe the "extraordinary lengths" that smugglers employ to evade discovery and how authorities are understaffed or lack the knowledge to identify illegal wildlife trade due to falsified paperwork such as listing "freshwater turtles" as "fisheries products" and listing animals as "farm bred" even though they have been "poached" [52 p. 114]. Consequently, they argue that the "most pressing priority" is to reduce "market demand" though media and education. Similarly with respect to birds, Beissinger says that "presently there is no "marking system … that can reliably distinguish legal from illegally harvested birds" and that "without strong controls, attempts at sustainable harvesting *could* increase conservation problems rather than solve them" [53 p. 197]. The head of the International Trade Centre in an editorial for the *Wall Street Journal* titled "Legal Trade Can Save Endangered Wildlife" cites the case of vicuna in Peru as a success where they have been brought "back from extinction" because local communities were given the right to shear and process wool from them and consequently communities have acted to protect them from poachers and the vicuna population has expanded to more than 400,000 [54]. However, she acknowledges that a "successful legal trade requires an enforceable system of export permits" and even then "animals will still require protection through enforcement." Gonzalez cites the case of Southeast Asian pythons in which they are trying to develop "transparency" in their international trade by working with the parent company of Gucci to deal with problems of the abuse of permit systems [54].

In January of 2014, China announced that it would destroy 6 tons of ivory [55]. This is the first time that China has done this and the hope among conservationists is that "this widely publicized event" would send a message to poachers and the public that the use of illegal ivory "is unacceptable" [55]. It is estimated by the Wildlife Conservation Society that China has 45 tons of intercepted ivory and they have called on China to destroy the rest of their ivory stock which they claim would have a "transformative effect" on illegal poaching [55]. The recent decisions by several countries (e.g., China, the United States, and the Philippines) emphasizes the importance of the debate over the impacts of the destruction of ivory – some believe that it will just serve to raise the price of ivory and thus encourage more poaching. Hilborn studied data on poaching of elephants and other wildlife from 1957 through the early 2000s and found that anti-poaching patrols had a marked effect on reducing poaching, with the population of elephants rapidly increasing during the period from 1977 to 1986 but much improved since 1993 with an increased patrol activity [56 p. 1266]. He also attributes the improvement of the elephant population to the reduction in the price of ivory due to the CITES ban on its sale.

There has been an expansion and shift in the types of animals being illegally trafficked as well as the markets for these products. Wassener says that mantas are now under threat, while "there was no market for them twenty years ago" according to Manta Trust, a conservation group [57]. There is now a demand for their "gill rakers" that filter their food from water because it is used as an ingredient for a "health tonic" sold in countries like the U.S. for several hundred dollars per kilogram" [57]. An expert at the WWF said that illegal animal trafficking used to be focused on "furs and skins" for clothes and boots for people in Western countries but is now aimed at demands from the growing Asian middle class [57]. According to a turtle expert, freshwater turtles are being threatened by demand from the Chinese food market despite the fact that China has a turtle "farming industry" because demand for wild turtles persists due to the preference of many for them because of their perceived "safety" and prestige [57]. China also has "thousands of Asiatic bears" in cages on farms with "a catheter ... draining bear bile" which is used in traditional medicine for functions such as "fighting fever and inflammations" [58 p. 29]. China "claims that farms ... reduce poaching of wild bears" but animal welfare organizations challenge this proposition [58 p. 29]. Recently, data from Traffic, an organization that tracks seizures of illegal trade including bear parts, reported that illegal trade in them had "nearly tripled in Asia between 2000 and 2011" [59]. The same report contended that it is virtually impossible to raise the bears in captivity and that wild bears are the source of the captive breeding for bile as evidenced by the fact that when bears from bile farms are "moved to sanctuaries," they have missing paws and snare wounds showing that they were taken from the wild [59]. The Animals Asia Foundation is a non-governmental organization (NGO) that is attempting to end bear farming in China (where it is legal) and also Vietnam (where it is illegal but done nevertheless) by convincing traditional Chinese medicine community to "replace it [bear bile] with herbal and synthetic alternatives" and they report that "nearly 2,000 traditional Chinese medicine shops have pledged never to prescribe or sell bear bile" [60].

Bryan Christy conducted an investigation for National Geographic of "ivory worship" and its consequences [61]. In the Philippines, "Catholics are fond of ivory images of saints" and thus they have become a market for illegal ivory trades [61]. According to Christy, CITES has "one enforcement officer to police more than 30,000 animal and plant species" [61]. A major problem is corruption of Philippines customs officers who in the past have routinely "lost tons of ivory." In June of 2013, the Philippines government announced they would destroy "five tons of ivory in public" which they hailed as a "message that the country is serious and would not tolerate illegal wildlife trade" [62].

In Thailand, elephants are revered in Buddhism; nevertheless, it also has an illegal ivory trade, much of it conducted by monks, according to Christy [61]. Thailand does allow some legal trade of ivory from "tusk tips" of domesticated elephants and those that die natural deaths but, according to Christy, illegal African ivory is smuggled in to mix with the legal ivory. In 2013, Thailand's Prime Minister promised to change the country's laws which have been accused of having "loopholes" that allow tusks to be moved into China [63]. This action was taken because it would "remove the threat of trade sanctions" due to their violation of CITES conventions [63]. In China, ivory objects are used as gifts to "superiors" in the military and businesses as well as to government regulators. He says that sales of "Buddhist jewelry reached 15.8 billion and is growing by 50 percent a year" and the government has thirty-five "carving factories and 130 ivory retail outlets" [61]. As for Japan, in 1999, Japan bought 55 tons of ivory as part of a onetime sale of ivory from Zimbabwe, Botswana, and Namibia [61]. Christy says that CITES attempted to identify the impact of these sales on illegal ivory activity in Japan by hiring Traffic, an NGO that claims to have historical data on the illegal ivory trade, but its numbers are based on an assumption of the relationship between the intercepted shipments and the total amount of illegal ivory traded. Christy says that many governments failed to "report their seizures" and the information was based mostly on data from the United States and other Western countries and consequently, due to the poor baseline, it makes it impossible to determine if the Japan sale was a "success." CITES concluded that there was no correlation between the sale and illegal trade and thus declared the Japan sale a success but Christy says that the Chinese thought that the sale created problems of more illegal ivory trade because the sale made it seem as though it was now "acceptable" [61]. In 2008, CITES approved the sale of 115 tons of ivory to China and Japan with about $15 million from the sales going to conservation projects in Africa. The assumption that CITES made was that flooding the market with cheaper legal ivory would drive out the illegal traders, but Christy claims that instead it led to more illegal trafficking according to "traders and international watchdogs" [61]. One of the safeguards instituted in China was the requirement for a photo face card but Christy says that illegal trades have turned this ID card system into a smuggling tool. Christy reports that the CITES official in charge changed his perspective by 2011 and now believes that the Japan experiment did exacerbate the situation especially in China where buyers now considered it "okay to buy ivory" [61]. One interesting development in China was the fact that a Chinese NGO, WildlifeRisk, reported a "shark slaughterhouse" in a "Marine Organisms Health Protection Foods Company in Puqi township near Wenzhou" [64]. "Activists reported that 600 whale sharks were being processed annually" in a factory setting [64]. The development of domestic NGOs that act to protect wildlife would be a major development for China and other developing countries that have up till now depended on Western NGOs and governments for such actions.

An interesting contrast with the ivory experience concerns the effort to preserve crocodiles. Thorbjarnarson says that the installation of farming of crocodiles has helped to stave off the extinction of crocodiles in "cash-strapped countries" such as Venezuela [65]. He claims that the farming programs also help to improve "the image of crocodiles." He acknowledges that farming will not deal with the problem of loss of habitat and that protection from illegal poaching has also been very effective. CITES has played a key role in the program by establishing a "Crocodile Specialist Group" to "plan and implement programs" that distinguish between skins from legal farms versus illegally-poached crocs [65 p. 467]. He claims that "traders and tanners who used to work with illegal skins in the 1970s have switched to legal sources" due to CITES pressures and programs. He notes that the case of caimans is more difficult but that a "universal tagging system has been adopted" that has helped to identify origins of skins and regulate trade. However, farming does not necessarily end threats to species. Greenberg points out that neither tiger farms in China nor "hundreds of millions of farmed Atlantic salmon" have avoided the decline in these species [9]. There are "only 450 Siberian tigers left in the wild most in Russia . . . and only 18 to 22 in China" but China has "some 5000 to 6000 tigers in captivity – some of them Siberians" [66]. Feng says that though China has ratified restrictions on "the domestic trade of tigers," they continue to "allow the trade" "in tiger parts from domesticated tigers." Japan has undertaken a major effort to farm Pacific bluefin tuna, of which the country consumes 70 percent of the worldwide catch for its consumption as sushi [67]. Nagano says that because CITES is considering the listing of the Pacific tuna as an endangered species, finding a way to farm the fish "has become of national importance" [67]. Other species are also threatened by demands of consumers in China. One example is the small porpoise "vaquita" that lives in the northern Gulf of California. Mexican fishermen are seeking to catch both shrimp and a fish named "totoaba" whose bladders are used in soup in China [68]. The vaquita get caught in gillnets used for fishing. The Mexican government announced it "will ban gillnets for two years across . . . the upper gulf and compensate the fishermen for their lost catch" [68]. Fishermen say that nets designed to preserve the vaquita do not allow them to catch enough fish to survive economically [68]. The totoaba bladders bring so much money that there is doubt that the ban can be enforced.

Some wildlife experts maintain that bans on selling products can be counterproductive to the preservation of the species because bans drive up the price of the product and reduce the incentive of private landowners and natives to preserve the species. They make an argument for what they call "market-led conservation" [69 p. 112]. For example, Leader-Williams cites the "spectacular increase in southern African white rhinos" "where limited use is allowed" including sports hunting and "live sales" [70 p. 97]. He identifies the conditions for success as "providing good protection . . . usually in small areas . . . use of fencing . . . strong biological management through monitoring, translocation and seeding." The fact that the rhinos are located in small, fenced enclosures means that free movement is impossible and thus inbreeding would occur without monitoring and translocation. However, one case found that the enforcement of ivory bans though seizures of ivory in the Democratic Republic of the Congo led to a 60 percent "price collapse" of ivory and attributed this to the sensitivity of traffickers to "risk calculations" [37 p. 22]. The researchers concluded that this area "had previously been a secure hub with low risk of enforcement but once denied a principal transit point" that "traders acknowledged that the immediate-term risks outweighed the benefits" [37 p. 22].

The CITES agreement was signed in March 1973 after the 1972 UN Conference on Human Environment held in Stockholm. CITES has three levels of listing: (1) Appendix I species are banned for wildlife trade for commercial purposes; (2) Appendix II bans trade unless it can be shown that it will not endanger the species; (3) Appendix III concerns species requested to be protected by specific countries [71 p. 328; 72 p. 421]. Discussions about decisions to list a species often involve arguments over the adequacy of data supporting the need to list as well as the interests of individual countries that will have to shoulder the major costs of listing. New data sometimes can lead countries to change their position. For example, Gehring and Ruffing discuss the case of the humphead wrasse, a fish that was listed in Appendix II by consensus when Indonesia changed its position due to the presentation of new information [73 p. 140–1]. There was also debate over the listing proposed by Australia and Madagascar of the great white shark in Appendix II. The data issue was paramount for the great white shark because it is "rare" and "catch records are scarce" for it [73 p. 143–4]. The possibility of listing the shark had been discussed by the CITES "Animals Committee" and "shark working group" since 1994. According to Gehring and Ruffing, Japan opposed the listing because they said the "information was insufficient" to show that it was endangered or that trade was a threat to it" [73]. Its listing in Appendix II was eventually approved with eighty-seven votes for it and thirty-four against. CITES has a very limited budget (about $5 million in 1999) and most of its budget goes to commissioned studies, staffing and very little to enforcement because individual governments are expected to enforce CITES regulations themselves but governments (especially developing countries) spend limited resources on it [74 p. 197]. Western governments also sometimes oppose listings. For example, Canada opposed the listing of hooded seals in 1985 on the basis of "inadequate biological justification" and because of the impact it would have on "native and non-native sealers" [74 p. 197]. Duffy has strongly criticized the "western bias" of CITES, arguing that the "blanket bans" under Appendix I "do not take into consideration local or national differences" [75 p. 50–1]. Duffy also contends that it is the demand from wealthier countries like the United States that drives the trade but "the fact is that wildlife trade is simply not a high priority for most countries" and thus the sheer size of the trade "overwhelms the existing enforcement structure" [75 p. 51].

There is a debate over whether CITES restrictions on trading of rhino horn is aiding or hurting the conservation of the rhinoceros [76 p. 15–17]. Biggs, Courchamp, Martin, and Possingham argue that the ban on trade in rhino horn means that "demand can only be met through the illegal market" and consequently that the retail "price of the horn increased from $4700 to $65,000 per kilogram from 1993 to 2012" resulting in the increased poaching of rhinos [77 p. 1038–9]. Biggs et al. claim that attempts to use "militarized enforcement" of the ban fail because it will simply drive the price higher for the product in the face of "inelastic and growing demand" [77]. They also state that enforcement will be ineffective due to "corrupt government officials" who are "coopted by criminal syndicates" [77]. They acknowledge that there are conditions that must be met if legal trading of rhino horn is to be successful in encouraging conservation including the two following points: (1) "Regulators must be able to prevent illegal laundering of horn"; (2) "Demand does not escalate to dangerous levels" [77]. They argue that the first condition (prevent laundering) can be handled by technology to track the selling of the horn through the "selling chain" and they propose a "Central Selling Organization" that would make it more cost effective to buy legal ivory and they argue increased demand could be met by increasing the supply of rhinos [77]. Prins and Okita-Ourma reply that the market could greatly increase by "reawakening demand in countries such as Japan and Singapore where it has declined some" and that the comparison to crocodile example is unwarranted because "farmed crocodiles number in the millions" compared to the 30,000 rhinos and rhinos reproduce much more slowly [78 p. 1167–8]. Collins, Gracer, and Snowball caution that South Africa's rhino population is based on a very small gene population with implications of potential genetic weakness, and question whether they could breed at the rate of wild populations [79 p. 1167].

The Politics of Whaling Treaties

Whales are animals that create fierce attachments among humans that result in international tensions and treaties aimed at preserving this particular species. Kalland criticizes the creation by preservationists of a mythical "super whale" that is "as intelligent as humans, friendly and caring, fond of music, capable of inter-species communication" in order to make the argument that the consumptive use of the whale as a resource should be replaced by recreational uses like a "watch in the wild" relationship [80 p. 159–163]. Two environmentalist organizations, Greenpeace and the Sea Shepherd Conservation Society, have gained their environmental reputations to a great degree by tracking and (in the Sea Shepherd's case) attacking whaling ships [81]. These two organizations have antagonism for each other but nevertheless Greenpeace often gave information to Sea Shepherd about the location of Japanese whalers and, according to Heller, were happy when their ship, the *Farley Mowat*, shows up because it "puts fear into the whalers" [81]. Indeed, Watson, the captain of the *Farley Mowat*, has "sunk eight whaling ships" [81 p. 5]. The main point of the Sea Shepherd and Greenpeace efforts is to bring attention from the media on the issue so as to force international pressure on whalers. Heller quotes Watson as saying "if you have an action and no one covers it, it didn't happen" [81 p. 22]. Japan did attribute its failure to take "only 507 minke whales instead of the planned 987" to obstructions by the Sea Shepherd according to the Japanese Ministry of Agricultural, Forestry, and Fisheries [82]. Greenpeace announced in 2008 their conversion to a "softer approach" in protesting Japanese whaling by not trailing Japanese sailing vessels but trying to win "support inside of Japan" through quieter protests [83]. The Associated Press cite a Japanese expert that Japanese are less "tolerant of deviant behavior" and consequently anti-whaling protests had received negative coverage in Japanese press [83]. As part of the Sea Shepherd's strategy, they film the death of whales, which is gruesome – Heller says that whales do not die when the harpoon hits but they "thrash and gush blood" and then are winched on to the ship where they are "jolted with thousands of volts of electricity" to hasten their death and the whale "screams and thrashes" for some 15–20 minutes before it dies while if it is a mother, its doomed calf swims around the boat [81 p. 27]. Heller contends that the "equivalent of the pain and destruction of ocean life" would "not be allowed . . . by land butchers." However, Norwegian vets on whaling vessels claim that 90 percent of whales "die instantaneously" from the grenade "blowing apart their brain" and the "remaining 10 percent are dispatched quickly by a rifle" and they report that Norwegians are so efficient that the United States has brought them to Alaska to show Inuit their "techniques" [84].

The decline of whales illustrates the impact of technology as a key contributing factor to endangering species. Kobayashi says that the creation of factory ships where whales are processed on board without having to go to "land stations" combined with devices to "pull large whales onto decks" allowed them to expand their operations beyond their territorial waters [85 p. 182–3]. Furthermore the development of faster ships allowed them to catch "faster species" of whales and the development of "shell harpoons that detonate inside the whale" greatly increased their killing capacity [85 p. 182–3]. Likewise, "sonar devices" allowed them to easily track whales. Kobayashi states that these development set off a "frantic race" among nations "to capture whales around the world" [85 p. 182].

Underlying the problem of managing whale populations is the tenet that "seas are free for any nation" and can be limited "only with the consent of the participating states through multinational or international agreements" [85 p. 184]. The attempt to control whale harvests dates back to the International Whaling Convention of 1931 which was run by the League of Nations. In 1948, the International Convention for the Regulation of Whaling (ICRW) went into effect which over the years has developed five types of regulation: (1) quotas on the size and species to be harvested; (2) areas open for whale hunting; (3) "seasonal" and "geographic" limitations; (4) treatment after killing whales; (5) "supervision and control" [85 p. 188–90]. The International Whaling Commission (IWC) has a scientific committee and science is supposed to be "the basis of all regulation." The effectiveness of the new technologies for capturing and killing whales plus the rise of the environmentalist movement in the 1970s along with the abandonment of whaling by nations such as the United States and Australia led to the moratoria on whaling [85 p. 193]. There is a consensus that the IWC has been ineffective from its very beginning in regulating whaling because it "lacks the ability to enforce its policies as members are given the opportunity to opt out of IWC regulations by giving notice" and it "lacks enforcement mechanisms to compel member compliance" [86 p. 836–8]. If a member nation rejects regulations within ninety days of their adoption, they do not have to adhere to them. In such cases, the only constraints on these countries have been the threat of sanctions and boycotts from non-whaling countries, though these may create a backlash from the whaling countries [86 p. 846]. Jordan contends that the requirement for a 75 percent vote to make changes in the schedule that regulates quotas and types of whales that may be caught makes compromise difficult [86 p. 850]. Dan Goodman, who works for the Japan Institute of Cetacean Research, has written that Japan offered several compromises at IWC meetings including a 50 percent reduction of "lethal research" in southern oceans as well as "acceptance of neutral observers on whaling ships" and satellite-based monitoring systems [87]. He argues that the United States was initially receptive to these proposals, but influenced by anti-whaling NGOs to oppose them, and he cites threats of "tourist boycotts against Caribbean nations" that voted in favor of pro-whaling proposals [87]. Mike Iliff, a well-known observer of IWC politics, related how a proposal by Australia on whaling changes "did not receive the support it deserved" due to Australia's "ongoing strident condemnation of Japan's permit whaling program" [88 p. 462–3]. Iliff concluded that the IWC meeting was a failure because despite the "enthusiasm for an alternative," "neither side had any new ideas" and the "same old dogmas" prevailed [88 p. 466]. The *New York Times* editorialized that the "U.S. should press for a complete ban" even at the risk of destroying the IWC and possible resumption of commercial whaling [89]. In short, there is no obvious room for compromise given the positions of the opposed groups.

There are significant differences among national attitudes concerning the hunting of whales. According to a survey done in the early 1990s about 60 percent of Australians and Germans opposed whaling "under any circumstances" while 61 percent and 57 percent of Norwegians and Japanese disagreed with this position [90 p. 294]. The IWC is heavily involved in politics over moratoria on whale hunting. Many of the voting nations have no direct interest in whaling issues but, according to critics of whaling, vote against the moratoria due to payments from Japan to countries such as Palau and Saint Kitts-Nevis [81 p. 275]. When the same accusation was made in 2004 that Nicaragua joined the IWC and voted with Japan to allow more whaling, Nicaragua and Japan rejected the accusation, arguing that they had been convinced by facts such as the whales constituting a threat to endangered fish because whales "eat five times as much as human populations" [91]. However, Estes et al., in an article in *Science*, state that "industrial whaling during the 20th century" "transferred 105 million tons of carbon ... into the atmosphere and that whale feces return ... nutrients ... enhancing productivity" of the sea [92 p. 305]. Norway also has been heavily engaged in international tensions over the whaling issue. In 1993, after a campaign by Greenpeace for a boycott of Norwegian products, the U.S. Secretary of Commerce threatened to impose sanctions on trade with Norway [93 p. 126]. This action was taken on the basis of the Pelly Amendment of the "Fishermen's Protective Act" (P.L. 92–219 (85 Stat. 786)) which states that when it is determined that nationals of a foreign country are diminishing the effectiveness of an international fishery conservation program, the president then is authorized to prohibit the importation of fish products from the offending nation. Conservatives and whaling nations accused Greenpeace with buying votes on the IWC, through paying the membership fees and costs of members attending commission meetings for countries such as Antigua and St. Lucia, and they suggest that the Japanese merely copied the Greenpeace strategy to sway IWC votes to their position [94].

One of the reasons allowed for exceptions to the ban on whaling concerns "aboriginals," for whom the hunting of whales is part of their historical culture and important to their subsistence. In 2009, Greenland asked permission to kill "50 humpbacks whales" – an endangered species – to feed its aboriginal population [95]. A *New York Times* editorial noted that their request was supported by Denmark which also employs an exception for the same reason but in Denmark's case, the *New York Times* argues, it is a "thinly disguised cover for commercial whaling." Sanderson criticized the attempt to eliminate Faroe Islanders from whaling. Anti-whaling groups contended that "Faroe Islanders have one of the highest living standards in the World" and thus do not need "to rely on pilot whales for their survival" [96 p. 198–9]. Sanderson defended their whaling which "they have done for centuries" on the basis that "other meat" would have to be imported from elsewhere to replace it and thus be environmentally harmful [96 p. 199].

Some reports cite Japanese experts as saying that the whaling industry and the eating of whale meat is no longer important to the country but they continue to support whaling because they view criticism of it as an example of "cultural imperialism" from the West and that the actions of the Sea Shepherd had "fanned the popular ire" making it impossible for the Japanese government to compromise because cutbacks would cause a "huge political outcry" [82]. The *Economist* reports that "whale is cheaper than beef in the Norway market" and that the Japanese "seem to have lost their taste for the delicacy" with only "one restaurant in Tokyo" specializing in whale meat [84]. However, Kobayashi describes how many "whalers in the small coastal whaling communities descend from generations of whalers" and maintain that whaling is a matter of "tradition" and respect for them [85 p. 195]. Another theory is that resistance is due to the secretive and powerful Ministry of Agriculture, Forestry and Fisheries because it wants to protect its cushy jobs including high-paying jobs after retirement in the government-owned fleet that does the "scientific whaling" [82]. Recently, the World Court ruled that Japan's "whaling is not scientific research" because it had resulted in only two peer-reviewed articles since 2005 based on "nine killed whales" while "3600 minke whales had been killed" during that time, and revoked its research whaling permits for the area around Antarctica [95]. However, Japan can continue "scientific whaling" in the Pacific where it has permits to kill "up to 200 minke whales, 100 Sei whales, 50 Bryde's whales and 10 sperm whales" [95].

One of the strategies for compromise is to focus on other causes of whale deaths such as collisions with ships. In 2008, the National Oceanic and Space Administration implemented rules to "limit ocean-going ships" to 10 knots or less "for certain times and locations" along the East Coast of the United States, which has cut the number of whale deaths due to collisions by an estimated 80 to 90 percent and "no right whale deaths" have occurred since the new rule had been implemented [97]. The Science Committee of the IWC claims that scientific data now show that some whale species such as minkes, pilot, gray, and large sperm whales have recovered sufficiently to be harvested [85 p. 200–2]. There is a big difference between the positions of conservationists, who are willing to allow sustainable whaling based on scientific data, and preservationists, for whom "scientific evidence has no impact" [85 p. 197]. However, since the moratorium has not stopped "scientific whaling," Kobayashi says that even preservationists may agree that "closely-regulated hunting is better" than unregulated hunting that could occur [85 p. 207]. For example, Iceland withdrew from the IWC in 1992, but it rejoined the IWC, though stipulating that it would "resume limited commercial whaling" and has recently increased its quota to 150 fin whales – an endangered species [98 p. 633]. Stoett argues that a proposed compromise revised management schedule (RMS) would substantially lower this quota but he says that adopting this compromise RMS is "beyond the ideological horizon of the preservationists" [98]. Stoett goes on to say that there is now a very limited market for whale meat and products and that the renewal of a large-scale commercial whaling is "simply not possible" [98 p. 633–4]. Evidence shows that countries such as Iceland and Japan "heavily subsidize" the whaling industry and that the rapidly growing popularity of whale watching generates more net revenue [99 p. 155]. In summary, the case of whaling illustrates the difficulties of reaching and enforcing international treaties because the clash between valued customs of whale hunting versus commitment to the intrinsic value of charismatic whales have made compromise unachievable.

War and Its Effects on Wildlife

Wildlife conservation has long been affected by armed conflicts. For example, Gray cites the importance of the buffalo to the "economy of the Plains Indians" and the strategy of white settlers was to defeat Indians by slaughtering buffalo [100 p. 35]. The effects of wars on wildlife are complex and often unexpected. In many cases, the existence of uprisings and separatist movements directly lead to the demise of wildlife populations. For example, poachers who killed thirteen rhinos in Kaziranga National Park in India were associated with a separatist movement that had "gotten involved in poaching in order to raise money" and employ automatic weapons such as the AK 47s [101]. In response, the park armed its "Assam Forest Protection force" with automatic weapons with authority to shoot poachers – they have killed thirteen poachers in the last three years. Hart says that the civil war that began in the Democratic Republic of the Congo in 1996 made an already inadequate capability to administer protected areas even weaker as guns and ammunition became widely available and armed gangs intimidated park guards [102 p. 251].

There are reports of situations where war has helped to protect some species. McConahay, writing in the Sierra Magazine, stated that "peace is hell for the environment" in Central America because the end of conflict leads to much more homesteading (often by former combatants) who "cut down and sell forests" [103 p. 48]. Similarly, Fallows, writing in the Audubon Magazine, wrote that "when Indonesia and Malaysia were fighting over border claims on the island of Borneo, they did relatively little damage to the environment" but after the end of the conflict, they are competing to cut and "sell the forests" [104 p. 95]. Bourne claims that if you want to find "big cats" in Mexico, look to land cultivated by drug lords because they cut off all access to these lands and thus "protect the habitat for species" [105 p. 94]. Peter Matthiessen notes that war in Cambodia led to planting of mines in jungles so that the end of the Pol Pot regime has opened up jungle areas because of the decreased threat from them [106 p. 64]. Cox also says that the brutal Khmer Rouge government sent so many people into slave camps that they emptied birding spots in savannas and forests of population and "wildlife prospered" [107 p. 52]. However, after the end of the regime, Cox says that ecotourism generated income from watching birds that villagers used to kill, as well as providing employment for park rangers in Cambodia. Matthiessen describes how the demilitarized zone between North and South Korea functioned as a reserve for the endangered hooded cranes which were disappearing otherwise in South Korea due to the "economic boom" as wetlands were "tied-up with concrete embankments for the 1988 Summer Olympics" [108 p. 189–91 & 195]. Wilcove said that the 1983 war in Sudan between Arab populations in the North and non-Arab populations in the South did not have the expected negative effects on the kob population (a type of antelope) because, scientists believe, the huge swampy "Sudd" area in Sudan proved to be impenetrable even to poachers [1 p. 101]. Oates observed that wildlife in "disordered societies" like Liberia and Equatorial Guinea "recovered," but "forest wildlife in Ghana" declined during years of "relative peace and prosperity" in the country [109 p. 225]. Kobayashi says that the whale population recovered somewhat during the years of World War II due to the fact that many whaling vessels were used for war purposes and whaling villages were attacked [85 p. 187].

On the other hand, the war in Viet Nam reportedly had a disastrous effect on cranes. Rome quotes a former guerilla leader recalling seeing many cranes when he was young but none after the war – he is now helping to restore the population [110 p. 60]. War in the Congo harmed gorillas in the Virunga National Park case cited above where "10 gorillas were killed" with some "shot in the back of the head" [111]. Rebel soldiers occupied high lands in the park and government troops directed fire at them thus "blowing up gorilla habitat." Moreover, they also "eat in the park" and thus kill wildlife for food such as machine-gunning hippopotamuses in one of the park's lakes [111]. The war between Tanzania and Uganda in 1978–9 resulted in both armies "grabbing as much ivory as they could" such as by throwing grenades at families of elephants [112 p. 142]. More recently, Gettleman reported on several military-related poaching attacks in Africa [113]. In Chad, government rangers "were killed by elephant poachers" in Zakouma National Park with evidence linking the poachers to the "Sudanese para-military organization" with stacks of elephant carcasses similar to what happened in Cameroon earlier. According to Gettleman, the Chad elephant population has been reduced from 4350 in 2002 to only 450 now, and only one elephant calf birth has been reported due to their inability to procreate under stress [113]. Chad has had "several rebellions" in recent years and its borders are not defended [113].

Davalos compared "advantages" (from a conservation point of view) as well as disadvantages of the armed conflict in Columbia and concedes that there were positive aspects such as the "slowing . . . rate of settlement . . . belligerence has curbed deforest-ation in San Lucas, especially in the west slope" [114 p. 76–7]. But she concludes that the overall effects are bad because conversion of forest to "cocoa production" and the "permanent state of belligerence" takes away from any incentive to manage natural resources for conservation and destroys the existence of the community dedicated to conservation [114 p. 77].

Dudley, Ginsberg, Plumptre, Hart, and Campos conducted a wide-ranging review of the effects of war on protection of wildlife habitat and conclude that any positive effects were largely the result of "cold war situations such as those present between North and South Korea" where the demilitarized zone between the two countries has served as a wildlife refuge [115]. They say that recent wars have tended to be "internal conflicts rather than international conflicts" though they often cause migrations across borders and create destabilization. They argue that wars (old and new) generally have a negative effect on wildlife because the militaries and guerilla forces use them as a source of food [115 p. 322]. They cite cases such as the 1979 Ugandan war and conflict in the Democratic Republic of the Congo as causing "massive declines in elephants" and conflict between Tamil separatists and government troops had caused declines in Asian elephants.

Domestically, the U.S. Military now has become a "wildlife protector" because "many of the country's 440 bases act as 'off limits' to development" and thus provide protection to many endangered species such as the California red-legged frog and the red-cockaded woodpecker [116]. An example of collaboration occurred when the Vandenberg Air Force Base "joined with the Land Conservancies" of San Luis and Santa Barbara Counties to buy about 170 acres of land that could serve as a base for launch of missiles. The military needed the area to serve as a buffer due to the possibility of falling debris and "toxic clouds" while the Land Conservancies had run out of money to purchase it alone [116]. According to Kesling, the Defense Department was ordered to protect "flora and fauna" on its bases in 1960 with the Sikes Act, and Kesling proceeds to document how a marine base in California acts to protect endangered desert tortoises and red-cockaded woodpeckers [117].

Conclusion

The international politics of wildlife are dominated by disputes over trafficking of animals (and parts of them) and the exploitation of wildlife such as fish and mammals that cross national boundaries. International bodies such as CITES and IWC have been developed to deal with these issues but their ability to solve problems related to them has been limited. Both CITES and the IWC have few enforcement resources of their own and thus have to rely upon the compliance of individual nations that may have little interest or may be opposed to CITES or IWC measures. Consequently, some of the more effective actions have involved threats of trade sanctions by the United States and/or other Western countries against countries that violate norms. Other steps such as burning of ivory stores and the banning of its sale have been taken by several individual nations to highlight the destruction of elephants. These actions may have had some effect but the demand for ivory and many other endangered species (and products from them) is so high that they unleash powerful economic incentives and even countries like the United States have not invested enough resources to stop this trade. Indeed, there exists underlying disagreement over the role of markets in wildlife conservation and whether the attempt to stop ivory trading through bans and burning helps or hurts conservation. With respect to issues such as whaling, there exists disagreement over underlying values such as should we consume whale species at all even if scientific studies show that there exist enough whales to sustain commercial whaling?

As with the ESA, science is supposed to be the determining factor in IWC decisions, but preservationists do not accept "sustainable whaling" period and thus values have trumped scientific data. The IWC has been completely hamstrung by the inability to achieve compromise on the issue so that its very existence is threatened. The essence of the conflict concerns the refusal of whale-protecting NGOs to modify their core beliefs. This case illustrates again how the core beliefs of wildlife interest groups are based on non-consumptive, emotional attachment to wildlife which, to them, makes science and concepts such as "sustainable takes" irrelevant. It again emphasizes that economic motivations are not important to these groups.

The differences between the evolution of wildlife policy in Western and non-Western states is marked. For the most part, wildlife policy in Western states evolved primarily due to internal national politics while in contrast, international forces have been a strong influence on the policies of African nations. For example, Brown and Davies state that bushmeat is "unusual among human foodstuffs" because it raises "high emotions" from people "far removed from the site of its consumption" with Western non-consumers being "the most vocal parties" [118 p. 1].

It is clear that strong and inevitable forces are overwhelming the ability of individual nations to deal with threats to species. Technological changes in fishing and hunting threaten species that were once considered inexhaustible. Demands for threatened species (or products made from them) in countries like the United States and China have grown and even wealthy nations have not been able to stop illegal trade. As a result, cohesive action by international organizations is required to address the problems but the experiences of organizations such as CITES and the IWC demonstrate mixed and limited success.

9 Wildlife Politics, Values, and Ethics

Introduction

Some disputes over wildlife involve differing contentions over empirical facts such as "how large must an endangered population be in order to be sustain itself over long periods of time?" or "does the sale of ivory lead to more or less poaching of elephants?" However, underlying the most passionate political struggles over wildlife are not disputes over empirical facts, but differences in values or priorities among values. A primary debate concerns whether consumptive or non-consumptive values should prevail in decision making about wildlife conservation. Gibbons points out that it is not utilitarian benefits that drives support for the Endangered Species Act (ESA) but "the beauty and exquisite mystery of nature" [1 p. 26]. Although environmentalists often argue that there are economic benefits to wildlife, economic returns from wildlife cannot be relied upon to justify their conservation [1 p. 26]. Beazley emphasizes that "intrinsic values" are needed to argue for the preservation of species because "most species on the endangered list ... could be lost for spaceship earth without threat of an ecosystem collapse" [2 p. 16]. Non-economic values affect wildlife policies. Cultural values and traditions drive opinions on what policies are appropriate for wildlife. For example, Alaskan natives look at subsistence hunting from the perspective that "animals are their brothers and sisters ... and deserve respect ... in return they allow themselves to be harvested by humans" and that "wild game meat is used in important cultural ceremonies such as funerals" and thus these natives believe that "short seasons and bag limits are inappropriate" because wildlife are an "integral part of their lives" [3 p. 332–46]. Conniff makes the point that conservationists are constantly seeking to prove the worth of wildlife to humans such as their use in the "first effective treatment for H.I.V." as well as for "the development of ACE inhibitors" [4]. But Conniff goes on to say that "most wildlife species ... are always going to be useless or occasionally annoying from the human perspective" and thus most wildlife are "useless in the same way that art, music, and poetry" that do nothing more than raise our spirits" [4].

Throughout much of history, humans have judged the value of wildlife based on its utility to humankind, but in the last century alternative ethical systems have been proposed. Minteer cites Aldo Leopold's "land ethic" as the equivalent of a "Copernican revolution ... in our conceptualization of man's place in the natural world" [5 p. 79]. The land ethic postulates a "worldview supporting a new set of moral claims that force us ... to take a more expansive and intelligent account of myriad interdependencies between natural and human communities" [5 p. 79]. Nash argues that the ecological concept of the "food chain" turns the traditional hierarchy of life "upside down" – "take away the top of the pyramid – a hawk or human say – and the system was hardly disturbed ... humans depended on the bacteria which sustained grass which fed the cattle which became steaks" [6 p. 57]. Nash describes how environmental ethics have gone through an "evolution" from narrow to broader focus beginning with self, and then evolving through "family, tribe, nation" to "humans, animals, plantings, life, ecosystems, planets and the universe" [6 p. 5]. From the ecosystem perspective, Nash says that humans are "moral agents who have the responsibility to articulate and defend the rights for other parts of the ecological world" that cannot defend themselves [6 p. 11]. There have been a variety of other ethical systems that have been developed as alternatives to the conventional "anthropocentrism" ethic in which humans are at the center of the universe. Bryan G. Norton has proposed a "weak anthropocentric" position in which humans take a more "environmentally enlightened worldview" that recognizes the "transformative value that nature offers" [5 p. 83]. Peter Singer's approach employs utilitarianism but extends it to include the "maximization of the utility of all sentient creatures" [5 p. 87]. Minteer describes the "ecocentric" ethics of J. Baird Callicott and Holmes Rolston III that emphasize "ecological communities rather than individual organisms," in contrast to Singer, who is "preoccupied with the welfare of individual animals" [5 p. 85]. Thus Singer specifically describes the idea of justifying "recreational hunting of individual animals for the good of the conservation" of the species as "environmental fascism" [7 p. 63]. Values have affected key court decisions about wildlife. Callicott hailed the Supreme Court's decision to uphold the ESA in the snail darter ruling because of the court's "refusal to value the snail darter economically" and thus holding that it has "value that cannot be expressed in terms of price" [8 p. 40]. Callicott's position contrasts with Singer's in arguing, for example, that there may be a moral imperative to kill species like white-tailed deer that harm the environment for other species [7 p. 68]. DiZerega quotes conservative Senator James Buckley from New York as arguing in favor of the ESA and the snail darter decision stating that it "represents a quantum jump in man's acknowledgement of his moral responsibility for the integrity of the natural world" [9 p. 107]. DiZerega uses this example to demonstrate that "environmental values do not easily fit into a liberal/conservative political spectrum" [9 p. 107].

There exist wide differences concerning priorities among animal rights organizations with "animal welfare" groups such as the Society for the Prevention of Cruelty to Animals "accepting most current uses of animals" but seeking to "minimize their pain and suffering" while "fundamentalists" believe that man "should not use animals for their own purpose regardless of benefits" [10 p. 8–9]. Garner argues that protection of wild animals has more political support as reflected in the size of membership in NGOs than "pure animal protection organizations" because protecting wildlife has possible anthropocentric rewards (e.g., tourism and recreation) and thus a broader constituency than those focusing on "domestic and lab animals" [11 p. 120]. As an example, The Fund for Animals "worked to stop fashion shows that included ... wolf furs" but "failed to condemn furs from ranch animals" [10 p. 63]. Indeed, many domesticated animals such as cows or sheep are viewed as having "a ruinous effect on the landscape" by many environmentalists [11 p. 134]. The gap between animal rights and environmental organizations is illustrated by their positions toward a 1991 proposal to ban leghold traps, which, according to Garner "was not supported by any wildlife groups" and indeed, was "vigorously opposed by the Nature Conservancy" [12 p. 114–19]. Conniff, a critic of animal rights organizations, claims that "even conservationists ... used padded leghold traps to trap lynx in Canada ... secure in their knowledge that animals of this size don't chew off their limbs and are even less likely to starve if left without food for ten or twelve hours" [13 p. 131]. There are also significant differences in priorities among environmental organizations dating back to the conflict between those who believe in "sustainable use," such as Gifford Pinchot, in contrast to those (e.g., John Muir) who believe in the preservation of nature "with minimal human intervention" [14 p. 11]. Decker, Brown, and Siemer point out that wildlife management agencies have been closely associated with Pinchot's "utilitarian" approach [14].

Values affect positions toward hunting. Garner says that hunting is viewed by many environmentalists as having positive conservation effects, such as providing habitat for game animals as well as funds for state natural resource agencies, and reducing over-abundant "nuisance species"; while most animal rights organizations strongly oppose hunting [12 p. 112]. Cambrone critiques deer lovers who "consider themselves environmentalists" but refuse to confront the ecological damage caused by overabundant deer and refuse to accept "even one deer harmed" [15]. Environmentalists support hunting to remove wildlife that are harmful to ecosystems, such as burros that were found by biologists to be harmful to soil and vegetation in the Bandelier National Monument (in New Mexico) during the 1970s – an action that was opposed by the animal rights organization Fund for Animals [16 p. 259]. The fund won agreement to attempt to remove the burros but it did not work so the burros were "eradicated" by the Park Service. However, sometimes hunters oppose environmentalists' efforts to eradicate "invasive species" that harm other species that hunters want to hunt, such as feral pigs and goats in Hawaii [17 p. 279]. In such cases, values have led to an unusual alliance between animal rights and hunters in opposition to environmentalists. Jane Goodall admits that she had "always been an advocate for the individual [animal]" but "had to rethink my position" after "efforts to save a unique and amazing species – the kakapo [a nocturnal, flightless owl] ... almost failed due to cat predation and the utter destruction caused by rabbits and goats" [18 p. 225].

Values and Invasive Species

Differences in values form the basis of disagreement among groups between those who view non-native, invasive species as harmful and those who defend them. If a non-native animal is attractive and quiet like the mute swan, it is likely to attract support from admirers and animal rights organizations. Hugh Raffles wrote an opinion piece in the *New York Times* protesting the proposal of the New York State Department of Environmental Conservation to kill "the entire population of mute swans" [19].

New York State wildlife officials report that "swans are now consuming large amounts of aquatic vegetation needed by native waterfowl and contaminating the water with their feces" [20]. Raffles claims that the proposal is based on "inconclusive science" and assumptions based on growing numbers of these swans in Michigan and Chesapeake Bay" and he argues that the New York population "has not been shown to be a threat" and praises them for being "mysterious, beautiful" creatures that "delight men's eyes," and … feel grateful for the otherworldly serenity that a mating pair … can bring to the neighborhood pond in this age of municipal austerity" [19]. Raffles characterizes the lumping together of "nonnative" species "an ideological grab bag of a category whose members are varied in their impacts and diverse in their contributions" [19]. The swans have also won the support of GooseWatch group that has "collected 20,000 signatures" and a bill proposed by a state senator to "put a two-year moratorium on any elimination effort" [20]. Perry and Perry describe the state of Vermont's Fish and Wildlife Department's decision to use "lethal control" after non-lethal methods such as egg-shaking had failed to eliminate "the nuisance species," but residents and animal rights organizations brought a legal challenge and the court ruled that "mute swans were Federally protected under the Migratory Bird Treaty" and thus the state was forced to obtain a "depredation permit" from the U.S. Fish and Wildlife Service (USFWS), which has jurisdiction over migratory birds [21 p. 30]. Perry and Perry also describe how Italy attempted to control the gray squirrel, an invasive species from the United States, but during the three-year legal struggle, the gray squirrel population had "become too large to control" [21 p. 29–30]. Macdonald, King, and Strachan point out that when invader and native species cannot coexist, it forces humans to decide "whether to stand by and let modified nature take its new course, or to act to prevent a foreseeable extinction" [22 p. 199]. They go on to argue that when the probability of restoring red squirrels is nil, the "biodiversity argument for control" collapses and pragmatically it is better to have gray squirrels "than no squirrels" [22].

Perry and Perry argue that conservationists and animal rights supporters could reach accommodation on these issues if conservationists were willing to employ "alternatives to lethal methods" and if animal rights organizations were willing to offer to pay for the extra expense of using them [21 p. 27]. One example of their use occurred in Hastings-on-Hudson (New York), where the city's mayor originally proposed that overpopulous deer be lured with bait and then killed with a "stun gun," such as used in slaughter-houses, but this proposal was "met with outrage" by many residents [23]. Consequently, the town developed a plan to spend $30,000 over the first two years to employ contraception – animal rights groups pledged to pay at least $12,000 of the cost [23]. Rutberg says that the "protein-based immunocontraceptives" have been proven effective in controlling wild horse populations on Assateague but have not been used often even though they have been around for "20 years" [24]. Problems with wild horses are much more serious in the West (as discussed in Chapter 5) where the BLM (Bureau of Land Management) says that rangelands can only sustain 26,000 horses but there are now 48,000 and this number is projected to increase to 100,000 within five years [25]. Due to the strength of wild horse and animal rights enthusiasts, the main strategy has been to round them up and put them into feedlots, but this is a temporary solution.

Animal rights advocates want fertility drugs administered to them but the BLM says this is impractical now because it would have to be done every two years (new drugs are trying to be developed that could last five years) [25]. A rancher suggested that 50,000 horses "be slaughtered and the meat put to use" but, as a professor of wildlife management said, "horses are so beloved in our society that no one wants to make a hard decision" [25].

Most conservation biologists have little patience for popular but exotic species. Estes et al. point out that one of the reasons why invasive species are able to multiply so quickly is due to the absence of major predators, thus demonstrating the importance of preserving apex predators [26]. Patten and Ericson make the general argument that "there are almost no instances in which non-native species should receive consideration for conservation concern" and that "at best, exotic species are neutral, in that they have no detectable effect on biota" [27 p. 817]. The authors of this argument, Patten and Ericson, advise the California Department of Fish and Game about what birds should be of "special concern." Another case of conflict between an exotic and popular species versus biologists is the action taken against pike in several states, including the state of Washington, because they can threaten native trout and salmon. However, many sports fishermen have protested these actions (e.g., poisoning of the pike) because they treasure the pike for "their fighting ability and size of up to 55 pounds" [28].

Recently some researchers identified with the "new conservation" movement have challenged many assumptions about invasive species. Emma Marris, in her book *Rambunctious garden*, cites research that oceanic island "invasions" greatly exceeded extinctions and that "extinctions due to introduced species are quite rare" [29 p. 104]. Indeed, she goes on to argue that introduced species could sometimes serve to replace animals that have long been extinct, such as feral burros and wild horses in the West replacing "Equus caballus, the extinct American horse" [29 p. 61]. Concerning pythons in the Everglades, Marris says that she wishes that their introduction had not happened, but since it has and nothing can change that, we might as well learn to "love them … rather than revile them" and describes them as "impressive beasts" [30]. The USFWS in March 2015 announced restrictions on the sale and importation of four snakes (the reticulated python, DeSchauensee's anaconda, green anaconda and Beni anaconda) but proposed removing the boa constrictor from being listed as an "injurious wildlife species" because "although the boa constrictor can be damaging to U.S. wildlife … widespread private ownership and domestic breeding, render importation and interstate transport prohibitions less effective" [31]. In effect, according to Revkin, the USFWS is accepting a fait accompli that it cannot control because the "snake is out of the bag" [32]. More generally, Marris says that we ought "to learn to love the inevitable changes … as nature adapts to humans" and respect its "dynamism and resilience" [30]. Macdonald, Collins, and Wrangham define invasive species as "introduced species recently trans- ported by man" and point out that these "biogeographical movements" are "escalating" due to human-made environmental changes [33 p. 199]. If it is decided that it is necessary to "remove the invaders," then Macdonald et al. hold that it should be done as humanely as possible, with major emphasis put on prevention of invasions. They point out that "consumers have to make 'nasty tradeoffs' between 'spotted hyenas and wild dogs, lions and cheetah, coyotes and swift foxes' because the larger carnivore endangers the smaller and there is only one defensible principle that 'no biodiversity' should avoidably be lost" [33 p. 278–83].

The International Union for the Conservation of Nature has a "Red list" of threatened species which presumes that all species are equally worthwhile in "intrinsic terms" but, as discussed extensively in Chapter 5, the general public has a bias in favor of mammals and invertebrates "that are pretty" [34 p. 98–9]. For example, the NGO Butterfly Conservation has 14,000 members in the United Kingdom while many invertebrates "don't even have names." Samways makes the point that the reason humans favor these animals is "utilitarian even though it is non-consumptive" because they make "people feel good" and when they are absent, "there is a feeling of loss" [34 p. 102]. However, the World Charter for Nature takes the position "every form of life" warrants respect "regardless of its value to man" including life that is an "anathema to man" such as mosquitoes [35 p. 123].

A movement known as "deep ecology" is related to the ecocentric movement, holding that "non-human life has inherent value independent of their usefulness to humans" and, indeed, that "the flourishing of non-human life may require a decrease [in the population of humans]" [36 p. 312]. Devall describes "the egalitarian ecosystem ethic" as "a thing is right when it tends to preserve the integrity, stability, and beauty of the biotic community" and "wrong when it tends otherwise" [37 p. 86]. Dave Foreman believes in deep ecology and supports "monkeywrenching" that aims to sabotage human-made developments that are harmful to the environment [38 p. 124]. Foreman responds to criticism about the destruction of private property by stating that "it boils down to the question of whether private property or . . . biological diversity . . . is more important?" [38 p. 124]. Foreman does distinguish between "strategic monkeywrenching" and "unwise monkeywrenching" in political terms – the latter gives "the entire environmental movement a bad name" such as putting spikes in trees without giving warning beforehand [38 p. 124–30]. In short, deep ecology rejects the attempt to value wildlife in economic terms. Foreman says that a "Grizzly bear snuffling along Pelican Creek in Yellowstone National Park with her two cubs has just as much right to life as any human has, and is far more important ecologically" [38 p. 4]. Foreman concludes that "their value is not determined by what they will ring up on the cash register of the GNP . . . they are good because they exist" [38 p. 4].

Eldredge states that since the "invention of agriculture" there is no limit on the number of people who can live in any local setting and consequently the "Malthusian cap on total human population" has been eliminated, with the consequence that humanity has been "degrading ecosystems and driving species to extinction at a rate not seen for 65 million years" [39 p. 283]. Leopold's "land ethic" generally "attributes more value to an endangered species than to an individual of a common species even if the endangered species is at a lower level of cognitive or sensory development" [40 p. 176]. Humans are not exempted from these comparisons. Some conservationists such as George Perkins Marsh compared humanity's role in nature with that of animal species, and argue that "no other species killed in such large quantities what it could not consume" and that "changes made by humans could not be counteracted by natural forces" [41 p. 35]. Dinerstein gives an account of how a warden in a Nepal park with endangered rhinoceros responded to demands that locals be allowed to take firewood and use the park for grazing and challenged him as to "who is more important – people or rhinoceros?" [42 p. 179]. Dinerstein says that the warden responded "there are 400 rhinoceros in Chitwan and over 80,000 human residents … my duty is to protect the minority" [42]. Similarly, ecologist Garret Hardin said "that in view of their relative numbers," if he were forced to choose, he would "choose one redwood tree over a baby" [43 p. 240]. As human populations across the world continue to increase while many species decline, this argument for giving priority to endangered species is likely to grow steadily in prominence, though whether the majority of affected humans will ever accept it is questionable. Other apex predators such as wolves, unlike humans, suffer from "boom and bust" periods because when they kill too many prey, their own numbers will decline from the lack of food [44 p. 114]. Thus the numbers of these other predators are controlled automatically by the force of nature. In short, from an ecocentric perspective, it can be argued that human beings are the most invasive predator species ever.

Drawing Lines

While many animal rights ethicists do not distinguish between the values of different animals in their systems, most humans and many members of ecological interest groups do make such distinctions. As noted above, environmentalists are especially concerned with the distinction between "native and outsider species," with most environmentalists viewing the latter as harmful "invasive species" or at least not deserving of protections [45 p. 143]. Adrian Franklin criticizes this "purist position" with respect to Australia, arguing, for example, that if "introduced rabbits were eradicated, the numbers of wedge-tailed eagles would plummet" [45 p. 147]. He also points out that brumbies (feral horses) were an introduced species that was viewed as a pest but when these charismatic animals were shot from helicopters "overnight" it changed an "environmental issue into an animal rights issue" and had powerful enough political support to become a "protected species" [45 p. 198]. Feral cats are viewed as invasives by those trying to restore the Everglades, but when they are "trapped in the Everglades, they may be neutered and released, but they are not killed" because "cat control generally is viewed through the lens of animal welfare rather than as a conservation issue" and they are often not even listed as an invasive species [46]. However, a comparison between cat-infested and cat-free islands in the South Pacific identified "at least 38 cases of population reduction threats due to cats" [33 p. 190]. Spain voted in 2008 to give "limited legal rights to our closest biological relatives, the great apes – chimpanzees, bonobos, gorillas and orangutans," an action that was supported by Peter Singer, who pointed out that chimpanzees share about 95 percent (or higher) DNA with humans [47]. Singer was not certain whether "lesser apes such as gibbons" deserved these protections because "the scientific evidence of human qualities is weaker" [47].

There has been a long and spirited debate over whether wildlife populations are better off if they are "able to be used as property" or whether they have intrinsic value and share human sensibilities so that treating them like property to be dispensed with is inherently cruel [48 p. 18]. Sugg and Kreuter argue that "denying the right of people to own, control and benefit from resources destroys the . . . incentive to invest in and care for them" [48]. In the conservation literature, Hardin's "tragedy of the commons" in which "open resources are doomed to over-exploitation and degradation" is widely cited as a fundamental problem that has to be faced [48 p. 20]. Sugg and Kreuter argue that "the lack of clear and enforceable property rights over whales" is a major factor in the threat to the species [48 p. 21]. Thus they contend that conservationism that allows "consumptive use of resources like whales" is superior to preservationism because it can provide incentives for conservation, in contrast to preservationists who want to "control the use of resources without incurring the costs of ownership" [48 p. 30]. They criticize the attempt to "attribute intrinsic value" to resources (such as wildlife), arguing that such an approach "negates the rights of people who do not share these values" and "humankind is the sole possessor of moral agency" [48 p. 30]. Doubleday goes further to say that the "right to life only has meaning legally in the context of human life, and whales are not human" [49 p. 251]. Critics of bans on trade in wildlife species hold that restrictions on trade actually "hasten the decline in species" because they reduce "the incentive to maintain wildlife habitat" [50 p. xvi]. They argue that international trade does not play a major role in species decline but that habitat loss will be greater if trade and consumptive use of wildlife are not allowed, because landowners will then convert their property to other "land-use options" [51 p. 16–17]. Webb acknowledges that CITES protections helped crocodile numbers to recover, but says that this increase was accompanied by increased attacks on humans and thus sustainable use is needed once the "immediate threat of extinction" has passed [52 p. 105].

It is no mystery, then, that advocates for whales have sought to portray them as "human-like" such as being friendly, living in families, intelligent, "composing music," playful, and caring [53 p. 162–3]. Similarly, Bradshaw reports that an elephant passed "the mirror self-recognition test," thus indicating they possess "self-awareness" [54 p. 3]. She also points out that elephants have a complex social hierarchy and have the ability to "distinguish among themselves" and have shown the ability to mimic sounds such as "trucks and lawnmowers" [54 p. 9]. Elephants also show "wrenching grief" over lost loved ones and make "repeated visits to the bones of relatives" [54 p. 10]. Culling of elephants is done by killing "whole families of elephants" to avoid leaving traumatized elephants, but Bradshaw says that elephants have "highly connected, multitiered social and psychological networks with communication systems capable of bridging miles" and that the only scientific study of the effects of elephant culls found "elevated stress levels over a decade later" [54 p. 234]. The purported similarity of whales to humans lies at the heart of the stalemate over whaling policies. If certain species of whales are numerous enough so that "sustainable whaling" can be conducted, is this the right thing to do? Angier reports that "many biologists who study whales and dolphins . . . urge that negotiators redouble efforts to abolish commercial whaling and dolphin hunting entirely" because "the evidence is high and mounting that the cetacean order includes species second only to humans in mental, social and behavioral complexity," and that "at the very least, you could put it [i.e. whaling] in line with hunting chimps" "according to Hal Whitehead, who studies sperm whales at Dalhousie University in Halifax" [55]. Whitehead says that "when you compare relative brain size, or levels of self-awareness, sociality, the importance of culture, cetaceans come out [ahead] on most of these measures compared to chimps" and concludes "they fit the philosophical definition of personhood" [55]. Angier also points out that "dolphins have passed the famed mirror test" and, "when presented with a mirror, dolphins take the opportunity to check their teeth and body parts they can't normally see, like their anal slit" [55]. Professor David N. Cassuto points out that the criterion humanity uses to determine whether "other beings" are "worthy of moral considerations" is based on "whether their essence sufficiently resembles our own" which "reflects a speciest bias" [56]. The essence of the question is, as Stephen M. Wise, a lawyer with the "Non-Human Rights Project," puts it, "where do you draw the line" between humans and animals and determining which animals (if any) should get rights? [57 p. 1283]. He is suing in the New York State court system on behalf of a chimpanzee kept in a cage. One issue he faces is "standing" to sue but Wise notes that lawyers are able to sue on behalf of "mentally handicapped" and thus this "relaxed standing requirement" could be extended to animals [58]. He also notes that since science has made it difficult to draw a clear line that animals can meet "sufficient requirements for legal personhood" [58]. Although scientific evidence contributes information to the debate over whether animals such as whales and chimpanzees possess self-awareness, the issue also involves legal and ethical morals that cannot be addressed by science.

There are scientific challenges to the attempt to draw sharp lines between invasive and native species. Klinkenborg cites research that "almost every habitat on earth has been affected by humans no matter how remote" and thus the distinction depends on when "the imaginary snapshot of the continent is taken" – for example, should it be "right before European contact?" [59]. One strategy to fight invasives is to harness humanity's destructive capacity. For example, Safina is an ecologist who is trying to encourage humans to consume lionfish, a species that is native to the West Pacific and Indian oceans but has now invaded coral reefs in the Atlantic and is a "super predator of native reef fishes" [60]. The lionfish is hard to catch, "holing up in small groups inside caves and under overhangs" so currently scuba diving is the main method used to catch them [60]. Safina argues that the only predator able to deal with this invasive species is humanity. However, to date, neither angling nor spear fishing "appear to have hindered them except perhaps locally" [46]. Canada had a controversy over whether to slaughter an entire herd of "hybrid bison" (hybrid of plains buffalo and the wood bison) in the Wood Buffalo National Park in order to help deal with diseases (brucellosis and bovine tuberculosis) as well as increase the "purity" of the bison [61 p. 204]. Area cattlemen sought out conservationists such as the Nature Conservancy who were concerned with purity of the herd to support the proposed slaughter, but local natives and other supporters of the bison opposed it and the plan was abandoned [61]. Debates over the role of hybrids have also occurred with respect to charismatic species such as the red wolf and Florida panther. There has been hybridization between red wolves and coyotes that is opposed by David Rabon, who heads the "Red Wolf Recovery" program. He argues that the hybridization would swamp the red wolf and thus it would disappear along with its unique ecological function, and humans need to preserve their identity by taking steps to prevent hybridization [62]. By way of contrast, a UCLA geneticist (Robert Wayne) argues that the red wolf already has coyotes genes in its past and that they should be allowed to interbreed and let "natural selection" determine the results [62]. Velasquez-Manoff points out that Texas panthers have been brought to Florida and encouraged to interbreed in order to save panthers in the state – the choice in this case being between hybrid panthers or no panthers at all.

The most coordinated effort to rid a nation of invasive species is that of New Zealand. The country's Department of Conservation is leading the effort to rid the country of all its "mammal predators" including rats, possums, stoats and other invasive species in order to protect threatened and highly-valued native species such as kiwis and kakapos (a flightless parrot) [63]. In order to achieve this goal, massive amounts of poison and traps are employed, along with an active program of recruiting the populace to join the campaign to rid the country of most of its mammals. As with many countries, animals deliberately imported by humans are now regarded as invasives and attempts are being made to kill them, including rabbits, "brushtail possums," and rainbow trout [63]. According to Kolbert, if "current trends continue" the country would eventually lose its iconic bird, the kiwi, and quotes one of the volunteer conservationists as saying that for them "conservation is all about killing things" [63].

Values, Place, and Religion

There is evidence that the perceptions and values humans hold toward wildlife vary across states in the United States. Teel and Manfredo developed a typology of humans based on two major "value orientations towards wildlife": (1) a domination belief that animals "should be managed for human benefits" with human wellbeing taking precedence over wildlife; (2) a mutualist orientation that views wildlife as capable of having "relationships of trust with humans" and also "deserving of rights and care" [64 p. 130]. They found that traditionalists, people who score high on domination and low on mutualism, were present in the highest percentages in states such as Alaska and South Dakota. Mutualists are people who score "high on mutualism and low on domination" are present in largest percentages in states like California, Nevada, Oregon, and Washington [64 p. 132–4]. Teel and Manfredo found that these differences in value orientations were correlated with views on wildlife management such as whether hunting is "an acceptable response to nuisance bears," with 68 percent of North Dakotans (a state high in traditionalists) taking this view compared to only "32 percent of California and Hawaii residents" [64]. Teel and Manfredo go on to speculate that the longer-term trend will be toward more mutualism and thus less "public acceptance" of "lethal control" [64 p. 138]. Indeed, one wildlife management expert criticized his profession for employing "the euphemisms of agriculture" such as "harvesting 50,000 elk" and its preoccupation with "populations" which, he argues, works for "soybeans" but to "ignore the welfare of an individual animal in a nation that . . . supports animal rights . . . does not work" [65 p. 23]. Based on my analysis in other chapters, this changing perspective is certainly true in states like California but, as revealed in the struggle over wolves, traditionalist and lethal control methods continue to dominate the wildlife policies in many of the states in the West such as Idaho, Wyoming, and Montana. Many people attribute the "dominance paradigm for wildlife use" to the impact of Christianity such as God's commands to men "to be fruitful and multiply" and "have dominion over the earth and all animals" [66 p. 77–81]. Some Christian theologians have developed a "Christian animal rights" philosophy challenging this belief system, but Stephen M. Vantassel has attempted to refute these arguments for a number of reasons including that they would "reduce human's freedom to enjoy the Earth's Bounty" [67 p. 613]. The growth in evidence for Darwin's theory of evolution would seem to eliminate a clear line between animals and humans, but Preece and Chamberlain say that the theory still placed humanity "at the pinnacle of nature" [68 p. 39]. It was not until the rise of the environmental movement in the 1960s that "non-consumptive uses" became an important competing force in the politics of the United States. Nash says that ancient Eastern Religions such as Janism, Buddhism, and Hinduism "honored life other than man's" and "feeling of compassion and code of ethical conduct for all that is alive" in contrast to the dominion belief of Christianity [43 p. 193]. Coggins describes how Henry Caldwell, a Christian missionary in China, hunted tigers in order to prove that they had no power and to counter "traditional Chinese customs" [69 p. 73]. However, Preece and Chamberlain say that despite their respect for animals, oriental religions tend to be "quietist rather than active" with a "resignation to things as they are approved" and thus "did little to create a societal order" that required ethical treatment of animals [68 p. 12–13].

Values and the Consumptive Uses of Wildlife

The impact of animal rights on the politics of natural resources has been significant in many developing countries due to the ability of these organizations to raise money that oppose activities such as hunting – for example a sports hunting ban in Kenya. The ban was supported by a "consortium of leading animal rights NGOs" "opposed to . . . consumptive wildlife utilization" [70 p. 135]. Supporters of consumptive uses of wildlife such as hunters argue that the staff of NGOs conduct campaigns to obtain funds for their organization rather than due to idealistic values. For example, Bonner claims that the United Kingdom's World Wildlife Fund group initially supported "sustainable utilization" of elephants but "received more letters supporting an ivory ban than any other issue" and feared that they would lose "20 percent of their members" if they supported hunting for ivory [71 p. 63–4]. Likewise, many Africans contrast "colonial era hunting allowed throughout the year" with the current situation where it is restricted to "safari trophy hunting" leading them to conclude that "animals are more important than humans" [72 p. 256]. Critics of preservationist positions say that in Africa it amounts to an "ecological apartheid" with rural people banned from legal bushmeat hunting when it is the only affordable source of protein and without it, "severe malnutrition" is common [73 p. 449].

The theme that purist preservationists from Western countries force the adoption of policies to protect wildlife at the cost of poor natives of developing countries has been contentious. For example, Schwartman, Moreira, and Nepstad criticize the attempt to create "people free parks" by removing indigenous people. They state that there is no conclusive evidence that indigenous people (e.g., through subsistence hunting) harm game species, and further argue that "even if they do drive to local extinction of large mammals" that this extinction would not threaten the majority of "other species" or harm other measures of forest integrity such as soil fertility and vulnerability to fire [74 p. 1351–5]. Moreover, they contend that there are other threats to species far more important than hunting or population growth, such as development and "inequitable land tenure" [74]. Redford and Sanderson take issue with their argument by citing specific studies that large human populations (e.g., those exceeding one person per square kilometer) do threaten game species. Redford and Sanderson agree that the natives have "rights to their lands" but caution that this does not mean that "conservationists have to count as conservation everything these people have done and wish to do" [75 p. 1362]. Western conservationists have not ignored this problem and have emphasized providing benefits to local communities for more than a generation, such as by replacing income from hunting with other sources, but Brown and Davies say that over the short term it will be hard to replace relatively high profits from hunting with tourism-related or agricultural income [76 p. 104]. Lindsey, Frank, Alexander, Mathieson, and Romanach claim that trophy hunting not only creates more "income per client" than ecotourism but also does not require costly infrastructure [77 p. 880–1]. They propose other methods to solve potential conflicts between values of wildlife conservation and equity to natives, such as having a certification process to select hunting operators who adhere to conservation standards. Similarly, Nuding says that the hunt for one elephant can generate as much income as thirty farms or livestock operations [78 p. 195]. Robert F. Jones also touts hunting as superior in preserving wild Africa, because tourism results in large hordes of minibuses and hot air balloons surrounding wildlife in African parks and consequently turning them into the equivalent of "Busch Gardens" [79 p. 51–4].

In a somewhat similar vein, the conservative Wise Use movement in the United States sought to portray environmentalists as "elitists" "more concerned with wildlife than whether the person on the street eats or not" [80 p. 84]. Actually, environmental organizations like the Audubon Society and Sierra Club are opposed to the "absolute protection of animals," arguing, for example, with respect to marine mammals that if "the survival of the species is assured, why not use the surplus for the benefit of people?" [6 p. 174]. Garner says the conflict between animal rights and environmental organizations is not surprising or new because their commitment to rights of "individual animal protection" is weak since many conservation organizations are closely associated with hunting [12 p. 42]. For example, the "Audubon Society was founded by a hunter" and the National Wildlife Federation "was dominated for several decades by hunting and fishing interests" [12 p. 42]. A representative from the National Wildlife

Federation opposed a bill banning leghold traps, arguing that "leg-hold traps can cause less painful and protracted deaths than those which wild animals might otherwise experience" [10 p. 85]. The European Union passed a regulation in 1991 banning import of furs from countries that used leghold traps, but did not enforce this ban because they "feared that it could be successfully challenged under GATT (General Agreement on Trades and Tariffs) rules" [81]. But Harrop and Bowles are concerned that establishment of the standards may create a "least common denominator approach" in which nations do not advance beyond the minimum requirements of the international standard [82]. Harrop and Bowles argue that it is difficult to resolve the tension between free trade and the desire of individual nations to pass environmental and animal welfare laws because the legislation protecting wildlife is often passed with overwhelming political support [82 p. 93–4]. The United States succeeded in pressuring nations into an agreement that set "humane standards" for use of traps including specific times by species from "capture to unconsciousness to death" – for example, 45 seconds for ermine but 2 minutes for martens [83 p. 87–8]. In setting such rules, exceptions are often made for native use of wildlife. For example, Harrop notes that indigenous groups are allowed to hunt whales due to their traditions and are not held to the same standards as whaling nations such as Japan which challenged this inconsistency and argued for the right of the whale to a "quick kill" [82 p. 127].

The spotted owl debate brought to the fore the conflict between the economic benefits of logging (and hence jobs for humans) versus preserving an endangered species. Yaffee quotes a person in Curry County (Oregon) whose "largest employer depended heavily on federal timber" as contending that "animals can learn to live under different conditions" and "if they die out – like the dinosaurs ... I think I could live without spotted owls too" [84 p. 54–5]. More recently, a conflict between protecting endangered species and human needs has been aggravated due to the severe drought in California. A *Wall Street Journal* opinion piece complained about the diversion of water to help smelt and California's GOP delegation "backed a bill that temporarily waives species protections so that farmers would be first in the water line when it rains" [85]. Similarly, a 2014 *Wall Street Journal* editorial warned against "ESA protection for the sage-grouse and prairie chicken" because, it argued, "the damage to humans would be enormous" because it would "limit oil drilling" [86].

The "survival of the fittest" is the normative criterion employed, which holds that extinction merely reflects the inability of the species to adapt to a changing environment. Environmentalists sometimes use this criterion to judge the value of activities to aid wildlife. Loftin, an environmentalist, criticizes "the medical treatment of wild animals," arguing that "unless it is returned to the breeding population, nothing has been done for the species" and these resources are better spent on preservation of "habitat for healthy animals" [87 p. 48]. Loftin also adds that "it may be propagating less fit genes such as turtles who don't know how to avoid shark attacks" [87]. However, humans can change the dynamics of the natural selection and the "struggle for survival." Recent studies show that "in stark contrast with most predators such as wolves and grizzlies, human hunters search not for the sick and infirm but the largest prey such as deer with big antlers" [88 p. 952–4]. In short, unlike other predators, humans are not constrained by the usual rules of nature. The consequence can be to "generate large and rapid changes … that can affect population persistence" such as smaller overall body size and smaller antlers as self-selection adapts the species to its main predator – humanity [88].

Norton says that the economic approach to protecting biodiversity is based on "the consumer's willingness to pay" with the view that "if there is no link between an organism and human production or consumption activity, there is no basis for establishing economic value" [89 p. 217]. Norton argues that this is too limited a view and proposes that the economic cost-benefit approach be replaced by a "safe minimum standard rule" that a species be preserved "if the costs are bearable," thus putting "the burden of proof" on those who would eliminate the species. Norton also says that the existence of a species like wolves should be judged "from a national view" because that species may have enough value "to outweigh" the losses to a local community [89 p. 225]. Some economists have adopted a broader framework for valuing "ecosystem services" by distinguishing among three different types of benefits: (1) "goods" (e.g., products obtained from ecosystems, such as resource harvests, water, and genetic material); (2) "services" (e.g., recreational and tourism benefits or certain ecological regulatory functions, such as water purification, climate regulation, erosion control, etc.); and (3) "cultural benefits" (e.g., spiritual and religious, heritage, etc.) [90 p. 2]. Critics such as Terborgh argue that ecosystem services "should not be confused with biodiversity conservation" [91 p. xiii]. McCauley [92 p. 39] provides a real-life example of such a conflict involving "the case of Africa's Lake Victoria, where the introduction of the invasive Nile perch … contributed significantly to the decimation of local biodiversity while dramatically boosting the economic value of the lake" [92 p. 39]. They say that local people viewed the perch introduction as a great success, whereas biologists have condemned the event as "the most catastrophic extinction episode of recent history" [92 p. 39].

There is disagreement over the role that market forces should play in conservation. Libertarian economists believe that the power of a free market can solve wildlife problems. Many people agree that a practical resolution of the conflict between the needs of people (especially the poor) and wildlife is the principle that "wildlife should pay for its survival," including threatened species such as black rhinos, through tourism and, if necessary, hunting. One "solution" to this dilemma is to breed a population of endangered species on farms so that the danger to wild members of the species are lessened. For example, Barun Mitra argues that China has "perfected breeding of tigers in captivity" and that the "tiger can pay for its survival" because China "if given a free hand could produce 100,000 tigers in 10 to 15 years" and thus provide a "supply of wildlife at affordable prices" and hence eliminate incentives for poaching of wild tigers [93]. Environmentalists concerned with saving poached species like tigers argue that the very existence and legalization of a market for trading tiger parts would "pose an unacceptable risk" to them [94 p. 464]. Nowell says that the existence of a ban on a legal trade of tiger parts led to a "steep decline in availability of tiger bone medicines" and increased awareness on the part of the public who were mostly "unwilling" to violate the law [94 p. 467]. Gratwicke, Bennet, and Broad also contend that "the world can't have wild tigers and eat them too," citing data that even if tigers were farmed for commercial use, it would still be much cheaper to poach a wild tiger than to raise them [95]. Nyhus, Tilson and Hutchins argue that though "private tiger ownership is justified as one way to save tigers" that the "cost ... of managing domestic tiger ownership in non-tiger range states" would draw resources away from saving the species [96 p. 237–8]. Nyhus et al. point out that there "are more captive tigers in the U.S. and China than in the wild" [96]. Thus, from these ecologists' perspectives, the destruction of markets for endangered species such as tigers is necessary to save them. In the United States, a similar argument has been made that in order to increase support for wildlife like wolves, they "should be made 'profitable' to increase support for them in rural areas" [97]. But Kellert goes on to say that there is little empirical research for this hypothesis and that some research shows that "the creation of legitimate markets" for threatened species often leads to increased poaching of them [97].

The same debate extends to other species such as crocodiles and rhinoceroses, though without the same concern about the inhumanity of farming them as in the cases of tigers and bears. Crocodile farming has been cited by supporters of farming-market solutions to prevent poaching as a model of success. Hutton and Webb describe how wild crocodile populations had declined radically by the 1970s which led CITES to place crocodile species on its Appendix I listing, which forbids international trade [98]. Hutton and Webb say that by the 1980s several countries had "reintroduced" farming of crocodiles and sought and achieved the transfer of crocodiles to Appendix II listing allowing legal trade which resulted, they claim, in illegal trade of crocs being replaced by farmed crocs [98 p. 112]. However, according to Hutton and Webb, one of the keys to the success was the willingness of CITES and the international community to take action against countries that allowed illegal trade of wild crocs; they cite specific pressures and/or actions taken against a number of countries including France, Italy, Paraguay, Bolivia, and Thailand [99 p. 7]. They claim that these pressures were successful in largely stopping the illegal trade. A second key to the success of this market approach was the implementation of a system for tagging crocodilian skins "at the point of origin and re-export" [99 p. 8]. The system has been hugely successful, according to Hutton and Webb, who conclude that the crocodile example shows that "conservation incentives can be generated by markets" and that "a regulated trade does not "inevitably stimulate illegal trade." Thorbjarnarson cautions that successes such as the recovery of the American crocodile are due as much or more to the increased "protective measures" taken and "commercial consumptive use" (CCU) should be viewed as a "supplementary tool for encouraging conservation of species [100 p. 11]. He claims that there is no "evidence that CCU is sufficient to affect decisions about the use of wetlands inhabited by crocodiles [100 p. 11]. Dutton et al. argue that Florida's alligator management program has created "political advocates for wetland preservation" that protects not just alligators but other species [101 p. 29]. Some supporters of international trade in wildlife, unlike conservation biologists, are not that worried about the possibility of international trade causing drops in species population. For example, Webb states that "no known species of crocodiles or sea turtles has become globally extinct in recent decades" despite heavy human use and "a few local extinctions" [52 p. 103]. They argue that when the population becomes so reduced in size, that it will no longer be economical to use them, so that the species will eventually recover [52 p. 105]. DuPlessis describes this as a "positive feedback" loop, though acknowledges that in the case of rhinos, "increasing rarity" adds to its allure leading to even "more investments in harvesting" of the horns and thus the principle may not work in such cases [51 p. 15].

Bulte and Damania reviewed the use of farming wildlife for conservation and argue that there are significant conditions that may make success impossible when demand for the "commodity" is growing rapidly such as animals used for "traditional Chinese medicine" due to the rapid expansion of wealth in China [102 p. 1224]. They note that the legal trading can help to reduce the stigma of using the resource and thus enhance demand. Still another danger is that legalizing trade may "facilitate laundering of illegal output." Moreover, Bulte and Damania argue that the establishment of populations on farms and ranches "completely separate from wild stock" may remove any "incentive to protect wild resources" at all – "why invest in wild resources when farmed substitutes are available?" [102]. Bulte and Damania do not object to the potential use of the farming approach but state that its success will depend on the "parameters of the market" that are not known in advance [102 p. 1232]. While Bulte and Damania explicitly "ignore the ethics of raising species like bears in captivity for their bile," animal rights and many biocentrists object to what they view as inhumane treatment [102 p. 1223].

Sanderson says that conservationists who hold to "the strong premise of property rights as a necessity for conservation" have not paid attention to the fact that these rights are very "diverse in their relation ... to wildlife," politically contested, and are not "commensurable across cultural divides" [103 p. 474]. He also contends that "nowhere in the literature has there been established a causal relationship between secure tenure and preferred environmental outcomes" [103 p. 474]. Geist says that the tragedy of the commons is not due to "public ownership" but to "absence of controls over exploitation" and that laissez faire would lead to "public disasters" [104 p. 48–52]. He points to the North American model of wildlife management as the most successful based on "four principles" including public ownership, elimination of commercial markets for game and birds, legal controls over hunting, and the "abolition of frivolous killing of wildlife" [104 p. 52]. Geist states that "policing of wildlife is terribly costly" and it is a mistake to allow "legal trafficking of wildlife parts" because it removes the most important protection and also because the "criminal element takes advantage" of it [104 p. 59]. Biologist Edward O. Wilson identifies an important limitation on the use of current prices to judge the value of wildlife because, he argues, the value assigned to it will likely change radically through time [105 p. 112–13]. He uses the example of the gigantic blue whale that was worth "close to zero" in Year 1000 but in Year 30000 would have "a virtually limitless value" and thus he believes we need to take into account "the gratitude of a [future] generation" to those who saved it from extinction.

Preserving Endangered Species and the Welfare of the Poor

Community-Based Natural Resources Management (CBNRM) was founded in part to deal with the ethical dilemma faced by Western countries and NGOs who wished to preserve wildlife in Africa and other developing countries. How could they justify encouraging limits on use of wildlife by the poor of these countries when Westerners had extinguished wildlife that presented any danger (e.g., wolves and bears) to their own lives and property as well as destroying habitat for agriculture, roads, and other forms of development? Adams and Hulme cite the argument that "fortress conservation should be abandoned because of its adverse effects on the living conditions of the rural poor" [106 p. 15]. Research showed that "wildlife users" (e.g., bushmeat consumers) were "less wealthy and secure" than non-users of wildlife [107 p. 132]. Hulme and Murphree sum up this view with the question: "Why should Africa or Africans be any different from the rest of the world?" [108 p. 286]. Hulme and Infield studied a community conservation project in Uganda and concluded that the main beneficiaries were "international" actors, "Ugandan conservationists," "foreign tourists," Ugandan conservation bureaucracy, "donor agencies" and "couch potato conservationists worried about African wildlife" [109 p. 127]. Many conservationists hope that the Maasai remain pastoralists because this lifestyle is compatible with conservation of wildlife, but Kangwana and Mako quote one Maasai elder as saying "we have discovered the new foods" and "now we went to grow crops and keep our cows" [110 p. 159]. From a biocentric perspective, although conservationists may sympathize with the poor of developing countries, this is not sufficient to deemphasize their conservation goals. Crist [111 p. 93] argues that protection of wildlife is not an "underlying cause of poverty" and Wuerthner [112 p. 136] says that "far more people are removed from their homes" for economic development such as dams and highways" than due to wildlife conservation. Kopnina holds that the attempt to help the most disadvantaged at the expense of wildlife will result in only short term gains with long-term negative consequences for environmental quality [113 p. 67]. It is not only Westerners who hold non-consumptive values about wildlife. Africans too hold non-consumptive values. Jones says that "many Africans value wildlife for its existence and wish their children and grandchildren to be able to enjoy seeing the wild animals they and their parents witnessed" [114 p. 166]. This is in contrast to the view that "wildlife must pay its way" [110 p. 158; 115].

Supporters of CBNRM and "sustainable development" hope to achieve their conservation goal while helping the poor at the same time. However, in practice, it has been challenging to achieve both goals simultaneously. The CBNRM theory assumes that "ownership rights are key to efficient management of wildlife resources" [116 p. 46–7]. Fraser et al. cite a Tanzanian CBNRM program that provided benefits to locals who "are responsible for protecting and living with wildlife" with a positive result that hunting revenues "increased eightfold" providing benefits to "stakeholders most strongly affected" [116 p. 50–1]. Rasker, Martin, and Johnson cite Zimbabwe and South African successes in using profit from selling rights to hunt elephants but note that in order to make this "property-based" approach work, they have to "put up a fence to keep the animals from wandering off, sell hunting permits to wealthy hunters, sell the ivory and hides, and use the proceeds to arm paramilitary-style park rangers" [117 p. 339–43]. A "State of the Knowledge" review of how biodiversity affects poverty in Africa concluded that "better off households" are more likely to participate in conservation projects and "capture the benefits" of these programs, thus leading to greater income disparity in rural areas [118 p. 155]. A study of the "great ape initiatives" in Africa was unable to determine their effect on poverty "due to a lack of data" [119 p. 188]. Homewood, Trench, and Brockington found that wildlife "brought little or nothing to the majority of Maasai" except to those who lived near Kenya's Mara National Reserve [120 p. 246]. A review of ten United Nations Development programs found limited economic benefits but emphasized that the projects did instill "community organization and empowerment" and they contend that these political, social and cultural impacts "can be more important than money" [121 p. 277–9]. A major problem is that Western countries and NGOs that fund many of the conservation efforts have little faith in local government in developing countries. For example, Hulme and Muphree summarize the widely shared view that in "sub-Saharan Africa, local government structures are in a sorry state" [122 p. 283]. In order for CBNRM to work satisfactorily (from a conservationist perspective), there must be a "genuine commitment of communities to sustainable use" so that the international community can feel certain that CBNRM will support biodiversity but "these conditions do not exist in much of East Africa" which is why wildlife management has emphasized protected areas [123 p. 72].

Values and Conflicts Between Species

Humans are sometimes placed in charge of killing one species to preserve another, which can lead to political turmoil. For example, in Washington State, the "Lake Washington steelhead were listed as endangered under the Endangered Species Act" and consequently "Washington state filed a petition to remove sea lions from the Ballard locks and kill them if all other methods to keep them from eating steelhead fail" [124 p. 120]. The National Research Council reviewed the issue and agreed that the sea lions do reduce steelhead populations but also noted that were other causes of the decline such as "the eight billion hatchery salmon that had been released since the late 1980s" [124 p. 119]. A Native American organization, the Columbia River Inter-Tribal Fish Commission (CRITFC), in Washington State has been trying to choose a "middle way" by shooting "explosive projectiles designed to scare away the sea lions from the salmon habitat" but they acknowledge that this is not a long-term solution [125]. Ironically, the sea lion versus salmon controversy has been caused in part by the success of the Marine Mammal Preservation Act that rescued the rapidly declining sea lions so they are more abundant than they have been in thousands of years [125]. Also, a mysterious "patch of warm water" in the Pacific has driven off their usual prey and helped to push the sea lions toward the River [125]. Fishermen complain that the lions steal their catch and in 2008, Washington and Oregon received Federal approval to "euthanize sea lions that ate salmon at the Bonneville Dam" which officials say has improved the situation. The passage of the Marine Mammal Protection Act was "amended in 1994 to allow the killing of marine mammals under particular conditions" [124 p. 120]. But this policy is opposed by a group dedicated to the sea lions, the Sea Lion Defense Brigade, as well as traditional animal rights groups such as the Humane Society. As is always the case with controversies over predators, there are multiple threats to an endangered species, and humans make the decisions as to which of the causes should be addressed and political support for species can be decisive.

Another interspecies struggle has developed between spotted owl populations and barred owls. Spotted owl populations have declined, despite the preservation of old growth forests for them due to competition from barred owls that "have been migrating into Northwestern forests and driving their smaller relatives from their ancestral territory" [126]. Consequently, in 2013, the USFWS issued an environmental impact statement concerning their plan "to shoot 3600 barred owls over a period of four years" because the barred owls were "outcompeting" the spotted owls and needed this assistance to endure [127].

Roemer and Wayne criticize the USFWS for their program to protect the loggerhead shrike (a bird) by taking predator control measures against foxes including the endangered San Clemente fox [128 p. 1251]. They argue that their approach was "species-centric" and that a "more balanced ecosystem approach" should have been used [128 p. 1251]. In Yellowstone Park, the Park Service along with an environmental group (The Greater Yellowstone Coalition) and sportsmen's organization (Trout Unlimited) are coordinating an effort to eliminate lake trout in order to save cutthroat trout, upon which they prey [129]. In Yellowstone, the cutthroat trout are viewed as a "keystone species" and are an important source of food for grizzlies and birds such as eagles and egrets. The lake trout "hide in the deep" and don't spawn in the streams where these other species can catch and eat them [129]. By way of contrast, Johnson points out that Great Lake states (where the lake trout are "natives") are often trying to replenish their stocks of lake trout and also lake trout are being bred and released by hatcheries just 100 miles south in Wyoming [129]. In short, "location" is central to determining whether a species is viewed as a harmful "invasive" by humans. In effect, much of wildlife conservation politics is "local."

In some cases, the killing of predators to preserve endangered species causes conflicts with animal rights organizations, such as the case where the BLM began to poison and kill ravens in order to preserve the endangered California desert tortoise [130 p. 84]. The Humane Society sued the BLM, arguing that the BLM was taking the path of least resistance by killing ravens rather than going after other major threats to tortoises such as all-terrain vehicles and construction of highways [130]. In Australia, there has been a conflict between "gray-headed flying foxes, a large species of bats and rare trees in country's Royal Botanic Gardens" [131]. The bats have killed twelve trees, and sixty others are threatened, so gardeners "want the bat removed" because they strip trees of their new buds. The bats have been defended by a bat conservation society but, according to Foley "so far, the tenor of the debate has been unfailingly polite, with both sides recognizing that each is merely trying to protect its own interests in an increasingly urbanized, populated world" [131].

There are several other examples of conflicts between two (or more) species. For example, the New Mexico Department of Game and Fish sanctioned "the removal of mountain lions in areas occupied by desert bighorn sheep through contracts with professional hunters" because desert bighorn sheep populations were at risk of extinction and are classified as "endangered" while mountain lions are listed only as a "protected" species [132 p. 1340]. The National Research Council acknowledges the fact that attempts to "improve conditions for a threatened or endangered species may affect dozens of non-targeted species in the same environments" [133 p. 114–16]. For example, they cite the plan to alter the "flow and control structures" of the Sacramento and San Joaquin River systems to assist both the non-native but popular striped bass as well as the threatened winter-run salmon. The problem is these actions would likely hurt the threatened delta smelt (fish) upon which the striped bass prey. They admit that bass are being supported "because of public interest." The National Research Council concluded that "tradeoffs have to be evaluated" and the need to take a broad ecosystems approach to potential conflicts among species [133 p. 116]. The decisions are not just biological because the public popularity of certain species makes it impossible for decision makers to ignore politics.

Even when the species in question is not endangered and, indeed, may be regarded as a pest, such as wild goose populations, many people with strong beliefs in animal rights resist lethal control. Lauber, Knuth, and Deshler describe how a "vocal segment of the population in Rockland County (New York) lobbied to reduce the goose population" because of threats to children from their droppings, but animal rights organizations instead called for preventive measures such as "changing landscaping to discourage geese from certain areas and setting aside certain areas for geese" [134 p. 586]. Thus many animal rights adherents admit to the existence of problems that need to be addressed from animals such as geese and wild horses, but object to what they view as too harsh methods of control. In the case of wild horses, an animal rights advocate agonized over the use of helicopters to "round up" the horses because they are "running at full speed for miles … with little babies and they don't let up on them … stressing them to the max" [135]. The man in charge of the roundup said that said that "you have to get them sore-footed and tired and there are a lot of problems with getting them really tired" but said that this method was better than the old method of using "rope and brawn" which injured both the horses and the roundup horsemen [135]. The BLM claims that the wild horses are a threat to other species such as the sage-grouse and pronghorn antelope because the horses strip the habitat of the vegetation they need to survive [136 p. 20]. There is also a conflict between wild horses and other wildlife on the Outer Banks of North Carolina where a herd of 140 horses live on a Federal parkland [137]. The horses have strong political supporters and this group is pushing Congress to pass legislation to allow the herd to be sustained at 120 [137]. Wildlife conservationists believe the herd is growing too large and threatening other wildlife such as birds. The director of the Wildlife Society that "opposes the bill" is quoted as saying "this is about values … I like horses … but I also deeply value what little we have of our native species and their habitats" [137]. Horse supporters have countered with the argument that the horses are a native species, with some evidence that they may be a remnant of an "Iberian breed that exists nowhere else." Beil says that "in the arena of politics and public sentiment, the horse wins hands down," as indicated by the fact that they have a citizen patrol dedicated to protecting them [137]. More recently, there is a plan to merge two separate groups of the horses in order to reduce inbreeding that has reduced their numbers to about 100 (from an estimated 6000) but it is opposed by the USFWS because they are concerned that growth in the herd would threaten endangered species living in the nearby Currituck National Wildlife Refuge [138]. The plan is supported by the Humane Society and ASPCA, and a nonprofit organization (The Corolla Wild Horse Fund) dedicated to footing the entire cost of the horse transfer, and Republicans who have passed a bill in the House of Representatives to force the USFWS to allow the horses to be moved. This case again illustrates the power of charismatic wildlife to draw human support and how animal rights groups often find themselves opposed to conservationists who place top priority on biodiversity. Fox hunts in Great Britain were banned in 2004. According to Moseley, both sides agreed that foxes "need to be culled because of their threat to lambs" but differ on whether fox hunts are the method that should be employed – possible alternatives include gassing, shooting, and trapping [139]. Opponents emphasize the stress of "being chased for miles and . . . then torn to bits" while supporters claim that "foxes die quickly with little pain" [139]. Supporters of the hunts claim that opponents are hypocritical because they do not "ban fishing as well" and also argue that fox hunting is a tradition dating back to the seventeenth century and that the ban "would infringe on their civil liberties" [139]. The fact that most persons engaged in fox hunts are wealthy is also key to the politics of the debate, with the Labour Party opposing the hunts.

Often people most concerned with development and those dedicated to conservation are at odds. As discussed in Chapter 5, there have been several challenges to wildlife management actions that have been viewed as "taking" the property of owners. However, sometimes there is evidence that conservation can help to enhance property values in many localities. In Scottsdale, Arizona, voters approved an increase in sales tax for land preservation and voters in a "right-leaning small town (Cave Creek) voted to tax themselves to . . . purchase land for conservation" – their mayor said "you could talk to the most hard-core Republicans in my community and . . . preservation is the most important thing" [140]. One of the underlying reasons for this interest in land preservation is growth in population "destroys the environmental amenities that made the place special" [140]. However, at the same time, as land in communities becomes more expensive, "increasing real estate prices and tendency for smaller parcels" makes it difficult for governments and environmental NGOs to purchase land and this makes it difficult for them to create "connectivity corridors" for wildlife such as mountain lions in Southern California [141 p. 280]. Nevertheless, the popularity of conservation among wealthy conservatives again demonstrates that wildlife politics does not exist on a strict liberal-conservative divide.

Economic Interests versus Wildlife Preservation

There is no question that development is often harmful to biodiversity. The importance of protecting wildlife on private lands is illustrated by the fact that the U.S. Geological Survey showed that while 95 percent of the Alpine habitat in California is protected, only "1 percent of the biologically rich riparian" habitat is [142]. Humans dominate the richest lands, especially those bordering water, leaving less biologically desirable lands for wildlife. One of the lessons from "island theory" is that larger areas withstand the threat of extinction better and that this theory applies to continental masses too because protected areas become isolated by roads and development, limiting habitat for wildlife, because the continent is broken up into a maze of islands separated by roads and human settlements [142]. Rick Bass says that "roadless areas contain great biological diversity and ecological function" and that building a road through a large "forested area is one of the most degrading things that humans can do to wilderness … worse than logging" for a number of reasons such as acting as "vectors for human caused fires and noxious weeds as well as channeling water away from forests" [143 p. 217]. In some cases, private industry has agreed to limitations to support these connections between "green areas." Wuerthner points out that Yellowstone was originally created for its "scenic and thermal features" – not to preserve wildlife – and corridors are necessary to connect even the largest of parks to other wildlife areas [142]. Wuerthner cites the Y2Y (Yellowstone to Yukon) coalition that wants to create a corridor along the entire Rockies and says that they have been able to win support in British Columbia from "outfitters, hunters, and even representatives from the timber, oil, and gas industries" which are given "limited oil and gas development rights" but are prohibited from using the "most biologically critical core areas" [142].

Sustainability: The New Value Criterion?

By 1950, a discussion begun over whether to "establish parks to protect species or benefit people" led to the concept of sustainable development as an attempt to encourage conservation programs that would at the same time support the needs of humans [144 p. 493–4]. However, some conservationists have become disenchanted with the merging of conservation and development because they feel that with limited resources for conservation, attempts to aid local people were "diverting resources from protection of diversity" [144 p. 496]. Conservationist George Schaller believes that the term "sustainability" is an "evasive euphemism" and that attempts to equate it with "conservation" are wrong [145 p. 10–11]. He emphasizes they are "two distinct concepts" but politicians assume that sustainability means that "everything (i.e., every species) must pay its own way" and that politicians accept the view that communities "will harvest resources sustainably on their own" even though Schaller has "yet to witness this" [145]. Sanderson likewise is concerned that "conservation is now almost universally associated with 'sustainable use,' whereas conservation that does not include human users has been relegated to 'preservation,' which strangely has taken on a very negative connotation, based on imperial models of preservation in Africa and Asia" [103 p. 468]. Macdonald, Collins, and Wrangham define sustainability as the "property of being continuable" with an emphasis on intergenerational equity meaning that "the needs of the present must not be allowed to out-compete the needs of future generations" [33 p. 282].

The calculation of what is a "sustainable take" is subject to disagreement, as has occurred with respect to whaling. For example, Iceland killed more than 100 fin whales during the summer of 2014 and exported most of the meat to Japan [146]. Iceland claims that this take is sustainable while Revkin argues that it is greater than "three times the level considered sustainable" according to "the best available science" [146]. The concept has also contributed to strife between conservationists who are open to consumptive use of wildlife and some preservationists who label them "traitors to Earth" [147 p. 468]. May says that even when the "intrinsic growth rate of a species (i.e., birth rate minus death rate) exceeds the economic discount rate, sustainability can fail due to the weakness of regulations" and he argues that in the case of "most whale species," purely economic logic would lead to "liquidating" the species [148 p. xv]. On the other hand, Brown [149 p. 116] contends that "continued preoccupation with animal welfare to the detriment of humans" is "untenable" and Roe reports that most NGOs now "include in their mission statements attention to local livelihood issues" [144 p. 498]. Adams et al. point out that the 2002 World Summit on Sustainable Development specified that it should take into consideration issues of "justice, equity, and poverty elimination" [150]. As a result of the tensions between economics and conservation, a distinction between "strong" and "weak" sustainability has developed. "Strong sustainability" signifies that "future generations" should inherit the same natural resources "as their forebears" and weak sustainability means that there will be "no loss in critical natural capital" [151 p. 235]. Pulgar-Vidal argues that the weak sustainability criterion is "more realistic in the context of developing nations" and suggests that conservationists will be forced to decide what trade-offs are acceptable. Economist Wilfred Beckerman has attacked both strong and weak concepts of sustainability, arguing that the concept of strong sustainability is "morally repugnant" because of the prevalence of "acute poverty" in the developing countries, it would mean "giving up vast resources" in order to "preserve several million species of beetles" when there are "more urgent environmental concerns such as increasing access to drinking water or sanitation" in these countries [152 p. 192–5]. Beckerman also derides the Brundtland Report that urged the conservation of plant and animal species for future generations, stating that "about 98 percent of all the species that have ever existed are believed to have become extinct, but most people do not suffer any great sense of loss as a result" [152]. Beckerman concludes that while strong sustainability would be unethical, he holds that "weak sustainability offers nothing beyond traditional economic welfare maximization" [152]. In short, although sustainability has become a popular concept, some traditional welfare economists have not accepted the validity or utility of this concept and it does not convince people who believe in preservation of a species to accept consumption even if it is sustainable.

Some new conservationists believe it is important to emphasize "benefits to humanity" and not just "species diversity" because to be effective, conservation needs human support; they cite data from the United States to show a big drop in the percentage of the population that considers itself "environmentalists" or "worries a great deal" about the environment [153 p. 1]. Kirby argues that it is a "moral imperative" to emphasize "the right of local people to self-determination" in light of the fact that their rights have been ignored in the past [154 p. 639]. Kareiva, Marvier, and Lalasz believe that the "new conservation" needs to create a more "human-friendly" vision and argues that by removing humans from protected areas while building hotels and wells "we are creating parks that are no less human constructions" [155]. Critics of the "new conservation" fear that the emphasis on "humanitarianism" is aimed at replacing the traditional conservation model that has focused on biodiversity [156 p. 895–7]. Doak, Baker, Goldstein, and Hale cite data that contradicts any weakening attachment to the environmental concerns in the United States and also disagree that "economic self-interest is the most potent motivator" because they cite "a great deal of research ... that social and moral factors strongly shape behavior and support for policies, often outweighing direct economic self-interest" [157 p. 77–80]. The new conservationists refer to our age as the "Anthropocene," given the dominance of humanity over other creatures, and hold that humanity can make "more nature" and "the Earth better" [29 p. 56]. Kareiva et al. state that "instead of pursuing the protection of biodiversity for biodiversity's sake, a new conservation should seek to enhance those natural systems that benefit the widest number of people, especially the poor" [155]. They also state that "instead of trying to restore remote iconic landscapes to pre-European conditions, conservation will measure its achievement in large part by its relevance to people, including city dwellers" [155]. Crist critiques the anthropocentrism of the new conservationists that prioritizes human needs over all others and regards "other life forms as resources" for human use [158 p. 17–18]. She argues that we need to become ecocentric, thus "scaling back humanity's presence enormously" including population and industrial food production [158 p. 30]. Likewise, Baskin argues that the Anthropocene concept elevates humanity above nature and is associated with a "number of prescriptive claims and normative assumptions" [159 p. 13 & 15]. The debate between the "old" and "new" conservationists has grown so "acrimonious" that a 2014 *Nature* opinion piece by Tallis and Lubchenco sought to defuse the controversy and called for an "inclusive conservation" that recognizes the worth of both "intrinsic" and "instrumental" values [160]. They contend that the "values need not be in opposition" but acknowledge that they do reflect the "hard choices that conservation often faces." In short, disputes over the primacy of values and goals (biodiversity versus benefits to humanity) is threatening to break up the unity of the conservation coalition.

Conclusion

There has been an impressive amount of scientific research concerning biodiversity and threatened species. Despite the abundance and quality of these empirical studies, the theme of this chapter is that core values continue to dominate wildlife politics despite the attempt to make policy based on science. People have strong (both positive and negative) feelings about wildlife that form the basis of passionate political struggles. Although the tendency has been for humans to value animals from a utilitarian perspective, non-consumptive, intrinsic values have always existed and have grown greatly in significance, especially with the advent of the environmentalist movement. Consequently, wildlife policy debates are based on struggles among groups that have different core values such as utilitarian views (e.g., ranchers and farmers) versus non-consumptive values (e.g., animal rightists and conservationists). Conservationists have adapted an "ecosystem" perspective that emphasizes preservation of biodiversity of species populations and native species, but they are willing to allow "sustainable" takes of species. Thus conservationists also differ in core values from animal rightists, with the former emphasizing species preservation and the latter concerned with the welfare of individual animals. New conservationists propose to emphasize benefits to humanity for both moral (e.g., protecting the rights of the poor living near protected areas) and practical political reasons. By attacking traditional conservationists and challenging the importance of maintaining pristine wilderness and the sanctity of native species (versus invasives), the new conservationists have shattered what used to be consensus on values of the conservation movement. The gap in values among new and old conservationists as well as animal rights groups creates potential political weakness for the coalition that favors protection for wildlife as it confronts challenges from opposed coalitions.

10   Hunting and Wildlife Politics

Introduction

Hunting and fishing are major ways in which humans benefit from consumption of wildlife. According to the U.S. Fish and Wildlife Service (USFWS) Survey of Fishing, Hunting and Wildlife Associated Recreation more than 33 million persons fished and almost 14 million hunted during 2011 [1 p. 4]. These hunters and fishers spent a total of nearly $90 billion on their sport. This was an increase from the USFWS's previous survey in 2006 in the number of hunters (about 12.5 million) while hunting expenditures increased from $25.5 billion to $33.7 billion during this same period. The number of people who traveled to watch but not consume wildlife was much larger by way of comparison – almost 72 million watched wildlife nearby their home while 22.5 million traveled away from home to do so. The expenditures made by those watching wildlife totaled nearly $55 billion in 2011. Many hunters (57 percent) report that they too enjoy just watching wildlife. Decker, Brown, and Siemer cite data that participation in hunting was stable over the 1990s [2 p. 292–3]. However, a report by the Wildlife Management Institute found the sale of duck stamps had dropped in recent years, resulting in a decline of the proceeds from these stamps that go into the Migratory Bird Conservation Fund [3]. The report estimates a "slow decline" in the average number of waterfowl stamps sold from 2.2 million in the 1970s to 1.4 million between 2004 and 2008. The report says that there used to be a rise and fall in waterfowl hunters based on the size of the annual duck population but that this relationship has "weakened considerably" in recent years [3]. "In Utah, the number of hunting licenses issued annually dropped precipitously from 1986 to 2013, to about 16,000 from 114,000" [4]. The percentage of residents who are hunters varies greatly by state – in Wisconsin hunters total about 14 percent. Kellert's 1980 data estimate a range of percentages of hunters from a high of 39 percent in Alaska to just over 6 percent in the Pacific Coast states [5]. Although hunters represent only a small fraction (that has been declining) of the U.S. population, as documented in other chapters, the influence of hunters over wildlife management policy has remained very strong. Laws have been passed to support the right to hunt in virtually all states. Mahoney and Jackson cite a 2010 survey that showed that about 78 percent of the public support "legal hunting" – a slight increase from 1995. Additional evidence of the political strength of hunters is that the Federal and state governments provide substantial funds to encourage recruitment of new hunters [6 p. 454]. There is a "huge network of hunter education programs" that is supported by more than $470 million (2010) from the Federal Aid in Wildlife Restoration Funds that are distributed to the states [7 p. 407]. The Utah Division of Wildlife Resources is purchasing thousands of partridge chicks from private growers to give them to families to raise and release, in order to recruit young new hunters; it holds special hunts only for youths younger than seventeen before the regular hunting season so they do not have to compete with adult hunters [4]. There are also many programs sponsored by hunting and gun rights organizations (e.g., the National Rifle Association) to counter long-term trends adverse to hunting such as urbanization and focus on video games among the young. Most states have "age minimums" for hunting but the firearms industry is working to overturn these and has succeeded in states such as Wisconsin (the minimum age dropped from twelve to ten), and Michigan, where the age limit was eliminated completely [8]. Most hunters prefer to hunt on private lands and consequently states like Illinois have formed organizations ("The Place to Hunt Committee") to solve "hunter–landowner conflicts" and thus improve hunter access to private lands [9 p. 280]. To summarize, hunter-related interest groups are actively seeking to counter the decline in overall percentage of hunters in the population.

Ethics and Hunting

There is evidence to show that the public support of hunting is conditional, based on its purpose. Kellert's research shows that the general public supports hunting that is of a practical nature such as subsistence hunting but "overwhelmingly" oppose hunting done only for "entertainment value" such as "trophy hunting" [10 p. 105]. When Illinois recently passed legislation to allow hunting of bobcats (banned since 1972), one of the objections of a Humane Society critic was that they are hunted only for their fur – not for their meat [11]. The sponsor of the bill cited the argument that he had heard "concerns" from hunters about "depleted game" and farmers about loss of chickens and pet cats [12]. As with many hunting measures, the bill received little attention until after it was passed. Data cited by Decker et al. show that hunting for "sport" receives substantially lower approval ratings than hunting for "meat" or "recreation" [13 p. 292]. Ethical issues concerning the acceptability of different types of hunting date back to English aristocratic sportsmen's "Code of Ethics" that originated the concept of "fair chase" [14 p. 135–6]. The concept of "fair chase" was central to sportsmen such as Teddy Roosevelt and his friends in the Boone and Crockett Club, and continues to this day. It also includes self-imposed restrictions on use of technology, demanding that hunters learn about the behaviors of prey [15 p. 89]. Those interested in "sportsmanlike" hunting criticize "slob hunters." Leader-Willams says that a fair chase is one in which it presents a "challenge to the hunter" who has to use skills to achieve success and that the methods used to kill the prey are more important than the outcome [16 p. 10]. One action of a slob hunter would be, for example, to wound an animal but not track it down, with the possibility that it takes days to die. One estimate is that bow hunters do not retrieve 50 percent of the prey they hit with arrows [17 p. 109]. An Audubon Magazine article states "there is a growing sentiment in this country that those who hunt should do it the hard way: tracking the animals and learning their habits" [18 p. 16]. The political salience of the issue extends to other countries, as is illustrated by the amount of time devoted to debate over hunting with dogs by England's parliament [16 p. 13]. Even in Alaska, there have been divisions among hunters with some supporting "fair chase" and opposing hunting of wolves by air [19 p. 123]. The difference between general public opinion and those in charge of governmental wildlife policy is illustrated in Alaska, as described in Chapter 5, where the public has voted against airborne hunting of wolves in ballot initiatives while the state's legislature and wildlife authorities have sought to override the ban [20]. Mech says that it is "difficult to take wolves fairly" without aids such as snowmobiles, airplanes, traps or snares but notes that the public "bitterly opposes" these measures because they are unaware of the difficulty of hunting wolves without them [21 p. 1422]. Some wolf supporters have come to support wolf-hunting measures they do not like, such as leghold traps, if these are done in place of practices that they dislike even more, such as air or snowmobile shooting [21 p. 1422]. In 1992, Colorado voted to ban the use of baiting and hounds in bear hunts by a seventy to thirty margin [22 p. 184]. The campaign over these bans involved the refusal to compromise by hunting groups (including an Archery Hunting organization) based on their belief that any compromise would lead to future banning of gun rights [22 p. 187]. A referendum to ban baiting, use of dogs, and trapping failed in Maine in 2004 and again in 2014. These three methods accounted for 90 percent of the bear kills, and state wildlife officials took an active role in the campaigns against the referendum, arguing that these methods are "all needed to control the bear population" though later they were banned from participating in the second campaign due to a court case brought by a group called "Mainers for Fair Bear Hunting" [23]. Maine is the only state that allows all three methods and there exists a wide variation in rules concerning bear hunting throughout the United States [23]. Manfredo, Pierce, Fulton, Pate, and Gill found that negative attitudes toward certain practices such as trapping were stable in Colorado with over 60 percent favoring a ban [24]. In Alaska, the issue of baiting raised controversy in 2012 when a hunter brought a horse carcass just outside the Denali National Park in an area that has previously been a state "buffer zone" protected against hunting until 2010 when Alaska "lifted the restriction" and the hunter killed two wolves, one the breeding alpha "female of a pack of wolves" [25 p. 115]. The killing created a public outcry but the state refused a petition to reinstate the buffer zone restrictions for the area [25].

Concern with public perception of hunters and unethical hunting has led to the formation of the Interstate Wildlife Violator Compact, which covers forty-two of the fifty states [26 p. 151]. It is aimed at cooperatively solving problems such as invasive species, but also outlaws non-ethical hunting procedures, such as the use of Internet cameras, and requires that states honor each other's suspension of hunting even when the state laws are not exactly the same [26]. California has outlawed hunting of bobcats with dogs [27]. When the National Park Service proposed a rule to ban certain hunting practices for wolves and bears in Alaska, they included electronics: "The use of airborne devices controlled remotely and used to spot or locate game with the use of a camera, video, or other sensing devices" [28]. On the other hand, many states have enacted "right to hunt" bans into their constitutions and several other states are considering adoption of such a requirement [29]. For example, the Alabama Dog Hunters Association is seeking a constitutional amendment on the right to hunt into the state constitution because they are worried that animal rights organizations might impose restrictions [27]. There has been no serious effort to ban all hunting, with proposed restrictions primarily focused on what many people regard as "unethical hunting" practices. Animal rights groups have tried to harass hunters with the result that all fifty states have laws prohibiting the harassment of hunters [30 p. 18]. One of the reasons for the high success rate of these laws is that environmental organizations have refused to join in protests about legal hunting – major environmental organizations like the Audubon Society and Sierra Club support legal hunting [30 p. 18]. State wildlife officials help to protect hunters from harassment – Krajick describes how one protester attempted to prevent the shooting of a bison by shouting "don't shoot" and was "shoved into a tree" by a Montanan state wildlife worker [30].

Some reports have found a lowering of norms among hunters with fewer hunters (in 1973–4) expressing satisfaction if no game were bagged, fewer believing that wounded game should always be tracked down, and fewer who say they would report "game law violators" [31 p. 53]. Hunter attitudes and practices vary depending on their motivations for hunting. Pierce, Manfredo, and Bright surveyed applicants for "antlerless deer licenses" in New York State and found that most had an "appreciative motivation" involving their desire to "become acquainted with wildlife and seek peace in the outdoors" while 24 percent had affiliative motivation to "share experiences with others" and only 11 percent had an "achievement orientation" to "bag an animal" [32 p. 47]. President Andrew Jackson had no patience for concern with ethical hunting and criticized "New England swells for their ridiculous notions of fair chase" [33 p. 3]. In England, hunting has also become involved with partisan politics because hunting is associated with "wealthy rural dwellers," and hence the Conservative party, while the blue-collar Labour party opposes fox hunts [34 p. 105]. There are major differences among hunters in the United States. Robbins and Luginbuhl point out that "in-state hunters" in Montana have an average income between $30–35,000 while out-of-state hunters average $50–$75,000 of income [35 p. 28].

Today ethical issues involving sportsmanship remain contentious. For example, the shooting of bison when they left Yellowstone Park became controversial. One of the objections of opponents was that they thought "hunting bison no more sporting than shooting a couch: bison normally do not try to evade or attack the threat represented by the hunter" and media coverage of the killing created a "national uproar" [36 p. 135]. However, research by Rudolph, Schecter, and Riley found that while a ban on the use of bait in hunting deer was being implemented, only about 22 percent of hunters agreed with the norm of not using bait [37 p. 15–25]. Cambrone says that both baiting and feeding are "more popular than ever" in Wisconsin, and baiting is legal in twenty-five states, but many municipalities and counties across the country have banned baiting and feeding because of the presence of problem deer in yards and roads [38 p. 88]. When Wyoming considered approving the use of silencers on hunting rifles, it ignited a debate with hunters who supported the ban because of the "bad image" that it would give hunters another unfair advantage in addition to other "high-tech" devices such as "night-vision goggles, ballistic scopes, GPS units, and four-wheelers" [39]. However, the use of silencers has been approved by more than twenty-four states such as Texas and Arizona. The use of lights for hunting has raised controversies in Wisconsin. The Ojibwe tribe petitioned to hunt deer at night with lights and the Great Lakes Indian Fish and Wildlife Commission approved this request, but the state's Department of Natural Resources sued to stop them from hunting at night with lights with the argument that it was dangerous; the state ultimately lost the case in the court [40].

There is some evidence that hunters who hunt a particular animal tend to have positive ideas about their "game animals" and will support conservation more than those hunters who do not hunt that mammal. This was found to be the case for bear hunters in East Texas [41 p. 407]. The president of the International Varmint Association says that they love the animals that they hunt like prairie dogs and consequently have acted to stop the poisoning of them [42 p. 28]. However, Jacobson and Marynowski found hunters in Florida less supportive than other recreational users of endangered species protection. They identified "subgroups of hunters" such as "stalk hunters," who are much more supportive of protections than those who hunted with dogs [43 p. 773–9].

Hunters and Conservationists

The relationship between hunters and conservation groups is complex. State conservation efforts in the United States originated as a way of countering declines in game from overhunting [35 p. 27]. For a long period of time, most "environmentalists" (with a few significant exceptions like John Muir) "fished and hunted for pleasure" and these activities were their first contact with nature that helped to spur their interest in preservation [44 p. 58]. It was a coalition of hunters and conservationists who helped to pass the Migratory Bird Act of 1918 that allowed the Federal government to protect waterfowl traveling across Canada and many U.S. states [45 p. 38]. By the 1870s there were almost 400 sportsmen's clubs that helped to establish hunting regulations such as quotas and seasons, and the Boone and Crocket Club helped to found environmental organizations like the Audubon Society [14 p. 140]. Environmental groups like the World Wildlife Fund have supported seal hunts of adult seals in Canada and other "sustainable hunts" [46 p. 13–16]. During the 2012 election campaign, a sports group, the Montana Hunters and Anglers Association, supported environmental programs and implicitly the Democratic candidate for Senate (Jon Tester) over the Republican candidate due to issues like access to streams in the state [47]. A Colorado College-conducted poll found that though most sports persons "identify as Republicans," a strong majority (66 percent of hunters) also describe themselves as "conservationists" [47]. The House of Representatives passed a bill (The Sportsman's Heritage Act) in 2012 "to entrench hunting, fishing and shooting on federal public lands" but the bill began to be opposed by groups such as Backcountry Hunters and Anglers organization because they feared that it would "open up wilderness areas to motorized recreation" [48].

In 2013, a coalition of "commercial fishermen and environmentalists" rose to oppose a plan to develop a huge mine in prime salmon habitat area of Alaska's Bristol Bay [49]. The use of "zoning" that sets aside areas where certain wildlife can be hunted versus restricted areas where they are protected has been one strategy used to achieve compromise between conservation groups and hunters, not only in the United States but also in other countries ranging from Bolivia to the Congo [50 p. 158]. Mackinnon claims that protected areas can help "enhance wildlife harvests" outside the protected areas [51 p. 162]. An underlying problem that causes overhunting is that trophy hunters' favorite prey are large mammals that reproduce slowly, in contrast to "prolific species like peccaries, large rodents, and game birds that can be hunted sustainably" [52 p. 142].

The Political Power of Hunters

In states like Wisconsin, hunters wield great power with 650,000 hunters (including many from other states) chasing deer during the season. Rauber says that the Forest Service creates "permanent clearings" for the deer to "congregate" in 3–5 percent of the Chequamegon-Nicolet National Forest in northern Wisconsin – helping the deer population to increase to more than twice the size it was during pre-colonial period [53 p. 52]. When Wisconsin sought to kill 20,000 deer in 2003 in order to fight "contagious brain-wasting disease," both hunters and conservation groups protested "emotionally" [54]. The National Rifle Association (NRA) pushed the National Park Service to open up national parks and national monuments to hunting and trapping in 1986 but the courts ruled they were "prohibited unless Congress specifically allowed them" [55 p. 44]. Hunting groups pressured the National Park Service in 1967 to allow them to participate in the elk "reduction programs," but Sellars says that the "public became uneasy" about the killing of elk in the parks and there was an agreement reached to stop the shooting of elk in the Yellowstone so that shooting would take place just outside the park – a compromise to deal with conflicting demands of the public versus those of hunters [56 p. 246–7]. Durbin tells how the Georgia-Pacific Corporation planned to log Admiralty Island in Alaska in 1955 but sportsmen, along with Field and Stream Magazine, fought to close the Admiralty area to logging and the corporation ultimately abandoned their quest for a mill in the area [57 p. 21]. Hunting is highly important in Alaska – it is the only state with a policy to protect the rights of residents to "harvest wildlife … considered vital to their physical and cultural well-being" [58 p. 205]. Initially, the law was intended to protect only the subsistence hunting rights of Native peoples but it was later interpreted so as to consider all Alaskans, in effect, as protected subsistence users under the law [58 p. 208]. However, there is not always unity among hunter and fisher groups in Alaska, with sometimes strong divisions among recreational, subsistence (both Native and non-Native) and commercial interests. For example, sometimes there are clashes between Natives and non-Natives over "priority protections given to subsistence users" because non-Natives fear these may hurt their own chances at hunting and fishing while commercial fishermen in Alaska view "subsistence users as competitors for limited stocks" [58 p. 215].

The influence of hunting and fishing groups over wildlife policy has been strong ever since licenses for these activities have provided most of the revenues of state wildlife agencies. The Pittman-Robertson Act, passed in 1937, required that proceeds from a tax on hunting equipment be used for "wildlife restoration" but DiSilvestro says that most of this money is spent to "benefit game animals" [59 p. 31]. Di Silvestro also cites the opening of the Loxahatchee National Wildlife Refuge after thirty years of closure to humans as an example of the influence of the "hunter-dominated Florida Wildlife Federation" [59 p. 84]. The American Humane Association has complained about how hunting interests dominate state wildlife decisions, despite the fact that hunters only constitute about 6 per cent of the population [60 p. 223]. Shivik says that it is no accident that about one third of "state wildlife agencies use the term 'game' in their titles rather than wildlife" [61 p. 65]. Recently, the Montana Fish, Wildlife and Parks Department (MFWPD) proposed creating a "wolf management stamp" that would broaden revenue support for the department and be used for a variety of activities including money for livestock, wolf-monitoring, habitat protection, scientific research, hiring of wardens, and educational outreach [62]. Although the proposal had supporters among both conservationist and hunters groups, it was shelved because of the controversy it created. Some hunting groups thought that limiting the money to "non-lethal methods was a dangerous precedent" and thought that sale of the stamps could give "pro-wolf interests" greater control over MFWPD to the detriment of hunting interests [62]. Due to the controversy, the MFWPD director postponed a decision on the stamp. Similarly, the Idaho Department of Fish and Game tried to organize a "summit" to discuss how funding for the department could be broadened, but this proposal brought a negative reaction from many hunters [62]. The difficulty of obtaining funding for non-game species is reflected in the history of the Fish and Wildlife Conservation Act of 1980 which targets non-game species. The legislation passed and it was supposed to be funded by excise taxes on non-consumptive uses of wildlife (e.g., excise taxes on birdfeed and recreational equipment) but these industries resisted and no Federal funding was provided until 2001 when "Congress actually appropriated money to the states through the State and Tribal Wildlife Grants program" [63 p. 147]. In short, hunters are aware of the importance of the fact that their dominance of funding dollars gives them control over wildlife policy and consequently many do not want a change in the status quo.

The Wildlife Management Institute, despite its strong pro-hunting policy, warns hunters that their opposition to the broadening of funding would not prevent other groups from influencing policy through legislative acts and referenda and encouraged them to compromise. The situation at the Federal level is significantly different. Culhane attributes the relative disinterest of Federal wildlife agencies in hunting and fishing recreation as being due to the fact that they do not receive hunting-related revenue as state agencies do [64 p. 119]. The USFWS announced in March of 2014 that it would open six wildlife refuges to new hunting programs and expand hunting and fishing in twenty other refuges [65]. Over time, competing demands for conservation funds from environmental groups have arisen in many states, and consequently other sources have been made available to certain state natural resource agencies such as "tax checkoffs" in states like West Virginia [66 p. 116]. In states like California, growing urbanization has led to- fewer hunters and fishers resulting in drops in "license sales from 480,000 in 1985 to 415,000 in 1988" [66 p. 116].

In the early years in the United States, there was a major division between "sports hunters" and commercial hunters that "sometimes approached the point of war" [44 p. 57]. In the 1800s, wealthy sportsmen who feared a decline in deer numbers supported the passage of hunting laws aimed at immigrants (e.g., Italians) [67 p. 28–29 & 48]. Dizard claims that hunters were often disliked by non-hunters because most hunters were "blue collar" which is why the Metropolitan District Commission in the Greater Boston Metropolitan Area took a long time to support hunting of deer [68 p. 111–16]. The Boone and Crockett Club was the first conservation group to "lobby effectively on behalf of large game" [33 p. 206]. The wealthier sports hunters prevailed in outlawing most commercial game hunting and fishing.

While many hunters are conservation minded, a large portion intensely dislike environmental groups and Federal agencies. Snell recounts how a rancher who discussed with the Nature Conservancy the possibility of establishing "conservation easements" on his ranch to preserve the open space lost many of his rancher friends [69 p. 24–8]. When the same rancher took action to oppose a Canadian company's plans to drill in the Blindhorse Outstanding Natural Area in Montana, he sought the support of the Boone and Crockett Hunting Club, many of whom are influentials from Texas (e.g., former President George W. Bush) and Florida to speak on behalf of conservation of the area.

One issue in which many hunters strongly conflict with environmentalists concerns the use of lead shot, which can cause death of waterfowl such as loons and swans [70]. Lead shot was banned for "waterfowl hunting" in 1991 but can still be employed for other game birds and mammals [70]. The use of lead sinkers for fishing is also a source of death for waterfowl. The sports fishing industry "does not dispute the fact" but argues that there are other much greater causes to mortality of waterfowl and thus the use of lead should not be banned [70]. The American Sportsfishing Association contends that despite the fact that lead can contribute to fish mortality, "sufficient data must exist to demonstrate that discarded lead tackle is an actual threat to the sustainability of loon or other water bird populations" [71]. According to research, lead shot is the "biggest exposure threat to condors" in California [72; 73 p. 283]. A five-year review by the Pacific Southwest branch of the USFWS found that deaths of condors in Arizona and California due to lead far outnumbered those of any other cause including predators, power lines, starvation, micro trash, fire, and shooting [74]. In a debate over whether to outlaw lead use in California, hunting-affiliated groups such as the California Waterfowl Association opposed the bill sponsored by the Audubon Society, and when the National Park Service said it would ban the use of lead ammunition in parks, they backed down when the NRA attacked them and consequently changed the policy to cover only "park personnel" [70]. So powerful and threatening is the gun lobby that Audubon's Ted Williams reported that a scientist who shared data with him (about the harmful effects of lead) asked for anonymity because he feared retribution. California banned the use of lead bullets in the fifteen counties that include condor country.

Many hunters believe that banning lead bullets is a violation of their property rights and a first step to restricting hunting [75]. In the 2014 election, Democratic senators facing tough reelections in conservative states, like Kay Hagan in North Carolina, Mark Begich in Alaska, and Mary Landrieu in Louisiana, cosponsored the bill to ban the U.S. Environmental Protection Administration (EPA) from regulating lead content. The House version of this proposed legislation (HR 3590) also proposed the "construction of shooting ranges on public lands" as well as to "prohibit frivolous lawsuits . . . by anti-hunting organizations when federal agencies move to open land to sportsmen" [76]. When liberal Democrats offered amendments such as striking the provision banning EPA from regulating ammunition and fishing gear, the bill was filibustered by Republicans. A Democratic senator from New Mexico, Martin Heinrich, proposed legislation (the "HUNT Act") that would expand hunting and fishing access to public lands by using money "earmarked for conservation projects" to use for "road and land purchase easements" [77]. Thus support of legislative acts favoring hunters has been a popular position for Democrats running in states that are rural and conservative. The final budget compromise reached between Congressional Republicans and Democrats in December of 2014 again demonstrated the political strength of the hunter lobby because it included the provision that "prohibited EPA from regulating the lead content in ammunition and fishing tackle" despite the scientific evidence that lead can be harmful [78]. Other conflicts occur between conservationists and some hunters. For example, one of the problems of preserving the reintroduced red wolf in North Carolina is that hunters, especially those from outside the area, mistake the red wolves for coyotes and shoot them, with the consequence that there has been a drop in mating pairs of wolves [79 p. 42].

Ecological Benefits and Costs of Hunting

A major benefit of hunting for wildlife concerns the fact that over a billion dollars (in 2006) were contributed to wildlife agencies based on the excise tax on hunting supplies as well license fees and other contributions from hunters [7 p. 403]. One possibly positive effect of hunting is to control overpopulations of species like deer that can become a threats to other species of life. Cambrone quotes Anthony Nicola, head of a team hired by many suburbs to reduce their deer populations, as saying that recreational hunters do not have a significant impact on reducing deer populations and, indeed, that deer hunters encourage growth in deer populations such as through their opposition to the hunting of does [80 p. 199]. Nicolai's teams have removed more than 10,000 deer from suburbs and are not concerned with "fair chase" but with achieving their "humane death."

The challenge for hunting to be "sustainable" is to only take as many prey as are added to the population through natural population growth [81 p. 77]. Certain strategies may contribute to adhering to this criterion. For example, trophy hunters can hunt lions sustainably if only male lions are taken [82 p. 114]. There is controversy in many developing countries on protections given to charismatic animals, due largely to demands by international non-governmental organizations. For example, a well-known Kenyan biologist (David Western) criticized the "emotional attachment" to "Dumbo . . . fairy tale . . . creatures" that blocked the hunting of elephants and rhinos in the Pilanesberg National Park (in South Africa) [83].

Although hunting is seen as having possibly positive benefits of reducing over-populations of some species, it has been the cause of tension between environmentalists and hunters because of the desire of many hunters for an overabundance of game, such as huge populations of caribou in Alaska. Consequently, wildlife officials in Alaska and some other states seek to reduce the numbers of "competitors of human hunters such as wolves and bears" as described in Chapter 5. It has also led to hunters supporting policies like banning the hunting of does in order to produce an "overpopulation of deer" [59 p. 29]. Another conflict has arisen over hunting in the National Wildlife Refuge system. Hunter organizations have pushed to allow hunting in the refuges though the Federal courts have stepped into block uses when they are seen as opposed to the "primary purpose" of the refuges of conservation of wildlife [84 p. 29–33]. Some famous conservationists such as William Hornaday considered hunting a primary threat to the loss of species, viewing hunters in states as "forty-eight armies" putting species at danger [85 p. 98]. However, environmentalists now see the loss of habitat as being much far more important cause than hunting [85 p. 97–8]. As discussed in Chapter 1, environmentalists such as Murie (and later David Brower) worked hard to get environmentalists to accept compromises on hunting and avoid contentious issues such as wolf control programs so they could form a powerful joint coalition to support conservation efforts [19 p. 109 & 123].

Both conservationists and many hunters have long been proud of the North American model of hunting, which is based on public ownership of wildlife. But, in recent years, this model has been challenged by the growth in private, commercial wildlife hunting. In states like Texas, "managed wildlife ranches" are popular and have encouraged what Sasser refers to as the "privatization of wildlife hunting" [86]. The Texas Parks and Wildlife Department (TP&W) allows special limits for hunting (e.g., deer) to be set for specific ranches including "lengthened seasons" and hunters may far exceed the usual quotas for deer per season (e.g., five). TP&W describes the program as follows: The Managed Lands Deer Permit (MLDP) program allows landowners involved in a formal management program to have the state's most flexible seasons and bag limits. Sasser says that TP&W did not try to create a management system that would allow the private-property deer herds to be balanced by more hunters but instead set-up the MLDP [86]. Privatization of hunting has occurred in other states. The State of Utah's Division of Wildlife Services has developed a system in which vouchers are allotted to ranchers and farmers for hunting licenses that can be "sold for thousands of dollars as part of a private hunt on their land" [87]. The State views this as an incentive to support wildlife on private land because ranchers have complained about elk eating food intended for cattle. Opponents of the voucher system argue that it violates the "North American model of hunting" in which wildlife belongs to everyone, not just those with money. Rasker, Martin, and Johnson cite examples where most landowners charging fees were not interested in wildlife and did not invest profits in habitat for them [88 p. 333–4]. Defenders of the system say that it is just "another way to conserve game" and, concerning the advantage given to the wealthy, they reply that "life is not fair" [87]. Another point of contention is that the groups that have benefited the most from the vouchers have spent about one quarter of their proceeds on lobbying for increased hunting of wolves. The case of Montana illustrates one other potential problem with private game farming – the state "largely eliminated the game farm industry in a 2000" voter initiative due to the fact it had contributed to the spread of chronic wasting disease [35 p. 32].

Recently, the North American model's contention that hunters contribute the lion's share of funding for wildlife conservation has been challenged by Smith and Molde, who argue that hunters only contribute about 14.5 percent [89 p. 8]. They say that previous calculations have ignored the contributions of Federal agencies that contribute to wildlife conservation such as by USFWS, Bureau of Land Management, the National Park System, and U.S. Forest Service [89 p. 3]. They argue that state wildlife managers' (e.g., the former Director of Nevada Department of Wildlife) claim that a high percentage (e.g., 79 percent in Nevada's case) derives from hunting is based upon false assumptions and has resulted in far much too attention given to the priorities of hunters [89 p. 10]. Clark and Milloy argue that Federal funding for wildlife based on the Pittman-Robertson Act is structured to favor the coalition of fishermen, hunters, government wildlife agencies, and industries that manufacture equipment for them, but that the "vast majority of the world's reptiles and amphibians that occur in the U.S. are not eligible for funding from the Sport Fish or Wildlife Restoration Acts because they are not huntable" [90 p. 294–300]. Consequently, the sportsman model has serious limitations for funding biodiversity. McShea points to another limitation of hunting for wildlife conservation – human hunters do not change the grazing habits of ungulates like carnivores because they avoid areas with deer populations "less than carrying capacity" [91 p. 149–50].

Government agencies generally tread lightly in regulating hunting in rural states. Papouchis cites evidence that setting of quotas for killing of mountain lions is not based on science but on the degree of hunter interest, the perception that lion numbers are increasing, and the belief that lions are decreasing the availability of game [92 p. 228–9]. These pressures led to increases in quotas for mountain lions in states such as Montana, Idaho, and Utah [92]. The USFWS and others are reluctant to take action against hunters. Rick Bass reports that there had been no arrests or prosecutions for killing of wolves in Montana because the "Feds don't want a backlash among the ranch and hunting communities" [93 p. 144]. Bass quotes Ed Bangs, a USFWS official, as saying "I have a motto … Don't piss off 200,000 people with guns, if they aren't doing anything wrong" [93]. Treves and Martin conducted surveys between 2000 and 2007, when controversy over listing of wolves was contentious, and found that a "plurality of all hunters" and a majority of all wolf and bear hunters would "oppose any restrictions on hunting" of wolves such as hunting with dogs, traps, or bait [94 p. 990].

Hunting can lead to genetic changes in the traits of exploited populations. Wildlife predators such as wolves and bears are more likely to kill weaker members of the population. Indeed, it has been found that cougars selectively hunt for deer that are suffering from chronic wasting disease and thus perform a "sanitation effect" on prey populations. By way of contrast, human hunters "always seek out the biggest bucks" which can cause changes in the genetics of the population leading to reduced size and smaller antlers [95 p. 112]. Darimont et al. found that "phenotype changes" were much more rapid in "human-exploited populations" outpacing "natural perturbations in nature" by as much as 300 percent and that the changes were quick, leading to declines in size of 20 percent [96 p. 952]. These changes were most dramatic in commercially exploited areas and, the authors argue, could "imperil ecosystems" [96 p. 952]. Hunting also can lead to huge "imbalances" in the sex ratios of populations. Research in India's Periyar Tiger Reserve found that "male-bias in hunting" elephants resulted in a ratio of 1 male to 122 females compared to a ratio of 1 male to 2 females in an area where "hunting was virtually absent" [97 p. 36]. Additionally, evidence shows that large mammals avoid areas that allow heavy hunting even though these areas are most appropriate for them, thus limiting the effective amount of habitat available to them. Thus hunting may push elephants and lions to expand their ranges so they come into conflict with villages and herders [97 p. 31–9].

The North American model does not apply very well in developing countries. Wall and Child point out that the North American model is dependent on a variety of preconditions including a strong economy, strong grass roots support for conservation, and an effective enforcement system, but these are lacking in countries that have "personalized economies" [98 p. 257–9]. Studies of South African game ranches demonstrate the complexities of "closely and actively" managing game resources on enclosed game ranches to counter the effects of inbreeding, and taking strong measures to prevent outside animals getting inside the preserves (or the reverse) [99 p. 233–6]. The financial attractiveness of privatized ranches is illustrated by the prices for trophy animals, which have jumped by 50 percent in the last six years and thus have attracted wealthy investors [100]. Hunters will pay $15,000 to shoot a cape buffalo and twice as much for individuals with especially large horns [100]. The game breeders for the ranches argue that by breeding for large horns and other characteristics that are attractive to hunters, they are "bringing back" the "magnificent specimens that were hunted out of existence" though some geneticists fear the effects of breeding to produce exotic hybrids and unusual colors in species because these could make them more susceptible to diseases [100].

According to Lindsey, Balme, Booth, and Midlane, the effects of trophy hunting on a species like lions varies greatly depending on the country involved [101]. In Tanzania, Lindsey et al. state that hunting of lions is important because relatively few elephants are hunted there, and that banning of trophy hunting could lead to serious negative consequences for conservation if "alternative land use" resulted; but they also acknowledge that current hunting levels are "excessive" and profits cannot be sustained. Tanzania has introduced minimum age requirements for lion "trophies" to make their hunting more sustainable, but Lindsey et al. acknowledge that the country has a "poor record of governance" [101]. In Namibia, lions are unimportant in trophy hunting due to "low quotas" and their numbers have increased as a result [101]. Their overall assessment is that banning of trophy hunting could have a worse impact on conservation than overhunting though this conclusion is contingent on "reform of hunting lion management" [102]. Since many countries have not demonstrated the ability to manage hunting effectively, the outlook for lions appears fragile.

Certain kinds of commercial fishing such as "bottom trawling" have negative effects on corals and sponges, and these effects take a long time to recover from even if bottom trawling is banned [103 p. 362]. Commercial fishers also waste and harm fish species they discard as "bycatch," though Kaiser and Jennings point out that certain kinds of "waste" by commercial fishers have become important to scavenging birds and that if this practice is stopped, it should be done gradually [103 p. 362]. Overfishing and depletion of fish due to increased population of fishers, boats, and use of technology have become problems. In Florida, a proposal to put fishing off limits in the Biscayne (Underwater) National Park divided fishermen [104]. Similar action banning fishing in the Dry Tortugas National Park (near Key West) has helped restore fish that had been depleted in part due to the increased use of technology such as GPS and other systems that make catching large fish easier [104]. State fishery management officials and some in the fishing industry oppose the step, favoring less radical measures. Law says that exploitation is "inherently selective" and cites the example of increasing occurrences of elephant tusklessness in areas with high poaching that are normalized when more effective protection is achieved [105 p. 324 & 332]. Indeed, because of the impacts of selection in hunting, some European countries implement "selective culling" policies to encourage the culling of "excess females," "sick individuals," and those with "malformed heads" [105 p. 338]. Hunters sometimes support exotic species that they like to hunt, such as mouflon sheep in Hawaii, even though these sheep are harmful to endangered species like the palila [106 p. 43–4].

Another fishing issue that can pit conservationists against anglers concerns trout removal in the West. The California Department of Fish and Wildlife is using gillnets to trap and kill "alien brook trout" in certain lakes in the High Sierra [107 p. 16]. Humans stocked some Sierra lakes with the fish after World War II but they began eating tadpoles and thus threaten the "mountain yellow-legged frog." Elimination of the trout also helps some other species revive such as mayflies and rosy finches that eat the mayflies [107]. But local anglers were described as being "apoplectic" about this removal and a local newspaper asked the question: "If the yellow-legged frog disappears, would anyone notice?" [107 p. 16]. Thus preservation of non-game and uncharismatic species is difficult if it involves elimination of game species with significant support from sportsmen.

The decline in a species usually has multiple causes and the contribution of any individual cause such as hunting is open to debate. The classic case of hunting contributing to the extinction of a species is the passenger pigeon, because the replacement rate dropped due to constant hunting, trapping, and "colony disturbance" [108 p. 2]. However, Bucher contends that loss of habitat was another important underlying cause [108]. The National Research Council cited data that found (mostly) unregulated hunting caused about 23 percent of known extinctions compared to 36 percent for habitat loss and 39 percent for "introduced animals" [109 p. 73]. Packer et al. studied the decline of lions in Tanzania (which has the most remaining lions in Africa) and found that the "intensity of trophy hunting" was the only factor consistently related to the decline; consequently they recommended lowering of hunting quotas for them [110]. The improvement of the technology of hunting has meant that hunters are achieving a much higher rate of success in the tropics [103 p. 343]. The passenger pigeon case is an early example of the impact of technology, because the combination of railroads and telegraph enabled hunters to quickly find the locations of flocks and then travel to them. Eisenberg points out that trappers used to be limited by the need to "use snowshoes and dogsleds" but now use snowmobiles; this allows them to have huge numbers of lines and go more deeply into the habitat of threatened species like wolverines [25 p. 156]. Drones present another technological advance that improves the effectiveness of hunters but raises ethical and conservation issues. Recently, an Illinois state senator proposed legislation that "would bar the use of drones to hunt and fish, building on existing Illinois law that prohibits using drones to interfere with hunters or fishermen and restricts their use by law enforcement" [111]. Dizikes cites one outfitter who supports the legislation because "I believe in doing things the old way, and it's not hunting to me if it's too easy ... Get out and do your legwork, that's what hunting is about" [111]. However, according to State Natural Resources Department officials, the legislation as originally worded would not ban the use of drones to "scout" for wildlife; another state legislator, who owns a hunting guide business, likened their use to "tree stands that allow hunters to see an area from a higher position" and rhetorically asks, "when does the cheating start?" [111].

As discussed in Chapter 7, American and other international sports hunters are important to countries such as Tanzania. The country's director of wildlife recently pleaded with the USFWS not to list the African lion as endangered because hunters pay nearly $10,000 in government fees to hunt lions; he calculates that these funds help "to support twenty-six game reserves" and the growing number of "wildlife management areas" owned by local communities in Tanzania [112]. In addition, he points out that these hunters pay many times as much as "regular tourists" and visit areas seldom frequented by photographic tourists. Schroeder reports that Tanzania is one of the few East African countries to allow "safari hunting" (of seventy "trophy species") but is "tough on poaching by natives" [113 p. 586]. However, a study of sports hunting for leopards in Mozambique showed that, although leopards produced significant revenue (about $24,000 per leopard), not enough of these revenues went to community members in order to discourage poaching, and revenue-sharing needs to be improved [114 p. 840]. On October 27, 2014, the USFWS announced that they were proposing to list lions due to three threats: habitat loss, loss of prey base, and increased human–lion conflict [115]. Although trophy hunting is not directly listed as one of the threats, the rule would require a permit to import a "sport-hunted trophy lion" into the United States, and will not allow such trophies into the United States unless the nation has a "conservation program that meets" USFWS criteria and is taken as part of a "scientific management program" that will provide benefits "to the overall lion population and local communities" [115].

Conclusion

The most direct consumption-oriented benefits to humans from wildlife involve hunting and fishing. Although the proportion of the population involved in hunting and fishing activities has declined in the past century, there are still billions of dollars of economic activity generated by these activities. However, more than five times as many people (including many hunters) enjoyed non-consumption activities such as watching of wildlife, and spent more than twice as much as hunters on these activities. Hunters are an unusual case of a group that has maintained a strong record of success in the politics of wildlife despite downward trends in their percentage of the U.S. population. Their political strength is a testimony to the continuing importance of "institutionalism" because fees from hunters have been a major source of funds for state wildlife agencies, which has enabled them to dominate the policies of these organizations. Also, although hunters are now a small percentage of the U.S. population, the saliency of hunting issues is extremely high for them and thus interest groups acting on their behalf have been successful in influencing state legislatures. Sports groups have proven to be highly effective in mobilizing their members to influence representatives and relevant agency officials. Thus the dynamics of interest groups remains extremely relevant to understanding wildlife politics.

The relationship between hunters and conservation is complex. Due to their concentration in rural areas and their love of guns, hunters would seem to be a prototype of anti-government conservatives and, on issues such as the right to hunt without restrictions, this image holds true. However, their love for wilderness and wildlife has often led to them to coalesce with conservationists against developers and extractive industries when they have threatened areas where they hunt and fish, which is a basic reason why the liberal-conservative continuum in politics does not adequately explain wildlife politics. Although the right to hunt is firmly ensconced in states, there have been many conflicts over hunting ethics such as the use of baiting, dogs, and lead bullets, and some states have successfully passed restrictions. Hunters have always been a varied group based on their motivations to hunt. Thus, in some states, animal rights groups and sometimes environmentalists have prevailed against hunters over issues of ethical hunting. There are also some divisions within the sportsmen coalition. Class differences have contributed to disagreements among hunters, with poorer subsistence hunters less concerned with "fair chase" and hunting ethics. The politics of hunting in developing countries is quite different. In such countries, native hunters usually are politically weak and hunting policies are most heavily influenced by foreign NGOs and governments, though heavy poaching by natives nevertheless occurs due to the weakness of the central governments of these countries and lack of enforcement on restrictions on hunting.

11   Tourism: Good or Bad for Conservation of Wildlife?

The Development of Ecotourism

A basic hope of many conservationists is that recreational use of wildlife in protected areas will have a positive impact on the preservation of biodiversity because humans will see value in preserving wildlife. Indeed, recreational use has built support for U.S. national parks and was the basic strategy employed by Gilbert Pinchot and George Hartzog, who built the U.S. park system [1 p. 66–7]. Tourists in U.S. national parks rate "wildlife viewing" as their most important reason for visiting them [2 p. 3]. On the other hand, long ago conservationists such as Adolph Murie were concerned about recreation in national parks unless it was restricted to "small groups" and Murie's brother (Olaus) opposed "the expansion of tourism" in Yellowstone National Park in favor of maintaining its "ecological integrity" [3 p. 36 & 43]. Although most parks are established with a view to attracting tourists, the Arctic National Wildlife Refuge (ANWR) in Alaska is an example of a park that had virtually no "record of recreational use" when it was established and thus "no constituency of visitors" [3 p. 53]. Some environmentalists wanted to impose size limits on parties visiting ANWR to no more than six, though the Sierra Club visited it in groups of twenty or more [3 p. 100]. The inherent dilemma for many conservationists is that building political support necessitates human use including hunting, wildlife viewing, and recreation but these very activities have the potential to harm the biodiversity that is being sought to be preserved. One example of pleasing tourists was "feeding garbage to grizzlies" in Yellowstone National Park in front of "grandstands" of humans [4 p. 146]. The same dilemma is also true in developing countries where research shows that the establishment of "protected areas" encourages tourism that brings with it capital investment and population growth attracted by jobs, roads, and educational and health facilities that often develop near these areas [5].

A major distinction has been made between consumptive uses of wildlife, such as hunting and fishing, and non-consumptive such as photo-tourism, where the individual wildlife are not taken. Actually, non-consumptive tourism can have a wide variety of negative impacts on wildlife such as disturbance of behavior (e.g., disrupting mating rituals), feeding patterns (providing food), "increasing vulnerability to poaching due to habituation," among others [6 p. 96]. Meyer says that even "low impact activities" may lead to the introduction of "alien species" to formerly safe areas [7 p. 57].

Roe, Leader-Williams, and Dalal-Clayton have analyzed the impacts of tourism systematically and distinguish between direct impacts (e.g., disturbance of feeding) and indirect impacts (habitat changes due to infrastructure developed to promote tourism) [8]. There are also less tangible effects such as "visual impacts." Roe et al. outline different strategies to minimize the detrimental effects of tourism on wildlife, such as limiting the number of persons in an area or zoning areas, with some areas off-limits to most tourist uses, using "fixed viewing points" or setting limits on how close viewing of wildlife can be as well as indirect methods such as visitor education [8]. Some of these restrictions are difficult to implement because most wildlife viewers like to see "big animals close up" with birdwatchers being the singular exception [8]. However, bird photographers can also cause significant harm to species. Ebersole contacted authorities about a nature photographer in Florida for "harassing a nesting female kite for nearly two hours" and he reports on many other instances where bird photographers disturbed birds during mating or nesting season [9]. Audubon is attempting to get a 100 ft buffer area established around the bird sanctuaries where anyone can be arrested for approaching too closely [9]. In Minnesota, Ebersole reported that photographers worked together to lure snowy owls with prey attached to a fishing line in order to get action photos – they did not allow the birds to capture and eat the prey. As a result, Minnesota is considering legislation to "forbid" anyone to bait owls [9].

Because of the dangers of tourism and other human uses, it has been argued that existence of pests such as the tsetse fly, that discourages both tourism and grazing, have done more to protect biodiversity in Mozambique by preventing conversion of habitat to grazing than "any national or international policies" [10 p. 158]. By way of contrast, the elimination of the tsetse fly and the building of roads have led to growth of tourism along with big population increases in Zimbabwe [11 p. 228]. Often pressure to restrict numbers of inhabitants and tourists comes from outside the country. For example, Ecuador's Galapagos Islands were put on the United Nation's Endangered Heritage sites in 2007 and Ecuador began limiting numbers of migrants to the islands, but these restrictions caused some migrants to complain that a "tortoise for a rich foreigner to photograph is worth more than an Ecuadorian citizen" [12].

Ecotourism has become a popular term used to denote tourism with the purpose of "interacting with nature" while at the same time minimizing negative impacts due to this interaction [8]. Another purpose of ecotourism is to ensure that local communities benefit from the tourism. The great hopes that surround the potential of ecotourism are reflected by the fact that the United Nations declared the year 2002 as the International Year of Ecotourism and encouraged governments and international organizations to support ecotourism activities [13 p. 103]. Unfortunately, much research shows that outsiders and a few natives are the ones who benefit the most from ecotourism. West, Fortwangler, Agbo, Simsik, and Sokpon point out conditions under which locals may be advantaged such as when they possess unique skills and knowledge "of local flora and fauna" or when they provide "support services" that do not directly compete with those of the outside operators [13 p. 112]. Roe et al. differentiate tourists into those that require little in the way of infrastructure support (e.g., backpackers and birdwatchers) versus the mass general public and the wealthy who require good facilities and much support [8]. One of the advantages of trophy hunters is that many of them do not require much supportive infrastructure.

One of the prerequisites for ecotourism to flourish is political stability. For example, Rwanda and Uganda both derive economically important benefits from gorilla tourism but when one country suffers from instability (e.g., Rwanda in the 1990s), the other country's gorilla tourism flourishes [14 p. 144]. However, even in Rwanda, the gorilla's importance has become evident as symbolized by being "displayed on postage stamps and idolized in popular radio tunes" [15 p. 48]. A recent World Wildlife Fund (WWF) report describes the Clouds Mountain Gorilla lodge in Nkuringo (Uganda) that employs forty people and has 1200 guests per year [16 p. 106–8]. The report states that income from the hotel and gorilla permits goes into a foundation that invests in support of projects such as tea plantations and vegetable growing. The WWF report also describes how the International Gorilla Conservation Program (IGCP) has been formed by the WWF and Fauna and Flora International that created a "gorilla water initiative" that provides water and sanitation to villages, thus avoiding the need for natives to collect water from within the gorilla parks, reducing threats to gorillas [16].

In the United States, tourism has helped to counter activities such as clear-cutting. For example, in Alaska, the growth of tourism industry pushed the U.S. Forest Service to halt clear-cutting of forests along shipping lanes frequented by tourist ships [17 p. 29]. In 1992, the Alaska Wilderness Tourism and Recreation Association was formed and "spoke out on conservation issues" including a threatened boycott if aerial shooting of wolves were allowed [17 p. 246]. Still, Durbin admits that tourism can be a double-edged sword because it sometimes overwhelms the carrying capacity of small towns like Sitka (Alaska) and sudden changes in routes of tourist ships can lead to a huge drop in visitors [17 p. 303]. Some groups benefit from ecotourism while others suffer. The U.S. Fish and Wildlife Service (USFWS) estimated in its Final Environmental Impact Statement that the restoration of wolves in the Yellowstone region would yield "23 million in tourism" dollars [18 p. 33]. A 2006 study by a University of Montana economist found that wolf-watching provided annually $70 million to the Yellowstone area [19 p. 87]. Wilcove observes that most of the job growth in the Yellowstone area has been due to service industries and that it is "surprising how minor a role logging and ranching play in the economy of the area" [20 p. 65].

It is difficult to estimate the value of wildlife viewing. The USFWS sought to estimate the economic benefits of visits to wildlife refuges to local communities [21]. They begin by acknowledging it is impossible to measure the value, for example, of "the survival of the endangered jaguarondi, or any of the other endangered or threatened creatures nurtured by refuges" [21]. They separated out the spending done by local versus non-resident visitors. Their results showed that in the fiscal year 2011, 46.5 million people visited refuges, spending $2.4 billion of sales in local economies with over 35,000 people employed. The refuge visitors resulted in about $343 million of tax revenue to local, state, and Federal governments. Non-consumptive activities accounted for the most expenditures (72 percent) versus those of fishing (21 percent) and hunting (7 percent). A total of 77 percent of the visitors were from outside the local areas of the refuges [21].

The Value of Ecotourism to Developing Countries

In developing countries, some researchers claim that tourism does not pay for native populations. Norton-Griffiths and Said argue that the fees paid to landholders in Africa for keeping their land undeveloped so that tourists can view wildlife are "vastly less than the rents" the landholders could obtain from "either livestock or agricultural production" [22 p. 370–8]. Moreover, they also state that wildlife can have harmful effects on agricultural and livestock profits so that profits could be cut in half, with the result that there would be major benefits to landholders to eliminating the wildlife in Kenya. In short, they recommend that the ban on "consumptive utilization of wildlife" in Kenya should be eliminated [22 p. 383].

Tourism has provided protection for wildlife in some Central American countries. In Costa Rica, tourism has become a "big earner of foreign currency" that has provided conservation forces with clout that is important because Central American parks are small and need the support of those who live on their borders [23 p. 45]. In Central American countries with violence and instability like Guatemala, tourism has not protected conservationists from being threatened with violence and death by logging and hunting interests [23 p. 48]. In Costa Rica, coastal communities like Tortuguero now act to protect sea turtles due to tourism – previously they used to catch them for food [23 p. 155]. Likewise, on the island of Trinidad, residents (including former poachers) now constitute the "Nature Seekers" group that acts to protect the turtles and guide ecotourists to view them [24]. Ecotourism at Mon Repos in Queensland (Australia) has been credited with positive impacts on the preservation of sea turtles [25 p. 1524–30]. This tourism is managed by the Queensland Park and Wildlife Service, with up to seventy people watching the turtles nesting and also for the hatchlings "to emerge," thus providing protection for them. Surveys of the tourists show a positive impact on their attitudes toward the preservation of sea turtles. The management of ecotourism is crucial because tourist developments can harm the turtles through the presence of distracting lights or large buildings that could prevent hatching, as well as general disturbance that can affect nesting. Thus properly managed ecotourism may help offset other harmful effects from humans on turtles, such as destruction of sea grass and other food sources due to pollution, hits by boats, and getting caught in fishing gear or crab pots [25]. In Borneo and Sumatra, the growth of oil palm industry has threatened the habitat of species like proboscis monkeys but the WWF's director for the region hopes that ecotourism can provide a "competitive alternative to logging and oil palm plantations" with more than 2 million visiting the area in order to view wildlife [26]. In Australia, dangerous crocodiles are tolerated because of the huge tourist trade, as symbolized by a hotel built in the shape of a crocodile [27 p. 24].

In Africa, the director of the Amboseli Research Project in Kenya ascribed the healthy number of elephants in the Amboseli National Park due to the tolerance of the Maasai and the presence of tourists [28 p. 24]. Likewise, Kabiri says that tourism had grown to 12 percent of Kenya's economy by 2006 so that the state gives the tourism industry "preferential treatment" in the competition for attention [29 p. 137]. In Tanzania, tourism has been its "fastest growing industry, increasing 600 percent from

1985 to 1990" [30 p. 369]. By 2008, the estimated value of tourism in the country had grown to US$1.6 billion [31 p. 272]. Victurine and Curtin describe one effective model of conservation in which "tour operators" (in the Tarangire Area of Tanzania) pay local villages to establish "conservation easements abolishing harmful practices toward wildlife in the area" even though the villages are not areas that the tours intend to visit because they are part of key "dispersal areas" that support wildlife of the region [32].

Tourism is the "central axis" around which South Africa, Zimbabwe, and Mozambique agreed to set up "Trans Frontier Conservation Areas" on the borders shared by these countries with the goal of creating jobs and helping to support stability of the countries [33 p. 8]. The negotiations to establish this agreement were notably led by the countries' tourism rather than environmental officials [34 p. 8]. Buckley cites several examples of positive effects from the agreement such as contributions to local schools as well as jobs in ecolodges that provide "30 times the income" paid by former agriculture properties [34 p. 9–22]. Arcese, Hando, and Campbell found a vicious circle existed in the Serengeti during the 1980s because poaching of elephants led to declines in tourism revenue which in turn led to less money for enforcement patrols [35 p. 510]. In Cambodia, villagers who used to be poachers of ibis say that now that they make $5 per day as guides to view the ibis and consequently they no longer poach because "hunting you only get big money one time a year" [36 p. 54–6]. Even critics of tourism such as Elizabeth Becker, author of *Overbooked: The exploding business of travel and tourism*, states that her interviews with "experts of all ideological persuasions" attest to the fact that without the presence of wildlife tourists, the "parks would disappear" [37 p. 213]. In Namibia, laws were passed in 1996 to give tribes rights to property for communally managed land that has resulted in a "rare success for African wildlife" [38]. The established conservancies have "tent chalets" and reportedly 90 percent of the employees are from local areas [38].

Whale watching is a fast growing worldwide industry even in countries that harvest whales. In 2008, there were more than 190,000 whale watchers in Japan and it is also popular in Iceland [39 p. 150–1]. Some research shows that dolphin- and whale-watching tourists hold strong environmental values and that countries that violate their norms can suffer loss of tourism. For example, tourists may boycott countries that allow whaling or seal culls resulting in lost revenues. An example of tourism helping to help preserve endangered manta rays occurred in Indonesia where they have been "newly protected under Indonesian law" [40]. They are caught for their "gill plates" that are "in high demand in China, where they are used as a health tonic in traditional Chinese medicine" [40]. There is now a rapidly growing tourism industry "based on manta ray watching" and Indonesia is listed as one of its "top 10 destinations" and hence the support for the new restrictions [40]. The Nature Conservancy has played a key role in building support for establishing protected areas in the Raja Ampat archipelago, where commercial fishing and employment of harmful fishing methods such as "blast fishing" had started to undermine the biodiversity of the fish and corals [41]. The Conservancy and other non-governmental organizations (NGOs) did research to identify critical spots and helped convince local communities and the government of Raj Ampat to set up six protected areas with the argument that these restrictions would help local subsistence fishing – they pointed out that 90 percent of the fish being caught were being taken by outside commercial vessels [41]. The problem of enforcement has been addressed by hiring and training local fishermen to patrol and report illegal activities such as catching sharks and manta rays. In coordination with the above, tourist facilities are being established which have already increased due to the attraction of divers to the newly protected areas with diverse sea life [41].

China's experience with pandas illustrates some of the difficulties of ensuring that ecotourism for a charismatic species contributes to long-term conservation. The USFWS has contributed "Panda Import Authorized Funds" that are to be used for "priority conservation projects" in China but, according to Allan, these monies went to "infrastructure related to tourism" such as "conservation stations, a boundary fence, monitoring and patrolling equipment ... roads" and she asserts that "these activities would jeopardize wild pandas by reducing available panda habitat" [42 p. 173]. Another issue is that China's developmental activities are encouraging "mass tourism" rather than small ecotourism and that "local people are leaving farming to make profits from tourism" and this large-scale tourism has already hurt biodiversity and the giant panda population in "Jiuzhaigou, a World Heritage Site and the first declared Scenic area in China" [42 p. 183–4].

Hunting and Ecotourism: Are They Compatible?

The relative benefits of hunting versus ecotourism have been argued concerning which is better for preserving biodiversity and, at the same time, assisting the native populations who live near the wildlife. The relative amounts earned through hunting versus tourism vary through time, especially due to political stability and wars. Rihoy, Chnirozva, and Anstey reported that ecolodges in Zimbabwe by 1997 had produced twice the income of hunting but unrest in the period after 2000 returned sports hunting as the top earner [43 p. 181]. Hunters are not bothered or scared off to the same degree as ecotourists, require less support, and may visit remote areas that are not of interest to ecotourists [8]. Hutton and Dickson argue that to preserve wild lands in countries such as Kenya, both tourism and hunting are needed in order to have a chance to compete with revenues that could be derived from farming the land [44 p. 449–51]. They cite the Zimbabwe CAMPFIRE case where they say that more than 90 percent of revenues were obtained from tourists who wanted to hunt elephants. Jones prefers hunting to tourism because it is "less obtrusive to the animals" while tourism leads to a "Busch Gardens effect." Jones describes poor behavior by minibuses of tourists harassing wildlife because they know that there is "big tip in it for them" while other animals flee from the hot-air balloons descending on them that especially bother elephants and rhinos [45 p. 81]. Lindsey, Frank, Alexander, Mathieson, and Romanach also state the advantages of hunting: it produces "more revenue per client with less impact" and can take place in areas with "low wildlife densities" that otherwise would be converted to livestock and farming [46 p. 880–3].

There is potential conflict between tourism and hunting. The shooting of wildlife can make them so afraid of humans that they will hide out of sight of visiting tourists, which is why Tanzania had its Game Division cease shooting wildlife that harmed farms around parks [47 p. 316]. Thus most national parks that emphasize ecotourism do not allow hunting. Hunters pay much more per person than ecotourists for services but the numbers of visits by the latter can greatly exceed those of hunters on a sustainable basis [48 p. 63–4]. However, for parks that are not highly popular, a small number of trophy hunts can provide substantial revenues. A number of game viewing areas in Zambia have demanded that there be no hunting around their lodges and some do not want hunting "even in adjacent areas" [48 p. 65]. In Tanzania, the Tanzanian Wildlife Division reportedly favors hunting over tourism interests because of the revenues they receive from hunting concessions. On the other hand, Snyder and Sulle state that villagers "marched on the Prime Minister's Office" to protest harassment of photo tourist outfits at the hands of hunting outfitters [49 p. 944].

With respect to the distribution of benefits to local natives, ecotourism has not been marked with great success as research shows (as discussed in detail in Chapter 7) because national governments and elites have taken much of the revenues for themselves. For example, Snyder and Sulle found little revenue (about US$85,000) went to the Ngorongoro District Council in this world-famous wildlife area [49 p. 935–40]. Likewise, small amounts of revenue from hunting makes it into local communities where hunting takes place, as Snyder and Sulle show, for similar reasons [49 p. 940].

In addition to foreign tourism, another major benefit of preserving wildlife is domestic tourism. For example, Jones says that many Africans want their "children and grandchildren" to be able to view the wildlife that they grew up with [50 p. 166]. In addition, cultural and some religious beliefs attached great importance to wildlife and conservation has value in maintaining these. On the other hand, tourism can also lead to begging that detracts from the values of the local residents and the experience of tourists as well. Jones cites that one safari group's solution in Puros (in Namibia) was to levy a fee per tourist that is distributed to the community (rather than allow begging) so that natives can see a link between dangerous wildlife such as lions and elephants and positive benefits [50 p. 164].

Advantages and Disadvantages of Tourism to Wildlife Conservation

Although tourism, especially by those interested in wildlife, has been viewed as a major device to preserve biodiversity, there can be downsides to ecotourism. Chase preferred tourists who stayed in their cars and hotel rooms to backpackers and hikers because the latter groups speed up "soil erosion", introduce invasive species such as through seeds on their boots, take trees for firewood, and disturb wildlife [51 p. 210]. There are disputes over the quality of jobs provided by tourism in wildlife areas, some arguing that they tend to be low paid compared to extractive industries, but others say that "gateway" cities gain well-paying jobs in real estate and other service industries that accompany the growing popularity of these areas [52 p. 85].

The growth of jobs in tourist areas in poor countries has been a major hope to compensate locals for negatives of protecting wildlife (e.g., damage to their farms and livestock, loss of access to protected areas). Unfortunately, many reports suggest that the majority of jobs go to outsiders, with "foreigners having a lock on high-paying jobs" and natives winding up "peons, busing tables or selling t-shirts." This was a problem with Paseo Pantera, a seven-nation Central American plan to cooperate on wildlife conservation including Guatemala, Belize, El Salvador, Honduras, Nicaragua, Panama, and Costa Rica that has received funding from the U.S. Agency for International Development [53 p. 78]. Similar concerns have been expressed by Mexican environmentalist Homera Arijidis about jobs in Mexico's whale-watching area (Magdalena Bay) where he says loggers and fishermen have been converted into "busboys" [54 p. 160]. In Belize, a report says that residents who did not benefit from ecotourism resented restrictions on their hunting and fishing, in contrast to those who received at least some small benefits [55 p. 98]. The Mexican government required (in 1990) that tourism developers hire Mexicans to drive the whale tour boats in Laguna San Ignacio [56 p. 43].

In Chapter 7, the difficulties of African and other countries in attempting to devolve benefits of tourism to local residents were detailed. One prominent example is Tanzania, which has experienced a huge and rapid growth in wildlife tourism such as in Loliondo near the Ngorongoro Crater. This rapid increase in value of tourism has, according to Ngoitiko, Senandei, Meitaya, and Nelson made Loliondo's lands "too valuable for communities to own" and they go on to say that as a result of their rich wildlife resources, the community's pastoralists members (e.g., Maasai) have been "marginalized" and consequently not many in the community pay much attention to local politics [31 p. 286]. Johnsen says that the only significant Maasai participation in tourism in the Ngorongoro area concerns their display of "dances and beadwork" at a village near the crater [57 p. 167].

Whale and dolphin-watching are booming industries worldwide including in "whaling countries" such as Japan and Iceland and may encourage "pro-conservation sentiments" but questions concerning their sustainability have been raised due to concerns about stress caused to them and harm to their habitats [39 p. 144–7] with reports of numerous boats congregating around a single whale. The growth of whale watching in Mexico has led to "competitive conflicts" and reportedly "reckless conduct" around whales [56 p. 41]. Elephant riding is a favorite tourist activity in Thailand and China, but has been depicted as cruel by organizations such as ResponsibleTravel.com because the elephants employed are usually wild elephants who have undergone "crushing the spirit" and negative reinforcement that is required for them to "perform" [58].

There have been reports of inappropriate tourism in Ranthambore National Park (in India), inhabited by tigers, with many more vehicles (often filled with thirty passengers each) than the sixteen officially allowed, and a slew of Land Rovers following tigers that are spotted [59 p. 69]. Ecotourism has encouraged Mexico to take some (albeit limited) steps to stop illegal logging that was destroying forests inhabited by wintering monarch butterflies, but excessive dust caused by vehicles bringing in tourists is harmful to the butterflies because it interferes with their "respiratory orifices" [60]. Brower and Aridjis say that, although a sign near the Piedra Herrada butterfly sanctuary stated that "no more than 20 people should be in the Sanctuary," there were "24 tourist buses in the lots" [60].

One of the most common disturbances by tourists is the feeding of wildlife. One example of this is illustrated by the Knapp et al. study of tourist feeding of Northern Bahaman rock iguanas that led to negative health consequences for the iguanas in tourist-visited areas compared with unvisited areas [61]. The authors nonetheless do not want to reduce tourism, because it provides economic benefits to locals as well as education for the tourists, but rather to focus on controlling the feeding by offering tourists healthier pelleted foods that will not be harmful combined with a general educational program. Another example of problematic feeding is the baiting of lions to provide sightings for tourists that has been associated with attacks by Asiatic lions on humans in India [62 p. 47].

Coastal areas are targeted by many tourists (e.g., 63 percent of Europeans) and consequently coastal environments have been especially harmed by tourism [63]. Not only the construction of huge hotels but the accompanying "vehicle emissions and sewage" have degraded the areas. Davenport points to the effects of "new forms of individual transport" such as off-road vehicles, "personal water craft," and "dune buggies" as well as scuba diving have contributed to the decline of populations of green, loggerhead, and leatherback turtles along the Mediterranean [63]. Even simple tourist activities such as walking on boulders and overturning of rocks harm some species of crabs and algae. Beach cleaning is mandated by some European nations but makes the areas unattractive to "many species" and thus reduces biodiversity [63]. Birdwatching of marine fowl may have both negative (e.g., disturbing natural behaviors) and positive (e.g., protection against hunting and vandalism of nests) effects [63]. An example of an accepted and fairly unobtrusive effect of tourists on biodiversity concerns the removal of sea shells from beaches. Kowalewski, Domenech, and Martinelli documented the decline in the "abundance of mollusk shells" on a stretch of the Iberian Peninsula along the Mediterranean Sea – the decline was correlated with a threefold increase in tourist visits [64]. Kowalewski et al. say that the removal has deleterious consequences because the shells performed important "functions such as nests for fish, protection for crabs and fish, and support for various other fora and fauna" [64]. They also note that the Bahamas, "a shell-fish rich country," has acted to "regulate the type and quantity" of shells that visitors are allowed to take out of the country [64].

A study of coral reefs in the Caribbean from 1970 to 2012 concluded that high numbers of tourists as well as population of island residents "are harmful to the reefs" and are the "best predictors of the decline in Caribbean coral" and these negative effects are inevitable unless environmental protections are in effect and enforced [65]. They also found that overfishing, especially of large parrot fish, has damaged coral reefs. Also, increased shipping since the 1960s is associated with the introduction of "pathogens" that have afflicted corals. Up until now, the only country in the region that has "progressive environmental regulations" is Bermuda where they have been in effect since the 1990s and contributed to it maintaining a significantly higher percentage of coral cover [65].

Recent research shows that areas with cross-country skiers and snowmobilers caused wolverines to move around much more in the winter, thus wasting valuable energy [66]. Likewise, research showed that even "quiet conservation activities like hiking" were associated with a "fivefold decline" in the presence of bobcats and other carnivores in protected areas of California [66]. Research by Harris, Nielson, Rinaldi, and Lohuis in Alaska found that, although snowmobiles cause more "disturbance events" due to the greater area they cover, skiers caused more "affect" per disturbance for moose than snowmobile use because it is more surprising and unpredictable and consequently "animals tend to move further from nonmotorized activity" [67]. Reed and Merenlender compared protected areas that allowed and did not allow recreation and found that "densities" of wildlife such as bobcats were "more than five times lower in protected areas that permitted recreation" [68 p. 150]. Although the authors acknowledge that access will have to continue to be provided in order to sustain support for conservation, they also state that "public access needs to be balanced with the protection of native species and ecosystems" [68 p. 153].

One of the strategies to combat the negative effects of tourists on the environment is to limit numbers. The problem is that many countries (e.g., Uganda and gorilla tourists) find it impossible to adhere to these limits [8 p. lxvi]. Also, it is discouraging to discover that even "small disturbances" can cause significant harm [69 p. 200]. Buckley illustrates the point with examples such as a single aircraft flight leading to the death of most of the chicks in a bird colony, a single car visit per week leading pink-footed geese in Denmark to leave the area, and a single boat driving away most birds [69 p. 200]. Likewise, Buckley says that grizzly bears stay "at least 250 meters from roads" and avoid trails even if they provide access to good habitat, and thus, consequently, the effective size of their habitat area is shrunk [70 p. 212]. Also, buffer zones between tourists and gazelles need to be at least 700 meters because gazelles avoid area with "human concentrations" and thus the presence of tourists, in effect, reduces the habitat available to them [71 p. 1688]. The growth of tourism around wildlife areas such as in Mfuwe in and around the South Luangwa National Park in Zambia brings new jobs, a positive impact of wildlife tourism, but Roe et al. say that each new job brings in ten or more people "in the immediate and extended family" [8 p. lii]. This population growth is also associated with the clearing of logs and increases in the snaring of wild animals such as impala [8]. Roe et al. also contend that the negative consequences of tourism and associated population growth establish the need to define "carrying capacity" of visitors for protected areas because of fragility of the ecology, infrastructure limits, and "aesthetic" reasons (e.g., so many tourists that enjoyment is lowered) [8 p. lxiii]. Peter Matthiessen contrasted the lack of enforcement of a law against shooting of wildlife passed in 1974 in the Ivory Coast with the situation in Kenya and Tanzania [72 p. 32–4]. In the latter countries, economic benefits from tourism were clear, but countries like the Ivory Coast without much tourism saw no reason to protect remaining wildlife and ignored the law.

The consequence is that ecotourism's positive effects on biodiversity occur only if there are strong legal and management controls "in place first" [73 p. 13]. These challenges exist in the United States as well as in developing countries. Buckley says that equipment manufacturers often build strong political lobbies, as in the cases of snowmobiles or off-road vehicles that resist controls [73]. A former Audubon Society president described how tour boats on Kauai (Hawaii) shot into the middle of "cavorting dolphins" so that "everyone could get a good look" [74 p. 6]. Berle cites Audubon ecotourism "codes of conduct" for their trips as a model to deal with such problems [74]. The code includes requirements to avoid disturbing wildlife, ensuring that areas visited will be "sustainable," respect for the cultures of locals, and the disposal of wastes so as not to affect the environment [74].

Conclusion

At the same time that diversity and abundance of wildlife have declined, there has been a steady increase in the tourism to view wildlife. The expenditures and jobs created by this wildlife tourism have been important to providing incentives to preserve wildlife and its habitat throughout the world. Conservationists have been especially hopeful about ecotourism because it is usually aimed at having as few impacts on nature as possible, while helping to provide benefits to those who live near the wildlife. There is evidence that ecotourism has often provided positive results for native populations, though the majority of benefits usually go disproportionately to foreigners or native elites. Tourists often disrupt wildlife by their very presence and may harm their habitat or try to feed them. Likewise, tourism usually brings development that has negative consequences for biodiversity such as hotels, roads, and other infrastructure to support the tourists. There are many approaches to minimizing or preventing these negative consequences such as limiting numbers of tourists, educating them on harmful practices, and setting and enforcing restrictions such as remaining at a proper distance from wildlife. These approaches require effective government action, and the strength of economic interests opposed to restrictions is often difficult to overcome. Still, the commerce of ecotourism creates businesses and employees who gain from the preservation of wildlife and thus notably broaden and strengthen the coalition for wildlife conservation that otherwise would consist mainly of NGOs and animal lovers.

12 Conclusion

Summary

The most basic finding of this book is that wildlife politics are important in virtually every country, ranging from the smallest and most primitive states to the most powerful. Moreover, due to the continuing and growing threat to species, wildlife politics are steadily becoming more salient. Until the twentieth century, the existence of abundant wildlife was taken for granted but the combination of species extinctions, along with the rise of the conservation movement, brought wildlife issues into mainstream politics. Wildlife have always played an important role in the lives of humanity, as evidenced by the drawings of animals in cave dwellings, but they were viewed as important for consumption purposes rather than a resource that should be preserved. As some iconic species vanished, interest groups in the early years of the twentieth century in the United States, composed of "elites" such as the Boone and Crockett Club as well as early conservationist organizations such as the Sierra Club and Audubon Society, began to bring attention to certain endangered species, albeit primarily game and charismatic animals such as birds. Internationally, many African and other developing countries followed the patterns of Great Britain and the United States by creating protected areas, with emphasis in the early years of protecting species for sports hunters. It was not until the rise of environmentalism in the 1960s that wildlife protection became an integral part of everyday policy concerns in the United States and the rest of the world. In short, as an important political topic, politics concerning wildlife conservation is a relatively recent phenomenon and its rapid ascent in prominence has been impressive. The growth in trade in wildlife and wildlife products has been extraordinary, with illegal wildlife trade now rivaling drugs in terms of size. International disputes over restrictions due to international regulations by the Convention on International Trade in Endangered Species of Wild Fauna and Flora (CITES) and the International Whaling Commission have led to continuing and often bitter disputes among nations. The attempts of nations to enact protections for wildlife sometimes run afoul of World Trade Organization (WTO) agreements. Sports hunting has long been important to many poor countries, but ecotourism to view wildlife has become a major source of income in the last generation in both poor and rich nations. However, its growth has helped to create tensions between those who benefit and those who suffer from the effects of wildlife, such as restrictions on living in protected areas and consumption of bush meat. In summary, wildlife politics are already important and are likely to become even more contentious and controversial in the future.

A second generalization is that wildlife politics are characterized by high levels of emotion. Many humans become emotionally attached to wildlife and have acted to protect these species by forming interest groups. Indeed, one of the major differences among species is the extent to which they are charismatic enough to attract organized support of humans. Such species are much more likely to be afforded protections from the government as well as private groups for their conservation. Non-consummatory viewing of wildlife has become a common activity engaged in regularly by people throughout the United States and the rest of the world. There are some species, especially wolves but also others, that threaten the interests of humans and arouse antipathy that is often based on emotions far exceeding the actual damage incurred by them. Through time, conservationists have emphasized the need to protect all species and ecosystems, but disputes over charismatic wildlife have dominated wildlife politics. Although wildlife have many significant economic impacts through hunting, fishing, and ecotourism, it is this visceral attachment which brings out the fierce emotions that characterize wildlife politics.

All of the frameworks and concepts outlined in Chapter 1 have assisted in providing insight into wildlife politics. However, one point that stands out concerning the passage of the Endangered Species Act (ESA) is the crucial importance of the political context of the time period and "naïveté" that allowed this "macho law" to be passed without any significant opposition. Moreover, the experience and controversy over the ESA affected the nature of similar legislation passed in Canada and Australia. Ever since the revolutionary implications of the law became apparent, wildlife conservation legislation has remained largely deadlocked in the United States. Given the growth of policy groups concerned with wildlife conservation (and every other policy field), every bill is scrutinized for its implications making the ESA a "one-off" type of law. Thus policy-making is a product of the political context of time period in which it developed. So far, interest in wildlife politics has not fallen into the "down cycle" predicted by Anthony Downs, though in times of economic downturns, public opinion shows more support for compromising conservation values.

Market incentives have been a central factor in causing threats to wildlife because they lead to increased hunting and fishing that goes far beyond the need to sustain local populations. Market incentives have been proposed as a solution to preservation of wildlife based on the proposition that landowners will seek to preserve them if they bring a satisfactory economic return. Community-based natural resources management (CBNRM) and more recently Payments for Environmental or Ecosystem Services (PES) have been experimented with to provide incentives on the behalf of rural populations in undeveloped countries to preserve species. CBNRM has proven to be difficult to implement successfully and PES experiments are too recent to draw firm conclusions.

Implementation is highly relevant to wildlife conservation policies throughout the world because conservation laws often exist on only "on paper" or, at best, are weakly implemented. Although the implementation problems are especially relevant in poor countries, they are also significant in the United States, with physical intimidation and threats employed, especially in Western states. Hundreds of habitat conservation plans and other forms of cooperation (e.g., land preservation agreements and credit exchange programs) have been established since the Clinton Administration began to use them as a major tool. Some conservationists are concerned about whether these plans will be implemented as promised, and have pointed to their weak monitoring requirements. Even if these plans are well implemented, it is entirely possible that the "uncontrollable" forces outlined in Chapter 1, such as development and its associated impacts including road building, may overwhelm the positive steps taken to preserve species. Thus monitoring of implementation and outcomes is necessary, but there is no clear national priority attached to the conduct of these activities, especially given the limited resources of agencies like the USFWS. The politics for U.S. administrations (including the Obama and Clinton Administrations) as well as the affected industries and landowners favors the assumption that these plans are working, and they do not want to reopen hard-won compromises to change agreements that required long and difficult political negotiations to reach.

Interest groups have been central in pushing wildlife politics into political prominence. In the early years of the twentieth century, these groups tended to be small but were made up of wealthy and often powerful individuals (e.g., Theodore Roosevelt) who were able to have impact on public policy despite their small numbers. Interest groups involved with wildlife sometimes struggle with each other, especially with conflicts between hunting and those focused on animal rights but they also have on important occasions coalesced to form powerful alliances countering those of development and extractive industries. Animal rights organizations have sometimes cooperated with environmental groups but also fought them on some policies. Thus a simple left–right continuum is not sufficient to explain wildlife politics. Although the staffs of conservation groups may receive important economic benefits from their employment by these organizations, the vast majority of members' attachments to the conservation groups are based on conservation purposes and emotion – not rational economic self-interest. Thus the exploration of wildlife politics provides a basis for understanding interest groups that form around non-economic concerns.

A focus on political institutions helps to understand some of the puzzles surrounding wildlife politics. I have documented a discrepancy between the attitudes of the general public and the mandated policies by wildlife agencies in the United States over issues such as hunting and trapping. The discrepancy is explained by the fact that wildlife agencies at the state level are dominated by those associated with hunting, due to the fact that much of their budget is derived from hunters and anglers, and also as a result of the prevalence of officials associated with hunting and fishing being placed in charge of state wildlife departments and policy-setting commissions. Although the general public has sometimes voted to limit certain hunting practices, the agencies and commissions overseeing wildlife policy have often been able to block these restrictions. Given the declining percentage of hunters in the overall population and the growth in ecotourism-related industry, it is notable that wildlife institutions have remained dominated by the hunting constituency. Wildlife politics thus once again affirms the fact that a minority group that is strongly attached to its core values can gain control over institutions and dominate a public policy area despite the contrary views of the larger general populace whose attachment to the issue is more diffuse. Still, wildlife politics in the United States (and elsewhere) do show that change can occur in institutions important to wildlife, such as the Bureau of Land Management (BLM), even in the face of strong opposing interests. Formerly dominated by extractive industries and ranchers and largely unconcerned with wildlife conservation, the BLM now must mediate between these traditional interests and conservation organizations.

Subgovernments continue to remain significant, but those involving wildlife conservation have lost some of their autonomy and power due to the rise of conservation and environmental movements. Prior to the 1960s, control over policies such as eradication of "pest" animals and grazing on public lands was so complete that these issues did not reach the national policy agenda. Western representatives and senators continue to flock to committees that oversee wildlife policies, as do rural legislators in states, and thus they exert significant control over policies. However, wildlife conservation issues are closely tracked by conservation interest groups so that the issues are no longer hidden, and they are sometimes able to form coalitions to challenge or block policies they find inimical to wildlife.

The Advocacy Coalition Framework (ACF) is especially valuable in studying wildlife politics because it focuses attention on how difficult it is to obtain compromise between opposing coalitions whose core values are at odds. This problem is especially problematic in wildlife conservation because of the emotional nature of the attachment of conservation groups – they are fighting for intrinsic values and are not interested in economic incentives. Hunters also are emotionally resistant to any effort to curtail their rights to hunt, and many people have strong negative emotions about wolves and other species that threaten humans. Since the 1980s, national wildlife politics has been paralyzed, with neither wildlife conservation groups nor the opposing coalitions (dominated by extractive industries, ranchers, and conservation property rights groups) able to forge a winning coalition to pass revised wildlife legislation. However, beginning with the Clinton Administration, the USFWS has been able to make use of a variety of mechanisms (e.g., habitat conservation plans) to achieve compromise agreements. The idea of using "stakeholder" approaches to achieve collaborative decisions about wildlife conservation is now common not only in the United States but throughout the world. Thus the study of wildlife politics shows how important policy change can occur despite legislative gridlock. Still, in the United States, the primary force underlying these successes has been the powerful "stick" of the threat of listing species under the ESA – an element that is generally missing in other countries. The movement to emphasizing early intervention and voluntary approaches faces what has been described in Chapter 6 as a "chicken-and-egg" dilemma – government and private actions only occur when the threat of regulatory action is perceived as real.

The study of organizational behavior provides important insights into agencies dealing with wildlife. It is characteristic not only of the USFWS but national wildlife agencies throughout the world that they are very underresourced when their mandated goals are compared with their limited staff and budgets. They are also faced with the difficult job of trying to implement measures that protect wildlife, often at the expense of humans living in their presence. In developing countries, these populations tend to be poor and have little political influence, but in the United States and other advanced countries these interests are often powerful landowners, extractive industries, and ranchers. Wildlife agencies consequently appear (from the perspective of wildlife conservationists) to act cautiously, often avoiding any substantive action, moving slowly and often only when forced by the courts. Although McFarland hypothesized that the existence of countervailing power "enhances agency autonomy," my review of the USFWS suggests that being stuck in the middle of strongly opposed coalitions is not an easy or desirable position – quite the contrary, they would like to defuse this tension [1 p. 67–8]. Wildlife agencies thus now must walk a "minefield" between bitterly opposed foes, and their behavior shows how organizations adapt to this uncomfortable environment. Another organizational issue concerns the conflict between large established national organizations like the Audubon Society and smaller, more radical organizations like Earth First! and the Center for Biological Diversity (CBD). Bevington's account reveals the disdain of the latter for what they view as the nationals succumbing to "professionalization" and priority given to Washington, D.C. insiders [2]. In contrast, the CBD engaged in controversial lawsuits that the nationals feared would be used by opponents to sabotage the ESA [2 p. 186–91]. These more radical organizations pride themselves on keeping salaries low and staffs small. Thus traditional assumptions about the dominance of economic motives are not effective in explaining behavior of many activist organizations related to wildlife conservation.

The case of U.S. wildlife politics highlights the importance of learning and science in conservation policymaking. ACF posits that science can be one of the vehicles that can facilitate "learning," with the possibility of changing coalition positions on secondary policy positions and thus potentially contributing to compromise. Indeed, because of the ESA's mandate to base decisions on "the best available science," political struggles over wildlife are now couched in terms of scientific analysis to a much greater extent than in other areas of politics. However, as discussed in Chapter 2, there remains plenty of room for disagreements among scientists and their research findings that weaken the impact of science. Nevertheless, the Federal courts have consistently acted on their interpretation of the "best science" mandate to favor wildlife conservation. Indeed, the success record of groups like the CBD demonstrates that expertise in wildlife conservation science has now become a major interest group asset in this policy area, outweighing other traditionally important resources such as budgets, membership numbers, and access to officeholders. Thus wildlife politics again provides new perspectives on traditional interest group theory. Other forms of learning, such as education to encourage preservation of endangered species, have achieved high visibility in countries such as China, where customs have fostered heavy consumption of ivory and tiger parts. The success of these educational efforts remains unclear and, if they are effective, it will take a long period of time to achieve major change in customs.

The impact of elections on wildlife policy has been moderated by the fact that the ESA law has remained in effect largely unchanged because no winning coalition has been able to revise the law, despite widespread dissatisfaction especially among conservatives. However, changes in control of the presidency have had a significant impact due to the manner in which they administer the law. Republican Administrations (those of Reagan and both Bushes) have largely avoided actions that threatened landowners, ranchers, or extractive industries unless they are forced to do so by the Federal courts. The irony is that, although collaboration and stakeholder approaches have been the preferred policy tools since the Clinton Administration, the biggest conservation advances during the Clinton, Bush and Obama Administrations have been forced either by presidents employing the Antiquities Act without consultation with Congress (or other "stakeholders") and rulings made by Federal courts. Thus "coercive" methods remain crucial in this era of "collaboration."

Federalism also remains important to conservation policy. In particular, although the ESA gives the USFWS theoretical authority to protect threatened species on state and private lands, the resources of the USFWS are far too limited to exert control over these areas. Indeed, even under Democratic Administrations of Clinton and Obama, the USFWS has emphasized reliance on their "partners" of state wildlife agencies rather than "top-down" mandates, and these administrations have also attempted to lure private corporations and landowners into agreements that provide some protections albeit with compromises. In the United States, Federal courts have been central to many of the best known clashes over wildlife involving the snail darter, the spotted owl, grizzly, and wolf cases. This central role of the courts in wildlife politics is peculiar to the United States, though courts in other countries do play a significant role with respect to their enforcement of penalties for violating wildlife preservation laws.

Wildlife politics take place daily throughout the world and are affected by the unique political, religious, and ethnic complexities of individual nations. However, my review found some general patterns. First, wildlife policies have been heavily influenced by the United States due to its establishment of national parks and passage of the ESA, while Great Britain influenced many developing countries due to its colonial policies with respect to wildlife. Countries following the patterns of the United States and colonial British policies tended to emphasize the use of protected areas as the major policy for preserving threatened species. There has been a consistent tension between residents of rural areas and conservation forces over these protected areas and threatened species, even in the United States and other advanced industrialized countries. However, in the West, those affected by wildlife protections (e.g., ranchers, sheep-herders, landowners, and extraction industries) tend to have strong enough political power to contest wildlife conservation policies. By way of contrast, those living near rural protected areas in developing counties tend to be poor and are not effective in their national politics. The major differences that appear to differentiate developing countries that are more successful in protecting species are the strength and quality of their governance systems. The central governments of many developing countries are simply too weak to enforce wildlife conservation even if they wanted to. Due to corruption, lack of transparency, and the dominance of personal politics and the power of elites, many attempts at implementing wildlife conservation that is "friendly" to the poor fail. Indeed, it is the case that in many developing countries, international wildlife organizations and even Western governments exert strong influence over their wildlife policies.

These developing countries often have rich wildlife resources that are of great interest to ecotourists, governments, and elites from wealthier countries. The United Nations and several of these wildlife conservation groups have attempted to address the accusation that the poor in these countries are suffering from the costs of wildlife preservation in a manner that would not be tolerated in the advanced countries. Consequently, many efforts have been attempted, such as community-based natural resources management (CBNRM) to achieve protection for species that also rewards those who might suffer costs. These efforts have often run afoul of the governance problems noted above, and though new efforts such as PES are trying to circumvent these problems by not relying on national governments, it is too early to determine if they will be more successful.

As noted in Chapter 7, one key factor omitted from the frameworks in Chapter 1 concerns the values and interests of dominant "political leaders." Strong leaders can have dramatic impacts in a relatively short periods of time when they push wildlife conservation. This is the case not only in dictatorships like Romania and Russia but also in the United States. In large part, the interests and values of leaders like (Teddy) Roosevelt, Putin, and Indira Gandhi are based on their life history and personal interests, but it does suggest that it is worthwhile for wildlife conservationists to appeal to strong leaders for assistance.

International action is becoming increasingly necessary to preserve species because of the huge growth in wildlife trade, much of it illegal, between wildlife "importing and exporting" countries as well as the spread of large-scale high technology fishing and hunting technologies. International actions have had some notable successes such as the recovery of certain whales. However, the resources of international conservation organizations like CITES are very limited and the success of conservation efforts still depends on individual countries taking action. Often, the only effective incentive to force reluctant countries to take action is pressure by the United States and other Western countries, though these pressures have to contend with rules prohibiting interference with free trade established by the WTO.

Despite the thousands of impressive attempts at international conservation, wildlife continue to be affected by hard-to-influence forces such as globalization, population growth, development, and technological advances. For example, technological advances in hunting and fishing have greatly increased the efficiency of hunting and fishing, making it impossible for wildlife to escape. Human population growth has slowed in many areas of the world, especially in developed countries, but Africa's population is increasing rapidly in the world with estimates that it will double to 2.5 billion people by 2050 [3]. Although much of that growth is in urban areas, it is also occurring in rural areas expanding populations into areas inhabited by lions and other wildlife, and thus precipitating conflict with humans. Vogt says that some parks in Kenya have become "so surrounded by people that animals can no longer migrate in or out" and they have become "fenced-in" parks [3]. Indeed, Rodgers, Hartley, and Bashir state that India's small-sized protected areas for wildlife "offer a snapshot of what Africa's conservation will look like fifty years from now" [4 p. 370]. Thus these underlying hard-to-change factors outlined at the beginning of the book will likely overwhelm efforts by both governments and non-governmental organizations (NGOs) to preserve the free movement of wildlife other than in tightly "zoo-like" protected areas.

If government and NGO efforts are to be effective, long-term preservation will be heavily influenced by attempts to change human customs and perspectives on wildlife. For example, many countries in the Far East have undertaken campaigns to combat use of ivory and tiger or rhino parts, not only via laws but also via the media, to change customs. Overall, there has been an evolution in ethical values with respect to wildlife with the growth in non-utilitarian values (e.g., admiring them for their beauty) and a movement to sustaining ecosystems rather than a "dominionistic" attitude that emphasizes human control and exploitation of other species [5 p. 91]. Media has the ability to affect human attitudes strongly, as evidenced by the uproar created over the killing of "Cecil the lion" in Zimbabwe by a U.S. trophy hunter. Perhaps, more impressive is the strong revulsion in China to a video showing a whale shark being sawed while still alive with blood gushing out of its mouth [6]. The video spread rapidly across the Internet with many Chinese calling it "inhumane." Thus communications technology may help to spur attitude change.

Still, as discussed further below, some believe that wildlife conservationists must demonstrate that humans benefit in practical ways if they are to win support for their preservation. Hunting, angling and ecotourism clearly provide significant benefits to many humans from wildlife and, indeed, without the existence of these activities, the conservation coalition would be much smaller and weaker than it is. Unfortunately, these activities can also have negative impacts on species that are just now becoming apparent.

The Best of Times or the Worst of Times?

It is impossible to spend nine years researching wildlife politics without attempting to come to some conclusion about the state of wildlife preservation. I was astonished to find two different narratives by those interested in wildlife conservation coexisting about the prognosis for threatened species: one is that we are in the last stages of apocalyptic extinction of species, primarily due to the harmful effects of humans, and the other is that the situation is satisfactory and promising for the future thanks to interventions by humans. These two alternative scenarios are the product of different political strategies, but also come out of different readings of science on wildlife. Below I explore both of these viewpoints as they are crucial to understanding the current state of wildlife politics.

Since the early twentieth century, much of the impetus for wildlife conservation has involved the raising of alarms by conservationists over disappearing species such as bison, birds, and whales. Indeed, it is this widely shared alarm that led to the passage of the U.S. ESA. Indeed, Chris Servheen, the head of the U.S. Interagency Grizzly Bear Committee, feared that once the grizzly bear began to experience some recovery that he was "concerned about losing the wind behind the sails" and that "people think,

'Well, it's not a crisis anymore, we'll go onto something else'" [7 p. 80]. John Fitzpatrick, the director of the Cornell Ornithology Lab, recently employed the extinction of the passenger pigeon once again as a primary warning that we need to save threatened species of birds [8].

By way of contrast, Emma Marris, author of *Rambunctious garden*, and the "new conservation movement" have expressed dissatisfaction with the "doom saying" of traditional conservation and have expressed optimism about the status of wildlife conservation and humanity's role in preserving species [9]. Marris says that humans can "make more nature" and "things on Earth better, not just less bad" [9 p. 56]. She goes on to say that monoculture fields like corn can have "native plants on their edges" and the effects of malls, buildings, and impervious surfaces can be offset by, for example, food planted in urban parks for "migrating butterflies" [9 p. 135]. She cites cases where "exotic-dominated ecosystems" outperform nearby native ecosystems in "terms of their biomass production" [9 p. 112]. Kareiva and Marvier argue that the "prevalence of recovery" is a very different story from the "apocalyptic collapse" that environmentalists predict [10 p. 967]. They also argue for finding "bright spots" of recovery that can be adopted elsewhere. Moreover, Kareiva, Marvier, and Lalasz contend that conservationists should support "the right kind of development" – development that is done "by design, done with the importance of nature to thriving economies foremost in mind," and "instead of scolding capitalism, conservationists should partner with corporations in a science-based effort to integrate the value of nature's benefits into their operations and cultures" [11].

One of their major arguments concerns the thesis that traditional conservation relies too completely on negative arguments involving predictions of disaster so that the general public will lose any enthusiasm for action. For example, Andrew Revkin, a science writer on conservation issues, praised a Public Broadcasting System documentary series titled "Earth: A New Wild" that follows the new conservation thesis that "the human presence is not just there, sometimes it's integral to either protecting it or making it function the way it is" [12]. One of positive stories reported in the film concerned the rebuilding of oyster reefs in New York City harbor, and the film shows "sea horses mating in City waters" [12]. The filmmaker, M. Sanjayan, says that "if I did a show just cataloging the worst destruction I wouldn't even be able to watch it. I wanted something fun to watch," and that "I don't think pessimism ever changed the world" [12]. Sanjayan admits that the challenges are enormous and that there is no assurance that the small-scale successes like the oyster restoration are "scalable" to deal with the magnitude of the problem [12]. Peter Kareiva et al. challenge pessimism about the survival of species like the polar bear due to climate change, arguing that the "the decline of sea ice" may be offset by the increase of "energy-rich" prey – both caused by climate change [11]. New conservationists also point to thriving wildlife in areas that suffered from human-made disasters, such as Chernobyl, the Gulf of Mexico, and the Bikini Atoll site of multiple nuclear bomb tests, that demonstrate that nature is resilient to negative effects of human actions [11]. Another optimistic account is by Diane Ackerman, who reports on the building of artificial reefs to make up for the loss of coral reefs worldwide [13]. One of the major differences between new and traditional conservationists concerns attitudes toward technology. This difference is not new – Gottlieb cites the director of the U.S. Geological Survey in the 1950s stating that "resource shortages would simply . . . inspire research and technical advances . . . to resolve such problems well in advance of the doom we are often prone to see" [14]. In short, the new conservation movement has made a significant point about the importance of positive success stories to stimulating belief in the value of conservation efforts among the general public.

However, in their attempt to counter pessimism of traditional conservationists, they have not confronted the existence of scientific findings that are much less optimistic about the state of conservation and the effects of humanity on biodiversity. Stuart Butchart and an international team of scientists reported that most of thirty-one indicators of biodiversity showed that "the rate of biodiversity loss has not declined" despite an international commitment to take action in 2002 [15 p. 1164]. They reported declines in vertebrates, "habitat specialist birds," shorebird populations, and in the condition of coral reefs worldwide. Moreover, they asserted that the "majority of pressure on biodiversity" is due to forces such as "increases in aggregate human consumption of the planet's ecological assets . . . alien species in Europe, fish stocks being overharvested, and the impact of climate change" [15 p. 1165]. They also state that there is a high "extinction risk for mammals, birds, and amphibian species used for food and medicine" and for birds that are "internationally traded." They do note the existence of some "local system exceptions with positive trends" that suggest that with "political will and adequate resources" that "biodiversity loss could be reduced or reversed" [15 p. 1168]. Michael Hoffmann et al. reported in another *Science* article that the "biodiversity decline" has occurred despite increasing use of "protected areas coverage and adoption of national legislation." They found that conditions were most serious in Southeast Asia due to "planting of perennial export crops (such as oil palm), commercial hardwood timber operations, agricultural conversion to rice paddies, and unsustainable hunting" [16 p. 1506–8]. Hoffman et al. did find improvement in 7 percent of the cases which mostly was due to "conservation action" and species that received the "bulk . . . of conservation funding and attention directed" to them [16]. They also posit that conservation actually made a much greater difference than these data suggest because declines would have been 18 percent greater without efforts, and that it takes time for conservation successes to "translate into improvements in status" [16]. They found that birds have been better protected from hunting than mammals, though there are some successes such as the vicuna (a relative of the llama) that has been protected by CITES and changed from "near threatened" to "least concern" status [16]. Rands et al. cite research showing the importance of maintaining "suitably managed habitats that should be large and connected" and argue that transaction-based solutions are "difficult" because those who damage biodiversity are "widely separated" from those who suffer the consequences and "have few incentives to change their behavior" [17 p. 1299–301]. Thus they conclude that "government will need to remove perverse subsidies" in "agriculture, forestry, and fisheries." Pikitch has reported on the "gathering wave of ocean extinction" with "huge declines of sharks, rays and skates" [18 p. 200]. For example, she cites the fact that just one percent of whitetip sharks. . .remain in the Gulf of Mexico" [18]. The 2014 report on the State of Birds compiled by the nation's leading bird conservation specialists, in collaboration with state and Federal wildlife agencies, documents conservation successes in the United States for certain species due to the effects of the ESA, but also states that "for every success story, a number of other birds ... are in serious danger" with 230 on the watch list as threatened to becoming extinct [8]. A study by a team of scientists from the WWF, the Zoological Society of London and others analyzed thousands of vertebrate species and concluded "that overall animal populations fell 52% between 1970 and 2010" [19]. The team ascribed the results mainly as due to "habitat destruction, commercial fishing, and hunting" [19]. The greatest declines were in rivers (76 percent decline) and Latin America (83 percent decline in mammals, birds, reptiles, and fish) [19]. The report goes on to state that humanity is consuming so many resources that it would take "1.5 Earths to supply these goods and services" and this is due to cutting trees "faster than they mature" and fishing "more than the ocean can replenish" [19].

Although new conservationists have pointed to successes in recovering from huge disasters like Chernobyl and atomic blasts, wildlife in these areas were assisted in their recovery by the fact that humanity avoided these areas after the disasters occurred. But wildlife may find it more difficult to deal with persistent problems such as changing chemical composition of water due to climate change or the steadily increasing pollution. Recently, Charles Moore reported on increasing accumulation of plastic particles in the sea with the result that "hundreds of species mistake plastic for natural food" and that major "bait fish" (for tuna and salmon) such as the "lantern fish" eat large amounts of plastic [20]. The plastic problem has been exacerbated by the "aquaculture industry" which employs "enormous amount of plastic in its floats, nets, lines and tubes" – huge sea-urchin and oyster farms are common, for example, in Hawaii. Moore claims that the cause of the plastic problem is an "economic model that thrives on wasteful products and packaging" and ignores the clean-up costs [20]. Mace contends that conservation has focused mostly on "direct drivers" of biodiversity loss such as local recreation and hunting that are "easily reversed" but that the "indirect drivers" are the underlying causes and need to be dealt with [21 p. 351]. These are "population and economic growth, technological development, land use change, and social and political change" [21].

Thus, although the new conservationists have succeeded in raising basic questions about the political viability of traditional conservation's overreliance on predictions of disaster, their optimism about humanity's impact on the state of biodiversity flies in the face of major international research. The bitterness of the dispute between new and traditional conservationists has been so strong and potentially destructive to the wildlife conservation coalition that rapprochement is being sought. Recently, Tallis and Lubchenko published an article in *Nature* that calls for an "inclusive conservation" and "that recognizes and accepts all values of nature, from intrinsic to instrumental, and welcomes all philosophies justifying nature protection and restoration, from ethical to economic, and from aesthetic to utilitarian" [22 p. 27–8]. They state that those dedicated to intrinsic arguments for conservation are correct in that overreliance on instrumental reasons for saving nature may negatively impact those parts of nature that have "no obvious value for people" [22]. But they also contend that instrumental arguments can be effective for other audiences and will help to "broaden support" [22]. Many conservationists from both sides signed on as agreeing with this "editorial," though traditional conservationists are still counterattacking against new conservationists positions such as in the book *Keeping the wild: Against the domestication of earth* [23]. Emma Maris and Greg Aplet also proposed a compromise based on the fact "both groups" (new and traditional conservationists) "love nature and want to save it" and state that we should pursue all three policies at once, including (1) "invest in keeping ecosystems in historical configurations"; (2) "engineer landscapes to be resilient to tomorrow's conditions"; (3) "let nature adapt on its own" [24].

Given the magnitude of the problems, one must agree that the conservation movement needs all of the help that it can get. However, conflict between intrinsic and instrumental values creates questions of priority – should governmental and conservation organizations focus on species and habitats that are of the greatest benefit to humans or species that are most in danger? Should new monies be directed more toward urban areas rather than remote protected areas? Would such a redirection of effort result in more human engagement with nature and hence support for overall wildlife conservation? Should we deemphasize concern with the spread of invasive and alien species, and indeed encourage such migration to make up for depletion of native species? In short, a commitment to encourage multiple approaches to wildlife conservation does not eliminate the need to set priorities and take positions on controversial issues such as invasive species that place new and traditional conservationists at odds with each other.

Klyza and Sousa have remarked on the fact that, despite the legislative gridlock at the national level, there has been a "green drift" in environmental area over the last generation [25 p. 16]. However, in large part, this drift has been due to the rulings of Federal courts and the clout posed by the ESA, whose language does not constrain protections with concerns about economic costs. Over the past two decades, the great successes of the environmental movement have been based on favorable Federal court decisions led by organizations like the CBD. The ESA has not been reauthorized since 1992 but the CBD has used it aggressively, sometimes over the objections of larger national conservation organizations fearful that these lawsuits would undermine political support for the ESA [2 p. 177–8]. In view of the Republican takeover of the Senate and hence Congress as a result of the 2014 election, the election of a Republican president would likely bring about a breaking of the gridlock, with changes made to the ESA that would subject protection efforts to cost-benefit analysis and/or give states more control over decisions [26 p. 22]. "Defanging the ESA" would be a top priority for conservatives. Pang and Greenwald found that by July 2015, there already had been sixty-six legislative attacks on the ESA compared to an average of five for the years 1996–2010, with many more attacks to come in the remainder of year [27 p. 1]. The attacks consist of "stand-alone" legislation to modify the ESA such as to "force consideration of short-term economics when designating critical habitat," and cut habitat from the Act's protections "whenever those impacts were deemed too high" [27 p. 3]. One of the Republican proposals would prevent the ESA from being used for species that do not cross state boundaries which would "roll back protections for plants and animals currently covered by the law" [28]. Another bill would prohibit the U.S.

Fish and Wildlife Service (USFWS) from listing the greater sage-grouse for at least six years [26]. Anticipating an attack on the ESA, the Obama Administration proposed a new rule that groups seeking to have a species listed as "endangered" would first have to send a petition to the relevant state agency and include that state agency's comments and data (if it provides any) when it later submits it to the Federal agency [29]. The purpose of this rule is to forestall more radical action by Republicans to weaken the ESA. Thus protection of endangered species promises to be one of the high-profile issues in U.S. politics. Conservatives such as the Pacific Legal Foundation hold that there is already an indication that the current Supreme Court is likely to overrule the regulation that forbids any take of listed species [30]. On the international level, the growing wealth of consumers in China, Japan, and other Pacific nations is negatively affecting wildlife such as elephants, tigers, rhinos, fish, and other wildlife throughout the world. China reacted by destroying a "third batch of contraband ivory in 18 months" in May of 2015 and as part of a publicity campaign against illegal ivory and a "renowned Chinese pianist urged travelers not to bring ivory back to China" [31]. These actions show again the sensitivity and importance of the wildlife politics internationally – China is not a nation that is easily influenced into taking actions that run counter to important domestic customs and economic interests. In short, wildlife politics is deserving of attention by political scientists and public policy researchers.

References

Chapter 1 References

1. Wilson, Kurt. Wolf advocates challenge delisting at Missoula hearing. *Missoulian* [Internet]. 2011 Jul 26 [cited 2012 Apr 14]; Available from: http://missoulian.com/news/local/article_5a6e734a-b780-11e0-9c31-001cc4c03286.html

2. Hansen, Heather. Who's afraid of the big, bad wolf? *High Country News* [Internet]. 2012 Apr 12 [cited 2012 Apr 12]; Available from: www.hcn.org/hcn/blogs/range/whos-afraid-of-the-big-bad-wolf

3. Bernacchi, Leigh A., Ragland, Chara J., Peterson, Tarla R. Engaging active stakeholders in implementation of community-based conservation: Whooping crane management in Texas, USA. *Wildl Soc Bull.* 2015; (August 5 online): 1–10.

4. Kamieniecki, Sheldon. Political parties and environmental policy. In: Lester, James P., editor. *Environmental politics and policy: Theories and evidence.* Durham: Duke University Press; 1995. p. 145–67.

5. Gratwicke, Brian, Bennett, Elizabeth L., Broad, Steven. The world can't have wild tigers and eat them too. *Conserv Biol.* 2008; 22(1): 222–3.

6. Raup, David M., Sepkoski, J. John, Jr. Mass extinctions in the marine fossil record. *Science.* 1982; 215(4539): 1501–3.

7. Pikitch, Ellen K. The gathering wave of ocean extinction. In: Guynup, Sharon, editor. *2006 state of the wild: A global portrait of wildlife, wildlands, and oceans.* Washington, D.C.: Island Press; 2005. p. 195–201.

8. Rands, Michael R., Adams, William M., Bennun, Leon, Butchart, Stuart H. M., Clements, Andrew, Coomes, David et al. Biodiversity conservation: challenges beyond 2010. *Science.* 2010; 329(5997): 1298–301.

9. Hoffmann, Michael, Hilton-Taylor, Craig, Angulo, Ariadne, Bohm, Monika, Brooks, Thomas M., Butchart, Stuart M. et al. The impact of conservation on the status of the world's vertebrates. *Science.* 2010; 330(December): 1503–9.

10. Butchart, Stuart H. M., Walpole, Matt, van Strien, Arco, Scharlemann, Jorn P. W., Almond, Rosamunde, E. A. et al. Global biodiversity: Indicators of recent declines. *Science.* 2009; 328 (5892): 1164–8.

11. Fitzpatrick, John W. Saving our birds. *New York Times* [Internet]. 2014 Aug 29 [cited 2014 Aug 31]; Available from: www.nytimes.com/2014/08/31/opinion/sunday/saving-our-birds.html?emc=edit_th_20140831&nl=todaysheadlines&nlid=10365419&_r=0

12. Meyer, Stephen M. *The end of the wild.* Cambridge: The MIT Press; 2006.

13. McNamee, Thomas. *The return of the wolf to Yellowstone.* New York: Henry Holt and Company; 1997.

14. Dizard, Jan E. *Going wild: Hunting, animal rights, and the contested meaning of nature.* Amherst: University of Massachusetts Press; 1999.

15. Illical, Mary, Harrison, Kathryn. Protecting endangered species in the US and Canada: The role of negative lesson drawing. *Can J Polit Sci.* 2007; 40(2): 367–94.

16. Foreman, Dave F. *Rewilding North America: A vision for conservation in the 21st century.* Washington, D.C.: Island Press; 2004.

17. Quammen, David. Island of the bears. *Audubon Magazine.* 1995; (March-April): 82–8.

18. Gaydos, Joseph K., Corn, Joseph L. Health aspects of large mammal restoration. In: Maehr, David, Noss, Reed F., Larkin, Jeffery L., editors. *Large mammal restoration: Ecological and sociological challenges in the 21st century.* Washington, D.C.: Island Press; 2001. p. 149–62.

19. Ackerman, Bruce B., Powell, James. Case 4: Can manatee numbers continue to grow in a fast-developing state? In: Maehr, David, Noss, Reed F., Larkin, Jeffery L., editors. *Large mammal restoration: Ecological and sociological challenges in the 21st century.* Washington, D.C.: Island Press; 2001. p. 313–20.

20. Adams, William N. *Against extinction: The story of conservation.* London: Earthscan; 2004.

21. Dorst, Jean. The remnants of European wilderness. In: Martin, Vance, editor. *Wilderness.* Moray, Scotland: Findhorn Press; 1980. p. 117–22.

22. Rawson, Timothy. *Changing tracks: Predators and politics in Mt. McKinley national park.* Fairbanks: University of Alaska Press; 2001.

23. Nash, Roderick. *Wilderness and the American mind.* 3rd ed. New Haven: Yale University Press; 1982.

24. Foreman, Dave. From scenery to Nature. In: Callicott, J. Baird, Nelson, Michael P., editors. *The great new wilderness debate.* Athens, GA: The University of Georgia Press; 1998. p. 568–84.

25. Krueger, Christopher, Senf, Christian, Durick, Janelle. Beef and backpackers: Grazing in the wilderness. In: Goodman, Doug, McCool, Daniel C., editors. *Contested landscape: The politics of wilderness in Utah and the west.* Salt Lake City: The University of Utah Press; 1999. p. 158–74.

26. Tobin, Mitch. *Endangered: Biodiversity on the brink.* Golden, CO: Fulcrum; 2010.

27. Dreitz, Victoria J., Knopf, Fitz L. Mountain plovers and the politics of research on private lands. *Bioscience.* 2007; 57(8): 681–7.

28. Noss, Reed F., O'Connell, Michael A., Murphy, Dennis D. *The science of conservation planning: Habitat conservation under the Endangered Species Act.* Washington, D.C.: Island Press; 1997.

29. Mangun, William R. Wildlife resources policy issues in the west. In: Smith, Zachary A., Freemuth, John C., editors. *Environmental politics and policy in the west.* Boulder: University Press of Colorado; 2007. p. 109–31.

30. Dinerstein, Eric. *The return of the unicorns: The natural history and conservation of the greater one-horned rhinoceros.* New York: Columbia University Press; 2003.

31. Nie, Martin A. *The governance of western public lands: Mapping its present and future.* Lawrence: University of Kansas Press; 2008.

32. Gibbons, J. W, McGlothlin, Karen L. A changing balance. In: Spray, Sharon L., McGlothlin, Karen L., editors. *Loss of biodiversity.* Lanham: Rowman & Littlefield Publishers, Inc.; 2003. p. 29–54.

33. Wilson, Edward O. *The future of life.* New York: Alfred A. Knopf; 2002.

34. Nyhus, Philip J., Tilson, Ronald. Panthera tigris vs homo sapiens: Conflict, coexistence, or extinction. In: Nyhus, Philip J., Tilson, Ronald, editors. *Tigers of the world: The science, politics, and conservation of panthera tigris.* 2nd ed. Amsterdam: Academic Press; 2010. p. 125–41.

35. Choudhury, Anwaruddin. Human-elephant conflicts in northeast India. *Hum Dimens Wildl.* 2004; 9(4): 261–70.

36. Parmesan, Camille, Yohe, Gary. A globally coherent fingerprint of climate change impacts across natural systems. *Nature.* 2003; 421(January 2): 37–42.

37. Bernazzani, Paola, Bradley, Bethany A., Opperman, Jeffrey J. Integrating climate change into habitat conservation plans under the U.S. Endangered Species Act. *Environ Manage.* 2012; 49(3): 1103–14.

38. Butler, Jessica S., Shanahan, James, Decker, Daniel J. Public attitudes toward wildlife are changing: A trend analysis of New York residents. *Wildl Soc Bull.* 2003; 31(4): 1027–36.

39. Bixby, Kevin. Predator conservation. In: Kohn, Kathryn A., editor. *Balancing on the brink of extinction: The Endangered Species Act and lessons for the future.* Washington, D.C.: Island Press; 1991. p. 199–213.

40. Manfredo, Michael J., Fulton, David C., Pierce, Cynthia. Understanding voter behavior on wildlife ballot initiatives: Colorado's trapping amendment. *Hum Dimens Wildl.* 1997; 2(4): 22–39.

41. Decker, Daniel J., Brown, Tommy L., Connelly, Nancy A., Enck, Jody W., Pomerantz, Gerri A., Purdy, Ken G., et al. Toward a comprehensive paradigm of wildlife management: Integrating the human and biological dimensions. In: Mangun, William R., editor. *American fish and wildlife policy: The human dimensions.* Carbondale: Southern Illinois University Press; 1992. p. 33–54.

42. Prince, Jennifer. Changing customs: Case of feathered hats, hats off to Audubon. *Audubon Magazine.* 2004; (November-December): 44–50.

43. Healy, Vikki Ortiz, Gregory, Ted. Shark fin soup: The predator has become the prey. *Chicago Tribune* [Internet]. 2012 Aug 9 [cited 2012 Aug 9]; Available from: www.chicagotribune.com/news/local/ct-met-shark-fin-soup-20120809,0,5669500.story

44. Roman, Joe. *Listed: Dispatches from America's Endangered Species Act.* Cambridge: Harvard University Press; 2011.

45. Kareiva, Peter. Ominous trends in nature recreation. *Proc Natl Acad Sci U S A.* 2008; 105(8): 2757–8.

46. Garner, Robert. *Political animals: Animal protection politics in Britain and the United States.* New York: St. Martin's Press, Inc.; 1998.

47. Krajick, Kevin. Free speech or harassment: Hunters and antihunters slug it out–in the forests and in court. *Audubon Magazine.* 1995; (July-August): 16–20.

48. Messmer, Terry A., Enck, Jody W. Human dimensions of wildlife use management. In: Decker, Daniel J., Riley, Shawn J., Siemer, William F., editors. *Human dimensions of wildlife management.* Baltimore: Johns Hopkins University Press; 2012. p. 203–19.

49. Smith, Bruce L. *Where elk roam: Conservation and biopolitics of our national elk herd.* Guilford, CT: Lyons Press; 2012.

50. Hackel, Jeffrey D. Community conservation and the future of Africa's wildlife. *Conserv Biol.* 1999; 13(4): 726–34.

51. Kellert, Stephen R. Public attitudes towards critical wildlife and natural habitat issues. Phase One. #024-010-00-623-4. U.S. Government Printing Office; 1979.

52. Matthiessen, Peter. *Wildlife in America.* New York: Viking Penguin, Inc.; 1987.

53. Neely, Nick. The salt pond puzzle: Restoring south San Francisco bay. *High Country News* [Internet]. 2012 Aug 6; Available from: www.hcn.org/issues/44.13/the-salt-pond-puzzle-restoring-south-san-francisco-bay/print_view

54. Dinerstein, Eric. *The kingdom of rarities.* Washington, D.C.: Island Press; 2012.

55. Fascione, Nina, Delach, Aimee, Smith, Martin E. Conclusion. In: Fascione, Nina, Delach, Aimee, Smith, Martin E., editors. *People and predators: From conflict to coexistence.* Washington, D.C.: Island Press; 2004.

56. Bodmer, Richard, Pueretas, Pablo, Tula, G. Comanaging wildlife in the Amazon and the salvation of the Pacaya-Samiria national reserve in Peru. In: Manfredo, Michael J., Vaske, Jerry J., Brown, Perry J., Decker, Daniel J., Duke, Esther A., editors. *Wildlife and society: The science of human dimensions.* Washington, D.C.: Island Press; 2009. p. 104–16.

57. U.S. General Accountability Office. Endangered species: Management improvement could enhance recovery program. 1988 Dec. Report No.: GAO/RCED-89-5.

58. Foster, Janet. *Working for wildlife: The beginning of preservation in Canada.* 2nd ed. Toronto: University of Toronto Press; 1998.

59. Matthiessen, Peter. *Tigers in the snow.* New York: North Point Press; 2000.

60. Rahmani, Asad R. Conservation outside protected areas: Case studies of bustard protection. In: Saberwal, Vasant K., Rangarajan, Mahesh, editors. *Battles over nature: Science and the politics of conservation.* New Delhi: Permanent Black; 2003. p. 117–35.

61. Kaye, Roger. *Last great wilderness: The campaign to establish the arctic national wildlife refuge.* Fairbanks: University of Alaska Press; 2006.

62. Theberge, John B. An ecologist's perspective on wolf recovery in the northeastern United States. In: Elder, John, editor. *The return of the wolf: Reflections on the future of wolves in the northeast.* Hanover: Middlebury College Press; 2000. p. 22–63.

63. Hanna, Susan. Transition in the American fishing commons: Management problems and institutional design challenges. In: Dolsak, Nives N.D., Ostrom, Elinor E.O., editors. *The commons in the new millenium.* Cambridge: The MIT Press; 2003. p. 61–76.

64. Roberts, Calllum. *The ocean of life: The fate of man and the sea.* New York: Viking; 2012.

65. Rigney, Matt. *In pursuit of giants: One man's global search for the last of the great fish.* New York: Penguin Group; 2012.

66. Roberts, Callum. *The unnatural history of the sea.* Washington, D.C.: Island Press; 2007.

67. Wines, Michael. Study finds large seabird toll From fishing nets. *New York Times* [Internet]. 2013 Jun 12 [cited 2013 Jun 12]; Available from: www.nytimes.com/2013/06/13/us/study-finds-large-seabird-toll-from-fishing-nets.html?emc=tnt&tntemail0=y&_r=0&pagewanted=print

68. Dean, Cornelia. The fall and rise of the right whale. *New York Times* [Internet]. 2009 Mar 16 [cited 2016 May 16]; Available from: www.nytimes.com/2009/03/17/science/17whal.html

69. Hames, Raymond. Wildlife conservation in tribal societies. In: Oldfield, Margaret L., Alcorn, Janice B., editors. *Biodiversity: Culture, conservation, and ecodevelopment.* Boulder: Westview Press; 1991. p. 172–199.

70. Harris, Melissa. With UIC technology, thwarting Africa's million dollar poaching. *Chicago Tribune* [Internet]. 2015 Mar 20 [cited 2015 Mar 20]; Available from: www.chicagotribune.com/business/ct-confidential-zebra-count-0319-biz-20150319-column.html

71. Nyhus, Philip J., Tilson, Ronald, Hutchins, Michael. Thirteen thousand and counting: How growing captive tiger populations threaten wild tigers. In: Tilson, Ronald, Nyhus, Philip J., editors. 2nd ed. *Tigers of the world: The science, politics, and conservation of panthera tigris.* Amsterdam: Academic Press; 2010. p. 223–38.

72. Geist, Valerius. Great achievements, great expectations: Successes of North American wildlife management. In: Hawley, Alex W.L., editor. *Commercialization and wildlife management: Dancing with the devil.* Malabar, FL: Krieger Publishing Company; 1993. p. 47–72.

73. Duffy, Rosaleen. *Nature crime: How we're getting conservation wrong.* New Haven: Yale University Press; 2010.

74. Ernst, Howard R. *Chesapeake Bay blues: Science, politics, and the struggle to save the bay.* Lanham: Rowman & Littlefield Publishers, Inc.; 2003.

75. Parenteau, Patrick A. NEPA at twenty: Great disappointment or whopping success? *Audubon Magazine.* 1990; (March): 104–7.

76. Repetto, Robert. Introduction. In: Repetto, Robert, editor. *Punctuated equilibrium and the dynamics of US environmental policy.* New Haven: Yale University Press; 2006. p. 1–23.

77. Dunlap, Riley E. Public opinion and environmental policy. In: Lester, James P., editor. *Environmental politics and policy: theories and evidence.* Durham: Duke University Press; 1995. p. 63–114.

78. Allin, Craig W. *The politics of wilderness preservation.* Westport: Greenwood Press; 1982.

79. Corn, M. Lynne, Alexander, Kristina. The Endangered Species Act (ESA) in the 113th Congress: New and recurring issues [Internet]. Congressional Research Service; [cited 2015 Feb 28]; Available from: http://nationalaglawcenter.org/wp-content/uploads/assets/crs/R42945.pdf

80. Pacific Legal Foundation. Policy positon on Endangered Species Act. In: Miller, Norman, editor. *Cases in environmental politics.* New York: Routledge; 2009. p. 20–3.

81. Warren, Louis. *The hunter's game: Poachers and conservationists in twentieth-century America.* New Haven: Yale University Press; 1997.

82. Rasker, Raymond, Martin, Michael V., Johnson, Rebecca L. Economics: Theory versus practice in wildlife management. *Conserv Biol.* 1992; 6(September): 338–49.

83. U.S. House of Representatives. H.R. 3824, Threatened and endangered species recovery act of 2005. Legislative hearing before the Committee on Resources. One-Hundred Ninth Congress, First Session. 2005.

84. Dixon, Lloyd, Sorensen, Paul, Wachs, Martin, Collins, Myles, Hanson, Mark, Kofner, Mark et al. Balancing environment and development. Costs, revenues, and benefits of the Western Riverside County multiple species habitat conservation plan. [Internet]. Rand Corporation; 2008 [cited 2016 Jun 8]; Available from: www.rand.org/content/dam/rand/pubs/monographs/2008/RAND_MG816.pdf

85. Donahue, Debra. A critical examination of economic incentives to promote conservation. In: Shogren, Jason F., editor. *Species at risk: Using economic incentives to shelter endangered species on private lands.* Austin: University of Texas Press; 2005. p. 147–71.

86. Pasquini, Lorena, Cowling, Richard M., Twyman, Chasca, Wainright, John W. Devising appropriate policies and instruments in support of private conservation areas: Lessons learned from the Klein Karoo, South Africa. *Conserv Biol.* 2009; 24(2): 470–8.

87. Duffy, Rosaleen. *Killing for conservation: Wildlife policy in Zimbabwe.* Oxford: International African Institute in association with James Curry; 2000.

88. Gibson, Clark C. *Politicians and poachers: The political economy of wildlife policy in Africa.* Cambridge: Cambridge University Press; 1999.

89. Ferraro, Paul J. The future of payments for environmental services. *Conserv Biol.* 2011; 25(6): 1134–8.

90. Conniff, Richard. What's wrong with putting a price on nature? Environment 360: Reporting, Analysis, and Debate [Internet]. 2012 [cited 2015 Mar 25]; Available from: http://e360.yale.edu/feature/ecosystem_services_whats_wrong_with_putting_a_price_on_nature/2583/

91. Alston, Lee J., Andersson, Krister, Smith, Steven M. Payment for environmental services: Hypotheses and evidence. January. Working Paper 18740. [Internet]. National Bureau of Economic Research; 2013; Available from: www.nber.org/papers/w18740

92. Zabel, Astrid, Engel, Stefanie. Performance payments: A new strategy to conserve large carnivores in the tropics? *Ecol Econ*. 2010; 70(2): 405–12.

93. Bowles, Samuel. Policies designed for self-interested citizens may undermine "the moral sentiments": Evidence from Economic Experiments. *Science*. 2008; 320(20): 1605–9.

94. Tierney, John. A tale of two fisheries. *New York Times Magazine* [Internet]. 2003, August 27 [cited 2015 Jan 24]; Available from: www.nytimes.com/2000/08/27/magazine/a-tale-of-two-fisheries.html?pagewanted=print

95. Dolsak, Nives, Ostrom, Elinor. The challenges of the commons. In: Dolsak, Nives, Ostrom, Elinor, editors. *The commons in the new millenium*. Cambridge: The MIT Press; 2003. p. 3–34.

96. Acheson, James M.;, Brewer, Jennifer F. Changes in the territorial system of the Maine lobster industry. In: Dolsak, Nives, Ostrom, Elinor, editors. *Large mammal restoration: Ecological and sociological challenges in the 21st century*. Cambridge: The MIT Press; 2003. p. 37–59.

97. Pressman, Jeffrey L., Wildavsky, Aaron. *Implementation: how great expectations in Washington are dashed in Oakland or, why it's amazing that federal programs work at all, this being a saga of the Economic Development Administration as told by two sympathetic observers who seek to build morals on a foundation of ruined hopes*. 3rd ed. Berkeley: University of California; 1984.

98. Rabinowitz, Alan. Helping a species go extinct; The Sumatran rhino in Borneo. *Conserv Biol*. 1995; 9(June): 486–7.

99. Arcese, Peter, Hando, Justine, Campbell, Ken. Historical and present-day anti-poaching efforts in Serengeti. In: Sinclair, A.R.E., Arcese, Peter, editors. *Serengeti II: Dynamics, management, and conservation of an ecosystem*. Chicago: The University of Chicago Press; 1995. p. 506–33.

100. Sing, Billy Arian. Tiger haven. In: Ward, Geoffrey, editor. *Tigers and Tigerwallahs*. New Delhi: Oxford University Press; 2002. p. 16–213.

101. Steinhart, Peter. Bear of the clouds. *Audubon Magazine*. 1989; (July): 92–103.

102. Zeigler, Harmon. *Interest groups in American society*. Englewood Cliffs, NJ: Prentice-Hall, Inc.; 1964.

103. McFarland, Andrew W. Interest groups and the policymaking process: Sources of countervailing power in America. In: Petracca, Mark P., editor. *The politics of interests: Interest groups transformed*. Boulder: Westview Press; 1992. p. 58–79.

104. Freeman, J. *Leiper. The political process*. New York: Random House; 1965.

105. Hoberg, George. The emerging triumph of ecosystem management: The transformation of federal forest policy. In: Davis, Charles, editor. *Western public lands and environmental politics*. Boulder: Westview Press; 2001. p. 55–85.

106. Davis, Charles. The politics of grazing on federal lands: A policy change perspective. In: Repetto, Robert, editor. *Punctuated equilibrium and the dynamics of US environmental policy*. New Haven: Yale University Press; 2006. p. 232–52.

107. Mangun, William R., Henning, Daniel H. *Managing the environmental crisis*. Durham: Duke University Press; 1999.

108. Nie, Martin. State wildlife policy and management: The scope and bias of political conflict. *Public Adm Rev*. 2004; 64(2): 221–33.

109. Adams, Jonathan S. *The future of the wild: Radical conservation for a crowded world*. Boston: Beacon Press; 2006.

110. Kraft, Michael E. *Environmental policy and politics*. 5th ed. Boston: Longman; 2011.

111. Ingram, Helen M., Colnic, David H., Mann, Dean E. Interest groups and environmental policy. In: Lester, James P., editor. *Environmental politics and policy: Theories and evidence.* Durham: Duke University Press; 1995. p. 115–45.

112. Rushefsky, Mark E. Elites and environmental policy. In: Lester, James P., editor. *Environmental politics and policy: Theories and evidence.* Durham: Duke University Press; 1995. p. 275–99.

113. Turner, James Morton. *The promise of wilderness: American environmental politics since 1964.* Seattle: University of Washington Press; 2012.

114. Williams, Ted. Giant strip mine threatens Alaska's Bristol Bay. *Audubon Magazine* [Internet]. 2012, November-December [cited 2016 Mar 22]; Available from: www.audubon.org/magazine/november-december-2012/giant-strip-mine-threatens-alaskas

115. Doremus, Holly, Pagel, Joel E. Why listing may be forever: Perspectives on delisting under the U.S. Endangered Species Act. *Conserv Biol.* 2001; 15(5): 1258–68.

116. Thomas, Craig W. *Bureaucratic landscapes: Interagency cooperation and the preservation of biodiversity.* New York: McGraw-Hill; 2003.

117. Selznick, Phillip. *TVA and the grassroots: A study of politics and organization.* Berkeley: University of California Press; 1949.

118. Sabatier, Paul A. An advocacy coalition framework of policy change and the role of policy-oriented learning therein. *Policy Sci.* 1988; 21: 129–68.

119. Jenkins-Smith, Hank, Silva, Carol L., Gupta, Kuhika, Ripberger, Joseph T. Belief system continuity and change in policy advocacy coalitions: Using cultural theory to specify belief systems, coalitions, and sources of change. *Policy Stud J.* 2014; 42(4): 484–508.

120. Keiter, Robert B. *Keeping faith with nature: Ecosystems, democracy, & America's public lands.* New Haven: Yale University Press; 2003.

121. Banerjee, Neela. Can black gold ever flow green? *New York Times* [Internet]. 2000 Nov 12 [cited 2016 Feb 10]; Available from: www.nytimes.com/2000/11/12/business/can-black-gold-ever-flow-green.html?pagewanted=all

122. Klyza, Christopher McGrory, Sousa, David J. *American environmental policy: Beyond gridlock.* Cambridge: MIT Press; 2013.

123. Sousa, David J., Klyza, Christopher McGrory. New directions in environmental policy making: An emerging collaborative regime or reinventing interest group liberalism? *Nat Resour J.* 2007; 47(Spring): 378–444.

124. Bevington, Douglas. *Rebirth of environmentalism: Grassroots activism from the spotted owl to the polar bear.* Washington, D.C.: Island Press; 2009.

125. Clarke, Jeanne Nienaber, McCool, Daniel C. *Staking out the terrain: Power and performance among natural resource agencies.* Albany: State University of New York Press; 1996.

126. Allin, Craig W. Wilderness policy. In: Davis, Charles, editor. *Public lands and environmental politics.* Boulder: Westview; 2001. p. 197–222.

127. Thompson, James D. *Organizations in action.* New York: McGraw-Hill; 1967.

128. Thomas, Craig. Public management as interagency cooperation: Testing epistemic community theory at the domestic level. *J Public Adm Res Theory.* 1997; 7(2): 221–46.

129. Nelson, Lisa. Wildlife policy. In: Davis, Charles, editor. *Western public lands and environmental politics.* Boulder: Westview Press; 2001. p. 223–50.

130. Robinson, Michael J. *Predatory bureaucracy: The extermination of the wolf and the transformation of the west.* Boulder: The University of Colorado Press; 2005.

131. Culhane, Paul J. *Public lands politics: Interest group influence on the forest service and the bureau of land management.* Baltimore: Johns Hopkins University Press; 1981.

132. Saberwal, Vasant K., Rangarajan, Mahesh. Introduction. In: Saberwal, Vasant K., Rangarajan, Mahesh, editors. *Battles over nature: Science and the politics of conservation.* New Delhi: Permanent Black; 2003. p. 1–28.

133. Saberwal, Vasant K. Conservation by state fiat. In: Saberwal, Vasant K., Rangarajan, Mahesh, editors. *Battles over nature: Science and politics of conservation.* New Delhi: Permanent Black; 2003. p. 240–63.

134. Yaffee, Steven Lewis. *Prohibitive policy: Implementing the federal Endangered Species Act.* Cambridge: MIT Press; 1982.

135. Jacobson, Cynthia A., Decker, Daniel J., Carpenter, Len. Securing alternative funding for wildlife management: Insights from agency leaders. *J Wildl Manag.* 2007; 71(6): 2106–13.

136. Yaffee, Steven L. Why environmental policy nightmares recur. *Conserv Biol.* 1997; 11(2): 328–37.

137. Clark, Tim W. *Averting extinction: Reconstructing endangered species recovery.* New Haven: Yale University Press; 1997.

138. Hoberg, George. How the way we make policy governs the policy we make. In: Salazar, Debra J., Alper, Donald K., editors. *Sustaining the forests of the Pacific coast: Forging truces in the war on the woods.* Vancouver: UBC Press; 2000. p. 25–53.

139. Cawley, R. McGreggor, Freemuth, John C. Science, politics, and federal Lands. In: Smith, Zachary A., Freemuth, John C., editors. *Environmental politics and policy in the west.* Boulder: University Press of Colorado; 2007. p. 69–88.

140. Doremus, Holly, Tarlock, A. Dan. *Water war in the Klamath basin: Macho law, combat biology, and dirty politics.* Washington, D.C.: Island Press; 2008.

141. Nie, Martin. *The governance of western public lands: Mapping its present and future.* Lawrence: University of Kansas Press; 2008.

142. VanNijnatten, Debora L. Participation and environmental policy in Canada and the United States: Trends over time. *Policy Stud J.* 1999; 27(2): 267–87.

143. Wood, Jonathan. Take it to the limit: The illegal regulation prohibiting the take of any threatened species under the Endangered Species Act [Internet]. Program for Judicial Awareness; 2015 Jul [cited 2015 Aug 25]. (Working Paper Series). Report No. 13–514; Available from: http://papers.ssrn.com/sol3/papers.cfm?abstract_id=2581766

144. Donahue, Debra L. *The western range revisited: Removing livestock from public lands to conserve native biodiversity.* Norman: University of Oklahoma Press; 1999.

145. Kareiva, Peter, Marvier, Michelle. What is conservation science? *BioScience.* 2012. 62(11): 962–9.

146. Kareiva, Peter, Marvier, Michelle, Lalasz, Robert. Conservation in the anthropocene: Beyond solitude and fragility. *The Breakthrough* [Internet]. 2012, Winter [cited 2014 Oct 20]; Available from: http://thebreakthrough.org/index.php/journal/past-issues/issue-2/conservation-in-the-anthropocene/

147. Gottlieb, Robert. *Forcing the spring: The transformation of the American environmental movement.* Washington, D.C.: Island Press; 2005.

148. Johns, David. With friends like these, wilderness and biodiversity do not need enemies. In: Wuerthner, George, Crist, Eileen, and Butler, Tom, editors. *Keeping the wild: Against the domestication of birds.* Washington, D.C.: Island Press; 2014. p. 31–44.

149. Anderson, James E. *Public policymaking: An introduction.* 7th ed. Boston: Wadsworth; 2011.

150. Dye, Thomas R. *Understanding public policy.* 13th ed. Boston: Longman; 2011.

151. Soulé, Michael. The "new conservation." In: Wuerthner, George, Crist, Eileen, Butler, Tom, editors. *Keeping the wild: Against the domestication of Earth.* Washington, D.C.: Island Press; 2014. p. 66–80.

152. Goble, Dale, D., Scott, J. Michael, Davis, Frank W., editors. *The Endangered Species Act at thirty: Volume I: Renewing the conservation promise.* Washington, D.C.: Island Press; 2006.

153. Greenwald, D. Noah, Suckling, Kieran F., Taylor, Martin. The listing record. In: Goble, Dale, D., Scott, J. Michael, Davis, Frank W., editors. *The Endangered Species Act at thirty: Volume I: Renewing the conservation promise.* Washington, D.C.: Island Press; 2006. p. 51–74.

154. Nie, Martin A. *Beyond wolves: The politics of wolf recovery and management.* Minneapolis: University of Minnesota Press; 2003.

155. Freeman, Milton R., editor. *Elephants and whales: Resources for whom?* Switzerland: Gordon and Breach Science Publishers; 1994.

156. Tilson, Ronald, Nyhus, Philip J. *Tigers of the world: The science, politics, and conservation of panthera tigris.* 2nd ed. Amsterdam: Academic Press; 2010.

157. Nie, Martin. State wildlife policy and management: The scope and bias of political conflict. *Public Adm Rev.* 2004; 62(2): 221–33.

158. Yaffee, Steven Lewis. *The wisdom of the spotted owl: Policy lessons for a new century.* Washington, D.C.: Island Press; 1994.

159. Nelson, Fred. *Community rights, conservation, and contested land: The politics of natural resources in Africa.* London: Earth; 2010.

160. Duffy, Rosaleen. *Nature crime: How we're getting conservation wrong.* New Haven: Yale University Press; 2010.

161. Babbitt, Bruce. *Cities in the wilderness: A new vision of land use in America.* Washington, D.C.: Island Press/Shearwater Books; 2005.

162. Leakey, Richard, Morell, Virginia. *Wildlife wars.* New York: St. Martin's Press, Inc.; 2001.

163. Sanderson, Steven. Getting the biology right in a political sort of way. In: Reynolds, John D., Mace, Georgina M., Redford, Kent H., Robinson, John G., editors. *Conservation of exploited species.* Cambridge: Cambridge University Press; 2001. p. 462–82.

Chapter 2 References

1. Sabatier, Paul A., Jenkins, Hank C. *Policy change and learning: An advocacy coalition approach.* Boulder: Westview Press; 1993.

2. Doremus, Holly, Tarlock, A. Dan. *Water war in the Klamath basin: Macho law, combat biology, and dirty politics.* Washington, D.C.: Island Press; 2008.

3. Nie, Martin. *Beyond wolves: The politics of wolf recovery and management.* Minneapolis: University of Minnesota Press; 2003.

4. Doremus, Holly. The purposes, effects, and future of the Endangered Species Act's best available science mandate. *Environ Law.* 2004; 34: 397–449.

5. Goodnough, Abby. Scientists say cod are scant; Nets say otherwise. *New York Times* [Internet]. 2011 Dec 10 [cited 2011 Dec 11]; Available from: www.nytimes.com/2011/12/11/us/conflicting-indicators-on-gulf-of-maine-cod-stocks.html?_r=1&nl=todaysheadlines&emc=tha23&pagewanted=print

6. Acheson, James M. The politics of managing the Maine lobster industry: 1860 to the present. *Hum Ecol.* 1997; 25(1): 3–27.

7. Sutherland, William J, Gill, Jennifer A. The role of behaviour in studying sustainable exploitation. In: Reynolds, John D., Mace, Georgina M., Redford, Kent H., Robinson, John G., editors. *Conservation of exploited species.* Cambridge: Cambridge University Press; 2001. p. 259–80.

8. Manfredo, Michael J. *Who cares about wildlife? Social science concepts for exploring human-wildlife relationships and conservation issues*. New York: Springer; 2008.

9. Clark, Douglas, Workman, Linaya, Slocombe, D. Scott. Science-based grizzly bear conservation in a co-management environment: The Kluane region case, Yukon. In: Clark, Susan G., Rutherford, Murray B., editors. *Large carnivore conservation: Integrating science and policy in the north American west*. Chicago: University of Chicago Press; 2014. p. 108–39.

10. Unger, Zac. Are polar bears really disappearing? *Wall Street Journal*. 2012 Feb 9; C3.

11. Boertje, Rodney D, Keech, Mark A., Paragi, Thomas F. Science and values influencing predator control for Alaska moose management. *J Wildl Manag*. 2010; 74(5): 917–28.

12. Nash, Roderick. *Wilderness and the American mind*. 3rd ed. New Haven: Yale University Press; 1982.

13. Bjerke, Tore, Retan, Ole, Kellert, Stephen R. Attitudes toward wolves in southeastern Norway. *Soc Nat Resour*. 1998; 11(2): 169–78.

14. Ames, Norma. Mexican Wolf Recovery Plan (Excerpts). In: Lynch, Tom, editor. *El lobo: Readings on the Mexican gray wolf*. Salt Lake City: The University Press; 2005. p. 107–29.

15. Alagona, Peter S., Pincetl, Stephanie. The Coachella valley multiple species habitat conservation plan: A decade of delays. *Environ Manage*. 2008; 41: 1–11.

16. Klyza, Christopher McGrory, Sousa, David J. *American environmental policy: Beyond gridlock*. Cambridge: MIT Press; 2013.

17. Chapron, Guillaume, Lopenz-Bao, Jose Vicente, Kjellander, Petter, Karlsson, Jens. Misuse of scientific data in wolf policy. *Science*. 2013; 339(6127): 1521.

18. Weber, Edward P. *Bringing society back in: Grassroots ecosystem management, accountability, and sustainable communities*. Cambridge: MIT Press; 2003.

19. Brick, Philip, Weber, Edward P. Will rain follow the play? Unearthing a new environmental movement. In: Brick, Philip, Snow, Donald, Van De Wetering, Sarah, editors. *Across the great divide: Explorations in collaborative conservation and the American west*. Washington, D.C.: Island Press; 2001. p. 15–24.

20. Mills, L. Scott. *Conservation of wildlife populations: demography, genetics, and management*. Malden, MA: Blackwell Publishing; 2007.

21. Miller, Brian J., Reading, Richard P., Biggins, Dean E., Detling, James K., Forrest, Steve C., Hoogland, John L. et al. Prairie dogs: An ecological review and current biopolitics. *J Wildl Manag*. 2007; 71(8): 2801–10.

22. Miller, Sterling D., Schoen, John W., Faro, Jim, Klein, David R. Trends in intensive management of Alaska's grizzly bears, 1980–2010. *J Wildl Manag*. 2011; 75(6): 1243–52.

23. Revkin, Andrew C. DNA study finds deeper antiquity of polar bear species. *New York Times* [Internet]. 2012 Apr 19 [cited 2012 Apr 20]; Available from: http://dotearth.blogs.nytimes.com/2012/04/19/dna-study-finds-deeper-antiquity-of-polar-bear-species/?pagemode=print

24. Welch, Craig. Oysters in deep trouble: Is Pacific Ocean's chemistry killing sea life? *Seattle Times* [Internet]. 2012 Oct 18 [cited 2013 Nov 25]; Available from: http://seattletimes.com/html/localnews/2009336458_oysters14m.html

25. Robbins, Jim. The year the monarch didn't appear. *New York Times* [Internet]. 2013 Nov 22 [cited 2013 Nov 24]; Available from: www.nytimes.com/2013/11/24/sunday-review/the-year-the-monarch-didnt-appear.html?_r=0&pagewanted=print

26. Urbigkit, Cat. *Yellowstone wolves: A chronicle of the animal, the people, and the politics*. Blacksburg, VA: The McDonald & Woodward Publishing Company; 2008.

27. Marris, Emma. *Rambunctious garden: Saving nature in a post-wild world*. New York: Bloomsbury; 2011.

28. Wuerthner, George. Why the working landscape isn't working. In: Wuerthner, George, Crist, Eileen, Butler, Tom, editors. *Keeping the wild: Against the domestication of earth*. Washington, D.C.: Island Press; 2014. p. 162–73.

29. Johns, David. With friends like these, wilderness and biodiversity do not need enemies. In: Wuerthner, George, Crist, Eileen, Butler, Tom, editors. *Keeping the wild: Against the domestication of birds*. Washington, D.C.: Island Press; 2014. p. 31–44.

30. Foreman, Dave. The myth of the humanized pre-columbian landscape. In: Wuerthner, George, Crist, Eileen, Butler, Tom, editors. *Keeping the wild: Against the domestication of Earth*. Washington, D.C.: Island Press; 2014. p. 114–25.

31. Soulé, Michael. The "new conservation." In: Wuerthner, George, Crist, Eileen, Butler, Tom, editors. *Keeping the wild: Against the domestication of Earth*. Washington, D.C.: Island Press; 2014. p. 66–80.

32. Locke, Harvey. Green postmodernism and the attempted highjacking of conservation. In: Wuerthner, George, Crist, Eileen, Butler, Tom, editors. *Keeping the wild: Against the domestication of Earth*. Washington, D.C.: Island Press; 2014. p. 146–61.

33. Ricciardi, Anthony, Simberloff, Daniel. Fauna in decline: First do no harm. *Science*. 2014; 345(6199): 884.

34. Schlaepfer, Martin A., Sax, Dov F., Oldens, Julian D. The potential conservation value of non-native species. *Conserv Biol*. 2011; 25(3): 428–37.

35. McCullough, Dale, R. The Craigheads' data on Yellowstone grizzly bear populations: Relevance to current research and management. *Ursus*. 1986; 6: 21–32.

36. Chase, Alston. *Playing God in Yellowstone: The destruction of America's first national park*. Orlando: Harcourt Brace and Company; 1987.

37. Vucetich, John A, Nelson, Michael P., Phillips, Michael K. The normative dimension and legal meaning of endangered and recovery in the U.S. Endangered Species Act. *Conserv Biol*. 2006; 20(5): 1383–90.

38. Vucetich, John A., Nelson, Michael Paul. Conservation, or curation? *New York Times* [Internet]. 2014 Aug 20; Available from: www.nytimes.com/2014/08/21/opinion/conservation-or-curation.html?emc=edit_tnt_20140820&nlid=10365419&tntemail0=y&_r=0

39. U.S. Fish and Wildlife Service. FAQs for gray wolf and delisting [Internet]. 2013 [cited 2013 Jun 13]; Available from: www.fws.gov/home/feature/2013/pdf/FAQsforGrayWolfandDelisting062013.pdf

40. Saberwal, Vasant K., Rangarajan, Mahesh. Introduction. In: Saberwal, Vasant K., Rangarajan, Mahesh, editors. *Battles over nature: Science and the politics of conservation*. New Delhi: Permanent Black; 2003. p. 1–28.

41. U.S. Fish and Wildlife Service. Final environmental impact statement: The reintroduction of gray wolves to Yellowstone national park and central Idaho [Internet]. 1994 [cited 2016 Mar 24]; Available from: www.fws.gov/mountain-prairie/species/mammals/wolf/eis_1994.pdf

42. Arizona Game and Fish Department. Letter from Arizona game and fish department director, Larry D. Voyles Dec. 10 to Benjamin N. Tuggle, director of southwest region, USFWS [Internet]. [cited 2013 Apr 27]; Available from: www.azgfd.gov/w_c/es/mexican_wolf.shtml

43. Mace, Georgina M., Reynolds, John D. Exploitation as a conservation issue. In: Reynolds, John D., Redford, Kent H., Robinson, John G., editors. *Conservation of exploited species*. Cambridge: Cambridge University Press; 2001. p. 3–15.

44. Wilhere, George F. The how-much-is-enough myth. *Conserv Biol*. 2008; 22(3): 514–7.

45. Reed, J. Michael et al. Critical habitat. In: Scott, J. Michael, Goble, Dale, D., Davis, Frank W., editors *The Endangered Species Act at thirty: Conserving biodiversity in human-dominated landscapes, Volume 2*. Washington, D.C.: Island Press; 2006. p. 164–80.

46. Farquhar, Brodie. New study questions how greater Yellowstone bears are counted. *High Country News* [Internet]. 2013 Aug 19; Available from: www.hcn.org/issues/45.14/new-study-questions-how-greater-yellowstone-bears-are-counted/print_view

47. Doak, Daniel F., Cutler, Kerry. Re-evaluating evidence for past population trends and predicted dynamics of Yellowstone grizzly bears. *Conserv Lett*. 2014; 7(3): 312–22.

48. van Manen, Frank T., Ebinger, Michael R., Haroldson, Mark A., Harris, Richard B., Higgs, Megan D., Cherry, Steve et al. Re-evaluation of Yellowstone grizzly bear population dynamics not supported by empirical data: Response to Doak & Cutler. *Conserv Lett*. 2014; 7(3): 323–31.

49. New York Times. Editorial: Counting bears. *New York Times* [Internet]. 2013 Jul 7 [cited 2013 Jul 8]; Available from: www.nytimes.com/2013/07/08/opinion/counting-bears.html?emc=tnt&tntemail0=y&pagewanted=print

50. Harbine, Jenny K. Gray wolves in the northern rockies again staring down the barrel at hostile state management. *Ecol Curr*. 2009; 36: 195–208.

51. Mech, L. David. Crying wolf: concluding that wolves were not restored. *Biol Lett*. 2009; 5(1): 65–6.

52. Leonard, J.A., Wayne, R.K. Native great lakes wolves were not restored. *Biol Lett*. 2008; 4(1): 95–8.

53. Leonard, Jennifer A., Wayne, Robert K. Wishful thinking: imagining that the current Great Lakes wolf is the same entity that existed historically. *Biol Lett*. 2009; 5: 67–8.

54. Adams, Jonathan S. *The future of the wild: Radical conservation for a crowded world*. Boston: Beacon Press; 2006.

55. Walker, Brian. Riding the rangelands piggyback: A resilience approach to conservation management. In: du Toit, John D., Kock, Richard, Deutsch, James C., editors. *Wild rangelands: Conserving wildlife while maintaining livestock in semi-arid ecosystems*. Oxford: Wiley-Blackwell; 2010. p. 15–29.

56. Keller, Sarah. The goat: grizzlies back from the brink? *High Country News* [Internet]. 2013 May 10 [cited 2013 May 14]; Available from: www.hcn.org/blogs/goat/grizzlies-back-from-the-brink

57. Rigney, Matt. *In pursuit of giants: One man's global search for the last of the great fish*. New York: Penguin Group; 2012.

58. Yaffee, Steven Lewis. *The wisdom of the spotted owl: Policy lessons for a new century*. Washington, D.C.: Island Press; 1994.

59. National Research Council. Science and the Endangered Species Act [Internet]. Washington, D.C.: National Academy Press; 1995 [cited 2016 Mar 24]; Available from: www.nap.edu/read/4978/chapter/1

60. Wilkinson, Todd. How real is the brucellosis threat? *Audubon Magazine*. 1997; (May-June): 46–7 & 108.

61. Clemons, Randy S., McBeth, Mark K. *A case approach for understanding policy and analysis*. 2nd ed. New York: Pearson Longman; 2009.

62. McKinley, Jesse. Horse advocates pull for underdog in roundups. *New York Times* [Internet]. 2010 Sep 5 [cited 2013 May 3]; Available from: www.nytimes.com/2010/09/06/us/06horses.html?pagewanted=all&_r=0

63. Peacock, Doug. The Yellowstone massacre. *Audubon Magazine*. 1997; (May-June): 41–9 & 102–10.

64. Loomis, Molly. Bison and boundaries: Can Yellowstone's signature mammal and the region's ranchers just get along? *Sierra Magazine* [Internet]. 2013; (November/December); Available from: www.sierraclub.org/sierra/201311/yellowstone-wildlife-free-roaming-bison.aspx

65. Gallatin Wildlife Association. Anti-Montana Bison Bill-SB 143 [Internet]. 2013 [cited 2013 Dec 25]; Available from: www.gallatinwildlifeassociation.org/sb%20143%20alert.htm

66. U.S. House of Representatives. Endangered species act implementation: Science or politics? Oversight hearing before the committee on natural resources. [Internet]. Government Printing Office; 2007 [cited 2016 Mar 24]; Available from: www.gpo.gov/fdsys/pkg/CHRG-110hhrg35221/html/CHRG-110hhrg35221.htm

67. Utah Division of Wildlife Resources. Hunting: Questions about Utah's predator control program [Internet]. 2015 [cited 2015 Jan 23]; Available from: http://wildlife.utah.gov/hunting-in-utah/118-hunting/big-game/892-questions-about-utahs-predator-control-program.html

68. Utah Division of Wildlife Resources. Utah's predator control program summary: Program activities and data from July 1, 2013 through June 30, 2014 [Internet]. 2014 [cited 2015 Jan 23]; Available from: http://wildlife.utah.gov/pdf/predator_program_summary_2014.pdf

69. Thuermer, Angus M. Critical mule deer research relies on fundraising [Internet]. *Wyofile*; 2015 [cited 2015 Jan 23]; Available from: www.wyofile.com/critical-mule-deer-research-relies-fundraising/

70. McBeath, Jerry. Greenpeace v. national marine fisheries service: Steller sea lions and commercial fisheries in the north pacific. *Alsk Law Rev*. 2004; 21(1): 1–42.

71. Fascione, Nina, Delach, Aimee, Smith, Martin E. Introduction. In: Fascione, Nina, Delach, Aimee, Smith, Martin E., editors. *People and predators: From conflict to coexistence*. Washington, D.C.: Island Press; 2004. p. 1–8.

72. Eisenberg, Cristinia. *The carnivore way: Coexisting with and conserving north America's predators*. Washington, D.C.: Island Press; 2014.

73. Kauffman, Matthew J., Brodie, Jedediah F., Jules, Erik S. Are wolves saving Yellowstone's aspen? A landscape-level test of a behaviorally mediated trophic cascade. *Ecology*. 2010; 91(9): 2742–55.

74. Mech, L. David. Is science in danger of sanctifying the wolf? *Biol Conserv*. 2012; 150(1): 143–9.

75. Ripple, William J., Beschta, Robert L. Trophic cascades in Yellowstone: The first 15 years after wolf reintroduction. *Biol Conserv*. 2012; 145(1): 205–13.

76. Shivik, John. *The predator paradox: Ending the war with wolves, bears, cougars, and coyotes*. Boston: Beacon Press; 2014.

77. Marshall, Kristin N, Hobbs, N. Thompson, Cooper, David J. Stream hydrology limits recovery of riparian ecosystems after wolf reintroduction. *Proc R Soc Lond B Biol Sci*. 2013; 280(1756): 1–7.

78. Rooney, Thomas P., Anderson, Dean P. Are wolf-mediated trophic cascades boosting biodiversity in the great lakes region? In: Wydeven, Adrian, Van Deelen, Timothy R., Heske, Edward J., editors. *Recovering of gray wolves in the Great Lakes region of the United States*. New York: Springer; 2009. p. 205–15.

79. Estes, James A., Terborgh, John, Brashares, Justin S., Power, Mary E., Berger, Joel, Bond, William J. et al. Trophic downgrading of planet Earth. *Science*. 2011; 333(6040): 301–6.

80. Estes, James A. Carnivory and trophic connectivity in kelp forests. In: Ray, Justina C., Redford, Kent H., Steneck, Robert S., Berger, Joel, editors. *Large carnivores and the conservation of biodiversity*. Washington, D.C.: Island Press; 2005. p. 61–81.

81. Boutin, Stan. Top carnivores and biodiversity conservation in the boreal forest. In: Ray, Justina C., Redford, Kent H., Steneck, Robert S., Berger, Joel, editors. *Large carnivores and the conservation of biodiversity*. Washington, D.C.: Island Press; 2005. p. 362–80.

82. Ray, Justina C. Large carnivorous animals as tools for conserving biodiversity: Assumptions and uncertainties. In: Ray, Justina C., Redford, Kent H., Steneck, Robert S., Berger, Joel, editors. *Large carnivores and the conservation of biodiversity*. Washington, D.C.: Island Press; 2005. p. 34–59.

83. Novaro, Andres J., Walker, R. Susan. Human-induced changes in the effect of top carnivores on biodiversity in the Patagonian steppe. In: Ray, Justina C., Redford, Kent H., Steneck, Robert S., Berger, Joel, editors. *Large carnivores and the conservation of biodiversity*. Washington, D.C.: Island Press; 2005. p. 268–88.

84. Miquelle, Dale, G. Tigers and wolves in the Russian far east: Competitive exclusion, functional redundancy, and conservation implications. In: Ray, Justina C., Redford, Kent H., Steneck, Robert S., Berger, Joel, editors. *Large carnivores and the conservation of biodiversity*. Washington, D.C.: Island Press; 2005. p. 179–207.

85. McClanahan, Tim R. Recovery of carnivores, trophic cascades, and diversity in coral reef marine parks. In: Ray, Justina C., Redford, Kent H., Steneck, Robert S., Berger, Joel, editors. *Large carnivores and the conservation of biodiversity*. Washington, D.C.: Island Press; 2005. p. 247–67.

86. Kerby, Jacob L, Richards-Hrdlicka, Kathryn L., Storfer, Andrew, Andrew, David K. An examination of amphibian sensitivity to environmental contaminants: Are amphibians poor canaries? *Ecol Lett*. 2010; 13(1): 60–7.

87. Cawley, R. McGreggor, Freemuth, John C. Science, politics, and federal Lands. In: Smith, Zachary A., Freemuth, John C., editors. *Environmental politics and policy in the west*. Boulder: University Press of Colorado; 2007. p. 69–88.

88. Weber, Bill. Culturally determined wildlife populations: The problem of the designer ark. In: Guynup, Sharon, editor. *2006 State of the wild: A global portrait of wildlife, wildlands, and oceans*. Washington, D.C.: Island Press; 2005. p. 233–9.

89. Nie, Martin A. The sociopolitical dimensions of wolf management and restoration in the United States. *Hum Ecol Rev* [Internet]. 2001 [cited 2013 Apr 6]; 8(1); Available from: www.humanecologyreview.org/pastissues/her81/81nie.pdf

90. Gehring, Thomas, Ruffing, Eva. When aguments prevail over power: The CITES procedure for the listing of endangered species. *Glob Environ Polit*. 2008; 8(2): 123–48.

91. Metrick, Andrew, Weitzman, Martin L. Patterns of behavior in endangered species preservation. *Land Econ*. 1996; 72(1): 1–16.

92. Wilcove, David S. *The condor's shadow: The loss and recovery of wildlife in America*. New York: W.H. Freeman and Company; 1999.

93. Swedlow, Brendon. Scientists, judges, and spotted owls: Policymakers in the pacific northwest. *Duke Environ Law Policy Forum*. 2003; 10(3): 187–288.

94. Florida Panther Recovery Team. Technical/agency draft: Florida panther recovery plan. (puma concolor coryi). [Internet]. 2006 [cited 2015 Apr 30]; Available from: http://digitalmedia.fws.gov/cdm/singleitem/collection/document/id/1123/rec/11#img_view_container

95. Suri, Manil. Mathematicians and blue crabs. *New York Times* [Internet]. 2015 May 2 [cited 2015 May 3]; Available from: www.nytimes.com/2015/05/03/opinion/sunday/manil-suri-mathematicians-and-blue-crabs.html?_r=0

96. Alston, Lee J., Andersson, Krister, Smith, Steven M. Payment for environmental services: Hypotheses and evidence. January. Working Paper 18740. [Internet]. National Bureau of Economic Research; 2013; Available from: www.nber.org/papers/w18740

97. Naeem, S., Ingram, J. C., Varga, A., Agardy, T., Barten, P., Bennett, G. et al. Get the science right when paying for nature's services: Few projects adequately address design and evaluation. *Science*. 2015; 347(6227): 1206–7.

98. Sommerville, Matt M., Milner-Gulland, E.J., Jones, Julia P.G. The challenge of monitoring biodiversity in payment for environmental service interventions. *Biol Conserv.* 2011; 144(12): 2832–41.

99. Pattanayak, Subhrendu K, Wunder, Sven, Ferraro, Paul J. Show me the money: Do payments supply environmental services in developing countries? *Rev Environ Econ Policy.* 2010; 4(2): 254–74.

100. Jackson, Peter. Fifty years in the tiger world: An introduction. In: Tilson, Ronald, Nyhus, Philip J., editors. *Tigers of the world: The science, politics, and conservation of panthera tigris.* Amsterdam: Academic Press; 2010. p. 1–15.

101. Tobin, Richard J. *The expendable future: U.S. politics and the protection of biological diversity.* Durham: Duke University Press; 1990.

102. Beatley, Timothy. Preserving biodiversity through the use of habitat conservation plans. In: Porter, Douglas R., Salvesen, David A., editors. *Collaborative planning for wetlands and wildlife: Issues and examples.* Washington, D.C.: Island Press; 1995. p. 35–74.

103. U.S. General Accountability Office. Endangered species act: The U.S. fish and wildlife service has incomplete information about effects on listed species from section 7 consultations [Internet]. U.S. General Accountability Office GAO-09–550; 2009 [cited 2016 Mar 24]; Available from: www.gao.gov/assets/290/289991.pdf

104. Kareiva, Peter, Adelman, Sandy, Doak, Daniel, Elderd, Bret, Groom, Martha, Hoekstra, Jonathan et al. Using science in habitat conservation plans [Internet]. 1999 [cited 2013 Jun 13]; Available from: www.nceas.ucsb.edu/files/Kareiva%20Using%20science %20in%20habitat%20conservation%20plans.pdf

105. Thomas, Craig W. Habitat conservation planning: Certainly empowered, somewhat deliberative, questionably democratic. *Polit Soc.* 2001; 29(1): 105–30.

106. Tilson, Ronald, Nyhus, Philip J., Franklin, Neil, Bastoni, Sriyanto, Yunus, Mohammad. Tiger restoration in Asia: Ecological theory vs. sociological reality. In: Maehr, David, Noss, Reed F., Larkin, Jeffery L., editors. *Large mammal restoration: Ecological and sociological challenges in the 21st century.* Washington, D.C.: Island Press; 2001.

107. Punt, Andre E., Smith, Anthony D.M. The gospel of maximum sustainable yield in fisheries management: birth, crucifixion and reincarnation. In: Reynolds, John D., Mace, Georgina M., Redford, Kent H., Robinson, John G., editors. *Conservation of exploited species.* Cambridge: Cambridge University Press; 2001. p. 41–66.

108. Arlinghaus, Robert, Cooke, Steven J. Recreational fisheries: Socioeconomic importance, conservation issues and management challenges. In: Dickson, Barney, Hutton, Jon, Adams, William N., editors. *Recreational hunting, conservation and rural livelihoods: Science and practice.* Oxford: Wiley-Blackwell; 2009. p. 39–58.

109. Sanderson, Steven. Getting the biology right in a political sort of way. In: Reynolds, John D., Mace, Georgina M., Redford, Kent H., Robinson, John G., editors. *Conservation of exploited species.* Cambridge: Cambridge University Press; 2001. p. 462–82.

110. Samways, Michael J. Conserving invertebrates: How many can be saved, and how? In: Leader-Williams, Nigel, Adams, William M., Smith, Robert J., editors. *Trade-offs in conservation: deciding what to save.* Oxford: Wiley-Blackwell; 2010. p. 97–117.

111. Economist. Obduracy in the face of hypocrisy. 2003;(December 30); Available from: www.economist.com/node/2313082

112. Wilhere, George. Adaptive management in habitat conservation plans. *Conserv Biol.* 2002;16(1):20–9.

113. Keller, Sarah Jane. Climate-based wolverine listing delayed by scientific disputes. *High Country News* [Internet]. 2014 Feb 25 [cited 2014 Mar 14]; Available from: www.hcn.org/blogs/goat/climate-based-wolverine-listing-delayed-by-scientific-disputes-1?utm_source=wcn1&utm_medium=email

114. McKelvey, K. S., Copeland, J. P., Schwartz, M. K., Littell, J. S., Aubry, K. B., Squires, J. R. et al. Climate change predicted to shift wolverine distributions, connectivity, and dispersal corridors. *Ecol Appl.* 2011; 21(8): 2882–97.

115. Copeland, J. P., McKelvey, K. B., Aubry, A. Landa, Persson, J., Inman, R.M., Krebs, J., et al. The bioclimatic envelope of the wolverine (Gulo gulo): Do climatic constraints limit its geographic distribution. *Can J Zool.* 2010; 88: 233–46.

116. Magoun, Audry J. Re: Extension of the comment period on the proposed wolverine listing determination [Internet]. 2013 [cited 2016 Mar 23]; Available from: www.fws.gov/mountain-prairie/science/PeerReviewDocs/10242013_docs/Aubry%20Review/MagounComments WolverineListingSecondRound.pdf

117. Inman, Robert M. Review of the United States fish and wildlife service's proposed rule to list wolverines as a threatened species in the contiguous United States, May 2013 [Internet]. 2013 [cited 2016 Mar 26]; Available from: www.fws.gov/mountain-prairie/science/PeerRe viewDocs/10242013_docs/Inman%20Review/1%20Summary%20of%20Comments%20on %20the%20Proposed%20Rule%20May%202013.pdf

118. Wuerthner, George. Montana fish wildlife and parks maintains wolverine trapping. *Wildlife News* [Internet]. 2012 Aug 2 [cited 2014 Mar 8]; Available from: www.thewildlifenews.com/2012/08/02/montana-fish-wildlife-and-parks-maintains-wolverine-trapping

119. U.S. Fish and Wildlife Service. Service determines wolverine does not warrant protection under Endangered Species Act. [Internet]. 2014 [cited 2014 Aug 15]; Available from: www.fws.gov/news/ShowNews.cfm?ID=CB5069E7-CFB9-BC06-C70E63988DF271A7

120. Wildlife Management Institute. FWS withdraws proposal to list wolverines under ESA. Outdoor News Bulletin [Internet]. 2014 Aug 14 [cited 2014 Aug 18]; 68(8); Available from: http://wildlifemanagementinstitute.org/index.php?option=com_content&view=article&id=762: fws-withdraws-proposal-to-list-wolverines-under-esa&catid=34:ONB%20Articles&Itemid=54

121. Jiminez, M.D. U.S. Fish and Wildlife Service review of the 2013 wolf population in the NRM [Internet]. 2014 [cited 2015 Dec 18]; Available from: www.fws.gov/mountain-prairie/species/mammals/wolf/NRM_DPS_2013_Review.pdf

122. Creel, Scott, Becker, Matthew, Christianson, David, Droge, E., Hammerschlag, Neil, Hayward, Matt W. et al. Questionable policy for large carnivore hunting. *Science.* 2015; 350(6267): 1473–5.

123. Cronin, Matthew A. The greater sage-grouse story: Do we have it right? *Rangelands.* 2015; 37(5): 200–4.

124. U.S. House of Representatives. Sound science for Endangered Species Act planning act of 2002 [Internet]. 2002 [cited 2016 Mar 24]; Available from: www.congress.gov/107/crpt/hrpt751/CRPT-107hrpt751.pdf

125. U.S. Fish and Wildlife Service. Endangered and threatened wildlife and plants: Threatened status for Gunnison sage-grouse. Final rule [Internet]. 2014 [cited 2014 Nov 19]; Available from: www.fws.gov/mountain-prairie/species/birds/gunnisonsagegrouse/GUSGFinalListin gRule_11122014.pdf

126. Vredenburg, Harrie, Westley, Frances R., Miller, Philip S. Strangers at the party: An industry strategy perspective on PHVS. In: Westley, Frances R., Miller, Philip S., editors.

Experiments in consilience: Integrating social and scientific responses to save endangered species. Washington, D.C.: Island Press; 2003. p. 298–320.

127. Hamilton, Joan. The owl and the scientist. *Sierra Magazine*. 1991; (July-August): 20–4.

128. Duffy, Rosaleen. *Killing for conservation: Wildlife policy in Zimbabwe*. Oxford: International African Institute in association with James Curry; 2000.

129. Matthiessen, Peter. *Tigers in the snow*. New York: North Point Press; 2000.

130. Dupree, Joe. Cat on a collision course. *National Wildlife Magazine* [Internet]. 2007 [cited 2012 Aug 13]; 45(3); Available from: www.nwf.org/News-and-Magazines/National-Wildlife/Animals/Archives/2007/Cat-on-a-Collision-Course.aspx

131. Carbyn, Lu. *The buffalo wolf: Predators, prey, and the politics of nature*. Washington, D.C.: Smithsonian Books; 2003.

132. Wildlife Management Institute. A comprehensive review and evaluation of the red wolf (*canis rufus*) recovery program. final report [Internet]. 2014 [cited 2014 Nov 25]; Available from: www.fws.gov/redwolf/reviewdocuments/WMI-Red-Wolf-Review-FINAL-11142014.pdf

133. Franklin, Adrian. *Animal nation: The true story of animals and Australia*. Sydney: University of New South Wales Press Ltd.; 2006.

134. Carolan, Michael S. The politics in environmental science: The Endangered Species Act and the Preble's mouse controversy. *Environ Polit*. 2008; 17(3): 449–65.

135. Yaffee, Steven Lewis. *Prohibitive policy: Implementing the federal Endangered Species Act*. Cambridge: MIT Press; 1982.

136. Symanski, Richard. Dances with horses: Lessons from the environmental fringe. *Conserv Biol*. 1996; 10(3): 708–12.

137. Schiff, Damien, MacDonald, Julie. The Endangered Species Act turns 40 – Hold the applause. *Wall Street Journal* [Internet]. 2013 Dec 27 [cited 2013 Dec 28]; Available from: http://online.wsj.com/news/articles/SB10001424052702303497804579240682942455964#printMode

138. U.S. Fish and Wildlife Service. Endangered and threatened wildlife and plants; revision to the regulations for the nonessential experimental population of the Mexican wolf [Internet]. 2015 [cited 2015 Jan 31]; Available from: www.gpo.gov/fdsys/pkg/FR-2015-01-16/pdf/2015-00436.pdf

139. Hull, Jeff. The grizzly truth. *Outside Magazine* [Internet]. 2012 June [cited 2012 May 19]; Available from: www.outsideonline.com/outdoor-adventure/natural-intelligence/The-Grizzly-Truth.html

140. Doremus, Holly, Tarlock, A. Dan. *Water war in the Klamath basin: Macho law, combat biology, and dirty politics*. Washington, D.C.: Island Press; 2008.

141. New York Times. Editorial: Wolves under review. 2013 Aug 15 [cited 2013 Aug 15]; Available from: www.nytimes.com/2013/08/16/opinion/wolves-under-review.html?emc=edit_tnt_20130815&tntemail0=y&_r=0&pagewanted=print

142. Cart, Julie. Plan to remove wolves from endangered species list on hold. *Los Angeles Times* [Internet]. 2013 Aug 12; Available from: www.latimes.com/news/science/sciencenow/la-sci-sn-wolf-delisting-on-hold-20130812,0,6991561.story

143. Maughan, Ralph. Some gray wolf peer review panel members axed by USFWS. *The Wildlife News* [Internet]. 2013 Aug 8 [cited 2013 Aug 16]; Available from: www.thewildlifenews.com/2013/08/08/gray-wolf-experts-axed-by-usfws/

144. U.S. Fish and Wildlife Service. Endangered and threatened wildlife and plants; designation of critical habitat for the fluted kidneyshell and slabside pearly mussel: A rule by the fish and

wildlife service on 09/26/2013 [Internet]. 2013 [cited 2013 Sep 26]; Available from: www.federalregister.gov/articles/2013/09/26/2013–23357/endangered-and-threatened-wild-life-and-plants-designation-of-critical-habitat-for-the-fluted

145. Greenwald, D. Noah, Suckling, Kieran F., Pimm, Stuart L. Critical habitat and the role of peer review in government. *BioScience*. 2012; 62(7): 686–90.

146. Hodges, Karen E, Elder, Jason. Critical habitat designation under the US Endangered Species Act: How are biological criteria used? *Biol Conserv*. 2008; 141(10): 2662–8.

147. Robinson, Michael J. *Predatory bureaucracy: The extermination of the wolf and the transformation of the west*. Boulder: The University of Colorado Press; 2005.

148. Meine, Curt. Early wolf research and conservation in the great lakes region. In: Wydeven, Adrian, Van Dee;em, Timothy R., Heske, Edward J., editors. *Recovering of gray wolves in the great lakes region of the United States*. New York: Springer; 2009. p. 1–13.

149. Leong, Kirsten M., Decker, Daniel J., Lauber, T. Bruce. Stakeholders as beneficiaries of wildlife management. In: Decker, Daniel J., Riley, Shawn J., Siemer, William F., editors. *Human dimensions of wildlife management*. 2nd ed. Baltimore: The Johns Hopkins University Press; 2012. p. 26–43.

150. Richie, Lauren, Oppenheimer, J. Daniel, Clark, Susan G. Social process in grizzly bear management: lessons for collaborative governance and natural resource policy. *Policy Sci*. 2012; 45(3): 265–91.

151. Williams, Ted. Bait and switch. *Audubon Magazine* [Internet]. 2008 March-April [cited 2016 Apr 20]; Available from: http://archive.audubonmagazine.org/incite/incite0803.html

152. Williams, Ted. Incite: Going catatonic. *Audubon Magazine*. 2004 September-October: 22–8.

153. Doremus, Holly. Scientific and political integrity in environmental policy. *Tex Law Rev*. 2008; 86: 1601–53.

154. Williams, Ted. Bad shot. *Audubon Magazine*. 2011 May-June: 50–8.

155. Rawson, Timothy. *Changing tracks: Predators and politics in Mt. McKinley national park*. Fairbanks: University of Alaska Press; 2001.

156. Wagner, Frederick H. *Yellowstone's destabilized ecosystem*. Oxford: Oxford University Press; 2006.

157. McPhee, John. *Encounters with the archdruid*. New York: Farrar. Straus and Giroux; 1971.

158. Kevin, Brian. Everybody hates Chuck Schwartz. *Sierra Magazine*. 2001 January-February: 26–31 & 102.

159. Decker, Daniel J., Chase, Lisa C. Stakeholder involvement: Seeking solutions in changing times. In: Decker, Daniel J., Brown, Tommy L., Siemer, William F., editors. *Human dimensions of wildlife management in North America*. Bethesda: The Wildlife Society; 2001. p. 133–52.

160. Lavelle, Marianne. Last dance? *Science*. 2015; 348(6241): 1300–5.

161. Ernst, Howard R. *Chesapeake Bay blues: Science, politics, and the struggle to save the bay*. Lanham: Rowman & Littlefield Publishers, Inc.; 2003.

162. Durbin, Kathie. *Tongass: Pulp politics and the fight for the Alaska rain forest*. 2nd ed. Corvallis: Oregon State University Press; 2005.

163. Goodall, Jane. *Hope for animals and their world: How endangered species are being rescued from the brink*. New York: Grand Central Publishing; 2009.

164. Keiter, Robert B. *Keeping faith with nature: Ecosystems, democracy, & America's public lands*. New Haven: Yale University Press; 2003.

165. Hunter Jr., Malcolm L., Bean, Michael J., Lindenmayer, David B., Wilcove, David S. Thresholds and the mismatch between environmental laws and ecosystems. *Conserv Biol*. 2009; 23(4): 1053–5.

166. Berger, Joel, Cain, Steven L. Moving beyond science to protect a mammalian migration corridor. *Conserv Biol*. 2014; 28(5): 1142–50.

167. Noss, Reed F., Dobson, Andrew P., Baldwin, Robert, Beier, Paul, Davis, Cory R., Della-Sala, Dominick A. et al. Bolder thinking for conservation. In: Wuerthner, George, Crist, Eileen, Butler, Tom, editors. *Protecting the wild: Parks and wilderness, the foundation for conservation*. Washington, D.C.: Island Press; 2015. p. 16–20.

168. Jenkins-Smith, Hank C., Sabatier, Paul A. Evaluating the advocacy coalition framework. *J Public Policy*. 1994; 14(2): 175–203.

Chapter 3 References

1. Edelman, Murray. *The symbolic uses of politics*. Urbana: University of Illinois Press; 1964.

2. Pressman, Jeffrey L., Wildavsky, Aaron. *Implementation: How great expectations in Washington are dashed in Oakland: Or, why it's amazing that federal programs work at all, this being a saga of the Economic Development Administration as told by two sympathetic observers who seek to build morals on a foundation of ruined hopes*. 3rd ed. Berkeley: University of California; 1984.

3. Okrent, Daniel. *Last call: The rise and fall of prohibition*. New York: Scribner; 2010.

4. Williamson, Elizabeth. GAO denounces bay cleanup efforts. *Washington Post* [Internet]. 2005 Nov 16 [cited 2016 Feb 10]; Available from: www.washingtonpost.com/wp-dyn/content/article/2005/11/15/AR2005111501506.html

5. Williams, Ted. The new guardians. *Audubon Magazine*. 1995 May-June: 34–9.

6. Tobin, Richard J. *The expendable future: U.S. politics and the protection of biological diversity*. Durham: Duke University Press; 1990.

7. Donahue, Debra L. *The western range revisited: Removing livestock from public lands to conserve native biodiversity*. Norman: University of Oklahoma Press; 1999.

8. Schorger, A.W. *The passenger pigeon*. Norman: University of Oklahoma Press; 1955.

9. Chase, Lisa C., Lamber, T. Bruce, Decker, Daniel J. Citizen participation in wildlife management decisions. In: Decker, Daniel J., Brown, Tommy L., Siemer, William F., editors. *Human dimensions of wildlife management in North America*. Bethesda: The Wildlife Society; 2001. p. 153–70.

10. Tresaugue, Matthew. Tiny lizard at center of big fight in the oil patch. *Houston Chronicle* [Internet]. 2015 Feb 19 [cited 2015 Mar 19]; Available from: www.mrt.com/news/article_1b412efc-b8a7-11e4-86ef-df1fa67f0cae.html

11. Gilman, Sarah. Fish and wildlife whistleblower retaliation case raises questions. *High Country News* [Internet]. 2015 Mar 9 [cited 2015 Mar 14]; Available from: www.hcn.org/articles/u-s-fish-and-wildlife-whistleblower-retaliation-case-raises-questions?utm_source=wcn1&utm_medium=email

12. Nelson, Fred. Introduction: The politics of natural resource governance in Africa. In: Nelson, Fred, editor. *Community rights, conservation and contested land: The politics of natural resource governance in Africa*. London: Earthscan; 2010. p. 3–31.

13. Steinhart, Peter. Bear of the clouds. *Audubon Magazine*. 1989 July: 92–103.

14. Wilkinson, Allie. Disappearing porpoise: Down to 97 and dropping fast. *New York Times* [Internet]. 2015 Jun 19 [cited 2015 Jun 19]; Available from: www.nytimes.com/2015/06/19/science/disappearing-porpoise-down-to-97-and-dropping-fast.html?emc=edit_tnt_20150619&nlid=10365419&tntemail0=y&_r=0

15. Rabinowitz, Alan. Helping a species go extinct; The Sumatran rhino in Borneo. In: Michael, Mark A., editor *Preserving wildlife: An international perspective*. New York: Humanity Books; 2000. p. 122–35.

16. Duffy, Rosaleen. *Nature crime: How we're getting conservation wrong*. New Haven: Yale University Press; 2010.

17. Tilson, Ronald, Nyhus, Philip J., Rubianto, Arief, Sriyanto. Poaching and poisoning of tigers in Sumatra for the domestic market. In: Tilson, Ronald, Nyhus, Philip J., editors. *Tigers of the world: The science, politics, and conservation of panthera tigris*. 2nd ed. Amsterdam: Academic Press; 2010. p. 101–12.

18. Arcese, Peter, Hando, Justine, Campbell, Ken. Historical and present-day anti-poaching efforts in Serengeti. In: Sinclair, A.R.E., Arcese, Peter, editors. *Serengeti II: Dynamics, management, and conservation of an ecosystem*. Chicago: The University of Chicago Press; 1995. p. 506–33.

19. Rigney, Matt. *In pursuit of giants: One man's global search for the last of the great fish*. New York: Penguin Group; 2012.

20. Gibson, Clark C. *Politicians and poachers: The political economy of wildlife policy in Africa*. Cambridge: Cambridge University Press; 1999.

21. Williams, Laura. Saga of the Saiga. *National Wildlife Magazine* [Internet]. 2004 [cited 2016 May 18]; 42(3); Available from: www.nwf.org/News-and-Magazines/National-Wildlife/Animals/Archives/2004/Saga-of-the-Saiga.aspx

22. Chivers, C.J. Corruption endangers a treasure of the Caspian. *New York Times* [Internet]. 2005 Nov 28 [cited 2016 Apr 7]; Available from: www.nytimes.com/2005/11/28/world/asia/corruption-endangers-a-treasure-of-the-caspian.html

23. Buchori, Damayati, Ardhian, David. Local involvement in emerging democracy: A case study of biodiversity management in Indonesia. In: O'Riordan, Tim, Stoll-Kleeman, Susanne, editors. *Biodiversity, sustainability and human communities: Protecting beyond the protected*. Cambridge: Cambridge University Press; 2002. p. 275–91.

24. Onishi, Norimitus. Humans intrude on an Indonesian park. *New York Times* [Internet]. 2009 Jun 14 [cited 2016 Apr 7]; Available from: www.nytimes.com/2009/06/14/world/asia/14borneo.html

25. Sturm, Michael. The mixed experience of private sector involvement in biodiversity management in Costa Rica. In: O'Riordan, Tim, Stoll-Kleemann, Susanne, editors. *Biodiversity, sustainability and human communities: Protecting beyond the protected*. Cambridge: Cambridge University Press; 2002. p. 243–59.

26. Duffy, Rosaleen. *Killing for conservation: Wildlife policy in Zimbabwe*. Oxford: International African Institute in association with James Curry; 2000.

27. Le Prestre, Philippe, Stoett, Peter, Beazley, Karen, Boardman, Robert. International initiatives, commitments, and disappointments: Canada, CITES, and the CBD. In: Beazley, Karen, Boardman, Robert, editors. *Politics of the wild: Canada and endangered species*. Oxford: Oxford University Press; 2001. p. 190–216.

28. Boardman, Robert. Risk politics in western states: Canadian species in comparative perspective. In: Beazley, Karen, Boardman, Robert, editors. *Politics of the wild: Canada and endangered species*. Oxford: Oxford University Press; 2001. p. 167–89.

29. Halpern, Benjamin S. Conservation: making marine protected areas work. *Nature*. 2014; 506 (February 13): 167–8.

30. Edgar, Graham J., Stuart-Smith, Rick D., Willis, Trevor J., Kininmonth, Stuart, Baker, Susan C., Banks, Stuart et al. Global conservation outcomes depend on marine protected areas with five key features. *Nature*. 2014; 506(February 13): 216–20.

31. Bielski, Vince. Armed and dangerous. *Sierra Magazine*. 1995 September-October: 33–4.

32. Williams, Ted. Fatal attraction. *Audubon Magazine*. 1997 September-October: 24–31.

33. Robinson, John. Response to David Brown: The view from Versailles contrasts with local reality. In: Guynup, Sharon, editor. *2006 state of the wild: A global portrait of wildlife, wildlands, and oceans*. Washington, D.C.: Island Press; 2005. p. 158.

34. Williams, Ted. The exclusion of sea turtles. *Audubon Magazine*. 1990 January-February: 24–33.

35. Russell, Sharman Apt. *Kill the cowboy: A battle of mythology in the new west*. Reading, MA: Addison-Wesley Publishing Company; 1993.

36. Bevington, Douglas. *Rebirth of environmentalism: Grassroots activism from the spotted owl to the polar bear*. Washington, D.C.: Island Press; 2009.

37. McCarthy, James. States of nature and environmental enclosures in the American. In: Peluso, Nancy Lee, Watts, Michael, editors. *Violent environments*. Ithaca: Cornell University Press; 2002. p. 117–45.

38. Keiter, Robert B. *Keeping faith with nature: Ecosystems, democracy, & America's public lands*. New Haven: Yale University Press; 2003.

39. Helvarg, David. *The war against the greens*. Boulder: Johnson Books; 2004.

40. Bass, Rick. The feds. In: Lynch, Tom, editor. *El lobo: Readings on the Mexican gray wolf*. Salt Lake City: The University of Utah Press; 2005. p. 156–63.

41. High Country News. Mapping threats on public land: Intimidation of federal officials is widespread across the West. 2014 Oct 27 [cited 2014 Oct 28]; Available from: www.hcn.org/issues/46.18/incidents-map/

42. Helvarg, David. "Wise Use" in the white house yesterday's fringe, today's cabinet official. *Sierra Magazine* [Internet]. 2004 September-October [cited 2016 Apr 7]; Available from: http://vault.sierraclub.org/sierra/200409/wiseuse.asp

43. McConahay, Mary Jo. Sweet waist of America. *Sierra Magazine*. 1993 January-February: 42–9 & 153–7.

44. Nagourney, Adam. A defiant rancher savors the audience that rallied to his side. *New York Times*. 2014 Apr 23 [cited 2014 Nov 10]; Available from: www.nytimes.com/2014/04/24/us/politics/rancher-proudly-breaks-the-law-becoming-a-hero-in-the-west.html?module=Search&mabReward=relbias%3As%2C%7B%221%22%3A%22RI%3A5%22%7D&_r=0

45. Wiles, Tay. An update on Nevada scofflaw Cliven Bundy. *High Country News* [Internet]. 2015 Mar 7 [cited 2015 Mar 15]; Available from: www.hcn.org/articles/cliven-bundy-rancher-nevada-scofflaw?utm_source=wcn1&utm_medium=email

46. O'Neill, Alan. Rancher in land dispute is a bully, not a hero. *Las Vegas Sun* [Internet]. 2014 Apr 6 [cited 2014 Nov 10]; Available from: www.lasvegassun.com/news/2014/apr/06/rancher-land-dispute-bully-not-hero/

47. Revkin, Andrew. Weighing Oregon standoff solutions, from arrests to birder invasion. *New York Times* [Internet]. 2016 Jan 5 [cited 2016 Jan 7]; Available from: http://dotearth.blogs.nytimes.com/2016/01/05/weighing-oregon-standoff-solutions-from-arrests-to-birdathons/?emc=edit_ty_20160105&nl=opinion&nlid=10365419

48. Neiwert, David. Not punishing the Bundys for the Nevada standoff led to the occupation in Oregon. *Washington Post* [Internet]. 2016 Jan 7 [cited 2016 Apr 7]; Available from: www.washingtonpost.com/posteverything/wp/2016/01/07/not-punishing-the-bundys-for-the-nevada-standoff-led-to-the-occupation-in-oregon/

49. Johnson, Kirk, Perez-Pena, Richard, Eckholm, Erik. Cautious response to armed Oregon protest. *New York Times* [Internet]. 2016 Jan 4 [cited 2016 Jan 7]; Available from:

www.nytimes.com/2016/01/05/us/in-oregon-law-enforcement-faces-dilemma-in-confronting-armed-group.html?emc=edit_th_20160105&nl=todaysheadlines&nlid=10365419

50. Thompson, Jonathan. The rise of the sagebrush sheriffs. *High Country News* [Internet]. 2016 Feb 2 [cited 2016 Feb 2]; Available from: www.hcn.org/issues/48.2/the-rise-of-the-sage brush-sheriffs

51. Johnson, Kirk. 25 plead not guilty in standoff at the Oregon wildlife refuge. *New York Times* [Internet]. 2016 Feb 24 [cited 2016 Feb 25]; Available from: www.nytimes.com/2016/02/25/us/25-plead-not-guilty-in-standoff-at-the-oregon-wildlife-refuge.html?emc=edit_th_20160225&nl=todaysheadlines&nlid=10365419&_r=0

52. Shogren, Elizabeth. Analyst: FBI let Malheur militants save face to end occupation. *High Country News* [Internet]. 2016 Feb 11 [cited 2016 Feb 12]; Available from: www.hcn.org/articles/fbi-analyst-says-the-remaining-occupiers-needed-a-surrender-ritual?utm_source=wcn1&utm_medium=email

53. Swearingen, Marshall. The BLM has armed up since 1978, but it's still outgunned. *High Country News* [Internet]. 2016 Jan 7 [cited 2016 Jan 8]; Available from: www.hcn.org/articles/bureau-of-land-management-outgunned-bundy-malheur-blm-sheriff?utm_source=wcn1&utm_medium=email

54. Klyza, Christopher McGrory, Sousa, David J. *American environmental policy: Beyond gridlock*. Cambridge: MIT Press; 2013.

55. Audubon Magazine. Is the ESA losing its bite? *Audubon Magazine*. 1991 July-August: 8–10.

56. Ernst, John P. *Federalism and the act. In:* Kohn, Kathryn A., editor. *Balancing on the brink of extinction: The Endangered Species Act and lessons for the future*. Washington, D.C.: Island Press; 1991. p. 98–113.

57. Wilcove, David S. *The condor's shadow: The loss and recovery of wildlife in America*. New York: W.H. Freeman and Company; 1999.

58. Biber, Eric, Brosi, Berry. Officious intermeddlers or citizen experts? Petitions and public production of information in environmental law. *UCLA Law Rev.* 2010; 58(2): 321–400.

59. Yaffee, Steven Lewis. *Prohibitive policy: Implementing the federal Endangered Species Act*. Cambridge: MIT Press; 1982.

60. Hunt, Constance Elizabeth. *Down by the river: The impact of federal water projects and policies on biological diversity*. Washington, D.C.: Island Press; 1988.

61. Arha, Kaush, Emmerich, John. Grizzly bear conservation in the greater Yellowstone ecosystem: A case study in the Endangered Species Act and federalism. In: Arha, Kaush, Thompson, Jr., Barton H., editors. *The Endangered Species Act and federalism: Effective conservation through greater state commitment*. London: RFF Press; 2011. p. 251–304.

62. Clarke, Jeanne Nienaber, McCool, Daniel C. *Staking out the terrain: Power and performance among natural resource agencies*. Albany: State University of New York Press; 1996.

63. Tennesen, Michael. Poaching, ancient traditions, and the law. *Audubon Magazine*. 1999 July-August: 90–7.

64. Bergman, Charles A. The bust. *Audubon Magazine*. 1991 May: 66–76.

65. Sachs, Jessica Snyder. Poisoning the imperiled. *National Wildlife Magazine* [Internet]. 2004 December-January [cited 2016 Apr 7]; Available from: www.nwf.org/News-and-Magazines/National-Wildlife/Animals/Archives/2004/Poisoning-the-Imperiled.aspx

66. Vucetich, John A., Nelson, Michael Paul. Conservation, or curation? *New York Times* [Internet]. 2014 Aug 20; Available from: www.nytimes.com/2014/08/21/opinion/conservation-or-curation.html?emc=edit_tnt_20140820&nlid=10365419&tntemail0=y&_r=0

67. Ashe, Dan, Sobeck, Eileen. Letter: Using scarce resources to save endangered species. *New York Times* [Internet]. 2014 [cited 2014 Sep 5]; Available from: www.nytimes.com/2014/09/

05/opinion/using-scarce-resources-to-save-endangered-species.html?emc=edit_tnt_20140904& nlid=10365419&tntemail0=y&_r=0

68. Nixon, Ron. Obama administration plans to aggressively target wildlife trafficking. *New York Times* [Internet]. 2015 Feb 11 [cited 2015 Feb 11]; Available from: www.nytimes.com/2015/ 02/12/us/politics/obama-administration-to-target-illegal-wildlife-trafficking.html?emc=edit_tnt_ 20150211&nlid=10365419&tntemail0=y

69. Alexander, Kristina. Warranted but precluded: What that means under the Endangered Species Act [Internet]. Congressional Research Service; 2010 [cited 2014 Oct 31]; Available from: http://ftp.ncseonline.org/NLE/CRSreports/10May/R41100.pdf

70. Smith, K. Mollie. Abuse of the warranted but precluded designation: A real or imagined purgatory. *Southeast Environ Law J* [Internet]. 2010 Fall [cited 2016 Apr 7]; Available from: http://works.bepress.com/k_smith/1/

71. WildEarth Guardians. On the waiting list [Internet]. 2011 [cited 2014 Oct 31]; Available from: www.wildearthguardians.org/site/PageServer?pagename=priorities_wildlife_ESA_listing_ waiting_list&AddInterest=1262

72. Rosner, Hillary. Rethinking the list. *Audubon Magazine* [Internet]. 2014 November-December [cited 2016 Apr 7]; Available from: www.audubon.org/magazine/november-december-2014/ rethinking-endangered-species-list

73. Beatley, Timothy. *Habitat conservation planning: Endangered species and urban growth*. Austin: The University of Texas Press; 1994.

74. Suckling, Kieran F., Taylor, Martin. Critical habitat and recovery. In: Goble, Dale, D., Scott, J. Michael, Davis, Frank W., editors. *The Endangered Species Act at thirty: Volume I: Renewing the conservation promise*. Washington, D.C.: Island Press; 2006. p. 75–89.

75. Seelye, Katharine Q. Ending logjam, U.S. reaches accord on endangered species. *New York Times* [Internet]. 2001 Aug 30 [cited 2013 Jul 13]; Available from: www.nytimes.com/2001/ 08/30/us/ending-logjam-us-reaches-accord-on-endangered-species.html

76. Wines, Michael. In Alaska, a battle to keep trees, or an industry, standing. *New York Times* [Internet]. 2014 Sep 27 [cited 2014 Sep 28]; Available from: www.nytimes.com/2014/09/28/ us/a-battle-to-keep-trees-or-an-industry-standing.html?ref=us&_r=0

77. Wildlife Management Institute. A comprehensive review and evaluation of the red wolf (*canis rufus*) recovery program. final report [Internet]. 2014 [cited 2014 Nov 25]; Available from: www.fws.gov/redwolf/reviewdocuments/WMI-Red-Wolf-Review-FINAL-11142014.pdf

78. Thirgood, Simon, Redpath, Steve. Hen harriers and red grouse: science, politics and human–wildlife conflict. *J Appl Ecol*. 2008; 45: 1550–4.

79. Huang, Shaojie. Trying to shield endangered animals from China's appetites. *New York Times* [Internet]. 2014 Apr 28 [cited 2014 Apr 28]; Available from: http://sinosphere.blogs .nytimes.com/2014/04/28/trying-to-shield-endangered-animals-from-chinas-appetites/?_php= true&_type=blogs&emc=edit_tnt_20140428&nlid=10365419&tntemail0=y&_r=0

80. Williams, Ted. The great butterfly bust. *Audubon Magazine*. 1996 March-April: 30–7.

81. Schueler, Donald G. Contract killers. *Sierra Magazine*. 1993 November-December: 70–6 & 96–7.

82. Robbins, Jim. Target green: Federal land managers under attack. *Audubon Magazine*. 1995 July-August: 82–5.

83. Bass, Rick. *The ninemile wolves*. New York: Ballantine Books; 1992.

84. Matthiessen, Peter. *Wildlife in America*. New York: Viking Penguin, Inc.; 1987.

85. Beatley, Timothy, Fries, T. James, Braun, David. The Balcones canyonlands conservation plan: A regional, multi-species approach. In: Porter, Douglas R., Salvesen, David A., editors.

Collaborative planning for wetlands and wildlife: Issues and examples. Washington, D.C.: Island Press; 1995. p. 75–92.

86. Wortman-Wunder, Emily. Do subdivisions designed for conservation actually help wildlife? *High Country News* [Internet]. 2012 Jun 11 [cited 2012 Jun 15]; Available from: www.hcn.org/issues/44.9/do-subdivisions-designed-for-conservation-actually-help-wildlife/print_view

87. Lenth, Buffy A., Knight, Richard L., Gilgert, Wendell C. Conservation value of clustered housing developments. *Conserv Biol.* 2006; 20(5): 1445–56.

88. Inslerman, Robert A. Wolf restoration in the Adirondacks: The perspective of the New York state department of environmental conservation. In: Sharpe, Virginia A., Norton, Bryan G., Donnelley, Strachan, editors. *Wolves and human communities: Biology, politics, and ethics.* Washington, D.C.: Island Press; 2001. p. 23–38.

89. Woinarski, J. C. Z., Fisher, Alaric. The Australian endangered species protection act 1992. *Conserv Biol.* 1999; 13(5): 959–62.

90. Nie, Martin. State wildlife policy and management: The scope and bias of political conflict. *Public Adm Rev.* 2004; 64(2): 221–33.

91. Nelson, Steve. Budget deal includes "de-listing" of wolves in Montana and Idaho. *The Daily Caller* [Internet]. 2011 Apr 12 [cited 2011 Apr 13]; Available from: http://dailycaller.com/2011/04/12/budget-deal-includes-de-listing-of-wolves-in-montana-and-idaho/

92. Elinson, Zusha. Shark-fin bans hard to police. *Wall Street Journal* [Internet]. 2014 Feb 25 [cited 2014 Feb 25]; Available from: http://online.wsj.com/news/articles/SB1000142405270230363640457939341096235346#printMode

93. Davis, Charles. The politics of grazing on federal lands: A policy change perspective. In: Repetto, Robert, editor. *Punctuated equilibrium and the dynamics of US environmental policy.* New Haven: Yale University Press; 2006. p. 232–52.

94. Koontz, Tomas, Bodine, Jennifer. Implementing ecosystem management in public agencies: Lessons from the U.S. bureau of land management and the forest service. *Conserv Biol.* 2008; 22(1): 60–9.

95. Peterson, Jodi. A recent history of land management in the Escalante region. *High Country News* [Internet]. 2015 Feb 16 [cited 2015 Feb 16]; Available from: http://www.hcn.org/issues/47.3/chainsaw-diplomacy/a-recent-history-of-land-management-in-the-escalante-region

96. Wyman, Katrina Miriam. Rethinking the ESA to reflect human dominion over nature. *N Y Univ Environ Law J.* 2008; 17: 490–528.

97. Brosi, Berry J., Biber, Eric G. Citizen involvement in the U.S. Endangered Species Act. *Science.* 2012; 337(6096): 802–3.

98. Achterman, Gail L, Doermann, Julia. Oregon coastal coho restoration and the ESA. In: Arha, Kaush, Thompson, Jr., Barton H., editors. *The Endangered Species Act and federalism: Effective conservation through greater state commitment.* London: RFF Press; 2011: 221–50.

99. Cashore, Benjamin, Howlett, Michael. Behavioral thresholds and institutional rigidities as explanations of punctuated equilibrium processes in Pacific northwest forest policy dynamics. In: Repetto, Robert, editor. *Punctuated equilibrium and the dynamics of US environmental policy.* New Haven: Yale University Press; 2006. p. 137–61.

100. Query, Shawn. Last dance? *Audubon Magazine.* 2008 March-April: 22.

101. Hoberg, George. How the way we make policy governs the policy we make. In: Salazar, Debra J., Alper, Donald K., editors. *Sustaining the forests of the Pacific coast: Forging truces in the war on the woods.* Vancouver: UBC Press; 2000. p. 25–53.

102. Nie, Martin. *The governance of western public lands: Mapping its present and future.* Lawrence: University of Kansas Press; 2008.
103. Murchison, Kenneth M. *The snail darter case: TVA versus the Endangered Species Act.* Lawrence: University of Kansas Press; 2007.
104. Wilson, Kurt. Wolf advocates challenge delisting at Missoula hearing. *Missoulian* [Internet]. 2011 Jul 26 [cited 2012 Apr 14]; Available from: http://missoulian.com/news/local/article_5a6e734a-b780-11e0-9c31-001cc4c03286.html
105. Herring, Hal. How the gray wolf lost its endangered status and how enviros helped. *High Country News* [Internet]. 2011 May 30 [cited 2011 Apr 24]; Available from: www.hcn.org/issues/43.9/how-the-gray-wolf-lost-its-endangered-status-and-how-enviros-helped.

Chapter 4 References

1. Scott, Douglas. In the national interest. *Sierra Magazine.* 1991 January-February: 40–4 & 121–37.
2. Robinson, Michael J. *Predatory bureaucracy: The extermination of the wolf and the transformation of the west.* Boulder: The University of Colorado Press; 2005.
3. Train, Russell E. *Politics, pollution, and pandas: An environmental memoir.* Washington, D.C.: Island Press/Shearwater Books; 2010.
4. Roman, Joe. *Listed: Dispatches from America's Endangered Species Act.* Cambridge: Harvard University Press; 2011.
5. Mann, Charles C., Plummer, Mark L. *Noah's choice: The future of endangered species.* New York: Alfred A. Knopf; 1995.
6. U.S. Senate. Committee on Environment and Public Works. Prepared by the Congressional Research Service of the Library of Congress. A legislative history of the Endangered Species Act of 1973, As Amended in 1976, 1977, 1978, 1979, and 1980 [Internet]. 1982 [cited 2016 Apr 10]. Report No.: Serial N. 97-6; Available from: www.eswr.com/docs/lh/leghist_1_10a.pdf
7. U.S. Senate. Senate Hearing 108–356 Endangered Species Act: Review of the consultation process required by section 7. Hearing Before the Subcommittee on Fisheries, Wildlife, and Water of the Committee on Environment and Public Works United States Senate 187th Congress First Session on an Examination of the Consulting Process required by Section 7 of the Endangered Species Act June 25, 2003 [Internet]. Sect. Hearing Before the Subcommittee on Fisheries, Wildlife, and Water of the Committee on Environment and Public Works United States Senat Washington, D.C.: Government Printing Office; Jun 25, 2003; Available from: https://bulk.resource.org/gpo.gov/hearings/108s/92378.pdf
8. U.S. House of Representatives. Endangered species act implementation: Science or politics? Oversight hearing before the committee on natural resources. [Internet]. Government Printing Office; 2007 [cited 2016 Mar 24]; Available from: www.gpo.gov/fdsys/pkg/CHRG-110hhrg35221/html/CHRG-110hhrg35221.htm
9. Strong, Douglas H. *Dreamers & defenders: American conservationists.* Lincoln: University of Nebraska; 1988.
10. Allin, Craig W. *The politics of wilderness preservation.* Westport: Greenwood Press; 1982.
11. Decker, Daniel J., Brown, Tommy L., Siemer, William F. Evolution of people-wildlife relations. In: Decker, Daniel J., Brown, Tommy L., Siemer, William F., editors. *Human dimensions of wildlife management in North America.* Lanham: The Wildlife Society; 2001. p. 3–22.

12. Satchell, M. The "wise use" movement. *US News & World Report*. 1991 Oct 21; 111(17): 74–7.

13. Balch, Alan, Press, Daniel, Spray, Sharon L., McGlothlin, Karen L. The politics of diversity. In: Spray, Sharon L., McGlothlin, Karen L., editors. *Loss of biodiversity*. Lanham: Rowman & Littlefield Publishers, Inc.; 2003. p. 119–55.

14. Cardwell, Diane, Krauss, Clifford. Frack quietly, please: Sage grouse is nesting. *New York Times* [Internet]. 2014 Jul 19 [cited 2014 Jul 23]; Available from: www.nytimes.com/2014/07/20/business/energy-environment/disparate-interests-unite-to-protect-greater-sage-grouse.html?emc=edit_th_20140720&nl=todaysheadlines&nlid=10365419

15. Repetto, Robert. Introduction. In: Repetto, Robert, editor. *Punctuated equilibrium and the dynamics of US environmental policy*. New Haven: Yale University Press; 2006. p. 1–23.

16. Davis, Charles. The politics of grazing on federal lands: A policy change perspective. In: Repetto, Robert, editor. *Punctuated equilibrium and the dynamics of US environmental policy*. New Haven: Yale University Press; 2006. p. 232–52.

17. Layzer, Judith A. *The environmental case: Translating values into policy*. Los Angeles: Sage; 2016.

18. Wuerthner, George. How the west was eaten. *Wilderness*. 1991; (Spring): 28–37.

19. Hartzog, Jr., George B. *Battling for the national parks*. Mt. Kisco: Moyer Bell Limited; 1988.

20. Prato, Tony, Fagre, Dan. *National parks and protected areas: Approaches for balancing social, economic, and ecological values*. Ames, IA: Blackwell Publishing Professional; 2005.

21. Nie, Martin. *The governance of western public lands: Mapping its present and future*. Lawrence: University of Kansas Press; 2008.

22. U.S. General Accountability Office. National wildlife refuges: Continuing problems with incompatible uses call for bold action [Internet]. 1989 [cited 2012 Oct 11]; Available from: www.gao.gov/assets/150/148073.pdf

23. Egan, Timothy. As easterners try to save west, westerners blanch. *New York Times* [Internet]. 1993 Aug 29 [cited 2016 Apr 9]; Available from: www.nytimes.com/1993/08/29/us/as-easterners-try-to-save-west-westerners-blanch.html?pagewanted=all

24. New York Times. For a wilder Rockies. *New York Times* [Internet]. 2009 Jul 7 [cited 2016 Jun 28]; Available from: www.nytimes.com/2009/07/07/opinion/07tue3.html?ref=topics

25. Keiter, Robert B. *Keeping faith with nature: Ecosystems, democracy, & America*. New Haven: Yale University Press; 2003.

26. Fleischner, Thomas L. Livestock grazing and wildlife conservation in the American west: Historical, policy and conservation biology perspectives. In: du Toit, John D., Kock, Richard, Deutsch, James C., editors. *Wild rangelands: Conserving wildlife while maintaining livestock in semi-arid ecosystems*. Oxford: Wiley-Blackwell; 2010. p. 235–65.

27. Schlickeisen, Roger. Overcoming cultural barriers to wolf reintroduction. In: Sharpe, Virginia A., Norton, Bryan G., Donnelley, Strachan, editors. *Wolves and human communities: biology, politics, and ethics*. Washington, D.C.: Island Press; 2001. p. 61–73.

28. Marvier, Michelle, Wong, Hazel. Resurrecting the conservation movement. *J Environ Stud*. 2012; 2: 291–5.

29. Gallup.com. Environment [Internet]. [cited 2016 Apr 12]; Available from: http://environment.research.yale.edu/documents/downloads/v-z/yale_enviro_poll.pdf

30. NBC/Wall Street Journal. Which do you think is more important: protecting endangered species from extinction even if some people may not be able to develop the land they own, or protecting the right of property owners to do what they want with their land, even though some species might become extinct as a result? [Internet]. 2005 [cited 2012 Oct 26];

Available from: www.publicagenda.com/charts/most-americans-say-protecting-endangered-species-more-important-protecting-property-rights

31. Gallup Survey. I'm going to read you a list of environmental problems. As I read each one, please tell me if you personally worry about this problem a great deal, a fair amount, or not at all [Internet]. 2008 [cited 2012 Oct 26]; Available from: www.publicagenda.com/charts/most-americans-say-protecting-endangered-species-more-important-protecting-property-rights

32. Cambridge Reports/Research International. National omnibus survey [Internet]. The iPOLL Databank, The Roper Center for Public Opinion Research, University of Connecticut; 1990 [cited 2007 May 22]; Available from: www.ropercenter.uconn.edu/ipoll.htm

33. Saad, Lydia. U.S. oil drilling gains favor with Americans [Internet]. 2011 [cited 2016 Apr 9]; Available from: www.gallup.com/poll/146615/oil-drilling-gains-favor-americans.aspx

34. Brailovskaya, Tatiana. Obstacles to protecting marine biodiversity through marine wilderness preservation: Examples from the New England region conservation biology. *Conserv Biol.* 1998; 12(6): 1236–40.

35. Wilcove, David S. *The condor's shadow: The loss and recovery of wildlife in America.* New York: W.H. Freeman and Company; 1999.

36. Williams, Ted. Waiting for wolves to howl in Yellowstone. *Audubon Magazine.* 1990 November-December: 32–41.

37. Mech, L. David, Keiter, Robert B., Boyce, Mark S. Returning the wolf to Yellowstone. In: Keiter, Robert B., Boyce, Mark S., editors. *The greater Yellowstone ecosystem: Redefining America's wilderness heritage.* New Haven: Yale University Press; 1991. p. 309–22.

38. Bruskotter, Jeremy T., Vaske, Jerry J., Schmidt, Robert H. Social and cognitive correlates of Utah residents' acceptance of the lethal control of wolves. *Hum Dimens Wildl.* 2009; 14: 119–32.

39. Osnos, Evan. Beaver laws trap towns –Surging numbers, state bans forge local dilemmas. *Chicago Tribune.* 2001 Aug 16.

40. DeVos, James. Managing wildlife by ballot initiative: The Arizona experience. *Hum Dimens Wildl.* 1998; 3(2): 60–6.

41. Amos, William, Harrison, Kathryn, Hober, George. In search of a minimum winning coalition: The politics of species-at-risk legislation in Canada. In: Beazley, Karen, Boardman, Robert, editors. *Politics of the wild: Canada and endangered species.* Oxford: Oxford University Press; 2001. p. 137–66.

42. Janega, James. Vote to consider wolf hunting triggers debate. As animals' numbers have increased in Wisconsin, so have attacks on livestock. *Chicago Tribune* [Internet]. 2008 Feb 26 [cited 2008 Apr 28]; Available from: www.chicagotribune.com/news/chi-wolfhuntapr 27,0,6970870.story

43. Helvarg, David. *The war against the greens.* Boulder: Johnson Books; 2004.

44. Hamilton, Joan. Babbitt's retreat. *Sierra Magazine.* 1994 July-August: 53–9 & 73–7.

45. Kraft, Michael E. *Environmental policy and politics.* 5th ed. Boston: Longman; 2011.

46. Mahoney, Shane P., Jackson, John J. Enshrining hunting as a foundation for conservation – the North American model. *Int J Environ Stud.* 2013; 70(3): 448–59.

47. Yeoman, Barry. Why the passenger pigeon went extinct. *Audubon Magazine.* 2014 May-June: 29–33.

48. Goldfarb, Ben. Should the humpback whale stay on the endangered species list? *High Country News* [Internet]. 2014 May 9 [cited 2014 May 14]; Available from: www.hcn.org/blogs/goat/should-the-humpback-whale-stay-on-the-endangered-species-list-1?utm_source=wcn1&utm_medium=email

49. Mattson, David J. State-level management of a common charismatic predator. In: Clark, Susan G., Rutherford, Murray B., editors. *Large carnivore conservation: Integrating science and policy in the North American west*. Chicago: University of Chicago Press; 2014. p. 29–64.

50. Pacelle, Wayne. Forging a new wildlife management paradigm: Integrating animal protection values. *Hum Dimens Wildl*. 1998; 3(2): 42–50.

51. Nie, Martin. *Beyond wolves: The politics of wolf recovery and management*. Minneapolis: University of Minnesota Press; 2003.

52. Hart, David. The hocus pocus of ballot box biology [Internet]. National Rifle Association: Institute for Legislative Action; 2005 [cited 2012 Oct 30]; Available from: www.nraila.org/hunting/articles/the-hocus-pocus-of-ballot-box-biology.aspx?s=ballot+box+biology&st=&ps

53. Herda-Rapp, Ann, Marotz, Karen G. Contested meanings: The social construction of the mourning dove in Wisconsin. In: Herda-Rapp, Ann, Goedeke, Theresa L., editors. *Mad about wildlife: Looking at social conflict over wildlife*. Leiden: Brill; 2005. p. 73–96.

54. Gray, Gary C. *Wildlife and people: The human dimensions of wildlife ecology*. Urbana: University of Illinois Press; 1993.

55. Vaske, Jerry J., Fulton, David C., Manfredo, Michael J. Human dimensions considerations in wildlife management planning. In: Decker, Daniel J., Brown, Tommy L., Siemer, William F., editors. *Human dimensions of wildlife management in North America*. Bethesda: The Wildlife Society; 2001. p. 91–108.

56. Russell, Sharman Apt. *Kill the cowboy: A battle of mythology in the new west*. Reading, MA: Addison-Wesley Publishing Company; 1993.

57. Nie, Martin. State wildlife policy and management: The scope and bias of political conflict. *Public Adm Rev*. 2004; 64(2): 221–33.

58. Vredenburg, Harrie. Strangers at the party: An industry strategy perspective on PHVS. In: Westley, Frances R., Miller, Philip S., editors. *Experiments in consilience: Integrating social and scientific responses to save endangered species*. Washington, D.C.: Island Press; 2003. p. 298–320.

59. Richie, Lauren, Oppenheimer, J. Daniel, Clark, Susan G. Social process in grizzly bear management: Lessons for collaborative governance and natural resource policy. *Policy Sci*. 2012; 45(3): 265–91.

60. Sabatier, Paul A. An advocacy coalition framework of policy change and the role of policy-oriented learning therein. *Policy Sci*. 1988; 21: 129–68.

61. Olson, Elizabeth A. Water management and the Upper Clark Fork steering committee. In: Brunner, Ronald D., Colburn, Christine H., Cromley, Christina M., Klein, Roberta A., Olson, Elizabeth A., editors. *Finding common ground*. New Haven: Yale University Press; 2002. p. 48–87.

62. Oppenheimer, J. Daniel, Richie, Lauren. Collaborative grizzly bear management in Banff national park. In: Clark, Susan G., Rutherford, Murray B., editors. *Large carnivore conservation: Integrating science and policy in the North American West*. Chicago: University of Chicago Press; 2014. p. 212–50.

63. Pym, William M., Rutherford, Murray B., Gibeau, Michael, Clark, Susan G., Rutherford, Murray B. Wolf management on ranchlands in southwestern Alberta: Collaborating to address conflict. In: Clark, Susan G., Rutherford, Murray B., editors. *Large carnivore conservation: Integrating science and policy in the north American west*. Chicago: University of Chicago Press; 2014. p. 140–76.

64. Clark, Susan G., Cherney, David N., Clark, Douglas. Large carnivore conservation: A perspective on constitutive decision making and options. In: Clark, Susan G., Rutherford,

Murray B., editors. *Large carnivore conservation: Integrating science and policy in the North American west*. Chicago: University of Chicago Press; 2014. p. 251–88.

65. Gilman, Sarah. Ranchers, enviros and officials seek a middle path on public-land grazing. *High Country News* [Internet]. 2014 Feb 17 [cited 2014 Feb 25]; Available from: www.hcn.org/issues/46.3/ranchers-enviros-and-officials-seek-a-middle-path-on-public-land-grazing-in-utah?utm_source=wcn1&utm_medium=email

66. Carrier, Scott. Chainsaw diplomacy. *High Country News* [Internet]. 2015 Feb 16 [cited 2015 Feb 16]; Available from: www.hcn.org/issues/47.3/chainsaw-diplomacy/

67. Beatley, Timothy. *Habitat conservation planning: Endangered species and urban growth*. Austin: The University of Texas Press; 1994.

68. Chase, Lisa C., Lamber, T. Bruce, Decker, Daniel J. Citizen participation in wildlife management decisions. In: Decker, Daniel J., Brown, Tommy L., Siemer, William F., editors. *Human dimensions of wildlife management in North America*. Bethesda: The Wildlife Society; 2001. p. 153–70.

69. Porter, Douglas R., Salvesen, David A. Introduction. In: Porter, Douglas R., Salvesen, David A., editors. *Collaborative planning for wetlands and wildlife: Issues and examples*. Washington, D.C.: Island Press; 1995. p. 1–6.

70. Beatley, Timothy. Preserving biodiversity through the use of habitat conservation plans. In: Porter, Douglas R., Salvesen, David A., editors. *Collaborative planning for wetlands and wildlife: Issues and examples*. Washington, D.C.: Island Press; 1995. p. 35–74.

71. McCreary, Scott T., Adams, Mark B., Porter, Douglas R., Salvesen, David A. Managing wetlands through advanced planning and permitting: The Columbia river estuary study taskforce. In: Porter, Douglas R., Salvesen, David A., editors. *Collaborative planning for wetlands and wildlife: Issues and examples*. Washington, D.C.: Island Press; 1995. p. 103–37.

72. Lauber, T. Bruce, Decker, Daniel J., Leon, Kirsten M., Chase, Lisa C., Schusler, Tania M. Stakeholder engagement in wildlife management. In: Decker, Daniel J., Riley, Shawn J., Siemer, William F., editors. *Human dimensions of wildlife management*. 2nd ed. Baltimore: The Johns Hopkins University Press; 2012. p. 139–56.

73. Committee to Review the Bureau of Land Management Wild Horse and Burro Management Program. Using science to improve the BLM wild horse and burro program: A way forward [Internet]. Washington, D.C.: National Academy Press; 2013 [cited 2013 Jun 20]; Available from: www.nap.edu/download.php?record_id=13511

74. Cashore, Benjamin, Howlett, Michael. Behavioral thresholds and institutional rigidities as explanations of punctuated equilibrium processes in Pacific northwest forest policy dynamics. In: Repetto, Robert, editor. *Punctuated equilibrium and the dynamics of US environmental policy*. New Haven: Yale University Press; 2006. p. 137–61.

75. Wildlife Management Institute. Gray wolves back on the endangered species list. *Outdoors News Bulletin* [Internet]. 2010 Aug 16 [cited 2010 Aug 25]; Available from: www.wildlifemanagementinstitute.org/index.php?option=com_content&view=article&id=467:grey-wolves-back-on-the-endangered-species-list&catid=34:ONB%20Articles&Itemid=54

76. Myers, Erik, Fischman, Robert, Marsh, Anne. Maryland Chesapeake Bay critical areas program: Wetlands protection and future growth. In: Porter, Douglas R., Salvesen, David A., editors. *Collaborative planning for wetlands and wildlife: Issues and examples*. Washington, D.C.: Island Press; 1995. p. 181–201.

77. Porter, Douglas R., Salvesen, David A. Conclusion. In: Porter, Douglas R., Salvesen, David A., editors. *Collaborative planning for wetlands and wildlife: Issues and examples*. Washington, D.C.: Island Press; 1995. p. 275–83.

78. Babbitt, Bruce. *Cities in the wilderness: A new vision of land use in America*. Washington, D.C.: Island Press/Shearwater Books; 2005.

79. Wicker, Tom. Waiting for an environmental president. *Audubon Magazine*. 1994 September-October: 49–54 & 102–5.

80. Yaffee, Steven Lewis. *The wisdom of the spotted owl: Policy lessons for a new century*. Washington, D.C.: Island Press; 1994.

81. Bevington, Douglas. *Rebirth of environmentalism: Grassroots activism from the spotted owl to the polar bear*. Washington, D.C.: Island Press; 2009.

82. Babbitt, Bruce. What the president can do right now for conservation. *High Country News* [Internet]. 2014 May 26 [cited 2014 May 26]; Available from: http://edition.pagesuite-professional.co.uk//launch.aspx?eid=7880409f-357f-4541-9590-334daf554402

83. Klyza, Christopher McGrory, Sousa, David J. *American environmental policy*. Cambridge: MIT Press; 2013.

84. McNamee, Thomas. *The return of the wolf to Yellowstone*. New York: Henry Holt and Company; 1997.

85. Cohen, Roger, Williams, Ted. Interview with Bruce Babbitt: Interior views. *Audubon Magazine*. 1993 May-June: 78–84.

86. Beatley, Timothy, Fries, T. James, Braun, David. The Balcones canyonlands conservation plan: A regional, multi-species approach. In: Porter, Douglas R., Salvesen, David A., editors. *Collaborative planning for wetlands and wildlife: Issues and examples*. Washington, D.C.: Island Press; 1995. p. 75–92.

87. Sousa, David J., Klyza, Christopher McGrory. New directions in environmental policy making: An emerging collaborative regime or reinventing interest group liberalism? *Nat Resour J*. 2007; 47(Spring): 378–444.

88. Beier, Colin M. Influence of political opposition and compromise on conservation outcomes in the Tongass national forest, Alaska. *Conserv Biol*. 2008; 22(6): 1485–96.

89. Sierra Magazine. 1994: Good and bad year for the environment. *Sierra Magazine*. 1995 January-February: 20.

90. Male, Timothy, Donlan, C. Josh. The future of pre-listing conservation programs for wildlife conservation. In: Donlan, C. Josh, editor. *Proactive strategies for protecting species*. Berkeley: University of California Press; 2015. p. 219–29.

91. Tobin, Richard J. *The expendable future: U.S. politics and the protection of biological diversity*. Durham: Duke University Press; 1990.

92. Hansen, Heather. Who's afraid of the big, bad wolf? *High Country News* [Internet]. 2011 Apr 12 [cited 2012 Apr 14]; Available from: www.hcn.org/hcn/blogs/range/whos-afraid-of-the-big-bad-wolf

93. Kingdon, John W. *Agendas, alternatives, and public policies*. 2nd ed. New York: Harper Collins Publishers; 1995.

94. Cohen, Michael D., March, James G.., Olsen, Johan F. A garbage can model of organizational choice. *Adm Sci Q*. 1972; 17(1): 2–15.

Chapter 5 References

1. Cioc, Mark. *The game of conservation: International treaties to protect the world's migratory animals*. Athens: Ohio University Press; 2009.

2. Yaffee, Steven Lewis. *Prohibitive policy: Implementing the federal Endangered Species Act*. Cambridge: MIT Press; 1982.

3. Beatley, Timothy. *Habitat conservation planning: Endangered species and urban growth.* Austin: University of Texas Press; 1994.

4. Alvarez, Lizette. Protecting a home where the puffer fish roam in Biscayne national park. *New York Times* [Internet]. 2014 Dec 21 [cited 2014 Dec 22]; Available from: www.nytimes.com/2014/12/22/us/protecting-a-home-where-the-puffer-fish-roam-in-biscayne-national-park.html?emc=edit_th_20141222&nl=todaysheadlines&nlid=10365419&_r=0

5. Turner, Pamela S. Struggling to save the seahorse. *National Wildlife Federation Magazine* [Internet]. 2005 [cited 2013 Mar 19]; 43(4); Available from: www.nwf.org/News-and-Magazines/National-Wildlife/Animals/Archives/2005/Struggling-to-Save-the-Seahorse.aspx

6. Greenberg, Paul. Tuna's end. *New York Times* [Internet]. 2010 Jun 21 [cited 2012 Jan 6]; Available from: www.nytimes.com/2010/06/27/magazine/27Tuna-t.html?th=&emc=th&pagewanted=prin

7. Mooallem, Jon. *Wild ones.* New York: The Penguin Press; 2013.

8. Bernacchi, Leigh A, Ragland, Chara J., Peterson, Tarla R. Engaging active stakeholders in implementation of community-based conservation: Whooping crane management in Texas, USA. *Wildl Soc Bull.* 2015; (August 5 online): 1–10.

9. Barcott, Bruce. *The last flight of the scarlet macaw: One woman's fight to save the world's most beautiful bird.* New York: Random House Trade Paperback; 2008.

10. Chadwick, Douglas. Whatever happened to "Save the Whales"? *Sierra Magazine.* 2008 July-August: 52–4 & 72.

11. Kalland, Arne. Whose whale is that? Diverting the commodity path. In: Freeman, Milton R., editor. *Elephants and whales: Resources for whom.* Switzerland: Gordon and Breach Science Publishers; 1994. p. 159–86.

12. Siebert, Charles. *The Wauchula Woods accord: Toward a new understanding of animals.* New York: Scribner; 2009.

13. Schaller, George B. *The last panda.* Chicago: University of Chicago Press; 1993.

14. Becker, Elizabeth. *Overbooked: The exploding business of travel and tourism.* New York: Simon & Shuster; 2013.

15. Bierman, Noah. Baby pandas born and bred at national zoo are not birthright citizens. *LA Times* [Internet]. 2015 Aug 25 [cited 2015 Aug 27]; Available from: www.latimes.com/nation/la-na-pandas-birth-national-zoo-20150825-story.html

16. Chen, Te-Ping. Pink dolphins face decline. *Wall Street Journal* [Internet]. 2013 Jun 19 [cited 2013 Jun 20]; Available from: http://blogs.wsj.com/chinarealtime/2013/06/19/hong-kongs-pink-dolphin-population-dwindles/tab/print/?KEYWORDS=Pink+Dolphins+Drop+Tied+to+Hong+Kong+Pollution

17. Capecchi, Christina, Rogers, Katie. Killer of Cecil the lion finds out that he is a target now, of internet vigilantism. *New York Times* [Internet]. 2015 Jul 29 [cited 2015 Jul 30]; Available from: www.nytimes.com/2015/07/30/us/cecil-the-lion-walter-palmer.html?emc=edit_th_20150730&nl=todaysheadlines&nlid=10365419&_r=0

18. Kareiva, Peter, Tear, Timothy H., Solie, Stacey, Brown, Michelle L., Sotomayor, Leonardo, Yuan-Farrel, Christopher. Nongovernmental organizations. In: Goble, Dale, D., Scott, J. Michael, Davis, Frank W., editors. *The Endangered Species Act at thirty: Volume I: Renewing the conservation promise.* Washington, D.C.: Island Press; 2006. p. 176–94.

19. Czech, Brian, Krausman, Paul R. *The Endangered Species Act.* Baltimore: Johns Hopkins University Press; 2001.

20. DiSilvestro, Roger L. *The endangered kingdom: The struggle to save America's wildlife.* New York: John Wiley & Sons, Inc.; 1989.

21. Krausman, Paul R. Mountain sheep restoration through private/public partnership. In: Maehr, David, Noss, Reed F., Larkin, Jeffery L., editors. *Large mammal restoration: Ecological and sociological challenges in the 21st Century.* Washington, D.C.: Island Press; 2001. p. 231–44.

22. Gugliotta, Guy. A glamorous killer returns. *New York Times* [Internet]. 2013 Jun 10 [cited 2013 Jun 10]; Available from: www.nytimes.com/2013/06/11/science/cougars-glamorous-killers-expand-their-range.html?emc=tnt&tntemail0=y&pagewanted=print

23. McClenachan, Loren, Cooper, Andrew B., Carpenter, Kent E., Dulvy, Nicholas K. Extinction risk and bottlenecks in the conservation of charismatic marine species. *Conserv Lett*. 2012; 5(1): 73–80.

24. Howard, Gregory D., Shogren, Jason F., Tschirhart, John. The nature of endangered species protection. In: Shogren, Jason F., Tschirhart, John, editors. *Protecting endangered species in the United States*. Cambridge: Cambridge University Press; 2001. p. 1–20.

25. Rauber, Paul. When nature turns nasty. *Sierra Magazine*. 1993 January-February: 28–32 & 121–3.

26. National Research Council. Science and the Endangered Species Act [Internet]. Washington, D.C.: National Academy Press; 1995 [cited 2016 Mar 24]; Available from: www.nap.edu/read/4978/chapter/1

27. Posner, Richard A. Animal rights: Legal, philosophical, and pragmatic perspectives. In: Sunstein, Cass R., Nussbaum, Martha C., editors. *Animal rights: Current debates and new directions*. Oxford: Oxford University Press; 2004. p. 51–77.

28. Nickens, T. Edward. There goes the neighborhood. *Audubon Magazine*. 2008 November-December: 77–82.

29. Roman, Joe. *Listed: Dispatches from America's Endangered Species Act*. Cambridge: Harvard University Press; 2011.

30. Bass, Rick. *The ninemile wolves*. New York: Ballantine Books; 1992.

31. Smith, Bruce L. *Where elk roam: Conservation and biopolitics of our national elk herd*. Guilford, CT: Lyons Press; 2012.

32. Kellert, Stephen R., Berry, Joyce K. *Phase III: Knowledge, affection and basic attitudes towards animals in American society*. Washington, D.C.: U.S. Government Printing Office; 1980. Report No.: #024-010-00–625-1.

33. Samways, Michael J. Conserving invertebrates: How many can be saved, and how? In: Leader-Williams, Nigel, Adams, William M., Smith, Robert J., editors. *Trade-offs in conservation: Deciding what to save*. Oxford: Wiley-Blackwell; 2010. p. 97–117.

34. Cambronne, Al. *Deerland: America's hunt for ecological balance and the essence of wildness*. Guilford, CT: Lyons Press; 2013.

35. Brant, Anthony. Not in my backyard. *Audubon Magazine*. 1997 September-October: 58–62, 86–7, 102–3.

36. Capek, Stella. Of time, space and birds: Cattle egrets and the place of the wild. In: Herda-Rapp, Ann, Goedeke, Theresa L., editors. *Mad about wildlife: Looking at social conflict over wildlife*. Leiden: Brill; 2005. p. 195–222.

37. Siemer, William F., Jonker, Sandra, A., Merchant, Matthew, Brown, Tommy L. *Attitudes toward beaver and norms about beaver management: Insights from baseline research in New York. Human Dimensions Research Unit Department of Natural Resources Cornell University*; 2004 Jul. Report No.: HDRU Series No. 04–5.

38. Freedman, Bill, Rodger, Lindsay, Ewins, Peter, Green, David M. Species at risk in Canada. In: Beazley, Karen, Boardman, Robert, editors. *Politics of the wild: Canada and endangered species*. Oxford: Oxford University Press; 2001. p. 26–48.

39. Brailovskaya, Tatiana. Obstacles to protecting marine biodiversity through marine wilderness preservation: Examples from the New England region conservation biology. *Conserv Biol*. 1998; 12(6): 1236–40.

40. Willison, Martin. Endangered marine species and marine protected areas in Canada. In: Beazley, Karen, Boardman, Robert, editors. *Politics of the wild: Canada and endangered species*. Oxford: Oxford University Press; 2001. p. 94–115.

41. Wilcove, David S. *The condor's shadow: The loss and recovery of wildlife in America*. New York: W.H. Freeman and Company; 1999.

42. Verissimo, Diogo, MacMillan, Douglas C., Smith, Robert J. Toward a systematic approach for identifying conservation flagships. *Conserv Lett*. 2011; 4: 1–8.

43. Graham, Jr., Frank. Winged victory. *Audubon Magazine*. 1994 July-August: 36–40.

44. Boutin, Stan. Top carnivores and biodiversity conservation in the boreal forest. In: Ray, Justina C., Redford, Kent H., Steneck, Robert S., Berger, Joel, editors. *Large carnivores and the conservation of biodiversity*. Washington, D.C.: Island Press; 2005. p. 362–80.

45. Tobin, Richard J. *The expendable future: U.S. politics and the protection of biological diversity*. Durham: Duke University Press; 1990.

46. U.S. General Accountabilty Office. Endangered species: Management improvement could enhance recovery program. Report to the Chairman, Subcommittee on Fisheries and Wildlife Conservation, and the Environment, Committee on Merchant Marine and Fisheries, House of Representatives. GAO/RCED-89-5. 1988.

47. Anderson, David A. Pricing protection. In: Spray, Sharon L., McGothlin, Karen L., editors. *Loss of biodiversity*. Lanham: Rowman & Littlefield Publishers, Inc.; 2003. p. 99–118.

48. Committee to Review the Bureau of Land Management Wild Horse and Burro Management Program. Using science to improve the BLM wild horse and burro program: A way forward [Internet]. Washington, D.C.: National Academy Press; 2013 [cited 2013 Jun 20]; Available from: www.nap.edu/download.php?record_id=13511

49. Committee to Review the Bureau of Land Management Wild Horse and Burro Management Program; Board on Agriculture and Natural Resources. Division on Earth and Life Studies. National Research Council. Using science to improve the BLM horse and burro program: A way forward [Internet]. Washington, D.C.: The National Academies Press; 2013 [cited 2013 Jun 20]; Available from: www.nap.edu/download.php?record_id=13511

50. Frosch, Dan. Report criticizes U.S. stewardship of wild horses. *New York Times* [Internet]. 2013 Jun 6 [cited 2013 Jun 10]; Available from: www.nytimes.com/2013/06/07/us/report-criticizes-us-stewardship-of-wild-horses.html

51. Zimmerman, Alexandra, Baker, Nick, Inskip, Chloe, Linnell, John D. C., Marchini, Silvio, Odden, John et al. Contemporary views of human-carnivore conflicts on wild rangelands. In: du Toit, John D., Kock, Richard, Deutsch, James C., editors. *Wild rangelands: Conserving wildlife while maintaining livestock in semi-arid ecosystems*. Oxford: Wiley-Blackwell; 2010. p. 129–51.

52. Williams, Ted. Incite: Saddle sores. *Audubon Magazine*. 2011 January-February: 28–36.

53. Gulliford, Andrew. Wild horses: Too much of a good thing. *High Country News* [Internet]. 2013 Apr 15 [cited 2013 Apr 23]; Available from: www.hcn.org/wotr/wild-horses-too-much-of-a-good-thing/print_view

54. U.S. General Accountability Office. Bureau of Land Management: Effective long-term options needed to manage unadoptable wild horses. Washington, D.C.: USGAO; 2008 Oct. Report No.: GAO-09-77.

55. Philipps, Dave. As wild horses overrun the West, ranchers fear land will be gobbled up. *New York Times* [Internet]. 2014 Sep 30 [cited 2014 Oct 1]; Available from: www.nytimes.com/2014/10/01/us/as-wild-horses-overrun-the-west-ranchers-fear-land-will-be-gobbled-up.html?emc=edit_th_20141001&nl=todaysheadlines&nlid=10365419

56. Schirtzinger, Alexa. Horse ills: A controversial new effort aims to protect the wild West. *Audubon Magazine*. 2010 March-April: 20.

57. Gray, Gary C. *Wildlife and people: The human dimensions of wildlife ecology*. Urbana: University of Illinois Press; 1993.

58. Rawson, Timothy. *Changing tracks: Predators and politics in Mt. McKinley national park*. Fairbanks: University of Alaska Press; 2001.

59. Robbins, Jim. Anger over culling of Yellowstone's bison. *New York Times* [Internet]. 2008 Mar 23 [cited 2013 May 2]; Available from: www.nytimes.com/2008/03/23/us/23bison.html?pagewanted=print

60. Nie, Martin. *Beyond wolves: The politics of wolf recovery and management*. Minneapolis: University of Minnesota Press; 2003.

61. Coleman, Jon T. *Vicious: Wolves and men in America*. New Haven: Yale University Press; 2004.

62. Russell, Sharman Apt. *Kill the cowboy: A battle of mythology in the new west*. Salt Lake City: University of Utah Press; 2005.

63. Parsons, Alexander. Strip mall lobos. In: Lynch, Tom, editor. *El lobo: Readings on the Mexican gray wolf*. Salt Lake City: University of Utah Press; 2005. p. p183–96.

64. Robinson, Michael J. *Predatory bureaucracy: The extermination of the wolf and the transformation of the west*. Boulder: The University of Colorado Press; 2005.

65. Russell, Sharman Apt. *Kill the cowboy: A battle of mythology in the new west*. Reading, MA: Addison-Wesley Publishing Company; 1993.

66. Shivik, John. *The predator paradox: Ending the war with wolves, bears, cougars, and coyotes*. Boston: Beacon Press; 2014.

67. U.S. Fish and Wildlife Service. Gray wolf [Internet]. 2003 [cited 2013 Feb 26]; Available from: http://digitalmedia.fws.gov/cdm/singleitem/collection/document/id/111/rec/16

68. Brinkley, Douglas. *The wilderness warrior: Theodore Roosevelt and the crusade for America*. New York: Harper Collins Publishers; 2009.

69. Urbigkit, Cat. *Yellowstone wolves: A chronicle of the animal, the people, and the politics*. Blacksburg, VA: The McDonald & Woodward Publishing Company; 2008.

70. Mattson, David J. State-level management of a common charismatic predator. In: Clark, Susan G., Rutherford, Murray B., editors. *Large carnivore conservation: Integrating science and policy in the North American west*. Chicago: University of Chicago Press; 2014. p. 29–64.

71. Williams, Ted. Doggone! *Audubon Magazine*. 2009 November-December: 66–72.

72. Franke, James. Rattlesnake roundups: Uncontrolled wildlife exploitation and the rites of spring. *J Appl Anim Welf Sci*. 2000; 3(2): 151–60.

73. Fernandez, Manny. Rattlesnake wranglers, armed with gasoline. *New York Times* [Internet]. 2014 Mar 30 [cited 2014 Mar 30]; Available from: www.nytimes.com/2014/03/31/us/rattlesnake-wranglers-armed-with-gasoline.html?emc=edit_tnt_20140330&nlid=10365419&tntemail0=y&_r=0

74. Angier, Natalie. Noble eagles, nasty pigeons, biased humans. *New York Times* [Internet]. 2008 Apr 29 [cited 2013 Apr 25]; Available from: www.nytimes.com/2008/04/29/science/29angi.html?ref=woodpeckers&pagewanted=print

75. Wallace, Richard L. The Florida manatee recovery program. In: Clark, Tim W., Reading, Richard P., Clarke, Alice L., editors. *Endangered species recovery: Finding the lessons, improving the process*. Washington, D.C.: Island Press; 1994. p. 134–56.

76. Peterson, Rolf O. Wolves as top carnivores: New faces in new places. In: Sharpe, Virginia A., Norton, Bryan G.., Donnelley, Strachan, editors. *Wolves and human communities: Biology, politics, and ethics*. Washington, D.C.: Island Press; 2001. p. 151–60.

77. Farquhar, Brodie. WY: Governor defends wolf stance. *Twin Observer* [Internet]. 2006 May 27 [cited 2013 Feb 9]; Available from: www.timberwolfinformation.org/?p=2717

78. Dupree, Joe. The most important fish in the sea. *National Wildlife Federation Magazine* [Internet]. 2008 [cited 2008 Feb 6]; 46(2); Available from: www.nwf.org/nationalwildlife/article .cfm?issueID=120&articleID=1556&utm_source=NationalWildlifeMagazine&utm_medium= Article&utm_term=Feb08&utm_content=MostImportantFishInSea&utm_campaign=1

79. Ferretti, Francesco, Myers, Ransom A., Serena, Fabrizio, Lotse, Heike K. Loss of large predatory sharks from the Mediterranean sea. *Conserv Biol.* 2008; 22(4): 952–64.

80. Baird, Julia. The great white shark's image problem. *New York Times* [Internet]. 2014 Nov 30 [cited 2014 Dec 1]; Available from: www.nytimes.com/2014/12/01/opinion/the-great-white-sharks-image-problem.html?emc=edit_ty_20141201&nl=opinion&nlid=10365419&_r=0

81. Bergman, Margareta, Akerberg, Sofia. Moose hunting, forestry, and wolves in Sweden. *Alces.* 2006; 42: 13–23.

82. Pym, William M., Rutherford, Murray B., Gibeau, Michael, Clark, Susan G., Rutherford, Murray B. Wolf management on ranchlands in southwestern Alberta: Collaborating to address conflict. In: Clark, Susan G., Rutherford, Murray B., editors. *Large carnivore conservation: Integrating science and policy in the north American west.* Chicago: University of Chicago Press; 2014. p. 140–76.

83. Schadler, Christine L. Reintroduction: Inspired policy or poor conservation? In: Sharpe, Virginia A., Norton, Bryan G., Donnelley, Strachan, editors. *Wolves and human communities: Biology, politics, and ethics.* Washington, D.C.: Island Press; 2001. p. 161–73.

84. Goodall, Jane. *Hope for animals and their world: How endangered species are being rescued from the brink.* New York: Grand Central Publishing; 2009.

85. U.S. Fish and Wildlife Service. Federal officials request assistance regarding latest red wolf killing [Internet]. 2013 [cited 2013 Nov 21]; Available from: www.fws.gov/southeast/news/ 2013/086.html

86. McAllister, Ian. *The last wild wolves: Ghosts of the rain forest.* Berkeley: University of California Press; 2007.

87. Williams, Ted. Alaska's war on the wolves. *Audubon Magazine.* 1993 November-December: 44–50.

88. Dunlap, Thomas R. *Saving America's wildlife.* Princeton University Press; 1988.

89. Dickie, Gloria. As delisting looms, grizzly advocates prepare for a final face-off. *High Country News* [Internet]. 2016 May 16 [cited 2016 May 24]; Available from: www.hcn.org/issues/ 48.8/as-delisting-looms-grizzly-advocates-prepare-for-a-final-face-off?utm_source=wcn1&utm_ medium=email

90. Tolmé, Paul. Sexy beasts. *National Wildlife Magazine* [Internet]. 2007 [cited 2013 Apr 5]; 45(2); Available from: www.nwf.org/News-and-Magazines/National-Wildlife/Animals/Arch ives/2007/Sexy-Beasts.aspx

91. U.S. Fish and Wildlife Service. Final environmental impact statement: The reintroduction of gray wolves to Yellowstone national park and central Idaho [Internet]. 1994 [cited 2016 Mar 24]; Available from: www.fws.gov/mountain-prairie/species/mammals/wolf/eis_1994.pdf

92. Forsgren, Harv, Talbott, Scott. Guest opinion: Hunting another step toward grizzly bear recovery. *Billings Gazette* [Internet]. 2012 Dec 29 [cited 2013 Feb 14]; Available from: http:// billingsgazette.com/news/opinion/guest/guest-opinion-hunting-another-step-toward-grizzly-bear-recovery/article_b7763b6e-2221–5c1b-91b9-dc05c3c35bb9.htm

93. Mech, L. David. Considerations for developing wolf harvesting regulations in the contiguous United States. *J Wildl Manag.* 2010; 74(7): 1421–4.

94. Kaufman, Leslie. After years of conflict, a new dynamic in wolf country. *New York Times*. 2011 Nov 4 [cited 2011 Nov 5]; Available from: www.nytimes.com/2011/11/05/science/earth/conflict-over-wolves-yields-new-dynamic-between-ranchers-and-conservationists.html?nl=todaysheadlines&emc=thab1&pagewanted=print

95. New York Times. Editorial: Wolves under review. 2013 Aug 15 [cited 2013 Aug 15]; Available from: www.nytimes.com/2013/08/16/opinion/wolves-under-review.html?emc=edit_tnt_20130815&tntemail0=y&_r=0&pagewanted=print

96. Peterson, Christine. Proposed Wyoming wolf quotas attract little public comment. *Casper Star Tribune* [Internet]. 2013 May 25 [cited 2013 Jun 12]; Available from: http://billingsgazette.com/news/state-and-regional/wyoming/proposed-wyoming-wolf-quotas-attract-little-public-comment/article_e14c8eac-1f61-5f39-b908-b7f7028088a1.html

97. Treves, Adrian, Martin, Kerry A. Hunters as stewards of wolves in Wisconsin and the northern Rocky Mountains, USA. *Soc Nat Resour*. 2011; 24: 984–94.

98. Wuerthner, George. The perverse argument for hunting grizzly bears. *Counterpunch* [Internet]. 2013 Jan 2 [cited 2013 May 23]; Available from: www.counterpunch.org/2013/01/02/to-the-save-the-grizzly-you-must-destroy-it/

99. Schanning, Kevin. Human dimensions: Public opinion research concerning wolves in the Great Lakes states of Michigan, Minnesota, and Wisconsin. In: Wydeven, Adrian, Van Deelen, Timothy R., Heske, Edward J., editors. *Recovering of gray wolves in the Great Lakes region of the United States*. New York: Springer; 2009. p. 251–65.

100. Downes, Lawrence. Wolf haters. *New York Times* [Internet]. 2013 Dec 28 [cited 2013 Dec 29]; Available from: www.nytimes.com/2013/12/29/opinion/sunday/wolf-haters.html?emc=edit_tnt_20131228&tntemail0=y&pagewanted=print

101. Barker, Rocky. Idaho Fish and Game turns to hired hunter. *Idahostatesman.com* [Internet]. 2013 Dec 17 [cited 2013 Dec 30]; Available from: www.idahostatesman.com/2013/12/17/2931287/fish-and-game-turns-to-hired-hunterpetition.html

102. Zuckerman, Laura. Judge won't block Idaho wolf, coyote-killing competition. Reuters [Internet]. 2013 Dec 27 [cited 2013 Dec 30]; Available from: www.reuters.com/article/2013/12/27/us-usa-hunt-idaho-idUSBRE9BQ0JO20131227

103. Askins, Renee. Releasing wolves from symbolism. *Harper's Magazine*. 1995 Apr; 290 (1739): 15–18.

104. Adaptive Management Oversight Committee. Mexican wolf Blue Range reintroduction project 5-Year Review: AMOC responses to public comment component [Internet]. 2005 [cited 2016 Apr 13]; Available from: http://azmemory.azlibrary.gov/cdm/ref/collection/statepubs/id/2423

105. Goble, Dale, D. Reintroducing the missing parts: The experimental population provisions of the Endangered Species Act. In: Lynch, Tom, editor. *El Lobo: Readings on the Mexican gray wolf*. Salt Lake City: University of Utah Press; 2005. p. 130–7.

106. Mexican Wolf Livestock Coexistence Council. 2014 strategic plan [Internet]. 2014 [cited 2014 Mar 31]; Available from: http://nebula.wsimg.com/44f097fc32f18ec546b4b7e11d1f4486?AccessKeyId=9B17E8A0ABBE291EE878&disposition=0&alloworigin=1

107. Reese, April. Can a grazing buyout program ease life for wolves and ranchers? *High Country News* [Internet]. 2014 Feb 17 [cited 2014 Aug 19]; Available from: www.hcn.org/issues/46.14/46.3/can-a-grazing-buyout-program-ease-life-for-wolves-and-ranchers

108. Orme, Wyatt. The latest: wild Mexican wolf pups born in Sierra Madre. *High Country News* [Internet]. 2014 Aug 18 [cited 2014 Aug 19]; Available from: www.hcn.org/issues/46.14/the-latest-wild-mexican-wolf-pups-born-in-sierra-madre?utm_source=wcn1&utm_medium=email

109. U.S. Fish and Wildlife Service. Final environmental impact statement: The reintroduction of gray wolves to Yellowstone national park and central Idaho [Internet]. 1994 [cited 2013 Mar 14]; Available from: http://westerngraywolf.fws.gov/EIS_1994.pdf

110. Klinkenborg, Verlyn. After years of progress, a setback in saving the wolf. *New York Times* [Internet]. 2013 Jun 1 [cited 2013 Jun 2]; Available from: www.nytimes.com/2013/06/02/opinion/sunday/after-years-of-progress-a-setback-in-saving-the-wolf.html?emc=tnt&tntemail0=y

111. Van Ballenberghe, Victor. Predator control, politics, and wildlife conservation in Alaska. *ALCES*. 2006; 42: 1–11.

112. Brown, Tommy L., Decker, Daniel J. Alaska residents' attitudes toward predator management statewide and in unit 13: executive summary [Internet]. 2003 [cited 2016 Apr 13]; Available from: https://ecommons.cornell.edu/bitstream/handle/1813/40386/HDRUReport03-4exec.pdf?sequence=1

113. Bruskotter, Jeremy T., Vaske, Jerry J., Schmidt, Robert H. Social and cognitive correlates of Utah residents' Acceptance of the lethal control of wolves. *Hum Dimens Wildl*. 2009; 14: 119–32.

114. Pate, Jennifer, Manfredo, Michael J., Bright, Alan D. Coloradans' attitudes toward reintroducing the gray wolf into Colorado. *Wildl Soc Bull*. 1996; 24(4): 421–8.

115. Wilson, Patrick Impero. Wolves, politics and the Nez Perce: Wolf recovery in central Idaho and the role of native tribes. *Nat Resour J*. 1999; 38: 543–64.

116. Willcox, Louis. Is the proposal to hunt Yellowstone grizzlies based on sound science and public support? [Internet]. *Saving Wildlife and Wild Places*. 2013 [cited 2013 Jan 10]; Available from: http://switchboard.nrdc.org/blogs/lwillcox/is_the_proposal_to_hunt_yellow.html

117. Williams, Christopher K. A quantitative summary of attitudes toward wolves and their reintroduction. *Wildl Soc Bull*. 2002; 30(2): 575–84.

118. Gadbow, Daryl. A bear's best friend. *Montana* [Internet]. 2010 Fall [cited 2013 Apr 20]; Available from: www2.umt.edu/montanan/f10/A%20Bears%20Best%20Friend.asp

119. Responsive Management. Public attitudes toward grizzly bear management in Wyoming [Internet]. Conducted for the Wyoming Game and Fish Department; 2001 Aug [cited 2013 Apr 24]; Available from: www.responsivemanagement.com/download/reports/grizzlydist.pdf

120. Roy, Johnna, Servheen, Christopher, Kasworm, Wayne, Waller, John. Restoration of grizzly bears to the Bitterroot wilderness: The EIS approach. In: Maehr, David, Noss, Reed F., Larkin, Jeffery L., editors. *Large mammal restoration: Ecological and sociological challenges in the 21st century*. Washington, D.C.: Island Press; 2001. p. 205–24.

121. Schoenecker, Kathryn A., Shaw, William W. Attitudes toward a proposed reintroduction of Mexican gray wolves in Arizona. *Hum Dimens Wildl*. 1997; 2(3): 42–55.

122. Brown, Wendy M., Parsons, David R. Restoring the Mexican gray wolf to the mountains of the southwest. In: Maehr, David, Noss, Reed F., Larkin, Jeffery L., editors. *Large mammal restoration: Ecological and sociological challenges in the 21st Century*. Washington, D.C.: Island Press; 2001. p. 169–86.

123. New York Times. For a wilder Rockies. *New York Times* [Internet]. 2009 Jul 7 [cited 2016 Jun 28]; Available from: www.nytimes.com/2009/07/07/opinion/07tue3.html?ref=topics

124. New York Times. Editorial: Wolf hunt. 2009 Dec 2 [cited 2013 May 18]; Available from: www.nytimes.com/2009/12/02/opinion/02wed3.html?pagewanted=print

125. Chicago Tribune. Editorial: "Killing wolves and democracy in Michigan. 2014 Aug 22 [cited 2014 Aug 22]; Available from: www.chicagotribune.com/news/opinion/editorials/ct-wolf-hunt-michigan-edit-0822-20140821-story.html

126. Kellert, Stephen R., Black, Matthew, Rush, Colleen Reid, Bath, Alistair J. Human culture and large carnivore conservation in North America. *Conserv Biol.* 1996; 10(4): 977–90.

127. Houston, Melanie J., Bruskotter, Jeremy T., Fan, David. Attitudes toward wolves in the United States and Canada: A content analysis of the print news media, 1999–2008. *Hum Dimens Wildl.* 2010; 15: 389–403.

128. Enck, Jody W., Brown, Tommy L. New Yorkers' attitudes towards restoring wolves to Adirondack park. *Wildl Soc Bull.* 2002; 30(1): 16–28.

129. Dizard, Jan E. In wolves' clothing: Restoration and the challenge to stewardship. In: Sharpe, Virginia A., Norton, Bryan G., Strachan, Donnelly, editors. *Wolves and human communities: Biology, politics, and ethics.* Washington, D.C.: Island Press; 2001. p. 75–92.

130. Enck, Jody W., Brown, Tommy L. Preliminary assessment of social feasibility for reintroducing gray wolves to the Adirondack park in northern New York [Internet]. Ithaca: Human Dimensions Research Unit, Cornell University; 2000 Mar [cited 2013 May 30]. Report No.: HDRU Series 00–3; Available from: www2.dnr.cornell.edu/hdru/pubs/HDRUReport00-3.pdf

131. Schneider, Bill. Idaho governor declares wolf public enemy number one. New West [Internet]. 2007 Jan 12 [cited 2013 Apr 27]; Available from: www.newwest.net/index.php/main/article/idaho_governor_declares_wolf_public_enemy_number_one/

132. Otter, C.L. Butch, Governor of Idaho. Letter to Ken Salazar, Secretary of the Interior [Internet]. 2010 [cited 2015 Apr 16]; Available from: https://fishandgame.idaho.gov/public/docs/wolves/letterGovernor1.pdf

133. Miller John. Idaho governor pulls state management of wolves in dispute over wolf hunt. Associated Press [Internet]. 2010 Oct 19 [cited 2013 Apr 27]; Available from: www.flatheadbeacon.com/articles/article/idaho_wont_manage_wolves_under_esa/20166/

134. Zuckerman, Laura. Idaho governor declares wolves a "disaster emergency." Reuters [Internet]. 2011 Apr 19 [cited 2013 Apr 27]; Available from: www.reuters.com/article/2011/04/20/us-wolves-idaho-idUSTRE73J0I120110420

135. Associated Press. Idaho governor offers his Oregon counterpart more wolves. 2012 Mar 10 [cited 2013 Feb 8]; Available from: http://earthfix.boisestatepublicradio.org/flora-and-fauna/article/idaho-governor-offers-his-oregon-counterpart-more-/

136. Miller, Sterling D., Schoen, John W., Faro, Jim, Klein, David R. Trends in intensive management of Alaska's grizzly bears, 1980–2010. *J Wildl Manag.* 2011; 75(6): 1243–52.

137. Browne-Nuñez, C., Treves, A., McFarland, D., Voyles, Z., Turng, C. Tolerance of wolves in Wisconsin: A mixed-methods examination of policy effects on attitudes and behavioral inclinations. *Biol Conserv.* 189(September): 59–71.

138. Treves, Adrian. Beyond recovery: Wisconsin's wolf policy 1980–2008. *Hum Dimens Wildl.* 2008; 13: 329–38.

139. Hudenko, Heather, Siemer, William F., Decker, Daniel J. Humans and coyotes in suburbia: Can experience lead to sustainable coexistence? Ithaca: Human Dimensions Research Unit, Cornell University; 2008 Dec. Report No.: HDRU Series No. 08–9.

140. Manuel, John. Red wolf showdown. *Audubon Magazine.* 1995; (March-April): 22–4.

141. U.S. House of Representatives. Endangered species Act implementation: Science or politics? Sect. sec. Oversight Hearing Before The Committee On Natural Resources, Serial No. 110–24 May 9, 2007.

142. Carroll, Carlos, Noss, Reed F., Schumaker, Nathan H., Paquet, Paul C. Is the return of the wolf, wolverine, and grizzly bear to Oregon and California biologically feasible? In: Maehr, David, Noss, Reed F., Larkin, Jeffery L., editors. *Large mammal restoration:*

Ecological and sociological challenges in the 21st Century. Washington, D.C.: Island Press; 2001. p. 25–46.

143. Duke, Danah L., Hebblewhite, Mark, Paquet, Paul C., Callaghan, Carolan, Percy, Melanie. Restoring a large-carnivore corridor in Banff national park. In: Maehr, David, Noss, Reed F., Larkin, Jeffery L., editors. *Large mammal restoration: Ecological and sociological challenges in the 21st century.* Washington, D.C.: Island Press; 2001. p. 261–75.

144. Maehr, David, Hoctor, Thomas S., Harris, Larry D. The Florida panther: A flagship for regional restoration. In: Maehr, David, Noss, Reed F., Larkin, Jeffery L., editors. *Large mammal restoration: Ecological and sociological challenges in the 21st century.* Washington, D.C.: Island Press; 2001. p. 293–312

145. Harris, Larry D., Duever, Linda C., Meegan, Rebecca P., Hoctor, Thomas S., Schortemeyer, James L., Maehr, David S. The biotic province: Minimum unit for conserving biodiversity In: Maehr, David, Noss, Reed F., Larkin, Jeffery L., editors. *Large mammal restoration: Ecological and sociological challenges in the 21st century.* Washington, D.C.: Island Press; 2001. p. 321–43.

146. Papouchis, Christopher M. Conserving mountain lions in a changing landscape. In: Fascione, Nina, Delach, Aimee, Smith, Martin E., editors. *People and predators: From conflict to coexistence.* Washington, D.C.: Island Press; 2004. p. 219–39.

147. Linn, Amy. Wild cats wild. *Audubon Magazine.* 1993 July-August: 22–5.

148. Beier, Paul. Cougar attacks on humans in the United States and Canada. *Wildl Soc Bull.* 1991; 19(4): 403–12.

149. Manfredo, Michael J., Zinn, Harry C., Sikorowski, Linda, Jones, Jim. Public acceptance of mountain lion management: A case study of Denver, Colorado, and nearby foothills areas. *Wildl Soc Bull.* 1998; 26(4): 964–70.

150. Meyer, Stephen M. *The end of the wild.* Cambridge: The MIT Press; 2006.

151. Derr, Mark. Growing bigger coyotes. *Audubon Magazine.* 1994 November-December: 20–1.

152. Sellars, Richard West. *Preserving nature in the national parks: A history.* New Haven: Yale University Press; 1997.

153. Chicago Tribune. Editorial: The cougar killed in Illinois was looking for love. 2013 Nov 26 [cited 2013 Nov 26]; Available from: www.chicagotribune.com/news/opinion/editorials/ct-saving-cougars-edit-1126–20131126,0,6065924.story

154. Miller, Marc. Illinois plans for return of wildlife like cougars. *Chicago Tribune* [Internet]. 2013 Dec 10 [cited 2013 Dec 10]; Available from: www.chicagotribune.com/news/opinion/editorials/ct-oped-1210-cougar-20131210,0,5880953.story

155. Johnson, Kirk. Study faults efforts at wolf management. *New York Times* [Internet]. 2014 Dec 3 [cited 2014 Dec 3]; Available from: www.nytimes.com/2014/12/04/us/washington-state-study-faults-efforts-at-wolf-management.html?emc=edit_tnt_20141203&nlid=10365419&tntemail0=y

156. Beyer, Dean E., Peterson, Rolf O., Vucetich, John A., Hammill, James H. Wolf population changes in Michigan. In: Wydeven, Adrian, Van Deelen, Timothy R., Heske, Edward J., editors. *Recovering of gray wolves in the Great Lakes region of the United States.* New York: Springer; 2009. p. 65–85.

157. Knuth, Barbara A., Siemer, William F., Duda, Mark D., Bissell, Steven J., Decker, Daniel J. Wildlife management in suburban environments. In: Decker, Daniel J., Brown, Tommy L., Siemer, William F., editors. *Human dimensions of wildlife management in North America.* Bethesda: The Wildlife Society; 2001. p. 219–42.

158. Hull, Jeff. The grizzly truth. *Outside Magazine* [Internet]. 2012 June [cited 2012 May 19]; Available from: www.outsideonline.com/outdoor-adventure/natural-intelligence/The-Grizzly-Truth.html

159. Abbey, Edward. *Beyond the wall: Essays from the outside*. New York: Holt, Rhinehart, and Winston; 1984.

160. Hornaday, William T. *Our vanishing wild life: Its extermination and preservation*. New York: Charles Scribner's Sons; 1912.

161. Romo, Rene. Divide widening over gray wolf program: Game panel hosts session. *Albuquerque Journal* (New Mexico). 2007 Mar 29; Available from: https://www.abqjournal.com/news/state/550460nm03-29-07.htm

162. Cart, Julie. Plan to remove wolves from endangered species list on hold. *Los Angeles Times* [Internet]. 2013 Aug 12; Available from: www.latimes.com/news/science/sciencenow/la-sci-sn-wolf-delisting-on-hold-20130812,0,6991561.story

163. Siemer, William F., Decker, Daniel J., Merchant, Matthew. Wildlife risk perception and expectations for agency action: Insights from a black bear management case study. Ithaca: Human Dimensions Research Unit Department of Natural Resources Cornell University; 2004 Jul. Report No.: HDRU Series No. 04–5.

164. Grose, Jessica. A death in Yellowstone. *Slate* [Internet]. 2012 Apr 2 [cited 2013 Apr 20]; Available from: _bear_attacks_how_wildlife_investigators_found_a_killer_grizzly_in_yellowstone_.single.html#pagebreak_anchor_2

165. Eisenberg, Cristinia. *The carnivore way: Coexisting with and conserving north America's predators*. Washington, D.C.: Island Press; 2014.

166. Thirgood, Simon, Redpath, Steve. Hen harriers and red grouse: science, politics and human–wildlife conflict. *J Appl Ecol*. 2008; 45: 1550–4.

167. Boertje, Rodney D, Keech, Mark A., Paragi, Thomas F. Science and values influencing predator control for Alaska moose management. *J Wildl Manag*. 2010; 74(5): 917–28.

168. Niemeyer, Carter C. The good, bad and ugly, depending on your perspective. *Transactions of the 72nd North American Wildlife and Natural Resources Conference*, p. 287–96. Available from: https://wildlifemanagement.institute/sites/default/files/2016-09/10-The_Good_Bad.pdf

169. Robbins, Jim. For wolves, a recovery may not be the blessing it seems. *New York Times* [Internet]. 2007 Feb 6 [cited 2013 Apr 13]; Available from: www.nytimes.com/learning/teachers/featured_articles/20070207wednesday.html

170. Bonner, Raymond. Crying wolf over elephants. *New York Times* [Internet]. 1993 Feb 7 [cited 2013 May 4]; Available from: www.nytimes.com/1993/02/07/magazine/crying-wolf-over-elephants.html?pagewanted=print&src=pm

171. Williams, Ted. Incite: Going catatonic. *Audubon Magazine*. 2004 September-October: 22–8.

172. Mooallem, Jon. Who would kill a monk seal? *New York Times Magazine* [Internet]. 2013 May 8 [cited 2013 May 12]; Available from: www.nytimes.com/2013/05/12/magazine/who-would-kill-a-monk-seal.html?hp&_r=0&pagewanted=print

173. Sharpe, Virginia A., Norton, Bryan G., Strachan, Donnelly. Introduction part IV: Lessons learned and applied. In: Sharpe, Virginia A., Norton, Bryan G., Donnelley, Strachan, editors. *Wolves and human communities: Biology, politics, and ethics*. Washington, D.C.: Island Press; 2001. p. 129–33.

174. Mech, L. David. Is science in danger of sanctifying the wolf? *Biol Conserv*. 2012; 150(1): 143–9.

175. Fascione, Nina, Delach, Aimee, Smith, Martin E. Introduction. In: Fascione, Nina, Delach, Aimee, Smith, Martin E., editors. *People and predators: From conflict to coexistence.* Washington, D.C.: Island Press; 2004. p. 1–8.

176. McGrath, Susan. The urchin keepers. *Audubon Magazine.* 2014 January-February: 38–45.

177. Opar, Alisa. Ghost dogs. *Audubon Magazine.* 2011 May-June: 76–81.

178. Gehrt Stanley D., Wilson, Evan C., Brown Justin L., Anchor, Chris. Population ecology of free-roaming cats and interference competition by coyotes in urban parks. *PLoS ONE* [Internet]. 2013 [cited 2014 Jun 24]; 8(9); Available from: www.plosone.org/article/info%3Adoi%2F10.1371%2Fjournal.pone.0075718

179. Foreman, Dave. *Rewilding North America.* Washington, D.C.: Island Press; 2004.

180. Judson, Olivia O. The wild side: Where tasty morsels fear to tread. *New York Times* [Internet]. 2009 Sep 28 [cited 2009 Sep 29]; Available from: http://opinionator.blogs.nytimes.com/2009/09/29/where-tasty-morsels-fear-to-tread/

181. Dugelby, Barbara L., Foreman, Dave, List, Rurik, Miller, Brian, Humphrey, Jack, Seidman, Mike, et al. Rewilding the sky islands region of the southwest. In: Maehr, David, Noss, Reed F., Larkin, Jeffery L., editors. *Large mammal restoration: Ecological and sociological challenges in the 21st century.* Washington, D.C.: Island Press; 2001. p. 65–81.

182. Ripple, William J., Wirsing, Aaron J., Beschta, Robert L., Buskirk, Steven W. Can restoring wolves aid in lynx recovery? *Wildl Soc Bull.* 2007; 35(4): 514–8.

183. Kaiser, Michel J., Jennings, Simon. An ecosystem perspective on conserving targeted and non-targeted species. In: Reynolds, John D., Mace, Georgina M., Redford, Kent H., Robinson, John G., editors. *Conservation of exploited species.* Cambridge: Cambridge University Press; 2001. p. 343–69.

184. Rauber, Paul. Illusions of wilderness. *Sierra Magazine.* 1992 July-August: 33–4.

185. Seideman, David. Out of the woods. *Audubon Magazine.* 1996 July-August: 66–75.

186. Duffield, John W., Neher, Chris J., Patterson, David A. Wolf recovery in Yellowstone: Park visitor attitudes, expenditures, and economic impacts. *Yellowstone Sci.* 2008; 16(1): 20–5.

187. Johnson, Kirk. Humans divided as wolves rebound in a changing West. *New York Times* [Internet]. 2008 Jan 2 [cited 2013 Apr 25]; Available from: www.nytimes.com/2008/01/02/us/02wolves.html?_r=0&pagewanted=print

188. Dax, Michael. Frontier anxiety for the 21st century. *High Country News* [Internet]. 2013 Apr 29 [cited 2013 May 8]; Available from: 5/8/13 from www.hcn.org/wotr/frontier-anxiety-for-the-21st-century/print_view

189. Wielgus, Robert B. Effects of wolf mortality on livestock depredations. *PLoS ONE* [Internet]. 2014 Dec 3 [cited 2014 Dec 5]; Available from: www.plosone.org/article/info%3Adoi%2F10.1371%2Fjournal.pone.0113505

190. Phillips, Michael K., Edward, Rob, Arapkiles, Tina. Restoring the gray wolf to the southern Rocky Mountains: Anatomy of a campaign to resolve a conservation issue. In: Fascione, Nina, Delach, Aimee, Smith, Martin E., editors. *People and predators: From conflict to coexistence.* Washington, D.C.: Island Press; 2004. p. 240–62.

191. Ando, Amy Whitenour. Waiting to be protected under the Endangered Species Act: The political economy of regulatory delay. *J Law Econ.* 1999; 42(1): 29–60.

192. Breining, Greg. Wolf pact: Will congress imperil the wolf again—and the very act that has saved it? *Audubon Magazine.* 2011 March-April: 22.

193. Barron, Joan. Wyoming governor: "Congressional fix" best way to resolve wolf issue. *Star-Tribune* [Internet]. 2011 Feb 18 [cited 2013 Feb 19]; Available from: http://trib.com/news/

state-and-regional/wyoming-governor-congressional-fix-best-way-to-resolve-wolf-issue/article_
a03d1469-12fa-53e8-b90d-d91d1e0a3c05.html?print=true&cid=print

194. Wildlife Management Institute. The ESA dances with wolves continues [Internet]. 2011 [cited 2011 May 19]; Available from: http://wildlifemanagementinstitute.org/index.php? option=com_content&view=article&id=525:the-esa-dances-with-wolves-continues&catid= 34:ONB%20Articles&Itemid=54

195. Mech, L. David. Wolf restoration to the Adirondacks: The advantages and disadvantages of public participation in the decision. In: Sharpe, Virginia A., Norton, Bryan G., Donnelley, Strachan, editors. *Wolves and human communities: Biology, politics, and ethics*. Washington, D.C.: Island Press; 2001. p. 13–22.

196. Parker, Warren T. Application of the experimental population designation to recovery of the endangered red wolves. *Wildl Soc Bull*. 1991; 19(1): 73–9.

197. Povilitis, Anthony, Parsons, David R., Robinson, Michael J., Baker, C. Dusti. The bureaucratically imperiled Mexican wolf. *Conserv Biol*. 2006; 20(4): 942–5.

198. Bixby, Kevin. Predator Conservation. In: Kohn, Kathryn A., editor. *Balancing on the brink of extinction: The Endangered Species Act and lessons for the future*. Washington, D.C.: Island Press; 1991. p. 199–213.

199. Mech, L. David. The challenge of wolf recovery: An ongoing dilemma for state managers. *The Wildlife Society News* [Internet]. 2013 Mar 22 [cited 2013 Jun 17]; Available from: http://news.wildlife.org/featured/the-challenge-of-wolf-recovery/

200. Cart, Julie. Recovery of Mexican gray wolves remains elusive: Federal efforts to bring back the endangered animal in the Southwest have backfired, critics say. *Chicago Tribune* [Internet]. 2009 Jul 26 [cited 2009 Jul 27]; Available from: www.chicagotribune.com/ news/nationworld/la-na-wolves26-2009jul26,0,1186726.story

201. Carswell, Cally. Mexican wolf restoration hits (another) snag. *High Country News* [Internet]. 2015 Sep 16 [cited 2015 Sep 19]; Available from: www.hcn.org/articles/new-mexico-resists-mexican-wolf-releases?utm_source=wcn1&utm_medium=email

202. Schlickeisen, Rodger. Overcoming cultural barriers to wolf reintroduction. In: Sharpe, Virginia A., Norton, Bryan G., Donnelley, Strachan, editors. *Wolves and human communities: Biology, politics, and ethics*. Washington, D.C.: Island Press; 2001. p. 61–73.

203. Conover, Michael R, Dinkins, Jonathan B. Human dimensions of abundant wildlife management. In: Decker, Daniel J., Riley, Shawn J., Siemer, William F., editors. *Human dimensions of wildlife management*. 2nd ed. Baltimore: Johns Hopkins University Press; 2012. p. 177–202.

204. Musiani, Marco, Muhly, Tyler, Callaghan, Carolan, Gates, C. Cormack, Smith, Martin E., Stone, Suzanne, et al. Wolves in rural agricultural areas of western North America: Conflict and conservation. In: Fascione, Nina, Delach, Aimee, Smith, Martin E., editors. *People and predators: From conflict to coexistence*. Washington, D.C.: Island Press; 2004. p. 51–75.

205. Vynne, Stacy J. Livestock compensation for the Mexican gray wolf: Improving tolerance or increasing tension? *Hum Dimens Wildl*. 2009; 14(6): 456–7.

206. Treves, Adrian, Jurewicz, Randle L., Naughton-Treves, Lisa, Wilcove, David S. The price of tolerance: Wolf damage payments after recovery. *Biodivers Conserv*. 2009; 18: 4003–21.

207. Naughton-Treves, Lisa, Grossber, Rebecca, Treves, Adrian. Paying for tolerance: Rural citizens' attitudes toward wolf depredation and compensation. *Conserv Biol*. 2003; 17(6): 1500–11.

208. McGregor, JoAnn. Crocodile crimes: People versus wildlife and the politics of postcolonial conservation on Lake Kariba, *Zimbabwe. Geoforum*. 2005; 36: 353–69.

209. Jonsing, A.J.T., Pandav, Bivash, Madhusudan, M.D. Status and conservation of tigers in the Indian subcontinent. In: Tilson, Ronald, Nyhus, Philip J., editors. *Tigers of the world: The science, politics, and conservation of panthera tigris.* 2nd ed. Amsterdam: Academic Press; 2010. p. 315–30.

210. Nyhus, Philip J., Tilson, Ronald. Panthera tigris vs homo sapiens: Conflict, coexistence, or extinction. In: Tilson, Ronald, Nyhus, Philip J., editors. *Tigers of the world: The science, politics, and conservation of panthera tigris.* 2nd ed. Amsterdam: Academic Press; 2010. p. 125–41.

211. Bulte, Erwin H., Rondeau, Daniel. Why compensating wildlife damages may be bad for conservation. *J Wildl Manag.* 2005; 69(1): 14–9.

212. Zabel, Astrid, Holm-Muller, Karin. Conservation performance payments for carnivore conservation in Sweden. *Conserv Biol.* 2008; 22(2): 247–51.

213. Defenders of Wildlife. Frequently asked questions: Transitioning wolf compensation [Internet]. 2010 [cited 2013 May 8]; Available from: www.defenders.org/publication/faq-transitioning-wolf-compensation

214. Metrick, Andrew, Weitzman, Martin L. Patterns of behavior in endangered species preservation. *Land Econ.* 1996; 72(1): 1–16.

215. Jasper, James M., *Nelkin, Dorothy. The animal rights crusade: The growth of a moral protest.* New York: The Free Press; 1992.

216. Nash, Roderick Frazier. *The rights of nature: A history of environmental ethics.* Madison: The University of Wisconsin Press; 1989.

Chapter 6 References

1. Nash, Roderick Frazier. *The rights of nature: A history of environmental ethics.* Madison: The University of Wisconsin Press; 1989.

2. Yaffee, Steven Lewis. *Prohibitive policy: Implementing the federal Endangered Species Act.* Cambridge: MIT Press; 1982.

3. U.S. Fish and Wildlife Service. Candidate conservation agreements (CCAs) [Internet]. 2013 [cited 2013 Aug 17]; Available from: www.fws.gov/endangered/what-we-do/cca.html

4. Phelps, Martha F. Candidate conservation agreements under the Endangered Species Act: Prospects and perils of an administrative experiment. *Boston Coll Environ Aff Law Rev.* 1997; 25(1): 175–212.

5. Murchison, Kenneth M. *The snail darter case: TVA versus the Endangered Species Act.* Lawrence: University of Kansas Press; 2007.

6. Mann, Charles C., Plummer, Mark L. *Noah's choice: The future of endangered species.* New York: Alfred A. Knopf; 1995.

7. Wyman, Katrina Miriam. Rethinking the ESA to reflect human dominion over nature. *N Y Univ Environ Law J.* 2008; 17: 490–528.

8. Tobin, Richard J. *The expendable future: U.S. politics and the protection of biological diversity.* Durham: Duke University Press; 1990.

9. VonHoldt, Bridgett M., Stahler, J. Daniel R., Bangs, J. Edward, Smith, Douglas W., Jimenez, Mike D., Mack, Curt M. et al. The genealogy and genetic viability of reintroduced Yellowstone grey wolves. *Mol Ecol.* 2008; 17(1): 252–74.

10. U.S. Senate. Listing and delisting processes under the Endangered Species Act [Internet]. Sect. Hearing before the Subcommittee on Fisheries, Wildlife, and Water of the Committee

on the Environment and Public Works. 137th Congress First Session on the Regulations and Procedures of the U.S. Fish and Wildlife Service Concerning the Listing and Delisting of Species Under the Endangered Species Act, S. HRG. 107–322 May 9, 2001; Available from: www.gpo.gov/fdsys/pkg/CHRG-107shrg78073/html/CHRG-107shrg78073.htm

11. U.S. Fish and Wildlife Service. News release: Endangered species act scores another success as Oregon chub becomes first fish delisted due to recovery [Internet]. 2015 [cited 2015 Feb 20]; Available from: www.fws.gov/pacific/news/news.cfm?id=2144375359

12. Wilson, Edward O. On silent spring. In: Matthiessen, Peter, editor. *Courage for the Earth: Writers, scientists, and activists celebrate the life and writing of Rachel Carson.* Boston: Houghton Mifflin Company; 2007. p. 27–36.

13. U.S. Fish and Wildlife Service. Endangered species. Defining success under the Endangered Species Act [Internet]. 2013 [cited 2013 Jun 20]; Available from: www.fws.gov/endangered/news/episodes/bu-04–2013/coverstory/index.html

14. Maile, C. Neel, Leidner, Allison K., Haines, Aaron, Goble, Dale, D., Scott, J. Michael. By the numbers: How is recovery defined by the US Endangered Species Act? *BioScience.* 2012; 62(7): 646–57.

15. Robinson, Michael J. *Predatory bureaucracy: The extermination of the wolf and the transformation of the west.* Boulder: The University of Colorado Press; 2005.

16. Nie, Martin. *Beyond wolves: The politics of wolf recovery and management.* Minneapolis: University of Minnesota Press; 2003.

17. Donlan, C. Josh. *Proactive strategies for protecting species.* Berkeley: University of California Press; 2015.

18. Male, Timothy, Donlan, C. Josh. The future of pre-listing conservation programs for wildlife conservation. In: Donlan, C. Josh, editor. *Proactive strategies for protecting species.* Berkeley: University of California Press; 2015. p. 219–29.

19. Vucetich, John A., Nelson, Michael Paul. Conservation, or curation? *New York Times* [Internet]. 2014 Aug 20; Available from: www.nytimes.com/2014/08/21/opinion/conservation-or-curation.html?emc=edit_tnt_20140820&nlid=10365419&tntemail0=y&_r=0

20. Ashe, Dan, Sobeck, Eileen. Letter: Using scarce resources to save endangered species [Internet]. 2014 [cited 2014 Sep 5]; Available from: www.nytimes.com/2014/09/05/opinion/using-scarce-resources-to-save-endangered-species.html?emc=edit_tnt_20140904&nlid=10365419&tntemail0=y&_r=0

21. Meyer, Stephen M. *The end of the wild.* Cambridge: The MIT Press; 2006.

22. Udall, James R. Launching the natural ark. *Sierra Magazine.* 1991 September-October: 80–9.

23. Kirst, Marian Lyman. BLM teams with researchers to protect midget faded rattlesnake. *High Country News* [Internet]. 2013 May 14 [cited 2013 May 14]; Available from: www.hcn.org/issues/45.8/blm-teams-with-researchers-to-protect-midget-faded-rattlesnake/print_view

24. Zollinger, Brett, Daniels, Steven E. We all can just get along: The social constructions of prairie dog stakeholders and the use of a transaction management approach in devising a species conservation plan. In: Herda-Rapp, Ann, Goedeke, Theresa L., editors. *Mad about wildlife: Looking at social conflict over wildlife.* Leiden: Brill; 2005. p. 253–77.

25. Beissinger, Steven R., Perrine, John D. Extinction, recovery, and the ESA. In: Shogren, Jason F., Tschirhart, John, editors. *Protecting endangered species in the United States.* Cambridge: Cambridge University Press; 2001. p. 51–71.

26. Watkins, T.H. What's wrong with the ESA? Not much – here's why. *Audubon Magazine.* 1996 January-February: 37–41.

27. Doremus, Holly, Pagel, Joel E. Why listing may be forever: Perspectives on delisting under the U.S. Endangered Species Act. *Conserv Biol*. 2001; 15(5): 1258–68.

28. National Research Council. Science and the Endangered Species Act [Internet]. Washington, D.C.: National Academy Press; 1995 [cited 2016 Mar 24]; Available from: www.nap.edu/read/4978/chapter/1

29. U.S. General Accountability Office. Endangered species: Many factors affect the length of time to recover select species. 2006 Sep. Report No.: GAO-06–730.

30. Roman, Joe. *Listed: Dispatches from America's Endangered Species Act*. Cambridge: Harvard University Press; 2011.

31. Ferraro, Paul J., McIntosh, Craig, Ospina, Monica. The effectiveness of the US Endangered Species Act: An econometric analysis using matching methods. *J Environ Econ Manag*. 2007; 54(3): 245.

32. Kerkvliet, Joe, Langpap, Christian. Learning from endangered and threatened species recovery programs: A case study using U.S. Endangered Species Act recovery scores. *Ecol Econ*. 2007; 63(2): 499–510.

33. Hagen, Amy N., Hodges, Karen E. Resolving critical habitat designation failures: Reconciling law, policy, and biology. *Conserv Biol*. 2006; 20(2): 399–407.

34. Greenwald, D. Noah, Suckling, Kieran F., Pimm, Stuart L. Critical habitat and the role of peer review in governmen. *BioScience*. 2012; 62(7): 686–90.

35. Rachlinski, Jeffery J. Noah by the numbers: An empirical evaluation of the Endangered Species Act. *Cornell Law Rev*. 1997; 82: 356–90.

36. Armsworth, Paul R., Cappel, Carie V., Micheli, Fiorenz, Bjorkstet, Eric P. Chapter Three: Marine species. In: Goble, Dale, D., Scott, J. Michael, Davis, Frank W., editors. *The Endangered Species Act at thirty: Volume I: Renewing the conservation promise*. Washington, D.C.: Island Press; 2006. p. 36–44.

37. Wilcove, David S. *No way home*. Washington, D.C.: Island Press; 2008.

38. Allin, Craig W. *The politics of wilderness preservation*. Westport: Greenwood Press; 1982.

39. Wolf, Clark. Sustainability, environmental policy, and the reintroduction of wolves. In: Sharpe, Virginia A., Norton, Bryan G., Donnelley, Strachan, editors. *Wolves and human communities: Biology, politics, and ethics*. Washington, D.C.: Island Press; 2001. p. 233–53.

40. Rauber, Paul. Maximizing profits. *Sierra Magazine*. 1994 July-August: 42–4.

41. Brooks, Richard O., Jones, Ross, Virginia, Ross A. *Law and ecology: The rise of the ecosystem regime*. Burlington, VT: Ashgate Publishing Company; 2002.

42. Grumbine, R. Edward. Using biodiversity as a justification for nature protection in the U.S. *Humboldt J Soc Relat*. 1995; 21(1): 35–59.

43. Colburn, Christine H. Forest policy and the Quincy library group. In: Brunner, Ronald D., Colburn, Christine H., Cromley, Christina M., Klein, Roberta A., editors. *Finding common ground*. New York: Yale University Press; 2002. p. 159–201.

44. Noss, Reed F., O'Connell, Michael A., Murphy, Dennis D. *The science of conservation planning: Habitat conservation under the Endangered Species Act*. Washington, D.C.: Island Press; 1997.

45. Boutin, Stan. Top carnivores and biodiversity conservation in the boreal forest. In: Ray, Justina C., Redford, Kent H., Steneck, Robert S., Berger, Joel, editors. *Large carnivores and the conservation of biodiversity*. Washington, D.C.: Island Press; 2005. p. 362–80.

46. Linnell, John D.C., Promberger, Christoph, Boitani, Luigi, Swenson, Jon E., Britenmoser, Urs, Andersen, Reidar. The linkage between conservation strategies for large carnivores and

biodiversity: The view from the "half-full" forests of Europe. In: Ray, Justina C., Redford, Kent H., Steneck, Robert S., Berger, Joel, editors. *Large carnivores and the conservation of biodiversity*. Washington, D.C.: Island Press; 2005. p. 381–99.

47. Noss, Reed F., Maehr, David S., Larkin, Jeffery L. Introduction: Why restore large mammals? In: Maehr, David S., Noss, Reed F., Larkin, Jeffery L., editors. *Large mammal restoration: Ecological and sociological challenges in the 21st century*. Washington, D.C.: Island Press; 2001. p. 1–21.

48. Tear, Timothy H. Recovery plans are the Endangered Species Act: Are criticisms supported by data? *Conserv Biol*. 1995; 9(1): 183–95.

49. Holt, Sidney. On loving whales, krill, and marine ecosystems. *Conserv Biol*. 1993; 7(3): 451–2.

50. Abbitt, Robbyn J.F., Scott, J. Michael. Examining differences between recovered and declining endangered species. *Conserv Biol*. 2001; 15(5): 1274–84.

51. Naeem, Shahid, Jouseau, Claire. Preserving ecosystem services. In: Scott, J. Michael, Goble, Dale, D., Davis, Frank W., editors. *The Endangered Species Act at thirty: Conserving biodiversity in human-dominated landscapes*. Washington, D.C.: Island Press; 2006. p. 80–96.

52. Roemer, Gary W., Wayne, Robert K. Conservation in conflict: The tale of two endangered species. *Conserv Biol*. 2003; 17(5): 1251–60.

53. Clark Jr., Howard O., Cypher, Brian L., Warrick, Gregory D., Kelly, Patrick A., Williams, Daniel F., Grubbs, David E. Challenges in conservation of the endangered San Joaquin kit fox. In: Fascione, Nina, Delach, Aimee, Smith, Martin E., editors. *People and predators: From conflict to coexistence*. Washington, D.C.: Island Press; 2004. p. 118–31.

54. DiSilvestro, Roger L. *The endangered kingdom: The struggle to save America's wildlife*. New York: John Wiley & Sons, Inc.; 1989.

55. Yaffee, Steven Lewis. *The wisdom of the spotted owl: Policy lessons for a new century*. Washington, D.C.: Island Press; 1994.

56. New York Times. Editorial: Wolves under review. 2013 Aug 15 [cited 2013 Aug 15]; Available from: www.nytimes.com/2013/08/16/opinion/wolves-under-review.html?emc=edit_tnt_20130815&tntemail0=y&_r=0&pagewanted=print

57. Plater, Zygmunt J.B., Abrams, Robert H., Goldfarb, William, Graham, Robert L. *Environmental law and policy: Nature, law, and society*. St. Paul, Minnesota: West Publishing Co.; 1998.

58. Bruskotter, Jeremy T, Enzler, Sherry A. Narrowing the definition of endangered species: Implications of the U.S. government's interpretation of the phase "A significant portion of its range" under the Endangered Species Act of 1973. *Hum Dimens Wildl*. 2009; 14: 73–88.

59. Adams, Jonathan S. *The future of the wild: Radical conservation for a crowded world*. Boston: Beacon Press; 2006.

60. Doremus, Holly. Restoring endangered species: The importance of being wild. *Harv Environ Law Rev*. 1999; 23(1): 1–92.

61. Sanderson, Eric W., Redford, Kent H., Weber, Bill, Aune, Keith, Baldes, Dick, Berger, Joel et al. The ecological future of the North American bison: Conceiving long-term, large-scale conservation of wildlife. *Conserv Biol*. 2008; 22(2): 252–66.

62. New York Times. Editorial: Another species in danger. 2008 Jul 19 [cited 2008 Jul 19]; Available from: www.nytimes.com/2008/07/19/opinion/19sat3.html

63. Mech, L. David. Wolf restoration to the Adirondacks: The advantages and disadvantages of public participation in the decision. In: Sharpe, Virginia A., Norton, Bryan G., Donnelley, Strachan, editors. *Wolves and human communities: Biology, Politics, and Ethics*. Washington, D.C.: Island Press; 2001. p. 13–22.

64. Beatley, Timothy. *Habitat conservation planning: Endangered species and urban growth.* Austin: The University of Texas Press; 1994.

65. Ruckelshaus, Mary, Darm, Donna. Science and implementation. In: Scott, J. Michael, Goble, Dale, D., Davis, Frank W., editors. *The Endangered Species Act at thirty Volume 2: Conserving biodiversity in human-dominated landscapes.* Washington, D.C.i: Island Press; 2006. p. 104–26.

66. Theberge, John B. An ecologist's perspective on wolf recovery in the northeastern United States. In: Elder, John, editor. *The return of the wolf: Reflections on the future of wolves in the northeast.* Hanover: Middlebury College Press; 2000. p. 22–63.

67. Goble, Dale, D. Reintroducing the missing parts: The experimental population provisions of the Endangered Species Act. In: Lynch, Tom, editor. *El lobo: Readings on the Mexican gray wolf.* Salt Lake City: University of Utah Press; 2005. p. 130–7.

68. Oko, Dan. Profiles in courage. *Sierra Magazine.* 2008 September-October: 44–7.

69. U.S. General Accountability Office. Endangered species: Management improvement could enhance recovery program. 1988 Dec. Report No.: GAO/RCED-89-5.

70. Seelye, Katharine Q. Ending logjam, U.S. reaches accord on endangered species. *New York Times* [Internet]. 2001 Aug 30 [cited 2013 Jul 13]; Available from: www.nytimes.com/2001/08/30/us/ending-logjam-us-reaches-accord-on-endangered-species.html

71. Williams, Ted. Incite: Last chance. *Audubon Magazine.* 2009 September-October: 36–44.

72. Czech, Brian, Krausman, Paul R. *The Endangered Species Act.* Baltimore: Johns Hopkins University Press; 2001.

73. Keiter, Robert B., Boyce, Mark S. Greater Yellowstone's future: Ecosystem management in a wilderness environment. In: Keiter, Robert B., Boyce, Mark S., editors. *The greater Yellowstone ecosystem: Redefining America's wilderness heritage.* New Haven: Yale University Press; 1991. p. 379–413.

74. Stokes, David L., Hanson, Marian F., Oaks, Deborah D., Straub, Jaime E., Ponio, Aileen V. Local land-use planning to conserve biodiversity: Planners' perspectives on what works. *Conserv Biol.* 2009; 24(2): 450–60.

75. Metrick, Andrew, Weitzman, Martin L. Conflict and choices in biodiversity preservation. *J Econ Perspect.* 1998; 12(3): 21–34.

76. Anderson, David A. Pricing protection. In: Spray, Sharon L., McGothlin, Karen L., editors. *Loss of biodiversity.* Lanham: Rowman & Littlefield Publishers, Inc.; 2003. p. 99–118.

77. U.S. General Accountabilty Office. Endangered species: Management improvement could enhance recovery program. Report to the Chairman, Subcommittee on Fisheries and Wildlife Conservation, and the Environment, Committee on Merchant Marine and Fisheries, House of Representatives. GAO/RCED-89-5. 1988.

78. Restani, Marco, Marzluff, John M. Avian conservation under the Endangered Species Act: Expenditures versus recovery priorities. *Conserv Biol.* 2001; 15(5): 1292–9.

79. Cardwell, Diane, Krauss, Clifford. Frack quietly, please: Sage grouse is nesting. *New York Times* [Internet]. 2014 Jul 19 [cited 2014 Jul 23]; Available from: www.nytimes.com/2014/07/20/business/energy-environment/disparate-interests-unite-to-protect-greater-sage-grouse.html?emc=edit_th_20140720&nl=todaysheadlines&nlid=10365419

80. Wildlife Management Institute. Montana adopts sage grouse strategy. Outdoor News Bulletin [Internet]. 2014 Sep 15 [cited 2016 Apr 19];68(9); Available from: www.wildlifemanagementinstitute.org/index.php?option=com_content&view=article&id=768%3Amontana-adopts-sage-grouse-conservation-strategy&Itemid=95

81. Beartooth NBC. Governor Bullock signs executive order establishing the sage grouse habitat conservation program. 2014 Sep 9 [cited 2014 Sep 16]; Available from: www.beartoothnbc.com/

home/headlines/Governor-Bullock-Signs-Executive-Order-Establishing-the-Sage-Grouse-Habi tat-Conservation-Program-274487431.html

82. Storrow, Benjamin. Feds adopt Wyoming sage grouse strategy for 2.4 million acres around Lander. *Casper Star Tribune* [Internet]. 2014 Jun 27 [cited 2014 Sep 16]; Available from: http://trib.com/business/energy/feds-adopt-wyoming-sage-grouse-strategy-for-million-acres-around/article_32f3fd37-c141-561c-99ae-3e38961ad086.html

83. Thuermer, Jr., Angus M. Conservation groups give BLM an "F" for sage grouse protection. [Internet]. Wyofile; 2014 [cited 2014 Sep 16]; Available from: http://wyofile.com/angus_thuermer/conservation-groups-give-blm-f-sage-grouse-protection/

84. Williams, Ted. Two flat tires on the sage grouse express. *High Country News* [Internet]. 2014 Sep 9 [cited 2014 Sep 16]; Available from: www.hcn.org/articles/two-flat-tires-on-the-sage-grouse-express

85. Ginger, Shauna, Vickerman, Sara, Taylor, Bruce. The greater sage-grouse, energy development, and pre-listing conservation. In: Donlan, C. Josh, editor. *Proactive strategies for protecting species*. Berkeley: University of California Press; 2015. p. 167–87.

86. Goldfarb, Ben. Are we smart enough to solve our raven problem? *High Country News* [Internet]. 2014 Jul 21 [cited 2014 Jul 25]; Available from: www.hcn.org/issues/46.12/are-we-smart-enough-to-solve-our-raven-problem

87. Zaffos, Joshua. Gunnison sage grouse gets divisive "threatened" listing: The decision upsets enviros and industry alike. *High Country News* [Internet]. 2014 Nov 14 [cited 2014 Nov 18]; Available from: www.hcn.org/articles/a-grouse-divided?utm_source=wcn1&utm_medium=email

88. U.S. Fish and Wildlife Service. Endangered and threatened wildlife and plants: Threatened status for Gunnison sage-grouse. Final Rule [Internet]. 2014 [cited 2014 Nov 19]; Available from: www.fws.gov/mountain-prairie/species/birds/gunnisonsagegrouse/GUSGFinalListingRule_11122014.pdf

89. Wildlife Management Institute. International sage-grouse forum held in Salt Lake. *Outdoor News Bulletin* [Internet]. 2014 Nov 17 [cited 2014 Nov 18]; 69(11); Available from: http://wildlifemanagementinstitute.org/index.php?option=com_content&view=article&id=779:international-sage-grouse-forum-held-in-salt-lake&catid=34:ONB%20Articles&Itemid=54

90. U.S. Fish and Wildlife Service. Endangered and threatened wildlife and plants: Threatened status for Gunnison sage-grouse. Final rule [Internet]. 2014 [cited 2014 Nov 19]; Available from: www.fws.gov/mountain-prairie/species/birds/gunnisonsagegrouse/GUSGFinalListingRule_11122014.pdf

91. Wilson, Reid. Western states worry decision on bird's fate could cost billions in development. *Washington Post* [Internet]. 2014 May 11 [cited 2014 May 19]; Available from: www.washingtonpost.com/blogs/govbeat/wp/2014/05/11/western-states-worry-decision-on-birds-fate-could-cost-billions-in-development/

92. Brown, Matthew, Gruver, Mead. Sage grouse plan aims for balance between industry, wildlife. *Seattle Times.com* [Internet]. 2015 Sep 22 [cited 2015 Sep 23]; Available from: www.seattletimes.com/nation-world/u-s-rejects-protections-for-greater-sage-grouse-across-west/

93. Gilman, Sarah. ESA changes could protect sage on private land. *High Country News* [Internet]. 2014 May 20 [cited 2014 May 20]; Available from: www.hcn.org/blogs/goat/esa-changes-could-help-protect-sage-grouse-on-private-land?utm_source=wcn1&utm_medium=email

94. U.S. Bureau of Land Management. Historic conservation campaign protects greater sage-grouse [Internet]. 2015 [cited 2016 Apr 19]; Available from: www.blm.gov/wo/st/en/info/newsroom/2015/september/nr_09_22_2015.html

95. Gilman, Sarah. Compromise on Colorado's Roan plateau. *High Country News* [Internet]. 2014 Nov 22 [cited 2014 Nov 25]; Available from: www.hcn.org/articles/compromise-on-colorados-roan-plateau?utm_source=wcn1&utm_medium=email

96. Boardman, Robert. Risk politics in western states: Canadian species in comparative perspective. In: Beazley, Karen, Boardman, Robert, editors. *Politics of the wild: Canada and endangered species*. Oxford: Oxford University Press; 2001. p. 167–89.

97. Donahue, Debra. The Endangered Species Act and its current set of incentive tools for species protection. In: Shogren, Jason F., editor. *Species at risk: Using economic incentives to shelter endangered species on private lands*. Austin: University of Texas Press; 2005. p. 25–63.

98. Ando, Amy Whritenour. Waiting to be protected under the Endangered Species Act: The political economy of regulatory delay. *J Law Econ*. 1999; 42(1): 29–60.

99. Wilhere, George F. The how-much-is-enough myth. *Conserv Biol*. 2008; 22(3): 514–7.

100. U.S. Senate. Senate Hearing 108–356 Endangered Species Act: Review of the consultation process required by section 7. Hearing Before the Subcommittee on Fisheries, Wildlife, and Water of the Committee on Environment and Public Works United States Senate 187th Congress First Session on an Examination of the Consulting Process required by Section 7 of the Endangered Species Act June 25, 2003 [Internet]. Sect. Hearing Before the Subcommittee on Fisheries, Wildlife, and Water of the Committee on Environment and Public Works United States Senat Washington, D.C.: Government Printing Office; Jun 25, 2003; Available from: https://bulk.resource.org/gpo.gov/hearings/108s/92378.pdf

101. U.S. House of Representatives. Land and money mitigation requirements in Endangered Species Act enforcement. Sect. Oversight Hearing before the Committee on Resources House of Representatives 106th Congress First Session, Serial No. 106–34 Washington, D.C.; May 26, 1999.

102. Campoy, Ana. Drought in Southwest fuels dispute over protections for silvery minnow. *Wall Street Journal* [Internet]. 2014 Feb 23 [cited 2014 Apr 23]; Available from: http://online.wsj.com/news/articles/SB10001424052702304626304579506182996143744#printMode

103. Cashore, Benjamin, Howlett, Michael. Behavioral thresholds and institutional rigidities as explanations of punctuated equilibrium processes in Pacific northwest forest policy dynamics. In: Repetto, Robert, editor. *Punctuated equilibrium and the dynamics of US environmental policy*. New Haven: Yale University Press; 2006. p. 137–61.

104. Williams, Ted. The new guardians: HCPs, private landowners incentive to help protect endangered species. *Audubon Magazine*. 1999 January-February: 34–9.

105. Williams, Ted. Bait and switch. *Audubon Magazine*. 2008 March-April: 60–6.

106. Beatley, Timothy. Preserving biodiversity through the use of habitat conservation plans. In: Porter, Douglas R., Salvesen, David A., editors. *Collaborative planning for wetlands and wildlife: Issues and examples*. Washington, D.C.: Island Press; 1995. p. 35–74.

107. Lueck, Dean. The law and politics of Federal wildlife preservation. In: Anderson, Terry L., editor. *Political environmentalism: Going behind the green curtain*. Stanford: Hoover Institution Press; 2000. p. 61–120.

108. Hoffman, Andrew J., Bazerman, Max H., Yaffee, Steven L. Balancing business interests and endangered species protection. *Sloan Manage Rev*. 1997; 39(1): 59–73.

109. Lueck, Dean, Michael, Jeffrey A. Preemptive habitat destruction under the Endangered Species Act. *J Law Econ*. 2003; 46(April): 27–60.

110. Stap, Don. Returning the natives. *Audubon Magazine*. 1996 November-December: 54–60 & 120–3.

111. Conover, Michael R., Messmer, Terry A. Wildlife and rural landowners. In: Decker, Daniel J., Brown, Tommy L., Siemer, William F., editors. *Human dimensions of wildlife management in North America*. Bethesda: The Wildlife Society; 2001. p. 243–68.

112. Tobin, Mitch. *Endangered: Biodiversity on the brink*. Golden, CO: Fulcrum; 2010.

113. Vongs, Pueng. The real woodpecker deal. *Audubon Magazine*. 1993 September-October: 28–9.

114. Stevens, William K. The future of Endangered Species Act in doubt as law Is debated. *New York Times* [Internet]. 1995 May 16 [cited 2013 Jul 30]; Available from: www.nytimes.com/1995/05/16/science/future-of-endangered-species-act-in-doubt-as-law-is-debated.html?pagewanted=all&src=pm

115. Meyer, Stephen M. Environmentalism and economic prosperity: Testing the environmental impact hypothesis [Internet]. Cambridge: MIT; 1992 Oct [cited 2016 Apr 18]; Available from: http://web.mit.edu/polisci/mpepp/Reports/eep.pdf

116. Prato, Tony, Fagre, Dan. *National parks and protected areas: Approaches for balancing social, economic, and ecological values*. Ames, IA: Blackwell Publishing Professional; 2005.

117. Wells, Ken. Environmentalists split over tortoise treatment at solar farms. *Business Week* [Internet]. 2012 Sep 20 [cited 2013 Jul 5]; Available from: www.businessweek.com/printer/articles/327914?type=bloomberg

118. Cart, Julie. Saving desert tortoises is a costly hurdle for solar projects. *Los Angeles Times* [Internet]. 2012 Mar 4 [cited 2012 Mar 14]; Available from: http://articles.latimes.com/print/2012/mar/04/local/la-me-solar-tortoise-20120304

119. Sullivan, Brian K. The greening of public lands grazing in the Southwestern U.S.A. *Conserv Biol*. 2009; 23(4): 1047–9.

120. Scott, J. Michael, Goble, Dale, D., Davis, Frank W. Introduction. In: Goble, Dale, D., Scott, J. Michael, Davis, Frank W., editors. *The Endangered Species Act at thirty: Volume I: Renewing the conservation promise*. Washington, D.C.: Island Press; 2006. p. 3–15.

121. Burgess, Bonnie B. *Fate of the wild: The Endangered Species Act and the future of biodiversity*. Athens: The University of Georgia Press; 2001.

122. Goble, Dale, D. Reintroducing the missing parts: The experimental population provisions of the Endangered Species Act. In: Lynch, Tom, editor. *El Lobo: Readings on the Mexican gray wolf*. Salt Lake City: University of Utah Press; 2005. p. 130–7.

123. Maehr, David S. Dispersal and colonization in the Florida panther: Overcoming landscape barriers – biological and political. In: Fascione, Nina, Delach, Aimee, Smith, Martin E., editors. *People and predators: From conflict to coexistence*. Washington, D.C.: Island Press; 2004.

124. Cioc, Mark. *The game of conservation: International treaties to protect the world's migratory animals*. Athens: Ohio University Press; 2009.

125. U.S. General Accountiability Office. Endangered Species Act: Information on species protection on nonfederal lands. 1994. Report No.: GAO/RCED-95-16.

126. Klyza, Christopher McGrory, Sousa, David J. *American environmental policy*. Cambridge: MIT Press; 2013.

127. Babbitt, Bruce. *Cities in the wilderness: A new vision of land use in America*. Washington, D.C.: Island Press/Shearwater Books; 2005.

128. Keiter, Robert B. *Keeping faith with nature: Ecosystems, democracy, & America's public lands*. New Haven: Yale University Press; 2003.

129. Hierl, Lauren A., Franklin, Janet, Deutschman, Douglas H., Regan, Helen M., Johnson, Brenda S. Assessing and prioritizing ecological communities for monitoring in a regional habitat conservation plan. *Environ Manage*. 2008; 42: 165–79.

130. Alagona, Peter S., Pincetl, Stephanie. The Coachella valley multiple species habitat conservation plan: A decade of delays. *Environ Manage*. 2008; 41: 1–11.

131. Adams, Jonathan S. *The future of the wild: Radical conservation for a crowded world*. Boston: Beacon Press; 2006.

132. Luoma, Jon R. Habitat conservation plans: Compromise or capitulation. *Audubon Magazine*. 1998 January-February: 36–43.

133. Greer, Keith A. Habitat conservation planning in San Diego county, California: Lessons learned after five years of implementation. *Environ Pract*. 2004; 6(3): 230–9.

134. Thomas, Craig W. Habitat conservation planning: Certainly empower, somewhat deliberative, questionably democratic. *Polit Soc*. 2001; 29(1): 105–30.

135. Goldstein, Bruce Evan. Epistemic mediation: Aligning expertise across boundaries within an endangered species habitat conservation plan. *Plan Theory Pract*. 2010; 11(4): 523–47.

136. Dixon, Lloyd, Sorensen, Paul, Wachs, Martin, Collins, Myles, Hanson, Mark, Kofner, Mark et al. Balancing environment and development. Costs, revenues, and benefits of the Western Riverside County multiple species habitat conservation plan. [Internet]. Rand Corporation; 2008 [cited 2016 Jun 8]; Available from: www.rand.org/content/dam/rand/pubs/mono graphs/2008/RAND_MG816.pdf

137. Brook, Amara, Zint, Michaela, De Young, Raymond. Landowners' responses to an Endangered Species Act listing and implications for encouraging conservation. *Conserv Biol*. 2003; 17(6): 1638–49.

138. Fox, Jessica, Scott, J. Michael, Goble, Dale, D., Davis, Frank W. Conservation banking. In: Scott, J. Michael, Goble, Dale, D., Davis, Frank W., editors. *The Endangered Species Act at thirty Volume II: Conserving biodiversity in human-dominated landscapes*. Washington, D.C.: Island Press; 2006. p. 228–42.

139. Li, Ya-Wei, Male, Timothy. Pre-listing conservation. In: Donlan, C. Josh, editor. *Proactive strategies for protecting species*. Berkeley: University of California Press; 2015. p. 73–93.

140. Williams, Ted. Free-range chickens. *Audubon Magazine* [Internet]. 2011 September-October [cited 2011 Dec 18]; Available from: www.audubonmagazine.org/articles/birds/free-range-chickens?

141. Rice, Nathan. Saving threatened Utah prairie dogs – on private property. *High Country News* [Internet]. 2012 Aug 20 [cited 2012 Aug 28]; Available from: www.hcn.org/issues/44.14/saving-threatened-utah-prairie-dogs-on-private-property/print_view

142. Wortman-Wunder, Emily. Do subdivisions designed for conservation actually help wildlife? *High Country News* [Internet]. 2012 Jun 11 [cited 2012 Jun 15]; Available from: www.hcn.org/issues/44.9/do-subdivisions-designed-for-conservation-actually-help-wildlife/print_view

143. Hannum, C.S., Laposa, Stephen, Reed, Sarah E., Pejchar, Liba, Ex, Lindsay. Comparative analysis of housing in conservation developments: Colorado Case Studies. *J Sustain Real Estate*. 2012; 4: 149–76.

144. Morrison, Scott A., Boyce, Walter. Conserving connectivity: Some lessons from mountain lions in southern California. *Conserv Biol*. 2008; 23(2): 275–85.

145. Wilcove, David S. *The condor's shadow: The loss and recovery of wildlife in America*. New York: W.H. Freeman and Company; 1999.

146. Doremus, Holly, Tarlock, A. Dan. *Water war in the Klamath basin: Macho law, combat biology, and dirty politics*. Washington, D.C.: Island Press; 2008.

147. Satija, Neena. It's not the rare birds they mind so much: It's the watchdogs. *New York Times* [Internet]. 2013 Sep 25 [cited 2013 Sep 27]; Available from: www.nytimes.com/2013/09/27/us/its-not-the-rare-birds-they-mind-so-much-its-the-watchdogs.html?emc=edit_tnt_2013 0926&tntemail0=y&pagewanted=print

148. Zaffos, Joshua. Conservation agreements try to head off endangered species listings. *High Country News* [Internet]. 2012 May 28 [cited 2012 Jun 15]; Available from: www.hcn.org/issues/44.9/conservation-agreements-try-to-head-off-endangered-species-listings?utm_source=wcn1&utm_medium=email

149. Baier, Lowell E. *Inside the equal access to justice act: Environmental litigation and the crippling battle over America's lands, endangered species, and critical habitats.* Lanham: Rowman & Littlefield Publishers, Inc.; 2016.

150. Woody, Todd. Wildlife at risk face long line at U.S. agency. *New York Times* [Internet]. 2011 Apr 20 [cited 2013 Jul 25]; Available from: www.nytimes.com/2011/04/21/science/earth/21species.html?pagewanted=print

151. Biber, Eric, Brosi, Berry. Officious intermeddlers or citizen experts? Petitions and public production of information in environmental law. *UCLA Law Rev.* 2010; 58(2): 321–400.

152. Mernit, Judith Lewis. The environmental lawsuit sue-and-settle spin cycle. *High Country News* [Internet]. 2013 Aug 19 [cited 2013 Oct 2]; Available from: www.hcn.org/issues/45.14/the-environmental-lawsuit-sue-and-settle-spin-cycle/print_view

153. Ruhl, J.B. The Endangered Species Act's fall from grace in the supreme court. *Harv Environ Law Rev.* 2012; 26: 488–532.

154. Mapes, Katharine. National Association of Home Builders v. Defenders of Wildlife. *Harv Environ Law Rev.* 2008; 32: 263–78.

155. McClintock, Tom. California Drains Reservoirs in the Middle of a Drought. *Wall Street Journal* [Internet]. 2014 May 24 [cited 2014 May 24]; Available from: http://online.wsj.com/news/articles/SB10001424052702304547704579565622649474370#printMode

156. Peterson, Jodi. Changing of the guard at the Department of Interior. *High Country News* [Internet]. 2013 Apr 16 [cited 2013 Apr 17]; Available from: www.hcn.org/blogs/goat/changing-of-the-guard-at-the-department-of-interior?utm_source=wcn1&utm_medium=email

157. Root, Jay. Oil lobbyists oversee protection of threatened lizard. *The Texas Tribune* [Internet]. 2013 Apr 24 [cited 2013 Jun 8]; Available from: www.texastribune.org/2013/04/24/oil-lobbyists-oversee-threatened-lizard-protection/

158. Denny, Jemma. The Texas conservation plan: The good, the bad and the lizard. *EcoSystem Marketplace* [Internet]. 2012 Jun 18 [cited 2013 Jun 7]; Available from: www.ecosystemmarketplace.com/pages/dynamic/article.page.php?page_id=9100&section=news_articles&eod=

159. Defenders of Wildlife. ESA policy white paper series: Dunes sagebrush lizard: The cautionary tale of a candidate [Internet]. 2013 [cited 2013 Sep 16]; Available from: www.defenders.org/sites/default/files/publications/defenders-esa-policy-dunes-sagebrush-lizard.pdf

160. McClure, Robert, Stiffler, Lisa. Flaws in habitat conservation plans threaten scores of species. *Seattle Post-Intelligencer* [Internet]. 2005 May 3 [cited 2016 Apr 18]; Available from: www.biologicaldiversity.org/news/media-archive/Flaws%20in%20Habitat%20Conservation%20Plans%20Threaten%20Scores%20of%20Species.pdf

161. Kareiva, Peter, Adelman, Sandy, Doak, Daniel, Elderd, Bret, Groom, Martha, Hoekstra, Jonathan et al. Using science in habitat conservation plans [Internet]. 1999 [cited 2013 Jun 13]; Available from: www.nceas.ucsb.edu/files/Kareiva%20Using%20science%20in%20habitat%20conservation%20plans.pdf

162. Schweik, Charles M., Thomas, Craig W. Using remote sensing to evaluate environmental institutional designs: A habitat conservation planning example. *Soc Sci Q.* 2002; 83(1): 244–62.

163. Callihan, David, Kleinman, Devra, Tirnaver, Jill. *An independent evaluation of the U.S. Fish and Wildlife Service's habitat conservation plan program. Management Systems International;* Washington, D.C., 2009.

164. U.S. Fish and Wildlife Service. Endangered species permits: HCPs – Frequently asked questions [Internet]. 2015 [cited 2015 Apr 25]; Available from: www.fws.gov/midwest/endangered/permits/hcp/hcp_faqs.html

165. Powell, Beth. Indian River County annual report to the USFWS for the Sebastian area-wide conservation plan [Internet]. Vero Beach, Florida: Indian River County; 2007 Aug; Available from: www.ircgov.com/Departments/General_Services/Parks/Conservation/scrub jayinfo/SJHCP_2007_USFWS.pdf

166. Monroe County (Florida) Growth Management. 8th Annual Report on the Habitat Conservation Plan for the Key Deer and Other Protected Species [Internet]. 2014 Aug [cited 2015 May 1]; Available from: http://fl-monroecounty.civicplus.com/DocumentCenter/View/8067

167. U.S. Fish and Wildlife Service. Spectacled eider (*Somateria fischeri*): 5-year review: Summary and evaluation [Internet]. Fairbanks; 2010 Aug [cited 2016 Apr 20]; Available from: www.adfg.alaska.gov/static/species/specialstatus/pdfs/spectacledeider_2010_5year_fws.pdf

168. Dwyer, Lynn E., Murphy, Dennis D., Ehrlich, Paul R. Property rights case law and the challenge to the Endangered Species Act. *Conserv Biol.* 1995; 9(4): 725–41.

169. Balch, Alan, Press, Daniel. The politics of diversity. In: Spray, Sharon L, McGlothlin, Karen L, editors. *Loss of biodiversity.* Lanham: Rowman & Littlefield Publishers, Inc.; 2003. p. 119–55.

170. Shogren, Jason F. Introduction. In: Shogren, Jason F., editor. *Species at risk: Using economic incentives to shelter endangered species on private lands.* Austin: University of Texas Press; 2005. p. 1–21.

171. Economist. *The overcrowded ark.* The Economist. 2007 Sep 8; 36.

Chapter 7 References

1. Sandlos, John. Nature's nations: the shared conservation history of Canada and the USA. *Int J Environ Stud.* 2013; 70(3): 358–71.

2. Foster, Janet. *Working for wildlife: The beginning of preservation in Canada.* 2nd ed. Toronto: University of Toronto Press; 1998.

3. Amos, William, Harrison, Kathryn, Hober, George. In search of a minimum winning coalition: The politics of species-at-risk legislation in Canada. In: Beazley, Karen, Boardman, Robert, editors. *Politics of the wild: Canada and endangered species.* Oxford: Oxford University Press; 2001. p. 137–66.

4. Illical, Mary, Harrison, Kathryn. Protecting endangered species in the US and Canada: The role of negative lesson drawing. *Can J Polit Sci.* 2007; 40(2): 367–94.

5. Johns, David. Editorial: Like it or not, politics is the solution. *Conserv Biol.* 2007; 21(2): 287–8.

6. Federalist Society. State attorneys general win fight to enforce roadless rule [Internet]. 2009; Available from: www.fed-soc.org/publications/detail/state-attorneys-general-win-fight-to-enforce-roadless-rule

7. Willison, Martin. Endangered marine species and marine protected areas in Canada. In: Beazley, Karen, Boardman, Robert, editors. *Politics of the wild: Canada and endangered species*. Oxford: Oxford University Press; 2001. p. 94–115.

8. Mooers, L.R., Prugh, L.R., Festa-Bianchet, M., Hutchings, J.A. Biases in legal listing under Canadian endangered species legislation. *Conserv Biol*. 2007; 21(3): 572–5.

9. Bocking, Stephen. The politics of endangered species: A historical perspective. In: Beazley, Karen, Boardman, Robert, editors. *Politics of the wild: Canada and endangered species*. Oxford: Oxford University Press; 2001. p. 119–36.

10. Salazar, Debra J., Alper, Donald K. Politics, policy, and the war in the woods. In: Salazar, Debra J., Alper, Donald K., editors. *Sustaining the forests of the Pacific Coast: Forging truces in the war in the woods*. Vancouver: UBC Press; 2000. p. 3–21.

11. Cioc, Mark. *The game of conservation: International treaties to protect the world's migratory animals*. Athens: Ohio University Press; 2009.

12. Scudder, G.G.E. Endangered species protection in Canada. *Conserv Biol*. 1999; 13(5): 963–5.

13. Clark, Susan G.; Rutherford, Murray B.; and Mattson, David J. Large carnivores, people, and governance. In: Clark, Susan G., Rutherford, Murray B., editors. *Large carnivore conservation: Integrating science and policy in the north American west*. Chicago: University of Chicago Press; 2014. p. 1–28.

14. Eisenberg, Cristinia. *The carnivore way: Coexisting with and conserving north America's predators*. Washington, D.C.: Island Press; 2014.

15. Nash, Roderick Frazier. *The rights of nature: A history of environmental ethics*. Madison: The University of Wisconsin Press; 1989.

16. Prato, Tony, Fagre, Dan. *National parks and protected areas: Approaches for balancing social, economic, and ecological values*. Ames, IA: Blackwell Publishing Professional; 2005.

17. Ray, Justina C., Ginsberg, Joshua R. Endangered species legislation beyond the borders of the United States. *Conserv Biol*. 1999; 13(5): 956–8.

18. Woinarski, J. C. Z., Fisher, Alaric. The Australian Endangered Species Protection Act 1992. *Conserv Biol*. 1999; 13(5): 959–62.

19. Gibbs, Walter. Sweden's welcome friend Is Oslo's big bad wolf. *New York Times* [Internet]. 2001 Jan 21 [cited 2015 Jan 9]; Available from: www.nytimes.com/2001/01/21/world/21WOLV.html January 21

20. Monbiot, George. Norway's plan to kill wolves explodes myth of environmental virtue [Internet]. George Monbiot's Blog. 2012 [cited 2013 Nov 8]; Available from: www.theguardian.com/environment/georgemonbiot/2012/nov/20/norway-predators-wolves

21. Castle, Stephen. Wolves, resurgent and protected, vex Swedish farmers. *New York Times* [Internet]. 2015 Aug 14 [cited 2014 Aug 16]; Available from: www.nytimes.com/2015/08/16/world/europe/wolves-resurgent-and-protected-vex-swedish-farmers.html?ref=topics&_r=0

22. Lande, Russell, Saether, Bernt-Erik, Engen, Steinar. Sustainable exploitation of fluctuating populations. In: Reynolds, John D., Mace, Georgina M., Redford, Kent H., Robinson, John G., editors. *Conservation of exploited species*. Cambridge: Cambridge University Press; 2001. p. 67–86.

23. Matti, Simon, Sandström, Annica. The rationale determining advocacy coalitions: Examining coordination networks and corresponding beliefs. *Policy Stud J*. 2011; 39(3): 385–410.

24. Zimmerman, Alexandra, Baker, Nick, Inskip, Chloe, Linnell, John D. C., Marchini, Silvio, Odden, John et al. Contemporary views of human-carnivore conflicts on wild rangelands. In:

du Toit, John D., Kock, Richard, Deutsch, James C., editors. *Wild rangelands: Conserving wildlife while maintaining livestock in semi-arid ecosystems.* Oxford: Wiley-Blackwell; 2010. p. 129–51.

25. McNamee, Thomas. *The return of the wolf to Yellowstone.* New York: Henry Holt and Company; 1997.

26. Campion-Vincent, Veronique. The restoration of wolves in France: Story, conflicts and uses of rumor. In: Herda-Rapp, Ann, Goedeke, Theresa L., editors. *Mad about wildlife: Looking at social conflict over wildlife.* Leiden: Brill; 2005. p. 99–121.

27. Geist, Valerius. Great achievements, great expectations: Successes of North American wildlife management. In: Hawley, Alex W.L., editor. *Commercialization and wildlife management: Dancing with the devil.* Malabar, FL: Krieger Publishing Company; 1993. p. 47–72.

28. Saberwal, Vasant K. Saving the tiger: More money or less power? *Conserv Biol.* 1997; 11(3): 815–7.

29. Jacoby, Karl. *Crimes against nature: Squatters, poachers, thieves, and the hidden history of American conservation.* Berkeley: University of Chicago Press; 2003.

30. Williams, Ted. Japan bashing reconsidered. *Audubon Magazine.* 1991 September-October: 26–36.

31. Francis, George. Governance for conservation. In: Westley, Frances R., Miller, Philip S., editors. *Experiments in consilience: Integrating social and scientific responses to save endangered species.* Washington, D.C.: Island Press; 2003. p. 223–43.

32. Ngoitiko, Maanda, Nelson, Fred. Political ecology of wildlife conservation in the Mt. Meru area of Northeast Tanzania. In: Nelson, Fred, editor. *Community rights, conservation and contested land: The politics of natural resource governance in Africa.* London: Earthscan; 2010. p. 269–89.

33. Kamins, A.O., Restif, O., Ntiamoa-Baidu, Y., Suu-Ire, R., Hayman, D.T.S., Cunningham, A.A. et al. Uncovering the fruit bat bushmeat commodity chain and the true extent of fruit bat hunting in Ghana, West Africa. *Biodivers Conserv.* 2011; 144(12): 3000–8.

34. Browne-Nuñez, Christine, Jonker, Sandra, A. Attitudes Toward Wildlife and Conservation Across Africa: A Review of Survey Research *Human Dimensions of Wildlife.* 2008; 13: 47–70.

35. Steinhart, Peter. Bear of the clouds. *Audubon Magazine.* 1989 July: 92–103.

36. Gupta, Sujata. Of sparrows and sodbusters. *High Country News* [Internet]. 2013 Sep 2 [cited 2013 Oct 12]; Available from: www.hcn.org/issues/45.15/western-and-mexican-conserva tionists-race-against-time-to-save-grasslands-and-the-bird-species-that-depend-on-them/print_ view

37. Friedman, Thomas L. Stampeding black elephants. *New York Times* [Internet]. 2014 Nov 22 [cited 2014 Nov 22]; Available from: www.nytimes.com/2014/11/23/opinion/sunday/ thomas-l-friedman-stampeding-black-elephants.html?emc=edit_tnt_20141122&nlid=103654 19&tntemail0=y&_r=0

38. Franklin, Adrian. *Animal nation: The true story of animals and Australia.* Sydney: University of New South Wales Press Ltd.; 2006.

39. Duffy, Rosaleen. *Killing for conservation: Wildlife policy in Zimbabwe.* Oxford: International African Institute in association with James Curry; 2000.

40. Neumann, R.P. Political ecology of wildlife conservation in the Mt. Meru area of Northeast Tanzania. *Land Degrad Rehabil.* 1992; 3(2): 85–98.

41. Barrow, Edmund, Gichohi, Helen, Infield, Mark. The evolution of community conservation policy & practice in East Africa. In: Hulme, David, Murphree, Marshall, editors.

African wildlife & livelihoods: The promise and performance of community conservation. Oxford: James Currey Ltd.; 2001. p. 59–73.

42. Cousins, Jenny A., Sadler, Jon P., Evans, James. The challenge of regulating private wildlife ranches for conservation in South Africa. *Ecol Soc* [Internet]. 2010 [cited 2016 Apr 21]; 15(2); Available from: www.ecologyandsociety.org/vol15/iss2/art28/

43. Sharp, Robin, Wollscheid, Kai-Uwe. An overview of recreational hunting in North America, Europe and Australia. In: Dickson, Barney, Hutton, Jon, Adams, William M., editors. *Recreational hunting, conservation and rural livelihoods: Science and practice.* Oxford: Wiley-Blackwell; 2009. p. 25–58.

44. Nash, Roderick. *Wilderness and the American mind.* 3rd ed. New Haven: Yale University Press; 1982.

45. Levin, Dan. From elephants' mouths, an illicit trail to China. *New York Times* [Internet]. 2013 Mar 1 [cited 2013 Mar 2]; Available from: www.nytimes.com/2013/03/02/world/asia/an-illicit-trail-of-african-ivory-to-china.html?nl=todaysheadlines&emc=edit_th_20130302&_r=0&pagewanted=print

46. Dinerstein, Eric. *The return of the unicorns: The natural history and conservation of the greater one-horned rhinoceros.* New York: Columbia University Press; 2003.

47. Schaller, George B. *The last panda.* Chicago: University of Chicago Press; 1993.

48. Harris, Richard B. *Wildlife conservation in China: Preserving the habitat of China's wild west.* Armonk, NY: M.E. Sharpe, Inc.; 2007.

49. Teer, James G. Commercial utilization of wildlife: Has its time come? In: Hawley, Alex W.L., editor. *Commercialization and wildlife management: Dancing with the devil.* Malabar, FL: Krieger Publishing Company; 1993. p. 73–83.

50. Rahmani, Asad R. Conservation outside protected areas: Case studies of bustard protection. In: Saberwal, Vasant K., Rangarajan, Mahesh, editors. *Battles over nature: Science and the politics of conservation.* New Delhi: Permanent Black; 2003. p. 117–35.

51. Saghal, Bittu, Scarlott, Jennifer. This heaven and this earth: Will India keep its promise to Panthera tigris? In: Tilson, Ronald, Nyhus, Philip J., editors. *Tigers of the world: The science, politics, and conservation of Panthera tigris.* 2nd ed. Amsterdam: Academic Press; 2010. p. 301–30.

52. Seidensticker, John, Christie, Sarah, Jackson, Peter. Approaches to tiger conservation: Overview. In: Seidensticker, John, Christie, Sarah, Jackson, Peter, editors. *Riding the Tiger: Tiger conservation in human-dominated landscapes.* Cambridge: Cambridge University Press; 1999. p. 193–7.

53. Kopnina, Helen. Of tigers and humans: The question of democratic deliberation and biodiversity conservation. In: Wuerthner, George, Crist, Eileen, Butler, Tom, editors. *Protecting the wild: Parks and wilderness, the foundation for conservation.* Washington, D.C.: Island Press; 2015. p. 63–71.

54. Cuevas, Carlos. Protected areas in Chilean Patagonia. In: Wuerthner, George, Crist, Eileen, Butler, Tom, editors. *Protecting the wild: Parks and wilderness, the foundation for conservation.* Washington, D.C.: Island Press; 2015. p. 226–41.

55. Promberger, Barabara, Promberger, Christoph. Rewilding the Carpathians: A present-day opportunity. In: Wuerthner, George, Crist, Eileen, Butler, Tom, editors. *Protecting the wild: parks and wilderness, the foundation for conservation.* Washington, D.C.: Island Press; 2015. p. 242–9.

56. Romig, Rollo. The hard life of celebrity elephants. *New York Times.* 2013 Aug 9; Available from: http://www.nytimes.com/2013/08/18/magazine/the-life-of-celebrity-elephants-in-india.html

57. Songorwa, Alexander N. Saving lions by killing them. *New York Times* [Internet]. 2013 Mar 17 [cited 2013 Mar 18]; Available from: www.nytimes.com/2013/03/18/opinion/saving-lions-by-killing-them.html?ref=opinion&pagewanted=print

58. Packer, C., Brink, H., Kissul, B.M., Maliti, H., Kushnir, H., Caro, T. Effects of trophy hunting on lion and leopard populations in Tanzania. *Conserv Biol.* 2011; 25(1): 142–53.

59. Osnos, Evan. Beaver laws trap towns – Surging numbers, state bans forge local dilemmas. *Chicago Tribune.* 2001 Aug 6; Available from: http://articles.chicagotribune.com/2001-08-06/news/0108060137_1_beaver-population-trapping-wildlife/2

60. Adams, William, Hulme, David. Conservation & community: Changing narratives, policies & practices in African conservation. In: Hulme, David, Murphree, Marshall, editors. *African wildlife & livelihoods: The promise and performance of community conservation.* Oxford: James Currey Ltd.; 2001. p. 9–23.

61. Adams, William N. *Against extinction.* London: Earthscan; 2004.

62. Wilshusen, Peter R., Brechin, Steven R., Fortwangler, Crystal L., West, Patrick C. Contested nature: Conservation and development at the turn of the twenty-first century. In: Brechin, Steven R., Wilshusen, Peter R., Fortwangler, Crystal L., West, Patrick C., editors. *Contested nature: Promoting international biodiversity with social justice in the twenty-first century.* Albany: State University of New York Press; 2003. p. 1–22.

63. Nelson, Fred. *Community rights, conservation, and contested land: The politics of natural resources in Africa.* London: Earthscan; 2010.

64. Nelson, Fred. Introduction: The politics of natural resource governance in Africa. In: Nelson, Fred, editor. *Community rights, conservation and contested land: The politics of natural resource governance in Africa.* London: Earthscan; 2010. p. 3–31.

65. Cowlishaw, Guy, Mendelson, Samatha, Rowcliffe, J. Marcus. Livelihoods and sustainability in a bushmeat commodity chain in Ghana. In: Davies, Glyn, Brown, David, editors. *Bushmeat and livelihoods: Wildlife management and poverty reduction.* Malden, MA: Blackwell Publishing; 2007. p. 32–46.

66. Murombedzi, James. Agrarian social change and post-colonial natural resource management interventions in southern Africa's "communal tenure" regimes. In: Nelson, Fred, editor, *Community rights, conservation and contested land.* London: Earthscan, 2010. p. 32– 54.

67. Murphree, Marshall W. The lesson from Mahenye. In: Hutton, Jon, Dickson, Barnabas, editors. *Endangered species threatened convention: The past, present and future of CITES, the Convention on International Trade in Endangered Species of wild fauna and flora.* London: Earthscan; 2000. p. 181–96.

68. Butler, Victoria. Is this the way to save Africa's wildlife? *Int Wildl.* 1995; 25(2): 38–43.

69. Gibson, Clark C. *Politicians and poachers: The political economy of wildlife policy in Africa.* Cambridge: Cambridge University Press; 1999.

70. McGregor, JoAnn. Crocodile crimes: People versus wildlife and the politics of postcolonial conservation on Lake Kariba, Zimbabwe. *Geoforum.* 2005; 36: 353–69.

71. Rihoy, Liz, Chnirozva, Chaka, Anstey, Simon. "People are not happy:" Crisis, adaptation and resilience in Zimbabwe's CAMPFIRE programme. In: Nelson, Fred, editor. *Community rights, conservation and contested land: The politics of natural resource governance in Africa.* London: Earthscan; 2010. p. 174–201.

72. Human Rights First. Zimbabwe suspended indefinitely from Commonwealth [Internet]. 2003; Available from: http://web.archive.org/web/20080610130413/www.humanrightsfirst.org/media/2003_alerts/1208.htm

73. Balint, Peter J., Mashinya, Judith. CAMPFIRE during Zimbabwe's national crisis: Local impacts and broader implications for community-based wildlife management. *Soc Nat Resour.* 2008; 21: 783–96.

74. Hulme, David, Murphree, Marshall. Community conservation as policy: Promise & performance. In: Hulme, David, Murphree, Marshall, editors. *African wildlife & livelihoods: The promise and performance of community conservation.* Oxford: James Currey Ltd.; 2001. p. 280–97.

75. Adams, William M. Path dependence in conservation. In: Leader-Williams, Nigel, Adams, William M., Smith, Robert J., editors. *Trade-offs in conservation: Deciding what to save.* Oxford: Wiley-Blackwell; 2010. p. 293–310.

76. Jones, Brian, Murphree, Marshall. The evolution of policy on community conservation in Namibia & Zimbabwe. In: Hulme, David, Murphree, Marshall, editors. *African wildlife & livelihoods: The promise and performance of community conservation.* Oxford: James Currey Ltd.; 2001. p. 38–58.

77. Hulme, David, Infield, Mark. Community conservation, reciprocity & park-people relationships: Lake Mburo national park Uganda. In: Hulme, David, Murphree, Marshall, editors. *African wildlife & livelihoods: The promise and performance of community conservation.* Oxford: James Currey Ltd.; 2001. p. 106–30.

78. Jones, Brian T.B. Community benefits from safari hunting and related activities in Southern Africa. In: Dickson, Barney, Hutton, Jon, Adams, William M., editors. *Recreational hunting, conservation and rural livelihoods: Science and practice.* Oxford: Wiley-Blackwell; 2009. p. 157–77.

79. Bergin, Patrick. Accommodating new narratives in a conservation bureaucracy: TANAPA & community conservation. In: Hulme, David, Murphree, Marshall, editors. *African wildlife & livelihoods: The promise and performance of community conservation.* Oxford: James Currey Ltd.; 2001. p. 88–105.

80. Emerton, Lucy. The nature of benefits & the benefits of nature: Why wildlife conservation has not economically benefited communities in Africa. In: Hulme, David, Murphree, Marshall, editors. *African wildlife & livelihoods: The promise and performance of community conservation.* Oxford: James Currey Ltd.; 2001. p. 208–26.

81. Rihoy, Liz, and Maguranyanga. The politics of community-based natural resource management in Botswana. In: Nelson, Fred, editor. *Community rights, conservation and contested land: The politics of natural resource governance in Africa.* London: Earthscan; 2010. p. 55–78.

82. Nelson, Fred, Agrawal, Arun. Patronage or participation? Community-based natural resource management reform in Sub-Saharan Africa. *Dev Change.* 2008; 39(4): 557–85.

83. Mordi, A. Richard. *Attitudes toward wildlife.* New York: Garland Publishing, Inc.; 1991.

84. Campbell, David J., Gichohi, Helen, Reed, Robin, Mwangi, Albert, Chege, Lucy, Sawin, Thor. Interactions between people and wildlife in Southeast Kajiado district Kenya [Internet]. LUCID Working Paper Series, Number: 18; 2003 [cited 2013 Dec 10]; Available from: www.lucideastafrica.org/publications/Campbell_LUCID_WP18.pdf

85. Leakey, Richard, Morell, Virginia. *Wildlife wars.* New York: St. Martin's Press, Inc.; 2001.

86. Homewood, Katherine, Thompson, D. Michael. Social and economic challenges for conservation in East African rangelands: Land use, livelihoods and wildlife change in Maasailand. In: du Toit, Johan T., Kock, Richard, Deutsch, James C., editors. *Wild rangelands: Conserving wildlife while maintaining livestock in semi-arid ecosystems.* Oxford: Wiley-Blackwell; 2010. p. 340–66.

87. Vira, Varun, Ewing, Thomas. Ivory's Curse: The militarization & professionalization of poaching in Africa [Internet]. 2014 [cited 2014 Jun 29]; Available from: http://media.wix.com/ugd/e16b55_7ccc46650a664e47b09709c97bc94933.pdf

88. Kabiri, Ngeta. Historic and contemporary struggles for a local wildlife governance regime in Kenya. In: Nelson, Fred, editor. *Community rights, conservation and contested land: The politics of natural resource governance in Africa.* London: Earthscan; 2010. p. 121–44.

89. Hackel, Jeffrey D. Community conservation and the future of Africa's wildlife. *Conserv Biol.* 1999; 13(4): 726–34.

90. du Toit, Johan T. Addressing the mismatches between livestock production and wildlife conservation across spatio-temporal scales and Institutional Levels. In: du Toit, Johan T., Kock, Richard, Deutsch, James C., editors. *Wild rangelands: Conserving wildlife while maintaining livestock in semi-arid ecosystems.* Oxford: Wiley-Blackwell; 2010. p. 30–52.

91. Victurine, Ray, Curtin, Charles. Financial incentives for rangeland conservation: Addressing the "show-us-the-money" challenge. In: du Toit, Johan T., Kock, Richard, Deutsch, James C., editors. *Wild rangelands: Conserving wildlife while maintaining livestock in semi-arid ecosystems.* Oxford: Wiley-Blackwell; 2010. p. 152–87.

92. Snyder, Katherine A., Sulle, Emmanuel B. Tourism in Maasai communities: A chance to improve livelihoods? *J Sustain Tour.* 2011; 19(8): 935–51.

93. Norton-Griffiths, M. Economic incentives to develop the rangelands of the Serengeti: implications for wildlife conservation. In: Sinclair, A.R.E., Arcese, Peter. editors. *Seregenti II: Dynamics, management, and conservation of an ecosystem.* Chicago: University of Chicago Press; 1995. p. 588–604.

94. Lubilo, Rodgers, Child, Brian. The rise and fall of community-based natural resource management in Zambia's Luangwa Valley: An illustration of micro- and macro-governance issues. In: Nelson, Fred, editor. *Community rights, conservation and contested land: The politics of natural resource governance in Africa.* London: Earthscan; 2010. p. 202–26.

95. Lewis, Dale, M., Alpert, Peter. Trophy hunting and wildlife conservation in Zambia. *Conserv Biol.* 1997; 11(1): 59–68.

96. Astle, W.L. *The fallacy of popular wisdom in African wildlife management: A history of wildlife conservation and management in the mid-Luangwa Valley,* Zambia. British Empire and Commonwealth Museum; 1999.

97. Schroeder, Richard A. Environmental justice and the market: The politics of sharing wildlife revenues in Tanzania. *Soc Nat Resour.* 2008; 21: 583–96.

98. Nelson, Fred, Foley, Charles, Foley, Lara S., Leposo, Abraham, Loure, Edward, Peterson, David et al. Payments for ecosystem services as a framework for community-based conservation in Northern Tanzania. *Conserv Biol.* 2009; 24(1): 78–85.

99. Nelson, Fred, Blomley, Tom. Peasants' forests and the king's game? Institutional divergence and convergence in Tanzania's forestry and wildlife sectors. In: Nelson, Fred, editor. *Community rights, conservation and contested land: The politics of natural resource governance in Africa.* London: Earthscan; 2010. p. 79–105.

100. Brockington, Dan. *Fortress conservation: The preservation of the Mkomazi game reserve Tanzania.* Bloomington, IN: Indiana University Press; 2002.

101. Fraser, John, Wilkie, David, Wallace, Robert, Coppolillo, Balas, Painter, R. E. Lilian, Zahler, Peter, et al. The emergence of conservation NGOs as catalysts for local democracy. In: Manfredo, Michael J., Vaske, Jerry J., Brown, Perry J., Decker, Daniel J., Duke, Esther A., editors. *Wildlife and society: The science of human dimensions.* Washington, D.C.: Island Press; 2009. p. 44–56.

102. Vaughan, Christopher, Long, Andrew. Bushmeat, wildlife management and good governance; rights and institutional arrangements in Namibia's community-based natural resources management programme. In: Davies, Glyn, Brown, David, editors. *Bushmeat and livelihoods: Wildlife management and poverty reduction*. Malden, MA: Blackwell Publishing; 2007. p. 125–39.

103. Boudreaux, Karol, Nelson, Fred. Community conservation in Namibia: Empowering the poor with property rights. *Community Conserv Namib Empower Poor Prop Rights*. 2011; 31(2): 17–24.

104. Jones, Brian. The evolution of Namibia's communal conservancies. In: Nelson, Fred, editor. *Community rights, conservation and contested land: The politics of natural resource governance in Africa*. London: Earthscan; 2010. p. 106–20.

105. Conniff, Richard. A trophy hunt that is good for rhinos. *New York Times* [Internet]. 2014 Jan 20 [cited 2014 Jan 21]; Available from: http://opinionator.blogs.nytimes.com/2014/09/13/useless-creatures/

106. Hamilton, A., Cunningham, A., Byarugaba, D., Kayanja, F. Conservation in a region of political instability: Bwindi impenetrable forest, Uganda. *Conserv Biol*. 2000; 14(6): 1722–5.

107. Lamprey, Richard H., Mugisha, Arthur. The re-introduction of recreational hunting in Uganda. In: Dickson, Barney, Hutton, Jon, Adams, William M., editors. *Recreational hunting, conservation and rural livelihoods: Science and practice*. Oxford: Wiley-Blackwell; 2009. p. 212–31.

108. Reuters. Uganda: Inquiry into ivory theft opens. *New York Times* [Internet]. 2014 Nov 18 [cited 2014 Nov 18]; Available from: www.nytimes.com/2014/11/19/world/africa/uganda-inquiry-into-ivory-theft-opens.html?emc=edit_tnt_20141118&nlid=10365419&tntemail0=y&_r=0

109. Whande, Webster. Windows of opportunity or exclusion? Local communities in the great Limpopo transfrontier conservation area, South Africa. In: Nelson, Fred, editor. *Community rights, conservation and contested land: The politics of natural resource governance in Africa*. London: Earthscan; 2010. p. 147–73.

110. Booth, Vernon R., Cumming, David H.M. The development of a recreational hunting industry and its relationship with conservation in Southern Africa. In: Dickson, Barney, Hutton, Jon, Adams, William M., editors. *Recreational hunting, conservation and rural livelihoods: Science and practice*. Oxford: Wiley-Blackwell; 2009. p. 282–95.

111. McGroarty, Patrick. A bull market of a different kind: Controversial but profitable, African-game breeding has become the new trophy investment for some. *Wall Street Journal* [Internet]. 2014 Mar 29 [cited 2014 Mar 29]; Available from: http://online.wsj.com/news/articles/SB10001424052702303563304579445382496815614?KEYWORDS=patrick+mcgroarty+and+trophy+investment&mg=reno64-wsj

112. Monjane, Marta, Nelson, Fred. External agency and local authority facilitating CBNRM in Mahel, Mozambique. In: Nelson, Fred, editor. *Community rights, conservation and contested land: The politics of natural resource governance in Africa*. London: Earthscan; 2010. p. 227–40.

113. Madzwamuse, Masego, Nelson, Fred. Adaptive or anachronistic? Maintaining indigenous natural resource governance systems in Northern Botswana. In: Nelson, Fred, editor. *Community rights, conservation and contested land: The politics of natural resource governance in Africa*. London: Earthscan; 2010. p. 241–68.

114. Duffy, Rosaleen. *Nature crime: How we're getting conservation wrong*. New Haven: Yale University Press; 2010.

115. Kellert, Stephen R., Mehta, Jain N., Ebbin, Syma A., Lichtenfeld, Laly A. Community natural resource management: Promise, rhetoric, and reality. Society and Natural Resources. *Soc Nat Resour.* 2000; 13: 705–13.

116. Hill, Catherine M. Working with communities to achieve conservation goals. In: Manfredo, Michael J., Vaske, Jerry J., Brown, Perry J., Decker, Daniel J., Duke, Esther A., editors. *Wildlife and Society: The science of human dimensions.* Washington, D.C.: Island Press; 2009. p. 117–28.

117. McKenna, Phil. It takes just one village to save a species. *New York Times* [Internet]. 2008 Sep 22 [cited 2013 Dec 13]; Available from: www.nytimes.com/2008/09/23/science/ 23monk.html?_r=0&pagewanted=print

118. Gratwicke, Brian, Shrestha, Mahendra, Seidensticker, John. Save the tiger fund's grantmaking strategy for recovering wild tiger populations. In: Tilson, Ronald, Nyhus, Philip J., editors. *Tigers of the world: The science, politics, and conservation of panthera tigris.* 2nd ed. Amsterdam: Academic Press; 2010. p. 188–99.

119. Bennett, Elizabeth L. Hunting, wildlife trade and wildlife consumption patterns in Asia. In: Davies, G, Brown, David, editors. *Bushmeat and livelihoods: Wildlife management and poverty reduction.* Malden, MA: Blackwell Publishing; 2007. p. 241–9.

120. Oates, John F. *Myth and reality in the rain forest: How conservation strategies are failing in West Africa.* Berkeley: University of California Press; 1999.

121. Poulsen, John R., Clark, Connie J., Mavah, Germain A. Wildlife management in a logging concession in Northern Congo: Can livelihoods be maintained through sustainable hunting. In: Davies, Glyn, Brown, David, editors. *Bushmeat and livelihoods: Wildlife management and poverty reduction.* Malden, MA: Blackwell Publishing; 2007. p. 140–57.

122. Francis, Tazoacha. Korup national park – The displacement of the indigenous people: Voluntary or by force? [Internet]. 2010 [cited 2013 Dec 26]; Available from: www.monitor .upeace.org/innerpg.cfm?id_article=740

123. Aveling, Rosalind, Anthem, Helen, Lanjouw, Annette. A fighting chance: Can conservation create a platform for peace within cycles of human conflict?". In: Leader-Williams, Nigel, Adams, William M., Smith, Robert J., editors. *Trade-offs in conservation: Deciding what to save.* Oxford: Wiley-Blackwell; 2010. p. 253–72.

124. Milner-Gulland, E.J. Institutional contexts. In: Davies, Glyn, Brown, David, editors. *Bushmeat and livelihoods: Wildlife management and poverty reduction.* Malden, MA: Blackwell Publishing; 2007. p. 107–10.

125. Cobb, Stephen, Ginsberg, Joshua, Thomsen, Jorgen. Conservation in the tropics: Evolving roles for governments, international donors and non-government organizations. In: MacDonald, David W., Service, Katrina, editors. *Key topics in conservation biology.* Oxford: Blackwell Publishing; 2007. p. 145–55.

126. Hurst, Andrew. Institutional challenges to sustainable bushmeat management in Central Africa. In: Davies, Glyn, Brown, David, editors. *Bushmeat and livelihoods: Wildlife management and poverty reduction.* Malden, MA: Blackwell Publishing; 2007. p. 158–71.

127. De Chant, Tim. Wild refuges pay price for protection: Study: National parks in developing nations are attracting the human encroachment and the conflict they were meant to be shielded from. *Chicago Tribune* [Internet]. 2008 Jul 4 [cited 2013 Dec 27]; Available from: http://articles.chicagotribune.com/2008-07-04/news/0807030640_1_national-parks-park-bound aries-population-growth

128. Wittemyer, George, Elsen, Paul, Bean, William T., Coleman, A., Burton, O., Brashares, Justin S. Accelerated human population growth at protected area edges. *Science.* 2008; 320(5): 123–5.

129. Maddox, Tom. The claws of a dilemma: Can big business contribute to tiger conservation in Indonesia? In: Tilson, Ronald, Nyhus, Philip J., editors. *Tigers of the world: The science, politics, and conservation of panthera tigris.* 2nd ed. Amsterdam: Academic Press; 2010. p. 395–402.

130. Cutter, Peter, Hean, Sun. Costs and benefits of sustaining wild tigers in Cambodia: A strategic economic perspective. In: Tilson, Ronald, Nyhus, Philip J., editors. *Tigers of the world: The science, politics, and conservation of panthera tigris.* 2nd ed. Amsterdam: Academic Press; 2010. p. 357–65.

131. Nyhus, Philip J., Tilson, Ronald. The next 20 years of science, politics, and conservation. In: Tilson, Ronald, Nyhus, Philip J., editors. *Tigers of the world: The science, politics, and conservation of panthera tigris.* 2nd ed. Amsterdam: Academic Press; 2010. p. 507–17.

132. Ferraro, Paul J., Kiss, Agnes. Direct payments to conserve biodiversity. *Science.* 2002; 298 (November 29): 1718–9.

133. Missrie, Mónica, Nelson, Kristen. Direct payments for conservation: Lessons from the monarch butterfly conservation fund [Internet]. 2005 [cited 2013 Dec 26]; Available from: www.forestry.umn.edu/prod/groups/cfans/@pub/@cfans/@forestry/documents/asset/cfans_asset_183624.pdf

134. Barry, Ellen, Kumarfeb, Hari. Tiger population grows in India, as does fear after attacks. *New York Times* [Internet]. 2014 Feb 11 [cited 2014 Feb 12]; Available from: www.nytimes.com/2014/02/12/world/asia/tiger-population-grows-in-india-as-does-fear-after-attacks.html?nl=todaysheadlines&emc=edit_th_20140212&_r=0

135. Karanth, K. Ullas, Madhusudan, M.D. Avoiding paper tigers and saving real tigers: Response to Saberwa. *Conserv Biol.* 1997; 11(3): 818–20.

136. Ward, Geoffrey C. The people and the tiger. *Audubon Magazine.* 1994 July-August: 62–9.

137. Goering, Laurie. Creativity helps save big cats: Indian tigers get a second chance when people are put first. *Chicago Tribune* [Internet]. 2007 Nov 8 [cited 2015 Jan 7]; Available from: http://articles.chicagotribune.com/2007-11-08/news/0711071077_1_big-cats-tiger-millions-of-hindu-pilgrims

138. Rodgers, W.A., Hartley, Dawn, Bashir, Sultana. Community approaches to conservation: Some comparisons from Africa and India. In: Saberwal, Vasant K., Rangarajan, Mahesh, editors. *Battles over nature: Science and the politics of conservation.* London: Earthscan; 2003. p. 324–82.

139. Dinerstein, Eric, Rijal, Arun, Bookbinder, Marnie, Kattel, Bijaya, Rajuria, Arup. Tigers as neighbours; Efforts to promote local guardianship of endangered species in lowland Nepal. In: Seidensticker, John, Christie, Sarah, Jackson, Peter, editors. *Riding the tiger: Tiger conservation in human-dominated landscapes.* Cambridge: Cambridge University Press; 1999. p. 316–33.

140. Kawanishi, Kawanishi, Gurmal, Melvin, Shepherd, Loretta Ann., Goldthorpe, Gareth, Shepherd, Chris R., Krishnasamy, Kanitha et al. The Malayan tiger. In: Tilson, Ronald, Nyhus, Philip J., editors. *Tigers of the world: The science, politics, and conservation of panthera tigris.* 2nd ed. Amsterdam: Academic Press; 2010. p. 367–76.

141. Wikramanayake, Erick, Manandhar, Anil, Bajamiya, Shiyam, Nepal, Santosh, Thapa, Gokama, Thapa, Kanchan. The Terai arc landscape: A tiger conservation success story in a human-dominated landscape. In: Tilson, Ronald, Nyhus, Philip J., editors. *Tigers of the world: The science, politics, and conservation of panthera tigris.* 2nd ed. Amsterdam: Academic Press; 2010. p. 163–73.

142. Jhala, Y.V., Qureshi, Q., Gopal, R. The status of tigers in India, 2014 [Internet]. National Tiger Authority, New Delhi and The Wildlife Institute of India, Dehradun; 2015 [cited 2015 Jan 22]; Available from: www.wii.gov.in/images/images/documents/Status_of_tiger_2014.pdf

143. Kumar, Hari. India's rebounding tiger population grows 30 percent in 4 years. *New York Times* [Internet]. 2015 Jan 20 [cited 2015 Jan 20]; Available from: www.nytimes.com/2015/01/21/world/asia/indias-rebounding-tiger-population-grows-30-percent-in-4-years.html?emc=edit_tnt_20150120&nlid=10365419&tntemail0=y&_r=0

144. Bodmer, Richard, Pueretas, Pablo, Tula, G. Comanaging wildlife in the amazon and the salvation of the Pacaya-Samiria national reserve in Peru. In: Manfredo, Michael J., Vaske, Jerry J., Brown, Perry J., Decker, Daniel J., Duke, Esther A., editors. *Wildlife and society: The science of human dimensions*. Washington, D.C.: Island Press; 2009. p. 104–16.

145. Nelson, Fred. Democratizing natural resource governance: Searching for institutional change. In: Nelson, Fred, editor. *Community rights, conservation and contested land: The politics of natural resource governance in Africa*. Leiden: Earthscan; 2010. p. 310–33.

146. Thomas, Stephen J. Seeking equity in common property wildlife in Zimbabwe. In: Freeman, Milton R., editor. *Elephants and whales: Resources for whom?* Switzerland: Gordon and Breach Science Publishers; 1994. p. 129–42.

147. West, Paige, Brockington, Daniel. Some unexpected consequences of protected areas: An anthropological perspective. *Conserv Biol*. 2006; 20(3): 609–16.

148. Corson, Catherine. Shifting environmental governance in a neoliberal world: US aid for conservation. *Antipode*. 2010; 42(3): 567–602.

149. Allan, Jaye B. People and pandas in Southwest China. *J Int Wildl Law Policy*. 2008; 11: 156–88.

150. Sanderson, Steven, Redford, Kent. The defence of conservation is not an attack on the poor. *Oryx*. 2004; 38(2): 148–9.

Chapter 8 References

1. Wilcove, David S. *No way home*. Washington, D.C.: Island Press; 2008.

2. Wilkinson, Tracy. U.S., Mexico and Canada are asked to protect monarch butterflies. *Los Angeles Times* [Internet]. 2014 Feb 14 [cited 2014 Feb 17]; Available from: www.latimes.com/world/worldnow/la-fg-wn-us-mexico-canada-monarch-butterflies-20140214,0,3481239.story#axzz2tb9mf6lN

3. Macdonald, David W., Collins, N. Mark, Wrangham, Richard. Principles, practice and priorities: the quest for "alignment." In: Macdonald, David W., Service, Katrina, editors. *Key topics in conservation biology*. Malden, MA: Blackwell Publishing; 2007. p. 275–90.

4. Brinkley, Douglas. *The wilderness warrior: Theodore Roosevelt and the crusade for America*. New York: Harper Collins Publishers; 2009.

5. Jones, Patrice M. Brazil grapples with animal trade: Smugglers imperil S. America species. *Chicago Tribune* [Internet]. 2001 Aug 20 [cited 2014 Jan 1]; Available from: http://articles.chicagotribune.com/2001-08-20/news/0108200184_1_animal-trafficking-animal-trade-exotic-animals

6. United Nations Environmental Programme. UNEP Year Book 2014 emerging issues update illegal trade in wildlife [Internet]. 2014 [cited 2016 Apr 28]; Available from: www.unep.org/yearbook/2014/PDF/chapt4.pdf

7. du Toit, Johan T. Addressing the mismatches between livestock production and wildlife conservation across spatio-temporal scales and institutional levels. In: du Toit, Johan T., Kock, Richard, Deutsch, James C., editors. *Wild eangelands: Conserving wildlife while maintaining livestock in semi-arid ecosystems.* Oxford: Wiley-Blackwell; 2010. p. 30–52.

8. Christie, Patrick, Buhat, Delma, Garces, Len R., White, Alan T. The challenges and rewards of community-based coastal resources management: San Salvador Island, Philippines. In: Brechin, Steven R., Wilshushen, Peter R., Fortwangler, Crystal L., West, Patrick C., editors. *Contested nature: Promoting international biodiversity with social justice in the twenty-first century.* Albany: State University of New York Press; 2003. p. 231–49.

9. Greenberg, Paul. Tuna's end. *New York Times* [Internet]. 2010 Jun 21 [cited 2012 Jan 6]; Available from: www.nytimes.com/2010/06/27/magazine/27Tuna-t.html?th=&emc=th&page wanted=prin

10. Roberts, Calllum. *The ocean of life: The fate of man and the sea.* New York: Viking; 2012.

11. Public Citizen. GATT-Zilla vs. flipper: Dolphin case demonstrates how trade agreements undermine domestic environmental, public interest policies [Internet]. 2003 [cited 2013 Oct 31]; Available from: www.citizen.org/Page.aspx?pid=2913

12. Knox, John H. The judicial resolution of conflicts between trade and the environment. *Harv Environ Law Rev.* 2004; 28: 1–78.

13. Williams, Ted. The last bluefin hunt. *Audubon Magazine.* 1992 July-August: 14–20.

14. Song, Yann-huei. The efforts of ICCAT to combat IUU fishing: The roles of Japan and Taiwan in conserving and managing tuna resources. *Int J Law.* 2009; 24: 101–39.

15. Pew Foundation. ICCAT takes positive action to rebuild Atlantic bluefin tuna populations, end illegal fishing, but ignores sharks [Internet]. www.pewenvironment.org; 2013 [cited 2014 Jan 1]; Available from: www.pewenvironment.org/news-room/press-releases/iccat-takes-positive-action-to-rebuild-atlantic-bluefin-tuna-populations-end-illegal-fishing-but-ignores-sharks-85899522599

16. World Wildlife Fund. Atlantic tuna commission sticks to science on bluefin tuna, fails to protect sharks [Internet]. 2013 [cited 2014 Jan 1]; Available from: http://wwf.panda.org/?212655/Atlantic-tuna-commission-sticks-to-science-on-bluefin-tuna-fails-to-protect-sharks

17. Ludwig, Donald. Can we exploit sustainably? In: Reynolds, John D., Mace, Georgina M., Redford, Kent H., Robinson, John G., editors. *Conservation of exploited species.* Cambridge: Cambridge University Press; 2001. p. 16–40.

18. Urbina, Ian. A renegade trawler hunted for 10,000 miles by vigilantes. *New York Times* [Internet]. 2015 Jul 28 [cited 2015 Jul 28]; Available from: www.nytimes.com/2015/07/28/world/a-renegade-trawler-hunted-for-10000-miles-by-vigilantes.html?emc=edit_tnt_20150728&nlid=10365419&tntemail0=y&_r=0

19. Kaiman, Jonthan. Pirate fishing's toll means high stakes on the high seas. *Los Angeles Times* [Internet]. 2015 Jul 25 [cited 2015 Jul 30]; Available from: http://amestrib.com/news/pirate-fishing-s-toll-means-high-stakes-high-seas

20. Huxley, Chris. CITES: The vision. In Hutton, Jon, Dickson, Barnabas, editors. *Endangered species threatened convention: The past, present and future of CITES, the convention on international trade in endangered species of wild fauna and flora.* London: Earthscan; 2000. p. 3–12.

21. Kievit, Henriette. Conservation of the Nile crocodile: Has CITES helped or hindered? In: Hutton, Jon, Dickson, Barnabas, editors. *Endangered species threatened convention: The past, present and future of CITES, the Convention on International Trade in Endangered Species of wild fauna and flora.* London: Earthscan; 2000. p. 88–97.

22. Martin, R.B. CITES and the CBD. In: Hutton, Jon, Dickson, Barnabas, editors. *Endangered species threatened convention: The past, present and future of CITES, the Convention on International Trade in Endangered Species of wild fauna and flora*. London: Earthscan; 2000. p. 125–33.

23. Webb, Grahame J.W. Are all species equal? A comparative assessment. In: Hutton, Jon, Dickson, Barnabas, editors. *Endangered species threatened convention: The past, present and future of CITES, the Convention on International Trade in Endangered Species of wild fauna and flora*. London: Earthscan; 2000. p. 98–106.

24. Hemley, Ginette, Mills, Judy A. The beginning of the end of tigers in trade? In: Seidensticker, John, Christie, Sarah, Jackson, Peter, editors. *Riding the tiger: Tiger conservation in human-dominated landscapes*. Cambridge: Cambridge University Press; 1999. p. 217–29.

25. Coggins, Chris. *The tiger and the pangolin: Nature, culture, and conservation in China*. Honolulu: University of Hawai'i Press; 2003.

26. Galster, Steven, Schaedla, William, Redford, Tim. Partnering to stop poaching: Developing cross-sector strategic responses to wildlife poaching. In: Tilson, Ronald, Nyhus, Philip J., editors. *Tigers of the world: The science, politics, and conservation of panthera tigris*. Amsterdam: Academic Press; 2010. p. 113–24.

27. U.S. Department of Justice. U.S. justice department efforts against wildlife trafficking [Internet]. 2013 [cited 2013 Nov 15]; Available from: http://iipdigital.usembassy.gov/st/english/texttrans/2013/09/20130910282535.html#axzz2kj8580CP

28. Wilson, Michael. In rhino horn case, judge sees a criminal instead of a "naïve kid." *New York Times* [Internet]. 2014 Jan 10 [cited 2014 Jan 10]; Available from: www.nytimes.com/2014/01/11/nyregion/in-rhino-horn-case-judge-sees-organized-crime-link-instead-of-naive-kid.html?emc=edit_tnt_20140110&tntemail0=y

29. Wilson, Edward O. *The future of life*. New York: Alfred A. Knopf; 2002.

30. Hulkrans, Andrew N. Greenbacks for greenery. *Sierra Magazine*. 1988 November-December: 43–6.

31. Schaller, George B. *The last panda*. Chicago: University of Chicago Press; 1993.

32. Zahler, Peter, Schaller, George. Saving more than just snow leopards. *New York Times* [Internet]. 2014 Feb 1 [cited 2014 Feb 1]; Available from: www.nytimes.com/2014/02/02/opinion/saving-more-than-just-snow-leopards.html?emc=edit_tnt_20140201&tntemail0=y

33. Frisina, Michael R., Tareen, Sardar Naseer A. Exploitation prevents extinction: Case study of endangered Himalayan sheep and goats. In: Dickson, Barnabas, Hutton, Jon, Adams, William M., editors. *Recreational hunting, conservation and rural livelihoods: Science and practice*. Oxford: Wiley-Blackwell; 2009. p. 141–56.

34. Eilperin, Juliet. Polar bear trade, hunting spark controversy. *Washington Post* [Internet]. 2012 Dec 25 [cited 2013 Jan 6]; Available from: http://mankatofreepress.com/community-news-network/x2056566049/Polar-bear-trade-hunting-spark-controversy

35. Platt, John. Proposal to ban trade in polar bear parts fails at international wildlife conference [Internet]. *Mother Nature Network*; 2013 [cited 2014 Feb 24]; Available from: www.mnn.com/earth-matters/animals/stories/proposal-to-ban-trade-in-polar-bear-parts-fails-at-international

36. Nash, Roderick. *Wilderness and the American mind*. 3rd ed. New Haven: Yale University Press; 1982.

37. Vira, Varun, Ewing, Thomas. Ivory's curse: The militarization & professionalization of poaching in Africa [Internet]. www.c4ads.org; 2014 [cited 2014 Jun 29]; Available from: http://media.wix.com/ugd/e16b55_7ccc46650a664e47b09709c97bc94933.pdf

38. Lovett, Jon C. Elephants and the conservation dilemma. *Afr J Ecol.* 2009; 47: 129–30.

39. Sas-Rolfes, Michael. Does destroying ivory really save elephants? [Internet]. Property and Environment Research Center; 2013 [cited 2013 Nov 15]; Available from: http://perc.org/articles/does-destroying-ivory-really-save-elephants

40. U.S. Department of Justice. Efforts against wildlife trafficking [Internet]. 2013 [cited 2013 Nov 15]; Available from: http://iipdigital.usembassy.gov/st/english/texttrans/2013/09/20130910282535.html#axzz2kj8580CP

41. U.S. Fish and Wildlife Service. U.S. destroys confiscated ivory stockpile, sends message that wildlife trafficking, elephant poaching must be crushed [Internet]. 2013 [cited 2013 Nov 15]; Available from: www.fws.gov/mountain-prairie/pressrel/2013/11142013_ivoryCrush.php

42. Finley, Bruce. As feds crush ivory in Denver to curb poaching, Kerry offers $1M reward to stop elephant killing. *The Denver Post* [Internet]. 2013 Nov 13 [cited 2013 Nov 15]; Available from: www.denverpost.com/environment/ci_24518193/u-s-government-crushing-ivory-save-elephants-and

43. Safina, Carl. Blood ivory. *New York Times* [Internet]. 2013 Feb 11 [cited 2013 Feb 12]; Available from: www.nytimes.com/2013/02/12/opinion/global/blood-ivory.html?emc=tnt&tntemail1=y&_r=0&pagewanted=prin

44. Maisels, Fiona, Strindberg, Samantha, Blake, Stephen, Wittemyer, George, Williamson, Elizabeth A., Aba's, Rosten et al. Devastating decline of forest elephants in central Africa. *PLoS ONE* [Internet]. 2013 Mar 4 [cited 2013 Dec 31]; Available from: www.plosone.org/article/info%3Adoi%2F10.1371%2Fjournal.pone.0059469

45. Strindberg, Samantha, Maisels, Fiona. Slaughter of the African elephants. *New York Times* [Internet]. 2013 Mar 16 [cited 2013 Mar 17]; Available from: www.nytimes.com/2013/03/17/opinion/sunday/slaughter-of-the-african-elephants.html?emc=tnt&tntemail1=y&pagewanted=print

46. Ogada, Darcy L. The poisoning of Africa's vultures. *New York Times* [Internet]. 2014 Aug 27 [cited 2014 Aug 27]; Available from: www.nytimes.com/2014/08/28/opinion/the-poisoning-of-africas-vultures.html?emc=edit_tnt_20140827&nlid=10365419&tntemail0=y

47. U.S. Fish and Wildlife Service. Eye on ivory: Investigations & inspections [Internet]. 2013 [cited 2013 Nov 15]; Available from: www.fws.gov/le/pdf/Elephant-Ivory-Investigations.pdf

48. Fuller, Thomas. In trafficking of wildlife, out of reach of the law. *New York Times Magazine* [Internet]. 2013 Mar 3 [cited 2013 Mar 4]; Available from: www.nytimes.com/2013/03/04/world/asia/notorious-figure-in-animal-smuggling-beyond-reach-in-laos.html?ref=world&pagewanted=print

49. Fuller, Thomas. Laos, destination in illegal ivory trade, so far eludes global crackdown. *New York Times* [Internet]. 2015 Aug 1 [cited 2015 Aug 1]; Available from: www.nytimes.com/2015/08/02/world/asia/laos-destination-in-illegal-ivory-trade-so-far-eludes-global-crackdown.html?emc=edit_tnt_20150801&nlid=10365419&tntemail0=y&_r=0

50. Scharf, Katie M., Fernandez-Gimenez, Maria E., Batbuyan, Batjav, Enkhbold, Suymiya. Herders and hunters in a transitional economy: The challenge of wildlife and rangeland management in post-socialist Mongolia. In: du Toit, John D., Kock, Richard, Deutsch, James C., editors. *Wild rangelands: Conserving wildlife while maintaining livestock in semi-arid ecosystems.* Oxford: Wiley-Blackwell; 2010. p. 312–39.

51. Dreifus, Claudia. A conversation with Patricia C. Wright: A lemur rescue mission in Madagascar. *New York Times* [Internet]. 2014 Aug 8 [cited 2014 Aug 8]; Available from: www.nytimes.com/2014/08/19/science/a-rescue-mission-in-madagascar.html?emc=edit_tnt_20140818&nlid=10365419&tntemail0=y

52. Compton, James, Lee, Samuel K.H. Wildlife trade within east Asia: Supply and demand for traditional oriental medicine. In: Guynup, Sharon, editor. *2006 State of the wild: A global portrait of wildlife, wildlands, and oceans*. Washington, D.C.: Island Press; 2005. p. 114–21.

53. Beissinger, Steven R. Trade of live wild birds: Potentials, principles and practices of sustainable use. In: Reynolds, John D., Mace, Georgina M., Redford, Kent H., Robinson, John G., editors. *Conservation of exploited species*. Cambridge: Cambridge University Press; 2001. p. 182–202.

54. Gonzalez, Arancha. Legal trade can save endangered wildlife. *Wall Street Journal* [Internet]. 2014 Mar 3 [cited 2014 Mar 3]; Available from: http://online.wsj.com/news/articles/SB10001424052702304709904579407232749368154?KEYWORDS=legal+trade+can+save+endangered+wildlife&mg=reno64-wsj

55. Wassener, Bettina. China destroys 6 tons of ivory. *New York Times* [Internet]. 2014 Jan 6 [cited 2014 Jan 6]; Available from: http://sinosphere.blogs.nytimes.com/2014/01/06/china-destroys-6-tons-of-ivory/?emc=edit_tnt_20140106&tntemail0=y&_r=0&pagewanted=print

56. Hilborn, Ray Arcese. Effective enforcement in a conservation area. *Science*. 2006; 314 (5803): 1266.

57. Wassener, Bettina. No species is safe from burgeoning wildlife trade. *New York Times* [Internet]. 2013 Mar 12 [cited 2013 Mar 12]; Available from: www.nytimes.com/2013/03/12/world/asia/no-species-is-safe-from-burgeoning-wildlife-trade.html?emc=tnt&tntemail1=y&_r=0&pagewanted=print

58. Rauber, Paul. Critter: Moon bear: Its bile fuels a multimillion-dollar industry. *Sierra Magazine*. 2013 May-June: 29.

59. Huang, Shaojie. Trying to shield endangered animals from China's appetites. *New York Times* [Internet]. 2014 Apr 28 [cited 2014 Apr 28]; Available from: http://sinosphere.blogs.nytimes.com/2014/04/28/trying-to-shield-endangered-animals-from-chinas-appetites/?_php=true&_type=blogs&emc=edit_tnt_20140428&nlid=10365419&tntemail0=y&_r=0

60. Levin, Dan. Q. and A.: Jill Robinson on animals and empathy in Asia. *New York Times* [Internet]. 2014 Dec 26 [cited 2014 Dec 26]; Available from: http://sinosphere.blogs.nytimes.com/2014/12/26/q-and-a-jill-robinson-on-animals-and-empathy-in-asia/?emc=edit_tnt_20141226&nlid=10365419&tntemail0=y

61. Christy, Bryan. Ivory worship. *National Geographic* [Internet]. 2012 October [cited 2013 Nov 15]; Available from: http://ngm.nationalgeographic.com/2012/10/ivory/christy-text

62. Tatlow, Didi Kirsten. Sending a signal, Philippines to destroy ivory stock. *International Herald Tribune* [Internet]. 2013 Jun 19 [cited 2013 Jun 19]; Available from: http://rendezvous.blogs.nytimes.com/2013/06/19/sending-a-signal-philippines-to-destroy-ivory-stock/?emc=tnt&tntemail0=y&pagewanted=print

63. Levin, Dan. From elephants' mouths, an illicit trail to China. *New York Times* [Internet]. 2013 Mar 1 [cited 2013 Mar 2]; Available from: www.nytimes.com/2013/03/02/world/asia/an-illicit-trail-of-african-ivory-to-china.html?nl=todaysheadlines&emc=edit_th_20130302&_r=0&pagewanted=print

64. Tatlow, Didi Kirsten. Mass slaughter of vulnerable shark species in China, wildlife group says. *New York Times* [Internet]. 2014 Jan 28 [cited 2014 Jan 28]; Available from: http://sinosphere.blogs.nytimes.com/2014/01/28/mass-slaughter-of-vulnerable-shark-species-in-china-wildlife-group-says/?_php=true&_type=blogs&emc=edit_tnt_20140128&tntemail0=y&_r=0

65. Thorbjarnarson, John. Crocodile tears and skins: International trade, economic constraints, and limits to the sustainable use of crocodilians. *Conserv Biol*. 1999; 13(3): 465–70.

66. Feng, Bree. Police find dead tiger in S.U.V. in Wenzhou. *New York Times* [Internet]. 2014 Jan 9 [cited 2014 Jan 9]; Available from: http://sinosphere.blogs.nytimes.com/2014/01/09/police-find-dead-tiger-in-s-u-v-in-wenzhou/?emc=edit_tnt_20140109&tntemail0=y&_r=0&pagewanted=print

67. Nagano, Yuriko. Japan's delicate search for a way to breed tuna on an industrial scale. *New York Times* [Internet]. 2013 Nov 11 [cited 2013 Nov 11]; Available from: www.nytimes.com/2013/11/11/business/energy-environment/japans-delicate-search-for-a-way-to-breed-tuna-on-an-industrial-scale.html?emc=edit_tnt_20131111&tntemail0=y&_r=0&pagewanted=print

68. Malkin, Elisabeth. Mexico moves to save endangered porpoise. *New York Times* [Internet]. 2015 Feb 28; Available from: www.nytimes.com/2015/03/01/world/americas/mexico-moves-to-save-endangered-porpoise.html?emc=edit_tnt_20150228&nlid=10365419&tntemail0=y&_r=0

69. Hutton, Jon, Webb, Grahame. Crocodiles: Legal trade snaps back. In: Oldfield, Sara, editor. *The trade in wildlife: Regulation for conservation.* London: Earthscan; 2003. p. 108–20.

70. Leader-Williams, Nigel. Regulation and protection: Successes and failures in rhinoceros conservation. In: Oldfield, Sara, editor. *The trade in wildlife: Regulation for conservation.* London: Earthscan; 2003. p. 89–99.

71. Brooks, Richard O., Jones, Ross, Virginia, Ross A. *Law and Ecology: The rise of the ecosystem regime.* Burlington, VT: Ashgate Publishing Company; 2002.

72. Matthews, Paul, Problems related to the convention on the international trade in endangered species. Int Comp Law Q. 1996; 45(2): 421–31.

73. Gehring, Thomas, Ruffing, Eva. When aguments prevail over power: The CITES procedure for the listing of endangered species. *Glob Environ Polit.* 2008; 8(2): 123–48.

74. Le Prestre, Philippe, Stoett, Peter, Beazley, Karen, Boardman, Robert. International initiatives, commitments, and disappointments: Canada, CITES, and the CBD. In: Beazley, Karen, Boardman, Robert, editors. *Politics of the wild: Canada and endangered species.* Oxford: Oxford University Press; 2001. p. 190–216.

75. Duffy, Rosaleen. *Nature crime: How we're getting conservation wrong.* New Haven: Yale University Press; 2010.

76. du Plessiss, Morne A. CITES and the causes of extinction. In: Hutton, Jon, Dickson, Barnabas, editors. *Endangered species threatened convention: The past, present and future of CITES, the Convention on International Trade in Endangered Species of wild fauna and flora.* London: Earthscan; 2010. p. 13–25.

77. Biggs, Duan, Courchamp, Frank, Martin, Rowan, Possingham, Hugh P. Science policy forum: Legal trade of Africa's rhino horns. *Science.* 2013; 339(March 1): 1038–9.

78. Prins, Herbert H.T., Okita-Ourma, Benson. Rhino poaching: Unique challenges. *Science.* 2013; 340(June 7): 1167–8.

79. Collins, Alan, Graser, Gavin, Snowball, Jen. Rhino poaching: Supply and demand uncertain. *Science.* 2013; 340(6137): 1167.

80. Kalland, Arne. Whose whale is that? Diverting the commodity path. In: Freeman, Milton R., editor. *Elephants and whales: Resources for whom.* Switzerland: Gordon and Breach Science Publishers; 1994. p. 159–86.

81. Heller, Peter. *The whale warriors. The battle at the bottom of the world to save the planet's largest mammals.* New York: The Free Press; 2007.

82. Fackler, Martin. Uncertainty buffets Japan's whaling fleet. *New York Times* [Internet]. 2010 May 15 [cited 2014 Jan 10]; Available from: www.nytimes.com/2010/05/16/world/asia/16whaling.html?pagewanted=print

83. Associated Press. Greenpeace changes tactic on whaling in Japan. www.nbcnews.com [Internet]. 2008 Dec 9 [cited 2014 Jan 23]; Available from: www.nbcnews.com/id/28141932/#.UuH5yxDnY0M

84. Economist. Obduracy in the face of hypocrisy. 2003 Dec 30; Available from: www.economist.com/node/2313082

85. Kobayashi, Lisa. Lifting the international whaling commission's moratorium on commercial whaling as the most effective global regulation of whaling. *Environs.* 2006; 29(2): 177–219.

86. Jordan, Tara. Revising the international convention on the regulation of whaling: A proposal to end the stalemate within the international whaling commission. *Wis Int Law J.* 2011–12; 29(4): 833–68.

87. Goodman, Dan. The future of the IWC: Why the initiative to save the international whaling commission failed. *J Int Wildl Law Policy.* 2011; 14: 63–74.

88. Iliff, Mike. Contemporary initiatives on the future of the International Whaling Commission. *Mar Policy.* 2010; 34: 461–7.

89. New York Times. Editorial: A non-ban on whaling. 2009 Jun 28 [cited 2014 Jan 10]; Available from: www.nytimes.com/2009/06/28/opinion/28sun3.html?pagewanted=print

90. Freeman, Milton M.R., Kellert, Stephen R. International attitudes to whales, whaling and the use of whale products: A six-country survey. In: Freeman, Milton R., editor. *Elephants and whales: Resources for whom?* Switzerland: Gordon and Breach Science Publishers; 1994. p. 293–300.

91. Dellios, Hugh. Intrigue and politics in world of whaling. Japan is accused of buying votes of poor nations like Nicaragua to promote its pro-hunting agenda. *Chicago Tribune* [Internet]. 2004 Dec 1 [cited 2011 Dec 9]; Available from: www.chicagotribune.com/news/yahoo/chi-0412010247dec01,1,399820.story

92. Estes, James A., Terborgh, John, Brashares, Justin S., Power, Mary E., Berger, Joel, Bond, William J. et al. Trophic downgrading of planet Earth. *Science.* 2011; 333(6040): 301–6.

93. Ellis, Richard. How much longer? *Audubon Magazine.* 1994 March-April :126.

94. Spencer, Leslie, Bollwerk, Jan, Morais, Richard C. The not so peaceful world of Greenpeace. *Forbes* [Internet]. 1991 November [cited 2014 Jan 11]; Available from: http://luna.pos.to/whale/gen_art_green.html

95. New York Times. Editorial: A ruling to protect whales. 2014 Apr 1 [cited 2014 Apr 1]; Available from: www.nytimes.com/2014/04/02/opinion/a-ruling-to-protect-whales.html?emc=edit_tnt_20140401&nlid=10365419&tntemail0=y&_r=0

96. Sanderson, Kate. Grind – ambiguity and pressure to conform: Faroese whaling and the anti-whaling protest. In: Freeman, Milton R., editor. *Elephants and whales: Resources for whom?* Switzerland: Gordon and Breach Science Publishers; 1994. p. 187–202.

97. Revkin, Andrew. The right rules for keeping ships from hitting right whales. *New York Times* [Internet]. 2013 Jun 5 [cited 2013 Jun 5]; Available from: http://dotearth.blogs.nytimes.com/2013/06/05/the-right-rules-for-keeping-ships-from-hitting-right-whales/?emc=tnt&tntemail0=y&pagewanted=print

98. Stoett, Peter. Irreconcilable differences: The international whaling commission and cetacean futures. *Rev Policy Res.* 2011; 28(6): 631–4.

99. Cunningham, Paul A., Huijbens, Edward H., Wearing, Stephen L. From whaling to whale watching: Examining sustainability and cultural rhetoric. *J Sustain Tour*. 2012; 20(1): 143–61.

100. Gray, Gary C. *Wildlife and people: The human dimensions of wildlife ecology*. Urbana: University of Illinois Press; 1993.

101. Agarwal, Vibhuti. India takes hard line on rhino kills. *Wall Street Journal* [Internet]. 2013 Mar 26 [cited 2013 Apr 1]; Available from: http://online.wsj.com/article/SB100014241278873247 8950457838348349338051 0.html#printMode?KEYWORDS=India+takes+hard+line+on +rhino+kill

102. Hart, John. Neither war nor peace: Protected areas still at risk in DR Congo, 2005. In: Guynup, Sharon, editor. *2006 State of the wild: A global portrait of wildlife, wildlands, and oceans*. Washington, D.C.: Island Press; 2005. p. 250–5.

103. McConahay, Mary Jo. Sweet waist of America. *Sierra Magazine*. 1993 January-February: 42–9 & 153–7.

104. Fallows, James. War and the environment. *Audubon Magazine*. 1991 September-October: 94–6.

105. Bourne, Joel. El tigre comes north. *Audubon Magazine*. 1997 September-October: 88–95.

106. Matthiessen, Peter. *Tigers in the snow*. New York: North Point Press; 2000.

107. Cox, Christopher. Paradise found. *Audubon Magazine*. 2011 July-August: 52–6.

108. Matthiessen, Peter. *The birds of heaven: Travels with cranes*. New York: North Point Press; 2001.

109. Oates, John F. *Myth and reality in the rain forest: How conservation strategies are failing in West Africa*. Berkeley: University of California Press; 1999.

110. Rome, Paul. Coming home: In Vietnam, a majestic bird rises from the ashes of war. *Sierra Magazine*. 1990 March-April: 58–64.

111. Gettleman, Jeffrey. Congo violence reaches endangered mountain gorillas. *New York Times* [Internet]. 2008 Nov 18 [cited 2014 Jan 16]; Available from: www.nytimes.com/2008/11/ 18/world/africa/18congo.html?pagewanted=print

112. Siebert, Charles. *The Wauchula Woods accord: Toward a new understanding of animals*. New York: Scribner; 2009.

113. Gettleman, Jeffrey. Rangers in isolated central Africa uncover grim cost of protecting wildlife. *New York Times* [Internet]. 2012 Jan 31 [cited 2013 Jan 7]; Available from: www.nytimes.com/ 2013/01/01/world/africa/central-africas-wildlife-rangers-face-deadly-risks.html?nl=todayshea dlines&emc=edit_th_20130106&_r=0&pagewanted=print

114. Davalos, Liliana M. The San Lucas mountain range in Colombia: How much conservation is owed to the violence? *Biodivers Conserv*. 2001; 10: 69–78.

115. Dudley, Joseph P., Ginsberg, Joshua, Plumptre, Andrew J., Hart, John A., Campos, Liliana C. Effects of war and civil strife on wildlife and wildlife habitats. *Conserv Biol*. 2002; 16(2): 319–29.

116. Sahagun, Louis. Defense department becomes a wildlife. *Los Angeles Times* [Internet]. 2013 Apr 27 [cited 2013 May 15]; Available from: http://articles.latimes.com/2013/apr/27/local/ la-me-pentagon-habitat-20130428

117. Kesling, Ben. The few, the proud, the tortoises: Marines protect endangered species. *Wall Street Journal* [Internet]. 2013 May 14 [cited 2013 May 14]; Available from: http://online .wsj.com/article/SB10001424127887323798104578452941180687984.html?mod=WSJ_WSJ_ US_News_10_1

118. Brown, David, Davies, Glyn. Introduction. In: Davies, Glyn, Brown, David, editors. *Bushmeat and livelihoods: Wildlife management and poverty reduction*. Malden, MA: Blackwell Publishing; 2007. p. 1–10.

Chapter 9 References

1. Gibbons, Boyd. Endangered thought, political animals. In: Shogren, Jason F., Tschirhart, John, editors. *Protecting endangered species in the United States.* Cambridge: Cambridge University Press; 2001. p. 23–31.

2. Beazley, Karen. Why should we protect endangered species? Philosophical and ecological rationale. In: Beazley, Karen, Boardman, Robert, editors. *Politics of the wild: Canada and endangered species.* Oxford: Oxford University Press; 2001. p. 11–25.

3. Muth, Robert M., Dick, Ronald E., Blanchard, Kathleen A. Subsistence use of wildlife and native peoples' wildlife issues. In: Decker, Daniel J., Brown, Tommy L., Siemer, William F., editors. *Human dimensions of wildlife management in north America.* Bethesda, MD: The Wildlife Society; 2001. p. 329–51.

4. Conniff, Richard. Useless creatures. *New York Times* [Internet]. 2014 Sep 13 [cited 2014 Sep 14]; Available from: http://opinionator.blogs.nytimes.com/2014/09/13/useless-creatures/

5. Minteer, Ben A. Valuing nature. In: Spray, Sharon L., McGothlin, Karen L., editors. *Loss of biodiversity.* Lanham: Rowman & Littlefield Publishers, Inc.; 2003. p. 75–98.

6. Nash, Roderick Frazier. *The rights of nature: A history of environmental ethics.* Madison: The University of Wisconsin Press; 1989.

7. Dickson, Barney. The ethics of recreational hunting. In: Dickson, Barney, Hutton, Jon, Adams, William M., editors. *Recreational hunting, conservation and rural livelihoods: Science and practice.* Oxford: Wiley-Blackwell; 2009. p. 59–72.

8. Callicott, J. Baird. Explicit and implicit values. In: Scott, J. Michael, Goble, Dale, D., Davis, Frank W., editors. *The Endangered Species Act at thirty: Conserving biodiversity in human-dominated landscapes.* Washington, D.C.: Island Press; 2006. p. 36–48.

9. DiZerega, Gus. Environmentalists and the new political climate: Strategies for the future. In: Brick, Philip D., Cawley, R. McGregor, editors. *A wolf in the garden: The land rights movement and the new environmental debate.* Lanham: Rowman & Littlefield Publishers, Inc.; 1996. p. 107–14.

10. Jasper, James M., Nelkin, Dorothy. *The animal rights crusade: The growth of a moral protest.* New York: The Free Press; 1992.

11. Garner, Robert. *The political theory of animal rights.* Manchester: Manchester University Press; 2005.

12. Garner, Robert. *Political animals: Animal protection politics in Britain and the United States.* New York: St. Martin's Press, Inc.; 1998.

13. Conniff, Richard. Fuzzy-wuzzy thinking about animal rights. *Audubon Magazine.* 1990 November: 120–32.

14. Decker, Daniel J., Brown, Tommy L., Siemer, William F. Evolution of people-wildlife relations. In: Decker, Daniel J., Brown, Tommy L., Siemer, William F., editors. *Human dimensions of wildlife management in North America.* Bethesda, MD: The Wildlife Society; 2001. p. 3–22.

15. Cambrone, Al. Can't see the forest for the deer. *Wall Street Journal* [Internet]. 2014 Mar 12 [cited 2014 Mar 12]; Available from: http://online.wsj.com/news/articles/SB10001424052702304704504579429583302400534#printMode

16. Sellars, Richard West. *Preserving nature in the national parks: A history.* New Haven: Yale University Press; 1997.

17. Anderson, Elizabeth. Animal rights and the values of nonhuman life. In: Sunstein, Cass R., Nussbaum, Martha C., editors. *Animal rights: Current debates and new directions.* Oxford: Oxford University Press; 2004. p. 277–98.

18. Goodall, Jane. *Hope for animals and their world : How endangered species are being rescued from the brink.* New York: Grand Central Publishing; 2009.

19. Raffles, Hugh. Speaking up for the mute swan. *New York Times* [Internet]. 2014 Feb 18 [cited 2014 Feb 18]; Available from: www.nytimes.com/2014/02/18/opinion/speaking-up-for-the-mute-swan.html?nl=opinion&emc=edit_ty_20140218

20. Cavaliere, Victoria. Protesters make noise over New York plan to kill off mute swans. Reuters [Internet]. 2014 Feb 22 [cited 2014 Feb 24]; Available from: http://news.yahoo.com/protesters-noise-over-york-plan-kill-off-mute-120237629.html

21. Perry, Dan, Perry, Gad. Improving interactions between animal rights groups and conservation biologists. *Conserv Biol.* 2008; 22(1): 27–35.

22. Macdonald, David W., King, Carolyn M., Strachan, Robert. Introduced species and the line between biodiversity conservation and naturalistic eugenics. In: Macdonald, David W., Service, Katrina, editors. *Key topics in conservation biology.* Malden, MA: Blackwell Publishing; 2007. p. 186–205.

23. Foderaro, Lisa W. A kinder, gentler way to thin the deer herd. *New York Times* [Internet]. 2013 Jul 5 [cited 2014 Sep 10]; Available from: www.nytimes.com/2013/07/06/nyregion/providing-birth-control-to-deer-in-an-overrun-village.html?_r=0

24. Rutberg, Allen. Yes, wildlife contraception works. *High Country News* [Internet]. 2014 Sep 3 [cited 2014 Sep 9]; Available from: www.hcn.org/articles/yes-wildlife-contraception-works?utm_source=wcn1&utm_medium=email

25. Philipps, Dave. As wild horses overrun the West, ranchers fear land will be gobbled up. *New York Times* [Internet]. 2014 Sep 30 [cited 2014 Oct 1]; Available from: www.nytimes.com/2014/10/01/us/as-wild-horses-overrun-the-west-ranchers-fear-land-will-be-gobbled-up.html?emc=edit_th_20141001&nl=todaysheadlines&nlid=10365419

26. Estes, James A., Terborgh, John, Brashares, Justin S., Power, Mary E., Berger, Joel, Bond, William J. et al. Trophic downgrading of planet Earth. *Science.* 2011; 333(6040): 301–6.

27. Patten, Michael A., Ericson, Richard A. Conservation value and rankings of exotic species. *Conserv Biol.* 2001; 15(4): 817–8.

28. Carlton, Jim. Predator fish in the cross hairs. *Wall Street Journal* [Internet]. 2013 May 14 [cited 2013 May 14]; Available from: http://online.wsj.com/article/SB10001424127887324059704578471213642371462.html#printMode?KEYWORDS=predator+fish+in+cross+hairs

29. Marris, Emma. *Rambunctious garden: Saving nature in a post-wild world.* New York: Bloomsbury; 2011.

30. Revkin, Andrew. Emma Marris: In defense of Everglades pythons. *New York Times* [Internet]. 2012 Aug 17 [cited 2015 Mar 16]; Available from: http://dotearth.blogs.nytimes.com/2012/08/17/emma-marris-in-defense-of-everglades-pythons/

31. U.S. Fish and Wildlife Service. Service lists four nonnative, large constrictor snakes as injurious wildlife [Internet]. 2015 [cited 2015 Mar 16]; Available from: www.fws.gov/news/ShowNews.cfm?ID=F0464D00-9BCE-0156-C88E1ADECD13395B

32. Revkin, Andrew C. U.S. constricts snake trade, but boa wriggles free. *New York Times.* 2015 Mar 6 [cited 2015 Mar 14]; Available from: http://dotearth.blogs.nytimes.com/2015/03/06/u-s-constricts-snake-trade-but-boa-wriggles-free/?emc=edit_tnt_20150306&nlid=10365419&tntemail0=y

33. Macdonald, David W., Service, Katrina, editors. *Key topics in conservation biology.* Malden, MA: Blackwell Publishing; 2007.

34. Samways, Michael J. Conserving invertebrates: How many can be saved, and how? In: Leader-Williams, Nigel, Adams, William M., Smith, Robert J., editors. *Trade-offs in conservation: deciding what to save*. Oxford: Wiley-Blackwell; 2010. p. 97–117.

35. Harrop, Stuart R. Trade-offs between animal welfare and conservation in law and policy. In: Leader-Williams, Nigel, Adams, William M., Smith, Robert J., editors. *Trade-offs in conservation: Deciding what to save*. Oxford: Wiley-Blackwell; 2010. p. 118–34.

36. Session, George, Devall, Bill. Deep ecology. In: Nash, Roderick Frazier, editor. *American environmentalism: Readings in conservation history*. New York: McGraw-Hill; 1985. p. 309–15.

37. Devall, Bill. *Deep ecology*. Layton, Utah: Gibbs Smith Publisher; 1985.

38. Foreman, Dave. *Confessions of an eco-warrior*. New York: Harmony Books; 1991.

39. Eldredge, Niles. A hard sell: The cultural-ecological context of reintroducing wolves to the Adirondacks. In: Sharpe, Virginia A., Norton, Bryan G., Donnelley, Strachan, editors. *Wolves and human communities: Biology, politics, and ethics*. Washington, D.C.: Island Press; 2001. p. 275–84.

40. Loftin, Robert W. The medical treatment of wild animals. *Environ Ethics*. 1985; 7(Fall): 231–9.

41. Strong, Douglas H. *Dreamers & defenders: American conservationists*. Lincoln: University of Nebraska; 1988.

42. Dinerstein, Eric. *The return of the unicorns: The natural history and conservation of the greater one-horned rhinoceros*. New York: Columbia University Press; 2003.

43. Nash, Roderick. *Wilderness and the American mind*. 3rd ed. New Haven: Yale University Press; 1982.

44. Eisenberg, Cristinia. *The carnivore way: Coexisting with and conserving north America's predators*. Washington, D.C.: Island Press; 2014.

45. Franklin, Adrian. *Animal nation: The true story of animals and Australia*. Sydney: University of New South Wales Press Ltd.; 2006.

46. National Research Council. *Progress towards restoring the Everglades: The fifth biennial review, 2014*. Washington, D.C.: National Academy Press; 2014.

47. McNeil Jr., Donald G. When human rights extend to nonhumans. *New York Times* [Internet]. 2008 Jul 13 [cited 2014 Feb 7]; Available from: www.nytimes.com/2008/07/13/weekinreview/13mcneil.html?pagewanted=print

48. Sugg, Ike C., Kreuter, Urgs P. Elephants and whales as resources from the noosphere. In: Freeman, Milton R., editor. *Elephants and whales: Resources for whom?* Switzerland: Gordon and Breach Science Publishers; 1994. p. 17–38.

49. Doubleday, Nancy. Arctic whales: Sustaining indigenous peoples and conserving arctic resources. In: Freeman, Milton R., editor. *Elephants and whales: Resources for whom?* Switzerland: Gordon and Breach Science Publishers; 1994. p. 241–62.

50. Hutton, Jon, Dickson, Barnabas, Hutton, Jon. Introduction. In: Hutton, Jon, Dickson, Barnabas, editors. *Endangered species threatened convention: The past, present and future of CITES, the Convention on International Trade in Endangered Species of wild fauna and flora*. London: Earthscan; 2000. p. xiii–xx.

51. du Plessis, Morne A. CITES and the causes of extinction. In: Hutton, Jon, Dickson, Barnabas, editors. *Endangered species threatened convention: The past, present and future of CITES, the Convention on International Trade in Endangered Species of wild fauna and flora*. London: Earthscan; 2000. p. 13–25.

52. Webb, Grahame J.W. Are all species equal? A comparative assessment. In: Hutton, Jon, Dickson, Barnabas, editors. *Endangered species threatened convention: The past, present and future of CITES, the Convention on International Trade in Endangered Species of wild fauna and flora*. London: Earthscan; 2000. p. 98–106.

53. Kalland, Arne. Whose whale is that? Diverting the commodity path. In: Freeman, Milton R., editor. *Elephants and whales: Resources for whom*. Switzerland: Gordon and Breach Science Publishers; 1994. p. 159–86.

54. Bradshaw, G. A. *Elephants on the edge: What animals teach us about humanity*. New Haven: Yale University Press; 2009.

55. Angier, Natalie. Save a whale, save a soul, goes the cry. *New York Times* [Internet]. 2010 Aug 26 [cited 2014 Feb 18]; Available from: www.nytimes.com/2010/06/27/weekinreview/27angier.html?sq=save%20a%20whale,%20save%20asoul,%20goes%20the%20cry&st=cse&scp=1&pagewanted=print

56. Revkin, Andrew C. A closer look at "nonhuman personhood" and animal welfare. *New York Times* [Internet]. 2013 Jul 28 [cited 2013 Jul 28]; Available from: http://dotearth.blogs.nytimes.com/2013/07/28/a-closer-look-at-nonhuman-personhood-and-animal-welfare/?emc=edit_tnt_20130728&tntemail0=y&pagewanted=print

57. Wise, Stephen M. Nonhuman rights to personhood. *Pace Environ Law Rev* [Internet]. [cited 2014 Feb 18]; 30(3); Available from: http://digitalcommons.pace.edu/pelr/vol30/iss3/10. 1278–90

58. Siebert, Charles. Should a chimp be able to sue its owner? *New York Times* [Internet]. 2014 Apr 23 [cited 2014 Apr 23]; Available from: www.nytimes.com/2014/04/27/magazine/the-rights-of-man-and-beast.html?emc=edit_tnt_20140423&nlid=10365419&tntemail0=y

59. Klinkenborg, Verlyn. After years of progress, a setback in saving the wolf. *New York Times* [Internet]. 2013 Jun 1 [cited 2013 Jun 2]; Available from: www.nytimes.com/2013/06/02/opinion/sunday/after-years-of-progress-a-setback-in-saving-the-wolf.html?emc=tnt&tntemail0=y

60. Safina, Carl. Scourge of the lionfish, part 3: The newest fish in the kitchen. *New York Times* [Internet]. 2012 Sep 10 [cited 2014 Feb 17]; Available from: http://bittman.blogs.nytimes.com/2012/09/10/scourge-of-the-lionfish-part-3-the-newest-fish-in-the-kitchen/?_php=true&_type=blogs&_r=0

61. Carbyn, Lu. *The buffalo wolf: Predators, prey, and the politics of nature*. Washington, D.C.: Smithsonian Books; 2003.

62. Velasquez-Manoff, Moises. Should red wolves be allowed to mate with coyotes. *New York Times* [Internet]. 2014 Aug 19 [cited 2014 Aug 19]; Available from: http://6thfloor.blogs.nytimes.com/2014/08/19/should-red-wolves-be-allowed-to-mate-with-coyotes/?_php=true&_type=blogs&emc=edit_tnt_20140819&nlid=10365419&tntemail0=y&_r=0

63. Kolbert, Elizabeth. The big kill: New Zealand's crusade to rid itself of mammals. *The New Yorker* [Internet]. 2014 Dec 22 [cited 2014 Dec 22]; Available from: www.newyorker.com/magazine/2014/12/22/big-kill

64. Teel, Tara L., Manfredo, Michael J. Understanding the diversity of public interests in wildlife. *Conserv Biol*. 2009; 24(1): 128–39.

65. Beck, Thomas. Citizen ballot initiatives: A failure of the wildlife management profession. *Hum Dimens Wildl*. 1998; 3(2): 21–8.

66. Gigliott, Larry M., Shroufe, Duane L., Gurtin, Scott. The changing culture of wildlife. In: Manfredo, Michael J., Vaske, Jerry J., Brown, Perry J., Decker, Daniel J., Duke, Esther A., editors. *Wildlife and Society: The science of human dimensions*. Washington, D.C.: Island Press; 2009. p. 75–89.

67. Hiller, Tim L. Book Review: Dominion over wildlife? An environmental theology of human–wildlife relations by Stephen M. Vantassel. *J Wildl Manag.* 2010; 73(3): 613–4.

68. Preece, Rod, Chamberlain, Lorna. *Animal welfare & human values.* Waterloo, Ontario, Canada: Wilfrid Laurier Press; 1993.

69. Coggins, Chris. *The tiger and the pangolin: Nature, culture, and conservation in China.* Honolulu: University of Hawai'i Press; 2003.

70. Kabiri, Ngeta. Historic and contemporary struggles for a local wildlife governance regime in Kenya. In: Nelson, Fred, editor. *Community rights, conservation and contested land: The politics of natural resource governance in Africa.* London: Earthscan; 2010. p. 121–44.

71. Bonner, Raymond. Western conservation groups and the ivory ban wagon. In: Freeman, Milton R., editor. *Elephants and whales: Resources for whom?* Switzerland: Gordon and Breach Science Publishers; 1994. p. 59–72.

72. Madzwamuse, Masego. Adaptive or anachronistic? Maintaining indigenous natural resource governance systems in northern Botswana. In: Nelson, Fred, editor. *Community rights, conservation and contested land: The politics of natural resource governance in Africa.* London: Earthscan; 2010. p. 241–68.

73. Hutton, Jon, Dickson, Barney. Conservation out of exploitation: a silk purse from a sow's ear? In: Reynolds, John D., Mace, Georgina M., Redford, Kent H., Robinson, John G., editors. *Conservation of exploited species.* Cambridge: Cambridge University Press; 2001. p. 440–61.

74. Schwartzman, Stephan, Moreira, Adriana, Nepstad, Daniel. Rethinking tropical forest conservation: Perils in parks. *Conserv Biol.* 2000; 14(5): 1351–7.

75. Redford, Kent H., Sanderson, Steven E. Extracting humans from nature. *Conserv Biol.* 2000; 14(5): 1363–4.

76. Brown, Taylor, Marks, Stuart A. Livelihoods, hunting and the game meat trade in Northern Zambia. In: Davies, Glyn, Brown, David, editors. Bushmeat and livelihoods: Wildlife management and poverty reduction. Malden, MA: Blackwell Publishing; 2007. p. 92–105.

77. Lindsey, Peter A., Frank, L. G., Alexander, R., Mathieson, A., Romanach, S. S. Trophy hunting and conservation in Africa: Problems and one potential. *Conserv Biol.* 2007; 24(3): 880–3.

78. Nuding, Markus A. Wildlife management in Namibia: The conservancy approach. In: O'Riordan, Tim, Stoll-Kleeman, Susanne, editors. *Biodiversity, sustainability and human communities: Protecting beyond the protected.* Cambridge: Cambridge University Press; 2002. p. 189–209.

79. Jones, Robert F. Farewell to Africa. *Audubon Magazine.* 1990 September-October: 51–104.

80. O'Callaghan, Kate. Whose agenda for America? *Audubon Magazine.* 1992 September-October: 84.

81. Stevenson, Peter. The world trade organisation rules: A legal analysis of their adverse impact on animal welfare [Internet]. The Food and Agricultural Organization of the United Nations; 2002 [cited 2014 Mar 15]; Available from: www.fao.org/fileadmin/user_upload/animalwelfare/world_trade_legal_analysis_2002.pdf

82. Harrop, Stuart, Bowles, David. Wildlife management, the multilateral trade regime, morals and the welfare of animals. *J Int Wildl Law Policy.* 1997; 1(3): 64–94.

83. EuroGroup for Animals. Areas of concern: Analysis of animal welfare issues in the European union [Internet]. 2010 [cited 2014 Mar 14]; Available from: http://eurogroupforanimals.org/files/publications/downloads/EurogroupForAnimals-AreasOfConcern2010.pdf

84. Yaffee, Steven Lewis. *The wisdom of the spotted owl: Policy lessons for a new century.* Washington, D.C.: Island Press; 1994.

85. Finley, Allysia. How the other California lives. *Wall Street Journal* [Internet]. 2014 Mar 7 [cited 2014 Mar 8]; Available from: http://online.wsj.com/news/articles/SB1000142405270 23037755045793960931192154448#printMode

86. Wall Street Journal. Editorial: Sage grouse rebellion will Obama use two small birds to limit oil drilling in the West? 2014 Mar 11 [cited 2014 Mar 11]; Available from: http://online.wsj.com/news/articles/SB10001424052702304858104579262383209254934#printMode

87. Loftin, Robert W. Loftin, Robert W. The medical treatment of wild animals. In: Michael, Mark A., editor Preserving wildlife: An international perspective. New York: Humanity Books; 2000. p. 47–56.

88. Darimont, Chris T., Carlson, Stephanie M., Kinnison, Michael T., Paquet, Paul C., Reimchen, Thomas E., Wilmers, Christopher C. Human predators outpace other agents of trait change in the wild. *Proc Natl Acad Sci U S A.* 2009; 106(3): 952–4.

89. Norton, Bryan G. What do we owe the future? How should we decide? In: Sharpe, Virginia A., Norton, Bryan G., Donnelley, Strachan, editors. *Wolves and human communities: Biology, politics, and ethics.* Washington, D.C.: Island Press; 2001. p. 213–31.

90. Barbier, Edward B., Heal, Geoffrey M. Valuing ecosystem devices. *Economists' Voice.* 2006; (February): 1–5.

91. Terborgh, John. Foreword. In: Wuerthner, George, Crist, Eileen, Butler, Tom, editors. *Protecting the wild: Parks and wilderness, the foundation for conservation.* Washington, D.C.: Island Press; 2015. p. xi–xvi.

92. McCauley, Douglas J. Fool's gold in the Catskill mountains: Thinking critically about the ecosystem services paradigm. In: Wuerthner, George, Crist, Eileen, Butler, Tom, editors. *Protecting the wild: Parks and wilderness, the foundation for conservation.* Washington, D.C.: Island Press; 2015. p. 36–40.

93. Mitra, Barun. Sell the tiger to save it. *New York Times* [Internet]. 2006 Aug 15 [cited 2014 Feb 24]; Available from: www.nytimes.com/2006/08/15/opinion/15mitra.html?_r=0

94. Nowell, Kristen, Tilson, Ronald, Nyhus, Philip J. Tiger farms and pharmacies: The central importance of China's trade policy for tiger conservation. In: Nyhus, Philip J., Tilson, Ronald, editors. *Tigers of the world: The science, politics, and conservation of panthera tigris.* 2nd ed. Amsterdam: Academic Press; 2010. p. 463–76.

95. Gratwicke, Brian, Bennett, Elizabeth L., Broad, Steven. The world can't have wild tigers and eat them too. *Conserv Biol.* 2008; 22(1): 222–3.

96. Nyhus, Philip J., Tilson, Ronald, Hutchins, Michael. Thirteen thousand and counting: How growing captive tiger populations threaten wild tigers. In: Tilson, Ronald, Nyhus, Philip J., editors. *Tigers of the world: The science, politics, and conservation of panthera tigris.* 2nd ed. Amsterdam: Academic Press; 2010. p. 223–38.

97. Kellert, Stephen R. A sociological perspective: Valuation, socioeconomic, and organizational factors. In: Clark, Tim W., Reading, Richard P., Clarke, Alice L., editors. *Endangered species recovery: Finding the lessons, improving the process.* Washington, D.C.: Island Press; 1994. p. 371–89.

98. Hutton, Jon, Webb, Grahame. Crocodiles: Legal trade snaps back. In: Oldfield, Sara, editor. *The trade in wildlife: Regulation for conservation.* London: Earthscan; 2003. p. 108–20.

99. Hutton, Jon, Webb, Grahame Legal trade Snaps Back: Using the experience of crocodilians to draw lessons on regulation of the wildlife trade. In: Hutton, Jon, Webb, Grahame, editors. *Crocodiles: Proceedings of the 16th working meeting of the crocodile specialist group,*

IUCN – *The World Conservation Union.* Gland, Switzerland, and Cambridge, UK: The World Conservation Union; 2002. p. 1–10.

100. Thorbjarnarson, John. Commercial consumptive use of crocodilians: A conservation panacea or pitfall? In: Hutton, Jon, Webb, Grahame, editors. *Proceedings of the 16th Working meeting of the crocodile specialist group, IUCN – The World Conservation Union* [Internet]. Gland, Switzerland, and Cambridge, UK: The World Conservation Union; 2002 [cited 2014 May 2]. p. 11; Available from: https://portals.iucn.org/library/efiles/edocs/NS-2002-001.pdf

101. Dutton, Harry J., Brunell, Arnold M., Carbonneau, Dwayne A., Hord, Lindsey J., Stiegler, Stephen G., Visscher, Christian H. et al. Florida's alligator management program: An update 1987 to 2001. In: *Crocodiles: Proceedings of the 16th working meeting of the crocodile specialist group, IUCN—The world conservation union* [Internet]. Gland, Switzerland, and Cambridge, UK: IUCN—The world conservation union; 2002 [cited 2014 May 12]. p. 23–30; Available from: https://portals.iucn.org/library/efiles/edocs/NS-2002-001.pdf

102. Bulte, Erwin H., Damania, Richard. An economic assessment of wildlife farming and conservation. *Conserv Biol.* 2005; 19(4): 1222–33.

103. Sanderson, Steven. Getting the biology right in a political sort of way. In: Reynolds, John D., Mace, Georgina M., Redford, Kent H., Robinson, John G., editors. *Conservation of exploited species.* Cambridge: Cambridge University Press; 2001. p. 462–82.

104. Geist, Valerius. Great achievements, great expectations: Successes of north American wildlife management. In: Hawley, Alex W.L., editor. *Commercialization and wildlife management: Dancing with the devil.* Malabar, FL: Krieger Publishing Company; 1993. p. 47–72.

105. Wilson, Edward O. *The future of life.* New York: Alfred A. Knopf; 2002.

106. Adams, William, Hulme, David. Conservation & community: Changing narratives, policies & practices in African conservation. In: Hulme, David, Murphree, Marshall, editors. *African wildlife & livelihoods: The promise and performance of community conservation.* Oxford: James Currey Ltd.; 2001. p. 9–23.

107. Vaughan, Christopher, Long, Andrew. Bushmeat, wildlife management and good governance; rights and institutional arrangements in Namibia's community-based natural resources management programme. In: Davies, Glyn, Brown, David, editors. *Bushmeat and livelihoods: Wildlife management and poverty reduction.* Malden, MA: Blackwell Publishing; 2007. p. 125–39.

108. Hulme, David, Murphree, Marshall. Community conservation as policy: Promise & performance. In: Hulme, David, Murphree, Marshall, editors. *African wildlife & livelihoods: The promise and performance of community conservation.* Oxford: James Currey Ltd.; 2001. p. 280–97.

109. Hulme, David, Infield, Mark. Community conservation, reciprocity & park-people relationships: Lake Mburo national park Uganda. In: Hulme, David, Murphree, Marshall, editors. *African wildlife & livelihoods: The promise and performance of community conservation.* Oxford: James Currey Ltd.; 2001. p. 106–30.

110. Kangwana, Kadzo, Mako, Rafael Ole. Conservation, livelihoods & the intrinsic value of wildlife: Tarangire national park, Tanzania. In: Hulme, David, Murphree, Marshall, editors. *African wildlife & livelihoods: The promise and performance of community conservation.* Oxford: James Currey Ltd.; 2001. p. 148–59.

111. Crist, Eileen. I walk in the world to live it. In: Wuerthner, George, Crist, Eileen, Butler, Tom, editors. *Protecting the wild: Parks and wilderness: The foundation for conservation.* Washington, D.C.i: Island Press; 2015. p. 82–95.

112. Wuerthner, George. Yellowstone as Model for the World. In: Wuerthner, George, Crist, Eileen, Butler, Tom, editors. *Protecting the wild: Parks and wilderness: The foundation for conservation.* Washington, D.C.: Island Press; 2015. p. 131–43.

113. Kopnina, Helen. Of tigers and humans: The question of democratic deliberation and biodiversity conservation. In: Wuerthner, George, Crist, Eileen, Butler, Tom, editors. *Protecting the wild: Parks and wilderness, the foundation for conservation*. Washington, D.C.: Island Press; 2015. p. 63–71.

114. Jones, Brian. The evolution of a community-based approach to wildlife management at Kunene, Namibia. In: Hulme, David, Murphree, Marshall, editors. *African wildlife & livelihoods: The promise and performance of community conservation*. Oxford: James Currey Ltd.; 2001. p. 160–76.

115. Keller, Bill. Africa thinks about making wildlife pay for its survival. *New York Times* [Internet]. 1992 Dec 27; Available from: http://www.nytimes.com/1992/12/27/weekinreview/the-world-africa-thinks-about-making-wildlife-pay-for-its-survival.html

116. Fraser, John, Wilkie, David, Wallace, Robert, Coppolillo, Peter, McNab, Roan Balas, Lilian, R. et al. The emergence of conservation NGOs as catalysts for local democracy. In: Manfredo, Michael J., Vaske, Jerry J., Brown, Perry J., Decker, Daniel J., Duke, Esther A., editors. *Wildlife and society: The science of human dimensions*. Washington, D.C.: Island Press; 2009. p. 44–56.

117. Rasker, Raymond, Martin, Michael V., Johnson, Rebecca L. Economics: Theory versus practice in wildlife management. *Conserv Biol*. 1992; 6(September): 338–49.

118. Leisher, Craig, Sanjayan, M., Blockhus, Jill, Larsen, S. Neil, Kontoleon, Andreas. Does conserving biodiversity work to reduce poverty? A state of knowledge review. In: Roe, Dilys, Elliott, Joanna, Sandbrook, Chris, Walpole, Matt, editors. *Biodiversity conservation and poverty alleviation*. West Sussex, UK: Wiley-Blackwell; 2013. p. 145–59.

119. Sandbrook, Chris, Roe, Dilys. Species conservation and poverty alleviation – The case of great apes in Africa. In: Roe, Dilys, Elliott, Joanna, Sandbrook, Chris, Walpole, Matt, editors. *Biodiversity conservation and poverty alleviation*. West Sussex, UK: Wiley-Blackwell; 2013. p. 173–90.

120. Homewood, Katherine, Trench, Pippa Chevenix, Brockington, Dan. Pastoralism and conservation – Who benefits? In: Roe, Dilys, Elliott, Joanna, Sandbrook, Chris, Walpole, Matt, editors. *Biodiversity conservation and poverty alleviation*. West Sussex, UK: Wiley-Blackwell; 2013. p. 239–52.

121. Berkes, Fikret. Poverty reduction isn't just about money: Community perceptions of conservation benefits. In: Roe, Dilys, Elliott, Joanna, Sandbrook, Chris, Walpole, Matt, editors. *Biodiversity conservation and poverty alleviation*. West Sussex, UK: Wiley-Blackwell; 2013. p. 270–85.

122. Hulme, David, Murphree, Marshall. Community conservation as policy: Promise & performance. In: Hulme, David, Murphree, Marshall, editors. *African wildlife & livelihoods: The promise and performance of community conservation*. Oxford: James Currey Ltd.; 2001. p. 280–97.

123. Barrow, Edmund, Gichohi, Helen, Infield, Mark. The evolution of community conservation policy & practice in East Africa. In: Hulme, David, Murphree, Marshall, editors. *African wildlife & livelihoods: The promise and performance of community conservation*. Oxford: James Currey Ltd.; 2001. p. 59–73.

124. National Research Council. *Science and the Endangered Species Act*. Washington, D.C.: National Academy Press; 1995.

125. Goldfarb, Ben. For sea lions, a feast of salmon on the Columbia. *High Country News* [Internet]. 2015 Jul 6 [cited 2015 Jul 7]; Available from: https://mail.google.com/mail/u/0/?tab=wm#inbox/14e6a1c7f1661af1

126. Raban, Jonathan. Losing the owl, saving the forest. *New York Times* [Internet]. 2010 Jun 25 [cited 2010 Jun 27]; Available from: www.nytimes.com/2010/06/27/opinion/27raban.html? th=&emc=th&pagewanted=print

127. Mast, Katie. The latest: Fish & wildlife to shoot thousands of barred owls. *High Country News* [Internet]. 2013 Aug 19 [cited 2013 Oct 2]; Available from: www.hcn.org/issues/ 45.14/the-latest-fish-wildlife-to-shoot-thousands-of-barred-owls/print_view

128. Roemer, Gary W., Wayne, Robert K. Conservation in conflict: The tale of two endangered species. *Conserv Biol.* 2003; 17(5): 1251–60.

129. Johnson, Kirk. In Yellowstone, killing one kind of trout to save another. *New York Times* [Internet]. 2011 Aug 23 [cited 2011 Aug 23]; Available from: www.nytimes.com/2011/08/ 24/us/24trout.html?_r=1&nl=todaysheadlines&emc=tha23&pa

130. Cohen, Andrew Neal. Weeding the garden. *Atlantic Monthly.* 1992; 270(5): 76–86.

131. Foley, Meraiah. Bats threaten their Australian paradise. *New York Times* [Internet]. 2009 Mar 15 [cited 2015 Jan 16]; Available from: www.nytimes.com/2009/03/15/world/asia/ 15bats.html

132. Rominger, Eric C.;, Bleich, Vernon C., Goldstein, Elise J. Bighorn sheep, mountain lions, and the ethics of conservation. *Conserv Biol.* 2006; 20(5): 1340–1.

133. National Research Council. *Science and the Endangered Species Act.* Washington, D.C.: National Academy Press; 1995.

134. Lauber, T. Bruce, Knuth, Barbara A., Deshler, J. David. Educating citizens about controversial issues: The case of suburban goose management. *Soc Nat Resour.* 2002; 15: 581–97.

135. McKinley, Jesse. Horse advocates pull for underdog in roundups. *New York Times* [Internet]. 2010 Sep 5 [cited 2013 May 3]; Available from: www.nytimes.com/2010/09/06/us/06horses .html?pagewanted=all&_r=0

136. Schirtzinger, Alexa. Horse ills: A controversial new effort aims to protect the wild West. *Audubon Magazine.* 2010 March-April: 20.

137. Beil, Laura. Herd's fate lies in preservation clash. *New York Times* [Internet]. 2012 May 7 [cited 2014 Feb 20]; Available from: www.nytimes.com/2012/05/08/science/wild-horses-fate-in-outer-banks-lies-in-preservation-clash.html?pagewanted=all&_r=0

138. Ferguson, Russ. Federal horse play in North Carolina: Washington is blocking a local initiative to save the state's wild Spanish mustangs. Why? *Wall Street Journal* [Internet]. 2015 Mar 30 [cited 2015 Apr 1]; Available from: www.wsj.com/articles/russ-ferguson-federal-horse-play-in-north-carolina-1427758948?KEYWORDS=russ+ferguson+and+span ish+mustangs

139. Moseley, Ray. Commons votes to ban fox hunts. *Chicago Tribune* [Internet]. 2001 Jan 28 [cited 2014 Feb 7]; Available from: http://articles.chicagotribune.com/2001-01-18/news/ 0101180239_1_hunting-supporters-prime-minister-tony-blair-commons

140. Phillips, Erica E. In Scottsdale, a quest to keep the West wild. *Wall Street Journal* [Internet]. 2013 Nov 22 [cited 2013 Nov 23]; Available from: http://online.wsj.com/news/articles/ SB10001424052702303559504579200460245513536#printMode

141. Morrison, Scott A., Boyce, Walter. Conserving connectivity: Some lessons from mountain lions in southern California. *Conserv Biol.* 2008; 23(2): 275–85.

142. Wuerthner, George. The core of the matter. *National parks.* 2001; 12: 1–32.

143. Bass, Rick. The land the wilderness act forgot. In: Guynup, Sharon, editor. *2006 State of the wild: A global portrait of wildlife, wildlands, and oceans.* Washington, D.C.i: Island Press; 2005. p. 215–21.

144. Roe, Dilys. The origins and evolution of the conservation-poverty debate: A review of key literature, evens, and policy processes. *Oryx*. 2008 ;42(4): 491–502.

145. Schaller, George B. Gold or flowers: One view on the state of the wild. In: Guynup, Sharon, editor. 2006 *State of the wild: A global portrait of wildlife, wildlands, and oceans*. Washington, D.C.: Island Press; 2005. p. 6–15.

146. Revkin, Andrew C. Should fin whales be a source of wonder or meat? *New York Times* [Internet]. 2014 Sep 13 [cited 2014 Sep 13]; Available from: http://dotearth.blogs.nytimes .com/2014/09/13/should-fin-whales-be-a-source-of-wonder-or-meat/?emc=edit_tnt_20140 913&nlid=10365419&tntemail0=y

147. Sanderson, Steven. Getting the biology right in a political sort of way. In: Reynolds, John D., Mace, Georgina M., Redford, Kent H., Robinson, John G., editors. *Conservation of exploited species*. Cambridge: Cambridge University Press; 2001. p. 462–82.

148. May, Sir Robert. Foreword. In: Reynolds, John D., Mace, Georgina M., Redford, Kent H., Robinson, John G., editors. *Conservation of exploited species*. Cambridge: Cambridge University Press; 2001. p. xiii–xvi.

149. Brown, David. Is the best the enemy of the good? Institutional and livelihoods perspectives on bushmeat harvesting and trade – Some issues and challenges. In: Davies, Glyn, Brown, David, editors. *Bushmeat and livelihoods: Wildlife management and poverty reduction*. Malden, MA: Blackwell Publishing; 2007. p. 111–24.

150. Adams, William M., Aveling, Ros, Brockington, Dan, Dickson, Barney, Elliott, Jo, Hutton, Jon et al. Biodiversity conservation and the eradication of poverty. *Science*. 2004; 306 (April 11): 1146–9.

151. Pulgar-Vidal, Manuel, Monteferri, Bruno, Dammert, Juan Luis. Trade-offs between conservation and extractive Industries. In: Leader-Williams, Nigel, Adams, William M., Smith, Robert J., editors. *Trade-offs in conservation: Deciding what to save*. Oxford: Wiley-Blackwell; 2010. p. 233–52.

152. Beckerman, Wilfred. "Sustainable development": Is it a useful concept? *Environ Values*. 1994; 3(3): 191–209.

153. Marvier, Michelle. New conservation is true conservation. *Conserv Biol*. 2014; 28(1): 1–3.

154. Kirby, Kathryn R. "New conservation" as a moral imperative. *Conserv Biol*. 2014; 28(3): 639–40.

155. Kareiva, Peter, Marvier, Michelle, Lalasz, Robert. Conservation in the anthropocene: Beyond solitude and fragility. *The Breakthrough* [Internet]. 2012 [cited 2014 Oct 20]; (Winter); Available from: http://thebreakthrough.org/index.php/journal/past-issues/issue-2/ conservation-in-the-anthropocene/

156. Soulé, Michael. The "new conservation." *Conserv Biol*. 2013; 27(5): 895–7.

157. Doak, Daniel F., Bakker, Victoria J., Goldstein, Bruce Evan, Hale, Benjamin. What is the future of conservation? *Trends Ecol Evol*. 2014; 29(2): 77–81.

158. Crist, Eileen. Ptolemaic environmentalism. In: Wuerthner, George, Crist, Eileen, Butler, Tom, editors. *Keeping the wild: Against the domestication of Earth*. Washington, D.C.: Island Press; 2014. p. 16–30.

159. Baskin, Jeremy. Paradigm dressed as epoch: The ideology of the anthropocene. *Environ Values*. 2015; 24: 9–29.

160. Tallis, Heather, Lubchenco, Jane. A call for inclusive conservation. *Nature*. 2014; 515 (November): 27–8.

Chapter 10 References

1. U.S. Fish and Wildlife Service. National survey of fishing, hunting, and wildlife-associated recreation [Internet]. 2012 [cited 2014 Jun 27]; Available from: www.census.gov/prod/2012pubs/fhw11-nat.pdf

2. Decker, Daniel J., Brown, Tommy L., Siemer, William F. Understanding hunting participation. In: Decker, Daniel J., Brown, Tommy L., Siemer, William F., editors. *Human dimensions of wildlife management in north America*. Bethesda, MD: The Wildlife Society; 2001. p. 289–306.

3. Wildlife Management Institute. As duck stamp goes on sale, new research spotlights decline of buyers. *Outdoor News Bulletin* [Internet]. 2013 Jul 15 [cited 2013 Jul 22]; Available from: http://wildlifemanagementinstitute.org/index.php?option=com_content&view=article&id=671:as-duck-stamp-goes-on-sale-research-spotlights-decline-of-buyers&catid=34:ONB%20Articles&Itemid=54

4. Dobner, Jennifer. Fostering pheasants to keep a tradition alive. *New York Times* [Internet]. 2014 Nov 5 [cited 2014 Nov 6]; Available from: www.nytimes.com/2014/11/06/us/fostering-pheasants-to-keep-a-tradition-alive.html?emc=edit_th_20141106&nl=todaysheadlines&nlid=10365419&_r=0

5. Kellert, Stephen R. Phase II: Activities of the American public relating to animals. 1980. Report No.: Government Printing Office. #024-020-00–624-2.

6. Mahoney, Shane P., Jackson, John J. Enshrining hunting as a foundation for conservation – the North American model. *Int J Environ Stud*. 2013; 70(3): 448–59.

7. Heffelfinger, James R., Geist, Valerius, Wishart, William. The role of hunting in north American wildlife conservation. *Int J Environ Stud*. 2013; 70(3): 339–413.

8. McIntire, Mike. Selling a new generation on guns. *New York Times* [Internet]. 2013 Jan 26 [cited 2013 Jan 28]; Available from: www.nytimes.com/2013/01/27/us/selling-a-new-generation-on-guns.html?nl=todaysheadlines&emc=edit_th_20130127&pagewanted=print

9. Brown, Tommy L, Messmer, Terry A., Decker, Daniel J. Access for hunting on agricultural and forest lands. In: Decker, Daniel J., Brown, Tommy L., Siemer, William F., editors. *Human dimensions of wildlife management in north America*. Bethesda: The Wildlife Society; 2001. p. 269–88.

10. Kellert, Stephen R. *Public attitudes towards critical wildlife and natural habitat issues*. Phase One. #024-010-00–623-4. U.S. Government Printing Office; 1979.

11. Strawbridge, Kristen. Bobcats are in peril in Illinois. *Chicago Tribune* [Internet]. 2014 Dec 19 [cited 2014 Dec 19]; Available from: www.chicagotribune.com/news/opinion/commentary/ct-bobcats-illinois-hunting-perspec-1219–20141218-story.html

12. Gutowski, Christy. Bobcat hunting may return to Illinois after 40-year hiatus. *Chicago Tribune* [Internet]. 2014 Dec 22 [cited 2014 Dec 22]; Available from: www.chicagotribune.com/news/ct-bobcat-hunting-met-20141220-story.html#page=1

13. Decker, Daniel J., Brown, Tommy L., Siemer, William F. Understanding human participation. In: Decker, Daniel J., Brown, Tommy L., Siemer, William F., editors. *Human dimensions of wildlife management in north America*. Bethesda, MD: The Wildlife Society; 2001. p. 289–306.

14. Brulle, Robert J. *Agency, democracy, and nature: The U.S. environmental movement from a critical theory perspective*. Cambridge: MIT Press; 2000.

15. List, Charles J. *Hunting, fishing, and environmental virtue: Reconnecting sportsmanship and conservation*. Corvallis: Oregon State University Press; 2013.

16. Leader-Williams, Nigel. Conservation and hunting: Friends or foes? In: Dickson, Barney, Hutton, Jon, Adams, William M., editors. *Recreational hunting, conservation and rural livelihoods: Science and practice*. Oxford: Wiley-Blackwell; 2009. p. 9–24.

17. Francione, Gary L. Animals – property or persons? In: Sunstein, Cass R., Nussbaum, Martha C., editors. *Animal rights: Current debates and new directions*. Oxford: Oxford University Press; 2004. p. 108–42.

18. Kurlansky, Mark. Humane hunting. Audubon Magazine. 1998; (January-February): 16.

19. Kaye, Roger. *Last great wilderness: The campaign to establish the arctic national wildlife refuge*. Fairbanks: University of Alaska Press; 2006.

20. Williams, Ted. Kill, baby, kill. *Audubon Magazine*. 2009 July-August: 36–44.

21. Mech, L. David. Considerations for developing wolf harvesting regulations in the contiguous United States. *J Wildl Manag*. 2010; 74(7): 1421–4.

22. Petersen, David. *Ghost grizzlies. Does the great bear still haunt Colorado?* Boulder: Johnson Books; 1998.

23. Calvert, Scott. Maine set to vote on bear-hunting methods. *Wall Street Journal* [Internet]. 2014 Oct 21 [cited 2014 Oct 22]; Available from: http://online.wsj.com/articles/maine-set-to-vote-on-bear-hunting

24. Manfredo, Michael J., Pierce, Cynthia L., Fulton, David, Pate, Jennifer, Gill, Bruce R. Wildlife and the public-public acceptance of wildlife trapping in Colorado. *Wildl Soc Bull*. 1999; 27(2): 499–507.

25. Eisenberg, Cristinia. *The carnivore way: Coexisting with and conserving north America's predators*. Washington, D.C.: Island Press; 2014.

26. Musgrave, Ruth S. Legal trends in fish and wildlife policy. In: Manfredo, Michael J.., Vaske, Jerry J., Decker, Daniel J., Duke, Esther A., editors. *Wildlife and society: The science of human dimensions*. Washington, D.C.: Island Press; 2009. p. 145–60.

27. Campo-Flores, Arian. More states aim to protect hunting. *Wall Street Journal* [Internet]. 2014 Apr 28 [cited 2014 Apr 29]; Available from: http://online.wsj.com/news/articles/SB100014 24052702304788404579519821058576310#printMode

28. U.S. National Park Service. Alaska: Hunting and trapping in national preserves [Internet]. 2014 Sep [cited 2014 Sep 7]. Report No.: 36 CFR Part 13 [NPS–AKRO–15122; PPAKAK-ROZ5, PPMPRLE1Y.L00000] RIN 1024–AE21; Available from: www.gpo.gov/fdsys/pkg/FR-2014-09-04/pdf/2014–20881.pdf

29. National Conference of State Legislatures. State constitutional right to hunt and fish [Internet]. 2014 [cited 2014 Jul 28]; Available from: www.ncsl.org/research/environment-and-natural-resources/state-constitutional-right-to-hunt-and-fish.aspx

30. Krajick, Kevin. Free speech or harassment: Hunters and antihunters slug it out–in the forests and in court. *Audubon Magazine*. 1995 July-August: 16–20.

31. Gray, Gary C. *Wildlife and people: The human dimensions of wildlife ecology*. Urbana: University of Illinois Press; 1993.

32. Pierce, Cynthia L., Manfredo, Michael J., Vaske, Jerry J. Social science theories in wildlife management. In: Decker, Daniel J., Brown, Tommy L., Siemer, William F., editors. *Human dimensions of wildlife management in north America*. Bethesda, MD: The Wildlife Society; 2001. p. 39–56.

33. Brinkley, Douglas. *The wilderness warrior: Theodore Roosevelt and the crusade for America*. New York: Harper Collins Publishers; 2009.

34. Garner, Robert. *The political theory of animal rights*. Manchester: Manchester University Press; 2005.

35. Robbins, Paul, Luginbuhl, April. The last enclosure: Resisting privatization of wildlife in the western United States. In: Heynen, Nik, MxCarthy, James, Prudham, Scott, Robbins, Paul, editors. *Neoliberal environments: False promises and unnatural consequences*. London: Routledge; 2007. p. 25–37.

36. Cromley, Christina M. Bison management in greater Yellowstone. In: Brunner, Ronald D., Colburn, Christine H., Klein, Roberta A., Olson, Elizabeth A., editors. *Finding common ground*. New Haven: Yale University Press; 2002. p. 126–58.

37. Rudolph, Brent A., Schecter, Michael G., Riley, Shawn J. Governance of wildlife resources. In: Decker, Daniel J., Riley, Shawn J., Siemer, William F., editors. *Human dimensions of wildlife management*. 2nd ed. Baltimore: Johns Hopkins University Press; 2012. p. 15–25.

38. Cambronne, Al. *Deerland: America's hunt for ecological balance and the essence of wildness*. Guilford, CT: Lyons Press; 2013.

39. Glionna, John M. Wyoming lawmakers to decide on silencers for hunting rifles. *LA Times* [Internet]. 2012 Dec 1 [cited 2012 Dec 14]; Available from: www.latimes.com/news/nation/nationnow/la-na-nn-wyoming-silencers-hunting-rifles-20121130,0,2356723.story

40. Wisconsin State Department of Natural Resources. Chippewa tribal night hunting [Internet]. 2015 [cited 2016 May 5]; Available from: http://dnr.wi.gov/topic/hunt/documents/tribalFAQ.pdf

41. Morzillo, Anita T., Mertig, Angela, Garner, Nathan, Liu, Jianguo. Evaluating hunter support for black bear restoration in east Texas. *Hum Dimens Wildl*. 2009; 14: 407–18.

42. Williams, Ted. No dogs allowed. *Audubon Magazine*. 1992 September-October: 26–35.

43. Jacobson, Susan K., Marynowski, Susan B. Public Attitudes and Knowledge about Ecosystem Management on Department of Defense Land in Florida *Conserv Biol*. 1997; 1(3): 770–81.

44. Reiger, John F. The sportsman factor in early conservation. In: Nash, Roderick Frazier, editor. *American environmentalism: Readings in conservation history*. New York: McGraw-Hill; 1990. p. 52–62.

45. Dunlap, Thomas R. *Saving America's wildlife*. Princeton University Press; 1988.

46. Knezevic, Irena. Hunting and environmentalism: Conflict or misperceptions. *Hum Dimens Wildl*. 2009; 14: 12–20.

47. Furshong, Gabriel. Secretly funded Montana sportsmen dive into political fray. *High Country News* [Internet]. 2012 May 28 [cited 2012 Jun 15]; Available from: www.hcn.org/issues/44.9/secretly-funded-montana-sportsmen-dive-into-political-fray?utm_source=wcn1&utm_medium=email

48. Wildlife Management Institute. Sportsmen's bill stirring controversy. *Outdoors News Bulletin* [Internet]. 2012 Jun 15 [cited 2012 Jun 18]; Available from: http://wildlifemanagementinstitute.org/index.php?option=com_content&view=article&id=593:sportsmens-bill-stirring-controversy&catid=34:ONB%20Articles&Itemid=54

49. Langlois, Krista. Final EPA report is the latest in a series of blows to Alaska's pebble mine. *High Country News* [Internet]. 2014 Jan 25 [cited 2014 Jan 29]; Available from: www.hcn.org/blogs/goat/final-epa-report-the-latest-in-a-series-of-blows-to-alaskas-pebble-mine?utm_source=wcn1&utm_medium=email

50. Robinson, John. Response to David Brown: The view from Versailles contrasts with local reality. In: Guynup, Sharon, editor. *2006 state of the wild: A global portrait of wildlife, wildlands, and oceans*. Washington, D.C.: Island Press; 2005. p. 158.

51. Mackinnon, Kathy. Through the looking glass: The tragedy of depleting wildlife resources: A response to John Robinson and David Brown. In: Guynup, Sharon, editor. *2006 state of the wild: A global portrait of wildlife, wildlands, and oceans*. Washington, D.C.: Island Press; 2005. p. 161–2.

52. Bodmer, Richard. Hunting for conservation in the Amazon rain forests: Lessons learned from Peru. In: Guynup, Sharon, editor. *2006 state of the wild: A global portrait of wildlife, wildlands, and oceans*. Washington, D.C.: Island Press; 2005. p. 139–45.

53. Rauber, Paul. Improving on nature. *Sierra Magazine*. 1995 March-April: 44–52 & 70–2.

54. Sachs, Jessica Snyder. The deer slayer. *National Wildlife Magazine* [Internet]. 2003 [cited 2014 Jun 28]; 41(3); Available from: www.nwf.org/News-and-Magazines/National-Wildlife/Animals/Archives/2003/The-Deer-Slayer.aspx

55. McManus, Reed. Home on the rifle range. *Sierra Magazine*. 1994 May-June: 42–4.

56. Sellars, Richard West. *Preserving nature in the national parks: A history*. New Haven: Yale University Press; 1997.

57. Durbin, Kathie. *Tongass: Pulp politics and the fight for the Alaska rain forest*. 2nd ed. Corvallis: Oregon State University Press; 2005.

58. Thornton, Thomas F. Subsistence: The politics of a cultural dilemma. In: Thomas, Clive S., editor. *Alaska public policy issues: Background and perspectives*. Juneau, Alaska: The Denali Press; 1999. p. 205–20.

59. DiSilvestro, Roger L. *The endangered kingdom: The struggle to save America's wildlife*. New York: John Wiley & Sons, Inc.; 1989.

60. Nie, Martin. State wildlife policy and management: The scope and bias of political conflict. *Public Adm Rev*. 2004; 64(2): 221–33.

61. Shivik, John. *The predator paradox: Ending the war with wolves, bears, cougars, and coyotes*. Boston: Beacon Press; 2014.

62. Wildlife Management Institute. Lessons from the Montana wolf management stamp. *Outdoor News Bulletin* [Internet]. 2014 Oct 17 [cited 2014 Oct 17]; Available from: http://wildlifemanagementinstitute.org/index.php?option=com_content&view=article&id=774:lessons-from-the-montana-wolf-management-stamp&catid=34:ONB%20Articles&Itemid=54

63. Mangun, William R., Henning, Daniel H. *Managing the environmental crisis*. Durham: Duke University Press; 1999.

64. Culhane, Paul J. *Public lands politics: Interest group influence on the forest service and the bureau of land management*. Baltimore: Johns Hopkins University Press; 1981.

65. U.S. Fish and Wildlife Service. Service announces 2014 expansion of hunting, fishing opportunities in national wildlife refuge system [Internet]. 2014 [cited 2014 Mar 7]; Available from: www.fws.gov/news/ShowNews.cfm?ID=93DA888D-FF13-4470-29232A2C80EF74E8

66. Steinhart, Peter. Who fired Harold Cribbs? *Audubon Magazine*. 1990 November-December: 113–9.

67. Warren, Louis. *The hunter's game: Poachers and conservationists in twentieth-century America*. New Haven: Yale University Press; 1997.

68. Dizard, Jan E. *Going wild: Hunting, animal rights, and the contested meaning of nature*. Amherst: University of Massachusetts Press; 1999.

69. Snell, Marilyn Berlin. Profile: Cowboys are their weakness. *Sierra Magazine*. 2005 July-August: 24–8.

70. Williams, Ted. Bad shot. *Audubon Magazine*. 2011 May-June: 50–8.

71. American Sportsfishing Association. Lead in fishing tackle [Internet]. 2015 [cited 2015 Jan 17]; Available from: http://asafishing.org/advocacy/legislative-action/lead-in-fishing-tackle/

72. McCamman, John. Region 8: Review finds lead exposure biggest threat to California condors [Internet]. U.S. Fish and Wildlife Service; 2013 [cited 2013 Sep 12]; Available from: www.fws.gov/fieldnotes/regmap.cfm?arskey=34216

73. Tobin, Mitch. *Endangered: Biodiversity on the brink*. Golden, CO: Fulcrum; 2010.

74. U.S. Fish and Wildlife Service. Pacific Southwest Region. California condor (*Gymnogyps californianus*). 5-year review: Summary and evaluation [Internet]. 2013 [cited 2014 Aug 14]; Available from: http://ecos.fws.gov/docs/five_year_review/doc4163.pdf

75. Associated Press. Top condor killer? It's still lead poisoning even with lead bullet ban, bird's death shows problem remains. 2009 May 22 [cited 2010 Nov 21]; Available from: www.msnbc.msn.com/id/30874063/ns/us_news-environment/

76. U.S. Sportsmen's Alliance. Critical federal hunting and fishing bill passes the House of Representatives [Internet]. 2014 [cited 2014 Oct 27]; Available from: www.ussportsmen.org/news/critical-federal-hunting-and-fishing-bill-up-for-a-vote/

77. Heinrich, Martin. The land grab out West. *New York Times* [Internet]. 2014 Oct 26 [cited 2014 Oct 27]; Available from: www.nytimes.com/2014/10/27/opinion/the-land-grab-out-west.html?emc=edit_th_20141027&nl=todaysheadlines&nlid=10365419

78. Cama, Timothy. Spending bill would block protection efforts for at-risk bird [Internet]. 2014 [cited 2014 Dec 19]; Available from: http://thehill.com/policy/energy-environment/226575-spending-bill-would-block-protection-efforts-for-at-risk-bird

79. DiSilvestro, Roger L. Saving the red wolf. *National Wildlife Federation Magazine*. 2014 August-September: 38–42.

80. Cambrone, Al. Can't see the forest for the deer. *Wall Street Journal* [Internet]. 2014 Mar 12 [cited 2014 Mar 12]; Available from: http://online.wsj.com/news/articles/SB10001424052702304704504579429583302400534#printMode

81. Milner-Guland, E.J., Bunnefeld, Niles, Proaktor, Gil. The science of sustainable hunting. In: Dickson, Barney, Hutton, Jon, Adams, William M., editors. *Recreational hunting, conservation and rural livelihoods: Science and practice*. Oxford: Wiley-Blackwell; 2009. p. 75–93.

82. Loveridge, Andrew J., Packer, Craig, Dutton, Adam. Science and the recreational hunting of lions. In: Dickson, Barney, Hutton, Jon, Adams, William M., editors. *Recreational hunting, conservation and rural livelihoods: Science and practice*. Oxford: Wiley-Blackwell; 2009. p. 108–24.

83. Keller, Bill. Africa thinks about making wildlife pay for its survival. *New York Times* [Internet]. 1992 Dec 27; Available from: http://www.nytimes.com/1992/12/27/weekinreview/the-world-africa-thinks-about-making-wildlife-pay-for-its-survival.html

84. Curtin, Charles C. The evolution of the U.S. national wildlife refuge system and the doctrine of compatibility. *Conserv Biol*. 1993; 7(1): 29–39.

85. Cioc, Mark. *The game of conservation: International treaties to protect the world's migratory animals*. Athens: Ohio University Press; 2009.

86. Sasser, Ray. TP&W proposal puts javelinas in crosshairs. *The Dallas Morning News*. 2007 Feb 18.

87. Barringer, Felicity. Utah hunters criticize market approach to licenses and conservation. *New York Times* [Internet]. 2012 Dec 1 [cited 2012 Dec 3]; Available from: www.nytimes.com/2012/12/02/us/auctions-introduce-market-forces-to-conservation-but-hunters-cry-foul.html?pagewanted=print

88. Rasker, Raymond, Martin, Michael V., Johnson, Rebecca L. Economics: Theory versus practice in wildlife management. *Conserv Biol*. 1992; 6(September): 338–49.

89. Smith, Mark E., Molde, Donald A. Wildlife conservation & management funding in the U.S. [Internet]. 2014; Available from: http://wyofile.com/wp-content/uploads/2014/11/SMITH-1.pdf

90. Clark, Susan G., Milloy, Christina. The north American model of wildlife conservation: An analysis of challenges and adaptive options. In: Clark, Susan G., Rutherford, Murray B., editors. *Large carnivore conservation: Integrating science and policy in the north American west*. Chicago: University of Chicago Press; 2014. p. 289–324.

91. McShea, William J. Forest ecosystems without carnivores: When ungulates rule the world. In: Ray, Justina C., Redford, Kent H., Steneck, Robert S., Berger, Joel, editors. *Large carnivores and the conservation of biodiversity*. Washington, D.C.: Island Press; 2005. p. 138–53.

92. Papouchis, Christopher M. Conserving mountain lions in a changing landscape. In: Fascione, Nina, Delach, Aimee, Smith, Martin E., editors. *People and predators: From conflict to coexistence*. Washington, D.C.: Island Press; 2004. p. 219–39.

93. Bass, Rick. *The ninemile wolves*. New York: Ballantine Books; 1992.

94. Treves, Adrian, Martin, Kerry A. Hunters as stewards of wolves in Wisconsin and the northern Rocky Mountains, *USA. Soc Nat Resour*. 2011; 24: 984–94.

95. Preece, Rod, Chamberlain, Lorna. *Animal welfare & human values*. Waterloo, Ontario, Canada: Wilfrid Laurier Press; 1993.

96. Darimont, Chris T., Carlson, Stephanie M., Kinnison, Michael T., Paquet, Paul C., Reimchen, Thomas E., Wilmers, Christopher C. Human predators outpace other agents of trait change in the wild. *Proc Natl Acad Sci U S A*. 2009; 106(3): 952–4.

97. Madhusudan, M.D., Mishra, Charudutt. Why big, fierce animals are threatened. In: Saberwal, Vasant K., Rangarajan, Mahesh, editors. *Battles over nature: Science and the politics of conservation*. New Delhi: Permanent Black; 2003. p. 31–55.

98. Wall, Bill, Child, Brian. When does hunting contribute to conservation and rural development? In: Dickson, Barney, Hutton, Jon, Adams, William M., editors. *Recreational hunting, conservation and rural livelihoods: Science and practice*. Oxford: Wiley-Blackwell; 2009. p. 255–81.

99. Davies, Richard, Hamman, Kas, Magome, Hector. Does recreational hunting conflict with photo-tourism? In: Dickson, Barney, Hutton, Jon, Adams, William M., editors. *Recreational hunting, conservation and rural livelihoods: Science and practice*. Oxford: Wiley-Blackwell; 2009. p. 233–51.

100. McGroarty, Patrick. A bull market of a different kind: Controversial but profitable, African-game breeding has become the new trophy investment for some. *Wall Street Journal* [Internet]. 2014 Mar 29 [cited 2014 Mar 29]; Available from: http://online.wsj.com/news/articles/SB10001424052702303563304579445382496815614?KEYWORDS=patrick+mcgroarty+and+trophy+investment&mg=reno64-wsj

101. Lindsey, Peter Andrew, Balme, Guy Andrew, Booth, Vernon Richard, Midlane, Neil. The significance of African lions for the financial viability of trophy hunting and the maintenance of wild land. *PLoS ONE* [Internet]. 2012 [cited 2015 Aug 13]; Available from: http://journals.plos.org/plosone/article?id=10.1371/journal.pone.0029332

102. Lindsey, Peter A., Frank, L. G., Alexander, R., Mathieson, A., Romanach, S. S. Trophy hunting and conservation in Africa: Problems and one potential. *Conserv Biol*. 2007; 24(3): 880–3.

103. Kaiser, Michel J., Jennings, Simon. An ecosystem perspective on conserving targeted and non-targeted species. In: Reynolds, John D., Mace, Georgina M., Redford, Kent H.,

Robinson, John G., editors. *Conservation of exploited species*. Cambridge: Cambridge University Press; 2001. p. 343–69.

104. Alvarez, Lizette. Protecting a home where the puffer fish roam in Biscayne national park. *New York Times* [Internet]. 2014 Dec 21 [cited 2014 Dec 22]; Available from: www.nytimes.com/2014/12/22/us/protecting-a-home-where-the-puffer-fish-roam-in-biscayne-national-park.html?emc=edit_th_20141222&nl=todaysheadlines&nlid=10365419&_r=0

105. Law, Richard. Phenotypic and genetic changes due to selective exploitation. In: Reynolds, John D., Mace, Georgina M., Redford, Kent H., Robinson, John G., editors. *Conservation of exploited species*. Cambridge: Cambridge University Press; 2001. p. 323–42.

106. Williams, Ted. Last chance. *Audubon Magazine*. 2009 May-June: 36–44.

107. Williams, Ted. Purging trout to save frogs. *National Wildlife Magazine*. 2015 August-September: 16.

108. Bucher, Enrique H. The causes and consequences of extinction of the passenger pigeon. *Curr Ornithol*. 1992; 9: 1–36.

109. National Research Council. Science and the Endangered Species Act [Internet]. Washington, D.C.: National Academy Press; 1995 [cited 2016 Mar 24]; Available from: www.nap.edu/read/4978/chapter/1

110. Packer, C., Brink, H., Kissul, B.M., Maliti, H., Kushnir, H., Caro, T. Effects of trophy hunting on lion and leopard populations in Tanzania. *Conserv Biol*. 2011; 25(1): 142–53.

111. Dizikes, Cynthia. Illinois bill would ban drones for hunting. *Chicago Tribune* [Internet]. 2015 Jan 28 [cited 2015 Jan 28]; Available from: www.chicagotribune.com/news/ct-hunting-drones-met-20150123-story.html

112. Songorwa, Alexander. Saving lions by killing them. *New York Times* [Internet]. 2013 Mar 17 [cited 2013 Mar 18]; Available from: www.nytimes.com/2013/03/18/opinion/saving-lions-by-killing-them.html?ref=opinion&pagewanted=print

113. Schroeder, Richard A. Environmental justice and the market: The politics of sharing wildlife revenues in Tanzania. *Soc Nat Resour*. 2008; 21: 583–96.

114. Agostinho, A. Jorge., Vanak, Abi T., Thaker, Maria, Begg, Colleen, Slotow, Rob. Costs and benefits of the presence of leopards to the sport-hunting industry and local communities in Niassa national reserve, Mozambique. *Conserv Biol*. 2013; 27(4): 832–43.

115. Ashe, Dan. Director's corner: The African lion needs our help [Internet]. 2014 [cited 2014 Oct 28]; Available from: www.fws.gov/director/dan-ashe/index.cfm/2014/10/27/The-African-Lion-Needs-Our-Help

Chapter 11 References

1. Hartzog, Jr., George B. *Battling for the national parks*. Mt. Kisco: Moyer Bell Limited; 1988.

2. Manfredo, Michael J. *Who cares about wildlife? Social science concepts for exploring human-wildlife relationships and conservation issues*. New York: Springer; 2008.

3. Kaye, Roger. *Last great wilderness: The campaign to establish the arctic national wildlife refuge*. Fairbanks: University of Alaska Press; 2006.

4. Allin, Craig W. *The politics of wilderness preservation*. Westport: Greenwood Press; 1982.

5. De Chant, Tim. Wild refuges pay price for protection: Study: National parks in developing nations are attracting the human encroachment and the conflict they were meant to be shielded from. *Chicago Tribune* [Internet]. 2008 Jul 4 [cited 2013 Dec 27]; Available from:

http://articles.chicagotribune.com/2008-07-04/news/0807030640_1_national-parks-park-boundaries-population-growth

6. Gray, Gary C. *Wildlife and people: The human dimensions of wildlife ecology.* Urbana: University of Illinois Press; 1993.

7. Meyer, Stephen M. *The end of the wild.* Cambridge: The MIT Press; 2006.

8. Roe, Dilys, Leader-Williams, Nigel, Dalal-Clayton, Barry. Take only photographs, leave only footprints: The environmental impacts of wildlife tourism [Internet]. London: Environmental Planning Group International Institute for Environment and Development; 1997 Oct [cited 2014 Apr 3]. (IIED Wildlife and Development Series). Report No.: 10; Available from: http://biblioteca.duoc.cl/bdigital/Documentos_Digitales/300/39709.pdf

9. Ebersole, Rene. Ethics: Too close for comfort. *Audubon Magazine* [Internet]. 2015 May-June [cited 2015 Apr 30]; Available from: www.audubon.org/magazine/may-june-2015/too-close-comfort

10. Metcalfe, Simon. Decentralization, tenure and sustainable use. In: Hutton, Jon, Dickson, Barnabas, editors. *Endangered species threatened convention: The past, present and future of CITES, the Convention on International Trade in Endangered Species of wild fauna and flora.* London: Earthscan; 2002. p. 153–60.

11. Bond, Ivan. CAMPFIRE & the incentives for institutional change. In: Hulme, David, Murphree, Marshall, editors. *African wildlife & livelihoods: The promise and performance of community conservation.* Oxford: James Currey Ltd.; 2001. p. 227–43.

12. Romero, Simon. Puerto Ayora journal: To protect Galápagos, Ecuador limits a two-legged species. *New York Times* [Internet]. 2009 Oct 5 [cited 2014 Aug 28]; Available from: www.nytimes.com/2009/10/05/world/americas/05galapagos.html?pagewanted=all&_r=0

13. West, Patrick C., Fortwangler, Crystal L., Agbo, Valentin, Simsik, Michael, Sokpon, Nester. The political economy of ecotourism: Pendjari national park and ecotourism concentration in northern Benin. In: Brechin, Steven R., Wilshushen, Peter R., Fortwangler, Crystal L., West, Patrick C., editors. *Contested nature: Promoting international biodiversity with social justice in the twenty-first century.* Albany: State University of New York Press; 2003. p. 103–11.

14. Adams, William M., Infield, Mark. Park outreach & gorilla conservation: Mgahinga gorilla national park, Uganda. In: Hulme, David, Murphree, Marshall, editors. *African wildlife & livelihoods: The promise and performance of community conservation.* Oxford: James Currey Ltd.; 2001. p. 131–47.

15. Salopek, Paul F. Gorillas and humans: An uneasy truce. In: Claggett, Hillary, editor. *Wildlife conservation.* New York: The H.W. Wilson Company; 1997. p. 46–53.

16. World Wildlife Fund. Species and places, people and places [Internet]. 2014 [cited 2014 Oct 2]; Available from: http://wwf.panda.org/about_our_earth/all_publications/living_planet_report/

17. Durbin, Kathie. *Tongass: Pulp politics and the fight for the Alaska rain forest.* 2nd ed. Corvallis: Oregon State University Press; 2005.

18. Nie, Martin. *Beyond wolves: The politics of wolf recovery and management.* Minneapolis: University of Minnesota Press; 2003.

19. Williams, Ted. Back off. *Audubon Magazine.* 2007 May-June: 50–3 & 84–7.

20. Wilcove, David S. *The condor's shadow: The loss and recovery of wildlife in America.* New York: W.H. Freeman and Company; 1999.

21. U.S. Fish & Wildlife Service. Executive summary: Banking on nature 2011: The economic benefits of national wildlife refuge visitation to local communities [Internet]. 2013 [cited 2014 Aug 15]; Available from: www.fws.gov/alligatorriver/images/2013BankingonNature.pdf

22. Norton-Griffiths, Michael, Said, Mohammed Y. The future for wildlife on Kenya's rangelands: An economic perspective. In: du Toit, John D., Kock, Richard, Deutsch, James C., editors. *Wild rangelands: Conserving wildlife while maintaining livestock in semi-arid ecosystems*. Oxford: Wiley-Blackwell; 2010. p. 367–92.

23. McConahay, Mary Jo. Sweet waist of America. *Sierra Magazine*. 1993 January-February: 42–9 & 153–7.

24. Tennesen, Michael. The secret to saving sea turtles. *National Wildlife Magazine* [Internet]. 2006 June-July [cited 2014 Aug 12]; Available from: www.nwf.org/nationalwildlife/article.cfm?issueID=107&articleID=1342

25. Tisdell, Clem, Wilson, Clevo. Ecotourism for the survival of sea turtles and other wildlife. *Biodivers Conserv*. 2002; 11: 1521–38.

26. Robbins, Michael W. Nose dive. *National Wildlife Magazine* [Internet]. 2007 August-September [cited 2014 Aug 8]; Available from: www.nwf.org/news-and-magazines/national-wildlife/animals/archives/2007/nose-dive.aspx

27. Klatchko, Joan. Life with croc. *Audubon Magazine*. 1995 May-June: 24.

28. Moss, Cynthia. Q&A. *Audubon Magazine*. 1995 March-April: 24 & 30.

29. Kabiri, Ngeta. Historic and contemporary struggles for a local wildlife governance regime in Kenya. In: Nelson, Fred, editor. *Community rights, conservation and contested land: The politics of natural resource governance in Africa*. London: Earthscan; 2010. p. 121–44.

30. Neumann, Roderick P. Local challenges to global agendas: Conservation, economic liberalization, and the pastoralists' rights movement in Tanzania. *Antipode*. 1995; 27(4): 363–82.

31. Ngoitiko, Maanda, Senandei, Makko, Meitaya, Partalala, Nelson, Fred. Pastoral activists: Negotiating power imbalances in the Tanzanian Serengeti. In: Nelson, Fred, editor. *Community rights, conservation and contested land: The politics of natural resource governance in Africa*. London: Earthscan; 2010. p. 269–89.

32. Victurine, Ray, Curtin, Charles. Financial incentives for rangeland conservation: Addressing the "show-us-the-money" challenge. In: du Toit, John D., Kock, Richard, Deutsch, James C., editors. *Wild rangelands: Conserving wildlife while maintaining livestock in semi-arid ecosystems*. Oxford: Wiley-Blackwell; 2010. p. 152–87.

33. Whande, Webster. Windows of opportunity or exclusion? Local communities in the great Limpopo transfrontier conservation area, South Africa. In: Nelson, Fred, editor. *Community rights, conservation and contested land: The politics of natural resource governance in Africa*. London: Earthscan; 2010. p. 147–73.

34. Buckley, Ralf. *Conservation Tourism*. Oxfordshire, UK: CAB International, 2010.

35. Arcese, Peter, Hando, Justine, Campbell, Ken. Historical and present-day anti-poaching efforts in Serengeti. In: Sinclair, A.R.E., Arcese, Peter, editors. *Serengeti II: Dynamics, management, and conservation of an ecosystem*. Chicago: The University of Chicago Press; 1995. p. 506–33.

36. Cox, Christopher. Paradise found. *Audubon Magazine*. 2011 July-August: 52–6.

37. Becker, Elizabeth. *Overbooked: The exploding business of travel and tourism*. New York: Simon & Shuster; 2013.

38. Scalza, Remy. In Namibia, conservation and tourism intersect. *New York Times* [Internet]. 2013 Oct 31 [cited 2013 Oct 31]; Available from: www.nytimes.com/2013/11/03/travel/in-namibia-conservation-and-tourism-intersect.html?emc=edit_tnt_20131031&tntemail0=y&_r=0&pagewanted=print

39. Cunningham, Paul A., Huijbens, Edward H., Wearing, Stephen L. From whaling to whale watching: Examining sustainability and cultural rhetoric. *J Sustain Tour*. 2012; 20(1): 143–61.

40. Maldarelli, Claire. In Indonesia, police stop sale of endangered manta rays. *New York Times* [Internet]. 2014 Sep 30; Available from: www.nytimes.com/2014/10/01/science/in-indonesia-police-stop-sale-of-endangered-manta-rays.html?emc=edit_tnt_20140930&nlid=10365419&tntemail0=y&_r=0

41. Seeger, Eric. Heart of the ocean. *Nature Conservancy Magazine* [Internet]. 2014 October-November [cited 2014 Oct 8]; Available from: http://magazine.nature.org/features/heart-of-the-ocean.xml

42. Allan, Jaye B. People and pandas in Southwest China. *J Int Wildl Law Policy*. 2008; 11: 156–88.

43. Rihoy, Liz, Chnirozva, Chaka, Anstey, Simon. "People are not happy:" Crisis, adaptation and resilience in Zimbabwe's CAMPFIRE programme. In: Nelson, Fred, editor. *Community rights, conservation and contested land: The politics of natural resource governance in Africa*. London: Earthscan; 2010. p. 174–201.

44. Hutton, Jon, Dickson, Barney. Conservation out of exploitation: A silk purse from a sow's ear? In: Reynolds, John D., Mace, Georgina M., Redford, Kent H., Robinson, John G., editors. *Conservation of exploited species*. Cambridge: Cambridge University Press; 2001. p. 440–61.

45. Jones, Robert F. Farewell to Africa. *Audubon Magazine*. 1990 September-October: 51–104.

46. Lindsey, Peter A., Frank, L. G., Alexander, R., Mathieson, A., Romanach, S. S. Trophy hunting and conservation in Africa: Problems and one potential. *Conserv Biol*. 2007; 24(3): 880–3.

47. Neumann, Roderick P. Disciplining peasants in Tanzania: From state violence to self-surveillance in wildlife conservation. In: Peluso, Nancy Lee, Watts, Michael, editors. *Violent environments*. Ithaca: Cornell University Press; 2002. p. 305–27.

48. Lewis, Dale, M., Alpert, Peter. Trophy hunting and wildlife conservation in Zambia. *Conserv Biol*. 1997; 11(1): 59–68.

49. Snyder, Katherine A., Sulle, Emmanuel B. Tourism in Maasai communities: A chance to improve livelihoods? *J Sustain Tour*. 2011; 19(8): 935–51.

50. Jones, Brian. The evolution of a community-based approach to wildlife management at Kunene, Namibia. In: Hulme, David, Murphree, Marshall, editors. *African wildlife & livelihoods: The promise and performance of community conservation*. Oxford: James Currey Ltd.; 2001. p. 160–76.

51. Chase, Alston. *Playing God in Yellowstone: The destruction of America's first national park*. Orlando: Harcourt Brace and Company; 1987.

52. Kurtz, Rick S. Public lands policy and economic trends in gateway communities. *Rev Policy Res*. 2010; 27(1): 77–88.

53. Royte, Elizabeth. Imagining paseo pantera. *Audubon Magazine*. 1992 November-December: 75–8.

54. Padgett, Tom, Begley, Sharon. Beware of humans. In: Claggett, Hillary, editor. *Wildlife conservation*. New York: The H.W. Wilson Company; 1997. p. 159–61.

55. Belsky, Jill M. Unmaking the "local": Gender, community, and the politics of community-based rural ecotourism in Belize. In: Brechin, Steven R., Wilshushen, Peter R., Fortwangler, Crystal L., West, Patrick C., editors. *Contested nature: Promoting international biodiversity with social justice in the twenty-first century*. Albany: State University of New York Press; 2003. p. 89–101.

56. Young, Emily H. Balancing conservation with development in marine-dependent communities. Is ecotourism an empty promise? In: Zimmerer, Karl S., Bassett, Thomas J., editors. *Political ecology: An integrative approach to geography and environment-development studies*. New York: The Guilford Press.; 2003. p. 29–49.

57. Johnsen, Nina. Placemaking, pastoralism, and poverty in the Ngoron goro conservation area, Tanzania. In: Broch-Due, Vigdis, Schroeder, Richard A., editors. *Producing nature and poverty in Africa*. Stockholm: Nordiska Afrikainstitutet; 2000. p. 148–72.

58. Responsibletravel.com. Breaking the spirit: How cruel is elephant trekking? [Internet]. 2014 [cited 2014 Aug 17]; Available from: www.responsibletravel.com/holidays/elephant-conser vation/travel-guide/

59. Ward, Geoffrey C. The people and the tiger. *Audubon Magazine*. 1994 July-August: 62–9.

60. Brower, Lincoln P., Aridjis, Homero. The winter of the monarch. *New York Times* [Internet]. 2013 Mar 15 [cited 2013 Mar 16]; Available from: www.nytimes.com/2013/03/16/opinion/ the-dying-of-the-monarch-butterflies.html?nl=todaysheadlines&emc=edit_th_20130316&_r=0& pagewanted=print

61. Knapp, Charles R., Hines, Kirsten N., Zachariah, Trevor T., Perez-Heydrich, Caro, Iverson, John B., Buckner, Sandra, D. et al. Physiological effects of tourism and associated food provisioning in an endangered iguana. *Conserv Physiol* [Internet]. 2013 [cited 2014 Aug 15]; 1(1); Available from: http://conphys.oxfordjournals.org/content/1/1/cot032.full

62. Madhusudan, M.D., Mishra, Charudutt. Why big, fierce animals are threatened. In: Saberwal, Vasant K., Rangarajan, Mahesh, editors. *Battles over nature: Science and the politics of conservation*. New Delhi: Permanent Black; 2003. p. 31–55.

63. Davenport, John, Davenport, Julia L. The impact of tourism and personal leisure transport on coastal environments: A review. *Coast Shelf Sci*. 2006; 67: 280–92.

64. Kowalewski, Michael, Domenech, Rosa, Martinelli, Jordi. Vanishing clams on an Iberian beach: Local consequences and global implications of accelerating loss of shells to tourism. *PLoS ONE* [Internet]. 2014 Jan 8 [cited 2014 May 22]; Available from: www.plosone.org/ article/info%3Adoi%2F10.1371%2Fjournal.pone.0083615

65. Jackson, Jeremy. Status and trends of Caribbean coral reefs: 1970–2012: Executive summary [Internet]. 2014 [cited 2014 Jul 8]; Available from: http://cmsdata.iucn.org/downloads/execu tive_summary_caribbean_status_report_eng.pdf

66. Solomon, Christopher. Leaving only footsteps? Think again. *New York Times* [Internet]. 2015 Feb 13 [cited 2015 Feb 13]; Available from: www.nytimes.com/2015/02/15/opinion/ sunday/leaving-only-footsteps-think-again.html?emc=edit_tnt_20150213&nlid=10365419& tntemail0=y&_r=0

67. Harris, Grant, Nielson, Ryan, Rinaldi, Todd, Lohuis, Thomas. Effects of winter recreation on northern ungulates with focus on moose (*Alces alces*) and snowmobiles. *Eur J Wildl Res* [Internet]. 2013 Jul 28 [cited 2015 Feb 14]; Available from: https://southwestnwrsnatresources .files.wordpress.com/2011/12/harrisnielsonrinaldilohuis_ejwr2013.pdf

68. Reed, Sarah E., Merenlender, Adina M. Quiet, nonconsumptive recreation reduces protected area effectiveness. *Conserv Lett*. 2008; 1(3): 146–54.

69. Buckley, Ralf. Impacts of ecotourism on birds. In: Buckley, Ralf, editor. *Environmental impacts of ecotourism*. Oxfordshire, UK: CABI; 2008. p. 187–210.

70. Buckley, Ralf. Impacts of ecotourism on terrestrial wildlife. In: Buckley, Ralf, editor. *Impacts of ecotourism on terrestrial wildlife*. Oxfordshire, UK: CABI; 2008. p. 211–28.

71. Manor, Regev, Saltz, David. Effects of human disturbance on use of space and flight distance of mountain gazelles. *J Wildl Manag*. 2005; 69(4): 1683–90.

72. Matthiessen, Peter. *African silences*. New York: Random House; 1991.

73. Buckley, Ralf. Impacts positive and negative: Links between ecotourism and environment. In: Buckley, Ralf, editor. *Environmental Impacts of ecotourism*. Oxfordshire, UK: CABI; 2008. p. 5–14.

74. Berle, Peter A. Two faces of eco-tourism. *Audubon Magazine*. 1990 March-April: 6.

Chapter 12 References

1. McFarland, Andrew W. Interest groups and the policymaking process: Sources of countervailing power in America. In: Petracca, Mark P., editor. *The politics of interests: Interest groups transformed*. Boulder: Westview Press; p. 58–79.

2. Bevington, Douglas. *Rebirth of environmentalism: Grassroots activism from the spotted owl to the polar bear*. Washington, D.C.: Island Press; 2009.

3. Vogt, Heidi. Human-population boom remains largest threat to Africa's lions in wake of Cecil's killing. *Wall Street Journal* [Internet]. 2015 Aug 7 [cited 2015 Aug 8]; Available from: www.wsj.com/articles/africas-growing-population-imperils-its-lions-1438939803

4. Rodgers, W.A., Hartley, Dawn, Bashir, Sultana. Community approaches to conservation: Some comparisons from Africa and India. In: Saberwal, Vasant K., Rangarajan, Mahesh, editors. *Battles over nature: Science and the politics of conservation*. London: Earthscan; 2003. p. 324–82.

5. Kellert, Stephen R. *Public attitudes towards critical wildlife and natural habitat issues*. Phase One. #024-010-00–623-4. U.S. Government Printing Office; 1979.

6. Tatlow, Didi. Footage of live whale shark being sawed prompts outcry in China. *New York Times* [Internet]. 2015 Aug 11 [cited 2015 Aug 11]; Available from: http://sinosphere.blogs.nytimes.com/2015/08/11/footage-of-live-whale-shark-being-sawed-prompts-outcry-in-china/?emc=edit_tnt_20150811&nlid=10365419&tntemail0=y&_r=0

7. O'Gara, Geoffrey. A grizzly's place. *Sierra Magazine*. 1992 September-October: 56–61 & 80–4.

8. Fitzpatrick, John W. Saving our birds. *New York Times* [Internet]. 2014 Aug 29 [cited 2014 Aug 31]; Available from: www.nytimes.com/2014/08/31/opinion/sunday/saving-our-birds.html?emc=edit_th_20140831&nl=todaysheadlines&nlid=10365419&_r=0

9. Marris, Emma. *Rambunctious garden: Saving nature in a post-wild world*. New York: Bloomsbury; 2011.

10. Kareiva, Peter, Marvier, Michelle. What is conservation science? *BioScience*. 62(11): 2012: 962–9.

11. Kareiva, Peter, Marvier, Michelle, Lalasz, Robert. Conservation in the anthropocene: Beyond solitude and fragility. *The Breakthrough* [Internet]. 2012 Winter [cited 2014 Oct 20]; Available from: http://thebreakthrough.org/index.php/journal/past-issues/issue-2/conservation-in-the-anthropocene/

12. Revkin, Andrew C. PBS series explores "A new wild" sustained, instead of wrecked, by people. *New York Times Magazine* [Internet]. 2015 Feb 4 [cited 2015 May 18]; Available from: http://dotearth.blogs.nytimes.com/2015/02/04/pbs-series-explores-a-new-wild-sustained-instead-of-wrecked-by-people/

13. Ackerman, Diane. *The human age: The world shaped by us*. New York: W. W. Norton and Company; 2014.

14. Gottlieb, Robert. *Forcing the spring: The transformation of the American environmental movement*. Washington, D.C.: Island Press; 2005.

15. Butchart, Stuart H. M., Walpole, Matt, Collen, Ben, van Strien, Arco, Scharlemann, Jorn P. W., Almond, Rosamunde, E.A. et al. Global biodiversity: Indicators of recent declines. *Science*. 2010; 328(5892): 1164–8.

16. Hoffmann, Michael, Hilton-Taylor, Craig, Angulo, Ariadne, Bohm, Monika, Brooks, Thomas M., Butchart, Stuart M. et al. The impact of conservation on the status of the world's vertebrates. *Science*. 2010; 330(December): 1503–9.

17. Rands, Michael R., Adams, William M., Bennun, Leon, Butchart, Stuart H. M., Clements, Andrew, Coomes, David et al. Biodiversity conservation: challenges beyond 2010. *Science*. 2010; 329(5997): 1298–303.

18. Pikitch, Ellen K. The gathering wave of ocean extinction. In: Guynup, Sharon, editor. *2006 state of the wild: A global portrait of wildlife, wildlands, and oceans*. Washington, D.C.: Island Press; 2005. p. 195–201.

19. Naik, Gautam. Wildlife numbers drop by half since 1970, report says. *Wall Street Journal* [Internet]. 2014 Oct 1 [cited 2014 Oct 1]; Available from: http://online.wsj.com/articles/report-wildlife-numbers-drop-by-half-since-1970-1412085197?KEYWORDS=gautam+naik

20. Moore, Charles J. Choking the oceans with Plastic. *New York Times* [Internet]. 2014 Aug 25 [cited 2014 Aug 26]; Available from: www.nytimes.com/2014/08/26/opinion/choking-the-oceans-with-plastic.html?emc=edit_ty_20140826&nl=opinion&nlid=10365419

21. Mace, Georgina M. Drivers of biodiversity change. In: Leader-Williams, Nigel, Adams, William M., Smith, Robert J., editors. *Trade-offs in conservation: Deciding what to save*. Oxford: Wiley-Blackwell; 2010. p. 349–64.

22. Tallis, Heather, Lubchenco, Jane. A call for inclusive conservation. *Nature*. 2014; 515 (November): 27–8.

23. Wuerthner, George. Why the working landscape isn't working. In: Wuerthner, George, Crist, Eileen, Butler, Tom, editors. *Keeping the wild: Against the domestication of earth*. Washington, D.C.: Island Press; 2014. p. 162–73.

24. Marris, Emma, Aplet, Greg. How to mend the conservation divide. *New York Times* [Internet]. 2014 Oct 31 [cited 2014 Nov 1]; Available from: www.nytimes.com/2014/11/01/opinion/how-to-mend-the-conservation-divide.html?emc=edit_tnt_20141031&nlid=10365419&tntemail0=y

25. Klyza, Christopher McGrory, Sousa, David J. *American environmental policy*. Cambridge: MIT Press; 2013.

26. Opar, Alisa. Attack mode. *Audubon Magazine*. 2015 September-October: 22 & 58.

27. Pang, Jamie, Greenwald, Noah. The politics of extinction: The unprecedented Republican attack on endangered species and the Endangered Species Act [Internet]. Center for Biological Diversity.; 2015 [cited 2015 Aug 13]; Available from: www.biologicaldiversity.org/campaigns/esa_attacks/pdfs/Politics_of_Extinction.pdf

28. Zaffos, Joshua. Prairie dog case challenges ESA. *Houston Chronicle* [Internet]. 2015 Jun 11 [cited 2015 Jun 16]; Available from: www.hcn.org/articles/prairie-dog-case-bites-back-at-endangered-species-act?utm_source=wcn1&utm_medium=email

29. Shogren, Elizabeth. Obama's preemptive strike to reform Endangered Species Act. *High Country News* [Internet]. 2015 May 20 [cited 2015 Jun 8]; Available from: www.hcn.org/articles/obama-administration-proposes-reforms-of-endangered-species-act

30. Wood, Jonathan. Take it to the limit: The illegal regulation prohibiting the take of any threatened species under the Endangered Species Act [Internet]. Program for Judicial

Awareness, Working Paper Series No. 13–514; 2015 [cited 2015 Aug 28]; Available from: http://papers.ssrn.com/sol3/papers.cfm?abstract_id=2581766

31. Piao, Vanessa, Chan, Cherie. Beijing destroys confiscated ivory in effort to curb illegal trade. *New York Times* [Internet]. 2015 May 29 [cited 2015 May 29]; Available from: http://sinosphere.blogs.nytimes.com/2015/05/29/beijing-destroys-confiscated-ivory-in-effort-to-curb-illegal-trade/?emc=edit_tnt_20150529&nlid=10365419&tntemail0=y&_r=0

Index